# Mecca and Eden

# Mecca and Eden

RITUAL, RELICS, AND TERRITORY IN ISLAM

*Brannon Wheeler*

THE UNIVERSITY OF CHICAGO PRESS *Chicago and London*

BRANNON WHEELER is director of the Center for Middle East and Islamic Studies and visiting distinguished professor of history and politics at the United States Naval Academy in Annapolis. He is the author or editor of seven books, including *Applying the Canon in Islam* (1996), *Moses in the Quran and Islamic Exegesis* (2002), *Prophets in the Quran* (2002), and *Teaching Islam* (2003).

The University of Chicago Press, Chicago 60637
The University of Chicago Press, Ltd., London

Printed in the United States of America

15 14 13 12 11 10 09 08 07 06     1 2 3 4 5

ISBN: 0-226-88803-7 (cloth)
ISBN: 0-226-88804-5 (paper)

Library of Congress Cataloging-in-Publication Data
Wheeler, Brannon M., 1965–
Mecca and Eden : ritual, relics, and territory in Islam / Brannon Wheeler.
p. cm.
Includes bibliographical references and index.
ISBN 0-226-88803-7 (cloth : alk. paper) — ISBN 0-226-88804-5 (pbk. : alk. paper)
1. Reliquaries, Islamic. 2. Islam—Rituals. 3. Civilization, Islamic. I. Title.
BP186.97.W48 2006
297.3—dc22

2005017331

∞ The paper used in this publication meets the minimum requirements of the American National Standard for Information Sciences—Permanence of Paper for Printed Library Materials, ANSI Z39.48-1992.

# *Contents*

# *Acknowledgments*

The ideas that eventually led me to write this book were given to me by Professor Bill Whedbee in a seminar on the history of religions in 1987 at Pomona College, when he introduced me to the works of Mircea Eliade and Jonathan Z. Smith on ritual and sacred space. Bill's dedication to developing the ideas of his students through careful, exhaustive study and the clear, ordered articulation of an argument continues to inspire me, although there is a long way to go before I begin to approach his standards.

The research and writing of this book have been supported by a number of individuals, institutions, grants, and fellowships in the years since the seminar at Pomona College. A large number of imaginative and sharp students have contributed to my thinking about the relationship of religion and the state. These include students in the courses "Government of Ritual" and "Utopia" at Macalester College (1991–1992) and Vanderbilt University (1992–1994), and different versions of my "Ritual and Territory in Islam" course, which I taught at the University of Washington (1996–2002). Without the insights of these students, this book would not have been possible.

My first attempt at putting to paper some of the ideas contained in this book was a paper I presented at the Islamic Area Studies Symposium "Beyond the Border" at the University of Kyoto in October 1999. Versions of this paper were also presented in lectures at Syracuse University and Yale University in December 1999. Helpful comments from a number of colleagues, including Michael Lecker, Dale Eickelman, Patricia Cox Miller, Gerhard Böwering, and Kazuo Morimoto, helped me to publish a revised version of this paper, "From Dar al-Hijra to Dar al-Islam: The Islamic Utopia," in *The Concept of Territory in Islamic Law and Thought*, edited by Yanagihashi Hiroyuki, Islamic Area Studies 2 (New York and London: Kegan Paul International, 2000), 1–36.

My interest in developing more specific and expanded interpretations of ritual, relics, and territory came from two contexts at the University of Washington. The first was a comparative religion colloquium with the theme "Ritual and (Sacred) Space," to which faculty and students from the University of Washington and visiting scholars contributed over a two-year period (2000–2002). Among the colleagues who most influenced my thinking in this colloquium were Jim Wellman, Kyoko Tokuno, Scott Noegel, Eugene Vance, and Philip Arnold. Instrumental in the success of this colloquium was Joel Walker, who organized the readings with me and helped to focus my attention on the historical contexts of the cases we examined. The second opportunity for reflection on these issues was a graduate seminar I cotaught with Joel Walker entitled "Holy Land in Late Antiquity and Early Islam." The erudition and enthusiasm of my coteacher and students urged forward my research in ways that go well beyond the confines of this book.

The four chapters of this book were written over a number of years and have gone through a series of modifications resulting from the countless insights of patient colleagues, students, and friends. Many of the concepts that found their way into chapter 1 were tried and tested on colleagues in various venues, including the comparative religion colloquium at the University of Washington (2002), the "Relics and Territory" consultation at the annual meeting of the American Academy of Religion (2003), and the School of Oriental and African Studies, University of London (2003). Especially valuable comments came from Michael Williams, Kristin Scheible, Gerald Hawting, Benjamin Fortna, and Robert Elgood.

Chapter 2 was developed from a number of talks and conference papers, including a paper presented at the annual meeting of the Middle East Studies Association (2001) and the Fourth International Islamic Legal Studies Conference in Murcia, Spain (2003). Most helpful to me were the comments of Michael Cook, Nasr Hamid Abu Zayd, Art Buehler, Jonathan Brockopp, Kevin Reinhart, and Everett Rowson. Students in my Arabic course "Ritual and Legal Texts" at the University of Washington aided me in thinking about some of the more convoluted and thorny issues in Islamic legal definitions of purity, especially Daryl Mutton and Dr. Ahmed Souaiaia. A modified version of chapter 2 appeared as "Touching the Penis in Islamic Law," *History of Religions* 44 (2004): 89–119 (© 2005 by The University of Chicago), and is reprinted here with permission.

Chapter 3 was largely compiled from references I was able to track down through the unparalleled library resources of Oxford University, especially at the Oriental and Indian Reading Rooms at the Bodleian Library, the Sackler Library of the Ashmolean Museum, and the library of the Oriental Institute. The librarians at the Bodleian were particularly helpful. A lecture at the University of Bristol gave me the chance to talk about some of the ideas in chapter 3 with a fantastic group of colleagues and graduate students in religion. I especially appreciate the comments of Robert Gleave and Rupert Gethin.

Chapter 4 was made possible only by the opportunity for me to travel throughout the Middle East and Central Asia during 2003–2004. During this time, I was afforded the chance to discuss with many colleagues and friends my ideas about the tombs of prophets. This included lectures at the Royal Institute for Interfaith Studies and Jordan Institute for Diplomacy, the American Center for Oriental Research in Amman, Yarmouk University, and the Institute for Islamic Sciences at the Grand Mosque in Muscat. An Arabic synopsis of my findings was published as "al-Anbiyāʾ al-ʿArabīyah wa Qubūr al-Jabābirah," *al-Nashra* 30 (Spring 2004): 19–23. A modified version of chapter 3 appeared as "Arab Prophets and the Tombs of Giants," *Bulletin of the Royal Institute for Inter-faith Studies* (2005), and is reprinted here with permission.

During the 2004–2005 academic year I had the opportunity to present an overview of my ideas in this book to colleagues and students in a number of different contexts, including invited lectures at Macalester College, the University of Oklahoma, Virginia Polytechnic Institute, the University of Bergen, and the University of Oslo. Special thanks to James Laine, Calvin Roetzel, Allen Hertze, William Ochsenwald, Peter Schmitthenner, Ananda Abeysekara, Brian Britt, Knut Vikor, and Albrecht Hofheinz for their insightful comments and help.

Much of the research, in libraries, archives, and fieldwork, was done during a two-year sabbatical from the University of Washington (2003–2005). I especially thank the Department of Near Eastern Languages and Civilization and the Comparative Religion Program for their support of my research during this period. I benefited greatly from a fellowship at the Institute for Ismaili Studies in London and was a Visiting Scholar at the Oxford Centre for Islamic Studies during the autumn of 2003. Christopher Melchert, Luke Treadwell, Jeremy Johns, and the other faculty of the Oriental Institute at Oxford University were gracious hosts and rousing colleagues. In September 2003, I had the good fortune to participate in a month-long exchange program in comparative religion and Islamic studies administered by the University of Washington (with five institutions of higher learning in Uzbekistan) and funded by the U.S. Department of State.

During the winter of 2004, a senior fellowship from the Council of the American Oriental Research Centers afforded me the occasion to spend four months at the American Center for Oriental Research in Amman. I am particularly grateful to Pierre and Patricia Bikai, Robert Rook, and Bjorne

Anderson at ACOR; Majed Nemy, Dr. Ghazi Bisheh, and Professors Omar al-Ghul and Hani al-Hawajaneh at Yarmouk University; and HRH Prince Ghazi bin Muhammad and HRH Prince Raʿad bin Zeid for their generosity, facilitation, and intellectual encouragement.

A regional Senior Fulbright Fellowship to Jordan, Egypt, and Oman during the 2004 academic year provided me with invaluable opportunities for research and academic cooperation with Arab colleagues. My sponsors in these countries were exceptionally hospitable and accommodating: HRH Prince El Hassan bin Talal, Bakr al-Hiyari and the other faculty and staff at the Royal Institute for Interfaith Studies in Jordan; Professor Muhammad al-Hawari at Ibn Saʿud University in Riyadh; Professors Jaʿfar ʿAbd al-Salam and ʿUmar al-Qadi at al-Azhar University; Professor Khalifah Hasan and the other faculty at the Center for Oriental Studies at Cairo University; Professor Amir al-Qadir from the University of Constantine, Algeria; Professors Isaac and Widad at the Coptic Studies Institute in Cairo; Professor Bahir ʿAbd al-Majid and the other faculty of the Department of Hebrew Language and Literature, and the faculty of the Center for the Dialogue of Civilizations at Ayn Shams University; the staff at the Sayyida Zaynab Manuscript Library; HE Mahmoud Hamdy Zaqzuq, Minister of Awqaf and Islamic Affairs in Egypt; ʿAli al-Shahri, Director General of Awqaf and Religious Affairs in Dhofar Region; Professor Ridwan al-Sayyid, Dr. ʿAbd al-Rahman al-Salmi and HE Shaikh Abdullah Bin Mohammed Bin Abdullah al-Salmi, Minister of Awqaf and Religious Affairs in Oman.

The whole manuscript of this book was carefully read and critiqued by David Powers, Janina Safran, Art Buehler, and Michael Feener. These four scholars provided enormous help to me in the historical detail, theoretical clarity, and structural organization of my writing. Other colleagues and friends have contributed by taking the time to answer my nagging questions about details I could otherwise never have tracked down: Carl Ernst, Richard Eaton, Walid Salih, Claude Gilliot, and Fred Donner. Nic Zakheim is to be thanked for proofreading the manuscript. I feel inadequate to respond to all the comments and questions they and others have raised, and I expect that future readers will compel me to think further about the difficult and perhaps unanswerable issues that are all too easily glossed over in the tidy narrative of a final draft. I hope that I have put forward my ideas, at this stage of their development, in a way that stimulates others to challenge and expand upon my conclusions.

Last but not least, I want to acknowledge the unwavering support of my three sons, Jeffry, Zachary, and Franklin, and my wife, Debbie, the smart one in the family, who put up with all of my many and long trips to visit tombs and relics, often driving around through nameless small villages and wandering for hours in what seemed to them like the middle of nowhere.

# *Notes on Conventions*

The transliteration of Arabic words follows the conventions used in the *International Journal of Middle East Studies* with the exception that the tā marbuṭā is indicated by a final "h" in the nonconstruct position. Common names of people and places (e.g., the prophet Muhammad, the Quran, Mecca) are given in standard English transliteration or simplified transliteration. All dates, unless otherwise indicated, are given according to the common era (BCE and CE).

# *Introduction*

Speaking on the topic of sacrifice and the origins of religion among the Semites, William Robertson Smith makes a number of insightful statements regarding the character of the "holy" and its relationship to certain locations and objects associated with those places. Perhaps his most fundamental contribution is his definition of holy places and objects as social conventions. He expresses this in explaining traditions concerning the Arabian concept of sanctuaries.

> On the whole, then, it is evident that the difference between holy things and common things does not originally turn on ownership, as if common things belonged to men and holy things to the gods. . . . The approach to ancient sanctuaries was surrounded by restrictions which cannot be regarded as designed to protect the property of the gods, but rather fall under the notion that they will not tolerate the vicinity of certain persons (e.g. such as are physically unclean) and certain actions (e.g. the shedding of blood). . . . Holy places and things are not so much reserved for the use of the god as surrounded by a network of restrictions and disabilities which forbid them to be used by men except in particular ways, and in certain cases forbid them to be used at all.[1]

Robertson Smith's emphasis on the common ownership of holy places and objects represents a significant shift away from the notion that the holy is perceived to be inherent in certain things. He recognizes that the rules regarding what actions may and may not be performed in relation to particular places and objects delineate the boundaries of what is holy and what is common.

The work of Robertson Smith, which had a profound influence on the early modern study of religion, is also important because of its interpretation of specifically Arabic and Islamic concepts.[2] He was one of the first and only scholars to draw general conclusions about religion based upon Arabic examples. He used a variety of classical Arabic sources and ethnographic accounts of beliefs and rituals among Arabs in the Arabian Peninsula and elsewhere. Unfortunately, since his work appeared, little attention has been given to the place of Arabic and Islamic materials in the more general conceptualization of religion.[3] This is particularly unfortunate given the great advances made in the knowledge of Islamic texts and history in the century since Robertson Smith.

Building upon Robertson Smith's definition of the Arabian sanctuary as a holy place, the larger project of this book is a description and analysis of the rituals and objects surrounding and associated with the sacred status of the sanctuary as delineated in Islamic exegetical and legal texts. Robertson Smith provides a useful starting point because of his insistence that the sacred status of certain locations and objects is primarily due not to their natural but rather to their social character. The following pages of the introduction provide a brief overview of Robertson Smith's approach to the concept of the holy with particular attention to his emphasis on its symbolic function. For Robertson Smith, the holy is a self-conscious symbolic representation of society based on a notion of communal ownership and restricted access. The social significance of the sacred is also stressed in Jonathan Z. Smith's examination of the bear hunt and its ritualization among different peoples in Central and East Asia. The examples of both the ancient Semites and of the bear hunters suggest how the actions that delimit the sacred status of objects and places can be interpreted as the result of societies reflecting upon their origins and displaying the need for the status quo of their social orders.

## RITUAL AND SOCIAL ORDER

Among the theoretical contributions made by Roberston Smith to the study of religion is his insistence that the sacred, and the rituals designed to delimit it, are symbolic representations of society. He defines the sacred, or the holy, as being generated by a system of restrictions on the human use of natural things: "[I]t would appear that common things are such as men have license to use freely at their own good pleasure without fear of supernatural penalties, while holy things may be used only in prescribed ways and under definite restrictions. . . . [H]oliness is essentially a restriction on the license of man in the free use of natural things."[4] That these prescriptions on the use of natural things are social in origin is evident from the notion that all objects and locations considered sacred are also considered to be held in common as the property of the society as a whole. The same restrictions placed upon the use of natural things such as locations, plants, and animals are also extended to objects owned by the whole of society, including items associated with the sanctuary (altars, candlesticks, idols, vessels), weapons and farming implements, food and drink, certain buildings, perfume, and treasures.[5]

For Robertson Smith, the sacred is that which is "set apart" by society not because it is "owned" by the gods or because of something intrinsic to any given location or object, but as a means of emphasizing the symbolic value of a location or object for society. The actual content of the rules restricting access to sacred things may be arbitrary, and the things set apart may appear to be no different from any other location or object. But sacred things pertain to that which society holds in common, and as such they are regarded as having special significance beyond the natural or generic attributes they share with other common items. Sacred things are conventions agreed upon by, and pertaining to, society.

That this symbolic character of the sacred represents a self-conscious attitude is also evident from a contradiction inherent in the restrictions and requirements relating society to the sacred. Referring to Robertson Smith's discussion of the sacred character of the camel, Émile Durkheim argues that the concept of the sacred is ironic: "Every sacred being is removed from profane touch by this very character with which it is endowed; but, on the other hand, they would serve for nothing and have no reason whatsoever for their existence if they could not come in contact with these same worshippers who, on another ground, must remain respectfully distant from them. At bottom, there is no positive rite which does not constitute a veritable sacrilege, for a man cannot hold commerce with the sacred beings without crossing the barrier which should ordinarily keep them separate."[6] Forbidding the private eating of camel flesh by an individual sets the camel apart from other animals as sacred. Public consumption of a camel that has been sacrificed in accordance with certain ritual regulations celebrates precisely that act which is prohibited to the private individual. According to Durkheim, recognizing that an act is sacrilege is what allows the group to perceive the social origins of the restrictions that make the camel sacred in the first place.[7] The gathering to eat the camel serves as a time for members of the group to focus on "their common beliefs, their common traditions, the memory of their great ancestors, the collective ideal of which they are the incarnation."[8] The ritual performance of this "sacrilege" by the group is what allows the camel to function as a symbolic representation of society.

Robertson Smith is also careful to point out that sacred things do not necessarily reflect an accurate image of society but are symbols with which society identifies itself. This is illustrated in his conception of the camel as a totem animal because it was, for the ancient Semites, the primary symbol for the domestication of animals, just as cattle were in other cultures.[9] The sacrifice of oxen among the Nuer is predicated on the significance of cattle as providing milk, carcasses for tools, ornaments, sleeping hides, and sun-dried dung to fuel smudges.[10] These domesticated animals are considered "sacred and kindred for they are the source of human life and subsistence."[11] The domesticated camel is used for its milk, transportation in the desert, and as a marker of status and wealth but not as a source of meat.[12] Society defines the camel as sacred by restricting access to it: no individual may kill and eat the camel privately. In those examples of the private eating of camel which do exist, it is clear that the camel is not regarded as sacred.[13]

According to Robertson Smith, the ancient Semitic notion that the domesticated camel was considered to be a part of human society further underlines the symbolic character of the camel.[14] The camel was regarded as part of society because of its close symbiotic relationship to desert society at its origins. Just as the domestication of the camel allowed for the survival of people in the desert, so a certain level of social development was necessary for the care and maintenance of the camel.[15] The domestication of animals is explicitly linked to that point in time when society first came into existence.

> [J]ust as in the Greek fable of the Golden Age, man, in his pristine state of innocence, lived at peace with all the animals, eating the spontaneous fruits of the earth; but after the Fall he was sentenced to earn his bread by agricultural toil. At the same time his war with hurtful creatures (the serpent) began, and domestic animals began to be slain sacrificially, and their skins used for clothing. . . . The original Hebrew tradition is that of the Jahvistic story, which agrees with Greek legend in connecting the sacrifice of domestic animals with a fall from the state of pristine innocence.[16]

Animal husbandry, like agriculture, became necessary only after the end of the golden age, when food no longer grew by itself and the cultivation of plant and animal products was required to provide clothing and shelter.[17]

Although not fully appreciated by all the followers of his work, this linkage made by Robertson Smith between the restrictions placed on the domesticated camel and the myth of a golden age is directly pertinent to defining the relationship of the sacred to society. For Robertson Smith, the camel was considered sacred because for certain groups it epitomized and may have been the only example of the domesticated animal.[18] The domesticated camel represented the one thing perceived to have allowed for the existence of present society and to link society with its mythical origins at the end of the utopia of the golden age. Claude Lévi-Strauss highlights this conception by emphasizing that the sacred character of the camel can only be understood by society as being futile: "While myth resolutely turns away from the continuous to segment and break down the world by means of distinctions, contrasts and oppositions, ritual moves in the opposite direction: starting from the discrete units that are imposed upon it by this preliminary conceptualization of reality, it strives to get back to the continuous, although the initial break with lived experience effected by mythic thought makes the task forever impossible. . . . [It is this] mixture of stubbornness and ineffectiveness which explains the desperate, maniacal aspect of ritual."[19] The apparent sacrilege of eating the camel in the context of the ritual is a recognition that present society does not live in the golden age without need for domesticated animals and agriculture.[20] It is a recognition that such a style of living is now impossible, and thus following the restrictions relating to sacred things is a conscious affirmation of the present social order.[21] For Roberston Smith, the definition of the sacred is self-conscious in the sense that it orients attention toward a lost utopian past which affirms, at least implicitly, the present social order, and the need for its government by the chieftain.[22]

In his detailed study of bear-hunting rituals, Jonathan Z. Smith points out an analogous dichotomy separating the utopia of the ritual to the social order of everyday life. He contends that the bear hunters he studies are conscious of the discrepancy between actual bear hunts and the way they talk about and ritualize the hunt. The hunters claim that the bear offers itself to be killed, as confirmed by the hunters' disclaiming their role in the bear's death.[23] The hunter must never kill a bear while it is sleeping in its den, for the hunter is said to address the bear face-to-face with poems of praise before dispatching it in hand-to-hand combat.[24] In reality, however, the bear is almost always killed in its den, or immobilized by a trap before the hunters approach.[25]

> [N]ot only ought we not to believe many of the elements in the description of the hunt as usually presented, but we ought not to believe that the hunters, from whom these descriptions were collected, believe it either. . . .
>
> . . . The hunter does not hunt as he says he hunts; he does not think about his hunting as he says he thinks. But, unless we are to suppose that,

as a "primitive," he is incapable of thought, we must presume that *he* is aware of this discrepancy, that he works with it, that he has some means of overcoming this contradiction between word and deed.[26]

That the hunter recognizes the utopian character of how he claims to hunt is evident from the fact that he does not actually hunt the way he claims to hunt. According to J. Z. Smith, scholars who fail to acknowledge this not only miss the point of the discrepancy but also attribute a kind of "cuckoo-land" irrationality to the hunters, construing them as "some other sort of mind, some other sort of human being."[27]

J. Z. Smith makes the case that it is the hunters' recognition of the discrepancy between what they say and what they do that typifies the ritual character of the hunt. Like Robertson Smith, J. Z. Smith shows how society acknowledges the conventional nature of the rituals it uses to talk about itself. The hunters ascribe meaning to their actions, performed in the context of the bear hunt, that differs from what these actions actually accomplish:[28] "[R]itual represents the creation of a controlled environment where the variables (i.e., the accidents) of ordinary life may be displaced precisely because they are felt to be so overwhelmingly present and powerful. . . . Ritual relies for its power on the fact that it is concerned with quite ordinary activities, that what it describes and displays is, in principle, possible for every occurrence of these acts. But it relies, as well, for its power on the perceived fact that, in actuality, such possibilities cannot be realized."[29] The ritual aspect of the hunt is found, for example, in addressing the bear and in "killing" it after it is already dead. Similar is the treatment of the bear carcass as a live bear in the later ceremonies, including feeding the bear, providing it special entrance into the tent, and giving it gifts, all while the bear is already dead. Only after it is dead may the people safely treat the bear as a guest, as a natural object upon which social significance may be placed.

This point is illustrated even more clearly in the special bear ritual practiced among the Ainu, Gilyak, Orochi, and Olcha, in which a bear is raised as a domesticated animal and slaughtered.[30] As with the wild bear, the domesticated bear is treated as though it has given itself up to be killed, though it is immobilized by being tied between stakes and poisoned by bow and arrow.[31] Because it is domesticated, the bear can be controlled and the killing staged in ways impossible in the wild. But although the ritual can control the domesticated bear to a greater degree, J. Z. Smith argues, following Lévi-Strauss's characterization of ritual, that people still recognize the futility of their actions: "It is not that 'magical' rituals compel the world through representation and manipulation; rather they express a realistic assessment of the fact that the world cannot be compelled."[32] For J. Z. Smith, the ritual is not an attempt to change the reality inherent in the natural relationship between bears and people, but rather a recognition of this reality. Even the more docile domesticated bear must still be tied up and poisoned before it can be killed, and the domesticated bear still needs to be dead before it will allow itself to be eaten.

Drawing on these examples, J. Z. Smith emphasizes the importance of seeing the rationality of ritual, the need to recognize that the hunters understand the incongruity between the ideal portrayed in the ritual and the experience of everyday life: "There is a 'gnostic' dimension to ritual. It provides the means for demonstrating that we know what ought to have been done, what ought to have taken place. But, by the fact that it is ritual action rather than everyday action, it demonstrates that we know what is the case."[33] J. Z. Smith contends that this incongruity is "recollected" in normal everyday life. Ritual marks certain actions, just as the "holy" marks certain objects and locations, as having social significance apart from their ordinary, natural character. As Robertson Smith points out with the camel sacrifice, bringing to mind the absence of the utopian past reaffirms the present social order, including the individual and group obligations made necessary by this loss. "Ritual is a means of performing the way things ought to be in conscious tension to the way things are in such a way that this ritualized perfection is recollected in the ordinary, uncontrolled, course of things."[34] It does not appear to be the case, however, that the ritual and the unrealistic talk about hunting depict a world in which the ideal hunt is possible or even desirable. The lost utopian existence imagined by the ritualized hunt is one in which there is no hunting, a world in which the first bear has never been killed.

The myths associated with bear rituals by the people who perform them suggest that the bear ritual and the description of the hunt are not understood only as evidence of an incongruity between perception and reality.[35] It is not so much that the world "should be" another way, but rather the recognition that the world "no longer is" the way it used to be. Talking about and ritualizing the bear hunt commemorates the natural hardships people have overcome to survive, by hunting and through social organization, in a non- or post-utopian existence.

The link between the practice of the hunt and the taming of bears for a ritualized hunt can be found in prehistoric times and is not limited to those groups that sacrifice domesticated bears.[36] In many of these cultures similar symbolic associations are made between the bear, whether tamed or dead, and the origins of civilization. Often the tame bear or the bear carcass is adorned with jewelry, including strips of copper for bracelets and collars marked with grass threads.[37] The bear is also given amulets, and amulets are made from the different body parts of the bear.[38] Around Hudson's Bay, pieces of the bear are attached to small objects such as saws, drills, and other implements of civilization.[39] A number of cultures associate planting and agriculture with the bear, planting posts in the ground, tied together with string.[40] The Eskimo attach the bear's bladder to a stick placed upright near the encampment for three days.[41] The Oroke set up spruce trees to which were tied special shavings (inau) in the dwellings of the tame bears, and they associated these trees with the cosmogonic and civilizing activities of the hero Khadau.[42]

The tamed bear and bear carcass are also treated as though they represent the king or leader of the society. Among the Nootka, the bear carcass is positioned opposite the chieftain at a ceremonial meal, dressed like the chieftain, and served a special tray of food.[43] Among the Koryak, food is presented to a wooden representation of the bear, while the Chukchi slaughter reindeer and serve it to the bear.[44] In several cultures, people refer to the bear as "king" of the animals.[45] Ostyak myths state that the bear is actually a divine being in human form wearing a bear skin.[46] In other cultures, people make the bear carcass smoke a pipe, and place tobacco in the bear's mouth.[47] Special burials are arranged for the bear in which the carcass is taken apart at the joints so that nothing of the bear's skeleton is broken or cut. The Evenk bundle the bear's dried bones and place them upon a high tree stump or a raised platform and place the head above them nearby.[48]

Tamed bears and carcasses are closely associated with gender segregation and sexual reproduction in human society.[49] Among the Turkic tribes of Siberia, hunters make movements in imitation of sexual intercourse over the body of the slain bear.[50] One of the older hunters stands behind the younger hunters and pushes them toward the bear with a stick opposite his penis (kocugan kan). In Lapland, the hunter who kills the bear thrusts his spear into the carcass three times following its death, for fertility and strength.[51] Similar cult sticks are used among the Ainu.[52] According to Irving Hallowell, all married women without children, young girls, and dogs are required to leave the camp and stay away during the time when the bear carcass arrives and is cooking. Among the Mistassini, unmarried women must cover their faces when the carcass is brought into the camp.[53] Some Even did not allow women to participate in any part of the eating of the bear.[54] The Nentsi, on their bear-hunting expeditions, took along pregnant women, from behind whom the men would shoot at the bear, believing that the bear would not attack pregnant women.[55] Other cultures regard the hunt and the bear feast as a punishment for men's killing the bear and therefore exempt women from eating certain parts of the bear (head, eyes, heart, entrails).[56]

In the mythology of the peoples who practice the bear hunt and its rituals, the bear is seen as an agent of civilization. Among the Yenisey Evenk the legend is told of a bear that sacrificed itself in order to provide humans with reindeer as domesticated herds.[57] In an Ainu myth, a bear gives to a human woman the gift of a son whose descendants become the Ainu people.[58] The Udegeys and other Lower Amur peoples also tell the story of the marriage of a human girl with a bear.[59] In other accounts, the bear is responsible for bringing gifts of civilization, and for instituting the ritualized bear hunt to commemorate its own death. A Ket legend tells how a "kaigus" (son of a woman by a bear) wanted to marry a human girl but was killed by the girl's people after issuing instructions for the bear ritual and the use of his carcass in divination.[60]

Several myths make explicit that the death of the bear represents a contest between the natural world of animals and the artificial world of human society. In Even folklore, a girl gives birth to two sons, one of them by a bear. The human son grows up to be Torgani, the legendary hero of the Even. This Torgani kills his brother, the bear, with the result that his people must now hunt the many bears that will stalk them, and must perform a special ceremony for the eating of the bears that are hunted. This ceremony ensures that the bears will not seek retribution for this initial killing of the brother bear.[61] The Ayan Evenk and Orochi have a similar myth, in which two rival brothers fight, one a bear and one a human, with the result that the bear is killed, but not before bequeathing the ritualized bear hunt to his brother and his people.[62] According to Vogul mythology, humans originally were covered with hair and had long nails and horns, like other animals.[63] In these accounts, the world before the killing of the bear is one in which animals and humans live together, and the killing of the bear represents the transition to human mastery of the natural world, marking the passage to a state of existence dominated by the use of tools, agriculture, and domesticated animals to maintain the growing size of human society.

That the ritualized hunt and the sacrifice of the domesticated bear might serve as a commemoration of the transition between nomadic and settled society is consistent with sacrificial practices in other cultures.[64] The bear is a symbol like the camel, kangaroo, and cattle in certain pastoral societies. Like these other animals, the bear is regarded as kin with the society that hunts and sacrifices it. Bears are referred to with various kinship terms including "cousin," "grandfather," "old man," "guest," and "four-legged human."[65] The bear is also called a spirit or god, one which disguises itself with black fur, sharp claws, and a large body, said to be the image of humans as they once lived.[66]

Bears are hunted as a source not only of food, but also clothing, shelter, and items of exchange.[67] More important than this, however, is the conception of the bear as prey or sacrificial victim, demonstrating the society's capacity to kill the bear (rather than be killed by it). Perhaps the bear was chosen because of its anthropomorphic features, because of the relative difficulty in subduing a bear in the wild, or from a memory of the bear's importance in prehistorical times. Note also that the bear hunt and ritual is found far outside the areas in which bears were common enough to serve as an easy source of food or would have been a significant nuisance to society.[68] Like the camel, the bear also appears to have been treated as a symbol of society's existence because it can best represent, through myth and ritual, the incongruity between the natural, utopian world and the social animal husbandry of settled society. It is not the animal itself, but the restrictions and prescriptions with which the animal is delimited and made sacred to communicate a message that concerns the origins of the social order and the need for establishment and governance of it.

## RITUAL, RELICS, AND THE MECCAN SANCTUARY

The observations of Robertson Smith and J. Z. Smith highlight some of the major theoretical issues relevant to the larger study of ritual and relics associated with Mecca and the origins of Islam. Of particular importance is how ordinary objects and actions are set apart and construed in terms of their conventional significance as symbols of society. The camel and the bear can be seen as natural objects that represent social concepts for the societies in which they serve as symbols. Certain locations and objects are likewise defined as sacred and protected from private trespass by both prohibiting and prescribing certain types of behavior in relation to these objects and locations. The examples of the ancient Semites and the bear hunters show that it is the process of restricting access, not only to the physical objects and locations themselves, but also to their conceptualization, that singles out such objects and locations as sacred. The face-to-face killing prescribed for bears and the designation of a given location as the abode of the god amount to fictions which, by virtue of their common acceptance as necessary social conventions, help to explain and legitimize the existence of society.

### MUSLIM EXAMPLES OF RITUAL AND RELICS

Muslim exegetical and legal traditions attribute special significance to everyday objects (clothing, utensils, hair and nails, weapons and armor, speech) as relics, and ordinary actions (sitting, standing, and not eating or having sex) as rituals. In the examples of J. Z. Smith, the discrepancy between what the hunters say they do and what they actually do in their hunting indicates that the hunters recognize the relationship between the bear, their hunt, and the origins of their society. According to Robertson Smith, the use of a domesticated camel in the sacrifice of the ancient Semites is an affirmation of the need for domesticated animals and the social order that accompanies it. Both the bear and the camel are symbols of the transition from nomadic to settled life. The killing of the camel and the bear epitomize a transition from a primeval, natural past to a constructed and social present.

Muslim scholarship also links selected objects, actions, and locations to the origins and development of Islamic civilization. One example, considered in chapter 1, is the accounts of the discovery of the treasure of the Kaʿbah, consisting of golden gazelles from pre-Islamic Arab and Iranian kings, and swords and armor from the Israelite prophets. Muslim accounts draw extensively on a number of ancient and late antique motifs, such as the burial of the temple implements, the divine origins of weapons, and the king as the guardian of the sanctuary. Analysis of how these motifs are appropriated into Muslim accounts shows that the objects contained in the treasure of the Kaʿbah are employed as part of larger narrative framework incorporating the prophet Muhammad and Islam into a history of prophets and kings going back to Adam following his expulsion from the garden of Eden. Specific descriptions associated with the golden gazelles, swords, and armor of the treasure portray these objects as symbols of the mythological origins of Islam within the context of the genesis of civilization on earth.

Not unlike the camel and the bear, the contents of the treasure of the Kaʿbah signify a transition between fundamentally different states of human existence and society. For both the bear hunters and the ancient Semites, the transition from nomadic to settled society is understood in light of the difference between a utopian golden age and the present social order. By tying the objects contained in the treasure of the Kaʿbah with particular pre-Islamic prophets and kings, Muslim accounts delineate a transition from the utopian existence in the garden of Eden to the current state of human civilization culminating in the prophet Muhammad and Islam. The accounts of the discovery of the treasure of the Kaʿbah link Islam with the origins of human civilization and the fall from Eden, just as accounts of the hunt tell of a contest between nature and culture that explains the absolute break between the world as it used to be and the world as it is now.

Central to both Robertson Smith's and J. Z. Smith's analyses is that the rituals surrounding the killing of the camel and the bear, and the objects associated with these rituals, function as regular physical reminders of the myth explaining the origins of present society as the result of a fall from a utopian golden age. Chapters 2, 3, and 4 examine how the definition of rituals, relics, and territory in Islamic exegetical and legal texts is related to the more general mythological depiction of the origins of Islamic civilization seen in the accounts of the recovery of the treasure of the Kaʿbah. In part, this is related to the centrality of the Meccan sanctuary in major rituals such as pilgrimage (ḥajj) and prayer (ṣalāt), and the symbolic link between Eden and Mecca in ritual purification (ṭahārah) and offering (zakāt).

Muslim rituals contrast civilization, focused on Mecca as the origin of human civilization (Adam) and Islamic civilization (Muhammad), with the garden of Eden where the activities of the rituals are unnecessary or impossible. The relics attributed to the prophet Muhammad (hair and fingernails, footprints, ḥadīth reports, clothing, other artifacts) are closely linked with the origins of civilization at Mecca and are said to have been dispersed by his followers from the Meccan sanctuary to the various locations which became outposts of Islamic civilization after the early Islamic conquests. Many of these relics were transported by Muslim rulers to centers within the area of Islamic civilization (Dār al-Islām) and were used in the establishment of buildings representative of Islam and the spread of knowledge from the prophet Muhammad, such as mosques and madrasas. The giant length of the tombs of certain prophets is also a physical reminder of the loss of Eden and the subsequent development of civilization. They testify to the existence of prophets, from before the time of Abraham and the Israelite prophets, including Adam, Seth, Idris, Noah, Hud, and Salih. These are prophets who played an integral role in the earliest development of human civilization and are thus described as being of giant size, representing the original stature of humanity before a decrease in size that accompanied an increase in technology and the arts of civilization.

## MYTHOLOGICAL ORIGINS OF CIVILIZATION

The way in which definitions of ritual, relics, and territory relate to the mythological origins of civilization is stressed in J. Z. Smith's insistence that ritual represents a rational process of thinking about the incongruity between the present social order and the utopian past. Robertson Smith likewise uses the example of the camel sacrifice to argue that the use of sacred actions, objects, and locations is how society is able to organize and maintain its structure. Similarly, my overarching aim in this book is to illustrate how the mythology of the fall from Eden and the origins of Islamic civilization represented by Muslim rituals and relics can be interpreted as a narrative expression of an ideology stipulating the necessity of religion and the state.[69]

This ideology and the mythology by which it is expressed can be uncovered from a combination of details concerning specific rituals and relics and how these actions and objects are related to particular episodes in the accounts of the origins of human and Islamic civilization. Muslim historical and exegetical texts describe the dispatch of prophets with different revelations over the course of civilization, from its origins in the fall from Eden to its culmination on the Day of Resurrection. Rituals and relics are described in Muslim legal texts and other sorts of sources as relating directly to the succession of prophets and their role in establishing religion and society to govern and guide humanity in its fallen existence. Taken individually, no single Muslim source provides a synthetic overview linking rituals, relics, and civilization, though state patronage of scholarship and religious sites might account for the confluence of these concepts. According to the ideology behind the definition of these concepts, the state is required to organize society in accordance with the stipulations of religion, which are themselves designed to remind people of the disjunction separating their current existence and the utopia of Eden.

In order to uncover some of the ways rituals and relics connect with a larger mythology and ideology of Islamic civilization, it is necessary to go beyond the confines of categories generated by attempts to fit Islamic materials into preconceived notions of the differences between Islam and other religions. Such an approach is similar to the attitude and method adopted by Robertson Smith in his eschewal of prejudices which excluded biblical religion, especially Christianity, from the comparative study of religion. Robertson Smith's wide-ranging combination of textual and ethnographic sources allowed him to recognize the outlines of a more general concept of sacrifice and religion that was otherwise obscured by what constituted the proper subjects for the study of the Bible. It should also be noted that although Robertson Smith did provide a model which could be applied in other contexts, he focused his attention on explaining the specific details of the ancient Semites rather than generalizing from a superficial understanding of the sources.

Following the example of Robertson Smith, this book pays careful attention to philological detail and the specific terminology and concepts of different Islamic textual genres as a means to transcend the categories of secondary scholarship and to open Islamic materials to fresh comparison. Such specialized research is to be combined with the insights of cultural anthropologists, art historians, and literary critics to help integrate the Islamic examples into the generic study of religion. The focus here is not on any particular instance of ritual or relic but rather on the synthesis of more general models of ritual and relics from a variety of Islamic sources.

It may be that the Islamic conception of ritual, relics, and territory, and their relation to myth and ideology, will challenge conventional, generic understandings of these terms. The goal of this book, however, is to provide a theory that is judged by whether it makes sense of and provides a rational explanation for the existence and use of rituals, relics, and territory in their Islamic contexts.

The following four chapters use a number of comparisons to highlight the distinctive character of Islamic conceptions of ritual, relics, and territory. Some of these examples might be related, as historical influences, to the earliest Islamic sources. These include late antique Christian traditions regarding relics and the recovery of sacred sites, inscriptions from the ancient Near East, and the Hellenistic accounts of the distribution of the relics of Horus in Egypt. Such examples help to explain the larger cultural context within which Islamic materials are situated. Other examples are treated as analogies and are not intended to indicate any historical influences. These include references to the ritual bear hunts, Taoist and Buddhist burials of bronze mirrors and texts, the Sumerian myth of the distribution of the "Me" by Enki, the distribution and burial of the parts of the Buddha's body, Iroquois conceptions of wampum and its relationship to land ownership, European and American curiosity shops compared with the patronage and display of relics as sites for visitation, Hindu and Hawaiian definitions of kingship based on different conceptions of the pure and the sacred, the worldview of contemporary surfing culture as a contrast to the utopian character of ritual, and the Lele Pangolin cult as described by Mary Douglas as displaying the conscious use of natural symbols to think about social issues.

It would be absurd to reduce the interpretation of the larger Islamic examples under consideration to the terms of these analogies, just as it would be a mistake to reduce an Islamic example to the sum of its historical influences. In his study of the ritual bear hunts, and in other contexts, J. Z. Smith insists on the need to use analogies which highlight not historical connections but the logical connections of different examples to theorize about religion. In part, this is to help make explicit the perspective and disciplinary framework which scholars employ in the selection and interpretation of their examples. It is also necessary in order to avoid too much reliance upon received categories that would hinder the distillation of more generic models from a wider variety of sources. Such comparisons are used in this book as heuristic models suggesting fresh patterns in the Islamic materials under consideration, and ultimately I consider the Islamic material itself as an example in the larger study of religion. This book will have served its purpose if it succeeds in stimulating new ways of thinking about the use of sacred objects, actions, and locations in the display of political power and religious authority in different cultural and historical contexts.

## CHAPTER OUTLINE

The four chapters in this book develop different issues related to ritual, relics, and territory in Islam. The chapters are not arranged according to types of sources, nor are they chronologically bounded. Each of the chapters might be seen as a transparency laid atop one another, and, as such, they are interrelated and meant to be read together, though each of the chapters addresses separately the larger thesis of the book. Chapter 1 provides an example of the mythology of the origins of human and Islamic civilization. Chapters 2, 3, and 4 show how this narrative mythology is reflected in Islamic definitions of ritual, relics, and the tombs of prophets. Various accounts of the stories of Adam and Eve in the garden of Eden, their fall, and the establishment of civilization at Mecca are present throughout all the chapters, as is the conclusion that a more general ideology of the necessity of the state underlies this mythology and its representation in ritual and relics. The relationship of the mythology and ideology is made explicit in the course of the four chapters through the uncovering of specific details of certain rituals and relics and the role of both rituals and relics in delineating the sacred status of the sanctuary at Mecca.

Chapter 1 provides an outline of the more general myth of the origins of Islamic civilization by examining the accounts of the recovery of the treasure of the Kaʿbah by ʿAbd al-Muṭṭalib, the paternal grandfather of the prophet Muhammad. The accounts are drawn from some of the earliest extant Islamic sources on Mecca, including Ibn Saʿd and Ibn Isḥāq's biography of the prophet Muhammad (extant in the recension of Ibn Hishām), the world histories of al-Ṭabarī and al-Yaʿqūbī, and al-Azraqī's history of Mecca. Section 1 compares ʿAbd al-Muṭṭalib's role in the recovery of the treasure and the details of its contents to ancient Near Eastern foundational and offering inscriptions, Jewish and Samaritan traditions regarding the loss and recovery of the tabernacle and temple vessels, and other examples of treasure burial, including the late antique and Islamic motif of the Cave of the Treasure associated with the tomb of Adam. Section 2 outlines the association of the treasure with the named swords and armor of the prophet Muhammad from Sunnī and Shiʿī collections of ḥadīth reports and their commentaries in the historical and biographical works of al-Wāqidī, Ibn Saʿd, Ibn al-Athīr, al-Dhahabī and in the Quran commentaries of Ibn al-Jawzī, Muḥammad b. Aḥmad al-Qurṭubī, and Ibn Kathīr. References to metalurgical texts, such as those attributed to al-Kindī and al-Bīrūnī, help to inform the discussion of the origins of certain metals and swords, and such information is also recorded in lexical and geographical works.

Chapter 2 focuses on definitions of certain obligatory rituals related to the garden of Eden and the origins of civilization at the sanctuary of Mecca. These definitions are drawn from a variety of Sunnī and Shiʿī texts from all the major legal schools, including collections of legal opinions, commentaries on these collections, and legal commentaries on ḥadīth reports. Section 1 examines the positions of various Sunnī and Shiʿī legal theorists regarding the opinion that touching the penis (and related genitalia) requires the performance of ritual purification (wuḍūʾ). This is supplemented by more general comparative works of legal theory, such as those of Ibn Rushd, Ibn Qudāmah, and Ibn Taymīyah. In section 2, the stories of Adam and Eve in the garden of Eden and their residence in Mecca after the fall are extracted from commentaries on the Quran, the stories of the prophets, and ḥadīth reports, including those of al-Ṭabarī, al-Thaʿlabī, al-Qurṭubī, and Ibn Kathīr. A comparison of these different genres and texts shows the close correspondence between the narrative of exegetical stories concerning the origins of civilization and the more systematic, technical definitions of purity and other obligatory rituals in legal scholarship.

Chapter 3 draws on a wide array of Islamic and non-Islamic sources for details about the treatment of the relics of the prophet Muhammad and how these relics relate to the sacred status of the sanctuary at Mecca. The dispersal and collection of the prophet Muhammad's hair and nails, footprints, ḥadīth reports, and various artifacts are recounted in ḥadīth collections, biographical dictionaries, and legal commentaries used in earlier chapters. These are examined in section 1. Section 2 highlights accounts from Quran commentaries and world histories concerning the relics of other prophets and the association of prophetic relics with the origins of human civilization. Section 2 also uses information on prophetic relics from the accounts of travelers, geographers, and pilgrimage guides, such as those of al-Maqdisī, Ibn al-Ḥawrānī, al-Harawī, Mujīr al-Dīn, al-Suyūṭī, ʿAbd al-Ghanī al-Nābulsī, and various European travelers. This is supplemented by certain state histories of different Middle Eastern and Asian Islamic dynasties to describe the identification and patronage of relics, highlighting attempts to demonstrate authority through linkages to the prophets and the locations of their activities.

Chapter 4 investigates the long tombs associated with the earliest prophets who are mentioned in the Quran and its exegesis. Section 1 outlines the depictions of these tombs found in the accounts of Muslim pilgrims, European travelers, and art historical and archaeological surveys done in the past two centuries. These sources describe long tombs of prophets, up to 150 meters in length, in the Middle East, Central Asia, and South Asia. The so-called "nine-yard" (nau-gaz) tombs of South and Southeast Asia, attributed primarily to the Muslims who died during the earliest conquests of Sind, are also included in this analysis. In order to contextualize these tombs and explain their extraordinary length, section 2 examines various accounts of giants and the recovery of their remains in the Quran, Muslim exegesis, the Bible, ancient Greek sources, and European folklore. These accounts demonstrate the Muslim appropriation of a widespread mythological motif in which giants represent a stage in human history away from which civilization has developed with the rise of technology and the law-based state.

A synthesis of these various sources suggests some more general conclusions relevant to the study of Islam and religion. The identification and patronage of relics, along with the mosques, madrasas, and tombs in which they are preserved, may be seen as resulting in the establishment of physical reminders of the loss of Eden and the concomitant need for religion and the social order maintained by the jurists and the state. Rules pertaining to purification and other obligatory rituals supply a map of the jurists' broad conception of the oppositions denoting the pure and impure, and the sacred and profane. Not unlike the physical symbols of relics, this categorization of the pure and impure, and the sacred and profane, reflects the separation of Eden and human civilization. The same separation between Eden and civilization is exemplified in the narrative accounts of the treasure of the Kaʿbah and the swords of the prophet Muhammad. The sort of ideology exhibited in this mythology, and its representation in relics and ritual, appears to be a justification for the existence of society and the state, necessitated by the loss of the Edenic utopia.

This book is not a systematic overview of relics and ritual in Islamic contexts, nor does it provide a full analysis of the history of the definitions of the sanctuary in Mecca. Rather, select concepts from diverse historical and geographical settings are highlighted to suggest the outlines of a larger theory of how certain objects and actions are defined in relation to the territorial origins and spread of Islamic civilization. In short, this book studies discrete examples of relics and rituals used to define the authority of the prophet Muhammad and the largely interpretive Muslim scholarship that is built upon that authority. It does so in order to raise larger questions about the definition of authority vis-à-vis religious myth and ritual. The following analyses suggest that this image of authority relies upon the myth of the fall from a utopia to justify the continued existence of an imperfect social structure based upon absolute notions of right and wrong perpetuated by the institutions of Quran exegesis and Islamic law.

CHAPTER ONE

# *Treasure of the Kaʿbah*

In his biography of the prophet Muhammad, ʿAbd al-Mālik Ibn Hishām (d. 834) cites a report, on the authority of Muḥammad b. Isḥāq (d. 768), regarding ʿAbd al-Muṭṭalib's recovery of the well of Zamzam and a buried treasure: "He [ʿAbd al-Muṭṭalib] continued digging until the top of the well appeared to him. He praised God because he knew that he had been right [about its buried location]. When he continued digging he found in it two gazelles of gold. These were the two gazelles which the Jurhum had buried in the well when they left Mecca. He also found in it Qalʿī swords and armor."[1] "ʿAbd al-Muṭṭalib made the swords into a door for the Kaʿbah, and pounded the two gazelles of gold into the door. This was the first gold ornamentation of the Kaʿbah. Then ʿAbd al-Muttalib began giving the water of Zamzam to the pilgrims."[2] The well of Zamzam is said to have been discovered originally by Ishmael and his mother Hagar at the place that would later be identified with the precincts of the sanctuary at Mecca. The Jurhum are said to have settled in Mecca with Ishmael and Hagar and continued as the guardians of the sanctuary until they were forced to leave by another group of people called the Khuzāʿah. An almost identical account is found in the history of Muḥammad b. Jarīr al-Ṭabarī (d. 923), and Aḥmad b. Abī Yaʿqūb al-Yaʿqūbī (d. 905) records that ʿAbd al-Muṭṭalib uncovered swords, weapons, and two gazelles of gold.[3] In his history of Mecca, Muḥammad b. ʿAbdallāh al-Azraqī (d. 921) mentions the two gazelles of gold that were in the Kaʿbah and the Qalʿī swords that were buried in the well of Zamzam.[4]

Aḥmad Ibn Saʿd (ca. 784–845) mentions another version of this account, which specifies the number of swords and armor and the type of armor uncovered by ʿAbd al-Muṭṭalib but does not indicate that the discovery was related to the well of Zamzam: "Ibn ʿUmar: When the Jurhum were preparing to leave Mecca they buried the two gazelles, seven Qalʿī swords, and five complete suits of armor. ʿAbd al-Muṭṭalib excavated this. It had been desecrated and was the cause of great abomination. He pounded the two gazelles, which were of gold, as a plating on the face of the Kaʿbah, and he hung the swords on the two doors by which he wanted to protect the treasury of the Kaʿbah [khizānat al-Kaʿbah], and he made keys and a lock from gold."[5] In this account and others there is agreement on the fact that the treasure consisted of the two golden gazelles, Qalʿī swords, and armor. The accounts also agree that this treasure was uncovered by ʿAbd al-Muṭṭalib, the paternal grandfather of the prophet Muhammad, and that the treasure had been buried by the Jurhum when they left Mecca. Most of the accounts also describe how ʿAbd al-Muṭṭalib used the treasure to adorn and protect the Kaʿbah.

Little attention has been paid to the details of the treasure. Later Muslim scholarship often mentions but does not elaborate on its significance, and there is no explicit connection among the recovery of the treasure, the recovery of the well, and the reestablishment of the sanctuary at Mecca under the prophet Muhammad. Recent scholarship interested in reconstructing the origins of the sanctuary at Mecca has focused on the significance of the well of Zamzam, especially the accounts of its rediscovery by ʿAbd al-Muṭṭalib, but has commented on the treasure only in passing.[6] G. R. Hawting studies some of the accounts of the recovery of the treasure and the well of Zamzam, also focusing not on the contents of the treasure but on how the accounts of its recovery are associated with Zamzam.[7] A number of details in the accounts of the treasure still require further comment, including the expression "Qalʿī swords" and the reason for the burial of arms and armor in the sanctuary at Mecca.

This chapter examines a number of issues related to the early Muslim accounts of the recovery of this treasure. The description of the treasure and its discovery is a part of and an example of the larger mythological conception of the origins of human and Islamic civilization. Section 1 focuses on the different accounts of the burial and recovery of objects at the sanctuary in Mecca, with reference to Hawting's theory concerning the origins of the Muslim traditions in Jewish eschatology. Analysis of various traditions about the burial of objects in the sanctuary in Mecca suggests that the Muslim accounts of the treasure are best understood as purposeful attempts to describe the origins of Islam in terms familiar from the ancient and late antique Near East. Section 2 concentrates on the particular contents of the treasure, especially the swords and the armor, to illustrate how these items are used in Muslim sources to link the origins of Islam with certain pre-Islamic kings and prophets. The golden gazelles, swords, and armor have specific symbolic associations upon which the Muslim accounts draw to delineate a certain conception of territory and its relation to the relics of the prophet Muhammad.

## 1: TEMPLE IMPLEMENTS AND TREASURE OF THE KAʿBAH

In his 1980 article, G. R. Hawting asserts that the Muslim accounts of the disappearance and rediscovery of Zamzam are derived from what he calls Jewish traditions regarding the loss and recovery of the temple implements or sacred sanctuary objects:

> There are, therefore, a number of obvious similarities between these [Jewish] traditions and the Muslim traditions associated with the loss of Zamzam. The loss of objects of great importance for the sanctuary and its cult, which is the main theme of the Jewish traditions, can be discerned in the Muslim traditions adduced to account for the loss of Zamzam. The recovery of the objects, which in Judaism is consigned to eschatology, has in Islam become an historical fact. The loss and recovery of the hiding place of the sacred objects, which is the main theme of the Muslim traditions, can also be seen in the Jewish traditions about the loss of the sacred objects.[8]

Hawting illustrates these close parallels with a number of examples—specifically, the account of the hiding of the temple implements by the prophet Jeremiah in 2 Maccabees 2:4–8 and several accounts involving Samaritan traditions regarding the loss and recovery of special objects.

These parallels might appear to suggest that the accounts of Zamzam and the buried treasure of the Kaʿbah found their way into Muslim sources by accident and that Muslim sources were at odds trying to explain their significance. Citing A. J. Wensinck, Hawting posits that the earliest Muslim conception associated the sanctuary of Mecca with a pit, related to the more general Semitic notion of the sanctuary as the "navel of the earth."[9] According to Hawting, this conception was derived from Jewish ideas, including the notion that this pit was the hiding place of the temple implements. When Muslim accounts associated the pit with the well of Zamzam, however, the original significance of the buried objects was forgotten or displaced.[10]

With its emphasis on the Jewish origins of the treasure motif and lack of attention to possible reasons for its purposeful inclusion in Muslim accounts of the sanctuary at Mecca, Hawting's explanation is misleading. His approach and conclusions are not unlike the explanations commonly given for the parallels between Jewish and Muslim interpretations of the Bible and

Quran. Scholars routinely cite Jewish (and Christian) parallels with Muslim texts as evidence that the Quran and Muslim exegesis is derived from the Bible and the interpretive traditions of Jews and Christians. Discrepancies between the parallels are used to demonstrate that the transmission from Jewish and Christian sources was garbled, and that the Muslim texts are unaware of the original or "correct" significance of the motifs and narratives they have adopted.[11]

The limitations of this approach are evident in the texts and traditions cited by Hawting as parallels for the Muslim accounts of the treasure and its recovery. Hawting cites two examples from Samaritan texts, in addition to an account recorded by Josephus.[12] The fullest example comes from a late chronicle, which is a continuation of an earlier chronicle composed in the fourteenth century CE.[13] In this and other late Samaritan texts, the recovery of the temple vessels is associated with the messianic figure called the Taheb.[14] Hawting also cites an earlier text, the Memar Marqah, a collection of sermons attributed to the Samaritan thinker Marqah, who lived in the third or fourth century CE.[15] Linguistic and textual analysis has shown, however, that the Memar Marqah was redacted multiple times over the centuries, and the extant text is difficult to date before the eleventh century CE.[16] Also, the account in the Memar Marqah is not about hiding the vessels of the Jerusalem temple, but rather about hiding the tabernacle and the tabernacle implements used by the Israelites in the wilderness of wandering.[17] This motif of hiding the tabernacle and its implements appears to be a separate tradition, perhaps related to the hiding of the temple vessels but attested separately in other contexts such as the Babylonian Talmud (Sotah 9a), which states that the implements from the wilderness tabernacle were stored in the crypts under the temple in Jerusalem.[18]

Limiting the origins of the motif of hiding the temple vessels to Judaism is too restricting. As does 2 Maccabees 2:4–8, the pseudepigraphical Lives of the Prophets (2:11–19) states that Jeremiah took the "Ark of the Law and the things in it" and caused them to be swallowed up by a rock.[19] The Babylonian Talmud (Keritot 5b, Yoma 53b, Sanhedrin 26b, Zebahim 62a, Horayot 12a) and Jerusalem Talmud (Sotah 8:22c) record that the temple vessels were hidden under a rock in Jerusalem by King Josiah.[20] Other rabbinic texts, such as the Mekhilta de Rabbi Ishmael (5:51b) and the Pesiqta de Rab Kahana (32a),[21] explicitly refer to the recovery of the objects in a messianic context, and one of the Sibylline Oracles (2:188) makes reference to Elijah as the one who will restore the objects to the temple in Jerusalem at the end of time.[22] In the Syriac 2 Baruch (6:7–9) an angel takes the veil, ephod, mercy seat, two tablets, priestly raiment, altar of incense, forty-eight precious stones, and all the "holy vessels of the tabernacle" and causes the earth to swallow them.[23] Eusebius, citing Alexander Polyhistor, states that the temple vessels were taken to Babylon, except for the ark and the tablets, which were left in the possession of Jeremiah.[24] These various texts demonstrate that the motif of the hidden temple vessels was widespread and can be found in a number of different religious traditions.

There are many examples of objects with religious significance being hidden that are not directly related to the motif of the temple vessels from Jerusalem or the tabernacle in the wilderness of wandering. The Copper Scroll (3Q15) from Qumran provides a list of some sixty items, including gold, silver, furniture, aromatics, utensils, scrolls, and a copy of a more detailed list of other things hidden in various underground locations.[25] Many of the hiding places are identified as "pits" or "cisterns," and the description of the treasure is given. The various explanations given for these buried treasures include that the Copper Scroll is from the library of the sectarians at Qumran, from the Jerusalem temple, from the Bar-Kokhba revolt, or from the medieval period and that it is a fraud designed to mislead treasure-hunting invaders.[26] Also found in the vicinity of Jerusalem but unconnected to the Israelite temple is a collection of artifacts from the so-called Cave of the Treasure discovered at Naḥal Mishmar. The buried cache, which dates to the Chalcolithic period, consists of both weapons and armaments (mace-heads, copper crowns, standards), numerous instruments representing gazelles, copper horns, and a variety of jars, ivory objects, and other miscellaneous objects.[27] Examples from further afield, such as the ritual burial of bronze mirrors in Han China, attest to the variety and widespread character of the purposeful burial of certain objects.[28]

A number of Jewish and Christian texts refer to the Cave of Treasures, in which Adam or his son Seth hid certain objects.[29] The Life of Adam and Eve mentions tablets of stone and clay which Eve commanded her children to make and bury.[30] These tablets are later uncovered by Solomon.[31] Josephus refers to these tablets or pillars erected by the children of Adam and Eve as containing astronomical secrets, and the Syriac Treatise of Shem attributes such calendrical and astrological knowledge to the son of Noah. The Abot de Rabbi Nathan (31), Genesis Rabbah (26), 2 Enoch 33:8–12, and Philo in his Life of Moses (2:36) also refer to this testament left by the children of Adam and Eve.[32] The Syriac Testament of Adam is an account of prophecies concerning the hours of the day, and the Coptic Three Steles of Seth contain the revelation of three pillars inscribed by Seth with hymns to a trinity of heavenly beings.[33] These texts are said to have been buried by Seth in the Cave of Treasures along with the things Adam had removed from the garden of Eden, including the gold, myrrh, and frankincense which the Magi would retrieve and offer as gifts to Jesus at the time of his birth.[34] Muslim sources mention a Cave of the Treasure in which Adam is supposed to be buried. The burial of secret books is also known from many other contexts, including the Arabic Hermetical tradition and Buddhism.[35]

## CONTENTS OF TREASURE AND VOTIVE OFFERINGS

None of these examples, however, seems to parallel closely or explain the particular description of the contents of the treasure recovered by ʿAbd al-Muṭṭalib. Nor do these parallels account for the specific mention that the treasure consisted in part of swords and armor. A more detailed examination of early Islamic accounts of the treasure and the history of the sanctuary at Mecca suggests that the treasure is understood to be linked with votive offerings made to the Kaʿbah and Zamzam by pre-Islamic kings. The contents of the treasure and its burial are also closely linked in Islamic sources to the custodianship of the sanctuary at Mecca. Emphasizing these elements, the Islamic accounts of the treasure associate ʿAbd al-Muṭṭalib with the widespread Near Eastern motif of the king as founder of the national sanctuary.

In some accounts, the foundation of the Kaʿbah by Abraham is specifically linked with the treasure. Hawting claims that "along with the gazelles and swords the Jurhum chief buried the *ḥajar al-rukn*" when the Jurhum were ousted by the Khuzāʿah.[36] The *ḥajar al-rukn* is the "foundation stone" usually connected with the building of the Kaʿbah by Abraham and Ishmael. The mention of the swords, however, does not occur in all of these accounts of the burial by the chief of the Jurhum. According to al-Ṭabarī, after the death of Nabt, the son of Ishmael, and Ishmael's Jurhumī wife, the Jurhum took control of the custodianship of the Kaʿbah. When the Jurhum began to misappropriate the belongings which had been given to the Kaʿbah as votive offerings and commit fornication inside the Kaʿbah itself, God sent plagues against the Jurhum and the Khuzāʿah attacked them. The leader of the Jurhum, ʿAmr b. al-Ḥārith b. Muḍāḍ, brought out the two gazelles of the Kaʿbah and the foundation stone (ḥajar al-rukn), asking God for forgiveness, but God did not respond. So he threw the two gazelles and the foundation stone into Zamzam, buried them, and left Mecca with the rest of the Jurhum who had survived.[37] A similar account is given by Ibn Hishām, though it states only that the leader of the Jurhum buried the two gazelles and the foundation stone, omitting the description of the Jurhum leader's use of the objects in the attempt to gain God's help.[38]

In another context, al-Azraqī links the burial of the objects with the son of the Jurhum leader featured in the accounts of al-Ṭabarī and Ibn Hishām, Muḍāḍ b. ʿAmr b. al-Ḥārith b. Muḍāḍ.

> When Muḍāḍ b. ʿAmr b. al-Ḥārith b. Muḍāḍ saw what the Jurhum were doing in the sanctuary [al-ḥaram], what they were stealing from the property of the Kaʿbah, both in secret and openly, he went for the two gazelles which were in the Kaʿbah, of gold, and the Qalʿī swords. He buried them in the place of the well of Zamzam. The water of Zamzam had dried up and disappeared when the Jurhum had done what they had done in the sanctuary, so that the place of the well had been hidden and obliterated. Muḍāḍ b. ʿAmr and his son got up in a dark night and dug deeply in the place of the well of Zamzam and then buried in it the swords and the two gazelles.[39]

In this account the burial of the gazelles and swords seems designed to hide them from the Jurhum, who were defiling the sanctuary, whereas in the accounts of al-Ṭabarī and Ibn Hishām the burial seems designed to hide the treasure from the invading Khuzāʿah. None of these accounts mentions armor as part of the treasure buried, although it is consistently mentioned as part of the items recovered by ʿAbd al-Muṭṭalib. These accounts do link the treasure with custodianship of the sanctuary.

Uri Rubin has noted a number of reports of votive objects' being cast into the well of Zamzam, many of which mention both golden gazelles (although not always two of them) and swords, often along with other items. Rubin uses these examples to dispute Hawting's denial that the treasure could have been, as the Muslim sources claim, items given to the Kaʿbah as votive offerings.[40] In one account cited by Abū al-Ḥasan ʿAlī al-Masʿūdī (d. 956), it is stated that the Sasanian Sāsān b. Bābāk put into Zamzam two gold gazelles, swords, and some gold.[41] Another report, cited on the authority of Ibn al-Kalbī, records that it was the Iranian king Bābāk b. Sāsān who buried swords and jewelry in the place of the well of Zamzam.[42] Other reports given on the authority of Saʿīd b. Jubayr, ʿIkrimah, Saʿīd b. al-Musayyab, and al-Zuhrī mention the swords and gazelles as having been votive offerings but do not associate them specifically with Iranian kings.[43]

Royal votive offerings to shrines and sanctuaries were widespread in the ancient Near East, and numerous examples are attested for the Arabian Peninsula. An inscription from Assur mentions the placing of precious stones and spices from the king of Saba in the foundation of a temple built for the New Year's Festival (bīt Akītu).[44] Other offerings included perishable items such as food and drink offerings but also figurines and statuettes in human or animal form made of stone, metal, and other substances.[45] The spoils of war, including arms and armor, and the spoils of the hunt, including live and slain animals and animal images, are attested as offerings to the gods.[46] Stelae and statues often portray gods clad in armor and armed with weapons, and the image of the deity as a warrior figure is widespread in the Near East and elsewhere.[47] That the burial of arms and armor was not uncommon in the Arabian Peninsula is demonstrated by archaeological finds such as the burial of armor in a second-century-CE grave at Janussan on the island of Bahrain.[48] An Aramaic inscription from North Arabia describes the dedication of two camel figurines to Dushara, and a Sabaean inscription records the offering of a bronze horse and rider to Almaqah.[49] Other Semitic inscriptions, such as the Temple of Baʿal inscription, provide evidence that gold and other items could be substituted for the offering of actual animals.[50]

Gazelles and horns associated with game are also widely attested as votive offerings in the Near East and in Arabia. In a Ḥaḍramī inscription from about the third century CE, the king of Ḥaḍramawt makes an offering of twenty-five gazelles on the occasion of his rebuilding of the temple and fortress in the city of Shabwah.[51] Offering the quarry from a ritual hunt at the founding of a sanctuary was a regular practice among the kings of South Arabia, as attested by numerous inscriptions and reliefs.[52] In both classical and more recent examples of hunting among the Arabs, the killing of gazelles and the distribution of meat is a ritual that reaffirms the authority of the chief and the loyalty of his subjects to him.[53] In classical Ḥaḍramī practice the head huntsman is the priest-king, and the ritual hunt involves purification and the circumambulation of cultic rocks both before and after the hunt.[54] Numerous horns are reported in connection with the Kaʿbah and the sanctuary at Mecca, including crescent horns of gold and the horns said to be from the ram offered by Abraham instead of his son Ishmael.[55]

According to Muḥammad b. Aḥmad al-Bīrūnī (d. 1048), ʿAbd al-Muṭṭalib's gift of the gazelles and swords to the Kaʿbah was an example of a royal votive offering that was imitated later by ʿUmar b. al-Khaṭṭāb, who hung two crescent moons or horns conveyed to him from the capture of Madaʾin along with his earnings and divination arrows made from gems.[56] That votive offerings were given to the Kaʿbah by South Arabian kings is also evident from the widespread tradition that the first covering (kiswā) was given to the Kaʿbah by the Tubbaʿ king of South Arabia identified as Asʿad Abū Karib al-Ḥimyarī. In his exegesis of Q 44:37, ʿImād al-Dīn Ismāʿīl Ibn Kathīr (d. 1373) relates that one of the kings of Tubbaʿ intended to destroy the Kaʿbah but was advised by two Jews that it had been built by Abraham and would be of great importance to a prophet sent at the end of time. The king of Tubbaʿ circumambulated the Kaʿbah and dressed it with fine cloths before calling all the people of Yemen to the religion of Moses.[57] Other accounts state that the Tubbaʿ king provided the Kaʿbah with a lock, as did ʿAbd al-Muṭṭalib, and it is reported that the ʿAbbasid caliph Muʿtaṣim presented the Kaʿbah with a gold lock (qufl) weighing a thousand mithqals.[58] According to al-Azraqī, the treasury of the

Kaʿbah used to hold all the votive offerings, including arrows used for divination, jewelry for adorning idols, and gold.[59] It is reported that the prophet Muhammad uncovered a large amount of gold in the well of the Kaʿbah. He left it there, and it was untouched until Ḥusayn b. ʿAlī removed it.[60]

Examples of weapons and armor sent as gifts are well known in the early Islamic period. The *Kitāb al-hadāyā wa al-tuḥaf* attributed to al-Qāḍī Ibn al-Zubayr (d. 1167) mentions the gift of a mounted horseman armed with a sword embossed with reptile skin and set with precious stones.[61] The king of Tibet is reported to have sent one hundred gilded Tibetan shields along with one thousand mana of musk (no. 3). Frequently, gifts of arms and armor are sent between rulers, such as the swords, girdles, spears, shields, and equipped beasts of burden sent from the ruler of Khurasān to the caliph Jaʿfar al-Muqtadir, and the swords, shields, and spears sent to al-Muktafī from a European queen (nos. 69, 70). The Byzantine emperor sent to the caliph al-Rāḍī a treasure of ornamented knives and a battle-ax studded with precious stones and pearls (no. 73). These treasures are also closely associated with ancient and famous kings. The Byzantine emperor is said to have sent al-Mustanṣir three heavy saddles of enamel inlaid with gold and saddles from Alexander the Great (no. 90). Another report mentions the discovery of saddles locked in a crate of palm fronds, one of them being one of the six saddles that had belonged to Dhū al-Qarnayn and later transferred from him to the Byzantine state treasuries (no. 99).

The Muslim accounts which describe ʿAbd al-Muṭṭalib's discovery of the treasure and subsequent gift to the sanctuary at Mecca closely parallel other ancient Near Eastern narratives of sanctuary foundations. The inscription on bricks found at Mari for the dedication of the Shamash temple mentions King Yahdun-Lim's securing and establishment of the house for Shamash, and the gift of a mighty weapon to the king by Shamash.[62] Other Near Eastern accounts also associate the establishment of the sanctuary with weapons, such as the Gudea inscriptions and the Ugaritic accounts of the sanctuary at Zaphon.[63] The Assyrian king Hammurabi also is depicted as securing the land, establishing sanctuaries, and providing water for his people.[64] Likewise, the accounts of Samsuiluna, the king of Babylon, the verse account of Nabonidus, the Moabite Stone, and the building inscription of Azitawadda of Adana link the civilizing activities of kings, primarily the conquest of peoples and the fortification of cities, with the establishment of sanctuaries.[65] A similar link between the establishing of the sanctuary and the construction of cities and the accoutrements of civilization can be found in South Arabian inscriptions, such as that found on the door of the Minaean capital at Maʿīn.[66]

Similarly, ʿAbd al-Muṭṭalib is portrayed as establishing his rightful claim to the custodianship of the sanctuary, as rebuilding the Kaʿbah, providing a door and a lock as well as ornamentation, and he provides water for the people of the area. The recovery of the treasure by ʿAbd al-Muṭṭalib is explicitly linked with the prophecies concerning the future prophethood and leadership of Muhammad.[67] Quṣayy is also closely associated with the reestablishment of the sanctuary at Mecca and with ʿAbd al-Muṭṭalib. He drives the Khuzāʿah out of Mecca, takes control of the sanctuary, and settles the Quraysh there.[68] Many sources describe Quṣayy in terms commensurate not only with ancient Near Eastern kings but also with other mythical civilizing figures such as the Greek Atlas or the Iranian king Oshahanj, who, according to al-Ṭabarī, was the first to build buildings, mosques, and the cities of Babylon and Susa.[69] Both Quṣayy and ʿAbd al-Muṭṭalib also establish themselves as hereditary custodians of the sanctuary, as did the priest-kings of South Arabia.[70] Akkadian texts prescribe certain rituals for the repair of temples, and Hittite texts describe special rituals for the erection of new buildings, including houses and palaces.[71] Quṣayy was responsible for the administration of the Dār al-Nadwah, providing pilgrims with food (rifāda) and drink (siqāyah), and with the supervision of the Kaʿbah (sidāna, ḥijāba). After his death these responsibilities reportedly were divided among his sons, but ʿAbd al-Muṭṭalib took control of both the provisions and the supervision of the Kaʿbah with his recovery of the treasure.

Muslim sources describe the Kaʿbah and the Meccan sanctuary in terms familiar from the descriptions of other temples of the ancient Near East. In his history of Mecca, al-Azraqī gives detailed measurements of the Kaʿbah and the surrounding sanctuary.[72] He also provides a number of traditions regarding the vessels of the Kaʿbah and its ornamentation, with particular attention to the dressing of the Kaʿbah with the *kiswā* cloth.[73] Such descriptions of the dimensions and accoutrements of temples is widespread and characteristic of temple registers in other Near Eastern contexts, including the accounts of the Israelite tabernacle in Exodus 26–40 and the Jerusalem temple in Ezekiel 40–42, the Temple Scroll, and the Mishnaic tractate Middot.[74] Elaborate and often striking descriptions of temple and city walls, and their connection with sovereignty, are common in the ancient Near East.[75]

It is important to note that in the various reports of his discovery of the treasure in Mecca, ʿAbd al-Muṭṭalib does not recover the black stone or "foundation stone" (ḥajar al-rukn) that is reported to have been buried along with the two gold gazelles by the Jurhum. Nor is such a foundation stone mentioned in the reports of the various votive offerings, outside the accounts of the burial of the implements by the Jurhum chieftain. The marked absence of this stone from the recovered treasure is significant. Such stones, especially black stones, were used as the main cult objects for the worship of other Arabian gods.[76] According to Epiphanius, the Nabataean god Dhushara (Dhū al-Shāra) was represented by something called a "khaabou," which represented the deity.[77] The Byzantine lexicographer Suidas reports that this was a black stone, roughly square, four feet high by two feet wide.[78] Antoninus Placentinus relates that in Sinai the local Arabs had an idol which changed from snow white to pitch black, perhaps related to the shedding of blood over it.[79] Q 5:3 refers to the food slaughtered on stone altars, and Ibn al-Kalbī relates that a number of Arab deities were represented by stones.[80]

In the accounts concerning ʿAbd al-Muṭṭalib's recovery of the treasure, however, the object uncovered at the establishment of the sanctuary is not the cult object but rather the well of Abraham and Ishmael, the swords of the Israelites, and the gifts of Arab and Iranian kings.[81] This is in striking contrast to the fact that ʿAbd al-Muṭṭalib is said to recover Zamzam in a location near the two idols where the Quraysh used to perform their sacrifices. In other Arabian contexts, the custodian of the sanctuary is often portrayed as gaining his office by establishing the altar or cult object. For example, a limestone stela from Tayma shows the priest-custodian of the god Salm performing the ritual installation of his cult object.[82] Often, the custodian is said to practice divination, and the foundation of the sanctuary sometimes includes receiving a dream from the deity, as is the case in the accounts of ʿAbd al-Muṭṭalib and Zamzam.[83] The many accounts of the recovery of the True Cross and the building of the churches in Palestine likewise emphasize the priority of the uncovering of the cult object.[84] Also evident in the legends of the True Cross is the close connection between the discovery of the cult object by the king figure and the establishment of cult sanctuaries.[85] In these legends of the True Cross, examples from the ancient Near East, and the accounts of ʿAbd al-Muṭṭalib, the establishment of the sanctuary is linked to the civilizing function of the royal or priestly figure who recovers lost territory. Similar examples can be adduced from ancient China, Rome, Egypt, and Southeast Asia.[86] The recovery of relics and the rituals accompanying the establishment of the sanctuary or state capital mark the origins of a new age of civilization.

## 2: SWORDS AND THE ORIGINS OF ISLAM

Although he does not develop the idea, Hawting does refer to the eschatological significance of the loss and recovery of the temple implements in the Bible and in Samaritan sources. It is possible that the early Muslim sources reflect a conscious attempt to use the account of the recovery of the treasure to signal the dawn of a new prophetic age. The swords and armor, in particular, are relevant to this attempt. According to a number of sources, pilgrims were not supposed to take swords or other weapons into the sanctuaries at Mecca and at other locations.[87] The rules for the visitation of other sanctuaries in the area also prohibited the carrying of weapons and required abstaining from sex while in the sanctuary.[88] Like other Semitic sanctuaries, the sanctuary at Mecca is said to have been a place, marked by stones, considered inviolable, a place of refuge, and a place in which blood was not to be shed.[89] This suggests that the swords and armor, as the two gold gazelles, were not understood as random objects buried in the sanctuary.

## LEXICAL REFERENCES TO SWORDS AND METALS

The specific designation of the recovered swords as "Qalʿī swords" is pertinent to the mythological significance of the accounts of the treasure. According to Abū ʿAbdallāh Yāqūt (d. 1229), the adjective "Qalʿī" may refer to a number of different things, including the name of a mountain in Syria:

> Qalʿah is the name of a tin mine from which the adjective is derived. It is also said that it is a mountain in Syria. Misʿar b. Muhlahal the poet says, in the account of his travels to China: "I returned from China to Kalah. It is the first city of India on the border with China. The caravan stopped there and did not go further. In it is a great fortress [qalʿah] in which is a tin [al-raṣāṣ al-qalʿī] mine which is only in this fortress. In this fortress are pounded the Qalʿī swords which are of ancient India [al-hindiyyah al-ʿatīqah]. The people of this fortress obey their king when they want and disobey him when they want, because there is a tin mine in this fortress. Between it and Sandābul the Chinese city is three hundred parsangs. Around it are well-ordered spread-out cities." Abū al-Riḥān says: "Tin is obtained from Sarnadīb, an island in the Indian Ocean." In al-Andalus is the region of al-Qalʿah from Kūrah Qabrah. I think the term "tin" [al-raṣāṣ al-qalʿī] is related to it because it is obtained from al-Andalus and therefore it is called after it or after some place else that is named al-Qalʿah there. Qalʿah is [also] a place in Yemen and it is from here that the legal scholar al-Qalʿī derives his name.[90]

The notion that "Qalʿah" refers to a mountain in Syria directly links the recovery of the treasure with the traditions about the hiding of the temple implements on a mountain outside Jerusalem.[91] That the term "Qalʿah" or the swords themselves are associated with a location in Syria is also mentioned by several sources cited by Ibn Manẓūr. Both Muḥammad b. Mukarram Ibn Manẓūr (d. 1312) and Yāqūt relate opinions that Marj Qalʿah is a village outside the district of Ḥulwān in Iraq, that it is in open country connected somehow with swords, and that it refers to a place in Yemen.[92] In his dictionary, Muḥammad b. Yaʿqūb al-Fīrūzābādī (d. 1415) locates Qalʿah in Yemen, and Yāqūt claims that the name is associated with Spain.[93] These multiple identifications may, in part, be due to the fact that the term "qalʿah" can refer in a generic sense to any fortress or stronghold, as indicated by Yāqūt's account of the fortress in which the tin is mined in Kalah.

The name Qalʿah and its relation to the adjective apparently formed from it as a descriptive of certain swords is unclear. In his work on minerology, al-Bīrūnī cites al-Bāhilī, who wrote a work on weapons, to demonstrate that the adjective "Qalʿī" refers to Qalʿah, just as the type of sword known as Mashrafī refers to Mishrāf.[94] Continuing with his descriptions of swords, al-Bīrūnī states that the term "Qalʿah" refers to a place and specifically to the type of sword which is made from the metal mined in that place, just as other swords are called Indian or Yemeni, referring to the origins of the materials used to make them.[95] He describes these swords as being broad, and explains that the association of the swords and the adjective "Qalʿī" with other apparently unrelated objects such as sails, types of boats, and mountains arises from the "white" color of the metal used to make the swords.[96] Ibn Manẓūr also explains that using the adjective "Qalʿī," as in "Qalʿī lead" (al-raṣāṣ al-qalʿī), is like saying "good lead" (raṣāṣ jayyid) or "tin," which is also called "white lead" (al-raṣāṣ al-abyāḍ) because it is white in color.[97] A number of other poetic sources mention "Qalʿī" swords, and some appear to identify these as being of Indian or Yemeni origins.[98]

In his work on swords, Yaʿqūb b. Isḥāq al-Kindī (d. ca. 866) lists "Qalʿī" swords as one of three types of "ancient" (ʿatīq) steel-bladed swords used by the Arabs, including "Yemeni" and "Indian" (Hindī or Hindiwānī) swords.[99] He explains that these swords are of non-Arab origin but does not specify the location of Qalʿah other than distinguishing it from Yemen and India.[100] A possible location for Qalʿah suggested by later sources is China or the eastern edge of India on the border with China. Yāqūt, citing Misʿar b. Muhlahal, identifies Qalʿah with the city of Kalah located in India on the border with China. Ibn Saʿīd says that the town of Kalah, in the thirteenth century CE, had a fortress in which a certain type of sword was forged.[101] According to Pliny, the Romans and Parthians used iron from China because it was best known, until exports from Europe increased.[102] The use of Chinese iron is also attested in Islamic times by Ibn Khurradādhbih and Muḥammad b. Muḥammad al-Idrīsī (d. 1165).[103] Others have identified Qalʿah with the region of Kalah in the Malay Peninsula, a successful trading center in later centuries, and have noted the use of the term in various forms to designate tin in other languages, such as Persian, Turkish, Greek, and Portuguese.[104]

Thus, it is possible that the sources reflect a lack of certainty about the origins of Qalʿī swords or the existence of multiple origins for swords given the "Qalʿī" adjective. The use of tin is one of the oldest metallurgical technologies for hardening metals and dates back to a stage immediately succeeding the use of copper. Tin is also one of the metals that is least durable but easiest to treat, and it was not used in the sword making described in Muslim sources such as al-Kindī and al-Bīrūnī.[105] The association of Qalʿī swords with tin, and their connection to the iron imports of China and the East in general, may signify an attempt to demonstrate the antiquity of the swords and the craft utilized to produce them. The uncertainty about the identification of Qalʿah in these later etymological and geographical sources may also be due to a lack of continuity with earlier historical sources that mention certain Qalʿī swords.

## SWORDS OF THE PROPHET MUHAMMAD

One of the swords attributed to the prophet Muhammad is said to be a Qalʿī sword or a sword named al-Qalʿī. In his section on the distribution of booty, Muḥammad b. Ismāʿīl al-Bukhārī (d. 870) cites a number of ḥadīth reports in which there is mention of items that belonged to the prophet Muhammad and were still in use after his death: "Section: What is mentioned concerning the arms of the prophet, his rod, his sword, his arrow, and his ring, and what the successors [khulafāʾ] used after him about which there is no mention that he apportioned it, and concerning his hair, his shoe, and his vessels [ānīyah] which his companions and others considered blessed after his death."[106] This section of al-Bukhārī includes six ḥadīth reports. The first ḥadīth report refers to the ring of the prophet Muhammad, the second to his shoes, the third to some of his clothing, the fourth to his arrow, the fifth to his sword, and the sixth to his giving of some alms (ṣadaqah). In his collection of ḥadīth reports, Muḥammad b. ʿĪsā al-Tirmidhī (d. 893) preserves a report that the prophet Muhammad had a sword of silver and gold.[107] He also cites a report that the pommel of the sword of the Prophet was of silver, and a similar report is recorded by Muḥammad b. ʿUthmān al-Dhahabī (d. 1348) in his biography of the prophet Muhammad.[108] Both Muḥammad b. Yazīd (d. 887) and al-Tirmidhī record a report, transmitted on the authority of Sulaymān b. Ḥabīb, that swords were ornamented with silver and gold.[109] There is also a report related by al-Tirmidhī and al-Dhahabī in which Ibn Sīrīn claims to have made his sword from the sword of Samurah b. Jundab, and that Samurah made his sword from the sword of the prophet Muhammad.[110]

There are a number of other swords attributed to the prophet Muhammad in Muslim sources. Nine swords are mentioned by name in verses recorded in the fifteenth century by al-Bulqīnī: "We gave nine swords: Rasūb, al-Mikhdham, Dhū al-Faqār, Qaḍīb, Ḥatf, al-Battār, ʿAḍb, Qalʿī, and Maʾthūr al-Fijār. They were decreed to be equivalent with the signs of Moses, all for the enemy the cause of ruin."[111] The names of many of these swords can be traced back to earlier sources, where other names are also provided. In the ninth century, Ibn Saʿd mentions Maʾthūr, Dhū al-Faqār, Battār, al-Ḥatf, al-Mikhdham, and a Qalʿī sword in the section of his work on the "swords of the apostle of God," along with various traditions related to the swords.[112] He follows this with several sections devoted to the armor, shield, spear, horses, camels, and other possessions of the prophet Muhammad.[113] In his biography of the prophet Muhammad, al-Dhahabī includes a section on the "weapons of the prophet Muhammad, his armor, and other war implements," in which he lists a number of traditions related to the named swords of the prophet Muhammad.[114] Among these, he cites the tenth-century scholar Ibn Fāris al-Qazwīnī as a source for eight named swords: "The weapons of the prophet Muhammad included Dhū al-Faqār, which was a sword he took as spoil on the day of Badr. He had a sword that was bequeathed to him by his father. Saʿd b. ʿUbādah gave him a sword called al-ʿAḍ b. He took as spoil from the weapons of the Banū Qaynuqāʿ a Qalʿī sword, and in another report he had one called al-Battār and al-Lakhīf. He had al-Mikhdham and al-Rasūb. There were eight swords."[115] According to the editor of al-Dhahabī's text, "al-Lakhīf" is Persian for "al-Ḥanīf," also related to "al-Ḥanf," another name given to this sword.[116] Based on the Arabic orthography, it is possible that the "al-Ḥanīf" mentioned here is to be identified with the "al-Ḥatf" mentioned by Ibn Saʿd and other sources.

Other items related to the military campaigns of the prophet Muhammad are mentioned in early Muslim sources. Ibn Saʿd has separate sections on the armor, shields, lances, riding animals, pack animals, and camels of the prophet Muhammad, and al-Bukhārī mentions a rod and arrows of the prophet Muhammad.[117] Ibn Mājah mentions his helmet, armor, bow, and lance.[118] In his collection of ḥadīth reports, al-Dārimī mentions the helmet of the prophet Muhammad and the silver pommel of his sword.[119] He is also reported to have owned and used a number of lances, armor, and rods known by name, and sources make reference to a number of banners, flags, and a tent (fusṭāṭ) that belonged to him.[120] In his work on the biography of the prophet Muhammad, Ibn Kathīr lists three lances, three bows, six swords, armor, a shield, a signet ring, an arrow, flags, and banners.[121] Abū al-Ḥasan ʿAlī b. al-Athīr (1160–1233) lists all of the named weapons of the prophet Muhammad:

> He had Dhū al-Faqār. He took it as spoil on the day of Badr. It belonged to Munabbih b. al-Ḥajjāj, and, it is said, to others. He took three swords as spoil from the Banū Qaynuqāʿ: a Qalʿī sword, a sword called Battār, and a sword called al-Khayf [ms. B: al-Ḥatf]. He had al-Mikhdham and Rasūb. He took two swords with him to Medina, one of which, named al-ʿAḍb, was present at Badr. He had three lances and three bows: a bow named al-Rawḥāʾ, a bow called al-Bayḍāʾ and a *nabʿ* wood bow called al-Ṣafrāʾ. He had armor called al-Saʿdīyah and he had armor called Fiḍḍah [i.e., "silver"]. He took it as spoil from the Banū Qaynuqāʿ. He had armor named Dhāt al-Fuḍūl, which he wore on the day of Uḥud. It was silver. He had a shield on which was a representation of the head of a ram.[122]

Many of these items are preserved in the Topkapi Museum in Istanbul and are mentioned as having been included in the treasuries of the ʿAbbasid, Fatimid, Mamluk, and Ottoman dynasties.[123]

*al-Maʾthūr* The first sword acquired by the prophet Muhammad was al-Maʾthūr, or Maʾthūr al-Fijār, bequeathed to him by his father, ʿAbdallāh b. ʿAbd al-Muṭṭalib.[124] Ibn Suhayl reports that the prophet Muhammad came to Medina at the time of the Hijrah with this sword, which had belonged to his father.[125] It is also reported that the prophet Muhammad accompanied the procession for the marriage of his daughter Fāṭimah to ʿAlī b. Abī Ṭālib with his sword unsheathed, protected by the swords of the Banū Hāshim.[126] Sharīf al-Dīn al-Dimyāṭī is cited by al-Dhahabī as reporting that the first sword owned by the prophet Muhammad was al-Maʾthūr and that people say it was made by the Jinn.[127] After the death of the prophet Muhammad, ownership of the sword is said to have been transferred to ʿAlī b. Abī Ṭālib, although the emphasis in all the reports appears to be upon the fact that the prophet Muhammad inherited the sword from his father. There is a sword preserved in the Topkapi Museum in Istanbul which is identified as the al-Maʾthūr sword. It is ninety-nine centimeters in length with a gold handle encrusted with emeralds and turquoise, shaped like two serpents. Inscribed on the handle is the inscription "ʿAbdallāh b. ʿAbd al-Muṭṭalib," in a Kufic script.[128] The close linkage of this sword with both ʿAbdallāh b. ʿAbd al-Muṭṭalib and ʿAbd al-Muṭṭalib, son of Hāshim, suggests that the sword is a symbol of the Hāshimī lineage of the prophet Muhammad and his association with the custodians of the sanctuary at Mecca.

*Dhū al-Faqār* The sword called "Dhū al-Faqār" is the best known of the named swords that are attributed to the prophet Muhammad.[129] Aḥmad b. Nūr al-Dīn ʿAlī b. Hajar (d. 1448) identifies the sword mentioned in al-Bukhārī's section on the weapons of the prophet Muhammad as Dhū al-Faqār, a sword which the prophet Muhammad took as spoil at the battle of Badr.[130] A sword taken by the prophet Muhammad as booty is also mentioned in the ḥadīth collection of Muslim b. al-Ḥajjāj b. Muslim (d. 875).[131] In his commentary on Q 8:41, Ibn Kathīr refers to this sword by name and cites al-Tirmidhī's report transmitted on the authority of Ibn ʿAbbās.[132] This is also reported by Ibn Mājah and al-Bayhaqī on the authority of Ibn ʿAbbās.[133] In his commentary on al-Bukhārī, Abū al-ʿAbbās Aḥmad b. Muḥammad al-Qasṭallānī (d. 1517) states that the sword mentioned in connection with the prophet Muhammad's weapons is Dhū al-Faqār, adding that the sword was given as a gift to ʿAlī b. Abī Ṭālib and was passed on to his descendants after his death, as indicated by the text of the ḥadīth itself.[134] According to al-Dhahabī, the name derives from the blade of the sword, which resembled the vertebrae of a spinal cord. He cites a description by al-Dimyāṭī in which the sword is said to have accoutrements of silver.[135]

According to a report transmitted on the authority of ʿIkrimah, Dhū al-Faqār belonged to al-ʿĀṣ b. Munabbih al-Sahmī, who was slain at the battle of Badr by ʿAlī b. Abī Ṭālib, and the sword was taken by the prophet Muhammad as spoil.[136] Al-Dimyāṭī explains that the sword had belonged to al-ʿĀṣ b. Munabbih, the brother of Nabīh b. al-Ḥajjāj b. Āmir al-Sahmī, who was killed along with his father and his paternal uncle while still unbelievers at the battle of Badr.[137] Other reports link a sword with al-ʿĀṣ b. Wāʾil of the Banū Sahmī, and with the revelation of Q 19:77–80.[138] Abū Dāʾūd al-Sijistānī (d. 889) cites a report which mentions that the prophet Muhammad killed Abū Jahl and took from him his sword.[139] In all of these reports the sword is closely associated with one of the more prominent of the Meccan opponents to the prophet Muhammad. Aḥmad b. Ḥanbal (d. 856) and Ibn Mājah preserve a report from Ibn ʿAbbās according to which the prophet Muhammad took his sword Dhū al-Faqār as spoil on the day of Badr, and that it was this sword in which he saw the vision on the day of Uḥud.[140] According to another report cited by al-Ṭabarī, on the authority of Abū Hurayrah, the sword had belonged to Munabbih b. al-Ḥajjāj, the father of al-ʿĀṣ b. Munabbih, who was also killed during the battle of Badr.[141]

Dhū al-Faqār is commonly associated with ʿAlī b. Abī Ṭālib and his descendants in later centuries. According to al-Ṭabarī, the sword is reported to have been used by ʿAlī b. Abī Ṭālib against a group of the unbelievers of the Quraysh at the battle of Uḥud: "Then the apostle of God saw another group of the unbelievers of the Quraysh and said to ʿAlī: 'Attack them!' ʿAlī attacked them, divided them, and killed Shaybah b. Mālik of the Banū ʿĀmir b. Luʾayy. Then Gabriel said: 'Apostle of God, this is for consultation.' The apostle of God said: 'He is of me and I am of him.' Gabriel said: 'I am of both of you.' They heard a voice saying: 'There is no sword but Dhū al-Faqār, and no companion but ʿAlī.'"[142] Ibn Mājah and al-Tirmidhī also cite reports of people hearing the voice making a statement about the sword and ʿAlī b. Abī Ṭālib.[143] It is also reported on the authority of Jaʿfar al-Ṣādiq that the prophet Muhammad saw a vision of God sitting on his throne and making this statement.[144] Later accounts closely associate Dhū al-Faqār with ʿAlī b. Abī Ṭālib and the leaders of the Shiʿah, including the Fatimid caliphs.[145] The Ismāʿīlī scholar al-Qāḍī al-Nuʿmān b. Muḥammad (d. 962) describes how the sword was taken from the caliphal palace in Baghdad after the murder of the ʿAbbasid al-Muqtadir in 932 and returned to its rightful owner, the Fatimid caliph, in Cairo.[146]

According to al-Dhahabī, the name "Dhū al-Faqār" is derived from the appearance of the sword, being the plural of "fiqrah," which means "vertebra," because the sword is said to have had notches or pits on the blade. He explains the source of the iron used to make the sword: "It is said that the source of the iron was found buried at the Kaʿbah, [taken] from that which the Jurhum buried. From it [the iron] was made Dhū al-Faqār. It was crafted by ʿAmr b. Maʿdī Karib al-Zubaydī and was given to Khālid b. Saʿīd b. al-ʿĀṣ."[147] The sword is tied to eschatological contexts in Ibn Ḥajar's commentary on al-Bukhārī, in which he compares the battles against Muslims at the end of time to the Meccan opposition to the prophet Muhammad.[148] A tradition cited by Abū ʿAbdallāh Muḥammad b. Shahrāshūb (d. 1192) states that this sword was a gift from Bilqīs the Queen of Sheba to Solomon the prophet and king of the Israelites.[149] These traditions connect Dhū al-Faqār to the burial and offering of swords at the sanctuary of Mecca and suggest a link between their recovery by ʿAbd al-Muṭṭalib and the prophet Muhammad.

*Swords Associated with ʿAlī b. Abī Ṭālib* Four other swords attributed to the prophet Muhammad are closely associated with ʿAlī b. Abī Ṭālib and later Shiʿī figures. Among these are the swords known as al-Rasūb and al-Mikhdham. According to some accounts, the prophet Muhammad sent ʿAlī b. Abī Ṭālib and 150 men on an expedition to al-Fuls, against the idol of the Ṭayyiʾ, and when ʿAlī b. Abī Ṭālib destroyed the idol he found in the treasury there the two swords al-Rasūb and al-Mikhdham.[150] Muḥammad b. ʿUmar al-Wāqidī (d. 822) mentions a third sword that was not given to the prophet Muhammad but was kept by ʿAlī b. Abī Ṭālib: "ʿAlī went out to al-Fuls, destroying and leveling it. He found in its temple three swords: Rasūb, al-Mikhdham, and a sword known as al-Yamānī."[151] Ibn Shahrāshūb mentions a report in which Gabriel commands ʿAlī b. Abī Ṭālib to destroy an iron idol in Yemen, and it is from this idol that two swords are made: Mikhdham and Dhū al-Faqār.[152] Both Rasūb and Mikhdham are mentioned by al-Dhahabī as having been made from the idol of the Ṭayyi'.[153] In another account, ʿAlī b. Abī Ṭālib discovers the swords when he is sent by the prophet Muhammad to raze Mināh. The two swords, said to have been in the possession of the Ghassānid king al-Ḥārith b. Shamr, had been offered as gifts to the local idols. Both swords were then given by the prophet Muhammad to ʿAlī b. Abī Ṭālib to pass down to his family.[154] There is a sword in the Topkapi Museum identified as al-Rasūb and bearing the name of Jaʿfar al-Ṣādiq,[155] and Aḥmad b. ʿAlī al-Maqrīzī (d. 1442) mentions swords of al-Ḥusayn b. ʿAlī b. Abī Ṭālib and Jaʿfar al-Ṣādiq in the treasuries from the Fatimids.[156] Another sword in the Topkapi Museum is identified as al-Mikhdham and bears the name ʿAlī Zayn al-ʿĀbidīn.[157]

The Shiʿī scholar al-Majlisī (d. 1698) preserves a tradition that the Shiʿah maintained a weapons storehouse (Dār al-Ṣilāḥ) for the weapons of the family of the prophet Muhammad, which included these swords, just as the Israelites kept their implements, like the Ark of the Covenant, in the storehouse of the ark (Dār al-Tābūt).[158] The swords known as al-Qaḍīb and al-ʿAḍb, the names of both of which mean "cutting," are also attributed to the prophet Muhammad and associated with ʿAlī b. Abī Ṭālib and his descendants.[159] A sword identified as the al-Qaḍīb sword is housed in the Topkapi Museum and is inscribed with the names of Muhammad, his father, and his grandfather.[160] A sword identified as the al-ʿAḍb sword is now kept in the Ḥusayn Mosque in Cairo.[161]

*Swords and Armor from the Israelites* The three remaining named swords of the prophet Muhammad—al-Qalʿī, al-Battār, and al-Ḥatf—are all said to have been taken as spoil by the prophet Muhammad from the Jewish tribal grouping of the Banū Qaynuqāʿ. According to al-Wāqidī, the prophet Muhammad took a number of weapons and armor from the Banū Qaynuqāʿ: "The apostle of God took their weapons: three bows, a bow called al-Katūm which he used at Uḥud, a bow called al-Rawḥā', and a bow called al-Bayḍā'. He took two suits of armor from their weapons, a suit of armor called al-Ṣaghdīyah, and another of silver, and three swords: a Qalʿī sword, a sword which is called Battār, and another sword, and three lances. They found many weapons in their strongholds and implements for smithing, for they were smiths."[162] The same statement is preserved by ʿAlī b. Aḥmad b. Ḥazm (d. 1064) in his collection of reports on the life of the prophet Muhammad, and al-Dhahabī mentions three swords and two suits of armor.[163]

Muslim sources mention that the raid against the Banū Qaynuqāʿ took place following the battle of Badr in the second year after the Hijrah to Medina. According to a report cited by al-Bukhārī, the Banū Qaynuqāʿ were smiths, and they left behind their tools and arms when they were expelled from Medina.[164] A number of exegetes claim that Q 3:12 refers to this confrontation between the prophet Muhammad and the Banū Qaynuqāʿ. According to Muḥammad b. Aḥmad al-Qurṭubī (d. 1273) and ʿAbd al-Raḥmān b. Abī Bakr al-Suyūṭī (d. 1505), both citing Ibn Isḥāq, the Jews refused to acknowledge the prophethood of Muhammad despite the fact that they knew of him from references in the Torah.[165] In his exegesis of Q 3:12, Maḥmūd b. ʿUmar al-Zamakhsharī (d. 1144) relates how the Jews acknowledged Muhammad to be the Gentile prophet (al-nabī al-ummī) about whom Moses had spoken, but they still refused to accept him.[166] Other exegetes link this incident to the revelation of Q 8:55–56. Muqātil b. Sulaymān (d. 767) states that the verses refer to the Jews, and ʿAbd al-Raḥmān b. ʿAli b. Muḥammad b. al-Jawzī (d. 1201) and al-Ṭabarī say that the verses refer to the Banū Qurayẓ ah.[167] It is known that the Muslims took a cache of weapons from the Banū Qurayẓah when they were killed, and the Banū Qurayẓah are said to have been Aaronites through their ancestor Qurayẓah the son of al-Khazraj b. al-Ṣarīḥ.[168] Given the parallels between the Banū Qaynuqāʿ and the Banū Qurayẓah, and the timing of the raid on the Banū Qaynuqāʿ immediately following the battle of Badr and the first division of spoils among the Muslims, it is possible that the traditions of taking arms and armor as booty from these Jewish groups overlap and may be conflated.

The swords and armor taken from the Jews of Medina, the Banū Qaynuqāʿ in particular, are closely linked with the history of the ancient Israelites. According to al-Dhahabī, the armor taken as spoil by the prophet Muhammad from the Banū Qaynuqāʿ originates with King David: "He [the prophet Muhammad] had a suit of armor, called Dhāt al-Fuḍūl because of its length, brought to him by Saʿd b. ʿUbādah when he campaigned at Badr. Also [he had] Dhāt al-Wishāḥ, which was ornamented, Dhāt al-Ḥawāshī, and two suits of armor from the Banū Qaynuqāʿ. They were al-Sughdīyah and al-Fiḍḍah. Al-Sughdīyah was the armor of ʿAkīr of the Qaynuqāʿ. It was the armor of David which he wore when he killed Goliath."[169] The swords taken by the prophet Muhammad also are said to have originated with King David and other Israelite prophets. The sword al-Battār, in particular, is said to be the sword of Goliath which David took from him after felling him with the sling, the sword with which he cut off the head of Goliath. One of the swords attributed to the prophet Muhammad and housed in the Topkapi Museum, identified as al-Battār, has on the blade a picture of David cutting off the head of Goliath.[170] It is inscribed with the names of the prophets David, Solomon, Moses, Aaron, Joshua, Zechariah, John, Jesus, and Muhammad.[171] The sword al-Ḥatf is said to have been made by David when he was old enough to make his own weapon for use in battle.

Exegesis on Q 2:251 explains that David slew Goliath with a sling and cut off Goliath's head with Goliath's own sword.[172] In some accounts David is not able to wear the armor or use the weapons given to him by Saul (Ṭālūt) because Saul was much taller than David, so instead David used the sling with which he protected the animals he shepherded.[173] According to ʿAlī b. Ibrāhīm al-Qummī (d. 940), it had been prophesized that Goliath would be defeated by someone wearing the armor of Moses, and David was wearing this armor when he confronted Goliath, who was mounted on an elephant.[174] According to Aḥmad b. Muḥammad al-Thaʿlabī (d. 1036), David cut off a signet ring from the hand of Goliath and presented the severed head to Saul.[175] The defeat of Goliath is compared to the victory of the prophet Muhammad at the battle of Badr in al-Thaʿlabī.[176] According to this tradition, David took the sword of Goliath after his defeat as spoil and as a symbol of his victory. That the sword was kept as spoil for David is also attested in 1 Samuel 21:9–10, where the priest Ahimelech explains that the sword of Goliath is being kept wrapped in a cloth behind the ephod.

David's defeat of Goliath is directly linked to his special knowledge, which included the making of swords and armor. According to Muqātil b. Sulaymān and al-Ṭabarī, it was upon the defeat of Goliath that God gave David the knowledge to make arms and armor. Al-Thaʿlabī explains that David was the first person to make chain mail, and that he could work the metal with his hands as though it were clay. He would sell the suits of armor he made and use the proceeds to feed his family and distribute food to the poor and homeless.[177] Similar accounts given in the exegesis of Q 34:10–11 emphasize that David was able to work with metal without heating it up in the forge.[178] In the exegesis on Q 21:79–80 it is stated that David's ability to make armor also included the making of weapons. Al-Ṭabarī says that David made all weapons and armor, including swords and lances. Al-Qurṭubī explains that the armor and weapons made by David include all the weapons of the Arabs, and al-Suyūṭī says that David is responsible for all arms and armor.

The swords and armor transferred from the Banū Qaynuqāʿ to the prophet Muhammad were the arms and armor of the Israelite prophets. The sword al-Battār is also called the "sword of the prophets" because it is said to have been passed from David to Solomon to Zechariah to John to Jesus, and finally to the prophet Muhammad. Exegesis on Q 19:6, in which Zechariah is described as being the custodian of the Jerusalem temple, states that the temple is where the Israelites kept their weapons under the guardianship of the Levites. When the temple was destroyed, a group of the Israelite tribes who were dispersed took the swords and armor and brought them to the

Arabian Peninsula, where they settled in Yathrib. The swords and armor then passed into the hands of the prophet Muhammad and his successors. It is one of these swords which will be used by Jesus at the end of time to defeat the anti-Christ al-Dajjāl. According to reports cited by al-Bukhārī and al-Tirmidhī, Jesus will wield a sword when he returns to slay the Dajjāl, and when he has defeated the Dajjāl, he will show the people his sword with the blood of the Dajjāl on it as a sign of his victory.[179]

*Weapons and Other Relics Associated with Prophets and Kings* Related to the swords of the prophet Muhammad are the swords of his companions and successors. It is reported that Abū Bakr had a special sword which he used at Uḥud to defend the prophet Muhammad.[180] A sword identified with this one is now housed in the Topkapi Museum.[181] ʿUmar b. al-Khaṭṭāb had a special sword called Dhāt al-Wishāḥ, also known as the Sword of the Rāshidūn.[182] This is said to be the sword he used to kill ʿAyyanah b. Ḥiṣn al-Fazārī at the time of the latter's apostasy.[183] In the Topkapi Museum there is a sword engraved with the name of ʿUthmān b. ʿAffān, which some sources say is related to the revelation of Q 2:137.[184] There are four different swords attributed to Khālid b. al-Walīd, one of which is famous for its use in his conquests.[185] Swords identified as those of Sharḥabīl b. Khusnah, ʿAmmār b. Yāsir, and al-Zubayr b. al-ʿAwwām are housed at the Topkapi Museum after having been acquired by Ottoman sultans.[186]

The association of the swords of the prophet Muhammad with earlier prophets is also evident from the discovery of other treasures associated with the Israelites. ʿIsā b. ʿAbdallāh reports on the authority of his uncle ʿAbdallāh b. ʿUmar that ʿAlī b. Abī Ṭālib narrated an account of a special mirror brought down from Eden:

> When Adam was brought down from the Garden, God raised him to the top of Abū Qubays and lifted the entire earth for him until he could see it. Then he said: "All this belongs to you and your children." Adam said: "Lord, how may I know what is in it?" So God created the stars for him and said: "If you see such and such a star it means such and such." Thus Adam used to know such things by means of the stars, and when that became too difficult for him, he complained about this to his lord. So God sent him a mirror [mirʾāh] from heaven, through which he could see whatever he wished on earth.

> When Adam died a devil called Faqṭash sought out the mirror, broke it, and built over it a city in the east called Jāburq. When Solomon b. David became king he already knew of the mirror, and he asked about it. He

was told that Faqṭash had taken it, so he summoned the devil and asked him about it. Faqṭash said: "It is beneath the foundations of Jāburq." Solomon said: "Bring it to me." Faqṭash said: "But who will destroy these foundations?" Solomon said: "You will." Solomon told him this and Faqṭash brought the mirror to Solomon. Solomon restored it piece by piece and shored it up on all sides with a leather band. Then he looked into it and saw whatever he wanted.

When Solomon died, the devils pounced on the mirror and bore it away. Only one fragment was left, which was inherited by the Israelites, until it reached the exilarch of the Jews [Ras al-Jālūt], who gave it as a gift to Marwān b. Muḥammad b. Marwān during his wars with the ʿAbbasids. Marwān would rub it, place it on top of another mirror, and see things that displeased him. When this had gone on for a while, he threw it away and beheaded the exilarch of the Jews. One of Marwān's slave girls then took it and kept it with her.

When Abū Jaʿfar al-Manṣūr became caliph, he already knew of it, and so he inquired about it. He was informed that it was in the possession of a slave girl of Marwān. He searched for it until he found it. It remained with him where he would look into it, and then remained in the caliph's treasuries for a long time until it was lost.[187]

Ibn al-Jawzī mentions the seven cities in Babylon, each of which had a wondrous object, including the fourth city, in which there was an iron mirror through which a family could see its absent members.[188] In his conquest of al-Andalus, Ṭāriq b. Ziyād is said to have recovered a "table" (māʾidah) which had belonged to Solomon b. David. It is said that it was brought to al-Andalus by a king of the Maghrib who had taken it from Jerusalem. The table was inlaid with gold, silver, and precious stones.[189]

There are also a number of traditions relating to the discovery of the remains of the prophet Daniel and relics associated with him. Ibn Isḥāq records that the Muslim conquerors who entered Tastar found the preserved corpse of Daniel and a book that was then transcribed into Arabic by Kaʿb al-Aḥbār. Abū al-Ashʿath al-Aḥmarī relates that Abū Mūsā discovered a box containing the nerves and veins of Daniel in Tastar, and Ibn Abī al-Dunyā reports that the box discovered by Abū Mūsā contained a book. Several accounts mention the discovery of a ring along with the corpse of Daniel. According to Abū Burdah and Ibn Abī Burdah, the ring depicted two lions licking Daniel. In another report, Abū Mūsā is said to have discovered the corpse of Daniel, a book, dirhems, a ring, and a jar of fat.

Numerous rings are associated with prophets and kings, indicating that the mention of prophetic and royal relics in early Islamic sources was part of a larger symbolism used to represent authority. Qāḍī Ibn al-Zubayr mentions rings that increase the sexual potency of the person wearing them, and rings of protection against illness.[190] Several rings are associated with a large ruby stone, including that of Ibrāhīm b. al-Mahdī, which was transferred to the Fatimid treasuries and later lost by ʿĪsā b. Abī Jaʿfar al-Manṣūr bi-Allāh.[191] Other rings with a similarly unusual ruby stone, called al-Jabal, al-Minqār, and al-Muṭṭalibī, are associated with the caliph al-Mutawakkil.[192] It is said that this large gemstone was originally owned by the Sasanian kings, who had it engraved with their names upon being enthroned. In his *Murūj al-dhahab,* al-Masʿūdī mentions nine signet rings owned by the Sasanian kings, and other Iranian rings are listed, each associated with a specific royal function.[193] Other unusual gifts are attributed to Iranian kings and later said to have been inherited by the ʿAbbasids, including a great throne, a fireproof turban, and a phoenix.[194]

Swords and their discovery are specifically linked to great kings of the past. Qāḍī Ibn al-Zubayr mentions the discovery of two cases and two leather bags in which were eleven swords, the armor of Khusraw, the armor of the Byzantine emperor, the armor of the Turkic Khāqān, the armor of the Indian Dāhir, the armor of Bahrām Chobin, the armor of King Siyāwukhs (grandson of Kaykāʾūs), and the armor of the Lakhmid king al-Nuʿmān. The swords were those of Khusraw, Hurmuz, Qubādh, Fayrūz, Heraclius, the Khāqān, the Dāhir, Bahrām, Siyāwukhs, and al-Nuʿmān.[195] Swords associated with the Tubbaʿ kings of Yemen are reported to have been discovered, such as the two dozen found by Abū al-Ḥasan, along with 160 other ancient Ḥimyarī swords, when he conquered the palace of Sayf b. Dhī Yazān in Ghumdān. The sword called al-Ṣamṣāma was in the possession of ʿAmr b. Maʿdīkarib al-Zubaydī and was said to have originated in South Arabia, where it once belonged to the people of ʿĀd and to Ibn Dhī Qayfān, the last of the Ḥimyar kings of the Dhū Jadan family.[196] The swords associated with the kings of Gurjjara (Arabic *malik al-juzar*) include a famous sword housed in the capital of Bhīamāla (Arabic *Bīlamān*) called Sulaymānīyah and a "sword of Japheth" (Yāfith).[197] Swords and weapons are mentioned as part of a treasury discovered, along with other emblems of kingship, such as girdles, thrones, and knives.[198] During the caliphate of al-Manṣūr, Hishām b. ʿAmr al-Taghlibī uncovered a treasure in his conquest of India: "There he found a thick iron column [sāriyah] 70 cubits long. He dug for its base and found it sunk 30 cubits into the ground. Its length was thus 100 cubits. He asked the people of al-Qundahar about it, and they replied: 'These are the swords of the Persians from the time when they, together with Tubbaʿ the Himyarite, defeated us and conquered the countries. When they entered al-Qundahar, they collected their swords, hammered them together, and formed this column.'"[199] Other accounts mention the private holdings of arms and armor and huge treasures of kings discovered by Muslim commanders when they conquered Iraq and Iran.[200]

## CONCLUSIONS: SWORDS AND THE ORIGINS OF CIVILIZATION

In many of these accounts, the discovery of treasure, and of swords and armor in particular, is closely associated with conquest and the passing on of royal authority. The association of swords with royal symbolism is found in many different cultural traditions. Swords are used in various cultures as symbols of investiture.[201] The sword, and the rod for which it is a substitute, is also used as a mark of religious authority.[202] Swords are used in Islamic law, deriving from ancient legal practices associated with kings and prophets, to conclude contracts. All of these are linked with the primary offices of civilization and its governance.[203]

Perhaps more directly pertinent to the account of ʿAbd al-Muṭṭalib's discovery of certain swords and armor in the treasure of the Kaʿbah is the use of swords and armor as marking the origins of civilization or the dawn of a new civilization.[204] Swords, armor, and other forged weaponry require a certain level of technology. A great deal of time and expertise is also necessary for the production of forged items. These conditions depend, in turn, upon a certain level of civilization having been achieved.[205] The divine origins of swords and their role in establishing civilization epitomizes the founding myth of many societies, especially in the ancient Near East. Linking the establishment of a new order to the recovery of an older order, one which has ties to the origins of civilization, is not uncommon. Accounts of the discovery of the hidden treasure in Zaphon at Ugarit tell how sacred weapons were given in order to aid in the reestablishment of the cosmic order.[206] The so-called Jewish tradition of the hidden vessels seems to be part of this larger Near Eastern motif in which the recovery of treasure heralds a new age.

A number of myths make the link between forged weapons and the origins of civilization, and they often include an account of the divine revelation of weapons and the conquest of chaos. The relationship of the divine smith and the first king is widespread in the cosmogonic mythologies of the ancient Near East.[207] Biblical tradition preserves this link in the accounts of Enoch bringing down swords and the other implements of civilization to a fallen humanity as reminders of their current state. Muslim exegesis on

Q 57:25 maintains that swords and metallurgy related to weapons were revealed by God because of humanity's fallen state.[208] Ibn Kathīr states that God gave iron to humanity to establish justice and civilization in the world, as demonstrated by the fact that God decreed fighting by the sword for the prophet Muhammad and his followers against those who reject the Quran.[209] Aḥmad b. Ḥanbal and Abū Dā'ūd both cite a ḥadīth report on the authority of Ibn ʿUmar according to which the prophet Muhammad said: "I was sent with the sword in my hands so that people would worship God alone without associating anything with him."[210]

Other exegetes relate Q 57:25 even more specifically to the swords of the prophet Muhammad. According to Ibn Shahrāshūb, the verse refers to Dhū al-Faqār: "The exegesis of al-Suddī on the authority of Ibn ʿAbbās concerning the word of God: 'We sent down the iron.' He [Ibn ʿAbbās] said: God sent down Adam from the Garden and with him was Dhū al-Faqār created out of the leaves of the myrtle tree in the Garden. Then God said: 'With it is great harm.' With it Adam fought his enemies from among the Jinn and Satans. On it was written that prophets would not cease to fight with it, prophet after prophet, righteous after righteous, until it was inherited by the Commander of the Faithful, who would fight with it on behalf of the Gentile Prophet."[211] Ibn Shahrāshūb reports that Gabriel caused Dhū al-Faqār to fall from the heavens, ornamented with silver.[212] Ibn ʿAbbās is reported to have said that God gave Dhū al-Faqār to Adam, and that the sword was sent from heaven to the prophet Muhammad, who then gave it to ʿAlī b. Abī Ṭālib. "It is also reported on the authority of other scholars that what is meant by this verse is that Dhū al-Faqār was sent down from heaven to the Prophet, who gave it to ʿAlī."[213] Other exegetes explain that the sending down of the sword in Q 57:25 indicates that victory comes only by the instruments of war.[214]

The divine origins and earthly dispersal of tools, weapons, and other implements and arts of civilization is found in other ancient Near Eastern conceptions of territory and civilization, like the dispersal of the Me in Sumerian myth. In the myth of Inanna and Enki, Inanna is said to acquire the Me from Enki at his Absu fortress in Eridu.[215] The list of Me provided in this text includes about a hundred different Me ranging from simple skills such as making bread and planting crops to more elaborate religious rituals and rules for war and diplomacy.[216] Among the items listed are the following relating to kingship, religion, state offices, war, music, and the sciences:

man.en = office of "en"
nam.lagar = office of "lagar"
nam.dingir = divine function

aga.zi.maḫ = legitimate coronation
gis.gu.za nam.lugal = royal throne
gidri.maḫ = great sceptre
tug.maḫ = great vestment
nam.sipa = pastoralism
nam.lugal = royalty
ni.gi.na = justice or stability
mar.uru = the deluge
gis.du.du = lovemaking
gis.ki.su.ub = penis
nam.se.er.ka.an = flattery
amalu = servant of cult of Inanna
nam.ni.erim = hostility
uru.laḫ.laḫ = sacking of cities
i.si.is.ga.ga = singing of lamentations
kur.ki.bala = rebel countries
nam.du.ge = prosperity
giz.zal = salvation
su.luḫ.ku.ga = purity ablutions
u.ma = victory
ub.ou.sem = trumpet
me.ze = tambourine
kus.a.la = trumpet
nam.tibira = metallurgy
nam.dub.sar = writing
nam.simug = foundry
nam.asgab = cooking
nam.sidim = art of construction[217]

Although more elaborate, the list of the Me given in Sumerian sources parallels the sorts of artifacts and arts of civilization associated with the fall of Adam from the garden of Eden, and the subsequent spread of civilization from Mecca. Like the knowledge of the prophet Muhammad dispersed in the form of ḥadīth reports, the Me are conceptualized as discrete written texts stored on tablets, one tablet for each civilizational skill. Other myths describe Enki's travels throughout the world and distribution of the Me in various locations, such as Ur and Egypt, leading to the origins of civilization in those places, not unlike the distribution and collection of ḥadīth reports at the centers of Islamic civilization.[218]

In the following chapter, the discovery of the treasure of the Kaʿbah is to be understood as an example of the mythology of the origins of civilization on earth, and the association of the sanctuary at Mecca with Adam and his fall from Eden. In this mythology, it is the prophets who establish the sanctuary at Mecca and act as its custodians, using the implements of civilization revealed to them by God: "It [the Kaʿbah] had not had a guardian since the time of Noah, when it was raised up. Then God commanded Abraham to settle his son Ishmael by the House of God intended as a mark of honor to the one whom he honored by his prophet Muhammad. Abraham and his son Ishmael were custodians of the House after the time of Noah. At this time Mecca was uninhabited, and the area around Mecca belonged to the Jurhum and Amalekites."[219] The founding of the sanctuary by Adam is the civilizing of the first place on the earth, and Adam's act of civilizing is connected with Abraham and the prophet Muhammad's subsequent re-establishment of the Meccan sanctuary. The recovery of Mecca by Quṣayy, the recovery of the treasure by ʿAbd al-Muṭṭalib, and the pilgrimage of the prophet Muhammad are successive episodes in the early Islamic account of the establishment of Mecca as the symbolic capital and center of Islamic civilization. Accounts of the recovery of the Meccan treasure draw upon Near Eastern mythological traditions to identify the gazelles, swords, and armor with the implements used by prophets and kings in the founding and development of civilization. These accounts link the founding of the sacred capital at Mecca and the origins of Islamic civilization with the beginnings of religion and society in human history.

CHAPTER TWO

# *Utopia and Civilization in Islamic Rituals*

Chapter 1 showed how the items in the treasure uncovered by ʿAbd al-Muṭṭalib had symbolic associations which link the prophet Muhammad with the origins of civilization. Muslim sources draw upon mythological accounts of the divine origins of weapons and other implements of civilization. The discovery of the treasure of the Kaʿbah is understood as a reference to the founding of the Meccan sanctuary by Adam as the first place of civilization on the earth after his fall from Eden. The swords and armor inherited by the prophet Muhammad are symbolic reminders of the fall from Eden and the role of prophets and kings in the development of civilization.

Chapter 2 shows how Muslim legal theorists interpret and define certain obligatory rituals as practicable symbols reminding people of this distinction between civilized life on earth and the utopian existence of Eden. Section 1 examines legal definitions of impurity, especially as the conception of impurity relates to genitalia and sex. Despite the variety of opinions, the general agreement of Muslim jurists on certain principles suggests that the impurity associated with touching the penis is logically related to other conditions that invalidate ablution (wuḍūʾ) and ritual washing (ghusl). These conditions defined by the jurists suggest a correspondence between purity laws and the detailed descriptions of the state of Adam and Eve in the garden of Eden. Building upon this explanation, section 2 focuses on how the rules pertaining to other rituals, such as the fast (ṣawm), offering (zakāt), and pilgrimage (ḥajj), relate to purity laws and Eden. The correspondences between these rituals and the descriptions of Eden suggest the outlines of a broad ideology expressed by Muslim jurists through two systems of oppositions between the pure and impure, and the sacred and profane.

## 1: TOUCHING THE PENIS

In the *Muwaṭṭaʾ*, there is an unusual report transmitted on the authority of Mālik b. Anas (d. 795), from the grandson of Saʿd b. Abī Waqqāṣ, Ismāʿīl b. Muḥammad.

> [Yaḥyāʾ] related to me, on the authority of Mālik, on the authority of Ismāʿīl b. Muḥammad b. Saʿd b. Abī Waqqāṣ, that Muṣʿab b. Saʿd b. Abī Waqqāṣ said: "I was holding a copy of the Quran [muṣḥaf] for Saʿd b. Abī Waqqāṣ, and I rubbed myself. Saʿd asked: 'Have your perhaps touched your penis?' I said: 'Yes.' So he said: 'Go and perform ablution [wuḍūʾ].' So I went and performed ablution, and returned."[1]

Although the *Muwaṭṭaʾ* includes five other reports in the same section with the heading "Ablution for Touching the Genitals" (wuḍūʾ min mass al-farj), this is the only report in which touching the penis appears to be accidental, or at least unintentional. It is also the only report in which the requirement to perform ablution is linked with touching the Quran. Other reports state that a person who touches his penis is to perform ablution, or that touching the penis requires ablution before prayer.[2] Discussions concerning the link between touching the penis and the requirement of ablution are to be found in all the different schools of Islamic law.

Despite the widespread acknowledgment of the regulations against touching the penis, there are few attempts to explain the connection between the touching of genitalia and impurity in Islamic law. Some Muslim jurists argue that "touching the penis" refers to masturbation, but others maintain that the impurity associated with "touching the penis" is attached to physical contact with impure substances that might be on the surface of, or emitted from, the penis and other genitalia. Still others hold that ablution is required for insouciant touching, touching the genitalia of a corpse, of certain animals, or of severed genitalia. What all of these opinions have in common, however, is the basic principle that contact with the genitalia or substances emitted from them results in impurity.

That touching the penis requires one to perform ablution is also found in later Mālikī texts, and in Shāfiʿī and Ḥanbalī texts. In many cases, this requirement is said to be based upon a report from Busrah bt. Ṣufwān concerning a statement made by the prophet Muḥammad. This is the first report listed in the *Muwaṭṭaʾ*, citing several early authorities:

> Yaḥyāʾ related to me, on the authority of Mālik, on the authority of ʿAbdallāh b. Abī Bakr b. Muḥammad b. ʿUrwah b. Ḥazm, that he heard ʿUrwah

> b. al-Zubayr say: "I came upon Marwān b. al-Ḥakam [b. Abī al-ʿĀṣī], and we were mentioning things which required ablution. Marwān said: 'Ablution is required for touching the penis.'" ʿUrwah said: "'I did not know that.' Marwān b. al-Ḥakam said: 'Busrah bt. Ṣufwān related to me that she heard the apostle of God saying: 'When one of you touches his penis [dhakar], let him perform the ablution.'"[3]

A variant of this report is given on the authority of Umm Ḥabībah, Abū Hurayrah, and Abū Ayyūb, replacing "penis" (dhakar) with "genitals" (farj).[4] All of the Sunnī schools of law cite these reports, although there is little agreement among or within the schools concerning the legal implications of the reports. Ḥanafī jurists cite the report of Busrah but do not require ablution for touching the penis.[5] Mālikī, Shāfiʿī, and Ḥanbalī jurists agree that ablution is required but have differing opinions about what qualifies as "genitals" (penis, vagina, anus, testicles), what kind of "touching" is intended (unintentional, purposeful, masturbation), and whether the impurity occurs when any genitalia are touched (those of the same or the opposite gender, genitalia of a hermaphrodite, animal genitalia) or only when persons touch their own genitalia.

One of the explanations given by Muslim jurists for the connection between touching genitalia and impurity is that "touching the penis" refers to masturbation. This is evident in the opinions of some jurists that only intentional and not accidental touching of the penis causes impurity. In his commentary on the *Muwaṭṭaʾ*, Muḥammad b. ʿAbd al-Bāqī al-Zurqānī (1645–1710) interprets the report of Ismāʿīl b. Muḥammad b. Saʿd b. Abī Waqqāṣ as an example of intentional touching. The comments of al-Zurqānī are made in reference to specific words and expressions from the original text quoted in the *Muwaṭṭaʾ*:

> ("... that he said: 'I was holding a copy of the Quran ...'") that is, "I took it ..." ("... to Saʿd b. Abī Waqqāṣ ..."), meaning his father. That is, [he took the copy of the Quran] in order that his father would be able to recite from it whether in private or in public view. ("... and I rubbed myself ...") that is, "under my robe." ("Saʿd said: 'Have you perhaps touched ...'") with a kasra on the first "sīn" is clearer than with a fatḥah. That is, "have you touched with your palm ..." ("... your penis?") that is, without a cover. ("He said: ...") Muṣʿab ("... I said: 'Yes.' And he ...") Saʿd ("... said: "Go and perform ablution.' So I went and performed ablution, and returned.")

By adding the details that Muṣʿab rubbed himself under his robe, with the palm of his hand, with nothing between the palm and the penis, al-

Zurqānī dismisses the accidental nature of the touching apparent from the plain text of the report and is able to use the text to reinforce the idea that ablution is required for intentional touching of the penis.

The reasoning for such an interpretation is given by al-Zurqānī in his interpretation of the report from Busrah:

> ("... that she heard the apostle of God say: 'If one of you touches his penis...") without anything in the way, with the palm of the hand, according to the report: "If a person causes his hand to come into contact with his genitals with nothing covering [them] ..." The "causing of the hand to come into contact with" [ifḍāʾ] is an expression for touching [mass] with the palm of the hand.[6]

Using more explicit language from the text of the report given on the authority of Abū Hurayrah, al-Zurqānī takes the phrase "touching the penis" as a reference to intentional touching, with the palm of the hand, and without anything between the hand and the penis.

In his discussion of the question, Abū al-Walīd Muḥammad b. Aḥmad b. Rushd (1058–1126) gives a similar explanation, linking intention, pleasure, and use of the palm of the hand:

> First there are those who distinguish between a person who does it [touches the penis] for pleasure and a person who does not do it for pleasure. Second there are those who distinguish between a person who touches it with the palm of his hand and a person who touches it with the back of the hand. They require ablution for the case of the person who does it for pleasure but not for the person who does not do it for pleasure. Likewise, the other group requires ablution for the person who does it with the palm of his hand but does not require ablution for the person who touches it with the back of his hand. Both of these opinions are transmitted by the followers of Mālik. Taking into account the palm of the hand is related to the consideration that it [the penis] is being touched for pleasure. There is also a group which distinguishes between intentional and accidental touching, requiring ablution for a person who touches intentionally, but not requiring it for a person who touches accidentally. This is transmitted on the authority of Mālik, and is the opinion of Dāʾūd and his followers.[7]

Ibn Rushd adds that some Mālikī jurists in the Maghrib regard performing ablution for touching the penis only as "customary" (sunnah) but not required (wājib). He also gives an account of the different reports used to support the view that touching the penis requires ablution but he does not mention the report, transmitted by Mālik on the authority of Ismāʿīl b. Muḥammad b. Saʿd b. Abī Waqqāṣ, which suggests that unintentional touching of the penis also results in impurity.

Ibn Rushd explains that the requirement of ablution for touching genitals is closely related to the requirement of ablution for noncoital sexual contact between a man and woman:

> One group holds that if a person touches a woman with his hand in an open area, and between her and him there is no covering or obstruction, then ablution is incumbent upon him. This is likewise the case if a person kisses a woman, because a kiss, according to this group, is a type of touching, whether for pleasure or not. This is the opinion of al-Shāfiʿī and his followers, except that on one occasion he made a distinction between the one touching and the one being touched, requiring ablution for the one touching but not for the one being touched; another time he required it equally for both of them. Also, one time he made a distinction between women who are forbidden to be married to the one touching and women eligible to be married to him. He required it for the one touching the woman eligible to be married to him but not the woman whom he is forbidden to marry; another time he required it equally for both of them.
>
> Others say that ablution is required for touching when the woman is accompanying the man for sexual pleasure or the intention of the touch is pleasure, when this occurs with or without an obstruction, with any part of the body. This does not include kissing unless pleasure is stipulated in this. This is the opinion of Mālik and some of his followers.
>
> Those who reject the requirement of ablution for touching women are the followers of Abū Ḥanīfah.[8]

The same distinctions seem to apply mutatis mutandis here as they do in relation to touching the penis. According to Ibn Rushd, the difference of opinion here also depends upon whether "touching" with the hand is to be understood metaphorically as "sexual contact," thus making ablution a requirement, according to the exegesis of Q 3:43, and in accordance with reports about the prophet Muhammad touching ʿĀʾishah with his hand during prayer without the intention of sexual pleasure.[9] The Shāfiʿī opinion also appears to rely on the presumption that the "touch" is sexual in nature, owing to the distinctions made for intention and marriageable women.

Aḥmad b. Taymīyah (1263–1328) agrees that the requirement of ablution for touching the penis is tied to the intention and sexual pleasure of the persons performing the act. Making the link between touching the penis and masturbation more explicit, Ibn Taymīyah states that if a person touches his penis, even with the palm of his hand and the tips of his fingers, but does not intend to do so, then ablution is not required of him. As an example of this, Ibn Taymīyah argues that touching the genitals of animals does not require ablution, presumably because the activity was not initiated with the intention of sexual pleasure but for some other reason. Like Ibn Rushd, Ibn Taymīyah follows this discussion with a review of the requirements of ablution for kissing and touching a woman, and also the issue of whether camel milk causes impurity.[10] The tenth-century jurist Ibn Abī Zayd al-Qayrawānī also puts "touching the penis" together with kissing and touching a woman for sexual pleasure.[11] In their commentaries on the *Risālah* of Ibn Abī Zayd, both Qāsim b. ʿĪsā b. Nājī (d. 1436) and Aḥmad b. Muḥammad Zarrūq (d. 1493) make a connection between touching genitalia and the intention of deriving sexual pleasure.[12]

In the *Kitāb al-umm,* Muḥammad b. Idrīs al-Shāfiʿī (767–820) makes the same connection as other jurists between the report of Busrah and the report of Abu Hurayrah, citing the two reports one after the other.[13] The *Mukhtaṣar* of Ibrāhīm al-Muzanī (791–878) provides a further interpretation of the reports in a summary of the Shāfiʿī position on actions and substances that invalidate and thus require ablution, illustrating Ibn Rushd's statement about Shāfiʿī's not stipulating intention in the act of touching genitals.

> (al-Shāfiʿī said:) That which requires ablution includes [contact with] feces and urine, sleep whether while leaning or sitting or bowing or prostrating, whether it is a lot or a little sleep, the mind being overcome by insanity, sickness whether it requires lying down or not, gas which comes out of the anus, sexual play between a man and woman, play that involves the man causing some part of himself to come into contact with [yufḍī] the body of the woman, her touching him without a barrier between them, his kissing her, touching [mass] the genitals [farj] of himself or someone else with the palm of the hand whether [the person whose genitals are touched] is old or young, alive or dead, male or female. It is the same whether the genitals are of the front or the rear, and [also applies to] touching her area around the anus. There is no ablution required for touching the genitals of beasts because it [such touching] is not forbidden. All that is emitted from the rear or the front, whether worms, blood, seminal fluid, or wetness, all of these things require ablution. There is no purification of the anus [istinjāʾ] for sleep or if gas is emitted from it.[14]

Note that al-Muzanī uses the term "causes to come into contact with" (yufḍī, ifḍāʾ) as a gloss upon the less specific "touch" (mass) and also specifies that touching the genitals is limited to using the palm of the hand. This limitation, and the explicit connection with other forms of sexual touching, like the linkage established by Ibn Rushd, seems to indicate that it is only intentional touching of genitals that requires ablution. In addition, however, al-Muzanī adds details that mitigate against the interpretation that "touching the penis" refers to masturbation or sexual stimulation. He states that ablution is also required when intentional contact is made with the anus, the area around the anus, and even touching the genitals of a youth or a corpse.

ʿAbdāllah b. Aḥmad b. Qudāmah (1147–1223) provides details on legal opinions that contradict the notion that the impurity caused by touching the penis is tied to masturbation or intentional contact. His section "Touching the Genitals" is divided into eleven different issues relating to the interpretation of the reports of Busrah, Umm Ḥabībah, and Abū Ayyūb. Ibn Qudāmah specifies the opinion of Aḥmad b. Ḥanbal: ablution is required for the intentional touching of one's own penis or vagina (or both) with the palm of the hand, with the intention of sexual pleasure. In each case, however, Ibn Qudāmah provides evidence of jurists and legal authorities who disagree with the Ḥanbalī interpretation. For example, some jurists hold that ablution is required for touching the penis unintentionally (as in the report of Ismāʿīl b. Muḥammad b. Saʿd b. Abī Waqqāṣ), while others maintain that any touching which has the intention of sexual pleasure (whether with the back of the hand or the arm) requires ablution.[15] Al-Shāfiʿī regards the penis of a youth, the anus, and the genitals of a corpse as requiring ablution, whereas Ibn Qudāmah argues that "if a person were to touch the foreskin which is cut from a circumcision before it [the foreskin] is cut, then it [touching] invalidates his ablution because it [the foreskin] is still part of the flesh of the penis, but if a person touches the foreskin after it is cut then it [touching] does not invalidate ablution because the foreskin ceases to be a penis in name and in being forbidden" once it is separated from the living human body.[16] ʿUmar b. al-Ḥusayn al-Khiraqī (d. 945) records the opinion of Isḥāq b. Ibrāhīm, according to whom touching a severed penis results in the requirement of ablution.[17] Ibn Qudāmah records that al-Layth b. Saʿd (b. ʿAbd al-Raḥmān) requires ablution for the touching of animal genitals, and ʿAṭāʾ b. Abī Rabāḥ holds that ablution is required for touching the penis-sheaf of a donkey but not for touching the teat of a camel.[18]

The opinions of some jurists seem to be at odds with the position that touching the penis requires ablution. The Ḥanafīs maintain that physical contact with the penis does not require ablution but touching the area of the genitals does when it causes a person to come into contact with substances which require ablution because they originate from the genitals (e.g., urine, feces, semen). Regarding the penis itself, Muḥammad b. al-Ḥasan al-Shaybānī (d. 804) cites several opinions from Abū Ḥanīfah:

> Abū Ḥanīfah related to me, on the authority of Ḥammād b. Ibrāhīm, on the authority of ʿAlī b. Abī Ṭālib, he said concerning touching the penis: "There is no harm [in that]. I touch it or the end of my nose."
>
> Abū Ḥanīfah related to me, on the authority of Ḥammād b. Ibrāhīm, that Ibn Masʿūd asked about ablution for touching the penis. He said: "It is impure [najas], so cut it off!" meaning that there is no harm in it.
>
> Abū Ḥanīfah related to me, on the authority of Ḥammād b. Ibrāhīm, that Saʿd b. Abī Waqqāṣ passed by a man who was washing his penis. He said: "What are you doing? This is not required of you." The opinion of Abū Ḥanīfah is that washing it [the penis] is preferred when one urinates.[19]

The first and second of these reports are related to the oft-cited report, transmitted on the authority of Ṭalq b. ʿAlī [b. al-Mundhir b. Qays], concerning what the prophet Muhammad said about the penis: "Ṭalq b. ʿAlī said: We were with the apostle of God when a man, like a Bedouin, came to him and said: 'Apostle of God, what do you think about a man touching his penis after performing ablution?' He [the prophet Muhammad] said: 'What is it but a piece of your flesh?'"[20] Many jurists consider this report to have been abrogated by later reports requiring ablution, such as those of Busrah, Abū Ayyūb, Abū Hurayrah, and Umm Ḥabībah, but it does continue to indicate for others that the penis itself is not the cause of the impurity. Imāmī Shiʿī jurists, some basing their opinions upon the opinion of ʿAlī b. Abī Ṭālib recorded in al-Shaybānī, likewise do not require ablution for touching the penis but do require it for a person who comes into contact with a monkey, dog, pig, or other thing which is considered to have an offensive smell.[21]

Many of the opinions held by Muslim jurists regarding the link between touching the penis and ablution are contradictory. Those jurists who limit ablution to cases of intentional touching do not agree whether the touching must also be for sexual pleasure, and many jurists include touching the anus and testicles as requiring ablution, which indicates that the impurity caused by touching the penis is not limited to the act of masturbation. The stipulation limiting ablution to persons touching naked genitals is also not wholly consistent with tying impurity to masturbation, for sexual pleasure may be sought without direct contact between the skin of the genitals and palm of the hand. Other anomalous cases include requiring ablution for touching the genitals of a corpse, a youth, animals, and severed penises, all acts which could be intentional but (presumably) not for the physical pleasure of the thing being touched. Another theory is that the impurity arises from the substances (and gas) which issue from genitalia. This too is contradicted by many cases in which the requirement of ablution is not dependent upon the presence of urine, feces, semen or other discharge.

Common to all of these cases, including the report of the apparently nonpremeditated rubbing by Muṣʿab b. Saʿd b. Abī Waqqāṣ, is a more basic concept: that any touching of genitals that makes one conscious of the genitals' existence requires ablution. The Ḥanafī and Imāmī Shiʿī position (i.e., that emissions from the genitals make ablution required for physical contact) basically understands the touching of genitalia as an extension or sign of the impurity that attaches to the physical results of other normal bodily functions (which exit the body from the genitals). It is not necessary that the touching be intentional or for sexual pleasure, or that there be an emission, but the penis and other genitalia are to be understood as features of the human body that are linked both physically and symbolically to the presence of substances and activities that require ablution and ritual washing. Note that touching the nose does not invalidate ablution even though the nose may be the source of recurrent bleeding, nor does touching the mouth require ablution, even though the mouth may be the source of vomiting. Unlike the nose and mouth, the genitals are features of the human body that regularly emit substances that require ablution, in addition to being features of the human body linked with sexual reproduction.

Ablution and ritual washing serve to separate a person from eating, bodily functions, and sex. Performance of ablution includes, in addition to the obligation of washing the face, hands, and feet, the customary practice (sunnah) of using the toothpick (siwāk), rinsing the mouth, snuffing, wiping the ears, and combing the beard with the fingers.[22] A Ḥanafī text describes the conditions that invalidate, or require, ablution, excluding the touching of genitals: "That which invalidates ablution is everything that comes out of the two apertures [urethral and anal], blood, pus, and purulent matter when it comes out of the body and comes into contact with a place [part of body] attached to the area of purity, vomit if it fills the mouth, and sleep while in a bed, reclining, or leaning against something that, if it were moved away from the sleeper, would cause him to fall, and the mind being overcome by unconsciousness, madness, and a guffaw during any prayer in which there is bowing and prostration."[23] These are all bodily functions that occur naturally, some regularly, in everyday human existence. Ibn Rushd classifies these substances and actions as being those that issue from the body, such as urine, feces, and gas.[24] Additional substances that exit the body with less regularity but still require ablution include blood, pus, and vomit.[25] Other activities unrelated to substances issuing from the body include sleeping and other forms of unconsciousness, touching a woman, eating something touched by fire, laughing during prayer, and carrying a corpse.[26]

Ritual washing is specifically associated with sexual reproduction in a list of actions that invalidate or require it. A list is given in a Ḥanafī legal text: "That which necessitates ritual washing [ghusl] is the ejaculation of semen in a gush, the passion of a man and woman, contact between genitalia without ejaculation, menstruation, and parturition."[27] Note that the actions and conditions requiring ritual washing are distinct from those requiring ablution. Ibn Rushd reiterates this distinction in his discussion of certain substances which require ritual washing (such as semen) that issue, in the case of male genitalia, from the same opening as substances that require ablution (such as urine and prostatic fluid).[28] He also lists the opinions of jurists and discusses the distinction between menstrual blood, which requires ritual washing, and nonmenstrual blood (such as blood from a nosebleed), which requires ablution.[29] Menstruation requires ritual washing because it is linked with sexual reproduction, as does semen, but a nosebleed and the release of prostatic fluid do not require ritual washing.

All the activities listed as requiring ablution and ritual washing, and the substances these activities produce, are natural occurrences necessary to the continued functioning of individual human beings and human society. Ablution relates to the continued existence of individuals and ritual washing to the continued existence of society. It is not so much that these activities and the production of substances cannot be controlled as that the natural human condition includes urination, defecation, and sleep. Certain actions that require ablution, such as touching the penis, carrying a corpse, and eating something touched by fire, are not outside human control to avoid. The actions and substances that require ritual washing, except for menstruation, are likewise susceptible to human control. But requiring ablution for things that cannot be controlled and for things such as sexual reproduction which are necessary for the continuation of the human species underlines the fact that the natural existence of human beings is a perpetual state of impurity. Ablution and ritual washing allow people to enter a temporary and artificial state of purity for specific ritual activities.[30]

## 2: ADAM AND EVE'S GENITALS

This same opposition between the natural state of impurity and the temporary state of purity effected by ablution and ritual washing is found in

Muslim exegesis of the accounts of Adam and Eve in the Quran. In the garden of Eden, Adam and Eve existed in a state of perpetual purity. In his exegesis of Q 2:36, al-Ṭabarī preserves a report to this effect, transmitted on the authority of Abū al-ʿĀlīyah: "Abū al-ʿĀlīyah said: Adam and Eve ate of the tree [of immortality]. It was a tree that made whoever ate from it impure [ḥadatha], but there was not allowed to be any impurity [ḥadath] in the garden, so God drove Adam out of the garden."[31] Muslim jurists use the term "ḥadath" as a reference to impurities which require ablution, but the term can also refer more specifically to defecation and feces. It could simply mean that eating from the tree was a condition that required ablution and thus that anyone being in a state requiring ablution was not allowed to be in the garden of Eden. Reports regarding the nature of the manna consumed by the Israelites in the wilderness of wandering indicate that the food of Eden did not cause defecation, and a number of exegetes relate accounts linking the manna of the Israelites with the food of Eden.[32]

According to the exegesis of Q 7:22–26, Adam and Eve did not have clothing in the garden of Eden but did not know they had genitals, because their bodies, and their genitals in particular, were covered with light, feathers, or fingernails.[33] Ibn Kathīr reports that Adam and Eve did not have sex while in the garden of Eden but did later after their expulsion, when they were taught the function of their genitals by Gabriel: "Adam did not have sex with his wife while in the garden, until he fell from there on account of the sin of eating from the tree. Both of them slept alone, side by side on the open ground, until Gabriel came and commanded Adam to produce his family. Gabriel taught him how to produce it. After Adam had sex with Eve, Gabriel asked: 'How did you find your wife?' He said: 'Upright.'"[34] Another account, reported on the authority of Ibn ʿAbbās, states that Adam fell to earth in India and Eve in Jedda, and the circumstances of their sexual meeting near Mecca account for the etymology of the names of Muzdalifah, ʿArafat, and Jamʿ.[35] According to Ibn ʿAbbās, after their fall, Adam and Eve fasted for forty days and Adam abstained from having sex with Eve for a hundred years.[36]

This account is consistent with the notion that Eve was punished with menstruation and the bearing of children in pain upon her fall from the garden of Eden.[37] Muslim exegesis of Q 2:34–38 preserves a report by Ibn Zayd to this effect: "When Adam blamed Eve for their sin, God said: 'It is incumbent upon me to make her bleed once every month just as she made this tree bleed, and I will make her foolish though I created her smart, and I will make pregnancy and childbearing reprehensible though I had made pregnancy and childbearing easy.' If it were not for the affliction that was set upon Eve, then the women of this world would not menstruate, they would be smart, and they would be pregnant and bear children with ease."[38] It is also reported that the water of Zamzam first appeared in Mecca so that Eve could purify herself from the blood of her menstruation. Another account, found in al-Ṭabarī and al-Thaʿlabī, states that God caused Eve to bleed because when she ate from the tree in the garden of Eden she caused it to bleed.[39] In the garden of Eden there would have been no need for Adam and Eve to be aware of using their genitals for sexual reproduction, since they were already immortal.

In another report, transmitted on the authority of Ibn ʿAbbās, the eating from the tree in the garden of Eden and the discovery of genitalia are specifically linked. Adam and Eve's genitalia appear to them as a result of their eating, not sex: "The tree that God forbade to Adam and his spouse was grain [sunbulah]. When they ate from it, their private parts were revealed to them, for their private parts had been hidden from them by their fingernails."[40] In another account, provided by al-Ṭabarī, Gabriel is said to have brought bags of wheat (ḥinṭah) or seven grains of wheat to Adam after his fall.[41] The fruit of the tree in Eden, the eating of which causes Adam and Eve to defecate and/or require them to perform ablution, is thus the same food Adam is compelled to cultivate on earth for sustenance. Adam and Eve did not use their genitalia for the release of bodily wastes in the garden of Eden because they had no cultivated produce and did not eat the meat of animals.[42] Adam is given seeds to grow fruit produce and is taught the skills necessary for the cultivation and preparation of it.[43] It is this earthly food, requiring tending and preparation, that produces the bodily wastes that require ablution.

These parallels between the temporary state of purity effected by ablution and ritual washing and the garden of Eden help to explain the linkage of impurity with touching the genitalia. Urination, defecation, bleeding, and other natural bodily functions require ablution because Adam and Eve's bodies did not produce these impure substances in the garden of Eden. When Adam and Eve fell from Eden, their punishment was to become human, and thus their descendants are required to perform ablution and ritual washing. In the garden of Eden, Adam and Eve were not aware of their genitals, did not need to defecate or urinate, and did not require sexual reproduction for their continued existence. Touching the penis seems to require ablution because performing ablution reminds people that their natural earthly state is a fallen state, that human nature is fallen. Becoming conscious of one's genitals, either as a source of impure substances or as the instrument of sexual reproduction, thus requires ablution as a reminder of the absence of genitals in the garden of Eden. Ablution is required for those conditions necessary for and definitive of earthly human existence, in sharp contrast to the state of Adam and Eve in the garden of Eden.

Some of these same stipulations are also found reflected in the restrictions and prohibitions applied in certain Muslim rituals. During the month of Ramaḍān, people are prohibited from activities (eating and having sex) that correspond directly with the activities that would require performance of ablution and ritual washing. Intentional sex breaks the fast just as sex and the bodily substances associated with it invalidate ritual washing. Breaking the fast by intentional eating, whether by consuming something normally eaten or not (such as a pebble), is considered equivalent to the conditions invalidating ablution, many of which are already closely associated with eating and the production of bodily wastes.

Other actions and conditions are also at issue for breaking the fast and correspond to the requirements of ablution and ritual washing. Thawbān and Rāfiʿ bt. Khudayj report that the prophet Muhammad said both the one letting blood and the one being bled break the fast.[44] This is the position held by a number of jurists, including Aḥmad b. Ḥanbal, Abū Dāʾūd, and al-Awzāʿī.[45] Mālik b. Anas also preserves a report that Ibn ʿUmar would not let his blood while fasting, although Mālik b. Anas appears to hold the position that letting blood is only reprehensible but does not break the fast.[46] The disagreement over the status of voluntary bloodletting contrasts with the unanimous agreement of the jurists that menstruation breaks the fast. Voluntary bloodletting is both intentional and temporary, whereas menstruation precludes any participation in the fast, since menstruating women would be in a perpetual state of breaking the fast because of their bleeding.[47] According to the Ayātallāh Khomeinī (d. 1989), the flowing of any nonmenstrual blood is reprehensible during fasting.[48] According to the laws of purity, menstrual blood requires ritual washing whereas nonmenstrual blood requires ablution.[49]

Vomiting breaks the fast, and it requires ablution under certain conditions. This position is based upon a number of ḥadīth reports, including one given on the authority of Abū al-Dardāʾ that the prophet Muhammad vomited and broke the fast. In a related account it is reported by Maʿdān b. Abī Ṭalḥah that Thawbān imposed ablution for vomiting during the fast. Abū Hurayrah reports that the prophet Muhammad stated that it is only when the vomiting is induced by the person fasting that the fast is broken but that a person vomiting uncontrollably does not break his fast.[50] Mālik b. Anas reports a similar opinion on the authority of Ibn ʿUmar.[51] Jurists argue from these reports that whether or not vomiting breaks the fast depends upon both the volume of the vomit and whether it was induced or due to sickness.[52]

The relationship between intentional vomiting and breaking the fast is also evident in the opinions concerning whether kissing results in breaking the fast. One report from Maymūnah bt. Saʿd states that when the prophet Muhammad was asked about kissing during fasting, he said that both people kissing break the fast.[53] Another report, transmitted on the authority of ʿĀʾishah and Umm Salamah, claims that the prophet Muhammad used to kiss when he was fasting, presumably without breaking his fast.[54] At issue among the jurists is whether the kissing is intentional in the sense that it leads to or is related to sex.[55] Mālik b. Anas cites a report on the authority of Ibn ʿAbbās that kissing is allowed for old men but reprehensible for young men.[56] Mālik b. Anas also cites reports which imply that the prophet Muhammad's kissing of his wives was a special allowance.[57] Ibn Qudāmah states that kissing breaks the fast only when it is accompanied by ejaculation, like masturbation that results in ejaculation and repeated looking or thinking about something that causes the emission of semen.[58]

In all three cases (bleeding, vomiting, kissing), breaking the fast is tied to the intention of the person fasting. The conditions that break the fast coincide with the conditions that invalidate ablution and ritual washing, but the actions that break the fast can be avoided temporarily. The conditions that invalidate ablution are unavoidable, whereas when bleeding and vomiting occur without artificial inducing they are not considered to break the fast. Demonstrating this same logic, Muḥammad b. ʿAlī Ibn Bābūyah (d. 991) states that a nocturnal emission does not break the fast but marriage does.[59] Kissing breaks the fast only insofar as it is consciously associated with sex. This relationship is stated succinctly in the Ḥanafī opinion described by Aḥmad b. Muḥammad al-Qudūrī (d. 1037):

> If he [the person fasting] sleeps and he has a nocturnal emission, looks at a woman and ejaculates, or anoints himself with oil, cups himself, applies kohl, or kisses, he has not broken the fast. If, by a kiss or touch, he ejaculates, then making up the fast is incumbent upon him without expiation. There is no harm in the kiss when he is in control of himself, but it is reprehensible if he is not in control of himself. If vomit overpowers him, he has not broken the fast. If he vomits on purpose, filling his mouth, then making up the fast is incumbent upon him without expiation.[60]

Unintentional ejaculation, like eating out of forgetfulness, does not break the fast, but the intentional eating of rocks or metal and having sexual intercourse with something other than the vagina of a woman (even without ejaculation) does break the fast.[61] The Ayātallāh Khomeinī adds the purposeful passing of gas and entering a bathhouse (ḥammām) as being reprehensible for the person fasting.[62] Likewise, the requirement to fast adheres even after the death of the person fasting, so that the statement of intention to fast obligates others to fast or otherwise redeem the deceased from the fast.[63] Because the fast is temporary, it allows the person fasting a relatively sustained but artificial state apart from human nature, analogous to that signified by the performance of ablution and ritual washing.

## OFFERING

A similar state separating people from regular human civilization is signified by the requirements for the offering (zakāt).[64] The laws of offering stipulate giving away a percentage of certain items, including domesticated animals, money, merchandise, and cultivated produce. Ibn Rushd provides the list of items upon which there is agreement among the jurists that offering should be given: "There is agreement that offering is given for two types of minerals: gold and silver not used for ornamentation; three types of animals: camels, cattle, sheep and goats; two types of grain: wheat and barley; and two types of produce: dried dates and raisins."[65] This list is specific, and a number of jurists insist that offering is to be given on these items only. There are disagreements regarding items that are judged by analogy to be included in the requirement of offering or are excluded for practical purposes.[66]

Among the items not agreed upon by the jurists are horses. Only Abū Ḥanīfah and his student Zufar require that offering be given on horses. The opinion is stated by al-Qudūrī: "When there are free-grazing horses, male and female, their owner has a choice. If he wants, he gives one dinar for every horse, or if he wants he appraises them and gives five dirhems for every one hundred dirhems [of their value]. There is no offering for male horses alone."[67] According to Ibn Rushd, this position actually requires offering for the offspring of horses and is based upon the treatment of the horses as a commodity.[68] That there is no offering for a person's mount is found in a ḥadīth report cited by numerous authorities, but the Ḥanafīs cite another ḥadīth report, on the authority of Zayd b. Thābit, which says that a dinar or ten dirhems is the offering for every horse.[69] To this, Ḥanafī authorities add the citation of a letter written from ʿUmar b. al-Khaṭṭāb to Abū ʿUbaydah b. al-Jarrāḥ requiring him to pay a dinar or ten dirhems for each free-grazing horse.[70] According to later Ḥanafī authorities, this ḥadīth report transmitted on the authority of Zayd specifies that the offering for horses is intended for horses used in war (fars al-ghāzī).[71]

There is no disagreement among the jurists regarding the requirement of giving offering on camels, cattle, and sheep and goats, but some jurists specify that offering is required only for free-grazing animals of these types.[72] It is possible that the Ḥanafī position on horses is based on an analogy with the requirement of offering for other free-grazing animals. Such an explanation is not offered by the Ḥanafīs, who claim that the requirement for offering on horses is in analogy with offering on other salable commodities. This is further evident from the opinions of Abū Yūsuf and al-Shaybānī, who state that there is no offering for horses, mules, or donkeys unless they are used for commerce.[73] Perhaps this is due to the recognition by the Ḥanafīs that horses (along with mules and donkeys) are not regularly used, as are animals of the other three types, to provide food and clothing.[74] Abū Yūsuf and al-Shaybānī support this logic by stating that there is no offering required for suckling camels (fuṣlān), lambs still carried by their mothers (ḥumlān), and calves under a year old (ʿajājīl).[75]

Jurists disagree on requiring offering for a number of different items of produce beyond the agreement that offering is required for wheat, barley, dried dates, and raisins. Some jurists, including Ibn Abī Laylā, Sufyān al-Thawrī, and Ibn al-Mubārak hold that offering is required for only the four items agreed upon by all jurists.[76] Mālik b. Anas and al-Shāfiʿī also require offering on other types of produce that is cut and stored.[77] Abū Ḥanīfah requires offering on everything that is cultivated by people, whether edible or not, including grass, wood, and stalks.[78] Despite these differences of detail, all of the jurists agree that offering is given only on products that are cultivated, just as offering is given only on domesticated animals.[79] The qualification that offering is given only for cultivated produce may also explain the almost unanimous rejection of requiring offering on honey, since it is produced by bees, just as milk and wool are produced by animals and are not subject to offering.[80] Abū Bakr b. ʿAlī al-Ḥaddād (d. 1398) limits Abū Ḥanīfah's requirement of offering on nonedible produce to produce that is cultivated and excludes items such as palm fronds and cane, which grow wild.[81] Similar questions are discussed regarding other items which may or may not be considered to be used as food, such as olive oil.

All of the jurists agree, however, that offering is not to be given on perishable produce. There is no offering for fresh fruits or leafy green vegetables.[82] Many of the disagreements over what produce is subject to offering is due to differing interpretations of what constitutes perishable and nonperishable produce, such as onions and figs.[83] Although some scholars have claimed that exempting perishable produce from offering is based upon practical considerations, it is remarkable that the categories used to determine which foods are subject to offering coincide with the foods pertaining to the garden of Eden and the fall of Adam and Eve. Foods subject to offering are cultivated foods.[84] Wheat in particular is associated with the forbidden tree in the garden of Eden, the fall to earth, and the cause of impurities requiring ablution. Fruit is also specifically linked with the garden of Eden and the special conditions enjoyed by Adam and Eve there.[85]

The same applies to the other items subject to offering. There were no domesticated animals in the garden of Eden, nor were animals used to provide foodstuffs and clothing for Adam and Eve before their fall.[86] Offering is also required on merchandise such as clothing, slaves, and other goods that were not present in the garden of Eden.[87] There was also no gold or silver in the garden of Eden: "ʿAlī b. ʿAbī Ṭālib: When God created the world he did not create in it any gold or silver. When he caused Adam and Eve to fall, he sent down with them gold and silver, that it would be passed down for use in buying and selling in the earth as an earthly benefit to their children after them. He established by this the dower [ṣadāq] of Eve, and it is thus necessary for everyone to give a dower when marrying."[88] Offering is also required on other precious minerals of the earth, and on money.[89] The practice of getting rid of certain items allows for a partial experience of existence in the garden of Eden, just as fasting provides a temporary experience of the prefall state of Adam and Eve.

Muslim scholars compare fasting and offering as both relate to conditions in the garden of Eden. Both the fast and the offering are said to give admittance to the garden of Eden. In a number of ḥadīth reports cited by al-Bukhārī, the prophet Muhammad states that the works required for entering the garden of Eden include the offering, fasting, and prayers.[90] Ibn Mājah preserves a ḥadīth report given on the authority of Abū Hurayrah in which the prophet Muhammad compares fasting and offering: "Abū Hurayrah said the apostle of God said: 'For everything there is offering. The offering of the body is the fast.'"[91] The breath of a person fasting is said to smell like the garden of Eden according to a number of ḥadīth reports preserved in al-Bukhārī, Muslim, and al-Tirmidhī.[92] Both fasting and offering are rituals oriented toward God, and are not to be performed or judged in terms of their actual natural and social effects.[93] Offering is required to be paid by a person even after death, just as the fast is still incumbent on a person who dies without completing it, both the offering and fasting owed as debts.[94] The offering and the fast are, like ablution and ritual washing, a means to subdue carnal connections, and the purification of one's body and belongings are specifically linked to the forgiveness of sins.[95]

### PILGRIMAGE

The pilgrimage is closely and explicitly linked to the garden of Eden. Adam is said to have instituted the rituals of the pilgrimage after his expulsion from the garden of Eden and his repentance for the sin that led to that expulsion. Ibn Isḥāq reports that when Adam fell to the earth he was sad because he missed the sights and smells of the garden of Eden, so God ordered him to go to Mecca.[96] According to Ibn ʿAbbās, because of Adam's sin God commanded him to build the Kaʿbah and circumambulate it, remembering God, just as the angels circumambulate the throne of God.[97] In his commentary on Q 2:39, Ibn Kathīr remarks that Adam's repentance after his fall was tied to his receiving the commands of religion, and al-Zamakhsharī links Adam's repentance to his prophethood.[98] The sanctuary at Mecca was to be an earthly substitute for the garden of Eden, made necessary by Adam's fall and allowed by Adam's repentance as part of that which was required for Adam and his descendants to return to the garden of Eden. Citing Ibn ʿAbbās, al-Ṭabarī reports that the establishment of the sanctuary and the pilgrimage were tied to God's acceptance of Adam's repentance, which included a fast of forty days and abstaining from sex with Eve for one hundred years.[99] Adam is made the custodian of the sanctuary at Mecca and is responsible for establishing the pilgrimage there for his descendants, emphasizing that these descendants no longer were living in the garden of Eden.[100]

The prohibitions established by Adam pertaining to the sanctuary at Mecca and the conduct of pilgrims correspond directly to conditions in the garden of Eden. An overview of the prohibitions is provided by al-Qudūrī: "He [a pilgrim] does not kill prey, nor does he motion toward it or point it out. He does not wear a shirt or trousers or a turban, tall hat [qalansūwah], or open garment [qabāʾ]. He does not wear enclosed shoes unless he does not find sandals; then he cuts out the lower part of the heels. He does not cover his head or his face, nor does he wear perfume. He does not shave his head or the hair of his body. He does not trim his beard or cut his nails. He does not wear clothes dyed with turmeric, saffron, or safflower unless they can be washed without fading."[101] In his description of the prohibitions connected to the pilgrim and the Meccan sanctuary, Ibn Qudāmah includes wearing a head covering, killing prey and pointing toward prey that is killed, eating prey, applying perfume, wearing dyed clothing, cutting the hair of the head and body, trimming the nails, eating certain foods, applying perfumed ointments, and applying kohl.[102] Ibn Bābūyah lists wearing certain types of clothes, hunting prey, applying perfume or odorific ointments, applying kohl, and ejaculation caused by looking at a woman's legs or genitals.[103] In addition, Ibn Rushd includes wearing enclosed shoes, certain clothes, coverings, and hats, applying perfume and marshmallow, hunting, marriage, cutting nails and hair, and various types of sexual relations.[104]

The condition prescribed for the pilgrim when in a state of sacralization (iḥrām) and within the sanctuary (ḥaram) at Mecca is not unlike the conditions in which Adam and Eve lived in the garden of Eden. There, Adam and Eve lived a noncivilized existence, without the need of clothing, shelter, or cultivated foods. Pilgrims are not allowed to cut their hair or fingernails or to wear perfume. Ibn Mājah and al-Tirmidhī preserve reports on the authority of Ibn ʿUmar that the prophet Muhammad defined the state of the pilgrim as being unkempt and ill-smelling: "A man came to the Prophet and said: 'Who is a pilgrim [ḥājj]?' He said: 'The unkempt [al-shaʿath] and ill-smelling [al-tifl].' Another came up and said: 'Which pilgrimage is better, Apostle of God?' He said: 'The crying [al-ʿajj] and bleeding [al-thajj].' Another came up and said: 'What is the way, Apostle of God?' He said: 'Provisions [al-zād] and luggage [al-rāḥilah].'"[105] Adam and Eve's bodies are also said to have been covered with fingernail, hair, or feathers like the bodies of wild animals before the discovery of their genitals and their fall. The prohibition against the application of perfume by a pilgrim inside the sanctuary may be linked with the notion that all perfume originated from the plants of the garden of Eden and as such did not exist before the fall.[106] Some jurists allow for the application of perfume before pilgrims enter their sacralized state (iḥrām), but once the pilgrim is inside the sanctuary, it may not be applied.[107] On the basis of a ḥadīth report, Mālik b. Anas requires that all perfume be washed from the pilgrim's body before entering into the sanctuary.[108] Some jurists likewise prohibit the application of marshmallow or other sweet-smelling items to the pilgrim's hair, and the prohibition against cloth dyed with turmeric and other spices is also related to their odor.[109] Ibn Qudāmah includes in this discussion the various positions on the prohibition against eating foods prepared with spices, such as saffron, or using scented creams.[110]

Pilgrims are not allowed to wear sewn clothing. Ibn Qudāmah specifies that the pilgrim cannot wear a shirt (qamīṣ), turban (ʿimāmah), trousers (sarāwīl), shoes (khifāf), hooded cloak (burūs), open garment (qabāʾ), covering (duwāj), long sleeves that cover the hands, or head covering.[111] This is based on a ḥadīth report, related by Ibn ʿUmar, in which certain items were prohibited to the pilgrim by the prophet Muhammad.[112] Ibn Rushd discusses the prohibition of gloves (quffāz), veils (niqāb, khimār), and open-fronted garments (durrāʿah) for women, also based on a ḥadīth report cited by Mālik b. Anas.[113] These prohibitions correspond to the conditions of Adam and Eve, who were naked in the garden of Eden. The origins of sewn clothing are specifically linked with Adam and Eve's becoming aware of their genitals, their fall, and the necessity of clothing themselves while living on earth.[114]

Pilgrims are not allowed to hunt wild prey or harvest wild plants growing in the sanctuary. Abū Yūsuf reports the opinion of Abū Ḥanīfah that it is reprehensible to graze animals on the grass of the sanctuary or to cut the grass but that there is no harm in removing dust and rocks from the area.[115] Aḥmad b. Muḥammad al-Ṭaḥāwī (d. 933) reports that it is not forbidden to hunt the prey of Medina or to cut down the trees there, as it is in the sanctuary around Mecca, although both Mālik b. Anas and al-Shāfiʿī categorize doing these things in Medina as reprehensible.[116] On the basis of a report from the prophet Muhammad, al-Shāfiʿī also considers hunting and cutting down trees in the nearby city of al-Ṭāʾif to be reprehensible.[117] Wild animals were not predatory in the garden of Eden, there were no domesticated animals, and Adam and Eve did not have a need to kill animals for food or clothing. The cultivation and harvesting of plants for food were not practiced in the garden of Eden, but were the punishment imposed upon Adam as a direct consequence of his fall to earth.

The penalties stipulated for the violation of the sanctuary or the pilgrim's sacralized state are also associated with food.[118] On the basis of the exegesis of Q 5:95, jurists stipulate three options for penalizing pilgrims who violate the rules of the pilgrimage or the area of the sanctuary, all of which involve food: fasting, feeding the poor, and animal sacrifice.[119] Ibn Abī Zayd provides the standard list: "If a person kills prey then incumbent upon him is a penalty like that which he killed from among grazing herd animals [naʿam], determined by two just people from among the Muslims jurists. . . . He has the choice of this or expiation by feeding the poor [an amount of food equal to] the value of the prey determined as food and given as alms for it, or equal to this is to fast a day for each measure of food [mudd], and for each portion of a measure a complete day."[120] Fasting is going without food and, like fasting during the month of Ramaḍān, suggests the possibility of existence without eating, sustained by God alone. Feeding the poor creates conditions, like those in the garden of Eden, in which people are not required to work the land for their sustenance. The sacrifice of domesticated animals is the symbolic elimination of animal food and by-products, an act by which pilgrims, in imitation of Adam and Eve, can renounce their reliance on the eating of meat and the existence of domesticated animals. Similar penalties are stipulated for breaking the fast during Ramaḍān, further strengthening the connection between the two rituals and the garden of Eden.[121]

Likewise, there is no sexual contact or marriage in the sanctuary, just as there was no sex in the garden of Eden, when Adam and Eve were ignorant of their genitals before their fall. Under this prohibition, Ibn Qudāmah includes marrying someone else, getting married, becoming engaged, sex both with and without ejaculation, sex with a vagina and with something other than a vagina whether ejaculating or not, kissing, and lustful looking.[122] Menstruating women or women who are still within the legal period following parturition are restricted from circumambulating the Kaʿbah.[123]

Ḥanafī authorities also specify lustful touching along with kissing, and they prohibit sex but do not further distinguish these actions or stipulate a distinction based on ejaculation.[124] The prohibition on sexual contact is specifically addressed to married couples, with the implication that it is the sexual contact as a function and consequence of marriage that is being prohibited in this context.[125] There are also a number of reports stating that a husband and wife performing the pilgrimage at the same time must separate for the period of the pilgrimage, suggesting that even a marriage already contracted is not valid for the period of the pilgrimage.[126]

## RELATED PURITY LAWS

Placing the restrictions on touching the penis in the context of these other rituals and the conditions of Eden allows for a more discerning interpretation of other unusual purity laws. According to Ibn Rushd, among the actions and conditions that are reported to require the performance of ablution are sleeping and unconsciousness, eating something touched by fire, and carrying a corpse.[127] That sleeping and unconsciousness require ablution is generally agreed, according to al-Shāfiʿī, Abū Ḥanīfah, and Mālik b. Anas, although some jurists do not require ablution for sleep outright.[128] In the *Kitāb al-umm,* it is stated that al-Shāfiʿī requires ablution if a person sleeps lying down or otherwise loses consciousness or the ability to reason due to insanity or sickness, whether lying down or not.[129] Drawing on the practice of different companions of the prophet Muhammad, al-Shāfiʿī states that there is no ablution required for sleeping while sitting.[130] But al-Shāfiʿī is also reported to have required ablution for any deep sleep:

> Equally for the rider on a boat, camel, riding animal, and riding while sitting on anything moving about the ground, sleeping standing or while prostrating, bowing, and lying down, ablution is required. When a person has doubt concerning whether he was asleep and he has the urge to urinate but does not know whether this urge was something he dreamed or related to himself awake, then he is not considered sleeping. If he is certain that he had the urge in a dream, but not certain he was asleep, then he is considered sleeping and ablution is incumbent upon him.[131]

Abū Ḥanīfah holds the same position with regard to the necessity of sleeping lying down, based on a report transmitted on the authority of ʿUmar b. al-Khaṭṭāb that sleeping while lying down requires ablution.[132] Mālik b. Anas also takes into consideration whether the sleep was heavy, the length of the sleep, and the position of the sleeper.[133] In all three cases, despite the differences of detail, the authorities agree that it is the loss of consciousness that invalidates ablution.

There are a number of ḥadīth reports going back to the prophet Muhammad and his companions which state that eating something touched by fire requires ablution, although almost all later jurists hold that this practice has been dropped. "Zayd b. Thābit said: I heard the apostle of God saying: 'Ablution [is required] for that which fire touches.'"[134] This report and similar ones are transmitted on the authority of Abū Hurayrah, ʿĀʾishah, Abū Ayyūb al-Anṣārī, Anas b. Mālik, Ibn Abī Mālik, Abū Mūsā, Umm Salamah, Ibn ʿUmar, ʿAbdallāh b. Zayd, Umm Ḥabībah, Ubayy b. Kaʿb, Jābir b. ʿAbdallāh, al-Ḥasan b. ʿAlī, al-Ḥusayn b. ʿAlī, and others.[135] To Mālik b. Anas and al-Shāfiʿī are attributed opinions that they specifically rejected the idea that eating cooked food invalidated ablution.[136] According to Ibn Rushd, Jābir b. ʿAbdallāh reported that the prophet Muhammad instructed his followers to cease observing the requirement of ablution for eating that which touched fire, thus abrogating his earlier practice.[137]

Carrying a corpse also requires ablution according to ḥadīth reports given on the authority of a number of companions of the prophet Muhammad, although some of the chains of transmission are considered weak.[138] The following is transmitted on the authority of Abū Hurayrah: "The Prophet said: 'For washing it [the corpse], ritual washing [is required]. For carrying it, ablution [is required].'"[139] Some of the opinions cited by al-Tirmidhī hold that ablution rather than ritual washing is required for the person who washes a corpse, but there is no further discussion of ablution's being required for the person who merely transports or handles the corpse.[140] Mālik b. Anas reports that Asmāʾ bt. Umays washed the corpse of Abū Bakr and was told that she was not required to perform ritual washing.[141] That a corpse would cause impurity might also be implied by the special category of animals thought to eat carrion, including allowances to kill carrion-eating animals in the Meccan sanctuary and restrictions on eating their flesh.[142] The Ayātallāh Khomeinī includes among substances that require ablution the urine of birds whose flesh is not eaten along with the sweat of certain animals and people affected by physical impurities.[143] The requirement of ablution for touching a corpse may also be related to the listing of carrion and skins of carrion in the category of physical impurity (najāsah).[144]

Although jurists proffer different accounts for these three cases individually, they do not provide a more general explanation encompassing how sleeping, cooked food, and corpse contact are related to other conditions that require ablution. Some scholars point to the fact that the impurity of cooked food may be due to the association of fire with the punishment of hell.[145] Ibn Qudāmah, though, cites a number of early Muslim authorities who required ablution for that which was altered (ghayyara) by fire, referring to cooked foods in general.[146] The notion that the requirement of ablution was intended to signify all food entering the body, by analogy to the impurity of food waste exiting the body through defecation and vomit, would not explain the ḥadīth report specifying food cooked with fire. It seems, rather, that the ḥadīth report refers to the eating of meat. Muslim records the following account transmitted on the authority of Jābir b. Samurah: "A man asked the apostle of God: 'Should I perform ablution from the meat of sheep?' He said: 'If you want perform ablution and if you want, do not perform ablution.' He [the man] said: 'Should I perform ablution from the meat of camels?' He [the Prophet] said: 'Yes, perform ablution from the meat of camels.'"[147] This ḥadīth report is discussed at some length by Ibn Taymīyah, who argues that the references to the meat of sheep and camels should be understood as references to cooked food.[148] The same point is made by Muḥammad b. ʿAlī al-Shawkānī (d. 1834), who cites an extensive list of authorities.[149] Note also that the necessity of performing ablution after touching raw meat is specifically denied.[150] Other jurists such as Ibn Rushd and Ibn Qudāmah also maintain that the requirement of ablution for eating food touched by fire should be understood to refer to the eating of the cooked meat of pigs.[151]

Food cooked with fire, and especially meat, is in the same category as touching the penis. Both are to be understood in relation to the existence of Adam and Eve in the garden of Eden. Just as touching the penis requires ablution because it makes one conscious of having genitalia (in contrast to Adam and Eve before their fall from Eden), so eating cooked meat required ablution as a reminder of the absence of cooking and the eating of meat in the garden of Eden. Muslim exegesis of Q 2:34–39 mentions that Adam had to be taught how to cultivate and prepare food after his fall from Eden.[152] The "oven" (tannūr) of Q 11:40 and 23:27 which God caused to boil forth the flood in the time of Noah is said to be this first oven which Adam and Eve used to cook their food.[153] Likewise, there was no death, sickness, or unconsciousness in the garden of Eden. Although the reasons behind the requirement of ablution for these conditions was perhaps lost on later jurists, contact with the dead and unconsciousness or sleep represent circumstances unknown in the garden of Eden, and thus ablution was required, at least for a time, to remind people of the separation between Eden and their current existence in a fallen state on earth.

## CONCLUSIONS: TABOO AND CONTAGION

In his essay "Taboo and Emotional Ambivalence," Sigmund Freud discusses what he calls the primitive concept of taboo and contagion.[154] He argues not that the taboo itself is contagious, but rather that a person who violates the taboo without consequence will encourage others to violate the taboo, with the result that the taboo loses its symbolic value and function in society. Requiring ablution for touching the penis holds a place in Islamic purity laws analogous to the sense of "taboo" as employed by Freud. Impurity is not "contagious," nor does the penis "transmit" impurity. Rather, the act of touching the penis is circumscribed to maintain the symbolic significance of ablution in its relationship with the loss of the garden of Eden and the necessity of religion and society.

Note also that purification and other rituals are symbolic acts. For example, the performance of ablution is not required before eating or after urination or defecation.[155] It is necessary only before performing ritual practices and thus not for hygenic reasons. Certainly the ritual offering is not a realistic means for the redistribution of wealth, just as fasting forever and never again urinating or sleeping would be impossible. Numerous ḥadīth reports and juristic definitions of ritual practices make it clear that people are not supposed to practice asceticism.[156] The control of eating and sex during the fast signifies a temporary state of purity apart from human nature and can only be temporary without resulting in starvation or ceasing the continuation of human existence through procreation. Also indicative of the symbolic but nonrepresentational dimension of the rituals is the timing of the rituals, which are tied not to seasonal or historical occurrences, but to artificial divisions of time.

It is important to keep in mind that the prohibitions on touching the penis are discussed in texts most commonly used in pedagogical contexts, not necessarily "how-to" manuals of Islamic law or texts that purport to describe actual or even normative practices. In these pedagogical contexts, the legal category of "touching the penis" serves as an example (of things that cause impurity and require ablution) that points to the general principles and reasoning behind all laws of purification and ritual. The link maintained between touching the penis and the existence of Adam and Eve in the garden of Eden can be extended to explain other laws of purification and the rituals made obligatory in Islamic law. Muslim definitions of purity and impurity emphasize the symbolic nature of ritual, that rituals are symbolic actions.[157] The symbolism of the purity laws is not only that ritual purity is equivalent to living in the garden of Eden, but also that such purity is no longer natural or even possible for humans living in a fallen existence. Definition and performance of rituals emphasize the distinction between this world, in which religion and its upkeep by jurists is necessary, and the utopian existence of Eden.

CHAPTER THREE

# *Relics of the Prophet Muhammad*

Chapter 2 showed how Muslim legal definitions of purity and impurity can be understood as symbolic references to conditions in the garden of Eden. The impurity associated with natural bodily functions and sexual reproduction emphasizes the absolute difference between earthly existence and the utopia of Eden. The definition and performance of other rituals, such as the fast, offering, and pilgrimage, are also tied to conceptions of Eden. Rituals are practicable references to the fallen human condition that is described in narrative form by the exegetical accounts of Adam and Eve's fall.

Chapter 3 focuses on the relics of the prophet Muhammad, and the relics of certain pre-Islamic prophets and kings, as they relate to the conception of the sanctuary at Mecca and the origins of civilization. Section 1 examines the prophet Muhammad's physical (hair, nails, footprints) and artificial (clothing, ḥadīth reports, various implements and artifacts) remains. The dispersal and collection of these remains represent different conceptions of territory based on a general model in which objects associated with the prophet Muhammad are transported by his followers from Mecca to the various outposts of Islamic civilization. Section 2 shows how Muslim exegesis links the relics of earlier prophets and kings to the origins of both Islamic and human civilization at the Meccan sanctuary established and visited as the earthly representation of the lost Eden. The state patronage of such relics, and the narrative description of their role in the development of civilization centered at Mecca, demonstrates the close connection between the mythological origins of civilization and an ideology which stipulates the existence of the state to administer religion required by the fallen state of humanity. Like ritual, relics serve to remind people of their fallen state by referring to the separation of earth and its civilization from existence in the garden of Eden.

## 1: RELICS OF THE PROPHET MUHAMMAD

In his history, al-Ṭabarī preserves an unusual report concerning the dying instructions of the first Umayyad caliph, Muʿāwiyah b. Abī Sufyān. The report is transmitted on the authority of ʿAbd al-Aʿlā b. Maymūn, on the authority of his father: "When he became sick with the illness from which he died, Muʿāwiyah said: 'The apostle of God clothed me with a shirt [qamīṣ], and I put it away. He pared his nails one day, and I took the parings and put them in a bottle. When I die, clothe me in that shirt, cut up and grind the parings, and scatter them on my eyes and mouth so that perhaps God might be merciful to me on account of the blessings [barakah] of these things.'"[1] A similar account is mentioned by Nasīm al-Riyāḍ in his commentary on the *Shifāʾ* of al-Qāḍī ʿIyāḍ, but in this account Muʿāwiyah is buried in two of the prophet Muhammad's cloaks (izār and ridāʾ), and both the hair and the fingernails of the prophet Muhammad are stuffed in Muʿāwiyah's mouth and nose in accordance with his bequest.[2]

Other reports indicate that the prophet Muhammad distributed his hair after shaving for the desacralization ritual (iḥlāl) after his pilgrimage to Mecca, suggesting that the nails belonging to Muʿāwiyah might also be connected to the prophet Muhammad's trimming of his nails at the conclusion of his pilgrimage and leaving his sacralized state as a pilgrim (iḥrām).[3] Both al-Bukhārī and Muslim cite a report in which it is said that the prophet Muhammad cut his hair upon completing the pilgrimage, instructed Abū Ṭalḥah to distribute one share of the hair to each of the male companions of the Prophet (ṣaḥābah), and instructed Abū Ṭalḥah's wife Umm Sulaym to distribute two shares to the women.[4] According to Ibn Ḥajar, it was this distribution which established the tradition of blessings (barakah) being associated with the hair of the Prophet.[5] Al-Qasṭallānī comments that the prophet Muhammad made this distribution at the completion of his pilgrimage so that his followers could keep the objects as relics.[6] Aḥmad b. Ḥanbal records a report that there was no hair that fell from the prophet Muhammad's head that was not collected by his followers.[7]

The link between these relics and the pilgrimage to Mecca is highlighted further by the context of the other prohibitions for pilgrims entering the Meccan sanctuary as a pilgrim, in a state of ritual sacralization (iḥrām). Pilgrims are not allowed to wear sewn garments, dyed clothes, shoes with enclosed heels, cloaks, or hats, nor are they allowed to apply perfume and oils. These items appear to represent both social status and products of civilization. Kissing, lustful touching, sexual intercourse, and marriage are prohibited, apparently as a means of separating the Meccan sanctuary from the space of everyday life and the bases for the continuity of human society.

The area of the Meccan sanctuary itself is a preserve of wilderness in which people are restricted from hunting for food and harvesting trees, grass, or rocks. On the basis of a saying of the prophet Muhammad recorded in Ibn Mājah and al-Tirmidhī, legal scholars stress that these prohibitions, and especially the restrictions on cutting hair and nails, keep the pilgrim in a wild, animal-like state for the duration of the stay in the territory of the Meccan sanctuary.[8]

The transportation of hair by the companions of the prophet Muhammad and the farther distribution of this hair through conquest is evident from the records of burial, especially at sites of martyrdom or conquest. The Umayyad Khālid b. al-Walīd is reported to have been buried in Ḥimṣ with a hair of the prophet Muhammad which he wore within or pinned to his hat when he conquered Damascus.[9] Abū Zamʿah al-Balawī, also known as ʿUbayd b. Arqam and ʿUbayd b. Adam, is reported to have been one of the companions present when the prophet Muhammad distributed his hair that was cut at the time of his desacralization (iḥlāl) on the day of Mina.[10] Al-Balawī is reported to have settled in Egypt but later traveled to Ifriqiyah on a raid with Muʿāwiyah b. Hudayj, during which he was martyred and buried in Qayrawan at a place later identified as al-Balawīyah. In his history of Qayrawan, ʿAbd al-Raḥmān b. Muḥammad al-Dabbāgh (d. 1300) describes how al-Balawī was buried with the hair of the prophet Muhammad: "He died in Qayrawan and was buried in a location known still today and called al-Balawīyah. He ordered them to cover over his grave and bury with him his tall hat [qalansūwah], in which was a hair from the Prophet."[11]

In another report cited by al-Dabbāgh, it is said that al-Balawī had three hairs of the prophet Muhammad, and he stated in his will that one should be placed on his tongue and one on each of his eyes.[12] ʿAbd al-Ghanī b. Ismāʿīl al-Nābulsī (d. 1731) states that the hairs of the prophet Muhammad are numerous in India, and some claim that such hairs move, grow, and multiply on their own.[13]

The mention of a special location marked as the burial site of al-Balawī is also known from other traditions regarding the hairs of the prophet Muhammad. For example, Abū Shaʿrah, who acquired some hairs of the prophet Muhammad, is said to have been buried in al-Zillaj in a spot marked with a dome around which was planted olive trees.[14] Ibn Ḥajar reports that the burial site of ʿAlī b. Muḥammad b. al-Ḥasan al-Khalāṭī, sometimes called "al-Rikābī" because of his possession of a stirrup (rikāb) and hair of the prophet Muhammad, is well known.[15] Anas b. Mālik is said to have requested that he be buried with a hair of the prophet Muhammad under his tongue.[16] Jaʿfar b. Khinzāb, the vizier of the Ikhshīdid Kāfūr, had three hairs of the prophet Muhammad, which he ordered to be placed in his mouth when he was buried in Medina.[17] The Zengid ruler Nūr al-Dīn Maḥmūd ordained that hairs of the prophet Muhammad be put on his eyes when he was buried in the madrasa he built in Damascus.[18]

In other cases, hairs of the prophet Muhammad are used at the foundation of a public building, such as the madrasa of Ibn al-Zaman, which was named for Shams al-Dīn Muḥammad b. ʿUmar b. Muḥammad b. ʿUmar al-Zaman, who is said to have possessed a hair of the prophet Muhammad.[19] In his work on this history of madrasas, ʿAbd al-Qādir b. Muḥammad al-Nuʿaymī mentions that the Naṣrid amir Sayf al-Dīn Manjak al-Yūsufī established the Madrasa al-Manjakīyah in Damascus with a hair from the prophet Muhammad.[20] Ottomans are recorded to have donated hairs of the prophet Muhammad to the Ayyubid Mosque in Cairo.[21] The public display and procession of hairs at mosques and madrasas, especially on the occasion of the birthday of the prophet Muhammad, is mentioned in a number of sources.[22]

This use of the remains of the prophet Muhammad in the establishment of pious endowments is consistent with reports preserved by Aḥmad b. ʿAlī al-Nasāʾī (d. 915) and Aḥmad b. Ḥanbal that the leftover water from the prophet Muhammad's ablution and mouth rinsing was used to mark the place of a mosque: "He [the prophet Muhammad] called for water. He performed his ablution, rinsed his mouth, and then poured it in a bucket. He instructed us, saying: 'Take this and when you come to your land, break your agreement, sprinkle this water in the place, and take it as a mosque.' We said: 'The city is far away and it is very hot. The water will dry up.' He said: 'Extend it with other water, for only the scent is necessary.' So we went out until we reached our city. We broke the agreement, then sprinkled in its place, and took it as a mosque."[23] In this case, the saliva of the prophet Muhammad, like his hair, is transported to a distant location as an extension of his authority for the foundation of Islamic worship. Many other mosques, such as the Masjid al-Ḥusayn in Cairo and the Masjid al-Jazzār Pasha in Acre, are said to be endowed with and founded upon hairs of the prophet Muhammad, as are other institutions such as the Ribāṭ al-Naqshbandīyah in Cairo, the Mashhad al-Ḥusaynī in Damascus, and the Jami Mosque in Bahubal.[24]

Abū ʿAbdallāh Muḥammad b. Abī Bakr al-Murshidī, who was born in Mecca (1368) and died in Medina (1435), is reported to have had twenty-six hairs of the prophet Muhammad which he acquired from an upright man on one of his three visits to Jerusalem. The account is given in Muḥammad b. ʿAbd al-Raḥmān's (d. 1497) biography of al-Murshidī: "[Al-Murshidī] was pious and staid among people. He visited the Prophet for more than fifty years, walking on his own feet. He also visited Jerusalem three times, where he met an upright man in whose possession were twenty-six hairs of the Prophet. He distributed them upon his death to six people in equal portions, and this one [al-Murshidī] was one of them."[25] In the biography of al-Murshidī's son, ʿUmar b. Muḥammad, al-Sakhāwī states that the hair was divided equally among three people, and that the hair brought blessings upon ʿUmar for fifty-six years.[26] Elsewhere in his work, al-Sakhāwī explains that the hairs were transferred from ʿUmar to his son, al-Murshidī's grandson, Abū Ḥamīd.[27] During his visit to Mecca in the sixteenth century, al-Qasṭallānī reported seeing the hair, then associated with al-Murshidī's grandson Abū Ḥamīd.[28] These reports point to the importance of the transmission of prophetic relics, not unlike the transmission of ḥadīth reports, among the pious and from father to son.

These hairs were acquired through travel away from Mecca and, in the case of al-Murshidī, travel in imitation of the prophet Muhammad's journey to Jerusalem. The transportation of the hair by al-Murshidī is an example of relic movement which facilitates the collection of the relics and their restoration to the place from which they were originally dispatched by the prophet Muhammad himself. The transfer of the hair to Mecca by al-Murshidī and his heirs represents a return of the prophet Muhammad's remains from their dispersal with his companions. It also establishes a chain of transmission not unlike that conceptualized in the dispersal and collection of ḥadīth reports and other relics. The hair transported by al-Murshidī provides a physical manifestation of the otherwise intangible link between the prophet Muhammad and later generations of followers.

## ḤADĪTH REPORTS AS TEXTUAL REMAINS

This dispatch of the relics with the companions and early followers of the prophet Muhammad, and the association of the relics with the establishment of civilizational centers in new territories, is also reflected in the distribution and collection of the Prophet's remains as text. The basic model of temporal succession and geographical distance is emphasized by the expansion of the companions (ṣaḥābah) and Islam to the civilizational centers or "camps" (amṣār) founded by the conquest, and by the necessity of travel among these civilizational centers in the search for knowledge of the prophet Muhammad. The Sunnah is represented by a textual record of the words and deeds of the prophet Muhammad as recorded by those of his followers who were in physical contact with him during his life. This textual corpus can be transmitted orally, in written form, or by the imitation of practices said to originate with the prophet Muhammad.

The dispersal of the Sunnah through four generations of scholarship, from the prophet Muhammad to the scholars of the third Islamic century, is traced by Muslim scholars concerned with identifying the lines of transmission of ḥadīth reports.[29] The first generations of followers are described as spreading the textual reports of the prophet Muhammad from the sanctuaries at Mecca and Medina in the Ḥijāz to Iraq, Syria, Iran, and Khurasan. The fourth generation of transmitters is identified with the local authorities whose opinions became the basis for the classical Sunnī schools of law.

| | | |
|---|---|---|
| First generation | Ṣaḥābah | Companions |
| Second generation | Tābiʿūn | Followers |
| Third generation | Tābiʿī al-Tābiʿīn | Followers of followers |
| Fourth generation | al-Aʾimmah | Founders of law schools |

With each generation the practicable and textual record of the prophet Muhammad's life was dispersed to a wider area and to greater numbers of people. According to ʿAbd al-Raḥmān Ibn Abī Ḥātim (d. 938), the authority of the textual record transmitted is due to the fact that the original transmitters had been in physical contact with the prophet Muhammad: "They [transmitters] preserve from the Prophet what he received from God, and what the Prophet practiced, defined as practice, decided, judged, delegated, commanded, proscribed, forbade, and suggested they memorized and acquired."[30] Those first transmitters, who were in physical contact with the prophet Muhammad—his companions (ṣaḥābah)—acquired his textual remains and became living examples of his words and deeds, which they imitated in their own sayings and actions. The Prophet was a physical manifestation of the revelation while he stayed in Mecca and Medina for twenty-three years and established the distinguishing characteristics (maʿālim) of the religion.[31] The practice of these first followers then became a physical manifestation of the prophet Muhammad's example. With each generation, this example became the example of new people in new locations, generations of followers who became themselves the distinguishing characteristics of Islam.[32]

A more detailed conception of the distribution of the example of the prophet Muhammad was mapped in later centuries. Abū Isḥāq al-Shīrāzī (1003–1083), for example, reconstructs the lines of transmission and the movement of the Sunnah from the Ḥijāz, where the prophet Muhammad lived, to the major civilizational centers in Iraq, Egypt, and Syria. The local authorities whose opinions became the basis for the classical schools of Sunnī law are tied not to particular people but to specific locations to which knowledge of the prophet Muhammad had spread.[33] Abū Ḥanīfah and his followers were identified with the transmission of the Sunnah to Kufah, al-Awzāʿī with the transmission to Syria, and Aḥmad b. Ḥanbal with the transmission to Baghdad.

According to this map of al-Shīrāzī, the classical Sunnī law schools grew from the example of a single individual in the Ḥijāz and spread to the widespread locations conquered by the earliest followers of the prophet Muhammad. Those who had been in physical contact with the Prophet brought reports of his life to the next generation of followers in Medina, Basrah, Mecca, Syria, Kufah, Nahiyah, Ṭāʾif, and Egypt. The next generation, larger in number than the first, spread the textual accounts of the prophet Muhammad to an even wider area: Medina, Mecca, Yemen, Syria and Jazirah, Egypt, Kufah, Basrah, Baghdad, and Khurasan.[34]

This dispersal of the successive generations of followers led to the necessity of traveling throughout these cities in order to collect the examples and reports of prophetic practice. The cities where the different scholars traveled and transmitted their knowledge of the Sunnah became depots for the textual record of the prophet Muhammad's life. Scholars had to journey, often great distances and over periods of many years within the far-flung area encompassed by the area constituted by the early conquests and subsequent expansion of Islamic civilization. Traveling among the cities established by those who had been in physical contact with the Prophet allowed scholars to connect themselves to the transmission of the Sunnah. This travel also allowed scholars to collect in one location, in one text, a complete textual record of the prophet Muhammad's life.[35] This travel also entailed the creation of specific chains of transmission, allowing that only the select who made this travel, or later those who could trace their knowledge to these select few, were in a position of legal authority having a physical link to the textual corpus of the prophet Muhammad's life.

With the culminating collection of the Sunnah into written texts and the concentration of knowledge of the prophet Muhammad in the cities of Islamic civilization, as centers of learning, the significance of the Prophet as text remained fundamental to the geographical model employed by Muslim ḥadīth and legal scholarship. The reports of prophetic practice collected from their dispersal throughout Islamic civilization were compiled into the "six books" (al-kutub al-sittah),[36] representing a single corpus of the sayings and actions of the prophet Muhammad.[37] This textualization allowed for a more detailed accounting of the chains of transmission and led to the development of the formal discipline of ḥadīth criticism (al-jarḥ wa al-taʿdīl) to examine the reliability of the reports claimed by various authorities on the basis of their localities.[38] Scholars began to compile biographical lists of the principle transmitters of this textual record which included the names of the transmitters in the six books,[39] but also lists in which were included only the names of either weak or trustworthy transmitters.[40] Although the interpretation of written texts might displace the necessity of travel, temporal and spatial considerations, such as when and where a particular transmitter died, became the primary basis for the evaluation of knowledge and the establishment of authority.[41]

## PRESERVED FOOTPRINTS OF THE PROPHET MUHAMMAD

The link between the distribution and collection of the prophet Muhammad's knowledge and the demarcation of territorial and civilizational boundaries is also illustrated by the transmission of other remains of the Prophet, such as his footprints. A number of his footprints are reported to be preserved in stone, each called *Qadam Rasūl Allāh* or *al-Qadam al-Sharīf.* These footprints preserved in stone are scattered throughout the area encompassed by the early conquests and places to which successive generations of the Prophet's followers traveled. Many of these footprints are still extant.[42]

Some of these footprints are preserved in situ, where they were left by the prophet Muhammad. Perhaps the best known of these is the footprint in Jerusalem, preserved in the rock that is under the Dome of the Rock.[43] This footprint is supposed to have been left by the prophet Muhammad when he visited Jerusalem during his Isrāʾ and Mirʿāj.[44] Other footprints are preserved in places that the prophet Muhammad is supposed to have visited during his life, such as the footprint in al-Ṭāʾif on Mount Abū Zubaydah.[45] Some sources report that the footprint is accompanied by the imprint left by a gazelle when the Jewish family that owned it converted to Islam.[46] In the Masjid al-Qadam, just south of Damascus on the pilgrimage road, is a footprint said to have been left by the prophet Muhammad when, half alighted from his camel, he was asked by Gabriel to choose between this world and the next.[47] Another report mentions the caliph al-Mahdī seeing a footprint of the prophet Muhammad upon his arrival in Medina.[48]

Other footprints of the prophet Muhammad, like his hair and ḥadīth reports, are distributed to areas farther afield than his actual footsteps. One of these footprints preserved in stone was brought to Constantinople by one of the first generation of the Prophet's followers, Abū Ayyūb al-Anṣārī, during the siege of the city, when he died, under the Umayyad caliph Yazīd b. Muʿāwiyah. As with the burial of the hair and nails of the prophet Muhammad, Abū Ayyūb al-Anṣārī left instructions that the footprint be buried with him.[49] The practice of collecting the footprints of the prophet Muhammad and their association with burial sites also extends to the preserved footprints of his followers, especially those claiming descent from him. The footprint of Sidi Shaykh is reported to be preserved in Algeria,[50] and the footprints of a marabout reportedly were seen when the first Muslims arrived in Senegal.[51]

The footprints of the prophet Muhammad are also used in the foundations of buildings. The Mujāhidīyah Madrasa in Damascus used to house a black stone on which was a footprint of the Prophet.[52] In Tanta, another black stone, on which are preserved the prints of both the feet of the prophet Muhammad, is built into the foundation of the domed shrine of Sayyid Aḥmad al-Badawī.[53] Other tombs contain footprints of the prophet Muhammad, such as that of Sultan Abū al-Naṣr Qāʾit Bay in Cairo,[54] that of Sultan ʿAbd al-Ḥamīd I in Istanbul,[55] and that of Fatḥ Khān, son of Fīrūz Shāh Rajab, in the Qadam Sharīf in Delhi.[56] There are also a number of mosques that were built specially to house footprints of the prophet Muhammad, such as the Masjid Āthār al-Nabī in Cairo and the Gawr Mosque.[57] Other footprints are kept in special buildings for exhibition, such as the six held in the Topkapi Palace in Istanbul or the footprint in the Qadam Rasul Building in Lucknow.[58]

Closely related to the footprints is the preserved shoe or "sandal" of the prophet Muhammad (naʿl al-nabī). In his catalog of a private Medinan library, C. Landberg mentions a book containing ḥadīth reports praising the preserved sandal of the Prophet.[59] Other literary descriptions of the sandal are known, and the sandal is mentioned by al-Dhahabī, Quṭb al-Dīn al-Ḥalabī, and Ibn Ḥajar.[60] As are the other relics of the prophet Muhammad, his sandals and their dispersion are traced back to his earliest followers. One of his sandals is said to have originated with Umm Kulthūm, the daughter of Abū Bakr.[61] Another sandal is reported to have been preserved in the mosque in Khalīl in the eleventh century.[62] A Mālikī *fatwā* from Aḥmad b. Yaḥyā al-Wansharīsī (d. 1508) in Fez on the veneration of the prophet Muhammad's sandal demonstrates that the practice was known in the Maghrib.[63] In his history of Egypt, Aḥmad b. ʿAbd al-Wahhāb al-Nuwayrī (d. 1333) records that a sandal of the Prophet was owned by an Egyptian named Aḥmad b. ʿUthmān, who was descended from Sulaymān Abū al-Ḥadīd, the companion of the prophet Muhammad.[64] Aḥmad b. ʿUthmān is reported to have put the sandal on his eyes and wanted it to be buried with him.

A number of accounts mention the sandal of the prophet Muhammad housed in the Ashrafīyah Madrasa. According to Mūsā b. Muḥammad al-Yūnīnī (d. 1326), the fourteenth-century ruler al-Mālik al-Ashraf wanted to visit a sandal he considered the sacred relic of the Prophet in the possession of Niẓām al-Dīn b. Abī al-Ḥadīd.[65] Ibn Abī al-Ḥadīd used to take the sandal on visits to various local rulers who would pay him, so al-Mālik al-Ashraf asked for a small piece of the sandal so that it could be buried with him. According to Muḥammad b. Shākir al-Kutubī (d. 1363), al-Mālik al-Ashraf wanted the sandal so that he could wear it around his neck like a talisman.[66] After the death of Ibn Abī al-Ḥadīd, the sandal was taken to Damascus by al-Mālik al-Ashraf, where it was housed in a special place for ḥadīth scholarship (dār al-ḥadīth) surrounded by books which contained scholarship devoted to the textual record of the prophet Muhammad's life.[67] According to ʿUthmān b. Aḥmad Ibn al-Ḥawrānī (d. 1705), the sandal was buried in the wall of the Dār al-Ḥadīth al-Ashrafīyah.[68] It was moved to Istanbul in the nineteenth century.[69] Other sandals are reported to have been placed in the foundations of buildings, such as the right sandal of the prophet Muhammad housed in the Madrasah al-Dāmāghīya, and another sandal in the mausoleum of the Sulṭān al-Ghūrī.[70]

## SYMBOLISM OF PROPHETIC RELICS

Despite the objections of scholars like Ibn Taymīyah, traditions relating to the footprints of the prophet Muhammad, like those related to his hair and ḥadīth reports, do not appear to be understood primarily as a means to venerate the prophet Muhammad's physical body. Different traditions do emphasize the miraculous physical character of the prophet Muhammad's feet, such as the reports attributed to ʿAlī b. Abī Ṭālib that when the Prophet walked his footsteps were so matched that it appeared as if he were walking on air.[71] There are also reports of other miraculous aspects of his body, such as that he cast no shadow, that fire could not burn his hair,[72] and that his sweat and spit had curative powers.[73] The footprints do not seem to be equated with the various traditions, especially in Sufism, of touching the feet of a venerable person as a sign of devotion and humility.[74] By contrast, the prophet Muhammad's relics and their distribution seem to reflect and stress his physical absence, and the concurrent spread of Islam to the widespread centers of civilization where these relics have been carried. Most of the footprints, even those made in situ by the prophet Muhammad in Jerusalem and Damascus, are outside the main area of his physical activity, as were the sites housing his hair and the far-flung civilizational centers which functioned as depots for the collection of ḥadīth reports.

The footprints, ḥadīth reports, and hair need to be seen as part of the larger context of all of the artifacts dispersed after the death of the prophet Muhammad. Most of these remains of the Prophet are artifacts lacking extraordinary attributes. There are items which were part of the prophet Muhammad's everyday life, such as his cup, shoes, cloak, a fragment of his bowl, his kohl pencil, an awl for patching shoes, an instrument for extracting thorns, his turban, his walking stick, and his bed.[75] Some of the artifacts relate to the practice of religion, including the prophet Muhammad's prayer mat, his pulpit (minbar), and his copy of the Quran.[76] Others were associated with the prophet Muhammad's role as a leader, such as his signet ring, his handwritten letters to certain families and other leaders, swords and bows, iron stirrup, armor, javelin, flags, and banners.[77] Aside from the hair and fingernails, and his body, which is buried in Medina, however, there are no other physical remains of the prophet Muhammad reported to be kept elsewhere.[78]

The relics of the prophet Muhammad are ordinary items the dispersal and collection of which, in his absence, reflect the spread of civilization and authority. Hair, footprints, and other artifacts of the Prophet are used in the foundation of buildings, such as mosques and madrasas, which are physical manifestations of the territorial distribution of Islam and of the preserved chain of transmission from him. These buildings are designated for the transmission of the example and textual record of the prophet Muhammad's life. The acquisition of ḥadīth reports was necessitated by the dispersal of the Prophet's knowledge but also represents a means by which certain scholars and institutions gained authority. The civilizational centers were founded upon the example of the prophet Muhammad and became collection depots for his dispersed remains. Footprints and other artifacts marked the tombs of special individuals and classes which had authority in the area in which the prophet Muhammad's relics were spread, such as sultans, jurists, saints, and martyrs. As such, the Prophet's relics served to mark and signify the territorial boundaries of civilization and the law of the revelation.

## 2: RELICS AND CIVILIZATION

Closely related to the dispersal and collection of the prophet Muhammad's relics and their link to the spread of civilization is the interpretation of the transportation and possession of the relics of earlier prophets and kings. In their sack of Mecca in the eleventh century, the Qarmaṭians are reported to have taken from the Kaʿbah a number of relics, including the rod of Moses, the horn of the ram sacrificed by Abraham, and a stone containing the footprint of Abraham (maqām Ibrāhīm).[79] Other accounts, mentioned in chapter 1, detail the survival of artifacts associated with David (swords and armor) and Solomon (horses, mirror, throne, table, signet ring), many of which are traced back to Adam and originated as gifts from heaven for the establishment of civilization.

One collection of prophetic relics that receives much attention in Muslim exegesis and histories is that of Moses and Aaron, said to be contained in the Ark of the Covenant. Early Muslim exegesis of Q 2:248 provides a context in which to understand the significance of the prophet Muhammad's relics, and in particular their link to the sanctuary at Mecca. ʿUbaydallah b. Sulaymān, on the authority of al-Ḍaḥḥāk, claims that the "remains" (baqīyah) said to be in the Ark of the Covenant are a reference to "fighting for God" (jihād fī sabīl allāh).[80] In another report, on the authority of ʿAṭāʾ b. Abī Rabāḥ, it is said that the "remains" refer to knowledge of the Torah.[81] As are the prophet Muhammad's artifacts, the ark is here linked to the spread of civilization and knowledge of the revealed law. In the broader context of the exegesis associated with Q 2:246–251, the ark itself is an artifact, linking its holder to the founding prophets and defining moments in the history of the Israelites. With its miraculous return, the ark is a sign of the authority of Ṭālūt, David, and Solomon and the locating of a civilizational and political center in Jerusalem.[82]

Although Q 2:248 uses the term "coffin" (tābūt) for the ark, and describes its contents as the "remains" of Moses and Aaron, Muslim exegesis is clear to point out that the relics of Moses and Aaron were not their physical remains:

> Ibn ʿAbbās said: The rod of Moses and the fragments of the tablets. This is the same as what was said by Qatādah, al-Suddī, al-Rabīʿa b. Anas, and ʿIkrimah, but they added: The Torah. Abū Ṣāliḥ said this meant the rod of Moses, the rod of Aaron, the two tablets of the Torah, and the Manna. ʿAṭīyah b. Saʿd said: The rod of Moses, the rod of Aaron, the garments of Moses, the garments of Aaron, and the fragments of the tablets.
>
> ʿAbd al-Razzāq said: I asked al-Thawrī about the verse, and he said: "There are those who say a measure of Manna and the fragments of the tablets, and others who say the rod and shoes."[83]

Various reports provide different accounts of the ark's contents, but they all identify the remains, with the exception of the manna, with ordinary objects.

Many of these objects parallel those associated with the prophet Muhammad, and Muslim exegesis associates the contents of the Ark of the Covenant with the stories of Adam and his fall from the garden of Eden. Moses's rod, for example, is said to have been brought by Adam when he was expelled from the garden of Eden. In the exegesis of the Moses narratives in the Quran, the rod is portrayed as a symbol of Moses's authority as a king and a prophet.[84] Moses used the rod to defeat the Egyptians, part the sea, bring water from the rock, and defeat the giant Og.[85] In one report, the rod was with Adam until his death, when Gabriel took guardianship of it and then passed it on to Moses in Midian.[86] Another report states that the rod was passed down through the prophets until it was passed from the prophet Shuʿayb to Moses in Midian, thus establishing a chain of transmission not unlike that found in the transmission of ḥadīth reports.[87]

Muslim exegesis also links the bringing of the rod from the garden of Eden with the origins of perfume and the arts of civilization. Adam is said to have taken the rod from one of the trees in the garden of Eden, sometimes identified with the Tree of Life, and taken with him pieces of the other trees when he fell to earth. Different reports of this are given by al-Ṭabarī in his exegesis of Q 7:22.

> Abū al-ʿĀliyah said: Adam left the Garden and took with him from there a rod from the trees of the garden. On his head was a crown or wreath from the trees of the garden. He fell to India, and from the crown came all the perfume in India. . . .
>
> It is also said that when Adam fell to earth he had a wreath on his head from the trees of the garden, when he reached the earth the wreath dried up and its leaves scattered, and from them grew the different types of perfume. Others say: This is what is meant when it is mentioned that Adam and Eve sewed leaves from the garden as clothes [Q 7:22]. When these leaves dried they scattered, and from them grew the types of perfume. Others say: When Adam learned that God was going to cast him to the earth, he began to pass by every tree in the garden and take branches from them. When he fell to the earth, these branches were with him, and when they dried up their leaves scattered. This is the origin of perfume.[88]

In his history, al-Ṭabarī reports that the origins of the rod are connected to other implements and arts of civilization:

> Adam caused some of the perfume of the garden to come down with him. He also brought down with him myrrh and incense, the black stone which used to be more white than snow, and the rod of Moses which was from the myrtle of the garden, ten cubits tall and equal to the height of Moses. After that, anvils, mallets, and tongs were sent down to him. When Adam fell upon the mountain, he looked and saw a rod of iron growing on the mountain. With the mallet, he began to break up the trees which had grown old and dry; then he heated the [iron] branch until it melted. The

first thing he pounded out was a knife with which he used to work. Then he pounded out an oven, the one which Noah inherited.[89]

In this account, Adam is supplied with the tools and raw materials necessary for working with iron, which he subsequently uses to create a knife and oven, implements used primarily for the preparation of food.

The manna is also supposed to have descended from heaven and is closely associated with the food eaten in the garden of Eden. On the authority of Ibn ʿAṭīyah, al-Jawharī, Mujāhid, and al-Zajjāj, Ibn Kathīr reports that the manna was like honey, the honey that flows in the garden of Eden.[90] There are numerous reports, based on the exegesis of Q 47:15, which associate honey with the garden of Eden.[91] Ibn Kathīr also reports, on the authority of ʿIkrimah, that the quail given to the Israelites in the wilderness of wandering were like the birds of the garden of Eden.[92] Consumption of the manna was not supposed to cause defecation, not unlike the food eaten by Adam and Even before they ate from the Tree of Life.[93] The manna represents food provided by God, food that requires no cultivation and harvesting, food for which the people did not have to work. This is in contrast with the punishment imposed on Adam: after his fall he was required to work the land for his food.[94]

Similarly, the clothing of Moses and Aaron is linked to the accounts of the garden of Eden and the fall of Adam and Eve. Ibn Kathīr reports, in his exegesis of Q 7:159, on the authority of al-Suddī, Ibn ʿAbbās, and others, that God provided special clothing to the Israelites in the wilderness: "[The Israelites asked]: 'Where are the clothes?' Their clothes used to grow with them, just as children grow. The clothes did not tear or wear."[95] These were clothes that did not need to be taken from animals, sheared, spun and woven, and sewn, like the coverings of Adam and Eve in the garden before the fall from Eden.[96] On the basis of the exegesis of Q 7:26, Muḥammad b. Qays reports that Adam and Eve were originally covered with feathers, like angels.[97] Wahb b. Munabbih claims that Adam and Eve's clothing was light which covered their genitals.[98] Others, on the basis of Q 7:22, report that it was Adam and Eve's fingernails that covered their "secret parts," and that after they ate of the tree, the fingernails fell off and they sewed together leaves as their clothing.[99]

The connection between the loss of Adam and Eve's coverings and the exposure of their genitals is related to the tradition that there was no sex in the garden of Eden. Gabriel's instructions in sex and reproduction are related to his other instruction of Adam in the arts of civilization such as farming and metal-working. Just as Adam's punishment was having to work the land for food, Eve's punishment was menstruation and the bearing of children in pain, for, before the fall, there was no need for Adam and Eve to reproduce themselves to overcome mortality.[100]

## MECCAN ORIGINS OF CIVILIZATION

It is in Mecca that Adam and Eve first meet after the fall and begin procreation and the issue of the human race. And it is from Mecca that civilization first develops and spreads, the location where Adam receives instruction in the arts of civilization along with the implements required to practice these arts. According to al-Thaʿlabī, Adam was the first person to coin dinars and dirhems, creating the money necessary for commerce.[101] Exegesis on Q 57:25 discusses the origins of iron and specifically the smithing of tools for agriculture and war, making the substances and the technical skills divine gifts to Adam as the first smith. Adam is also credited with having invented the different languages of the world. According to ʿAlī b. Burhān al-Dīn al-Ḥalabī (d. 1635), Adam knew the twelve different types of writing systems used in the world, and al-Kisāʾī claims that Adam spoke seven hundred languages.[102]

Much of the exegesis related to the establishment of the Meccan sanctuary and the pilgrimage to it portray Mecca as the center of the world and the location from which religion originated. In some exegesis, the Meccan sanctuary is associated with all the prophets. It is reported that when Adam arrived in Mecca, the Kaʿbah was already in place, a jewel from the garden of Eden that was later raised up into heaven as the Bayt al-Maʿmūr before the flood in the time of Noah.[103] In other accounts, Adam set up the first Kaʿbah as a tent (ʿarīsh) similar to the tabernacle that would later be built by the Israelites under Moses in the wilderness.[104] Several exegetes mention the account in which Adam builds the Kaʿbah when he arrives in Mecca out of five mountains: Mount Sinai, the Mount of Olives, Lebanon, al-Jūdī, and al-Ḥirāʾ. Each of these mountains is associated with future prophets: Moses, Jesus, Solomon, Noah, and Muhammad.[105]

Adam's role in instituting the rituals of the pilgrimage, and in particular the boundaries of the sanctuary, establishes a link between Mecca and the lineage of prophets. The observance of the pilgrimage rites and prohibitions of the sanctuary by the prophets reiterates the association of Mecca and Eden. The prohibition against the application of perfume in the sanctuary is related to the idea that perfume originated from the plants of the garden of Eden and thus would naturally provide a sweet smell to visitors. There is no sexual contact or marriage in the sanctuary, just as there was no sex in the garden of Eden, where Adam and Eve were ignorant of their genitals. Similarly, no sewn clothing is allowed for the pilgrim, just as Adam and Eve were naked in Eden and learned how to sew clothes only after their fall. Wild animals were not predatory in the garden of Eden, nor did Adam and Eve need to kill them for food or clothing. The cultivation and harvesting of plants for food was not practiced in the garden of Eden; they are tied directly to Adam's fall and the necessary origins of human food production.

The association of different prophetic relics with the fall from Eden is tied directly to the territory of the Meccan sanctuary as an earthly counterpart of the garden of Eden. Muslim exegesis states that the sanctuary was established by Adam in imitation of the garden of Eden. According to different reports, when Adam first fell to the earth he was tall enough that, standing on Mount Budh, or "Nod," in India, his head reached into heaven, where he enjoyed the sweet perfume of the garden and could see and hear the angels crowding around God's throne.[106] After the angels complained to God, Adam was reduced in size, but he was still large enough that his step was said to cover the distance it would take a normal-sized man to travel in three days.[107] Because he could no longer hear and smell the garden of Eden, God instructed Adam to make a pilgrimage to Mecca and establish the sanctuary there as a substitute for the garden of Eden. As Adam made his way to Mecca from India, his footsteps demarcated wild from civilized territory: "Adam went on the pilgrimage to Mecca from India. Every place his foot stepped became a city [qurā] and the territory between his steps became barren desert until he arrived at the House and circumambulated it."[108] In this account, Adam's footsteps mark out the future cities of the world, ending at the metropolis or "mother city" (umm al-qurā) of Mecca.[109]

Each of the gifts and actions of Adam relate directly to different aspects of civilization, and to the various prophets and kings who succeed him. Adam is cast as the first smith, who is taught the divine secrets of alchemy and metallurgy to create the implements of civilization, including tools, weapons, and money. He is portrayed as the first king, who demarcates the boundaries of cities and settled lands and who establishes language and commerce. Drawing upon all of these aspects, Adam is made to be the first prophet, who establishes the sanctuary at Mecca and performs the pilgrimage which is to be repeated by all successive prophets, culminating in the prophet Muhammad.

A similar link between relics and the Meccan sanctuary is made in many Muslim eschatological traditions. For example, the sword of the prophets is supposed to return to the earth in the hand of Jesus to defeat the Dajjāl. The Kaʿbah will be destroyed and the sanctuary devastated as knowledge of the Quran and Islamic law disappears. The old landscape of the earth will be replaced with a new one, such as that envisioned with the appearance of the prophet Muhammad's pool. Judgment will be on the basis of the laws of the fallen earth, but paradise will be different, governed by a set of rules between those of the earth and heaven.[110]

## STATE PATRONAGE OF RELICS

That these narratives about the origins of civilization and the artifacts that accompanied them had religious and political significance in later Muslim societies is evident from the collection of relics and sanction of rituals directed at their recognition, transportation, display, and preservation. Many of these relics were associated with the pilgrimage to Mecca from the major cities throughout the Middle East and North Africa. Local leaders provided accommodation and protection for pilgrims and maintained shrines, tombs, and other religious sites along the pilgrimage routes that passed through the areas within their jurisdiction. As seen from the examples above, states also patronized Islamic legal scholarship, often by establishing special buildings which housed the various relics of the prophet Muhammad.

Some of the earliest Muslim rulers, such as Muʿāwiyah b. Abī Sufyān, kept and used artifacts and relics associated with the prophet Muhammad. The Fatimids appear to be the first state to collect and display relics associated with Shiʿī or ʿAlid figures.[111] According to an inscription on a pulpit from the mashhad in ʿAsqalān, the head of Ḥusayn b. ʿAlī b. Abī Ṭālib was discovered by Badr al-Jamālī in the twelfth century.[112] The head is said to have been kept originally in Syria by the Umayyad caliph Yazīd until its disappearance.[113] After its discovery in ʿAsqalān, the head was cleaned up, perfumed, and transported to Cairo in a basket to be housed in the Ḥusayn Mosque.

In Fatimid Cairo a number of mausoleums were established to contain the bodies of Fatimid predecessors from North Africa, including ʿUbaydallāh al-Mahdī, al-Qāʾim, the grandfather, and al-Manṣūr, the father of al-Muʿizz.[114] A special building was built over the site of the rediscovered burial site of the head of Zayd b. ʿAlī Zayn al-ʿĀbidīn b. al-Ḥusayn in the thirteenth century.[115] These shrines and mosques, all dating from the last period of Fatimid rule, seem to be part of an attempt to provide physical evidence of the Fatimid claim of descent from the prophet Muhammad through Ḥusayn b. ʿAlī.[116] Other sites in Cairo included the mausoleum of the brothers of Joseph, on the site of what is said to have been a Jewish cemetery containing the relics of Moses.[117] The origins of special rituals designated for the visitation of relics can also be found in relation to some of these early buildings.[118]

Roughly concurrent with this work of the Fatimids was the attempt by the twelfth-century Zengid ruler Nūr al-Dīn Maḥmūd and the later Ayyubids to create centers of prophetic authority in Syria. Unlike the Fatimids, the Zengids and Ayyubids focused on the textual artifacts of the prophet Muhammad and the building of madrasas for ḥadīth and law scholarship and shrines for figures prominent in the transmission and study of these textual artifacts.[119] In Aleppo, Nūr al-Dīn built three madrasas, several caravansaries, a hospital, a number of mosques, a Dār al-ʿAdl, a Dār al-Ḥadīth, a shrine for the Ḥanbalīs and a shrine for the Mālikīs.[120] In Damascus, he built another hospital, a Dār al-ʿAdl, seven madrasas, the Dār al-Ḥadīth al-Nūrīya, the Ribāṭ of Abū al-Bayān, and a number of mosques, and he worked on the great mosque of the Umayyads.[121] Nūr al-Dīn also built a Shāfiʿī madrasa in Hama and a Shāfiʿī madrasa in Baʿalbek.[122] The breadth of his patronage and claim to territory are evidenced by his having built a pulpit for the al-Aqṣā Mosque in Jerusalem[123] and his commissioning of projects in Daraya, Hama, Mecca, Medina, and Mosul.[124] By laying emphasis upon the textual artifacts of the prophet Muhammad, Zengid buildings could counter the threat of the Shiʿī Fatimid ideology and of the Crusader states.

Under the Ayyubids and Mamluks certain cities became significant centers for the display of relics associated with the prophets and the origins and spread of Islam. Once established as sites for the collection and display of relics, cities such as Hama and Damascus continued to develop new pilgrimage sites, including those associated with artifacts, locations of special events, and bodies of important people. Ibn al-Ḥawrānī cites traditions according to which there are said to be 500 or 1,700 tombs of prophets in Damascus, including the tomb of Moses.[125] Compilations of ḥadīth reports and traditions concerning the virtues (faḍāʾil) and wonders (ʿajāʾib) of Damascus and its surroundings emphasize the importance of the area as a center for pilgrimage. This patronage included a major building program on the Ḥaram al-Sharīf in Jerusalem as one of the pilgrimage sites in Syria.[126]

Among the locations and items catalogued in medieval guides as pilgrimage sites in and around Damascus are the following: the cave at Mount Qāsiyūn where Abel was killed by Cain, the site of the birth of Abraham and the place where he observed the celestial phenomena, the tomb of Moses, the footprint of Moses in the al-Qadam Mosque, the rock struck by Moses in the wilderness of wandering, the place where Jesus and Mary took refuge, the minaret upon which Jesus will descend at the end of time, the head of John the Baptist, the throne of Bilqis the Queen of Sheba, the tomb of Hud, the place where Khiḍr prayed, the tomb of the mother of Mary, the footprints of ʿAlī b. Abī Ṭālib, the tombs of the prophet Muhammad's wives, the tombs of the prophet Muhammad's companions (Bilāl b. Hamāmah, Abū al-Dardāʾ, Faḍālah b. ʿUbayd, Sahl b. Hanzaliya, Wāthilah b. al-Aṣqaʿ, Aws b. Aws al-Thaqafī, Kaʿb al-Aḥbār, and Muʿāwiyah), the tombs of other prominent figures (Umm ʿAṭiyyah, Ṣuhayb al-Rūmī, ʿAbdallāh b. Masʿūd, Ubayy b. Kaʿb, and Jaʿfar al-Ṣādiq), the tombs of famous scholars (Ibn Kathīr, Shams al-Dīn al-Dhahabī, Ibn Rajab, Ibn Qayyim al-Jawzīya, Ibn Qudāmah, Ibn Mālik), the mashhads of ʿAlī, Ḥusayn, and Zayn al-ʿĀbidīn, the oratory of ʿUmar b. al-Khaṭṭāb or ʿUmar b. ʿAbd al-ʿAzīz, the tomb of ʿĀʾishah, the lance of Khālid b. al-Walīd, and the "Tomb of the Six" (ṣaḥābah) (containing the remains of Ḥughr b. ʿAdī, Khālid b. Saʿīd, Abū Muslim al-Khawlānī, Saʿd b. ʿUbādah, Daḥya al-Kalbī, Mudrik, and Kannāz).[127]

In and around Hama are attested a number of small shrines (mazārāt) connected with saints and prophetic figures: the maqām of Zayn al-ʿĀbidīn, the maqām of Jaʿfar al-Ṭayyār, the tomb of Jonah in the Ḥasanayn Mosque, the tomb of Ham the son of Noah, the maqām of David, the tomb of the Emīr Ṣārim al-Dīn al-Nābulsī, the tombs of soldiers who fought with Salāḥ al-Dīn (Shaykh Muḥammad Nahār and Shaykh Suweyd), the tombs of famous Muslim scholars (Abū al-Layth al-Samarqandī, Shaykh ʿAlwān Abū Muḥammad ʿAlī b. ʿAṭīya, al-Shīrāzī, Shaykh Khallūf, al-Birmawī, al-Sālūsī, al-Muẓaffar, Shaykh Maʿrūf, Umays al-Qaranī, Shaykh ʿAmbar, Abū al-Wafā al-Ḥawrānī, Shaykh ʿAbash, Sayyida Nafīsa, Shaykh Abū al-ʿAdīmnāt, Shaykh Ḥasan, Shaykh Masʿūd, Shaykh Maknūn, and Shaykh Bashīr), the mazār of al-Ḥusayn, and the maqām of ʿAbd al-Qādir al-Kīlānī.[128]

The existence of conflicting traditions concerning the location of some relics demonstrates that acknowledging the authenticity of the relics and accuracy of the site was less important than being able to claim patronage of the relics and the site. The rivalry over the location of the tomb of Moses resulted in the identification and patronage of three different sites.[129] In other cases, such as the complex of sites at Khalīl or Hebron, the competition among different groups included exegetical and physical claims.[130] Other sites and relics were destroyed rather than allowed to fall into the hands of a competing patron, as was not uncommonly practiced by the Crusaders around Jerusalem.[131] The different tombs of Ezra in Iraq and Syria were recognized and visited by both Jews and Muslims,[132] and a number of Buddhist relics were transformed into relics of ʿAlī b. Abī Ṭālib by Muslims in India.[133]

In other cases, relics and sites seem to have been produced without an attempt to trace their history. According to ʿAbd al-Raḥmān al-Jabartī (d. 1825), a number of relics including hairs, shoes, and a handwriting sample from the prophet Muhammad were discovered suddenly in the mausoleum of Sulṭān al-Ghūrī.[134] Aḥmad b. Muḥammad Ibn Khallikān (d. 1282) reports that Tāj al-Dīn b. Ḥinna constructed the Ribāṭ Dayr al-Ṭīn near Cairo for a cache of relics he had purchased from the family of the Banū Ibrāhīm for one hundred thousand dirhems.[135] Others claim that the Ribāṭ of relics is said to have contained only a piece of wood and a piece of iron.[136] Shams al-Dīn b. Muḥammad b. ʿAlī Ibn Ṭūlūn (d. 1546) reports that prophetic relics were taken in procession from Jerusalem to Damascus, including a cup (qadaḥ) and walking stick (ʿukkāz) of the prophet Muhammad.[137] Ibn Ṭūlūn doubts the authenticity of these relics but recognizes the significance of their acquisition and transport to Damascus by local authorities.[138] The identification of the tomb of Noah near Baʿalbek also appears to have been anticipated.[139] Nūr al-Dīn is reported to have taken a piece of the special saw of Shaykh Arslān Nūr al-Dīn and stipulated that it be placed in his burial shroud.[140]

The symbolic character of such relics is illustrated by a *fatwā* included in the collection of al-Wansharīsī. In response to a question about the permissibility of visiting a shrine which housed a shoe of the prophet Muhammad (naʿl karīmah), the author of the *fatwā* states that there is no sensible reason to venerate a shoe: "If this relic [al-āthār] is considered great and sacred, it is not because it has any particular form nor any particular smell, but because a person considers it great on account of his [the prophet Muhammad's] sacred character, from its connection to his noble house."[141] After this, the *fatwā* goes on to cite a number of ḥadīth reports concerning the veneration of objects. Permission for people to wear, touch, and wipe the shoe relic is based upon this veneration, a veneration that is supposed to focus the mind of the visitor on the prophet Muhammad and the sacred places where he walked. It is about bringing to mind the temporal and physical distance separating the visitor from the Prophet when he wore the shoe.

More important than the relics themselves was the relationship represented by the patronage of relics by the state. The Ottoman treasury housed one of the greatest collections of prophetic artifacts, now kept in the Topkapi Palace in Istanbul. Perhaps this collection, like the collection of relics by earlier local states, was intended to demonstrate the legitimacy of the Turkish state among the largely non-Turkish Arab population of the Middle East. In addition to the swords of the prophet Muhammad and his followers, the Topkapi includes the cloak (burdah) and hairs of the prophet Muhammad, a number of footprints, the silver keys of the Kaʿbah,[142] the cover (maḥfaẓah) for the black stone, an inscribed signet ring of the prophet Muhammad, and a letter from the prophet Muhammad to Muqawqas written on the cover of a Coptic Gospel.[143]

A large number of relics were brought to Samarqand by Timur from his conquests in the Middle East and were later transferred to Mughal India. These included a copy of the ʿUthmān Qurʾān, taken from Baghdād and stained with the blood of ʿUthmān,[144] the body or just the hand of the prophet Daniel,[145] and a large number of Arabic and Persian manuscripts. The Pādishāhī Mosque in Lahore is reported to contain twenty-eight different relics of the prophet Muhammad, ʿAlī b. Abī Ṭālib, Fāṭimah, al-Ḥusayn, and Shawth al-Aʿẓam ʿAbd al-Qādir Gīnānī and miscellaneous items, including a tooth of Uways al-Quranī. This cache is said to have been taken from Damascus by Timur and later brought to India and held by Babur until it was transferred by the British to the mosque at Lahore.[146]

The link between the patronage of relics and the legitimacy of the state is not limited to Islamic examples. In Ptolemaic Egypt, the Hellenistic rulers were able to assert their authority vis-à-vis local identity through a sort of pilgrimage to different cities in which were said to be interred the dismembered body parts of Osiris.[147] The modern state of Israel has attempted to lay claim to certain parts of historical Palestine on the basis of the identification of archaeological remains with the biblical narrative of the ancient Israelites.[148] The Hashemite Kingdom of Jordan has invested millions of dinars and many years of work in the renovation of the tombs and shrines attributed to prophets, companions of the prophet Muhammad, and other sites of religious significance among Muslims and Christians. This patronage and renovation has also included the upgrading of roads and other local infrastructure to facilitate the visits of pilgrims and tourism.

A map of the holy sites of Jordan, produced in conjunction with the Ministry of Religious Endowments and the Ministry of Tourism, lists fifty-three holy sites.

PROPHETS:

(1) Maqām of Noah in Karak
(2) Maqām of Hud near Jerash
(3) Maqām of Lot in Ghur al-Safi
(4) Maqām of Khidr in Karak, ʿAjlun, Mahis, and Bayt Ras
(5) Tomb of Shuʿayb near al-Salt
(6) Tomb of Aaron near Petra
(7) Maqām of Moses on Mount Nebo
(8) Tomb of Joshua b. Nun near al-Salt
(9) Maqām of David in al-Mazar al-Shamali
(10) Maqām of Solomon in Sirfa
(11) Maqām of Job near al-Salt

(12) Maqām of John in Mukawir
(13) Maqām of Jesus at Jordan River
(14) Maqām of Muhammad near al-Safawi

ṢAḤĀBAH:

(15) Tomb of Jaʿfar b. Abī Ṭālib
(16) Tomb of Zayd b. Ḥāritha
(17) Tomb of ʿAbdallāh b. Rawāḥa
(18) Tomb of Abū ʿUbaydah ʿĀmir b. al-Jarrāḥ
(19) Tomb of Muʿādh b. Jabal
(20) Tomb of Shurḥabīl b. Ḥasna
(21) Tomb of ʿĀmir b. Abī Waqqāṣ
(22) Tomb of Ḥirār b. al-Aqwar
(23) Tomb of al-Ḥārith b. ʿUmayr al-Azdī
(24) Tomb of Abū Dharr al-Ghiffārī
(25) Tomb of Abū al-Dardāʾ
(26) Maqām of Bilāl b. Rabāh
(27) Tomb of Maysara b. Masrūq
(28) Tomb of ʿIkrimah b. Abī Jahl
(29) Maqām of Abū Mūsā al-Ashʿarī
(30) Tomb of Farwa b. ʿUmayr al-Judhamī
(31) Maqām of ʿAbd al-Raḥmān b. ʿAwf
(32) Tomb of Jābir b. ʿAbdallāh

OTHER RELIGIOUS FIGURES AND SITES:

(33) Cave of Seven Sleepers near Amman
(34) Maqām of Zayd b. ʿAlī in Karak
(35) Maqām of Seth in Tafilah
(36) Site associated with Jādūr (biblical Gad) in al-Salt
(37) Khirbat Hazzir in al-Salt
(38) Springs of Moses
(39) Baths of Moses

ISLAMIC HISTORICAL SITES:

(40) Site of battle of Muʾtah
(41) Site of battle of Faḥl (Pella)
(42) Site of battle of Yarmouk
(43) Mount al-Taḥkīm (where ʿAlī and Muʿāwiyah met)
(44) Mosque of ʿUthmān
(45) al-Ḥumaymah

CHRISTIAN SITES:

(46) Place of baptism of Jesus
(47) Place of beheading of John
(48) Pella
(49) Copper mines of Feinan
(50) Cave of Lot
(51) Steps of Muʿab (Livias)
(52) Sanctuary of Wine
(53) Umm al-Rasas (Mayfaʿah)

Some of the sites are listed more than one time (13 and 46, 12 and 47, 41 and 48, 3 and 50) as Islamic and Christian sites, and the map includes a separate list of six places designated by the Vatican as pilgrimage sites.[149]

It is important to note that the historical and mythological significance attributed to the relics patronized by Islamic states seems to differ from the significance of the sort of oddities displayed in so-called curiosity shops. The oddities of curiosity shops are not symbols that refer to sovereignty, but are instead designed to encourage commerce. Marsh's Free Museum lists among its contents freaks of nature (Jake the alligator man, a two-headed baby, a one-eyed lamb, an eight-legged lamb), artificially produced oddities (a shrunken head, Morris the freeze-dried cat, a bowl made of human skin), and merchandise (antiques, souvenirs, candy, fudge, resort wear, fresh salt-water taffy, collectibles, glass floats, black lights; see fig. 1). Like the shrines and other structures built upon or housing relics, the curiosity shop does attract tourists with exhibits that cannot be missed—"You gotta' see Jake the alligator man"—without fear of having missed something integral to the visit. And both the oddities and the relics provide the reason for a visit to the place. Both the curiosity shop and relic shrine give the opportunity to take home a "souvenir" of the place visited.

The designation of the souvenir store as a curiosity shop or a "free museum" is intended perhaps to mask the real reason for the exhibits, just as relics provide an alternate and indirect explanation for the existence of the state that collects and displays them. Viewing the exhibition of oddities becomes an excuse for buying merchandise, just as visiting a relic is an implicit recognition of the legitimacy of the state patronage that identifies it as a relic. But relics are significant because they are defined in a way that links them to a recognized figure or event in the past, whereas the "relics" of curiosity shops do not appear to have an existence independent of the curiosity shop in which they are displayed. Jake the alligator man does not have a history, but relics provide a tangible link to the development of civilization and past prophets who established religion. As such, relics are a reminder

FIGURE ONE. Flyer for Marsh's Free Museum (Long Beach, Wash.) featuring "Jake the Alligator Man," other oddities, and souvenirs. (Author's photograph.)

of the fall from Eden, and the patronage of the relic is an attempt to assert a claim to what the relic represents, the need for the state to administer religion to humanity in its fallen condition.

## CONCLUSIONS: RELICS AND PORTABLE TERRITORY

It is possible that the prohibitions of cutting fingernails and hair in the context of the pilgrimage are related to the wild state of the pilgrim in the

Meccan sanctuary. These prohibitions appear to stress the connection of the Meccan sanctuary to life beyond or before civilization, in the wilderness of wandering and the garden of Eden. Pilgrims are required to let their hair grow all over their bodies, and to let their nails become long. There are numerous traditions associating a pilgrimage and religious retreat with a return to a wild or beastlike state of existence.[150] These traditions stress the distinctions separating civilization with its temptations and regulations from the Edenic state lacking the concomitant society and sin. In the garden of Eden, Adam and Eve were said to be covered with fingernail. The loss of the fingernail coincided with their fall from Eden, the recognition of sex, and the origins of civilization. Marking movement from one type of area to another, the prohibitions and practices of the pilgrimage to Mecca signify the transition from one type of existence to another. It is this transition that is highlighted by the treatment of the prophet Muhammad's hair, nails, and other relics.

Within the context of Muslim scholarship, the link between the prophet Muhammad's remains and civilization is of cultural rather than natural significance. The cutting of nails and hair at the conclusion of the pilgrimage is a sign of not being in the garden of Eden, of having to leave a location that allowed for only the temporary experience of what was lost with the fall of Adam and Eve. Similarly, the contents of the Ark of the Covenant signify the break between the wilderness and the Holy Land, the wilderness being like an Eden, flowing with milk and honey, whereas the Holy Land was to be a place of conquest, laws, building, farming, and social hierarchy. The relics of the prophet Muhammad are symbolic references to the fall and the separation of the utopian existence in the garden of Eden from the social realities of civilized life on earth.

The hair, nails, footprints, and ḥadīth reports are portable symbols linked to the Meccan sanctuary and the pilgrimage instituted by the prophets. By patronizing the collection and display of prophetic relics, states and local authorities could lay claim to a tangible link between their state and the origins of Islamic civilization. Just as obligatory Muslim rituals symbolize an acknowledgment of the break between Eden and earth, relics serve to remind people of the necessity of religion and its administration by the state in a postfall world.

In some cases, pieces of the territory itself might serve, as the relics do, as souvenirs of the place. Shiʿī pilgrims in Iraq and Syria purchase tablets of soil from the tomb of Ḥusayn and are given torn pieces of the shroud covering the tombs visited.[151] The transportation of water from Zamzam and earth from the Meccan sanctuary by pilgrims is also reported.[152] In his pilgrim guide, ʿAlī b. Abī Bakr al-Harawī (d. 1215) mentions the use of soil to cure a scorpion bite near Ḥimṣ.[153] According to Muḥammad b. Aḥmad al-Muqaddasī (d. 964), women in Syria were known to wear the shavings of a disinterred coffin dug up and identified as the coffin of the prophet Joseph.[154] Visitors to tombs of the Ahl al-Bayt in Damascus are given small pieces of the cloths covering the tombs. Yaḥyā Ḥaqqī (d. 1992) describes how people would put in their eyes kerosene from the lamps at the tomb of Sayyidna Zaynab in Cairo.[155] Pilgrims from other sites in the ancient world apparently took home scrapings from the temples and shrines they visited.[156] The Hashemite Kingdom of Jordan has advertised for companies to bid for a contract to bottle, market, and distribute holy water from the site of the baptism of Jesus at the Jordan River.[157] This notion of territory made portable by pilgrims visiting the location is analogous to the conception of relics as reminders of a place and time now absent. The analogy between portable territory and relics must also take into account that the acquisition of relics is usually limited to officials, perhaps because it is some sort of official patronage that signifies the object as a relic and testifies to its connection with the place of its origins.

Certain Indian notions relating to the distribution of the remains of the Buddha and the notion of the multiple Buddha bodies parallel, in some respects, the concept of the pieces of the prophet Muhammad associated with the Meccan sanctuary and the origins of civilization.[158] In a manner similar to that in which the dispersal of ḥadīth reports is linked to the early conquests and the establishment of Muslim centers of civilization, the Buddha's textual and physical remains are distributed to every large city throughout the earth.[159] The distribution of the Buddha's remains is a reconstruction of the physical body of the Buddha (rupa-kaya) and the legal body of the Buddha (dharma-kaya), just as the hair and nails of the prophet Muhammad are accompanied by his textual remains in their distribution and collection.[160] The stupas built atop the distributed remains of the Buddha are physical monuments to the dharma (dharmarājikā) and mark the boundaries of the civilized Buddha-world within which the dharma applies. Madrasas and mosques are built upon and contain the physical remains of the prophet Muhammad, functioning as centers for the collection and study of his textual remains in the formulation of the Sunnah and Islamic law.

The distribution of the pieces of the Buddha and the prophet Muhammad emphasize that which separates civilization from utopia: the absence of the Buddha and the loss of Eden.

| | |
|---|---|
| Nibbana | Eden |
| Buddha | Prophet Muhammad |
| (relics) | (relics) |
| civilization | civilization |

The utopian Nibbana and Eden are mediated to civilization through the relics of the Buddha and the prophet Muhammad. Asoka's distribution of the Buddha's body asserts the relationship of his kingdom and the dharma of the Buddha. The spread of the prophet Muhammad's relics affirms the legitimacy of the state, which preserves the relics and administers religious law. Asoka disperses the relics of the Buddha and performs a pilgrimage identifying himself and the civilization which he administers with the physical body and dharma teachings of the Buddha. Just as the physical body of the Buddha parallels his dharma body, so the physical relics and artifacts of the prophet Muhammad are equivalent to his textual remains, the ḥadīth reports that are instrumental in the formation of the Sunnah and Islamic law. The dispersal of the bodies is what provides for the establishment of the state, a dispersal made necessary because of the fallen state of humanity.

It is important to note that the assertion that the Muslim state is necessary is not based upon the absence of the prophet Muhammad, as the analogy with Buddhism might suggest. It is, rather, an indirect assertion. The Muslim state is necessary because of the loss of Eden. The prophet Muhammad's distribution of his hair and nails at the boundaries of the Meccan sanctuary and the completion of his pilgrimage underlines the link between Mecca and the origins of civilization. Mecca works as a symbol of the origins of civilization because, as the earthly substitute for the lost garden of Eden, it represents what was made necessary by the fall of Adam and Eve. In this respect, the Islamic example might be comparable to the Iroquois conception of wampum as a symbol of the disjunction of creation and humanity.[161] The wampum belt is integral to the Iroquois social structure, providing authority to speak in the longhouse and title to its bearer as a link to an ancestral past. As the first object discovered on earth by Haiawatha at the time of creation, the wampum marked the beginning of civilization, a prototype of the objects required for social governance and an economy of exchange. The relics of the prophet Muhammad also reflect back to the break between heaven and earth, and the need for the first objects of civilization.

In substance, the relics of the prophet are no different from the raw materials of the wampum. Pieces of hair, wood, metal, and ceramics and ordinary objects such as shoes, clothing, and a bed can be as arbitrary and common as a given seashell or the actions which might be labeled ritual: walking, standing, and speaking. Indeed, the symbolic nature of certain actions and objects is heightened by the fact that they are employed in a manner unlike what would be expected.[162] The Islamic legal definition of impurity, for example, marks bodily functions which are shared by all human beings on a daily basis. What makes a given object, action, or condition special is the attention paid to it. As a given text is canonized by its interpretation, objects are rendered sacred by their use as symbols to demonstrate the authority of the patron. Performing a given action as a "ritual" or visiting a given object as a "relic" is an acknowledgement, or at least a tacit recognition, of the authority that designates the actions and objects as rituals and relics.[163] In this sense, relics and ritual are not best understood as a supernatural link to the presence of the prophet Muhammad, but rather as reminders that the existence of the Prophet and the law he brought was made necessary by the loss of Eden.

In the Islamic context, relics mark the land with mosques and madrasas, as reminders of the loss of Eden and the necessity of rituals and the law. Collection and possession of the prophet Muhammad's relics were a means to demonstrate authority in the social organization of the postfall world. Likewise, burial with the prophet Muhammad's relics was a statement of the recognition of the break between the utopia of Eden and this life. Use of the relics was a recognition of the necessity of the state in providing the means for fallen humanity to follow the example of the prophet Muhammad and reenter paradise at the end of time.

CHAPTER FOUR

# *Tombs of Giant Prophets*

Chapter 3 focused on the relics associated with the prophet Muhammad and the territorial spread of Islamic civilization. The Prophet's hair and nails refer to the symbolism of the Meccan sanctuary as the earthly substitute for the garden of Eden and the origins of Islamic civilization. The spread of these physical remains, as well as ḥadīth reports and other artifacts such as the prophet Muhammad's footprints, clothing and weapons, delineate the boundaries of Islamic civilization. Relics were carried by the early conquests and their successor states to outposts and cities which then served as centers for the study and implementation of Islamic law. Official collection and preservation of these relics allowed local states to assert their legitimacy as patrons of the religious law necessary for the development of civilization in a postfall world.

Chapter 4 examines the locations and objects associated with the tombs of prophets mentioned in the Quran and Muslim exegesis. The identification and development of these tomb sites epitomize the sort of state patronage associated with the collection and preservation of prophetic relics. Particular attention is given to those tombs which are of extraordinary length, up to 175 yards long. Little has been written on these long tombs despite their frequent mention in both Islamic and European sources, and despite the many references to the giant size of early prophets in Muslim exegetical and historical accounts.[1] European scholars have noted the existence of the so-called "nine-yard" (nau-gaz) long tombs in South and Southeast Asia, usually associated with the Muslim warriors (ghāzī) involved in the earliest conquests of India and identified primarily in northwest India and Pakistan but also as far east as Bengal and Java.[2]

The following pages suggest that the extraordinary size of the nau-gaz tombs and the tombs of prophets is linked with the larger Muslim conception of the origins and development of civilization as outlined in previous chapters. Section 1 provides an overview of some of the nau-gaz and long tombs of prophets from archaeological evidence and travelers' accounts. These sources show that the phenomenon of long tombs is widespread throughout Asia but appears to be specific to Islamic conceptions of tomb symbolism. Section 2 shows how this symbolism is connected to the existence of giants in Muslim accounts of the earliest civilizations after the flood and before the Israelite conquest of the Holy Land. Various sources provide accounts in which a direct correlation is made between the technological development of civilization and a physical reduction in human size. Comparisons of Muslim and other ancient accounts concerning giants and the recovery of their remains indicate that the long tombs, like other prophetic relics, are understood as physical reminders of the fall from Eden and the progress of civilization toward the prophet Muhammad and Islam.

## 1: LONG TOMBS

In the description of his travels in southern Arabia, Theodore Bent (1852–1897) makes a remarkable observation concerning the tomb of the Arab prophet Salih:

> A short ride of two hours brought us nearly to the head of the Wadi Khonab, and there, situated just under the cliff, in an open wilderness, is the celebrated tomb. It consists simply of a long uncovered pile of stones, somewhat resembling a potato-pie, with a headstone at either end, and a collection of fossils from the neighbouring mountains arranged along the top. . . . The tomb is from 20 to 40 feet in length, and one of the legends concerning it is that it never is the same length, sometimes being a few feet shorter, sometimes a few feet longer. The Bedouin have endless legends concerning this prophet. He was a huge giant, they said, the father of the prophet Houd, or Eber; he created camels out of the rock, and hence is especially dear to the wandering Bedou; and he still works miracles, for if even unwittingly anyone removes a stone from this grave, it exhibits symptoms of life, and gives the possessor much discomfort until it is returned. Once a domed building was erected over the tomb, but the prophet manifested his dislike of being thus enclosed and it was removed.[3]

Of particular significance in Bent's description is the claim that the extraordinary length of the tomb was due to the gigantic size of the prophet Salih. Some forty years later, W. H. Ingrams (d. 1897) visited this same tomb of Salih and reported that it was sixty-four feet long and was contained in a long, low building.[4] Ingrams also mentions visiting the nearby tomb of the prophet Hud which he estimated measured some ninety feet long, stretching up the side of the hill behind the dome which housed the cleft in the rock into which Hud is supposed to have disappeared when pursued by his people.[5] Other travelers likewise mention the ninety-foot length of Hud's tomb[6] and describe the annual Muslim pilgrimage to it.[7] Tombs of other prophets in the area are also reported to be of enormous length, said to house the bodies of giants; these include the tomb of al-Galsad in the Ḥaḍramawt, another near the tomb of Hud, and a giant tomb near Shabwah.[8]

## TOMBS OF THE PROPHETS

Various structures at Islamic sanctuaries and shrines are associated with burials and tombs. According to Muqātil b. Sulaymān, there are seventy prophets, including Hud, Salih, and Ishmael, buried in the sanctuary of Mecca.[9] In his commentary on Q 2:125, al-Suyūṭī relates that along with Hud, Salih, and Ishmael, the prophets Noah and Shuʿayb are also said to be buried in the sanctuary of Mecca.[10] In his biography of the prophet Muhammad, al-Ḥalabī relates a report that three hundred prophets were buried around the Kaʿbah.[11] The Kaʿbah itself and the well and the pit associated with the Kaʿbah are interpreted as structures associated with and marking the sanctuary of Mecca not unlike how stelae, pillars, and cairns mark sacred areas in pre-Islamic Arab contexts.[12] Many of the rites associated with the pilgrimage to Mecca and visitation of other shrines parallel funerary and mourning practices attested in other contexts, such as circumambulation of the tomb, the wearing of certain sorts of clothing, and restrictions on certain types of behavior.[13]

Many of the long tombs found throughout the Middle East include pillars and resemble cairns, and the tombs themselves could represent the sorts of structures associated with the various terms used to designate shrines and places of burial. In the middle of the shrine dedicated to the prophet Hud in the Ḥaḍramawt is a structure like the base of a thick pillar built upon the rock into which Hud is supposed to have disappeared.[14] The long tombs on the Swahili coast of Kenya feature prominent pillars, and the local mosque there is sometimes called the "mosque of the pillar" because of this architectural feature.[15] Central Asian tombs often include rock structures built atop the main tomb resembling small cairns or pyramid-like pillars.[16] The tombs of Salih and Hud are described as cairnlike mounds of rocks, and the large area designated as the "tomb" of Seth is regarded by some to designate a larger sanctuary within which the body is buried.

Muslim pilgrims and European travelers report on the existence of a number of other long tombs associated with prophets from the Quran and its exegesis. General Alexander Cunningham (d. 1893), in his published reports on the various northwest provinces of India, mentions the tombs of the prophets Seth and Job, called Ayub Paigambar and Sis Paigambar by local tradition, at Ajudhya.[17] He also refers to a nau-gaz tomb in Lamghān, beyond the Indus, which is ascribed to Lamek Paigambar, or the prophet Lamech, the father of Noah.[18] W. Crooke (d. 1923), honorary director of the ethnographic survey of the northwest provinces and Oudh, also refers to the tombs of Seth and Job at Ajudhya, giving their measurements as seventeen and twelve feet long, respectively.[19] In his book on the early Arab conquests, Aḥmad b. Yaḥyā al-Balādhūrī (d. 892) reports an account of the people of Sind venerating an image of the prophet Job: "The temple [budd] of Multan received rich presents and offering, and the people of Sind considered it a place of pilgrimage. They circumambulated it and shaved their heads and beards. They conceived that the image there was that of the prophet Job."[20] Other tombs of the prophet Job can be found in Central Asia, including one in Bukhāra and the Mazar of Hazrett Ayyub Paigambar near Jalabad in Turkestan, the guardians of which claim descent from Job.[21] Both of these shrines in Central Asia include water sources said to be related to what is mentioned in Q 38:42.

The shrine of the prophet Daniel, or the Mazar of Saint Daniel, in Samarqand also contains an extralong tomb. Joseph Castagné measures the tomb of Daniel as twenty meters in length. Some local tradition claims that what is buried in this tomb is the remains of the prophet Daniel brought to Samarqand by Timur from the city of Sūs, or Shūsh, the ancient Susa in Iran.[22] According to some accounts, the tomb holds only the hand of Daniel, since the rest of the parts of Daniel's body had been plundered from his tomb in Sus by the time of Timur's visit.[23] Others claim that it is not the tomb of Daniel the prophet but Daniel, or Daniar, who was one of the followers of Qussām b. ʿAbbās, the prominent companion of the prophet Muhammad who is also buried in Samarqand, in the Shah-i-Zindah necropolis.[24]

Daniel, Job, and Seth also have tombs associated with them in the Middle East.[25] There is a tomb of Job in Palestine near Ayn Silwān in Jerusalem, and another tomb of Job near Jabal Qara in Dhofar, Oman.[26] Neither the tombs of Job or Daniel in the Middle East are of extraordinary length. The tomb of Job in Dhofar is about five meters in length, but the tomb of Seth in the Baqāʿa Valley of Lebanon is one the longest on record.[27] According to ʿAbd al-Ghanī al-Nābulsī, the tomb is forty meters in length: "Then we visited the tomb of the prophet of God Seth. . . . I saw that the tomb was very large, majestic and wondrous. The length of the tomb was about forty meters and its width was about two meters. We stopped there and prayed to God."[28] In the account of his travels, Muḥammad b. Aḥmad b. Jubayr (1134–1217) mentions the tombs of the prophets Seth and Noah in the Baqāʿa Valley, but he did not visit them in person.[29] The tomb of Noah is described to Ibn Jubayr as being thirty meters in length, and the tomb of Seth as being forty meters in length.[30] According to an anonymous medieval Hebrew travel account, the tomb of Noah was twenty-four cubits long, and the British traveler Lord Curzon (d. 1925) reports that when he visited the tomb of Noah it measured forty yards in length.[31]

In the same vicinity as the tombs of Seth and Noah is the long tomb of Abel, the son of Adam, on a mountaintop along the same range of the Anti-Lebanon Mountains as the tomb of Seth, just on the Syrian side of the border near the town of Sūq Wādī Barādah.[32] The tomb is roughly nine to ten meters in length. This tomb is not mentioned in classical Muslim pilgrimage guides but is mentioned along with the tomb of Cain in the anonymous Hebrew travel account entitled *Eleh ha-Massaʿot.* Ibn al-Ḥawrānī and al-Harawī both describe the Cave of Blood (maghārat al-dam) on the slope of the nearby Mount Qāsiyūn, where Cain is supposed to have killed Abel.[33] According to a Greek legend cited in Stephanus Byzantinus and reflected in Jerome's account of Cain and Abel, it was at this location that Hermes killed the giant Askos at the founding of the city of Damascus, possibly linking the status of Abel as a giant with the founding myth of the city.[34]

Further south, in the hills above the Jordan Valley, are the long tombs of Joshua and Aaron. The tomb of Joshua is located in the city of Zayy, near the city of al-Salṭ in Jordan.[35] This tomb is described by John Lewis Burckhardt (d. 1817), who identifies the tomb as that of the prophet Hosea, in his travels through Syria:

> The Mezar Osha is supposed to contain the tomb of Neby Osho, or the prophet Hosea, equally revered by Turks and Christians, and to whom the followers of both religions are in the habit of offering prayers and sacrifices. . . . [T]he tomb is covered by a vaulted building, one end of which serves as a mosque; the tomb itself, in the form of a coffin, is thirty-six feet long, three feet broad, and three feet and a half in height, being thus constructed in conformity with the notion of the Turks, who suppose that all our forefathers were giants, and especially the prophets before Mohammed. The tomb of Noah in the valley of Coelo-Syria is still longer. The coffin of Osha is covered with silk stuffs of different colours, which have been presented to him as votive offerings.[36]

FIGURE TWO. Tomb of the Arab prophet Salih in the Dhofar region of Oman, two hundred kilometers east of Salalah, between Hasik and Hadbeen, October 2004. (Author's photograph.)

Still further south is the tomb of the prophet Aaron on the top of Jabal Hārūn, just to the southwest of the Nabataean site of Petra.[37] Burckhardt did not visit the tomb when he was in Petra but had it described to him as being "a large coffin, like that of Osha in the vicinity of Szalt."[38]

There are a number of long tombs also found and reported in the Arabian Peninsula ascribed to prophets. Of those known from Oman is the tomb of the prophet ʿUmrān, located in the Dhofar region, in Salalah, measuring thirty meters in length.[39] ʿAlī al-Shaḥrī has cataloged other tombs of this type found in the monsoon mountains, the coastal area, and Solot, some of which may be pre-Islamic and resemble other prehistoric tombs in the area (see fig. 2).[40] It is possible that the ʿUmrān of Salalah is ʿImrān, mentioned in the Quran as the father of Mary the mother of Jesus (Q 3:33–35) and also identified in Muslim exegesis as the father of Moses.[41] According to al-Shaḥrī, ʿUmrān is a local Arab prophet like the prophet Raḍwā mentioned in connection with al-Jabal al-Akhḍar near Muscat. Perhaps the longest tomb of all reported is that of Eve, the wife of Adam, located in Jedda, on the Red Sea coast of the Ḥijāz. Charles Doughty (d. 1926) gives a rousing description of the tomb.

> There are graves, set out in many places, in the Arabian wilderness, more than twenty feet in length; and such are said to be of the B. Helál. In like sort, we may see the graves of certain biblical patriarchs and prophets in Palestine, now in the custody of the Moselmîn, that are drawn out to a demesurate length, after their higher age and dignities, some sixty, some a hundred feet long. Eve's grave is sought out (for is she not called mother of mankind?) to almost as many paces at Jidda; to the oratory upon our great mother's navel, being more than the height of a tall cedar;—her babes, at the birth (saving her reverence) should be greater than elephants. If thus were the first woman, what should Adam be?[42]

According to Lord Curzon, the tomb of Eve measured 173 yards in length, and D. Van der Meulen reports that the tomb, located near the entrance to Wadi Māder, was 175 yards long.[43]

There are various Islamic traditions regarding the location of the tombs of Adam and Eve. According to Ibn Kathīr, different accounts claim that Adam is buried on the mountain to which he fell in India, that he is buried in Mount Abū Qubays in Mecca, or that Noah took the bodies of Adam and Eve on the ark and reburied them in Jerusalem.[44] ʿAlī b. Abī Muḥammad al-Ḥasan Ibn ʿAsākir (d. 1176) says that the head of Adam is at the Mosque of Abraham in Khalīl and his legs at the Dome of the Rock in Jerusalem. In his history, al-Ṭabarī reports that Noah took Adam and Eve with him on the ark but then returned them both to the cave on Mount Abū Qubays, also called the Cave of the Treasure, in which they had originally been buried.[45] Although the actual tomb of Adam is not described, his great size is mentioned in a number of different sources, including a ḥadīth report related by Ubayy b. Kaʿb on the authority of the prophet Muhammad: "Your father Adam was as tall as a very tall palm, that is, sixty cubits. He had much hair, and his private parts were concealed. . . . When Adam was dead, the angels washed him separately with lotus and water and dressed him in separate layers of shrouds. then they prepared a grave and buried him. They said: This will be the custom of the children of Adam after him."[46] Both Qatādah and Ibn ʿAbbās also report that, after his fall from the garden of Eden, Adam was reduced in size to sixty cubits—about thirty meters—before he made his first pilgrimage to Mecca.[47]

The extraordinary lengths of the tombs of these prophets is largely a matter of speculation to most of the observers whose opinions are preserved. The local guardian of the shrine at the tomb of Noah reports that some think the length of the tomb is due to its holding an example of the "missing link" in the evolution of human beings.[48] Other travelers attribute the size of the tombs to pre-Islamic traditions, perhaps related to nature and fertility cults,[49] as Ingrams does in describing the grave of the giant Nebi Mola Matar, from whom the mountain takes its name:

> This was the first of the many giants' tombs we saw in the Hadhramaut. High up on the face of the opposite mountain is a weather-worn rock which our Badawin said represented their prophet's camel. The spot is sacred to the Badawin who hold there an annual fair, and I wondered whether the place was not a relic of one of the old sanctuaries of the pre-Islamic nature gods, particularly as the name [maṭar] means rain. To try and make this prophet more orthodox, a somewhat apologetic effort was later taken to identify him with ʿAli, the son-in-law of the Prophet Muhammad.[50]

Ingrams also reports that one of the giant tombs was situated near a lone sumar tree, perhaps representing a connection between the planting of trees and the shrines of certain prophets.[51] Bent postulates that the tombs associated with prophets were originally "heathen sites of veneration, which have, under Moslem influence, been endowed with orthodox names."[52]

Others attribute the length of the tombs to a mistaken identification of an earlier structure. One modern guidebook states that the long tomb of Noah in the Baqāʿa Valley is probably just the remains of a Roman aqueduct: "Au centre du village, ancienne mosquée que les habitants prétendent être le tombeau de Noé (Nouh) et qui n'est qu'un fragment d'aqueduc antique."[53] A local source in the town of Nebi Shith claims that the length of Seth's tomb is due to the fact that because the exact location of Seth's body was not known a large area was declared the "tomb" to protect the sanctity of the actual spot.[54] The local imam of the tomb of Joshua says that although the tomb is ten meters in length, Joshua was only four or five meters tall, but it is unknown which part of the tomb contains the body.[55] It is not uncommon for tombs to be enlarged by later patrons, and for the form of the architecture to produce a tomb that is larger than the body it is supposed to contain.[56]

## NAU-GAZ TOMBS

In addition to the large tombs located in the Arabian Peninsula, a number of different sources refer to the nau-gaz tombs located in South, Central, and Southeast Asia. Some of the earliest references to these tombs in South Asia are recorded in the archaeological surveys commissioned by the British in the middle and late nineteenth century. Cunningham lists the locations and measurements of a number of them. In Multan, he mentions eighteen such tombs, including those of well-known saints and their relatives, a converted Hindu, ghazis known by name and anonymous, and unidentified people.[57] The tombs range in size from twenty-one feet to fifty-four feet in length and are clustered around the gates of the old fort and city, though many were buried under the ruins of the fort before Cunningham's arrival in 1853. Five were near the fort:

1. Near the Sikki gate, tomb of Lâl Husen Bairâgi, a converted Hindu.
2. Near the De gate, tomb of Miran King Shamar, 4 gaj in length.
3. Near the Rehri gate, tomb of Sabz Ghazi, 3½ gaj in length.
4. Near the De gate, outside, tomb of unknown Ghâzi.
5. Near the Jâmi Masjid, tomb of Kazi Kutb Kushâni. There was no trace of this in 1854.[58]

The other tombs were near the gates of the city:

6. Near the Bor gate and inside the city, tomb of Pir Adham.
7. Near the Bor gate and outside the city, tomb of Pir Dindâr, 54½ feet long.
8. Above Husen Gai, in the Nandh Mohalla, tomb of Pir Ramzân Ghazi, 21 feet 3 inches long.
9. Outside the Delhi gate, 450 feet distant, tomb of Pir Gor Sultân. This tomb is 35½ feet in length.

10 and 11. near Sâgar, two tombs, each 3½ gaj in length. Names not known.

12 and 13. At Shâdana Shâhîd, tombs of the Shâdana himself, and of some unknown martyr, each 3½ gaj in length.

14. In Sajjika Mahalla, unknown tomb.
15. In Mangar-ka-Mahalla, unknown tomb.[59]

Cunningham also records the forty-six-foot-long tomb of Nūr Shah in Harapa,[60] the thirty-two-foot-long tomb of Muḥammad Shah in Bavanni,[61] and seven tombs in the Punjab measuring from twenty-nine feet to thirty-eight feet in length.[62]

Nau-gaz tombs are also reported in Rajputana and Ahmadabad. In Ahmadabad there are nine nau-gaz tombs to the south of the Hindu Narayan temple, near the Rauza to the northwest of the city. There is no record of their exact measurements, and they are not identified with particular people.[63] Crooke records one nau-gaz tomb at Nagaur, in Rajputana, and makes reference to the tombs listed by Cunningham in the Punjab.[64]

Crooke does not elaborate on the size of this tomb in Rajputana but describes the nau-gaz tombs as "where the giants of olden time rest."[65] Cunningham similarly does not provide any details on the gigantic size of the tombs and does not question the local traditions that the nau-gaz tombs date back to the earliest Muslim invasions of the area, although he identifies a number of them with later saints. He reports that the tomb of For Sultan in Multan is 1,300 years old, as is the tomb of Muhammad Shah in Bavanni, both belonging to warriors who fell under the command of the Arab general Muhammad b. al-Qāsim al-Thaqafī in 711 CE.[66]

Long tombs associated with the introduction of Islam to Southeast Asia have also been recorded in Java. Hasan Muarif Ambary describes four "long tombs" (makam panjang) in the village of Leran in Java, all roughly equivalent in length to the nau-gaz tombs found in South Asia, measuring 8.77, 9.25, 9.28, and 9.61 meters in length.[67] Local tradition identifies three of the tombs with known followers of Raja Cermin, the brother of Malik Ibrahim, who came to Java in 1385 and died in 1419 according to his grave marker.[68] The earliest Muslim burials on the island are recorded in the eleventh century on grave markers imported from further west, such as the tomb of Faṭimah bint Maimūn near the four long tombs in Leran.[69]

It is not possible to verify that the long tombs in Java or the nau-gaz tombs in South Asia—either the location or the structures themselves—date back as far as local tradition maintains. One of the earliest dated Muslim tombs from Sādan, near Muzaffargarh, has an inscription which states that the saint died in 674 AH, or 1275 CE.[70] This dates the tomb to the period of the Mongol attacks in the area, and local tradition claims that the tomb is that of a descendant of a companion of the prophet Muhammad who came to Multan with the army of Muhammad b. al-Qāsim in the eighth century. The tomb is constructed of baked bricks and is identical in design to other nau-gaz tombs but is roughly square (twenty-one feet by twenty-nine feet), and the casket itself is just over ten feet long.[71] A number of tombs, both dated and undated, in Central Asia and China are associated with companions of the prophet Muhammad and are not reported to be of extraordinary length.[72]

In addition to the indeterminacy of the tombs' dates, there is scant information regarding the length of the tombs beyond the scattered reports of their measurements and undocumented comments concerning local claims of the giant size of those buried in the tombs. Several observers do remark on the possibility that the length of the tombs might be influenced by local, non-Islamic traditions. Cunningham makes indirect comparisons between the nau-gaz tombs and the large stupas in Ajudhya,[73] and Crooke discusses possible Buddhist influences on the nau-gaz tombs.[74] Henry Cousens, who made a number of surveys of the antiquities of the Sind and western India, directly relates the architecture and materials used in the construction of Muslim tombs to those used in Buddhist and Hindu monuments in the same area.[75]

Of particular note is the fact that all the nau-gaz tombs are constructed of special baked bricks characteristic of stupas and Hindu temples.[76] The use of the baked mud brick in Muslim tombs may represent more than practical concerns, as Cousens notes in relation to the building of mosques: "The Muhammadan, on the other hand, looks upon every stone of his mosque, even when the latter is totally ruined, as having been consecrated to God's use, and it is a desecration to use it in any other way."[77] Cousens appears to be describing a notion shared with other traditions in the region regarding the individual stones or bricks each as representing the building as a whole in the construction of which they are employed. The bricks are thus said to signify or take on the substance of the structure in which they are employed and individually represent the significance of the building as a whole.[78]

This connection between the individual bricks and the body contained in the tomb is expressed in a number of ways. Buddhist stupas are built over the distributed remains of the Buddha's body, so that each stupa and each brick in the stupa represent the larger rupa-kaya, or physical body, of the absent Buddha.[79] In the case of the Hindu temple, the building is a physical manifestation of the deity to whom the temple is dedicated, an embodiment of the otherwise absent god or goddess.[80] Stella Kramrisch explains how the Hindu temple is a representation of the fire altar, in which the bricks represent the different pieces of the body of the sacrifice (yajna-tanu).[81] The foundation bricks of the temple are laid with mantras imbuing them with the symbolism of the body of the deity, so that the bricks become the limbs of Agni.[82] The installation of the bricks (istaka-nyasa) is the main foundation rite of the temple. In its design, the temple is the likeness of Purusa, the primal being whose body is dismembered for the creation of the cosmos and society.[83] The temple plan represents Purusa and Agni to the extent that the temple is regarded as the stone body of these beings.[84]

Muslim practices also connect the physical character of the tomb with the body of the deceased. For example, in both South and Central Asia stones are placed on the top of tombs in the shape of a pyramid, with the top stone supposed to represent a miniature version of the tomb or an image representing the body of the person in the tomb.[85] This is similar to the practice of the Turkic peoples of Siberia and the steppes of Central Asia, who erect figurines representing the dead person at the site of the tomb.[86] Certainly, the extraordinary length of the nau-gaz tombs is supposed to represent the gigantic size of the ghazi or saint encased in the brick structure of the tomb. The concept of the dismembered and buried body parts of the deity marked by the building of a temple is not unlike the example of shrines built over the distributed body parts of Horus in Egypt or the distribution and housing of the remains of the prophet Muhammad in mosques, mausoleums, madrasas, and other buildings associated with the transmission of ḥadīth reports and the study of Islamic law. Insofar as the Hindu temple and the stupa represent the bodies over which they are built, it is possible that the bricks of the Muslim tomb also embody and signify the fallen ghazi or saint who is entombed within it.[87]

## 2: GIANTS

Consistent throughout the accounts of the nau-gaz tombs and the long tombs of the prophets is the claim that the extraordinary length of the tombs is due to the gigantic size of the bodies buried in them. A number of travelers report that local Bedouin told them that the people buried in the long tombs were from the giants responsible for building the huge monuments now in ruins around the Arabian Peninsula: "Stories of antiquity tell of the people of ʿĀd and Thamūd. They were giants to whom the beduin to-day attribute the buildings and monuments of which they see the ruins that consist of huge blocks of stone. Only giants, people much taller and stronger than living mankind, could have put such colossal stones on top of each other."[88] The city of Sanʿa is also reported to have been built by the giant people of ʿĀd to whom Hud was sent as a prophet.[89] In his geography, Ibn al-Faqīh (fl. 903) reports on the authority of Ibrāhīm b. Abī al-Mahājir that the city of Mecca, originally called "Bakkah," as recorded in Q 3:96, used to be in the possession of the giants (jabābirah).[90] Doughty also reports that giants are said to be responsible for the wells, water pits, and large standing stones and mentions a number of long tombs supposed to belong to the tribe of the Banū Hilāl, who are associated with heroic feats.[91]

### RECOVERY OF GIANT REMAINS IN GREEK AND ROMAN SOURCES

That the people of long ago, especially the prophets and heroes, were giants is a motif known from other religious traditions and cultures. Numerous examples of the discovery of the bones of giants exist in Greek and Roman sources.[92] Solinus reports that massive bones washed ashore by streams at Pallene, site of a battle between the gods and giants, were found and collected.[93] Pausanias mentions the giant-sized bones at Megalopolis in the sanctuary of Asklepios, said to be from one of the giants called upon by

Hopladamos to defend Rhea: "Under this hill there is another sanctuary of Asclepius. His image is upright and about a cubit in height, that of Apollo is seated on a throne and is not less than six feet high. Here are also kept bones, too big for those of a human being, about which the story ran that they were those of one of the giants mustered by Hopladamus to fight for Rhea, as my story will relate hereafter."[94] In his work on the cult of Protesilaus, Philostratus mentions corpses from different locations attributed to giants such as Hyllos of the Aloadai brothers Otos and Ephialtes in Thessaly, Alkyoneus at Phlegra, and other giants buried by Vesuvius at Pallene.[95]

Plutarch narrates how the Athenian soldier Cimon brought back to Athens a giant body found beside bronze weapons at Skyros, said to be the bones of Theseus, son of Poseidon.[96] According to Plutarch and Strabo, the burial mound of the giant Antaios, the son of Poseidon and Gea, was dug up at Tingis (Tangier) by Sertorius, who found a body sixty cubits in length.[97] The body of Asterios, son of the giant Anax, who was the son of Gea, was reported to be at least ten meters in length when his tomb was opened.[98] A coffin eleven cubits in length containing a giant body was found in the Orontes River, and according to Philostratus,[99] a body dug from the Orontes River was the giant Aryades, measuring thirty cubits in length.[100] Phlegon reports that digging on an island near Athens uncovered a coffin one hundred cubits in length bearing an inscription identifying the giant body as that of Makroseiris.[101]

Greek and Roman sources also report on the large bones and tombs of heroes.[102] According to Diodorus and Pausanius, when the tomb of Ajax was unearthed at Troy near Thoiteion, his kneecaps were found to be as large as the discuses used by athletes.[103] The body of Ajax discovered in the tomb was sixteen feet in length, and the Iliad portrays him as being of enormous size.[104] The body of Orestes, recovered by the Spartans, was found at Tegea in a coffin seven cubits long.[105] Pausanius describes the retrieval of the bone of Pelops:

> When the war of the Greeks against Troy was prolonged, the soothsayers prophesied to them that they would not take the city until they had fetched the bow and arrows of Heracles and a bone of Pelops. So it is said that they sent for Philoctetes to the camp, and from Pisa was brought to them a bone of Pelops—a shoulder-blade. As they were returning home, the ship carrying the bone of Pelops was wrecked off Euboea in the storm. Many years later than the capture of Troy, Damarmenus, a fisherman from Eretria, cast a net into the sea and drew up the bone. Marveling at its size he kept it hidden in the sand. At last he went to Delphi, to inquire

whose the bone was, and what he ought to do with it. It happened that by providence of Heaven there was then at Delphi an Elean embassy praying for the deliverance from a pestilence. So the Pythian priestess ordered the Eleans to recover the bones of Pelops, and Damarmenus to give back to the Eleans what he had found. He did so, and the Eleans repaid him by appointing him and his descendants to be guardians of the bone. The shoulder-blade of Pelops had disappeared by my time, because, I suppose, it had been hidden in the depths so long, and besides its age it was greatly decayed through the salt water.[106]

Phlegon also reports the discovery of a broken jar containing three skulls and two jawbones, identified as the remains of Idas, the strongest man on earth.[107] The great size of Heracles is referred to numerous times, including the mention of a huge bone identified with the finger of Heracles bit off by the Nemean lion.[108]

The bones and bodies of giants are also found in other European contexts. In Egil's saga, the leg bone of Egil is described as being so large that it required several men to carry it. The first time a dinosaur bone was discovered in Oxfordshire, some said the bone was from a giant.[109] Giant bones were also identified with monsters and giants in other parts of Britain, such as the giant "Dun Cow" slain by Sir Guy of Warwick whose relics are kept in the Warwick Castle.[110] Saint Stephen's cathedral in Vienna contains a "Giant's Door" (Riesentor), so named on account of a giant bone found during the building of the church in the thirteenth century and displayed as the remains of a giant killed during the flood of Noah's time.[111] Trolls and giants are also common in European folklore.[112] In the Don Valley is the city of Kostienki, meaning "bone village," where large bones were uncovered and attributed to a giant named Inder in Russian folklore.[113]

## GIANTS AND THEIR REMAINS IN THE QURAN AND BIBLE

The accounts concerning giants in the Quran and Bible parallel and may be related to these Greek and Roman motifs but are more specific in how giant size is related to the origins and end of civilization. This specificity is reflected in the Muslim exegesis that attributes gigantic size to certain prophets mentioned in the Quran. According to al-Qurṭubī, the reference in Q 7:69 to God's increasing the stature of the people of ʿĀd is to the physical height of the people: "The ʿĀd were tall in stature and great in body size. Ibn ʿAbbās says their height was one hundred cubits and then God shortened them to sixty cubits. This was the extra [size] which he added to the natural size of their forefathers. It is also said that this verse means they were increased in size over the people of Noah."[114] A report given on the authority of Wahb b. Munabbih states that the heads of the people of ʿĀd were so large that they were like great domes, and their eyes were so large that they could scare away predatory animals.[115] Others report that the people of ʿĀd ranged from sixty to one hundred cubits in height.[116] The city of Iram dhāt al-ʿImād, in which the ʿĀd lived, is also described as being gigantic:

> It is said that Iram was a city unlike any other ever created. It was situated in Yemen between the Ḥaḍramawt and Sanʿa. In it were castles of gold and silver and dwelling places under which flowed rivers. It is also said that the people gathered all the gold, silver, pearls, gems, and precious stones in the world and brought them to one place, and from these things were built the city of Iram. The length and the width of the city was twelve parsangs on each side. In it were three hundred thousand castles all made of jewels. After the people of ʿĀd were destroyed, the city disappeared and no person has ever entered it except for one man during the days of Muʿāwiyah whose name was ʿAbdallāh b. Qilābah.[117]

Exegesis on the building of signs on every "high place" and "artifices" mentioned in Q 26:128–129 explains that the people of ʿĀd had great castles and tall towers, more magnificent than the ruins of ancient Egypt, that reached into the sky.[118]

The long tomb of Salih in the Ḥaḍramawt is also attributed to the gigantic size of the prophet and his people. Muslim genealogists state that Salih, like Hud, was a descendant of Shem the son of Noah but several generations removed from that of Hud.[119] Though it appears to contradict the sequence of the Quran in which Salih comes after Hud, local tradition of the Ḥaḍramawt claims that Salih was the father of Hud, perhaps identifying Hud with the biblical "Eber" and Salih with the biblical "Shelah" the father of Eber in Genesis 10:22–24 and Luke 3:35. Muslim exegetes also explain that Hud and Salih were the first two in a series of "Arab" prophets which also includes Shuʿayb and the prophet Muhammad: "The prophet Muhammad said to me: 'Abū Dharr, four [prophets] were Syrian: Adam, Seth, Noah, and Idris. He was the first to write with a pen. God revealed to Idris thirty scriptures. Four [prophets] were Arab: Hud, Salih, Shuʿayb, and your prophet.'"[120] The close relationship between the antediluvian "Syrian" prophets and the "Arab" prophets is also highlighted by the direct succession of the accounts of Noah, Hud, and Salih in Q 7, 11, and 26. Muslim exegesis on Q 19:57 states that Idris did not die, but tall stature and long tombs are attested for the other three antediluvian prophets.

The link between Hud and Salih, and the attestation of long tombs for both of these prophets, may be related to their special status as the original Arabs. Of the four Arab prophets, only Hud and Salih are considered to be from the "original Arabs" (al-ʿarab al-ʿāribah), also called the "extinct" or "long-ago Arabs" (al-ʿarab al-bāʿidah), while Shuʿayb and the prophet Muhammad are from the "arabicized Arabs" (al-ʿarab al-mustaʿribah):[121]

> Aram b. Shem b. Noah begat Uz b. Aram, Gether b. Aram, and Hul b. Aram. Then Uz b. Aram begat Gether b. Uz, ʿĀd b. Uz, and ʿUbayl b. Uz. Gether b. Aram begat Thamūd b. Gether and Judays b. Gether. They were an Arab people speaking the Muḍarī language. The Arabs called these nations the "original Arabs" because Arabic was their original language, but they called the descendants of Ishmael b. Abraham the "arabicized Arabs" because they spoke the language of these people after they had settled among them. The ʿĀd, Thamūd, Amalekites, Umaym, Jāsim, Judays, and the Ṭasm are the original Arabs.[122]

Ibn Kathīr records a number of reports that associate the origins of the Arabic language with Hud, his father, Noah, or Adam.[123] The Arabic language of Ishmael (al-ʿarabīyah al-fuṣḥā) and his descendants, who formed the tribes from which the prophet Muhammad descended, is said to have been learned from the original Arabs with whom Ishmael settled in Mecca: the Jurhum, the Amalekites, the people of Yemen, and the Arab peoples who preceded Abraham.[124]

In Muslim exegesis, the gigantic size attributed to certain figures appears to be limited to the early prophetic figures, the Syrian prophets, and the Arab prophets of the original Arabs.[125] The size of these early peoples might also be related to the notion that the life span of human beings was reduced after the great flood, which marked a division between the mythical era of primeval times and the origins of human civilization in historical time.[126] Genesis 5 lists the ten generations from Adam to Noah, attributing extraordinary long lives to the patriarchs:

> Adam (930 years)
> Seth (912 years)
> Enosh (905 years)
> Kenan (910 years)
> Mahalalel (895 years)
> Jared (962 years)
> Enoch (365 years)
> Methuselah (969 years)

Lamech (777 years)
Noah (950 years)

After the flood, the life spans decrease drastically:

Shem (Gen 11:10, 600 years)
Arpachshad (Gen 11:12, 438 years)
Shelah (Gen 11:14, 433 years)
Eber (Gen 11:16, 464 years)
Peleg (Gen 11:18, 239 years)
Reu (Gen 11:20, 239 years)
Serug (Gen 11:22, 230 years)
Nahor (Gen 11:24, 138 years)
Terah (Gen 11:31, 205 years)
Abraham (Gen 25:7, 175 years)

A similar pattern exists in the Sumerian King List, in which the reigns of the antediluvian kings (tens of thousands of years in length) are replaced after the flood by reigns lasting no more than 1,500 years.[127] Flood stories from the ancient Near East, Greece, and India also portray the flood as a measure to control population, and the immortality of the heroes is contrasted with the shortened lives of postdiluvian humanity.[128]

That the people who lived before the flood were of gigantic size is a common motif indicated in a variety of sources. A number of verses in the Quran use the term "giant" (jabbār, pl. jabābirah, jabbārīn) as an accusation against people who put their own importance over God.[129] References to particular giants are found in Muslim exegesis on the various Quran passages mentioning the flood.

> Some exegetes allege that Og [ʿAwj] b. ʿAnāq, also called Ibn ʿAnāq, was alive from before the time of Noah to the time of Moses. They say he was an unbeliever, a giant, and a tyrant. They say he was not rightly guided but he was the offspring of his mother, a daughter of Adam, out of wedlock. On account of his height he used to take fish from the depths of the sea and fry them on the face of the sun. He used to say to Noah while he was on the ark: "What is that large bowl you have there?" It is mentioned that he was 3,333⅓ cubits in height.[130]

This same giant is again mentioned by Muslim exegetes as being present at the time when the Israelites arrived in the Holy Land (al-arḍ al-muqaddisah) (Q 5:20–26). According to al-Ṭabarī, the giant Og captured the twelve chiefs sent out by Moses to reconnoitre the land.[131] A report given on the authority of Nawf b. Faḍālah claims that Moses defeated the giant Og: "The height of Og was eight hundred cubits. The height of Moses was ten cubits, and his rod was ten cubits. Moses jumped into the air ten cubits and hit Og, hitting his anklebone, and Og fell down dead. His body was a bridge for the people to cross."[132] Ibn Kathīr reports that there was another giant who called on Moses, named Balaam b. Beor (Baʿawra), who is said to have been the tallest of the giants encountered in the Holy Land.[133]

Muslim exegesis also connects the giants in the Holy Land with the original Arab peoples related to Hud and Salih. Ibn al-Jawzī and others explain that the giants inhabiting the Holy Land in the time of Moses were the Amalekites, and the giant Goliath whom David defeated in Q 2:251 was from the Amalekites who had conquered Gaza and Ashkelon.[134] In Numbers 13:27–33, the twelve representatives sent by Moses into the land report back concerning the giants inhabiting the land:

> 27. They told him saying: We came to the land to which you sent us. It flows with milk and honey, and this is its fruit. 28. Nevertheless, the people who are settled in the land are great and the cities are walled and very big. Also, the descendents of ʿAnaq we saw there. 29. The Amalekites have settled in the land of the Negev. The Hittites, Jebusites, and Amorites have settled in the mountains. The Canaanites have settled by the sea and by the side of the Jordan. 30. Caleb quieted the people before Moses and said: Let us go up now so that we might take it, for we are able to do it. 31. But the people who had gone up with him said: We are not able to go up against the people because they are stronger than we. 32. So they brought a bad report of the land which they had spied to the Israelites, saying: The land through which we have crossed to spy is a land that eats its settlers, and all the people that we saw in it were people of great stature. 33. There we saw the Nephilim, the descendants of ʿAnaq who are from the Nephilim. In our own eyes we were as grasshoppers, and likewise we were in their eyes.

The inhabitants of Moab are called the Emim (Deut 2:10) and the territory of Ammon was known as the land of the Rephaim, who were also called the Zamzummim by the Ammonites (Deut 2:20–21). Both of these peoples are described as being giants, like the descendants of ʿAnaq, the Anakim.[135] In 2 Samuel 21:16–20 and 1 Chronicles 20:4–8 there are references to the Rephaim (ha-rāpâ) as "giants," and several passages mention Og of Bashan as one of the last of the Rephaim.[136] The Nephilim mentioned in Numbers

13:33 as being descendants of ʿAnaq, like the Anakim, are also mentioned in Genesis 6:1–4 as the offspring of the sons of God (ha-elōhîm) and daughters of Adam—a description similar to that of Og b. ʿAnāq in Muslim exegesis.[137]

Such traditions regarding giants were current in later periods and were identified with particular locations visited by pilgrims in late antiquity. Josephus mentions a place near Hebron where the Israelites are said to have destroyed a race of giants: "So they [the Israelites] moved their camp to Hebron, took that town and massacred all those in it. There remained yet a race of giants who, by reason of their huge frames and figures were in no way like the rest of humanity, and were an amazing sight and a tale of terror to be heard. Their bones are shown to this day, bearing no resemblance to any that have been known to people."[138] In his account of Christian pilgrimage sites, Jerome identifies a number of Palestinian cities with giants, including Ashdod, Hebron, and Gaza.[139] Eucherius also mentions that Hebron was once a city of giants, as does Adomnan.[140] Theodosius mentions the city of Paran, near Mount Sinai, where Moses is supposed to have fought with Amalek.[141] In the account of his pilgrimage to the Holy Land, Bernard the Monk mentions on the Plain of Tanis the bodies of people who fell in the time of Moses, which look like three walls.[142]

The gigantic size of certain prophets may also be related to a larger soteriological history beginning with the garden of Eden and culminating in the Day of Judgment. According to a report given on the authority of Ibn ʿAbbās and Qatādah, Adam was reduced in height to thirty cubits when he fell from the garden of Eden.[143] This corresponds to the reduction in size and life span of people after the flood. The tombs of Adam and Eve are reported to be the longest, followed by those of the antediluvian and Arab prophets, and then by the tombs of later prophets and the nau-gaz tombs of the ghazis and saints. Local tradition holds that the body of Daniel, in the tomb in Samarqand, continues to grow, and that the tomb is enlarged to accommodate this growth.[144] It is possible that the growth of Daniel's corpse relates to his special role in eschatological traditions—that the growth of his body is his gradual restoration to the original size of humanity in its prefall, Edenic state.[145] From this perspective, the body of Daniel can be expected to reach its full primordial size just before the Day of Resurrection. According to a ḥadīth report given on the authority of Anas b. Mālik, the bodies of all the people who enter Eden are given the height of Adam, sixty cubits.[146] The giant size of other eschatological figures, such as the Dajjāl, the Dabbat al-Arḍ, and Jesus, is also mentioned in traditions about the end of time.[147]

Several of the long tombs, such as those ascribed to Salih and Hud in the Ḥaḍramawt, are described as mounds of rocks resembling cairns. Cairns and burial mounds are well attested in the Near East, especially the ancient burial mounds on Bahrain and in the Gulf, and the cairns with Safaitic inscriptions from the basalt desert region of eastern Jordan.[148] According to Edward Westermarck, the cairnlike appearance of some tombs may be due to pilgrims' throwing stones at a roadside shrine when passing it in lieu of a personal visit.[149] The tomb of the prophet Muhammad in Medina is described by Richard Burton (d. 1890) as an oblong mound of earth covered with small stones laid by pilgrims visiting the site.[150] The domelike structure of the cairn is considered to be a more primitive form of the later dome (qubbah) that covers many enclosed tombs. Both the dome and the cairn, as the pyramids or the tholoi—the beehive-shaped tombs of the Mycenaean Greeks—are thought to represent artificial mountains, the construction of an artificial cave in which the body may be interred.[151]

Many tombs, including the long tombs of prophets, contain or are endowed with objects of value and thus resemble artificial versions of caves associated with the burial of treasure. Some of these objects are buried with the body, often under the mound or cairn, and other times the objects are depicted on the tombs themselves.[152] Castagné mentions a host of objects which accumulate at the tombs of saints and prophets, including horns of goats and rams, skulls of horses, lamps, swords, mosaic fragments, written prayers, Quran codices, rugs, and metal balls sometimes as large as cannonballs.[153] Burckhardt describes the treasures reported to have been kept in the tomb of the prophet Muhammad in Medina, including jewelry and an original copy of the ʿUthmān Quran.[154] The more important the person buried, the more numerous and valuable the items left at the tomb. Jewelry buried in the tombs, portrayed on them, or left at the tomb by visitors is also used to indicate the importance of the deceased.[155] Cunningham reports on giant-size jewelry up to two feet in diameter, said to be the thumb rings linked to a nearby nau-gaz tomb, at Multan.[156] Weapons are also linked with tombs, often signifying the heroic stature of the deceased though not necessarily associated only with warriors.[157]

The status of the deceased can also be displayed through the construction of elaborate tombs and necropolises. Such necropolises are often built and patronized by the state for the burial of ruling family members and appear to serve as monuments to the greatness of the dynasty.[158] Towers, pillars, and other accoutrements are added to tombs to indicate status, including huge piles of stones, perhaps associated with cairns, for the burial of nobles and royal figures.[159] Also demonstrating the continued importance of the tombs is how the size of many of the nau-gaz and other long tombs appear to increase over time with additions from pilgrims and local patronage. The nau-gaz tomb of Nūr Shah is recorded to have grown from eighteen to forty-six feet in length.[160] Cunningham and Crooke describe the tombs of Seth and Job at Ajudhya as growing from ten and a half to seventeen and nine to twelve feet in length "through the frequent repairs of pious Musulmâns."[161]

Such examples suggest that much tomb architecture and size results not from the physical requirements of the corpse but rather from the attempt to express the historical and social significance of the interred person. The relative lengths of the long tombs in the Arabian Peninsula are described as reflecting a hierarchy among the prophetic figures: "We soon passed some tombs arranged around a larger one that is believed to be the last resting-place of the Prophet Handala and is twenty-five yards long. The longer the tomb the greater the importance attached to the person believed to have been buried in it. The tomb of Hūd the Prophet of Allah, six days' travel by camel to the east, is tens of yards longer than that of Handala. In Jidda, the Red Sea port of Mecca, the tomb of our Mother Eve is 175 yards in length."[162] One of the most striking tombs in India is the Dargah of Shah Amīn al-Dīn Aʿla (d. 1675) which bears the shahādah, numerous ḥadīth reports, names of the twelve imams, and a ghazal of fifteen couplets culminating in the saint's being identified with God.[163] Often, the relative importance of the dead is expressed in the relative position and size of their tombs. In the Deccan, tombs were rebuilt by later adherents to ensure that the tombs of certain Sufi saints and the founders of orders were larger than those of later followers.[164] Crooke mentions the tomb of a disciple of Sayyad Mahmud at Jhanjhana, in Muzaffarnagar, whose tomb is said to continuously sink below the earth so that it is lower than the tomb of his master.[165] Tomb construction also reflects ordinary social and gender distinctions, such as the custom of burying religious leaders near mosques, burying women deeper than men, or using separate areas in cemeteries for children and non-Muslims.[166]

The special status signified by the size of tombs is also found associated with other large remains, including the relics of prophets. The preserved footprints of the prophet Muhammad discussed in chapter 3, for example, are relatively large, roughly eighteen to twenty-four inches in length. Large footprints are also attributed to other prophetic figures, such as the enormous footprint of Adam in Sri Lanka.[167] According to al-Nābulsī, the tomb of Job in a village near Nawī has a running spring and a footprint of the prophet.[168] There are numerous Greek examples of large footprints attributed to Perseus (two cubits long), Dionysius (one hundred feet long), and Heracles (just shorter than the footprint of Dionysius).[169] Extra-large footprints of the Buddha and giant-size teeth attributed to the Buddha are attested.[170] These large remains, like the long tombs, appear to represent the special status of the figure with which they are connected rather than an attempt to display a more literal interpretation of giant body size.

It is the association of such locations and objects with the prophets and their followers, and thus their definition as sacred, that is accomplished by the state's authorization of their veneration through both narrative and visual discourse.[171] The building of mosques, madrasas, and tombs demonstrates the state's support for religious learning, the scholars, and the institutions that develop from the prophet Muhammad. By using the ruins of earlier tombs and monuments in its own constructions, the state can show its building upon and supercession of earlier regimes.[172] The identification and patronage of tombs, in particular, coincides with territorial claims.[173] Duplication of tomb locations and the use of shrines (maqāmāt) illustrate state and local competition for claims of identity and sovereignty.[174] The patronage of prophetic relics and tombs has the effect of grafting the current regime into the continuity of authority stemming from the prophet Muhammad and the line of prophets that stretches back to Adam.

## CONCLUSIONS: TECHNOLOGY AND HUMAN SIZE

The state patronage of certain objects and locations as relics and tombs of the prophets helps provide legitimacy to the current social order by reminding people of the fall from the garden of Eden and the necessity of civilization. Tombs serve to signify the break between this world and the utopian existence of Eden, in part by reference to the physical remains of those no longer present.[175] The association of tombs and relics with miracles relating especially to sickness and infertility can signify the disjunction between current human existence and how it was in Eden. To tombs and relics are also attributed cosmogonic significance, such as the tomb as a representation of the world mountain which once linked heaven and earth, and the tombs of prophets and saints are closely tied to the establishment of sanctuaries built in imitation of Eden.[176]

The attribution of long tombs to the antediluvian and Arab prophets is understood as a direct reference to the origins of Islamic civilization in

Mecca. Muslim exegetes explain that the sanctuary in Mecca was established by Adam as an earthly substitute for the garden of Eden, and it is from Mecca that the civilization established by the prophet Muhammad spreads. The antediluvian Syrian prophets and the successive Arab prophets are the direct successors to Adam and the direct predecessors to the prophet Muhammad. The complicated history of the multiple prophets sent to the Israelites is in stark contrast to the stories of Noah, Hud, Salih, and Shuʿayb, which illustrate a basic pattern of the prophet sent from God with a simple message that is rejected by the people, who are then destroyed.[177]

Size matters in the symbolism of the long tombs and their relation to the progress of civilization. That the giant bodies said to be housed in the long tombs are much larger than regular people evinces the size reduction of later humanity. Aḥmad b. Ḥanbal preserves a ḥadīth report, given on the authority of Abū Hurayrah, that God gradually decreased the size of humans from the original sixty-cubit height of Adam.[178] This reflects an inverse relationship between the technological advances accompanying the progress of civilization and the size of people. The size of grain is said to have shrunk from giant size in the time of Adam to the size of an ostrich egg in the time of Idris, a hen's egg in the time of Elijah, a hazelnut in the time of Jeremiah, a pea in the time of Ezra, and its current small size in the time of Jesus.[179] As farming and agricultural technology advanced, the size of grain diminished, just as giant people were reduced when advances in medicine, housing, and weapons made such great stature and strength unnecessary to human survival.

Along with advances in technology comes increased social interaction and the need for more laws that address the regulation of an increasingly populous society in its many aspects. The reduction of Adam's size corresponds to his fall from Eden and receiving of the many tools and arts of civilization, including language, agriculture, clothes production, weapons, and religion. Likewise, the elimination of the giants from the Holy Land is accompanied by God's revelation of the Torah, with its complex of laws to be applied in the land, for the Israelites. The simple message given to Hud, that his people acknowledge the oneness of God, is addressed to an age far removed from the more developed society to which are addressed the Quran and the example of the prophet Muhammad.

After the fall from Eden, human beings were compelled to develop agriculture, harvesting, kneading, baking, and other techniques in order to eat, just as they needed to develop artificial cover and weapons to compensate for their unprotected bodies. Perhaps the early people on the earth required gigantic size in order to build, travel, and protect themselves before the development of adequate technology and the full realization of human civilization. Human civilization and religion culminate in the stage of civilization initiated by the prophet Muhammad, the last in a series of ages preceding the Day of Resurrection and a return to Eden.[180] The long tombs thus appear to be symbols of a bygone age reminding people of the prophets, religion, and civilization made necessary by the fall of humanity from the garden of Eden.

CONCLUSION

# *The Pure, the Sacred, and Civilization*

The preceding chapters outlined the symbolic significance of rituals, relics, and territory as understood in certain Muslim contexts. Chapter 4 related the long tombs of prophets to the giant size associated with the earliest development of civilization. Chapter 3 showed how the distribution and collection of prophetic relics is connected to the origins and spread of Islamic civilization from the Meccan sanctuary. Chapter 2 focused on how legal definitions of impurity and other obligatory rituals make reference to the lost conditions of the garden of Eden. Chapter 1 examined the accounts of the treasure of the Kaʿbah as an example of the narrative motif linking Islamic civilization with the founding of the Meccan sanctuary by Adam after his fall from Eden.

The examples in these chapters illustrate how sacred status is attributed to selected objects, actions, and places which refer to the mythological origins of human and Islamic civilization. Muslim exegetical and historical sources articulate in narrative form the mythology which is represented in practicable and physical form by ritual and relics. In its various forms, this mythology expresses an ideology that makes necessary the existence of the state as the means to administer religion to humanity in its fallen condition. Official patronage of the scholarship and facilities designed to promote this mythology allows local states to assert their legitimacy as the guardians of Islamic civilization.

By way of conclusion, the following pages detail how Muslim definitions of ritual, relics, and territory delineate the authority and structure of a social order based upon two complementary systems of difference. The conception of these two systems provides more generic significance to the mythological symbolism exemplified by specific Muslim rituals and relics. Section 1 outlines how Muslim scholarship defines these two systems of difference. On the one hand, the Muslim scholars propose the opposition between the pure and impure, marking the absolute distinction between existence in Eden and humanity in its fallen state. On the other hand, Muslim jurists construct an opposition between the sacred and profane, delineating the relative distinctions at work in human civilization made necessary by the fact of humanity's fallen state.

Section 2 emphasizes the particular conception of agency characteristic of the specific Muslim examples of ritual and relics examined in the previous chapters. Mary Douglas's study of the Lele pangolin cult highlights the importance of society's recognition of the symbolism of the objects and actions it categorizes as sacred. Muslim definitions of ritual and relics evince a conscious attempt to demonstrate the conventional character of the sacred. This conventional character of ritual is illustrated further in contrast to the popular conception of surfing and its relationship to society. Unlike surfing, ritual is typified by its attitude of futility: that the break between Eden and earth is absolute and beyond human agency. These comparisons help to clarify the integral link between the sacred and a lost utopia.

## 1: STATUS AND POWER

The use of oppositions to generate and authorize hierarchical structures is evident in other cultural contexts. Providing a close reading of Louis Dumont's magisterial work on the caste system of India, J. Z. Smith distinguishes status from power, each constructed by separate sets of systemic oppositions:

> Status is founded on the absolute dichotomy of the pure and the impure, and is expressed as a relative hierarchy of degrees of purity and impurity, with the priest at its summit. It is, essentially, a sacerdotal system. Power is dominance—a hierarchy of degrees of legitimate force, with the king at its summit. It is, essentially, a juridical system. The two systems exhibit a necessary complementarity. The king will always be impure with respect to the priest (largely, though not exclusively, due to corpse pollution); but the priest will be inferior to the king with respect to authority. The priest legitimates the power of the king; the king supports, protects, and preserves the power of the priests.[1]

Smith concludes that Dumont's opposition between pure and impure is associated with the "hierarchy of status and priestly function," while the distinction between sacred and profane is defined as a "hierarchy of power associated with the royal function."[2]

Muslim definitions of certain obligatory rituals employ a similar distinction between the absolute opposition of the pure and impure, and the relative degrees separating the sacred and profane. This is evident from the stark contrast between the laws of purity and the laws relating to other rituals, such as prayer (ṣalāt).

Muslim legal definitions of impurity refer to the complete separation of earth and Eden, caused by the fall, and thus do not recognize distinctions within earthly existence. Certain differences that are taken into account affect the actual performance of the purification rites. It is not necessary for an injured person to remove a splint in order to perform purification, nor are pregnant and nursing women or old and sick people required to fast.[3] Menstruation affects only women, and women are allowed practical considerations, such as exemptions for long hair and dress when performing purification rituals.[4] Jurists also exempt persons without sufficient reasoning capacity, such as children and the insane, from ritual purification. Such mentally immature and infirm persons are excluded not because they are incapable of performing the rituals, but precisely because the value of the ritual is to remind people, through their activity, of their current separation from existence in Eden.

Similarly, Muslim purity law does not allow for relative states of purity, but only different types of impurity and the attendant rituals for purification relative to the basic cause of the impurity. A person cannot transmit impurity, nor is impurity contagious in a physical sense. Menstruating women, for example, do not infect other people or objects with which they come into contact.[5] The ablution (wuḍūʾ) relates to the natural bodily state and functions of individual human beings, and the ritual washing (ghusl) relates to the natural continuation of human society through sexual reproduction. Impurities arising from sexual reproduction require ritual washing, and those arising from everyday bodily functions, such as sleep, eating, and drinking, require ablution. Other impurities related to contact with physical substances are also assigned their place in this system. Physical impurities (najāsah, anjās) include semen, blood, urine, and corpses.[6] Such impurities do not involve a lack of bodily control; rather, as substances and conditions unknown in Eden, they are markers and reminders of the fall and the perpetual state of human impurity.[7]

In sharp contrast to the laws of purity are the many earthly distinctions recognized and required in the definition of other ritual practices. Certain restrictions emphasize social distinctions, such as those that distinguish men and women. Women are not to attend the group prayer (jumʿah) on Fridays and are not allowed to pray in mixed groups with men, and virgins, according to some, are not allowed to perform any prayers or fast during the month of Ramaḍān.[8] The qualifications of the prayer leader delineate a social standing according to age, piety, and learning: "The best person for leading the prayer is the most learned of the people praying in customary practice. If they [candidates] are equal in learning, then the best reader among them [is chosen]. If they are equal, then the most pious of them [is chosen]. If they are equal, then the oldest of them [is chosen]. It is reprehensible to put forward a slave, a nomad, a sinner, a blind person, or a child of fornication, but if they are put forward it is permitted."[9] These criteria set up oppositions between the free person and slave, city dweller and nomad, pious person and sinner, the healthy and the handicapped, and heir and bastard. Similar distinctions are made in describing the standing order for a group prayer: "The pure person does not pray following a person who has incontinence of urine, nor does a pure woman pray following a woman with an irregular discharge, nor a literate person following an illiterate person, nor a clothed person following the naked person. It is permitted for the person purified by purification without water to lead in prayer people purified by ablution, and the person who has wiped his slippers [to lead in prayer] the people purified by washing."[10] In these examples, the absolute and nonrelative rules for purification demarcate social differences, as do markers of social status, such as clothing and education. Other rituals are restricted to certain segments of society. Offering (zakāt) is required only of people possessing wealth over and above that required for their regular upkeep, just as the pilgrimage to Mecca and fighting in defense of the community (jihād) are not required for a people who do not have the means to both perform the duty and provide for their families during their absence.

Spatial and temporal distinctions are also demarcated through ritual. For example, when traveling outside a civilizational center (miṣr), people are not allowed to perform the congregational prayer.[11] Nor is purification without water (tayammum) allowed within the confines of a civilizational center.[12] People traveling more than three days distance from their home are required to pray only three daily prayers.[13] Parallel commercial and criminal laws, such as the prohibition against a city dweller's selling goods for a desert dweller and the stipulation that a bailed defendant be deposited in a market (sūq) but not in open country, also illustrate such social and geographical differentiation.[14] The rules pertaining to fighting in defense of the community (jihād, siyār) that apply outside the boundaries of Islamic civilization—such as killing, looting, and setting free slaves—are serious crimes inside Muslim society.[15] These territorial distinctions establish a kind of social mapping of Islamic society (see fig. 3). This can be extended to take into account the position of Mecca and its relation to the garden of Eden. The mosque refers to Mecca and Mecca to Eden, just as

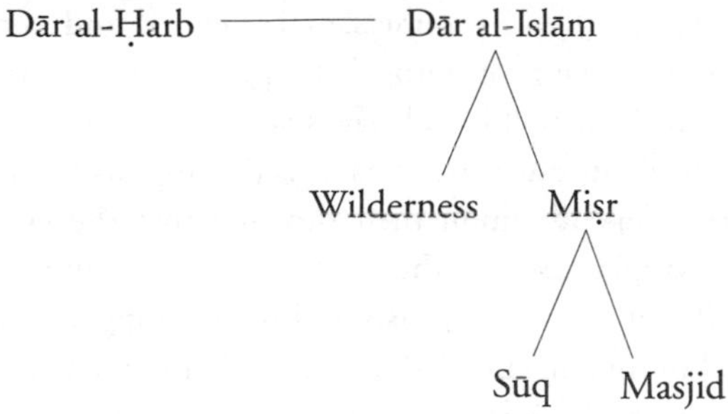


FIGURE THREE. The hierarchy of territory according to distinctions in Islamic legal practices.

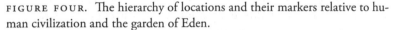

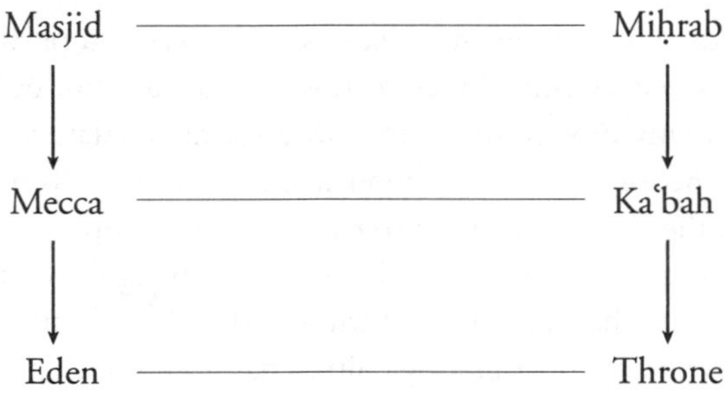


FIGURE FOUR. The hierarchy of locations and their markers relative to human civilization and the garden of Eden.

the indication of the direction of prayer (miḥrab) points to the Kaʿbah and the Kaʿbah to the throne of God (see fig. 4).

Muslim jurists define two realms, that of Eden and that of the earth. The earth is the realm of civilization, the laws of which are determined by the jurists and enforced by the state. As in the Indian case, where the king is separated from the priests through purity laws, the Muslim state does not have access to the legislative process of the jurists.[16] In the realm of civilization, the state ensures that people have the facilities to fulfill the ritual obligations of the law (ʿibādāt) and are bound by the social obligations of the law (muʿāmalāt). According to Abū al-Ḥasan ʿAlī al-Māwardī (d. 1058), the head of the state is intended as a representative of the prophets in upholding the faith and managing the affairs of the world.[17] Citing Q 4:59 and a ḥadīth report transmitted on the authority of Abū Hurayrah, al-Māwardī states that Muslims are to obey those in authority over them, even if the authorities themselves are impious, as long as the authorities uphold that which is according to the law (wāfiq al-ḥaqq).[18]

The area of Islamic civilization, the Dār al-Islām, is the realm of caliphs, judges, laws, mosques, and prophets. It is defined and constituted by a hierarchy of ranks—marks of status that represent the spectrum of human existence in the real, postfall world. The state is responsible for upholding a law which is outside its purview. The law is the responsibility of the jurists, whose authority depends upon their showing that the law they ask the state to uphold originates with the revelation and example of the prophet Muhammad. Patronage of the jurists and the learning associated with the transmission of prophetic knowledge ensures that the state is granted legitimacy. The jurists provide a law that provides for the existence of the state.

## 2: SYMBOL AND AGENCY

In her well-known study of the relationship between impurity and social order, Mary Douglas contributes to the central question of how certain rituals, and the myths with which they are associated, relate to the structure and maintenance of social order.[19] Douglas's insistence on distinguishing the impure from the sacred allows her to recognize that people are conscious of the symbolic character of their rituals: "[The Lele pangolin cult epitomizes] cults which invite their initiates to turn round and confront the categories on which their whole surrounding culture has been built up and to recognize them for the fictive, man-made, arbitrary creations that they are."[20] According to Douglas, ritual directs attention to the conventional character of religious definitions, such as the pure and impure, culminating in an activity that confirms the necessary shared nature of these conventions: "Then comes the inner cult of all their ritual life, in which the initiates of the pangolin, immune to dangers that would kill uninitiated men, approach, hold, kill and eat the animal which in its own existence combines all the elements which Lele culture keeps apart."[21] Echoing the camel sacrifice described by Robertson Smith and the Intichiuma described by Durkheim, Douglas uses the Lele initiation rite to underline that the social significance of these rituals and rules is to be found in the recognition of their symbolic value. What matters is not the particular animals that are prohibited or the particular actions prescribed. What matters is the fact that certain animals and actions are recognized by society as having symbolic value, and that this symbolic value is recognized as having been attributed to these animals and actions by society. It is this recognition that allows for the animals and actions related to natural phenomena to communicate a message that is of a social character. Douglas contends that this message, communicated also by other definitions of impurity, is the disjuncture between the ideal cosmic order and the actual state of the world.[22]

Such a conception of the disjunction between society and the natural world is also found in Islamic rituals and the treatment of relics. Except for the extraordinary attention given to them, relics are natural objects and artifacts coming from everyday life. Rituals are actions from everyday life given symbolic value. Just as the Lele pangolin cult uses definitions of impurity to highlight the symbolism of the sacred, so Islamic definitions of purity and impurity provide a conceptual contrast against which to perceive the symbolic value of other rituals.

The contrast between status and power displayed in the undifferentiation of purification rituals and the highly differentiated structure of other rituals (e.g., ṣalāt) illustrates this point. People performing the ritual prayer are defined on one level as humans, reminded of their fallen state, while on another level they are defined as males or females, city dwellers or nomads, learned or illiterate, healthy or infirm. These two axes are also evident in the symbolism of the rituals themselves. Facing Mecca during the group prayer, people direct their attention toward Mecca and its symbolism as a substitute for the lost Eden, while standing in rows and thus delineating their social and economic standing in the society of the postfall world.

Like the Lele pangolin cult, Muslim rituals also display a conscious attempt to demonstrate the conventional character of the rules by which they are governed. The close parallels between Muslim rituals and other rites of mourning and celebration in contemporary and neighboring cultures indicates that Muslim rituals are an assertion of a new identity based on social convention rather than shared history or seasonal patterns. The timing of the rituals is specifically nonnatural. Although prayer times are set according to the position of the sun, legal discussion of prayer times makes clear that the use of the sun's position is only to create convention, and the prayers are not to be performed in such a fashion as to link them organically with natural phenomena.

Likewise, the Muslim calendar, based on the lunar cycle without intercalation, is not based upon seasonal patterns. Despite the original link of fasting, offering, and pilgrimage to seasonal festivals, as in Judaism, Christianity, and other ancient Near Eastern contexts, these Muslim rituals are not fixed according to the natural cycle of fertility. The nonhistorical character of Muslim rituals is also striking. Although all of the rituals are said to have been performed by earlier prophets, only the seclusion during Ramaḍān (iʿtikāf) and the pilgrimage partly correspond to concrete historical events.[23]

Douglas emphasizes the need to pay attention to the agency of the rituals and rules. The "danger" of impurity is not the superstitious beliefs of individual harm coming from the violation of a rule. To the contrary, as Douglas observes, much of so-called purity law concerns what people must do when they become impure. Impurity is a natural consequence of everyday life, and as such is not dangerous, but failure to recognize the conventional rules of society concerning what is pure and impure is dangerous. Such a failure is dangerous because it threatens the common conception of the society. The execution of the apostate is an example of this principle, protecting society from the contagion of the individual who, in theory, would repudiate all social conventions. Impurity as defined by Islamic law is a result of the fall from Eden, and as a result all people are de facto impure. The purpose of purification rituals is not to eliminate impurity or its causes. This could be accomplished only by an actual, physical return to the conditions of Eden. The obligation of all people to perform regular purification rituals serves to "protect" society from the lack of attention to its fallen existence, and thus to confirm its need for organization and rule.[24]

In this sense, the relationship of ritual to the social order, as described by Douglas, is not unlike the relationship between surfing and society. Like ritual, surfing creates a social group through initiation rites, technical language, special clothing, and certain repeated actions.[25] Surfing is performed in designated areas, following in the footsteps of earlier surfers, and the act of surfing itself is performed in imitation of kings in a mythic setting.[26] The use of specialized objects—including boards and wax—based on mythic archetypes also parallels the use of sacred objects in ritual contexts.[27]

Surfing resembles the bear ritual described by J. Z. Smith: the activity of surfing and the culture accompanying it are based on a consciousness that life is not what it should or could be. Surfing epitomizes the notion that the everyday world of work, school, and cold weather is discontinuous from the idealized world of an endless summer of cranking waves.[28] Surfing is a temporary condition in the sense that most surfers eventually have to return to work, the summer ends, the waves are not always big, and you get old and die (and can't surf anymore). But whereas the bear ritual is utopian, surfing is unrealistic. The bear ritual is utopian because the real hunt can never take place as it is enacted in ritual, but it is not impossible to surf on the same beach as King Kealoha in Hawaii. As attested in movies and by professional surfers, it is possible, however unrealistic for most surfers, to surf continuously, following the summer around the world, never going back to work or school.[29]

Surfing differs from ritual in another significant way. The recognition of the disjunction between the ideal world of surfing and the real world of work and school does not serve to legitimate the status quo, as ritual does. On the one hand, the artifacts and body parts that are recognized as relics, and the actions that are stipulated as ritual, are officially sanctioned and supported by the state. Surfing may be a popular fad, but it is an activity that creates a subculture distinct from the larger social setting in which it is performed.[30] The culture of surfing can be an outlaw, punk culture.[31] On the other hand, although surfing makes a distinction similar to that made by ritual between the ideal and real world, ritual makes this distinction to authorize and underline the need for society and the state. The activity of surfing does not recall a primordial utopia whose loss requires the existence of society. There is a futility to ritual, a "helpless" attitude not shared by surfing: the attitude that regardless of the ritual performed there is really nothing that can be done by human beings to change the fundamental condition of their existence.

This helpless attitude of ritual is captured, in part, by Lévi-Strauss's insistence that the utopian existence described in myth and displayed in ritual cannot be recovered by society.[32] The participants in both surfing and ritual realize that their actions do not magically transport them to a place and time that does not exist, but only in ritual are the participants reminded of a utopia to which they cannot return through their own activity. Ritual legitimizes the existence of the state because it is designed to emphasize the ineffectiveness of human activity in overcoming humanity's fallen condition. Surfing is imitative, and surfers can actually accomplish the feats of Hawaiian kings and ancestral heroes, but ritual purification does not stop the need for sleep or defecation. Ritual and relics are about absence.

This futile attitude, contained in the notion that the break between Eden and earth is absolute and beyond the realm of human agency, is found in the Islamic context. The futility of ritual is that the actions performed do not actually accomplish physical change. Only God can return humanity to its prefallen state, and this will happen only if people follow the rules God has established in the postfall world. Rituals communicate this basic message using symbols that turn attention toward the sharp discontinuity between the actual and the ideal human condition. Surfing is escapist and is not unlike certain soteriological traditions in Buddhism, so-called gnosticism, and the beliefs and practices of groups like the Branch Davidians of Waco that treat the break between a utopia and the real world as a problem from which it is possible to escape through secret knowledge, initiatory experiences, or physical transport. This escapist view makes the sharpest break between the ideal and the real, abandoning the real to the extent that it is the real world that becomes the no-place, a demiurgic creation, or product of false consciousness.

At the opposite extreme is the apocalyptic ideology associated with so-called fundamentalism and religious activism. The apocalyptic view is one in which the break between heaven and earth is seen as a problem that can be fixed through human action or initiative. Various "fundamentalist" religious groups urge people to actions that are said to lead to immediate and real change in the world so that it might become like the utopia. Such an apocalyptic view mistakes the utopian ideal as a literal goal, something that can be achieved through human agency. There is no "utopia" (no-place) that justifies the way things are in a fallen world, but rather a "eutopia" (good-place) into which this world must be changed.

For the apocalyptic view, the sacred is not a symbol or a social convention but rather an attribute of objects and locations that are an intermediate stage in the transformation of this world into the next. Rituals are seen not as symbolic acts but as utilitarian activities designed to transform or correct the here and now into the then and there. Whereas the surfer opts to escape temporarily from the world, the fundamentalist seeks to restore the world to its "utopian" state, thus erasing, ultimately, the distinction between the ideal and the real. Both the apocalyptic and escapist ideologies represent radical critiques of what might be called the civilizational view that relies upon the conception of an unattainable utopia to legitimize the status quo of existing religious and state institutions.

## GENERAL CONCLUSIONS

ʿAbd al-Raḥmān b. Muḥammad Ibn Khaldun (d. 1382) writes that civilization is the necessary condition of humanity after the fall from Eden: "God created and fashioned humanity in a form that can live and subsist only with the help of food. He guided humanity to a natural desire for food and instilled in it the power than enables humanity to obtain food."[33] Human beings must develop agriculture, harvesting, kneading, baking, and other techniques in order to survive. God also did not provide humans with natural defenses, great strength, or tough hides, long nails, and sharp teeth. This means that human beings must organize themselves socially: "Social organization is necessary to the human species. Without it, the existence of human beings would be incomplete. God's desire to settle the world with human beings and leave them as his representatives on earth would not materialize."[34] God designed human beings, in their fall from Eden, to require social organization, the use of tools, and the governance of religion. Civilization is, for Ibn Khaldūn, God's soteriology for humanity. It is not that civilization leads to salvation, but rather that living in the conditions of this world reminds people of the way things were and can be again at some point in the future.

The conception of Islamic rituals and relics examined in this book fits a model of religion in which an absolute distinction is made between heaven and earth. The examples from Islamic contexts exemplify what appears to be the general motif of reflecting upon the break between a utopia and the real world. Muslim jurists and exegetes think about this break from what might be called a civilizational perspective, in which the utopia serves not as a realistic goal to be achieved through human agency, but as a concept invoked to remind people of the fall and of the need for the necessities of this world: religion and its administration by the state. This conception is eschatological in the sense that the utopia is to be realized at some point in the future and can be realized only through changes of radical and divine nature. Human beings are able to think about the break only in such a way as to justify waiting for God to heal it while living in the conditions of this world.

Muslim scholars define rituals and relics as symbols reminding people that their salvation depends upon adherence to a state whose legitimacy depends upon its patronage and administration of a religious law derived by Muslim scholars from revelation and the example of the prophet Muhammad. Certain actions, objects, and places are accorded sacred status because of their function as symbols referring to the loss of utopia and the need for civilization. These sacred things are physical manifestations of a mythology that is expressed in historical, legal, and exegetical discourses. Patronage of the textual and physical expression of this mythology allows the state and the religious elite to assert indirectly their own legitimacy as the necessary custodians of a postfall civilization.

It is certainly the case that this assertion by the state and religious elite, whether the claim to sovereignty or the particular justification of its existence, is not always accepted by those who might not appear to reject this ideology openly. Historical and ethnographic research demonstrates that people visit relics, follow the restrictions of sanctuaries, and perform rituals for a wide variety of reasons.[35] The use of conceptual oppositions (pure and impure, sacred and profane) to explain the need for religion and the state represents a strategy to assert authority, a strategy that exists in dynamic tension with the people who are governed by the social structure in which the assertion is made.

The reliance upon notions of absence and loss in Islamic conceptions of the significance of ritual, relics, and territory suggests a more generic understanding of how assigning categories of the pure and the sacred to specific actions and objects is related to the organization and maintenance of social order. In this sense, religion is a type of social theory, providing not only the means but also the reason for the organization of society and its governance. Jurists maintain a theory of civilization that authorizes their own position and the rule of the state on a model of absolute opposition between this world and the next, a model that requires sheer obedience. The rituals and relics that make up religion are about this utopia of the next world whose absence legitimizes the existence of society by insisting upon its necessity.

# *Notes*

## INTRODUCTION

1. William Robertson Smith, *Lectures on the Religion of the Semites: The Fundamental Institutions,* 3d ed., ed. Stanley A. Cook (London, 1927), 147–149. The first edition was published in November 1889, revised in May 1894 (with Smith's notes edited by John Sutherland Black, James Frazer, and A. A. Bevan), and subsequently reprinted in April 1901, July 1907, 1914, and 1923. A German translation by R. Stübe, *Die Religion der Semiten* (Freiburg, 1899), modified the format of the book and revised the text by expanding references and making other additions and omissions. The third edition includes extensive notes (495–692) by Stanley Cook and has a table comparing its pagination to the German edition (693).

The lectures on which this volume are based were originally delivered by Robertson Smith between 1888 and 1891, though only the first nine chapters were actually delivered at Aberdeen, and the last two were added later. The second and third series of Burnett Lectures (March 1890 and December 1891) were not published by Robertson Smith but were later discovered in manuscript at Cambridge University and published as *The Religion of the Semites: Lectures on the Religion of the Semites (Second and Third Series) by William Robertson Smith*, ed. John Day, Journal for the Study of the Old Testament Supplemental Series 183 (Sheffield, 1995). On this discovery, see John Day, "William Robertson Smith's Hitherto Unpublished Second and Third Series of Burnett Lectures on the Religion of the Semites," in *William Robertson Smith: Essays in Reassessment*, ed. William Johnstone, Journal for the Study of the Old Testament Supplemental Series 189 (Sheffield, 1995), 190–202.

2. Much has been written on Robertson Smith, primarily with regard to his contributions to biblical studies and anthropological theory. On his life, see John Sutherland Black and George Chrystal, *The Life of William Robertson Smith*

(London, 1912). Essays evaluating Roberston Smith's contribution to different disciplines can be found in Johnstone, *William Robertson Smith: Essays in Reassessment.*

3. Important exceptions to this statement include Arent Jan Wensinck, "The Ideas of the Western Semites Concerning the Navel of the Earth," *Verhandelingen der Koninklijke Akademie van Wetenschappen te Amsterdam*, Afdeling Letterkunde, n.s., 17, no. 1 (1916); Geo Widengren, *The Great Vohu Mana and the Apostle of God*, Uppsala Universitets Årsskrift 1951:4 (Uppsala, 1945); idem, *Mespotamian Elements in Manichaeism: King and Saviour 2*, Uppsala Universitets Årsskrift 1946:3 (Uppsala, 1946); idem, *The Ascension of the Apostle and the Heavenly Book: King and Saviour 3*, Uppsala Universitets Årsskrift 1950:7 (Uppsala, 1950); idem, *The King and the Tree of Life in Ancient Near Eastern Religion: King and Saviour 4*, Uppsala Universitets Årsskrift 1951:4 (Uppsala, 1951); idem, *Sakrales Königtum im Alten Testament und im Judentum* (Stuttgart, 1955); idem, *Muhammad, the Apostle of God, and His Ascension: King and Saviour 5*, Uppsala Universitets Årsskrift 1951:4 (Uppsala, 1955); idem, *Religionens värld: Religionsfenomenologiska studier och översikter* (Stockholm, 1952), trans. into German by Rosemarie Elgnowski as *Religionsphänomenologie* (Berlin, 1969). Also see Henri Corbin, *Cyclical Time and Ismaili Gnosis*, trans. Nancy Pearson (London, 1983); idem, *Terre céleste et corps de résurrection* (Paris, 1979), trans. Nancy Pearson as *Spiritual Body and Celestial Earth: From Mazdean Iran to Shiʿīte Iran* (Princeton, 1977); idem, *L'homme de lumière dans le soufisme iranien* (Paris, 1971), trans. Nancy Pearson as *The Man of Light in Iranian Sufism* (Boulder, Colo., 1978).

For analysis of the state of Islamic studies and the study of religion, see Steven Wasserstrom, *Between Muslim and Jew: The Problem of Symbiosis under Early Islam* (Princeton, 1995); idem, *Religion after Religion: Gershom Scholem, Mircea Eliade, and Henry Corbin at Eranos* (Princeton, 1999); Carl Ernst, *Following Muhammad: Rethinking Islam in the Contemporary World* (Chapel Hill, 2003); Azim Nanji, ed., *Mapping Islamic Studies: Genealogy, Continuity and Change* (Berlin, 1997); and J. Waardenburg, *L'Islam dans le miroir de l'Occident*, 3d ed. (Paris, 1970).

4. Robertson Smith, *Lectures on the Religion of the Semites*, 150. This same definition is repeated on 152: "Rules of holiness in the sense just explained, i.e. a system of restructions on man's arbitrary use of natural things, enforced by the dread of supernatural penalties, are found among all primitive peoples."

5. On references to these items, see ibid., s.v. in index. For another example of artificial objects denoting communal property as an extension of a given location, see Emanuel Marx, "Communal and Individual Pilgrimage: The Region of Saints' Tombs in South Sinai," in *Regional Cults*, ed. R. P. Werbner, ASA Monograph 16 (London, 1977), 29–51, esp. 45.

6. Émile Durkheim, *The Elementary Forms of the Religious Life*, trans. Joseph Ward Swain (London, 1915; reprint, New York, 1957), 338. For a fuller discussion

of Durkheim's critique of Robertson Smith, see 336–340. On Robertson Smith and the study of religion, see Gillian Bediako, *Primal Religion and the Bible: William Robertson Smith and His Heritage* (Sheffield, 1997); Carol Emma Burnside, "W. Robertson Smith and Louis Dumont: 'Fundamental Institutions' and 'Ideologies'" (PhD dissertation, Committee on the History of Culture, University of Chicago, 1987); O. Beidelman, *W. Robertson Smith and the Sociological Study of Religion* (Chicago, 1974); and al-Sayyid ʿĀmid, *al-Qarābah ʿinda Ibn Khaldūn wa Rūbirtsūn Smith* (Alexandria, 1984).

7. See Durkheim, *The Elementary Forms of the Religious Life,* 338–339: "But the important thing is that the sacrilege should be accompanied with precautions which attenuate it." Also see his comment that sometimes the prohibited item is so unrealistic, as in the case of the water totem (130–131), as to preclude literal adherence.

8. Durkheim, *The Elementary Forms of the Religious Life,* 348–349. It can be argued that Durkheim sees a more direct relationship between the act of sacrifice and society in his critique of Robertson Smith: "[S]acrifice was not founded to create a bond of artificial kinship between a man and his gods, but to maintain and renew the natural kinship which primitively united them" (340). Also see his longer critique on 344–350.

9. See Robertson Smith, *Lectures on the Religion of the Semites,* 295–303.

10. See E. E. Evans-Pritchard, *Nuer Religion* (Oxford, 1956), 248, although he appears to reject Robertson Smith's conclusions about the social function of sacrifice (273–274). For a fuller evaluation of Evans-Pritchard's work, see Luc de Heusch, *Sacrifice in Africa: A Structuralist Approach* (Bloomington, 1985). On the sacrifice of oxen among the ancient Egyptians, see Porphyry, *On Images,* trans. A. H. Armstrong (Cambridge, Mass., 1966): "They did not, however, believe the animals to be gods, but regarded them as likenesses and symbols of gods; and this is shown by the fact that in many places oxen dedicated to the gods are sacrificed at their monthly festivals and in their religious services. For they consecrated oxen to the sun and moon" (fragment 10).

11. Robertson Smith, *Lectures on the Religion of the Semites,* 296–297.

12. On this, see William Robertson Smith, *Kinship and Marriage in Early Arabia* (Cambridge, 1885). For the value of camels as pack animals and to carry cavalry, see Herodotus, *The Histories,* ed. and trans. A. D. Godley (London, 1924–1928), 1:80–81, 7:88–90.

13. See Robertson Smith, *Lectures on the Religion of the Semites,* 281–284. He also cites Imru al-Qays; see *Dīwān Imruʾ al-Qays wa muhḥaqātuh: Bi-sharḥ Abī Saʿīd al-Sukkarī,* ed. Anwār ʿAylān Abū Suwaylam (al-ʿAyn, 2000), vv. 10–12; and ʿAmr b. al-Ahtam, *Die Mufaḍḍalîjât,* ed. Heinrich Thorbecke (Leipzig, 1885), poem 12, vv. 12ff., p. 283. Simeon the Stylite forbade his Arab converts to eat the flesh of camels and wild asses: Theodoret, *Interpretatio Quatuordecim Episto-*

*larum s. Pauli Apostoli,* ed. Jacques Sirmond and Johann August Nösselt (Halae Magdeburgicae, 1771), 3:1274; also see references to feasts of camel flesh in Julius Wellhausen, *Reste arabischen Heidentums: Gesammelt un Erläutert* (Berlin, 1897), 117; Robertson Smith, *Kinship and Marriage in Early Arabia,* 60; and Campbell Thompson, *Semitic Magic: Its Origins and Development* (London, 1908), 201n1.

14. See Robertson Smith, *Lectures on the Religion of the Semites,* 285–289; idem, *Kinship and Marriage in Early Arabia,* passim.

15. See Richard Bulliet, *The Camel and the Wheel* (Cambridge, Mass., 1975). On domesticated animals in other contexts, see Bruce Lincoln, *Priests, Warriors, and Cattle: A Study in the Ecology of Religions* (Berkeley, 1981).

16. Robertson Smith, *Lectures on the Religion of the Semites,* 307. On the relations between animals and human, he cites Isa 11:6. On the need for animals for clothing, see Gen 2:16, 3:15, 4:4. Also appropriate to this context is Robertson Smith's statement "[P]opular tradition and ancient ritual alike bore testimony that the life of the swine and the sheep, but above all of the ox, was of old regarded as sacred, and might not be taken away except for religious purposes, and even then only with special precautions to clear the worshippers from the guilt of murder" (304).

17. See ibid., 300–309, citing Hesiod. On the fall from the garden of Eden and other biblical notions of this utopian golden age, see 305–309. The conclusion made by Robertson Smith about the need for agriculture following the golden age is particularly evident from his discussion of the sacrifice of firstfruits from agricultural products and firstlings from domesticated animals. See 458–465, although his discussion there centers on the sacrifice as tribute.

18. See ibid., 310–311: "[I]n the most ancient nomadic times, to which the sanctity of domestic animals must be referred, the same clan or community will not generally be found to breed more than one kind of domestic animal."

19. Claude Lévi-Strauss, *The Naked Man,* trans. J. and D. Weightman (New York, 1981), 679. On this opposition, although from what appears to be an inverted perspective, see also Lévi-Strauss, *The Savage Mind,* The Nature of Human Society Series (London, 1966; reprint, London, 1976): "As I have already suggested, ideas and beliefs of the 'totemic' type particularly merit attention because, for the societies which have constructed or adopted them, they constitute codes making it possible to ensure, in the form of conceptual systems, the convertibility of messages appertaining to each level, even of those which are so remote from each other that they apparently relate solely to culture or solely to society, that is, to men's relations with each other, on the one hand, or, on the other, to phenomena of a technical or economic order which might rather seem to concern man's relations with nature. This mediation between nature and culture, which is one of the distinctive functions of the totemic operator, enables us to sift out what may be true from what is partial and distorted in Durkheim's and

Malinowski's accounts. They each attempted to immure totemism in one or the other of these two domains. In fact however it is pre-eminently the means (or hope) of transcending the opposition between them" (90–91).

20. On the relationship between the mythical time of the Alcheringa and the Intichiuma among the Aborigines, see Durkheim, *The Elementary Forms of the Religious Life,* 247–248, 327–333.

21. See Lévi-Strauss, *The Savage Mind,* 54–72, for the description of ritual which imagines the equivalence of two beings whose inequality is absolute and unable to be overcome (i.e., God and humanity).

22. On the role of the chieftain, and later the priests, in the rituals and organization of society, see Robertson Smith, *Lectures on the Religion of the Semites,* 60–83.

23. See Jonathan Z. Smith, "The Bare Facts of Ritual," in his *Imagining Religion: From Babylon to Jonestown* (Chicago, 1982), 59. Smith cites D. K. Zelenin, *Kul't ongonov v Sibiri* (Moscow, 1936), trans. into French by G. Welter as *La culte des idoles en Sibérie* (Paris, 1952); and Eveline Lot-Falck, *Les rites de chasse chez les peuples sibériens* (Paris, 1953). On the bear offering itself to the hunters, see A. Irving Hallowell, "Bear Ceremonialism in the Northern Hemisphere," *American Anthropologist,* n.s., 28 (1926): 1–175, esp. 53–61. See Leopold von Schrenck, *Reisen und Forschungen im Amur-Lande in den Jahren 1854–1856,* vol. 3, *Die Völker des Amur-Landes,* Geographisch-historischer und anthropologisch-ethnologischer Theil (St. Petersburg, 1881), 715, on the Gilyak.

24. See J. Z. Smith, "The Bare Facts of Ritual," 59. See E. A. Alekseenko, "The Cult of the Bear among the Ket (Yenisei Ostyaks)," in *Popular Beliefs and Folklore Tradition in Siberia,* ed. V. Diószegi (Budapest, 1968), 175–192, esp. 180. Alekseenko relates that the Ket claim not to be hunting the bear but rather paying a visit to an aged relative.

25. J. Z. Smith, "The Bare Facts of Ritual," 61, discusses the use of traps and shotguns, citing M. G. Levin and L. P. Potapov, *Narody Sibiri* (Moscow, 1956), trans. Stephen P. Dunn as *The Peoples of Siberia* (Chicago, 1964). Henry Lansdell, *Through Siberia,* 4th ed. (London, 1883), 209–210, describes how the Yenesei in Yeneseysk Province hunt bears by fixing a platform to the trunk of tree in such a way that the bear has to stand on its hind legs to get at the bait. The platform is barbed with iron spikes so that the bear's paw becomes stuck on the raised platform when it goes for the bait. When the bear puts its other paw on the platform to free the first and it too becomes stuck, the bear is trapped in an upright, standing position, allowing the hunters to attack without fear.

26. J. Z. Smith, "The Bare Facts of Ritual," 61, 63.

27. Ibid., 61. The best-known interpretations of the bear hunt rituals appear to take this view of the hunters. See, for example, Hallowell, "Bear Ceremonialism in the Northern Hemisphere," 9: "It becomes apparent, for example, that the

categories of rational thought, by which we are accustomed to separate human life from animal life and the supernatural from the natural, are drawn upon lines which the facts of primitive cultures do not fit." Heonik Kwon, "Play the Bear: Myth and Ritual in East Siberia," *History of Religions* 38 (1999): 373–387, on 374, quotes J. G. Frazer (*The Golden Bough* [New York, 1922], 517): "[T]he act of killing and eating an animal must wear a very different aspect from that which the same act presents to us." See also Carleton S. Coon, *The Hunting Peoples* (London, 1971), 342: "But the emotional crisis of seeing an adopted member of the family killed, and then eating the flesh of a half-tame creature that they had nursed, may have helped give some of the women nervous breakdowns, and it may also have helped the men believe the fanciful explanation of the whole cycle which they had been taught."

From another perspective, see Kyōsuke Kindaichi, "The Concepts behind the Ainu Bear Festival (Kumamatsuri)," trans. Minori Yoshida, *Southwestern Journal of Anthropology* 5 (1949): 345–350, originally published in *Gakusō Zuihitsu* (Kyoto: Jinbun Shoin, 1936). He reports that the Ainu kill the bear in midwinter, when the fur is thickest and the meat is sweetest because of the fat in it.

28. On the eastern Siberian conception of the ritual hunt as "play" and the location of the ritual as "playground" (*aracu*), see Kwon, "Play the Bear," 378–379. Also see Levin and Popatov, *The Peoples of Siberia,* where the bear festival (*chkhyfle-kherno*) is reported to literally mean "bear game" (779). For related comments, see E. A. Kreinovich, "Rozhdenie i smert' cheloveka po vozzreniiam giliakov," *Etnografiia* 9 (1930): 89–113; T. Obayashi and H. Paproth, "Das Bärenfest der Oroken auf Sachalin," *Zeitschrift für Ethnologie* 91 (1966): 218; and C. Schaeffer, "The Bear Foster Parent Tale: A Kutenai Version," *Journal of American Folklore* 60 (1947): 286–288, on fostering and play.

29. J. Z. Smith, "The Bare Facts of Ritual," 63.

30. On the distinction between the bear hunt and the ritual of slaughtering a domesticated bear among the Ainu, Gilyak, Orochi, and Ulchi, see Alekseenko, "The Cult of the Bear among the Ket," 175–192. On the Ainu, see Coon, *The Hunting Peoples,* 340–344; and Hallowell, "Bear Ceremonialism in the Northern Hemisphere," 119–131. On the Gilyak, see Coon, *The Hunting Peoples,* 106–119; Sternberg, "Die Religion der Giljaken," *Archiv fur Religionswissenschaft* 8 (1905): 244–274, 456–473; and Joseph Deniker, *Les Ghiliaks: D'après les derniers renseignements* (Paris: E. Leroux, 1884). On the Gold, Olcha, and Orochi bear festivals, see Hallowell, "Bear Ceremonialism in the Northern Hemisphere," 119–131; A. M. Zolotarev, "The Bear Festival of the Oltcha," *American Anthropologist* 39 (1939); and Alexander Slawik, "Zur Etymologie des japanischen Terminus marebito 'Sakraler Besucher,'" *Wiener Völkerkundliche Mitteilungen* 2 (1954): 44–58. On the Oroke practice of rearing a bear cub in a cave near the village, see Levin and Popatov, *The Peoples of Siberia,* 764–765. For comparisons, on the Ainu and Gilyak, see von

Schrenck, *Reisen und Forschungen im Amur-Lande in den Jahren 1854–1856*, vol. 3, *Die Völker des Amur-Landes*, 11–91; Ivar Paulson, *Schutzgeister und Gottheiten des Wildes (Der Jagdtiere und Fische in Nordeurasien): Eine religionsethnographische und religionsphänomenologische Untersuchung jägerischer Glaubensvorstellungen*, Acta universitatis stockholmiensis 2 (Stockholm, 1961), 69–74; and Alexander Slawik, "Zum Problem des Bärenfestes bei den Ainu und Giljaken," *Kultur und Sprache: Wiener Beiträge zur Kulturgeschichte und Linguistik* 9 (1952): 189–203.

31. Coon, *The Hunting Peoples*, 343, describes how the Ainu wait until the bear is dead before strangling it.

32. J. Z. Smith, "The Bare Facts of Ritual," 65. On this lack of control, also see Kustaa Vilkuna, *Volkstümliche Arbeitsfeste*, FF Communications, no. 191 (Helsinki, 1963), where the "magic" of the feast is interpreted as the produce of the harvest, supplied not by people but by God.

33. J. Z. Smith, "The Bare Facts of Ritual," 63. Also see J. Z. Smith, *To Take Place: Toward Theory in Ritual* (Chicago, 1987).

34. J. Z. Smith, "The Bare Facts of Ritual," 63; all italics in the original. Also see his remark "It is conceivable that the northern hunter, while hunting, might hold the image of this perfect hunt in his mind. I would assume that, at some point, he reflects on the difference between his actual modes of killing and the perfection represented by the ceremonial killing" (64). For a more general discussion of the close correspondence between the ritual of the hunt and the slaughtering of the bear, see Carl-Martin Edsman, "Bärenfest," in *Die Religion in Geschichte und Gegenwart*, ed. Kurt Galling and Hans Campenhausen (Tübingen, 1957).

35. Joseph Kitagawa, "Ainu Bear Festival (Iyomante)," *History of Religions* 1 (1961): 95–151, recognizes the link between the ritual and the myth, but this is unmentioned by J. Z. Smith, perhaps because of the ultimate conclusion reached by Kitagawa (151): "It is the most significant communal ritual that solidifies the organic unity of the Ainu people since in this rite the people are made to realize that they are not simply men confined to the bondage of this earthly existence. Rather, they are made to feel the organic unity between this world of man and all other worlds of the kanui, so that 'the participants recover the sacred dimension of existence, by learning again how the gods [kamui] or the mythical ancestors [Okikurumi, Ainu-rak-kur, or Aeoina kamui] created man and taught him the various kinds of social behaviour and of practical work.'" The last part is a quote from Mircea Eliade, *The Sacred and the Profane*, trans. Willard R. Trask (New York, 1959), 90.

36. On the spread of the bear cult, see Alexandr A. Petrov, "The Bear Taboo in Even Language and Folklore," *Inuit Studies* 13, no. 1 (1989): 131–133, concerning the Even, Evenk, Oroke, Nanay, Olcha, Mansi, and Ket. B. A. Vasil'ev, "Medvezhii prazdnik," *Sovetskaia etnografiia* 4 (1948): 78–104, says that the bear cult cov-

ered a large area, including Scandinavia, the Kola Peninsula, northwest Europe, the taiga region of Siberia, the Amur region, and the taiga belt of North America. Also see Slawik, "Zum Problem des Bärenfestes bei den Ainu und Giliaken."

On prehistoric practices linking the hunt and taming, see Cristian Lascu and others, "A Mousterian Cave Bear Worship Site in Translyvania, Roumania," *Journal of Prehistoric Religion* 10 (1996): 17–27; and O. Abel and G. Kyrle, *Die Drachenhöhle bei Mixnitz* (Vienna, 1931). Also see K. Meuli, "Griechische Opferbräuche," in *Phyllobolia für Peter von der Muhll zum 60. Geburstag am 1. August 1945,* ed. Olof Gigon and others (Basel, 1945), 185–288; W. Schmidt, "Das Primitialopfer in der Urkultur," in *Corona Amicorum: Festgabe für Emil Bächler,* ed. Emil Egli (St. Gallen, 1948), 81–92; Karl J. Narr, "Bärenzeremoniell und Schamanismus in der Älteren Steinzeit Europas," *Saeculum* 10 (1959): 233–272; and Adrian Pârvulescu, "The Name of the Great Bear," *Journal of Indo-European Studies* 16 (1988): 95–120.

37. See, for example, K. Donner, *Ethnological Notes about the Yenisei Ostyaks* (Helsinki, 1933), esp. 96.

38. See Lot-Falck, *Les rites de chasse chez les peuples sibériens,* esp. 94–102.

39. See Franz Boas, *The Jesup North Pacific Expedition,* vol. 5, pt. 2: *The Kwakiutl of Vancouver Island* (Leiden: E. J. Brill, 1898; reprint, New York: AMS Press, 1975), esp. 501. Also see Wiliam Thalbitzer, "Die kultischen Gottheiten der Eskimos," *Archiv für Religionswissenschaft* 26 (1928); and Eric Juel, "Notes on Seal-Hunting Ceremonialism in the Arctics," *Ethnos* (1945): 2–3.

40. Hallowell, "Bear Ceremonialism of the Northern Hemisphere," 77–81.

41. See Boas, *The Kwakiutl of Vancouver Island,* 500. On a similar practice among the Gilyak, see Sternberg, "Die Religion der Giljaken," esp. 260–262; and Deniker, *Les Ghiliaks,* esp. 308.

42. See Levin and Popatov, *The Peoples of Siberia,* 764–765.

43. See the account in J. R. Jewitt, *A Narrative of the Adventures and Suffering of J. R. Jewitt* (London, 1820), 95–96. On the association of bears and kingship in the ancient world, see Y. Kurokawa, "A Newly Found Sasanian Silver Plate with Royal Bear Hunt," *Kodai oriento Hakubutsukan Kiyo* [Bulletin of the Ancient Orient Museum] 17 (1996): 65–87.

44. See Hallowell, "Bear Ceremonialism in the North Hemisphere," 82–84.

45. See the many references in Alekseenko, "The Cult of the Bear among the Ket," 175–192. Also see M. A. Castrén, "Journey into Siberia in 1845–1849," *Magazin zemlevedenia u pyteoestvia* 6.2 (1860); and Vasil'ev, "Medvezhii prazdnik."

46. See Alekseenko, "The Cult of the Bear among the Ket," 182–186.

47. See Hallowell, "Bear Ceremonialism in the Northern Hemisphere," 80–84.

48. See H. Paproth, *Studien über Bärenzeremoniell,* vol. 1, *Bärenjagdriten und Bärenfest bei den Tungusischen Völkern* (Uppsala, 1976), esp. 92–101.

49. For a general overview of the connection between bear hunting and

reproduction, see Othenio Abel and Wilhelm Koppers, "Eiszeitlich Bärendarstellungen und Bärenkult in paläobiologischer und prähistorisch-ethnologischer Beleuchtung," *Palaeobiologica* 7 (1939): 7–64.

50. See, for example, N. P. Dyrenkova, "Bear Worship among Turkish Tribes of Siberia," *Proceedings of the 23rd International Congress of Americanists* (New York, 1928–1930), 437–445.

51. See J. Abercromby, *The Pre- and Proto-historic Finns* (London, 1898), esp. 1:161; J. Scheffer, *History of Lapland* (Frankfort, 1673; reprint, London, 1704), esp. 95; and Carl-Martin Edsman, "Bear Rites among the Scandinavian Lapps," in *Proceedings of the 9th International Congress for the History of Religions* (Tokyo, 1960), 25–32.

52. See Taryo Obayashi, "On the Origin of the 'Inau' Cult-Sticks of the Ainu," *Japanese Journal of Ethnology* (Tokyo) 24 (1960): 16–27.

53. See Hallowell, "Bear Ceremonialism in the Northern Hemisphere," 86; and A. Gahs, "Kopf-, Schädel- und Langhochenopfer bei Rentiervölkern," in *Festschrift: Publication d'hommage offerte au P. W. Schmidt*, ed. W. Koppers (Vienna, 1928), 231–268.

54. See D. K. Zelenin, "Tabu slov u narodov vostochnoi Evropy: Severnoi Azii," *Sbornik Muzeia antropologii i etnografii* (Leningrad) 8 (1929): 1–144.

55. See L. V. Khomich, "Religioznye kul'ti nentsev," *Pamiatniki kul'tury narodov Sibiri i severa* (Leningrad) (1977): 5–28.

56. See Petrov, "The Bear Taboo in Even Language and Folklore." For other food restrictions relative to women, see Levin and Popatov, *The Peoples of Siberia*, 565. Also see Alekseenkso, field report, Archives of the Institute of Ethnography of the Academy of Sciences of the USSR 416, 34, for the claim that some women tell the bear to leave them alone because they are "not guilty" of killing it.

57. Levin and Popatov, *The Peoples of Siberia*, 649.

58. See Kitagawa, "Ainu Bear Festival," 135; and John Batchelor, *The Ainu and Their Folklore* (London, 1901), 9–10.

59. See Levin and Popatov, *The Peoples of Siberia*, 743; Waldemar Bogoras, "Le mythe de l'animal-dieu mourant et ressuscitant," *XXIIIe Congrès International des Américanistes, Rome 1926* (Rome, 1926); and Carl-Martin Edsman, "The Story of the Bear Wife in Nordic Tradition," *Ethnos* (Stockholm) 21 (1956): 1–2.

60. See Alekseenko, "The Cult of the Bear among the Ket," 178–180.

61. See See K. A. Novikova, *Evenskii fol'klor* (Magadan, 1958), 89–98.

62. See Alekseenko, "The Cult of the Bear among the Ket," 180.

63. See A. Veselovskii, *Razyskaniia v oblasti russkago dukhovnykh stikhov* (St. Petersburg, 1889), 12.

64. See J. Z. Smith, "The Domestication of Sacrifice," in *Violent Origins*, ed. G. Hamerton-Kelly (Stanford, 1987), 85–93.

65. On some of this terminology, see Hallowell, "Bear Ceremonialism of

the Northern Hemisphere," 43–53; Kwon, "Play the Bear," esp. 374; and Slawik, "Zum Problem des Bärenfestes bei den Ainu und Giljaken," 57. On cattle kinship, see See Evans-Pritchard, *Nuer Religion,* 250; H. C. Jackson, *Behind the Modern Sudan* (London, 1955), 94, 96; and C. G. Seligman, *Pagan Tribes of the Nilotic Sudan* (London, 1932), 169.

66. See S. M. Shirokogoroff, *Psychomental Complex of the Tungus* (London, 1935); R. Hamayon, *La chasse à l'âme: Esquisse d'une théorie du chamanisme sibérien* (Nanterre, 1990); and Kindaichi, "The Concepts behind the Ainu Bear Festival (Kumamatsuri)."

On the deification of domesticated animals in the ancient Near East and in connection with Robertson Smith, see Harriet Lutzky, "Deity and the Social Bond: Robertson Smith and the Psychoanalytic Theory of Religion," in Johnstone, *William Robertson Smith: Essays in Reassessment,* 320–330. On the kinship and deification of kangaroos among the Arunta, see Durkheim, *The Elementary Forms of the Religious Life,* 139.

67. On the uses of bears mentioned here, see Alekseenko, "The Cult of the Bear among the Ket," 176; Irving Goldman, *The Mouth of Heaven: An Introduction to Kwakiutl Religious Thought* (London, 1975), 121–125, on the giving of grizzly bear skins as gifts and items of exchange; and Franz Boas, *The Religion of the Kwakiutl Indians,* Columbia University Contributions to Anthropology 10 (New York, 1930).

68. See the comments of Hallowell, "Bear Ceremonialism of the Northern Hemisphere," 148–149.

69. On the use of the concept and phrase "mythology is ideology in narrative form," see Bruce Lincoln, *Theorizing Myth: Narrative, Ideology, and Scholarship* (Chicago, 1999).

## CHAPTER ONE

1. ʿAbd al-Mālik Ibn Hishām, *al-Sīrah al-nabawīyah,* ed. Ṭaha ʿAbd al-Rūf Saʿd (Beirut, n.d.), 1:281. See the English translation in A. Guillaume, *The Life of Muhammad* (Karachi, 1955; reprint, 1982), 64/94.

2. Ibn Hishām, *al-Sīrah al-nabawīyah,* 1:281; Guillaume, *The Life of Muhammad,* 64/94. I have omitted the few lines, between the discovery of the treasure and its use in the ornamentation of the Kaʿbah, in which ʿAbd al-Muṭṭalib and the Quraysh draw lots for the treasure.

3. See Muḥammad b. Jarīr al-Ṭabarī, *Taʾrīkh al-rusul wa al-mulūk,* ed. M. J. de Goeje (Leiden, 1879–1901), 1088. See the English translation in William Montgomery Watt and M. V. McDonald, trans., *The History of al-Ṭabarī: Muḥammad at Mecca* (Albany, 1988), 15. See Aḥmad b. Abī Yaʿqūb al-Yaʿqūbī, *Taʾrīkh al-Yaʿqūbī,* ed. ʿAbd al-Amīr Muhannā (Beirut, 1993), 1:298.

4. See Muḥammad b. ʿAbdallāh al-Azraqī, *Akhbār Makkah,* ed. Rushdī al-Ṣāliḥ Malḥas (Beirut, 1983), 92. For a modern account, see Fawād ʿAlī Riḍā, *Umm al-Qurā: Makkah al-Mukarramah* (Beirut, 1987), 210–212, who mentions the two gazelles and describes the swords and armor as being valuable (thamīnah).

5. Aḥmad Ibn Saʿd, *al-Ṭabaqāt al-kubrā,* ed. Muḥammad ʿAbd al-Qādir ʿAṭā (Beirut, 1990), 1:69.

6. See, for example, Uri Rubin, "The Kaʿba: Aspects of Its Ritual Functions and Position in Pre-Islamic and Early Islamic Times," *Jerusalem Studies in Arabic and Islam* 8 (1986): 97–131, esp. 115–117, where Rubin discusses a number of variant accounts of the treasure. Points related to the origins of the sanctuary at Mecca are also found in Uri Rubin, "Ḥanīfiyya and Kaʿba: An Inquiry into the Arabian Pre-Islamic Background of Dīn Ibrāhīm," *Jerusalem Studies in Arabic and Islam* 13 (1990): 85–112. Also see Yehuda D. Nevo and Judith Koren, "The Origins of the Muslim Descriptions of the Jāhilī Meccan Sanctuary," *Journal of Near Eastern Studies* 49, no. 1 (1990): 23–44, esp. 36–37, where the burial of objects is mentioned.

7. G. R. Hawting, "The Disappearance and Rediscovery of Zamzam and the 'Well of the Kaʿba,'" *Bulletin of the School of Oriental and African Studies* 43 (1980): 44–54. Hawting also refers to the treasure in his "The 'Sacred Offices' of Mecca from Jāhiliyya to Islam," *Jerusalem Studies in Arabic and Islam* 13 (1990): 62–84, esp. 80–81. The fuller implications of his conclusions can be found in Hawting, *The Idea of Idolatry and the Emergence of Islam: From Polemic to History,* Cambridge Studies in Islamic Civilization (Cambridge, 1999), esp. 20–44.

8. Hawting, "The Disappearance and Rediscovery of Zamzam and the 'Well of the Kaʿba,'" 48.

9. Ibid., 50, 53–54. Hawting cites Wensinck, "The Ideas of the Western Semites Concerning the Navel of the Earth." A related discussion on the association of the sanctuary with a hole in the earth can be found in parts of Arent Jan Wensinck, "The Ocean in the Literature of the Western Semites," *Verhandelingen der Koninklijke Akademie van Wetenschappen te Amsterdam,* Afdeling Letterkunde, n.s., 19, no. 2 (1918). Hawting also refers to the Syriac tradition of the Cave of Treasures (meʿārath gazzē) in C. Bezold, ed. and trans., *Die Schatzhöhle (Meʿārath Gazzē)* (Leipzig, 1883–1888; reprint, Amsterdam, 1981); and E. A. W. Budge, ed. and trans., *The Book of the Cave of Treasures* (London, 1927).

10. See Hawting, "The Disappearance and Rediscovery of Zamzam and the 'Well of the Kaʿba,'" 53–54.

11. For an overview and critique of this type of scholarship and the theoretical perspective it represents, see Reuven Firestone, *Journeys in Holy Lands: The Evolution of the Abraham-Ishmael Legends in Islamic Exegesis* (Albany, 1990), esp. 3–21; Jacob Lassner, *Demonizing the Queen of Sheba: Boundaries of Gender and Culture in Postbiblical Judaism and Medieval Islam* (Chicago, 1993), esp. 120–155; Roberto

Tottoli, *I profeti biblici nella tradizione islamica* (Brescia, 1999), trans. Michael Robertson as *Biblical Prophets in the Qur'ān and Muslim Literature* (Richmond, 2002); and Brannon Wheeler, *Moses in the Quran and Islamic Exegesis* (London, 2002), esp. 1–6.

12. For the account, see Josephus, *Jewish Antiquities,* ed. and trans. H. Thackeray and others (Cambridge, Mass., 1962–1965), 18.4.1. This account and others are examined in Marilyn F. Collins, "The Hidden Vessels in Samaritan Traditions," *Journal for the Study of Judaism* 3, no. 1 (1972): 97–116, which contains a more detailed overview of the hidden vessels motif in Samaritanism and other traditions.

The Sefer Yosippon also mentions this incident, with some small differences. See D. Flusser, *The Josippon* (Jerusalem, 1978–1980); and H. Huminer, ed., *Josiphon* (Jerusalem, 1971). For the Arabic recension, see Julius Wellhausen, *Der arabische Josippon* (Berlin, 1897).

13. On this text and other Samaritian chronicles written in the fourteenth and later centuries, see P. Stenhouse, "Samaritan Chronicles," in *The Samaritans,* ed. A. D. Crown (Tübingen, 1989), 218–265; and idem, *The Kitab al-Tarikh of Abu'l-Fath* (Sydney, 1985) . Also see J. Macdonald, *The Samaritan Chronicle II* (Berlin, 1969); and J. A. Cohen, *A Samaritan Chronicle* (Leiden, 1981).

14. On the Taheb, see Arthur Cowley, "The Samaritan Doctrine of the Messiah," *Expositor,* 5th ser., 1 (1895): 161–174; Adalbert Merx, *Der Messias oder Ta'eb der Samaritaner,* Beihefte zur Zeitschrift für die alttestamentliche Wissenschaft 17 (Giessen, 1909), 50–67 (biblical), 68–79 (Hibat b. Hajm), 80–91 (Midrash); J. Bowman, "Early Samaritan Eschatology," *Journal of Jewish Studies* 6 (1955): 63–72; and idem, "Samaritan Studies," *Bulletin of the John Rylands Library* 40 (1957–1958): 298–300. Bowman cites a fourteenth-century Samaritan text in which the Taheb recovers the ark, the tabernacle, and all of its furnishings. Also see H. G. Kippenberg, *Garizim und Synagoge* (Berlin, 1971), 276–305: and S. J. Isser, *The Dositheans* (Leiden, 1976), esp. 127–142.

15. For the text and English translation of the Memar Marqah, see J. Macdonald, *Memar Marqah* (Berlin, 1963).

16. On the dating of the Memar Marqah, see A. Tal, "Samaritan Literature," and P. Stenhouse, "Samaritan Chronicles," in Crown, *The Samaritans,* 313–367; and Robert T. Anderson, *Studies in Samartian Manuscripts and Artifacts: The Chamberlain-Warren Collection* (Cambridge, Mass., 1978); and idem, "Samaritans," in *The Anchor Bible Dictionary,* ed. David Noel Freedman and others (New York, 1992), 5:940–947.

17. See Memar Marqah 5:3; English translation, 206. Also see the specific reference to the hiding of the tabernacle in Memar Marqah 4:11; English translation, 179–180.

18. All citations from the Babylonian Talmud are taken from the text published as *The Babylonian Talmud,* ed. I. Epstein (London, 1948).

19. See D. R. A. Hare, "The Lives of the Prophets," in *The Old Testament Pseudepigrapha,* ed. James H. Charlesworth (Garden City, N.Y., 1983), 2:379–399. This text is extant in Greek, Syriac, Ethiopic, Latin, and Armenian recensions. The earliest Greek manuscript dates to the sixth century CE, though some scholars believe the Greek is a translation of an earlier Semitic original. For the Greek text, see C. C. Torrey, *The Lives of the Prophets: Greek Text and Translation* (Philadelphia, 1946); and T. Schermann, *Prophetarum Vitae Fabulosae Indices Apostolorum Discipulorumque Domini Dorotheo, Epiphanio, Hippolyto Aliisque Vindicate* (Leipzig, 1907). A critical analysis of the text and its context can be found in S. Klein, "ʿAl ha-sefer Vitae Prophetarum," in *Sefer Klozner,* ed. H. Torczyner (Tel Aviv, 1937), 189–208; and M. de Jonge, "Christelijke Elementen in de Vitae Prophetarum," *Nederlands Theologisch Tijdschrift* 16 (1961–1962): 161–178.

20. All citations from the Jerusalem Talmud are taken from the text published as *Talmud Yerushalmī,* 7 vols. (Jerusalem, 1998). In addition, see the references in Tosefta Sota 13:1 and Yoma 3:7. The Gemara on Yoma 53b says that the ark was buried in Jerusalem. Some of these references are cited in M. F. Collins, "The Hidden Vessels in Samaritan Traditions," 104–106.

For an overview of the motif of the hidden temple vessels in Judaism and Islam, see Scott Noegel and Brannon Wheeler, *Historical Dictionary of Prophets in Islam and Judaism* (Lanham, Md., 2002), 136–137. Hawting, "The Disappearance and Rediscovery of Zamzam and the 'Well of the Kaʿba,'" 47, mentions the reference to King Josiah in rabbinic literature, citing Louis Ginzberg, *The Legends of the Jews* (Philadelphia, 1909–1938; reprint, Baltimore, 1998).

21. All citations from the Mekhilta de Rabbi Ishamel are to the text and translation published as *Mekhilta de Rabbi Ishmael,* ed. and trans. Jacob Lauterbach (Philadelphia, 1933; reprint, Philadelphia, 2001). All citations from the Pesiqta de Rab Kahana are from the text published as *Pesikta de Rab Kahana,* ed. Bernard Mandelbaum (New York, 1962). Also see the reference to the rod held by every king, which was hidden away only to reappear in the hands of the Messiah at the end of time in Genesis Rabbah 18:23.

22. For the Sibylline Oracle on Elijah, see J. J. Collins, "Sibylline Oracles," in *The Old Testament Pseudepigrapha,* 1:317–472. On the relationship of Elijah to the Messiah and the end times, see W. Bousset, *The Antichrist Legend* (London, 1896); and Michael Stone and John Strugnell, eds. and trans., *The Books of Elijah* (Missoula, 1979), esp. fragments 2 and 5.

23. See A. F. J. Klijn, "2 (Syriac Apocalypse of) Baruch," in *The Old Testament Pseudepigrapha,* 1:615–652. The text of 2 Baruch, known from a single Syriac manuscript, is dated to the sixth or seventh century CE and is attested in a

number of excerpts from manuscripts dated to the thirteenth through fifteenth centuries. There are also an Arabic version (Sinai 589) and one fragment of a Greek version dated to the fourth or fifth century. On the redaction of the text, see A. F. J. Klijn, "The Sources and the Redaction of the Syriac Apocalypse of Baruch," *Journal of Semitic Studies* 1 (1970): 65–76. For the Syriac text of the Apocalypse, see S. Dedering, *Apocalypse of Baruch,* Peshiṭta Institute 4.3 (Leiden, 1973). The Syriac text of the letter in the Apocalypse can be found in M. Kmosko, *Epistola Baruch filli Neriae,* Patrologia Syriaca 1.2 (Paris, 1907), cols. 1215–1236. For the text in relation to its larger Jewish and Christian context, see L. Ginzberg, "Apocalypse of Baruch (Syriac)," in *Jewish Encyclopedia,* ed. I. Singer (New York, 1902), cols. 551–556; and W. Harnisch, *Verhängnis und Verheissung der Geschichte: Untersuchungen zum Zeit- und Geschichtsverständnis im 4. Buch Esra und in der syr. Baruchapokalypse* (Göttingen, 1969).

24. See *Eusebii Pamphili Evangelicae Preparationis,* ed. and trans. E. H. Gifford (Oxford, 1903), 9.39.454d. On this citation, see J. Freudenthal, *Alexander Polyhistor und die von ihm erhaltenen Reste jüdischer und samaritanischer Geschichtswerke* (Breslau, 1874); G. F. Chesnut, *The First Christian Histories: Eusebius, Socrates, Sozomen, Theodoret, and Evagrius,* 2d ed. (Macon, Ga., 1986); A. A. Mosshammer, *The Chronicle of Eusebius and Greek Chronographic Tradition* (Lewisburg, Pa., 1979); and A. Momigliano, "Pagan and Christian Historiography in the Fourth Century A.D.," in *The Conflict between Paganism and Christianity in the Fourth Century,* ed. A. Momigliano (Oxford, 1963), 79–99. This reference is cited in M. F. Collins, "The Hidden Vessels in Samaritan Traditions," 101.

25. For a thorough study and translation of the Copper Scroll, see Judah K. Lefkovits, *The Copper Scroll 3Q15: A Reevaluation: A New Reading, Translation, and Commentary* (Leiden, 2000).

26. A summary of these positions can be found in Lefkovits, *The Copper Scroll 3Q15,* 455–459. Also see Albert M. Wolters, "Apocalyptic and the Copper Scroll," *Journal of Near Eastern Studies* 19 (1990): 145–154; and idem, "History and the Copper Scroll," *Annals of the New York Academy of Sciences* 722 (1994): 285–298. On the theory that the scroll originated in the medieval period, see Solomon Zeitlin, "The Dead Sea Scrolls," pt. 1, "The Lamech Scroll: A Medieval Midrash"; pt. 2, "The Copper Scrolls"; pt. 3, "Was Kando the Owner of the Scrolls?" *Jewish Quarterly Review,* n.s., 47 (1956–1957): 245–268.

27. On the cave, the objects, and the date of the burial, see Pessaḥ Bar-Adon, *The Cave of the Treasure: The Finds from the Caves in Naḥal Mishmar* (Jerusalem, 1980).

28. On the Taoist burial of bronze mirrors, see Suzanne Cahill, "The Word Made Bronze: Inscriptions on Medieval Chinese Bronze Mirrors," *Archives of Asian Art* 38 (1985): 62–70. On the burial of objects (e.g., paper and clay sheets

inscribed with sutras, mirrors, swords, knives, or containers) in Japanese Buddhism (esp. in the tenth to thirteenth centuries), see Gregory Schopen, *Bones, Stones, and Buddhist Monks* (Honolulu, 1997); and Brian Rupert, *Jewel in the Ashes: Buddha Relics and Power in Early Medieval Japan* (Cambridge, 2000). Also see Paul Harrison, trans., *The Pratiyutpanna Samadhi Sutra* (Berkeley, 1998); and Daniel Boucher, "The Pratityasamutpadagatha and Its Role in the Medieval Cult of the Relics," *Journal of the International Association of Buddhist Studies* 14 (1991): 399–411. See also James Benn, "Where Text Meets Flesh: Burning the Body as an Apocryphal Practice in Chinese Buddhism," *History of Religions* 37, no. 4 (1998): 295–321; and Paul Mus, *Barabadur: Esquisse d'une histoire du bouddhisme fondée sur la critique archéologique des textes* (Hanoi, 1935–1955).

29. For the Syriac text entitled "The Book of the Cave of Treasures" [meʿārath gazzē], attributed to Ephraim the Syrian, see Budge, *The Book of the Cave of Treasures*; and Bezold, *Die Schatzhohle (Meʿārath Gazzē).*

30. For the Life of Adam and Eve, see M. D. Johnson, "Life of Adam and Eve," in *The Old Testament Pseudepigrapha,* 2:249–295; and L. S. A. Wells, "The Books of Adam and Eve," in *The Apocrypha and Pseudepigrapha of the Old Testament,* ed. R. H. Charles (Oxford, 1913), 2:123–154; Lucas Van Rompay, "Memories of Paradise: The Greek 'Life of Adam and Eve' and Early Syriac Tradition," *Aram* 5 (1993): 555–570.

31. See Life of Adam and Eve 51:3–9.

32. For the Abot de Rabbi Nathan, see *Maseket Abōt de-Rabbi Natan,* ed. Schechter (Vienna, 1887), which includes manuscripts A and B. For an English translation of A, see *The Fathers according to Rabbi Nathan,* trans. J. Golden (New Haven, 1955). For an English translation of B, see *The Fathers according to Rabbi Nathan,* trans. A. Saldarini (Leiden, 1975). All citations from the Midrash Rabbah are taken from M. Mirkin, ed., *Midrash Rabbah: Bereshit-Devarim,* 11 vols. (Tel Aviv, 1986). For an English translation of the Genesis Rabbah see *Genesis Rabbah: The Judaic Commentary to the Book of Genesis,* trans. Jacob Neusner (Providence, 1985). For 2 Enoch, see the composite text in F. I. Andersen, "2 (Slavonic Apocalypse of) Enoch," in *The Old Testament Pseudepigrapha,* 1:91–221. For Philo's *De Vita Mosis,* see the Greek text edited by F. H. Colson and G. H. Whitaker, Loeb Classical Library (Cambridge, Mass., 1929–1953). For an English translation, see C. D. Yonge, *The Works of Philo,* new ed. (Peabody, Mass., 1993). For an overview of some of the rabbinic legends connected with Adam and Eve, see Ginzberg, *The Legends of the Jews,* 5:22–53.

33. For the Testament of Adam, see S. E. Robinson, "Testament of Adam," in *The Old Testament Pseudepigrapha,* 1:989–995; and idem, *The Testament of Adam: An Examination of the Syriac and Greek Traditions* (Chico, Calif., 1982). For the Arabic text, see M. D. Gibson, *Apocrypha Arabica,* Studia Sinaitica 8 (London,

1901), 1–58. For the Three Stelae of Seth, see James M. Robinson and Frederik Wisse, "The Three Steles of Seth (NHC VII,5)," in *The Nag Hammadi Library,* ed. James M. Robinson (San Francisco, 1978), 362–367.

34. For this reference, see Testament of Adam 3:6.

35. On the hiding and recovery of secret books in the Arabic hermetical tradition, see some of the traditions associated with Appolonius of Tyre and Alexander the Great, in J. Ruska, *Tabula Smaragdina* (Leipzig, 1926); and the *Kitāb al-ʿilal; or, Sirr al-khalīqah,* ed. and trans. Sivestre de Sacy, *Notices et Extraits* 4 (1798–1799): 108ff.; and *Kitāb al-ʿilal; or, Sirr al-khalīqah,* ed. and trans. Ursula Weisser (Aleppo, 1979). Also see Ibn Wahshiyya, *al-Filāḥa al-Nabaṭīyah* (Damascus, 1993), containing an account of the secret knowledge revealed by the Sun, Moon, and Saturn to Adam and Seth. On the burial and recovery of texts in Buddhism, see Richard Salomon, *Ancient Buddhist Scrolls from Gandhara* (Seattle, 1999); and Karl Jettmar, "The Gilgit Manuscripts: Discovery by Installments," *Journal of Central Asia* 4, no. 2 (1981): 1–18.

36. Hawting, "The Disappearance and Rediscovery of Zamzam and the 'Well of the Kaʿba,'" 46. He cites al-Ṭabarī and Ibn Hishām as the source for this information.

37. See al-Ṭabarī, *Taʾrīkh al-rusul wa al-mulūk,* 1131–1132; Watt and McDonald, *The History of al-Ṭabarī: Muḥammad at Mecca,* 52–53. On the general history of the Kaʿbah in pre-Islamic and early Islamic times, see G. Alexander, "The Story of the Kaʿba," *Muslim World* 28 (1938): 43–53; and K. A. C. Creswell, "The Kaʿba in A.D. 608," *Archaeologia* 94 (1951): 97–102. Also compare Vera B. Moreen, "Is(h)maʿīliyat: A Judeo-Persian Account of the Building of the Kaʿba," in *Judaism and Islam: Boundaries, Communication, and Interaction: Essays in Honor of William M. Brinner,* ed. Benjamin H. Hary and others (Leiden, 2002), 185–202.

38. See Ibn Hishām, *al-Sīrah al-nabawīyah,* 1:244; Guillaume, *The Life of Muhammad,* 43/73.

39. al-Azraqī, *Akhbār Makkah,* 92. This passage is not cited by Hawting, "The Disappearance and Rediscovery of Zamzam and the 'Well of the Kaʿba,'" 46.

40. See Rubin, "The Kaʿba," 115–117, but esp. 116n133. On the account of the serpent in the well of the Kaʿbah, sent by God to guard its treasury in the time before the Kaʿbah was secured with doors and a lock, see Giovanni Canova, "Il serpente della Kaʿba: Una nota sulla Mecca preislamica," *Annali di Carl Foscari: Rivista della Racolta di lingue e letterature straniere dell'Università di Venezia* 25 (1994): 421–425.

41. See Abū al-Ḥasan ʿAlī al-Masʿūdī, *Murūj al-dhahab wa maʿādin al-jawhar,* 7 vols. (Beirut, 1965–1966), 1:242. This reference is cited in Rubin, "The Kaʿba," 117.

42. See Mughulṭāy, *al-Zahr al-bāsim,* MS Ledien, Or. 370, 57a, cited by Rubin, "The Kaʿba," 116.

43. See the citations in Rubin, "The Kaʿba," 117, which are taken from a variety of sources including al-Fākihī, *Taʾrīkh Makkah,* MS Leiden, Or. 463, 338a–339a; Ibn Hammām al-Ṣanʿānī ʿAbd al-Razzāq, *al-Muṣannaf fī al-ḥadīth* (Beirut, 2000), 5:315–316; al-Azraqī, *Akhbār Makkah,* 282–283; Aḥmad b. al-Ḥusayn al-Bayhaqī, *Dalāʾil al-nubuwwah* (Cairo, 1970), 1:72.

44. See VA (Staaliche Museen, Berlin) 8248, lines 48–51. See the reference in Israel Ephʿal, *The Ancient Arabs: Nomads on the Borders of the Fertile Crescent, 9th–5th Centuries B.C.* (Leiden, 1982), 123–124; and the discussion in W. L. Martin, *Tribut und Tributleistungen bei den Assyrern* (Helsinki, 1936), 24–25.

45. For examples, see Robert Hoyland, *Arabia and the Arabs: From the Bronze Age to the Coming of Islam* (New York, 2002), 163–166. Also see Joseph Henninger, "Le Sacrifice chez les Arabes," *Ethnos* (Stockholm) 13 (1948): 1–16; idem, "Das Opfer in den altsüdarabischen Hochkulturen," *Anthropos* 37–40 (1946–1947): 779–810; G. Ryckmans, "Le sacrifice DBH dans les inscriptions safaîtiques," *Hebrew Union College Annual* 23 (1950–1951): 431–438; and Jacques Ryckmans, "Sacrifices, offrandes et rites connexes en Arabie du Sud pré-islamique," in *Ritual and Sacrifice in the Ancient Near East,* ed. J. Quaegebeur (Louvain, 1993), 355–380. For a discussion of animal sacrifices and their relation to hunting and the origins of society, see Walter Burkert, *Homo Necans: The Anthropology of Ancient Greek Sacrificial Ritual and Myth* (Berkeley, 1983), esp. 1–83.

On the offerings of silver and gold bowls among late antique Arabs, see Ted Kaizer, *The Religious Life of Palmyra,* Oriens et Occidens 4 (Stuttgart, 2002), 248–249; H. J. W. Drijvers, "Inscriptions from Allât's Sanctuary," *Aram* 7 (1995): 109–119; and J. T. Milik, *Dédicaces faites par des dieux (Palmyre, Hatra, Tyr) et des thiases sémitiques à l'époque romaine,* Recherches d'épigraphie proche-orientale 1 (Paris, 1972).

46. See, for example the alabaster stela in the National Musum of Sanʿa on which is depicted the Tubbaʿ king with his bow, spear, and sword presenting spoils consisting of a horned gazellelike animal and a container of some sort. This stela is described in Hoyland, *Arabia and the Arabs,* 164. Other examples of dedications at Arab sanctuaries can be found in Milik, *Dédicaces faites par les dieux (Palmyre, Hatra, Tyr),* passim. Useful comparative analyses may also be found in Gary Anderson, *Sacrifices and Offerings in Ancient Israel: Studies in Their Social and Political Importance* (Atlanta, 1987).

47. For an example, see the basalt stela, from second-century-CE Kharaba, in the Hawran portraying Allāt with armor, a shield, and a spear. This stela is in the Louvre, AO 11215. See Hoyland, *Arabia and the Arabs,* 187. On the warrior image of deities, see the comparative material in S. M. Kang, *Divine War in the Old Testament and in the Ancient Near East* (Berlin, 1987); H. Fredricksson, *Jahwe als Krieger* (Lund, 1945); and P. D. Miller, *The Divine Warrior in Early Israel* (Cambridge, Mass., 1973).

48. See Hoyland, *Arabia and the Arabs,* 189; and D. T. Potts, "Some Issues in the Study of Pre-Islamic Weaponry of Southeastern Arabia," *Arabian Archaeology and Epigraphy* 9 (1998): 182–208. Potts includes a short discussion of the evolution of the sword in southeastern Arabia.

49. For the Aramaic inscription, see *Corpus Inscriptionum Semiticarum* (Paris, 1881–), 2:157. For the Sabaean inscription, see A. Jamme, *Sabaean Inscriptions from Mahram Bilqis* (Baltimore, 1962), 745. These inscriptions are also mentioned in Hoyland, *Arabia and the Arabs,* 186.

50. For this inscription, see James Pritchard, ed., *Ancient Near Eastern Texts Relating to the Old Testament,* 3d ed. (Princeton, 1969), 656–657. Also see *Corpus Inscriptionum Semiticarum,* 1:165; M. Lidzbarski, *Handbuch der nordsemitischen Epigraphik* (Weimar, 1898), 428; idem, *Kanaanäischen Epigraphik* (Giessen, 1907), 47–51; and G. A. Cooke, *A Text-Book of North-Semitic Inscriptions* (Oxford, 1903), 112–122.

51. See Pritchard, *Ancient Near Eastern Texts Relating to the Old Testament,* 669–670. This inscription is engraved on a cliff near Shabwah. For more on this inscription, see A. F. L. Beeston, "Appendix on the Inscriptions Discovered by Mr. Philby," in *Sheba's Daughters,* ed. H. St. J. B. Philby (London, 1939), 448–452; and A. Jamme, *The al-ʿUqlah Texts* (Washington, D.C., 1963), 949.

52. See the many examples cited in J. Ryckmans, "La chasse rituelle dans l'Arabie du Sud ancienne," in *al-Bahit: Festschrift Joseph Henninger,* ed. Joseph Henninger, Studia Instituti Anthropos 28 (St. Augustin bei Bonn, 1976), 259–308; A. F. L. Beeston, "The Ritual Hunt: A Study in Old South Arabian Religious Practice," *Le Muséon* 61 (1948): 183–196; and R. B. Serjeant, *South Arabian Hunt* (London, 1976).

Rubin, "The Kaʿba," 116–117, contends that the wild animal as a votive offering is related to the Arabian sanctuary as a refuge for wild animals. He also contends that the burial of the offerings is a sign of the treatment of the sanctuary as a burial site of prophets including Hud, Salih, and Ishmael. Hoyland, *Arabia and the Arabs,* esp. 188–189, remarks that the burial of offerings for the dead usually did include arms and armor but not gazelles or other animal offerings.

53. See Serjeant, *South Arabian Hunt,* 30–31, 56–57.

54. See the examples cited by Serjeant, *South Arabian Hunt,* 69–74.

55. On the gifts of golden crescent moons or horns, and the ram horns, see al-Azraqī, *Akhbār Makkah,* 156. Also see the brief comment in Rubin, "The Kaʿba," 117–118. In relation to this, see al-Jāḥiẓ, who mentions the two gazelles of Mecca connected with the sacrifices brought to the Kaʿbah in his *Kitāb al-ḥayawān,* ed. ʿAbd al-Salām Muḥammad Hārūn (Beirut, 1992), 3:192–195.

56. See Muḥammad b. Aḥmad al-Bīrūnī, *Kitāb al-jawāhir fī maʿrifat al-jawāhir* (Hyderabad, 1355), 66.

57. See Ibn Kathīr, *Tafsīr al-Qurʾān al-ʿaẓīm* (Beirut, n.d.), on Q 44:37. Similar reports are given on the authority of Ibn ʿAbbās and Saʿīd b. Jubayr.

58. On Tubbaʿ, see Muḥammad b. Aḥmad al- Khawarizmī, *Mafātīḥ al-ʿulūm* (Cairo, 1978), 67. On the gift of the ʿAbbasid caliph, see al-Qāḍī al-Rashīd Ibn al-Zubayr, *Kitāb al-Hadāyā wa al-Tuḥaf*, trans. Ghāda al-Ḥijjāwī al-Qaddūmī as *Book of Gifts and Rarities* (Cambridge, Mass., 1996), #41. On the identity of Ibn al-Zubayr as the author of this work, see al-Qaddūmī, 11–13.

59. See al-Azraqī, *Akhbār Makkah,* 119–124. The role of ʿAbd al-Muṭṭalib in providing security for the temple treasury of the Kaʿbah is also relevant to the existence of a serpent cult at the site in pre-Islamic times. See Canova, "Il serpente della Kaʿba"; B. Mundkur, *The Cult of the Serpent: An Interdisciplinary Survey of Its Manifestations and Origins* (Albany, 1983); W. Atallah, "Aymu-l-Lāh: Vestige d'un culte chtonien," *Arabica* 22 (1975): 166; Toufic Fahd, *Le panthéon de l'Arabie centrale à la veille de l'Hégire* (Paris, 1968), esp. 40–41; and Th. Nöldeke, "Die Schlange nach arabischem Volksglauben," *Zeitschrift für Völkerpsychologie* 1 (1860): 416.

60. See al-Azraqī, *Akhbār Makkah,* 124; and al-Qaddūmī, *Book of Gifts and Rarities,* no. 175.

61. See al-Qaddūmī, *Book of Gifts and Rarities,* no. 1.

62. See Pritchard, *Ancient Near Eastern Texts Relating to the Old Testament,* 556–557. The original is published by G. Dossin, "L'inscription de fondation de Iahdun-Lim, roi de Mari," *Syria* 32 (1935): 1–28, pls. 1–2. Also see A. Malamat, "Campaigns to the Mediterranean by Iahdunlim and Other Early Mesopotamian Rulers," *Assyriological Studies* 16 (1965): 365–372.

63. For the Gudea cylinder, statue, and mace-head inscriptions, see Pritchard, *Ancient Near Eastern Texts Relating to the Old Testament,* 268–269. For the original, see E. de Sarzec and L. Heuzey, *Découvertes en Chaldée* (Paris, 1884), pls. 16, 33–35. For another recent translation, see G. A. Barton, *The Royal Inscriptions of Sumer and Akkad* (New Haven, 1929), 181–261. The "Statue B" text states that when Gudea was building the temple of Ningirsu he gave two weapons to the king, the "SAR.UR" and the "SAR.GAZ." The "Macehead A" inscription states that Enlil fashioned the mace-head for king Ningirsu. On Gudea, see A. Falkenstein, *Die Inschriften Gudeas von Lagash* (Rome, 1966); and related materials in E. Sollberger, "The Temple in Babylonia," in *Le temple et le culte* (Leiden, 1975), 31–34.

64. See Pritchard, *Ancient Near Eastern Texts Relating to the Old Testament,* 269–271, for the list of date formulas of the reign of Hammurabi. The list was compiled by A. Ungnad in "Datenlisten," in *Reallexikon der Assyriologie,* ed. Erich Ebelling and Bruno Meissner (Berlin, 1928), 1:178–187.

65. For the account of Samuiluna, see Pritchard, *Ancient Near Eastern Texts Relating to the Old Testament,* 271. This is contained in the British Museum,

Bu 91-5-9,284, and is published in *Cuneiform Texts from Babylonian Tablets . . . in the British Museum* (London, 1896), 6, pls. 9ff.; and L. W. King, *Letters and Inscriptions of Hammurabi* (London, 1898), 2:101, 217ff. For the verse account of Nabonidus, preserved on a tablet in the British Museum, 38,299, see Pritchard, *Ancient Near Eastern Texts Relating to the Old Testament,* 312. The text is published in Sidney Smith, *Babylonian Historical Texts Relating to the Capture and Downfall of Babylon* (London, 1924), pls. 5–10. For the Moabite Stone, housed in the Louvre, see Pritchard, *Ancient Near Eastern Texts Relating to the Old Testament,* 320–321. The text is found in René Dussaud, *Les monuments palestiniens et judaïques* (Paris, 1912), 4–22. For the Northwest Semitic building inscription of Azitawadda of Adana, found in Phoenician and Hittite versions, see Pritchard, *Ancient Near Eastern Texts Relating to the Old Testament,* 653–654.

66. See Pritchard, *Ancient Near Eastern Texts Relating to the Old Testament,* 666–667.

67. See al-Bayhaqī, *Dalāʾil al-nubuwwah,* 1:85–92.

68. On Quṣayy, see al-Ṭabarī, *Taʾrīkh al-rusul wa al-mulūk,* 1092–1100; Watt and MacDonald, *The History of al-Ṭabarī: Muḥammad at Mecca,* 19–26; and Ibn Hishām, *al-Sīrah al-nabawīyah,* 1:247–249; Guillaume, *The Life of Muhammad,* 52/79–56/84.

69. See al-Ṭabarī, *Taʾrīkh al-rusul wa al-mulūk,* 1:170; trans. Franz Rosenthal as *The History of al-Ṭabarī: From the Creation to the Flood* (Albany, 1989), 340–341. Also see the extensive discussion of these myths in Arthur Christensen, *Les types du premier homme et du premier roi,* Archives d'études orientales 14.2, 2 vols. (Stockholm, 1917; Leiden, 1934). On Quṣayy as a civilizing hero, see Caetani, *Annali dell'Islam* (Milan, 1905–1926), 1:73–75, 99–106. For a general discussion on the role of kings in civilizing, see the extended discussion in Bruce Lincoln, *Myth, Cosmos, and Society: Indo-European Themes of Creation and Destruction* (Cambridge, Mass., 1986), esp. 156–169.

70. On the South Arabian "Mukarrib" as custodian of the sanctuary and the founding of sanctuaries in ancient Arabia, see J. F. Breton and C. Robin, "Le sanctuaire préislamique du Gabal al-Lawd (Nord-Yémen)," *Comptes Rendus de l'Académie des Inscriptions et Belles-Lettres* (1982): 590–629; and L. Tholbecq, "Les sanctuaires des Nabatéens," *Topoi* 7 (1997): 1069–1095. On temples, see J. F. Breton, "Religious Architecture in Ancient Hadramawt," *Proceedings of the Seminar for Arabian Studies* 10 (1980): 5–16; idem, "Les temples de Maʿin et du Jawf (Yémen): État de la question," *Syria* 75 (1998): 61–80; H. Crawford and others, eds., *The Dilmun Temple at Saar* (London, 1997); P. Hammond, *The Temple of the Winged Lions, Petra* (Fountain Hills, Ariz., 1996); Leila Nehmé and C. Rubin, "Le temple de Nakrah à Yathill (Baraqish)," *Comptes Rendus de l'Académie des Inscriptions et Belles-Lettres* (1993): 427–496; and A. V. Sedov and A. Batayiʿ,

"Temple of Ancient Hadramawt," *Proceedings of the Seminar for Arabian Studies* 24 (1994): 183–196.

On the possible relation of Mecca to the Macoraba of Ptolemy (Geography, vi, 7), which may be the equivalent of the South Arabian and Ethiopic *mikrab,* meaning "temple," see E. Glaser, *Skizze der Geschichte und Geographie Arabiens von den ältesten Zeiten bis zum Propheten Muḥammad* (Berlin, 1890), 2:235. Also see the discussion of these associations in Patricia Crone, *Meccan Trade and the Rise of Islam* (Princeton, 1987), esp. 134–136 on Ptolemy's Macoraba as Makka Rabba or Mikrab or Moka (a town in Arabia Petraea also cited in the *Geography* of Ptolemy).

71. For the Akkadian ritual, see F. .H. Weissbach, ed., *Babylonische Miscellen* (Leipzig, 1930), 12; F. Thureau-Dangin, *Rituels accadiens* (Paris, 1921), 34–36; and Pritchard, *Ancient Near Eastern Texts Relating to the Old Testament,* 339–342. For the Hittite ritual texts, see H. H. Figulla and others *Keilschrifttexte aus Boghazköi* (Leipzig, 1921), 4:1; Akademie der Wissenschaft und der Literatur, *Keilschrift-urkunden aus Boghazköi* (Berlin, 1921), 2:2, 9:33, 29:1–3; Pritchard, *Ancient Near Eastern Texts Relating to the Old Testament,* 356–358; M. Witzel, *Perlen sumerischen Poesie,* Keilinschritfliche Studien 5 (Fulda, 1925): 76–87; and B. Schwartz, *Orientalia,* n.s., 16 (1947): 23–55.

72. For the measurements of the sanctuary at Mecca, see al-Azraqī, *Akhbār Makkah,* 1:288–293.

73. On the *Kiswā,* see ibid., 1:249–257. For the vessels and other items placed inside the Kaʿbah, see ibid., 1:223–243, immediately preceding the section on the pit (jubb) of the Kaʿbah in 1:244–248.

74. On the tabernacle, see F. M. Cross, "The Priestly Tabernacle," *Biblical Archaeologist Reader* 1 (1961): 201–228; M. Haran, "The Priestly Image of the Tabernacle," *Hebrew Union College Annual* 36 (1965): 191–226; and Y. Aharoni, "The Solomonic Temple, the Tabernacle, and the Arad Sanctuary," in *Orient and Occident: Essays Presented to Cyrus H. Gordon on the Occasion of His Sixty-fifth Birthday,* ed. H. A. Hoffman, Alter Orient und Altes Testament 22 (Neukirchen, 1973), 1–8.

On the Jerusalem temple, see T. Busink, *Der Tempel von Jerusalem. Von Salomo bis Herodes,* 2 vols. (Leiden, 1970–1980); and J. M. Lundquist, "The Common Temple Ideology of the Ancient Near East," in *The Temple in Antiquity,* ed. T. G. Madsen (Provo, Utah, 1984), 53–76. For the temple in Ezekiel, see K. Elliger, "Die grosser Tempelsakristeien im Verfassungsentwurf des Ezechiel," in *Festschrift Albrecht Alt zum 70. Gebrutstag gewidmet,* ed. A. Alt (Leipzig, 1954), 79–103; and J. Levenson, *Program of Restoration in Ezekiel 40–48* (Missoula, Mont., 1976). For the temple scroll, see Y. Yadin, *The Temple Scroll,* 3 vols. (Jerusalem, 1977–1983).

75. On the general significance of the temple's measurements and construction, see H. Nissen, *Das Templum: Antiquarische Untersuchungen* (Berlin, 1869);

L. Mumford, *The City in History* (New York, 1961); and J. Z. Smith, *To Take Place*, esp. 47–73. Smith cites the opening and closing lines of the *Epic of Gilgamesh*, examples of chronologies dating from the completion of walls, and the royal symbolism of wall destruction. For the Babylonian chronicles of Hammurabi and Samuilina dating from the construction of the city and temple, see Pritchard, *Ancient Near Eastern Texts Relating to the Old Testament*, 269–271.

76. On cult objects in Arabian contexts, see H. M. al-Tawil, "Early Arab Icons: Literary and Archaeological Evidence for the Cult of Religious Images in Pre-Islamic Arabia" (PhD dissertation, University of Iowa, 1993); and J. B. Connelly, "Votive Offerings from Hellenistic Failaka," *L'Arabie préislamique et son environement historique et culturel*, ed. T. Fahd (Strasbourg, 1989), 145–158.

77. Epiphanius, *Haereses*, ed. Karl Holl (Berlin, 1980–1985), 5. See the mention of this in Arent Jan Wensinck and J. Jomier, "Kaʿba," in *Encyclopaedia of Islam*, 2d ed., ed. H. A. R. Gibb and others (Leiden: E. J. Brill, 1960–2002), 4:317–322, esp. 321–322. Wensinck and Jomier also cite Abū ʿUbayd ʿAbdallāh al-Bakrī, *Kitāb muʿjam mā istaʿjam*, ed. F. Wüstenfeld (Göttingen, 1876–1877), published in German as *Das Geographische Wörterbuch des Abu ʿObeid ʿAbdallah*, ed. F. Wüstenfeld (Göttingen, 1876–1877), 46, who reports that the tribe of Bakr b. Wāʾil had its center of worship in Sindād in the region of Kufa and that their holy tent (bayt) was called Dhāt al-Kaʿabāt.

78. See Suidas, *Lexicon*, ed. A. Adler (Leipzig, 1928–1938), s.v. "Theus Ares." This passage is translated and cited in Hoyland, *Arabia and the Arabs*, 183.

79. See Antoninus Placentinus, "Itinerarium," in *Itinera Hiersolymitana saeculi IV–VIII*, ed. Paul Geyer, Corpus Scriptorum Ecclesiasticorum Latinorum (Vindobonae, 1949; reprint, New York, 1964), 157–218, trans. in J. Wilkinson, *Jerusalem Pilgrims before the Crusades* (Warminster, 1977), 79–89. This passage is cited in Hoyland, *Arabia and the Arabs*, 183.

80. See Hishām Ibn al-Kalbī, *Kitāb al-aṣnām*, ed. and trans. into French by W. Atallah as *Les idoles de Hicham Ibn al-Kalbi* (Paris, 1969), 12d, 32c. See Hoyland, *Arabia and the Arabs*, 186, who also cites C. Clermont-Ganneau and Jean-Baptise Chabot, eds., *Répertoire d'épigraphie sémitique* (Paris, 1900–1968), 1088; and M. R. Savignac, "Le sanctuaire d'Allat à Iram," *Revue Biblique* 41 (1932):413; 43 (1934): 588. On the meaning of the "stone altars" in Q 5:3, see Crone, *Meccan Trade and the Rise of Islam*, 189–192; and Th. Nöldeke, "Der Gott mrʾ bytʾ und die kaʿba," *Zeitschrift für Assyriologie* 23 (1909): 184–186.

81. On the relationship of the sanctuary at Mecca in pre-Islamic times with other Arab sanctuaries and their custodians, see Toufic Fahd, "Une partique cléromantique à la Kaʿba préislamique," *Semitica* 8 (1958): 55–79, originally published in *Proceedings of the 27th International Congress of Orientalists* 24 (1957): 246–248; Nöldeke, "Der Gott mrʾ bytʾ und die kaʿba"; and Shahabuddin Ansari, "How Kaʿba Came to Be Defiled with Idols," *Studies in Islam* 19 (1982): 39–45.

82. See Louvre AO 1505, cited in Hoyland, *Arabia and the Arabs,* pl. 21, p. 160.

83. See the examples cited in Hoyland, *Arabia and the Arabs,* 159–161. On the role of divination and dream interpretation in the office of the sanctuary custodian, see Toufic Fahd, *La divination arabe* (Leiden, 1966); A. F. L. Beeston, "The Oracle Sanctuary of Jar al-Labbaʾ," *Le Muséon* 62 (1949): 207–228; and Drijvers, "Inscriptions from Allat's Sanctuary."

84. On the relationship of Mecca and Jerusalem in the establishment of sanctuaries, see H. Busse, "Jerusalem and Mecca, the Temple and the Kaaba: An Account of Their Interrelation in Islamic Times," in *The Holy Land in History and Thought,* ed. M. Sharon (Leiden, 1988), 236–246; and Nuha N. N. Khoury, "The Dome of the Rock, the Kaʿba and Ghumdan: Arab Myths and Umayyad Monuments," *Muqarnas* 10 (1993): 57–65.

85. On the relationship of the discovery of the cult object and the founding of the sanctuary, see (on Protonike) G. Howard, *Doctrina Addai,* Texts and Translations 16, Early Christian Literature Series 4 (Chico, Calif., 1981); (on Judas Kyriakos) H. J. W. Drijvers and J. W. Drijvers, *The Finding of the True Cross: The Judas Kyriakos Legend in Syriac,* Corpus Scriptorum Christianorum Orientalium 565, Subsidia 93 (Louvain, 1997); (on Eudoxia) H. A. Drake and others, *Eudoxia and the Holy Sepulchre: A Constantinian Legend in Coptic,* Testi e documenti per lo studio dell'antichità 47 (Milan, 1980). Also see J. W. Drijvers, *Helena Augusta: The Mother of Constantine the Great and Her Finding of the True Cross* (Leiden, 1992); S. Borgehammar, *How the Holy Cross was Found: From Event to Medieval Legend* (Stockholm, 1991), H. A. Drake, "Eusebius and the True Cross," *Journal of Ecclesiastical History* 36 (1985): 1–22; and M. Van Esbroek, "Hélène à Èdesse et la Croix," in *After Bardaisan: Studies on Continuity and Change in Syriac Christianty in Honour of Professor Han J. W. Drijvers,* ed. G. J. Reinink and A. C. Klugkist (Louvain, 1999), 107–115.

86. For China and a general overview of the significance linking the rituals establishing capital and its territory, see Paul Wheatley, *The Pivot of the Four Quarters: A Preliminary Enquiry into the Origins and Character of the Ancient Chinese City* (Chicago, 1971), esp. 465–476.

For examples pertaining to Rome, see Bruce Lincoln, *Myth, Cosmos, and Society,* esp. 41–64. Lincoln makes a number of careful distinctions regarding natural and artificial cosmogonies. Also see the comparisons in Jaan Puhvel, "Remus et Frater," *History of Religions* 15 (1975): 146–157. For further reflection on the distinction of natural and social cosmogony, see C. Grottanelli and others, eds., "Sacrificio, organizzazione del cosmo, dinamica sociale," *Studi storici* 25 (1984): 829–956.

On Egypt, and the pharaoh's ritual performance of the circuit of the wall as Menes had performed the circuit of the wall when he first laid out the sacred city, see Henri Frankfort, *Kingship and the Gods* (Chicago, 1948), esp. 124; and K. Sethe, *Beiträge zur ältesten Geschichte Ägyptens* (Leipzig, 1903), esp. 121–141.

On Cambodia and circumambulation of the new capital, see Paul Mus, "Symbolisme à Angkor Thom: Le 'grand miracle' du Bayon," *Académie des Inscriptions et Belles-Lettres: Comptes-Rendus des Séances* (1936): 57–68; George Coedès, *Pour mieux comprendre Angkor* (Paris, 1947); and Jean Przyluski, "Pradakshina et prasavya en Indochine," *Festschrift für Moriz Winternitz, 1863–23. Dezember 1933*, ed. Otto Stein and Wilhalm Gampert (Leipzig, 1933). On Thailand, see H. G. Quaritch Wales, *Siamese State Ceremonies: Their History and Function* (London, 1931), 106–107.

For the role of Mecca in the symbolism of Islamic cities, see Gustave E. von Grunebaum, "The Sacred Character of Islamic Cities," in *Mélanges Ṭāhā Ḥusain: Offerts par ses amis et ses disciples a l'occasion de son 70ième anniversaire,* ed. Abdurrahman Badawi (Cairo, 1962). On the Kaʿbah and its image in pre-Islamic and early Islamic times in relation to city symbolism, see R. Ettinghausen, "Die bildliche Darstellung der Kaʿba im islamischen Kulturkreis," *Zeitschrift der Deutschen Morgenländischen Gesellschaft* 12 (1933): 111–137; and M. Gaudefroy-Demombynes, "La Voile de la Kaʿba," *Studia Islamica* 2 (1954): 5–21. See also J. Hjärpe, "The Symbol of the Centre and Its Religious Function in Islam," in *Religious Symbols and Their Functions,* ed. H. Biezais (Stockholm, 1979), 30–40.

87. See, for example, the comments attributed to Muḍāḍ b. ʿAmr b. al-Ḥārith in al-Azraqī, *Akhbār Makkah,* 1:91, and the description of the pilgrimage to Mecca in pre-Islamic times on 1:179–194. See Ibn Hishām, *al-Sīrah al-nabawīyah,* 1:201–213; Guillaume, *The Life of Muhammad,* 50/35–56/39, for a list of sanctuaries in pre-Islamic Arabia. Also see H. Lammens, "Les sanctuaires préislamites dans l'Arabie occidentale," *Mélanges de l'Université Saint-Joseph* 11 (1926): 39–173; Fahd, *Le panthéon de l'Arabie centrale à la veille de l'Hégire*; and R. B. Serjeant, "Ḥaram and Ḥawṭah: The Sacred Enclave in Arabia," in *Mélanges Ṭāhā Ḥusain,* 41–58.

88. See, for example, the inscriptions in *Corpus Inscriptionum Semiticarum,* 4:548, 4:533. On these inscriptions and the regulations for visiting sanctuaries, see Hoyland, *Arabia and the Arabs,* 161. For more general references to pre-Islamic Arabian sanctuaries, see Joseph Henniger, "La religion bédouine préislamique," in *L'antica società beduina,* ed. Gabrieli Francesco (Rome, 1959), published in English as "Pre-Islamic Bedouin Religion," in *The Arabs and Arabia on the Eve of Islam,* ed. F. E. Peters (Brookfield, Vt., 1999), 109–128; Henniger, *Arabica sacra: Aufsätze zur religionsgeschichte Arabiens und seiner Randgebiete* (Göttingen, 1981); A. Muḥyī al-Dīn, "ʿIbādat al-arwāḥ fī al-mujtamaʿ al-ʿarabī al-jāhilī," in *Studies in the History of Arabia,* ed. A. T. Ansary (Riyadh, 1984), 2:153–164; G. Ryckmans, *Les religions arabes préislamiques* (Louvain, 1951); Wellhausen, *Reste arabischen Heidentums,* passim; and Robertson Smith, *Lectures on the Religion of the Semites,* esp. chap. 4.

89. According to al-Azraqī, *Akhbār Makkah,* 1:111, there was a "handle" on the Kaʿbah to which fugitives sometimes clung to declare their use of the sanctuary as a place of refuge. Sacrifices were performed at Mina so as to avoid the spilling of blood in the sanctuary at Mecca. See Wensinck and Jomier, "Kaʿba"; and Wensinck, "The Ideas of the Western Semites Concerning the Navel of the Earth," passim.

90. Abū ʿAbdallāh Yāqūt, *Muʿjam al-buldān* (Beirut, 1979), 4:379, s.v. "al-Qalʿah."

91. This is the interpretation put forward in Brannon Wheeler, *Moses in the Quran and Islamic Exegesis,* 90–91.

92. See Muḥammad b. Mukarram Ibn Manẓūr, *Lisān al-ʿArab* (Beirut, 1990), 8:290–293, s.v. "Q-L-ʿ."

93. See Muḥammad b. Yaʿqūb al-Fīrūzābādī, *Qāmūs al-muḥīṭ,* 4 vols. (Cairo, 1971–1973), s.v. "Q-L-ʿ." Also see the overview in M. Streck, "Kalah," in *Encyclopaedia of Islam,* 4:467–468.

94. al-Bīrūnī, *Kitāb al-jawāhir fī maʿrifat al-jawāhir,* 253. Similar comments can be found in Abū ʿUbayd al-Qāsim b. Salām, *Kitāb al-silāḥ,* ed. Ḥātim Ṣāliḥ al-Dāmin (Beirut, 1985), 17–18, in his section on swords and their descriptions.

95. See al-Bīrūnī, *Kitāb al-jawāhir fī maʿrifat al-jawāhir,* 248. For an overview of Indian metallurgical terminology, see Richard Garbe, *Die indischen Mineralien ihre Namen und die ihnen zugbeschriebenen Kräfte* (Hildesheim, 1974). For some examples of Indian weapons close to the areas mentioned here, see G. N. Pant, *A Catalogue of Arms and Armours in Bharat Kala Bhavan* (Delhi, 1995), esp. 14–33 on examples of swords.

96. See al-Bīrūnī, *Kitāb al-jawāhir fī maʿrifat al-jawāhir,* 248–250.

97. See Ibn Manẓūr, *Lisān al-ʿArab,* 8:290–293, s.v. "Q-L-ʿ." On the Latin use of "white lead" (plumbum album) to refer to tin, see Pliny, *Historia Naturalis,* ed. and trans. H. Rackham (Cambridge, Mass., 1938–1963), 4.30.

98. See some of the references in F. W. Schwarzlose, *Die Waffen der alten Araber aus ihren Dichtern dargestellt* (Leipzig, 1886; reprint, Hildesheim, 1982), esp. 127–128; and M. Streck, "Kalah," 4:467–468. Also see Abdussattar Siddiqi, *Studien über die persischen Fremdwörter im klassischen Arabisch* (Göttingen, 1919), 88–89.

99. See Yaʿqūb b. Isḥāq al-Kindī, "al-Suyūf wa ajnāsu-hā," Arab. Mss. Leiden 287, published by A. R. Zaki in *Bulletin of the Faculty of Arts, University of Cairo* 14, no. 2 (December 1952): 1–36. Also on this manuscript and the description of the different types of swords al-Kindī provides, see A. R. Zaki, "Islamic Swords in Middle Ages," *Bulletin de l'Institut d'Egypte* 36 (1954): 365–397.

100. On swords, armor and other weapons in South Arabia, see A. F. L. Beeston, *Warfare in Ancient South Arabia (2nd-3rd Century AD)* (London, 1976); D. T. Potts, "Late Sasanian Armament from Southern Arabia," *Electrum* 1 (1997):

127–137; and idem, "Some Issues in the Study of the Pre-Islamic Weaponry of Southeastern Arabia." On swords and other weapons in India, see G. Oppert, *On the Weapons, Army Organization, and Political Maxims of the Ancient Hindus* (Madras, 1880); V. R. Dikshitar, *War in Ancient India* (Calcutta, 1944); and P. E. P. Deraniyagala, "Sinhala Weapons and Armour," *Journal of the Ceylon Branch of the Royal Asiatic Society* 35 (1942): 57–142, plates I–V.

Zaki states that "Yemeni" swords were actually imported steel blades from Sri Lanka and Beilman. He identifies the Beilman blades as coming from a small town on the border between Sind and India. See A. R. Zaki, "Centres of Islamic Sword Making in Middle Ages," *Bulletin de l'Institut d'Egypte* 38 (1955–1956): 285–295. A "Baylman" is identified by Aḥmad b. Yaḥyā' al-Balādhūrī, *Futūḥ al-buldān,* ed. M. J. de Goeje (Leiden, 1968), 440–442, as a city in Yemen.

Zaki claims that the "Indian" blades mentioned by al-Kindī were made of Narmahen iron, noted for brightness, an iron which was also called "mandali." He cites al-Qazwīnī as identifying Mandal as a city in India where "al-nad" is found in large quantities, also called "al-mandali" or Indian Kameroni. See A. R. Zaki, "Islamic Swords in Middle Ages," 365–397; and Zakarīyā b. Muḥammad al-Qazwīnī, *Āthār al-bilād wa akhbār al-ʿibād,* ed. Ferdinand Wüstenfeld (Göttingen, 1848; reprint, Beirut, 1960–1961), s.v. "Mandal." Also see Yāqūt, *Muʿjam al-buldān,* 5:209, s.v. "Mandal"; Yāqūt also says that Mandal is a city in India and relates it to the adjective *Mandalī* used in Arab poetry. On Indian steel in sword-making technology, see M. Faraday, "An Analysis of Wootz, or Indian Steel," *Quarterly Journal of Science, Literature and the Arts* 7 (1819): 288–290.

101. See Ibn Saʿīd in G. Ferrand, *Relations de voyages et textes géographiques arabes, persans et turcs relatifs a l'Extrême-Orient* (Paris, 1914), 2:344. Zaki, "Islamic Swords in Middle Ages," 368, mentions this reference. On the trade between India and the Arabian Peninsula, see S. D. Goitein, "From Aden to India: Specimens of the Correspondence of Indian Traders of the Twelfth Century," *Journal of the Economic and Social History of the Orient* 23 (1980): 43–66.

102. See Pliny, *Historia Naturalis,* 30.14. Also see the discussion of Chinese mines in Zaki, "Centres of Islamic Sword Making in Middle Ages," 289–290. Richard F. Burton, *The Book of the Sword* (London, 1884; reprint, New York, 1987), 54 and 77–79, attempts to identify the "Cassiterids" (Oestrymnides) with a number of different locations in Europe on the basis of Herodotus (3.115), Strabo (3.5.11), and Diodorus Siculus (5.21–22).

103. Ibn Khurradādhbih, cited in Muḥammad b. Muḥammad al-Idrīsī, *Kitāb nuzhat al-mushtāq fī ikhtirāq al-afāq,* trans. P. A. Jaubert as *Géographie d'Edrisi traduite de l'arabe en français d'après deux manuscrits de la Bibliothèque du roi et accompagnée de notes* (Paris, 1836–1840), 1:51. See Zaki, "Centres of Islamic Sword Making in Middle Ages," 290. On Chinese weapons and their relation to the trade in tin, see Yang Hong, ed., *Weapons in Ancient China* (New York, 1993).

104. See the references in Streck, "Kalah," 4:467–468; R. P. A. Dozy, *Supplément aux dictionnaires arabes* (Leiden, 1927), s.v. "Kalah"; Johann Augustus Vullers, *Lexicon Persico-Latinum Etymologicum* (Bonn, 1855–1864), ii, 735; R. P. A. Dozy and Engelmann, *Gloss. des mots espagnols et portugais dérivés de l'arabe* (Leiden, 1869), 245; and Henry Yule and A. C. Burnell, *Hobson-Jobson: A Glossary of Colloquial Anglo-Indian Words and Phrases,* 2d ed. (New Delhi, 1986), 143. For geographical identification of Kalah in the Malay Peninsula, see Hugh Kennedy, ed., *An Historical Atlas of Islam,* 2d ed. (Leiden, 2002), esp. maps 8, 11, 60. On the later trade of weapons between the Middle East and Malaysia, see S. Q. Fatimi, "Malaysian Weapons in Arabic Literature: A Glimpse of Early Trade in the Indian Ocean," *Islamic Studies* (Karachi) 3, no. 2 (1964): 199–228.

105. See Burton, *The Book of the Sword,* 74–85.

106. Muḥammad b. Ismāʿīl al-Bukhārī, *Ṣaḥīḥ* (Damascus, 1981), 57:4; this text is also found in Aḥmad b. ʿAlī Ibn Ḥajar, *Fatḥ al-bārī bi-sharḥ Ṣaḥīḥ al-Bukhārī* (Cairo, 1301; reprint, Beirut, 1408), 6:160–163.

107. See Muḥammad b. ʿĪsā al-Tirmidhī, *al-Jāmiʿ al-ṣaḥīḥ* (Delhi, 1937), 21:16.

108. See al-Tirmidhī, *al-Jāmiʿ al-ṣaḥīḥ,* 21:16; and Shams al-Dīn al-Dhahabī, *Siyar aʿlām al-nubalāʾ*, ed. Bashār ʿAwwād Maʿrūf (Beirut, 1992), 2:429.

109. See Muḥammad b. Yazīd Ibn Mājah, *Sunan,* ed. Fūʾād ʿAbd al-Bāqī (Cairo, 1952), 24:18; and al-Tirmidhī, *al-Jāmiʿ al-ṣaḥīḥ,* 21:16. For traditions related to the ornamentation of swords with gold and silver, see al-Bukhārī, *Ṣaḥīḥ,* 56:83; Ibn Mājah, *Sunan,* 24:18; Muslim b. al-Hajjāj b. Muslim, *al-Jāmiʿ al-ṣaḥīḥ* (Beirut, n.d.), 52:34; and Ibn Abī Shaybah, *Kitāb al-muṣannaf al-aḥādīth wa al-āthār* (Beirut, 1989), 4:584 (no. 157) and 6:71 ( no. 2). Also see ʿAbd al-Raḥmān al-Awzāʿī, *Sunan al-Awzāʿī,* ed. and compiled by Marwān Muḥammad al-Shaʿār (Beirut, 1993), 382–383.

110. See al-Tirmidhī, *al-Jāmiʿ al-ṣaḥīḥ,* 21:14; and al-Dhahabī, *Siyar aʿlām al-nubalāʾ*, 2:429.

111. See the text as printed in Muḥammad Ḥasan Muḥammad al-Tihāmī, *Suyūf al-rasūl wa ʿuddah ḥarbi-hi* (Cairo, 1992), 26; and ʿUmar b. Raslān al-Bulqīnī, *Maḥāsin al-iṣṭilāḥ wa tadmīn kitāb Ibn al-Ṣalāḥ*, in *Muqaddimat Ibn al-Ṣalāḥ wa Maḥāsin al-iṣṭilāḥ* (Cairo, 1974). For another tradition mentioning nine swords, see al-Bukhārī, *Ṣaḥīḥ,* 64:44.

112. See Aḥmad Ibn Saʿd, *al-Ṭabaqāt al-kubrā* (Beirut, 1990), 1:376–378. A number of the names given to the swords of the prophet Muhammad are mentioned as generic "types" of swords in other sources such as Ibn Salām, *Kitāb al-silāḥ*, 17–18, in his section on swords and their descriptions.

113. See Ibn Saʿd, *al-Ṭabaqāt al-kubrā,* 1:378–384.

114. See al-Dhahabī, *Siyar aʿlām al-nubalāʾ*, 2:428–435.

115. Aḥmad b. Fāris al-Qazwīnī cited in ibid., 2:428.

116. See al-Dhahabī, *Siyar aʿlām al-nubalāʾ*, 2:428n1. Also see Yusūf b. ʿAbd al-

Raḥmān al-Mizzī, *Tahdhīb al-kamāl* (Damascus, n.d.), 1:212. Many of the names given to these swords are also adjectives commonly applied to swords, such as Battār and Qaḍīb, which mean "cutting" or "sharp" referring to the blades of the swords. See, for example, Ibn Manẓūr, *Lisān al-ʿArab*; and Muḥammad Murtaḍā al-Zabīdī, *Tāj al-ʿarūs min jawāhir al-qāmūs* (Kuwait, 1965), s.v. "B-T-R," "Q-D-B," and "ʿ-D-B."

117. See Ibn Saʿd, *al-Ṭabaqāt al-kubrā* (Beirut, 1990), 1:378–384; and al-Bukhārī, *Ṣaḥīḥ*, Farḍ al-Khums 4.

118. Ibn Mājah, *Sunan*, 24:18.

119. See ʿAbdallāh b. ʿAbd al-Raḥmān al-Dārimī, *Sunan al-Dārimī*, ed. Khālid al-Sabʿ al-ʿAlamī (Beirut, 1407), 1:20–21.

120. For an overview of these items, see al-Tihāmī, *Suyūf al-rasūl wa ʿuddah ḥarbi-hi*, 26, and 55–108 for the list of items used and acquired as booty in the different campaigns of the prophet Muhammad. Ibn Shahrāshūb, *Manāqib Āl Abī Ṭālib* (Najaf, 1956), 1:183, cites al-Wāqidī in a listing of four hundred suits of armor, four hundred lances, and five hundred swords.

121. See Ibn Kathīr, *al-Fuṣūl fī sīrah al-rasūl*, ed. Muḥammad al-ʿĪd al-Khaṭrāwī and Muhī al-Dīn Matū (Beirut, 1999), 260.

122. Abū al-Ḥasan ʿAlī b. al-Athīr, *Kāmil fī taʾrīkh*, ed. C. J. Tornberg (Leiden, 1868; reprint Beirut, 1995), 2:316.

123. For the Topkapi weapons treasury, see Hans Stöcklein, "Die Waffenschätze im Topkapu Sarayi Müzesi zu Istanbul," *Ars Islamica* 1 (1934); 200–218; O. Sermed Muhtar, *Müze-i Askeri-i Osmani-Rehber*, 3 vols. (Istanbul, 1920–1922); and Zaky, "Baʿḍ qaṭʿa al-islaḥah al-islāmīyah fī Istānbūl," *al-Muqataṭaf* 97 (April 1940): 393–397. On the swords in particular, see Ünsal Yücel, *Islamic Swords and Swordsmiths* (Istanbul, 2001), trans. into Arabic by Taḥsayn ʿAmr Tahaoglu as *al-Suyūf al-islāmīyah wa ṣannāʿu-hā* (Kuwait, 1988). For the "Treasuries of Weapons" in Cairo, see Aḥmad b. ʿAlī al-Maqrīzī, *Kitāb al-khiṭaṭ al-Maqrīzī* (Cairo, n.d.), 2:268–269. Al-Maqrīzī mentions a number of swords attributed to specific individuals, swords ornamented with silver and gold, iron swords, different types of lances, bows, and armor.

124. This sword is commonly referred to simply as al-Maʾthūr. The term al-Fijār refers to the "sacrilegious" war during which the sword was used. The Quraysh and the Kinānah fought against the tribe of Qay ʿAylān, and the war is said to have taken place when the prophet Muhammad was twenty years old (ca. 590 CE), although other sources give his age as anywhere from fourteen to twenty-eight years old. See the references in Ibn Hishām, *al-Sīrah al-nabawīyah*, 1:324–327; Guillaume, *The Life of Muhammad*, 82/119; al-Ṭabarī, *Taʾrīkh al-rusul wa al-mulūk*, 1130, 1255; Watt and McDonald, *The History of al-Ṭabarī: Muḥammad at Mecca*, 49–50, 161; and H. Lammens, "La Mecque à la veille de l'Hégire," *Mélanges de l'Université Saint-Joseph* 9 (1924): 97–439, esp. 326.

125. See Ibn Saʿd, *al-Ṭabaqāt al-kubrā,* 1:376–377.

126. See the reference to this in al-Tihāmī, *Suyūf al-rasūl wa ʿuddah ḥarbi-hi,* 113–114. On the accounts of the marriage of Fāṭimah and ʿAlī, see ʿAbd al-Raḥmān al-Nasāʾī, *Sunan* (Beirut, n.d.), 26:81; Ibn Mājah, *Sunan,* 9:24; Ibn Rustam al-Ṭabarī, *Dalāʾil al-imāmah* (Najaf, 1949), 1–58; Ḥusayn ʿAbd al-Wahhāb, *ʿUyūn al-muʿjizāt* (Najaf, 1950), 46–51; and Ibn Shahrāshūb, *Manāqib Āl Abī Ṭālib,* 3:101–140. Also see Ibn Hishām, *al-Sīrah al-nabawīyah,* 389/588, where it is reported that the prophet Muhammad handed his sword to Fāṭimah, asking her to wash the blood from it, and then ʿAlī handed her his sword, asking her to wash the blood from it too.

127. See al-Dhahabī, *Siyar aʿlām al-nubalāʾ*, 2:428. Also see Ibn Manẓūr, *Lisān al-ʿArab,* s.v. "ʾ-Th-R." This sword is also mentioned in Marḍī b. ʿAlī b. Marḍī al-Ṭarsūsī, *Mawsūʿah al-islaḥah al-qadīmah: al-Mawsūm tabṣirat arbāb al-albāb,* ed. Karen Sader (Beirut, 1998), 50.

128. For pictures and a general description of this sword, see Yücel, *Islamic Swords and Swordsmiths,* 15–16; and al-Tihāmī, *Suyūf al-rasūl wa ʿuddah ḥarbi-hi,* 113–117.

129. See David Alexander, "Dhu al-fakār" (PhD dissertation, Institute of Fine Arts, New York University, 1984). Because of this sword, the name Dhū al-Faqār (also pronounced "Dhū al-Fiqār") is well known in later Islamic prosopography, e.g., in Zulfiqar Ali Bhutto (1928–1979), the president and prime minister of Pakistan. See Annemarie Schimmel, *Islamic Names* (Edinburgh, 1989), 34; T. E. Colebrooke, "On the Proper Names of the Mohammadans," *Journal of the Royal Asiatic Society of Great Britain and Ireland* 11 (1879): 210; and Salahuddin Ahmed, *A Dictionary of Muslim Names* (New York, 1999), 231–232.

130. See Ahmad b. Nūr al-Dīn ʿAlī b. Ḥajar, *Fatḥ al-bārī,* 2:162.

131. See Muslim, *Ṣaḥīḥ,* 52:33–34. Ibn Shahrāshūb lists six suits of armor and eight swords as having been used in the raid of Badr. See Ibn Shahrāshūb, *Manāqib Āl Abī Ṭālib,* 1:162.

132. See Ibn Kathīr, *Tafsīr al-Qurʾān al-ʿaẓīm,* on Q 8:41; and al-Tirmidhī, *al-Jāmiʿ al-ṣaḥīḥ,* 21:14. Ibn Kathīr refers to the sword and the larger question of the distribution of spoils at the beginning of his exegesis of Surah al-Anfāl, "the Spoils." In his exegesis of Q 8:1, Ibn Kathīr cites a report transmitted on the authority of Saʿd b. Abī Waqqāṣ that the sword in question belonged to Saʿīd b. al-ʿĀṣ and was called Dhū al-Katīfah. Another report mentioned by Ibn Isḥāq states that the sword was the one taken by Mālik b. Rabīʿah from Ibn ʿĀʾidh and was called al-Marzabān.

133. See Ibn Mājah, *Sunan,* 24:18; and al-Bayhaqī, *Dalāʾil al-nabuwwah,* 3:136.

134. See Aḥmad b. Muḥammad al-Qasṭallānī, *Irshād al-sārī li-sharḥ Ṣaḥīḥ al-Bukhārī* (Cairo, 1304), 5:200–201. There may be a reference to this in the account of ʿAlī b. Abī Ṭālib's giving his sword to Fāṭimah. See al-Ṭabarī, *Taʾrīkh al-rusul*

*wa al-mulūk,* 1426; and M. V. McDonald and W. Montgomery Watt, *The History of al-Ṭabarī: The Foundation of the Community* (Albany, 1987), 138.

135. See al-Dhahabī, *Siyar aʿlām al-nubalāʾ,* 2:429.

136. Ibn Hishām lists al-ʿĀṣ b. Munabbih b. al-Ḥajjāj as one of five people from the Banū Sahm b. ʿAmr who were killed at the battle of Badr. See Ibn Hishām, *al-Sīrah al-nabawīyah,* 2:269; Guillaume, *The Life of Muhammad,* 338/510. Guillaume's translation does not specify that it was ʿAlī b. Abī Ṭālib who killed al-ʿĀṣ b. Munabbih.

137. See al-Dhahabī, *Siyar aʿlām al-nubalāʾ,* 2:428–429.

138. See al-Bukhārī, *Ṣaḥīḥ,* 65, on Q 19:4, where it is reported that Khabbāb worked as a blacksmith in Mecca and made swords for al-ʿĀṣ b. Wāʾil of the Banū Sahmī ,who refused to pay him until Khabbāb renounced his belief in the prophethood of Muhammad. Also see Ibn Hishām, *al-Sīrah al-nabawīyah,* 1:132; Guillaume, *The Life of Muhammad,* 162/234–235. Other commentaries on these verses do not mention the sword. See, for example, Muḥammad b. Aḥmad al-Qurṭubī, *al-Jāmiʿ li-aḥkām al-Qurʾān* (Beirut, 1997), on Q 19:77–80, who cites Wakiʿ, al-Aʿmash, al-Kalbī, and Muqātil b. Sulaymān as relating that Khabbāb was a blacksmith. Ibn Kathīr, *Tafsīr al-Qurʾān al-ʿaẓīm,* on Q 19:77–80, cites the report from al-Bukhārī that mentions the sword. See Muḥammad Ḥusayn al-Ṭabāṭabāʾī, *al-Mīzān fī tafsīr al-Qurʾān* (Beirut, 1970–1974), on Q 19:77–80, who omits mention of the sword, citing Ibn Ḥanbal, al-Bukhārī, Muslim, al-Tirmidhī, al-Bayhaqī, Ibn Ḥibbān, Ibn Abī Ḥātim, and others.

139. See Abū Dāʾūd al-Sijistānī, *Sunan,* ed. Muḥammad Muḥyī al-Dīn ʿAbd al-Ḥamīd (Beirut, 1980), 15:139.

140. See Aḥmad b. Ḥanbal, *Musnad* (Cairo, 1895), 1:271; Ibn Mājah, *Sunan,* 24:18; and Ibn Kathīr, *al-Bidāyah wa al-nihāyah fī al-taʾrīkh* (Cairo, 1351–1358), 6:5. Also see the ḥadīth reports stating that the prophet Muhammad took as spoils the sword of Abū Jahl, whom he killed on the day of Badr, in al-Dārimī, *Sunan,* 16:139; and Ibn Ḥanbal, *Musnad,* 3:497.

141. See al-Ṭabarī, *Taʾrīkh al-rusul wa al-mulūk,* 1359; and McDonald and Watt, *The History of al-Ṭabarī: The Foundation of the Community,* 84.

142. al-Ṭabarī, *Taʾrīkh al-rusul wa al-mulūk,* 1402; and McDonald and Watt, *The History of al-Ṭabarī: The Foundation of the Community,* 119–120.

The phrase spoken by the voice, and variants of it, are commonly inscribed on sword blades. See, for example H. J. Braunholtz and A. S. Fulton, "An Inscribed Turkish Sword," *British Museum Quarterly* 1 (1927): 106–107. For specific examples from collections, see David Alexander, *The Arts of War: The Nasser D. Khalili Collection of Islamic Art* (Oxford, 1992); Bernd Augustin, "Arms," in *Oriental Splendour: Islamic Art from German Private Collections,* ed. Claus-Peter Haase and others (Hamburg, 1993), 182–224; Robert Elgood, *Arms and Armour of Arabia in the 18th, 19th, and 20th Centuries* (London, 1994); and idem, ed.,

*Islamic Arms and Armour* (London, 1979). For a general overview of the decoration of swords and other weapons, see George Cameron Stone, *A Glossary of the Construction, Decoration and Use of Arms and Armor in All Countries and in All Times* (New York, 1934). Similar inscriptions became popular on firearms. See, for example, the North African, Balkan, and Indian guns cataloged in Robert Elgood, *Firearms of the Islamic World in the Tareq Rajab Museum, Kuwait* (London, 1995), esp. guns 44, 67, and 114.

143. See al-Tirmidhī, *al-Jāmiʿ al-ṣaḥīḥ*, 21:16; Ibn Mājah, *Sunan*, 24:16; and Ibn Kathīr, *al-Bidāyah wa al-nihāyah fī al-taʾrīkh*, 6:5.

144. See Ibn Shahrāshūb, *Manāqib Āl Abī Ṭālib*, 3:82. Ibn Shahrāshūb cites a number of reports, on the authority of ʿIkrimah and others, saying that it was an angel who called this phrase from the sky.

145. For the use of the sword by the Fatimids, see Heinz Halm, *The Empire of the Mahdi: The Rise of the Fatimids*, trans. Michael Bonner (Leiden, 1996), esp. 313–355. On the general significance of Dhū al-Faqār in its association with ʿAlī and in Shiʿī contexts, see S. M. Swemer, "The Sword of Mohammed and Ali," *Moslem World* 21, no. 2 (1931): 109–121. Swemer (111–112) cites a Chinese depiction of Dhū al-Faqār with the phrase "There is no companion like ʿAlī and no sword like Dhū al-Faqār." A Chinese text describes how the sword was passed to ʿAlī from the prophet Muhammad, who had received it from the angel Gabriel.

146. See al-Qāḍī al-Nuʿmān, *al-Majālis wa al-musāyarāt*, ed. al-Ḥabīb al-Faqqī and others (Tunis, 1978), par. 53; and ʿImād al-Dīn Idrīs, *ʿUyūn al-akhbār*, ed. M. Ghālib (Beirut, 1975), 5:265. Also see Halm, *The Empire of the Mahdi*, 352–353. For the reports of the sword's being with the ʿAbbasids, see Ignaz Goldziher, *Muhammedanische Studien* (Halle, 1889–1890), trans. C. R. Barber and S. M. Stern as *Muslim Studies* (London: Allen and Unwin, 1971), 2:324/259. On the presence of the sword of al-Ḥusayn b. ʿAlī b. Abī Ṭālib in the treasuries of the Fatimids, see al-Maqrīzī, *Kitāb al-khiṭaṭ al-Maqrīzī*, 2:268–269. On this sword and other weapons in the treasuries of the Fatimids, see Zakī M. Ḥasan, *Kunūz al-Fāṭimiyyīn* (Cairo, 1937), 54–57. On the later Ayyubid and Mamluk treasuries, see Nabīl Muḥammad ʿAbd al-ʿAzīz, *Khizānat al-silāḥ: Maʿa dirāsah ʿan khazāʾin al-silāḥ wa muhtawīyagi-hā ʿalā ʿasr al-Ayyūbīyīn wa al-Mamālik* (Cairo, 1978).

147. See al-Dhahabī, *Siyar aʿlām al-nubalāʾ*, 2:429.

148. See Ibn Ḥajar, *Fatḥ al-bārī*, 13:26–28, on 92:4.

149. See Ibn Shahrāshūb, *Manāqib Āl Abī Ṭālib*, 3:81.

150. This raid is mentioned in Ibn Hishām, *al-Sīrah al-nabawīyah*, 6:54; Guillaume, *The Life of Muhammad*, 916/1000; and in Ibn al-Kalbī, *Kitāb al-aṣnām*, 15–16, 61–62. See the English translation in *The Book of Idols: Being a Translation from the Arabic of the Kitāb al-Aṣnām by Hishām Ibn-al-Kalbi*, trans. Nabih Amin Faris (Princeton, 1952), 13–14, 52–53. The two swords are mentioned in a line of

pre-Islamic poetry by ʿAlqamah. See W. Ahlwardt, ed., *The Divans of the Six Ancient Arabic Poets* (London, 1870), 2:27, p. 107. Also see al-Tihāmī, *Suyūf al-rasūl wa ʿuddah ḥarbi-hi,* 197–198.

151. Muḥammad b. ʿUmar al-Wāqidī, *Kitāb al-maghāzī,* ed. Marsden Jones (Oxford, 1966), 3:988. He states that the first two swords were given to the prophet Muhammad but the third sword was kept by ʿAlī b. Abī Ṭālib.

152. See Ibn Shahrāshūb, *Manāqib Āl Abī Ṭālib,* 3:82.

153. See al-Dhahabī, *Siyar aʿlām al-nubalāʾ,* 1:378.

154. See al-Tihāmī, *Suyūf al-rasūl wa ʿuddah ḥarbi-hi,* 197–198. Ibn Hishām, *al-Sīrah al-nabawīyah,* 5:276–277; Guillaume, *The Life of Muhammad,* 636/946–639/950, records this expedition and its capture of the sister of ʿAdī b. Ḥātim, who was the chief of the Ṭayyiʾ and had fled to Syria in advance of the Muslim armies.

155. See Yücel, *Islamic Swords and Swordsmiths,* 38–39, who attributes this sword to Jaʿfar al-Ṭayyār; and al-Tihāmī, *Suyūf al-rasūl wa ʿuddah ḥarbi-hi,* 193–195.

156. See Aḥmad b. ʿAlī al-Maqrīzī, *Kitāb al-khiṭaṭ al-Maqrīzī,* 2:268.

157. See Yücel, *Islamic Swords and Swordsmiths,* 34, who attributes the sword to Zayn al-ʿĀbidīn on the basis of the inscription; and al-Tihāmī, *Suyūf al-rasūl wa ʿuddah ḥarbi-hi,* 197–199.

158. See Muḥammad al-Majlisī, *Biḥār al-Anwār* (Tehran, 1887), 7:448.

159. See al-Ṭarsūsī, *Mawsūʿah al-islaḥah al-qadīmah,* 47–48.

160. See Yücel, *Islamic Swords and Swordsmiths,* 17–18; and al-Tihāmī, *Suyūf al-rasūl wa ʿuddah ḥarbi-hi,* 119–124.

161. See al-Tihāmī, *Suyūf al-rasūl wa ʿuddah ḥarbi-hi,* 125–127. For references to the acquisition of this sword by the prophet Muhammad, see Ibn Ḥanbal, *Musnad* (from Anas); Muslim, *Ṣaḥīḥ*; and Sulaymān b. Aḥmad al-Ṭabarānī, *al-Muʿjam al-kabīr* (Baghdad, 1978) (from ʿIbādah al-Nuʿmān). It is thought that, since Dhū al-Faqar was given to ʿAlī b. Abī Ṭālib at Uḥud, the prophet Muhammad used al-ʿAḍb at that battle, although it was sent to him before Badr by Saʿd b. ʿIbādah al-Anṣarī.

162. al-Wāqidī, *Kitāb al-maghāzī,* 1:178–179.

163. See Abū Muḥammad ʿAlī Ibn Ḥazm, *Jawāmiʿ al-sīrah al-nabaqīyah,* ed. Nāʾyf al-ʿAbbās (Beirut, 1986), 123–124; and al-Dhahabī, *Siyar aʿlām al-nubalāʾ,* 1:378. Al-Dhahabī gives the names of the swords as Qalʿī, al-Battār, and al-Ḥanif.

164. See al-Bukhārī, *Ṣaḥīḥ,* 57:1, 64:12. Also see Arent Jan Wensinck and R. Paret, "Kaynukāʿ," in *Encyclopaedia of Islam,* 4:824. On relations between the prophet Muhammad and the Jews of Medina, see Arent Jan Wensinck, *Mohammed en de Joden te Medina* (Leiden, 1908), esp. 39, 146–151; R. Leszynsky, *Die Juden in Arabien zur Zeit Mohammeds* (Berlin, 1910), esp. 60–63; H. Z. Hirschberg, *Yisraʾel be-ʿArav* (Tel Aviv, 1946); William Montgomery Watt, *Muḥammad at Medina* (Oxford, 1956); Moshe Gil, "The Medinan Opposition to the

Prophet," *Jerusalem Studies in Arabic and Islam* 10 (1987): 65–96; and idem, "The Origin of the Jews of Yathrib," in *Jerusalem Studies in Arabic and Islam* 4 (1984): 203–224.

165. See al-Qurṭubī, *al-Jāmiʿ li-aḥkām al-Qurʾān*, on Q 3:12; and ʿAbd al-Raḥmān b. Abī Bakr al-Suyūṭī, *al-Durr al-manthūr fī tafsīr al-maʾthūr* (Beirut, 1990), on Q 3:12. Also see the citation of Ibn Isḥāq in Ibn Hishām, *al-Sīrah al-nabawīyah,* 3:313–316; Guillaume, *The Life of Muhammad,* 363/545.

166. See Maḥmūd b. ʿUmar al-Zamakhsharī, *al-Kashshāf ʿan ḥaqāʾiq ghawāmiḍ al-tanzīl wa ʿuyūn al-aqāwīl fī wujūh al-taʾwīl,* ed. Muḥammad ʿAbd al-Salām Shāhīn, 5 vols. (Beirut, 1995), on Q 3:12.

167. See ʿAbd al-Raḥmān b. ʿAlī Ibn al-Jawzī, *Zād al-musīr fī ʿilm al-tafsīr,* ed. ʿAbd al-Razzāq al-Mahdī (Beirut, 2001), on Q 8:55–56, citing Abū Ṣāliḥ on the authority of Ibn ʿAbbās. Muḥammad b. Jarīr al-Ṭabarī, *Jāmiʿ al-bayān fī tafsīr al-Qurʾān* (Beirut, 1412), on Q 8:55–56, cites Mujāhid as saying the verses refer to the Banū Qurayẓah and their enmity toward the prophet Muhammad at the time of the battle of Khandaq. Ibn Kathīr, *Tafsīr al-Qurʾān al-ʿaẓīm,* on Q 8:55–56, cites reports by Ibn ʿAbbās, Ḥasan al-Baṣrī, Ḍaḥḥāk, al-Suddī, and others who state that the verses refer to killing the enemies among the Arabs.

168. See ʿAlī b. ʿAbdallāh al-Samhūdī, *Wafāʾ al-wafā* (Beirut, 1971), 1:159–165. On the Banū Qurayẓah and their weapons, see M. J. Kister, "The Massacre of the Banū Qurayẓa: A Re-examination of a Tradition," *Jerusalem Studies in Arabic and Islam* 8 (1986): 61–96, reprinted in his *Society and Religion from Djāhiliyya to Islam* (Brookfield, Vt., 1990), chap. 8. For general remarks on the weapons of the Jews, see F. Altheim and R. Stiehl, *Die Araber in der alten Welt* (Berlin, 1968), esp. 5:366. On the armor of the Prophet being equivalent to the Ark of the Covenant, see Uri Rubin, *Between Bible and Quran: The Children of Israel and the Islamic Self-Image* (Princeton, 1999), 188–210. Also see Michael Lecker, *Muslims, Jews and Pagans: Studies on Early Islamic Medina* (Leiden, 1995), esp. 10–11.

169. al-Dhahabī, *Siyar aʿlām al-nubalāʾ*, 2:429–430. Also see the restatement of these traditions in al-Tihāmī, *Suyūf al-rasūl wa ʿuddah ḥarbi-hi,* 155–179.

170. On the sword of Goliath, see Stanley Isser, *The Sword of Goliath: David in Heroic Literature,* Studies in Biblical Literature 6 (Atlanta, 2003), esp. 34–37.

171. For this picture, the inscription and discussion, see Yücel, *Islamic Swords and Swordsmiths,* 19–20; and al-Tihāmī, *Suyūf al-rasūl wa ʿuddah ḥarbi-hi,* 155–179. The *Sefer ha-Zohar ḥadash,* ed. Daniyel Frish (Jerusalem, 1999), trans. Harry Sperling and Maurice Simon as *The Zohar* (London, 1970), Shemoth, sec. 2, p. 108a, states that David swore an oath using a sword engraved with the Tetragrammaton.

172. See, for example, the reports that David cut off the head of Goliath with the sword in al-Ṭabarī, *Jāmiʿ al-bayān fī tafsīr al-Qurʾān,* on Q 2:251. Also see al-Suyūṭī, *al-Durr al-manthūr,* on Q 2:251.

173. See Abū al-Layth Samarqandī, *Tafsīr al-Qurʾān al-Karīm* (Baghdad, 1985), on Q 2:251.

174. See ʿAlī b. Ibrāhīm al-Qummī, *Tafsīr al-Qummī* (Beirut, 1991); and also Muḥsin al-Malaqqab al-Ghayḍ Kashāni, *Tafsīr al-ṣāfī* (Tehran, n.d.), on Q 2:251. Al-Samarqandī states that one of the stones David used was the stone of Moses. Al-Ṭabarī, *Jāmiʿ al-bayān fī tafsīr al-Qurʾān,* on Q. 2:251, cites a number of reports that the stones David used were named after Abraham, Isaac, Jacob, and the Israelites. Al-Suyūṭī, *al-Durr al-manthūr,* on Q 2:241, cites a report in which one of the stones was the stone of the Israelites. Al-Qummī claims that David was a Levite; but al-Qurṭubī, *al-Jāmiʿ li-aḥkām al-Qurʾān,* on Q 2:251, states that David was from the tribe of Judah and that Goliath was the leader of the Amalekites. Al-Zamakhsharī, *al-Kashshāf ʿan ḥaqāʾiq ghawāmiḍ al-tanzīl wa ʿuyūn al-aqāwīl fī wujūh al-taʾwīl,* on Q 2:251, explains that Goliath was one of the Amalekites and was a descendant of the people of ʿĀd.

175. See Aḥmad b. Muḥammad al-Thaʿlabī, *Qiṣaṣ al-anbiyāʾ* (Cairo, n.d.), 274.

176. See al-Thaʿlabi, *Qiṣaṣ al-anbiyāʾ*, 274. The fight is also to be compared with ʿAlī b. Abī Ṭālib's defeat of the Jewish giant at Badr which resulted in the capture of the sword Dhū al-Faqār. See Burton's citation of ʿAlī b. Abī Ṭālib's killing a Jewish giant with Dhū al-Faqār. For the role of the sword in biblical narrative, see Isser, *The Sword of Goliath,* 34–51.

177. See al-Thaʿlabī, *Qiṣaṣ al-anbiyāʾ*, 281. On Islamic armor, see A. R. Zaki, "Islamic Armour: An Introduction," *Gladius* 2 (1963): 69–74; idem, "Introduction to the Study of Islamic Arms and Armour," *Gladius* 1 (1961): 17–29; J. Wallace, "Islamic Arms and Armour," *Discovering Antiques* 23 (1993): 548–552; L. A. Mayer, *Islamic Armourers and Their Works* (Geneva, 1962); and Michael Gorelik, "Oriental Armour of the Near and Middle East from the Eight to the Fifteenth Centuries as Shown in Works of Art," in R. Elgood, *Islamic Arms and Armour,* 30–63. On the different types of armor, see Ibn Salām, *Kitāb al-silāḥ*, 28–30.

178. See al-Zamakhshari, *al-Kashshāf ʿan ḥaqāʾiq ghawāmiḍ al-tanzīl wa ʿuyūn al-aqāwīl fī wujūh al-taʾwīl,* on Q 21:79–80, who states that David sold each suit for four thousand dinar. Al-Suyūṭī, *al-Durr al-manthūr,* on Q 21:79–80, cites a report on the authority of Qatādah that David did not have to use fire or a hammer to make the armor, and that he used the armor of David to protect the Israelites from their enemies.

179. On Jesus and the Dajjāl, see Q 18:94–99. Al-Bukhārī, *Ṣaḥīḥ,* 92, gives an overview of events (76–77) and describes how Jesus uses a sword (88–89) and the Dajjāl is killed by Jesus (93). Also see the section "Do not give unsheathed swords" in al-Bukhārī, *Ṣaḥīḥ,* 20:76–77, 20:88–89, 20:92—also see al-Tirmidhi, *Jāmiʿ al-ṣaḥīḥ,* 31:5, 31:10, describes how Jesus comes as morning prayer is called

to slay the Dajjāl with his hand, and he shows the people the blood of the Dajjāl on his sword. See Ibn Mājah, *Sunan,* 36:11. See al-Tirmidhi, *Jāmiʿ al-ṣaḥīḥ,* on Gog and Magog (31:23), the sword used (31:33), Jesus returning (31:54), breaking crosses and killing pigs (31:54), the Dajjāl (31:55–62), and Jesus killing the Dajjāl (31:1, 62).

180. See ʿAlī b. Burhān al-Dīn al-Ḥalabī, *al-Sīrah al-Ḥalabīyah* (Cairo, 1300), 2:303–309; and Muslim, *Ṣaḥīḥ,* 44.

181. See Yücel, *Islamic Swords and Swordsmiths,* 21; and al-Tihāmī, *Suyūf al-rasūl wa ʿuddah ḥarbi-hi,* 207–213.

182. See al-Ḥalabī, *al-Sīrah al-Ḥalabīyah,* 2:70, 309.

183. See Muḥammad b. Idrīs al-Shāfiʿī, *Kitāb al-umm* (Beirut, 1996); Ibn Ḥajar, *al-Iṣābah fī tamyīz al-ṣaḥābah* (Cairo, 1970–1972); and al-Tihāmī, *Suyūf al-rasūl wa ʿuddah ḥarbi-hi,* 215–218.

184. See Yücel, *Islamic Swords and Swordsmiths,* 27–32; and al-Tihāmī, *Suyūf al-rasūl wa ʿuddah ḥarbi-hi,* 219–223.

185. See Yücel, *Islamic Swords and Swordsmiths,* 40–47; and al-Tihāmī, *Suyūf al-rasūl wa ʿuddah ḥarbi-hi,* 225–235.

186. See Yücel, *Islamic Swords and Swordsmiths,* 49–50; and al-Tihāmī, *Suyūf al-rasūl wa ʿuddah ḥarbi-hi,* 237–347.

187. Al-Qaddūmī, *Book of Gifts and Rarities,* 203.

188. ʿAbd al-Raḥmān b. ʿAlī. Ibn al-Jawzī, *Mirʾāt al-zamān fī taʾrīkh al-aʿyān* (Beirut, 1985), 1:119. Also see al-Qaddūmī, *Book of Gifts and Rarities,* 209.

On the significance of mirrors, see Annemarie Schimmel, *Deciphering the Signs of God: A Phenomenological Approach to Islam* (Albany, 1994), esp. 21–29. See also A. E. Crawley, "Mirror," in *Encylopedia of Religion and Ethics,* ed. James Hastings and others (New York, 1951), 8; and T. Burckhardt, "The Symbolism of the Mirror," *Symbolon* 4 (1954): 117–123.

189. See al-Qaddūmī, *Book of Gifts and Rarities,* 211–212. On these and other relics of Solomon, see al-Suyūṭī, *al-Durr al-Manthūr,* on Q 21:78–82.

190. See al-Qaddūmī, *Book of Gifts and Rarities,* 102, 103, 104. On the rings and relics of Daniel, see al-Thaʿlabī, *Qiṣaṣ al-anbiyāʾ,* 340–345.

191. See al-Qaddūmī, *Book of Gifts and Rarities,* 227.

192. See al-Qaddūmī, *Book of Gifts and Rarities,* 230–235.

193. See al-Masʿūdī, *Murūj al-dhahab,* 1:307–308.

194. See al-Masʿūdī, *Murūj al-dhahab,* 1:307–308; and al-Qaddūmī, *Book of Gifts and Rarities,* appendix.

195. See al-Qaddūmī, *Book of Gifts and Rarities,* 186; al-Masʿūdī, *Murūj al-dhahab,* 1:299; and Muḥammad b. Aḥmad al-Khawarizmī, *Mafātīḥ al-ʿulūm,* 69.

196. See Ibn Badrūn, *Jawāhīr al-afkār wa maʿdin al-asrār,* ed. Zuhayr al-Shāwīsh

(Beirut, 1999), 84; and Muḥammad Murtaḍā al-Zabīdī, *Tāj al-ʿarūs*, 6:229, s.v. It is reported that the Umayyad Khālid b. Saʿīd b. al-ʿĀṣ, one of the companions of the prophet Muhammad, acquired the sword after routing ʿAmr in battle, but it is also said the ʿAmr gave it to the caliph ʿUmar, who passed it to his nephew, who then lost it defending the caliph ʿUthmān. The sword is later reported to have been found by a Bedouin tribe and is said to have existed in the later ʿAbbasid period. See Ibn al-Kalbi's remark in al-Balādhūrī, *Futūḥ al-buldān,* 119–120; and in a poem in Aḥmad b. Muḥammad Ibn Khallikān, *Wafayāt al-aʿyān,* ed. Iḥsān ʿAbbās (Beirut, 1968–1972). 5:329.

197. On the Sulaymānīyah sword, see al-Kindī, *al-Suyūf wa ajnāsu-hā,* ed. ʿAbd al-Raḥmān Zakī (Cairo, 1952), 9–10; M. L. Nigam, "Some Literary References to the History of the Gujara-Pratihāras Mahendrapāla and Mahipāla," *Journal of the Royal Asiatic Society* (1964): 14–17; and K. M. Munshi, *Glory That Was Gujara-Desa,* 2 vols. (Bombay, 1955). For the sword of "Japhet" and other South and Southeast Asian weapons, see W. E. G. Solomon, "The Sword of Aurangzebe: A Study of Arms and Art," *Islamic Culture* 8 (1934): 179–199; Firoz Mahmud, "A Sword of Nawab Siraj-ud-Davlah in the Dacca Museum," *Bangladesh llalil Kal J. Dacca Museum* 1 (1975): 127–130; and G. N. Pant, "A Study of Indian Swords," in "Itihasa-Chayanika: Dr. Sampurnanand Felicitation Volume," special issue, *Journal of the Uttar Pradesh Provinces Historical Society* 11–13, pt. 2 (1965): 75–86.

198. See al-Qaddūmī, *Book of Gifts and Rarities*, 255–333.

199. Al-Qaddūmī, *Book of Gifts and Rarities*, 221. Also see 222 for a report of the discovery of swords by Khālid b. Barmak during his conquest of Tabaristan and Dinawand.

200. See al-Qaddūmī, *Book of Gifts and Rarities*, 240, on the Indian spearheads, Tibetan armor, and Tarkhūniyyah plate mail. See also 196 for the treasure of Nihāwand, which had belonged to one of Khusraw's companions. On this, also see al-Ṭabarī, *Taʾrīkh al-rusul wa al-mulūk,* 197–198. Ṭabarī also reports that Aḥmad b. Ṭūlūn is said to have discovered a million dinars in the desert identified as the "treasure of bygone [al-awāʾil] peoples" (369).

201. For some of the many studies in the area of court ceremony, see for example, Hilāl b. al-Muḥassin al-Ṣābī, *Rusūm dār al-khilāfa,* ed. M. ʿAwwād (Baghdad, 1964), 90–98, trans. Elie A. Salem as *The Rules and Regulations of the ʿAbbasid Court* (Beirut, 1977); also on Umayyads, see Oleg Grabar, "Notes sur les ceremonies umayyades," in *Studies in Memory of Gaston Wiet*, ed. M. Rosen-Ayalon (Jerusalem, 1977), 51–60; al-Qāḍī al-Nuʿmān, *Kitāb al-Himma fī ādāb atbāʿ al-aʾimmah,* ed. M. Kāmil Ḥusayn (Cairo, n.d.); A. M. Mājid, *Nuẓūm al-Fāṭimiyyīn wa rusūmu-hum fī Miṣr* (Cairo, 1973); and F. W. Hasluck, "The Girding of the Sultan," in *Christianity and Islam under the Sultans* (Oxford, 1929; reprint, New York, 1973), 2:604–622.

On Indian swords, see Solomon, "The Sword of Aurangzebe"; Mahmud, "A Sword of Nawab Siraj-ud-Davlah in the Dacca Museum"; Pant, "A Study of Indian Swords"; and P. S. Rawson, *The Indian Sword* (Copenhagen, 1967; rev. ed., London, 1968). Also see the wide-ranging and extremely useful work of Robert Francis Willard Elgood, "A Study of the Origin, Evolution and Role in Society of a Group of Chiselled Steel Hindu Arms and Armour from Southern India, c. 1400–1865 A.D." (PhD dissertation, Linacre College, Oxford University, 1998). For African Muslim practices, see J. Sauvaget, "Notes preliminaires sur les epitaphes royales de Gao," *Revue des Études Islamiques* 21 (1948): 5–12; and idem, "Les epitaphes royales de Gao," *Bulletin de l'Institut Français d'Afrique Noire* 13 (1950): 418–440. For other cultural influences, see Alexander Slawik, "Kultische Geheimbünde der Japaner und Germanen," *Wiener Beiträge zur Kulturgeschichte* (Salzburg and Leipzig) 4 (1936): 675–764; and ʿAlī Akhbar Salmāsīzāda, *Taʾrīkhca-i wakf dar Islām* (Tehran, 1964). For some illustrations, see Bishr Farès, *Une miniature religieuse de l'École arabe de Baghdad* (Cairo, 1948), Livre des Chansons d'Abul' Faraq al-Asfahani (National Library, Cairo, Litt. 579), fig. 7; D. S. Rice, "The Aghānī Miniatures and Religious Painting in Islam," *Burlington Magazine* 45 (April 1953): 128–136; and Oscar Löfgren, "Ambrosian Fragments of an Illustrated Manuscript Containing the Zoology of Al-Gahiz," *Uppsala Univerity Årskrift,* 1946, vol. 5, pls. 1, 10, 13.

202. On the rod and sword as symbols of religious authority, see C. H. Becker, "Die Kanzel im Kultus des alten Islam," *Islam* 3 (1912): 451–469, reprinted in his *Islam Studien* (Leipzig, 1924; reprint, Hildesheim, 1967); I. Goldziher, "Der Chatib bei den alten Arabern," *Weiner Zeitschrift für die Kunde des Morgenlandes* 6 (1892): 97–102; M. Hammad, "L'evolution de la chaire dans la vie religieuse en Egypte," *Cahiers d'Histoire Egyptienne* 8 (1956): 117–129; E. Mittwoch, "Zur Entstehungs-geschichte des islamischen Gebets und Kultus," *Abhandlungen der preussischen Akademie der Wissenschaft* 2 (1913); and C. Miles, "Miḥrāb and ʿAnazah," *Archaeologica Orientalia in Memoriam Ernst Herzfeld*, ed. C. Miles (Locust Valley, N.Y., 1952), 156–171.

On ancient examples of sword as rod, see Burton, *The Book of the Sword*, esp. 199–208.

203. On the relationship of the cosmos and the built environment, see Wheatley, *The Pivot of the Four Corners*; idem, *The City as Symbol* (London, 1969); Robert von Heine-Geldern, "Weltbild und Bauform in Südostasien," *Wiener Beiträge zur Kunst- und Kulturgeschichte Asiens* (Vienna) 4 (1930):28–78; and Walter Krickeberg, "Bauform und Weltbild im alten Mexico," in *Mythe, Mensch und Umwelt,* Beiträge zur Religion, Mythologie und Kulturgeschichte, ed. Adolf Jensen (Bamberg, 1950), 295–333. See also Eric Voegelin, *Order and History* (Baton Rouge, 1956), esp. vol. 1 and 4; and, related, Frankfort, *Kingship and the Gods.*

204. On the role of the sword in establishing territorial boundaries and civi-

lization in ancient cultures, see C. Scott Littleton, "From Swords in the Earth to the Sword in the Stone: A Possible Reflection of an Alano-Sarmatian Rite of Passage in the Arthurian Tradition" in *Homage to Georges Dumézil,* ed. Edgar C. Polomé (Washington, D.C., 1982), 53–68; and E. Vinaver, "King Arthur's Sword," *Bulletin of the John Rylands Library* 60 (1958): 511–520. D. Yonge, *The Roman History of Ammianus Marcellinus* (London, 1902), 31.4.22, describes the Alanic custom of thrusting swords into the earth and worshipping them as Mars. A similar custom is reported among the Sarmatians. See T. Sulimirski, *The Sarmatians* (New York, 1970), 36. Also see, on the relation of swords and burial in Ottoman contexts, D. S. Brookes, "Of Swords and Tombs: Symbolism in the Ottoman Accession Ritual," *Turkish Studies Association Bulletin* 17 (1993): 1–22.

205. Sword combat also requires special training and, unlike missile combat, requires certain norms of behavior. Swords are implements of conscious intentions. On the use of the bow, which differs from the norms of hand-to-hand combat, see F. R. Baqi, "Kitāb faḍā'il al-ramy fī sabīl Allāh," *Islamic Culture* 34, no. 3 (1960): 195–218; A. Boudot-Lamotte and F. Vire, "Contribution a l'étude de l'archerie musulmane: Notes complémentaires," *Arabica* 17, no. 1 (1970): 47–68; and J. J. Modi, "Archery in Ancient Persia," *Journal of the Royal Asiatic Society* 25 (1917–1921): 175–186. Also see the wider-ranging but pertinent study of Allen J. Frantzen, *Bloody Good: Chivalry, Sacrifice, and the Great War* (Chicago, 2004).

206. See J. de Savignac, "Le sens du terme Ṣâphôn," *Ugarit Forschungen* 16 (1984): 273–278; R. J. Clifford, *The Cosmic Mountain in Canaan and the Old Testament* (Cambridge, Mass., 1972); and O. Eissfeldt, *Baal Zaphon, Zeus Kasios und der Durchzug der Israeliten durchs Meer* (Halle, 1932).

207. See, for example, Mircea Eliade, *Forgerons et alchimistes* (Paris, 1956), trans. Stephen Corrin as *The Forge and the Crucible,* 2d ed. (Chicago, 1956), esp. 87–96; G. Dieterlen and S. de Ganay, "Le génie des eaux chez les Dogons," *Miscellanaea Africana* 5 (Paris, 1942): 61ff.; Harry Tegnaeus, *Le héros civlisateur: Contribution à l'étude ethnologique de la religion et de la sociologie Africaines* (Uppsala, 1950); C. Scott Littleton, "Susa-nö-wo versus Ya-mata nö woröti: An Indo-European Theme in Japanese Mythology," *History of Religions* 20 (1981): 269–280; and Rudolf Thurneysen, *Die irische Helden- und Königsage bis zum siebzehnten Jahrhundert,* 2 vols (Halle, 1921). Also related is Diego Velázquez, *Apollo in the Forge* (Littleton, Colo., n.d.); and idem, *The Forge of Vulcan* (New York, 1965).

The connection between smithing and cosmogony is particularly pronounced in Indian contexts, for which see the excellent work of R. Elgood, "A Study of the Origin, Evolution and Role in Society of a Group of Chiselled Steel Hindu Arms and Armour from Southern India, c. 1400–1865 A.D." Also see Alf Hiltebeitel, *The Ritual of Battle* (Ithaca, 1976); and Heather Elgood, *Hinduism and the Religious Arts* (London: Cassells, 1998). On smiths and their position in South and Southeast Asian contexts, see Stella Kramrisch, "The Rgvedic Myth of the

Craftsmen (the Rbhus)," *Artibus Asiae* 22 (1959): 113–120; and R. Goris, "The Position of the Blacksmiths," *Studies in Bali Life, Thought and Ritual,* ed. W. F. Wertheim (The Hague, 1960), 291–297.

On the significance of sword-making and weapon metallurgy in Islamic contexts, see Marḍī b. ʿAlī b. Marḍī al-Ṭarsūsī, "Tabṣirah al-albāb fī kaifayah al-nijjāh min al-ḥurūb min al-aswāʾ," in "Tabṣirah al-albāb fī kaifayah al-nijjāh min al-ḥurūb min al-aswāʾ: Un traité d'Armurerie composé pour Saladin," by Claude Cahen, *Bulletin d'Etudes Orientales* (Beirut) 12 (1947–1948): 103–163; Ada Bruhn Hoffmeyer, "Middelalderens islamiske svaerd," *Vaabenhistoriske Aarboger* 8 (1956): 63–80; J. Piaskowski, "Metallographic Examination of Two Damascene Steel Blades," *Journal of the History of Arab Science* 2 (1973): 3–30; C. Panseri, "Damascus Steel in Legend and in Reality," *Gladius* 4 (1965): 5–66; Colonel N. Belaiew, "Damascene Steel," pts. 1 and 2, *Journal of the Iron and Steel Institute* 97 (1918): 417; 104 (1921): 181; A. Cour, "Jaysh," in *Encyclopaedia of Islam,* 2:504; Bréant, "Description à un procédé à l'aide duquel on obtient une espèce d'acier fondu, semblable à celui des lames damassées orientales," *Bulletin de la Société d'Encouragement pour l'Industrie Nationale* 21 (1823): 222–227; and M. Lombard, *Les metaux dans l'ancien monde du Ve au XIe siècle* (Paris, 1979).

On sword technology in general, see Kenneth Macksey, *The Penguin Encyclopedia of Weapons and Military Technology: Prehistory to the Present Day* (New York, 1993); and Leonid Tarassuk and Claude Blair, eds., *The Complete Encyclopaedia of Arms and Weapons* (London, 1979).

208. See, for example, al-Qurṭubī, *al-Jāmiʿ li-aḥkām al-Qurʾān,* on Q 57:25, in which a number of ḥadīth reports are cited. Al-Suyūṭī, *al-Durr al-manthūr,* on Q 57:25, states that the verse refers to shields and weapons. Abū ʿAlī al-Faḍl b. al-Ḥasan al-Ṭabarsī, *Majmaʿ al-bayān fī tafsīr al Qurʾān* (Beirut, n.d.), on Q 57:25, cites al-Zajjāj, who says that the verse means vessels used for defense and offense, and Mujāhid, who says it means a shield and weapons. Some useful material can also be found reviewed in E. Kohlberg's article "Some Shiʿi Views of the Antediluvian World," *Studia Islamica* 52 (1980): 41–66. Isser, *The Sword of Goliath,* 36–37, cites 2 Macc 15:11–16, where Judah Maccabeus has a dream in which the prophet Jeremiah gives Judah a gold sword from God. In 1 Macc 3:12 Judah takes as booty and uses the sword of the Seleucid general Apollonius.

On the tradition of bows and arrows transported to Adam, see al-Ṭaybughā, "Kitāb ghunyat al-ṭullāb fī maʿrifat ramī al-nushshāb," Ms. Add. 233489, British Museum, esp. fol. 4b–5b; and Yücel, *Islamic Swords and Swordsmiths,* 5. Also see J. D. Latham and W. F. Paterson, eds. *Saracen Archery: An English Version and Exposition of a Mameluke Work of Archery (c. AD 1368)* (London, 1970), 3.

209. See Ibn Kathīr, *Tafsīr al-Qurʾān al-ʿaẓīm,* on Q 57:25.

210. See Aḥmad b. Ḥanbal, *Musnad,* 1:178; and Abū Dāʾūd, *Sunan,* 15:144.

211. Ibn Shahrāshūb, *Manāqib Āl Abī Ṭālib,* 3:339.

212. See al-Ṭabāṭabā'ī, *al-Mizān fī tafsīr al-Qur'ān,* on Q 57:25.

213. See al-Ṭabarsī, *Majma',* on Q 57:25.

214. See G. Zawadowski, "Note sur l'origine magique de Dhou-Faqar," in *En Terre d'Islam* 1 (1943): 36–40.

215. The scholarship on this myth is extensive. For an overview and references to further sources, see G. Farber-Flügge, "Inanna und Enki," in *Der Mythos "Inanna und Enki" unter besonderer Berücksichtingung der Liste der Me,* ed. G. Farber-Flügge, Studia Pohl 10 (Rome, 1973), 16–65; and W. R. Sladek, "Inanna's Descent to the Netherworld" (PhD dissertation, Johns Hopkins University, 1974). There is a brief overview of the myth in S. H. Hooke, *Middle Eastern Mythology: From the Assyrians to the Hebrews* (New York, 1963), 23–29.

216. The most complete overview of the Me in relation to Inanna is Jean-Jacques Glassner, "Inannat et les me," in *Nippur at the Centennial: Papers Read at the 35e Rencontre Assyriologique Internationale, Philadelphia, 1988,* ed. Maria deJong Ellis (Philadelphia, 1992), 55–76.

217. For the full list and comments on the individual features, see Glassner, "Inanna et les me," 57–73, passim; and Farber-Flügge, *Der Mythos "Inanna und Enki" unter besonderer Berücksichtingung der Liste der Me,* passim.

218. On Enki and the origins of the world, see C. Benito, "Enki and Ninmah and Eni and the World Order" (PhD dissertation, University of Pennsylvania, 1969).

219. Al-Ṭabarī, *Ta'rīkh al-rusul wa al-mulūk,* 146.

## CHAPTER TWO

1. Mālik b. Anas, *al-Muwaṭṭa',* ed. Muḥammad Fu'ād 'Abd al-Bāqī (Beirut, n.d.), 1:42.

2. See ibid., 1:42–43.

3. Ibid., 1:42. Among the six authoritative collections of ḥadīth, this report is also cited in Abū Dā'ūd, *Sunan,* 1:69; al-Tirmidhī, *al-Jāmi' al-ṣaḥīḥ,* 1:61; al-Nasā'ī, *Sunan,* 1:118; and Ibn Mājah, *Sunan,* 1:63. The report is also cited in al-Shāfi'ī, *Kitāb al-umm,* 1:33–34.

4. For the report transmitted on the authority of Umm Ḥabībah, see Ibn Mājah, *Sunan,* 1:162; Aḥmad b. Muḥammad al-Ṭaḥāwī, *Sharḥ ma'ānī al-āthār,* ed. Muḥammad Sayīd Jādd al-Ḥaqq (Cairo, 1391), 1:75; Aḥmad b. al-Ḥusayn al-Bayhaqī, *Musnad* (Beirut, n.d.), 1:130; and al-Khaṭīb al-Baghdādī, *Ta'rīkh Baghdād,* ed. 'Abd al-Raḥmān b. Yaḥyā' al-Mu'allimī (Hyderabad, 1959), 11:73. For the report transmitted on the authority of Abū Hurayrah, see al-Shāfi'ī, *Kitāb al-umm,* 1:34; al-Ṭaḥāwī, *Sharḥ ma'ānī al-āthār,* 1:74; and Ibn Ḥanbal, *Musnad,* 2:333. For the report transmitted on the authority of Abū Ayyūb, see Ibn Mājah, *Sunan,* 1:162; and Abū Muḥammad 'Abdallāh b. Aḥmad Ibn Qudāmah, *al-Mughnī,* ed. 'Abdallāh b.

ʿAbd al-Muḥsin al-Turkī and ʿAbd al-Fattāḥ Muḥammad al-Ḥilw (Cairo, 1986; reprint, Beirut, 1992), 1:240.

5. See, for example, Aḥmad b. Muḥammad al-Qudūrī, *Mukhtaṣar fī al-fiqh* (Cairo, 1324), 20; ʿAlī b. Abī Bakr al-Marghīnānī, *al-Hidāyah: Sharḥ bidāyat al-mubtadā* (Multān, 1980), 1:15–33; Muḥammad b. Aḥmad al-Sarakhsī, *Kitāb al-mabsūṭ* (Cairo, 1378), 1:5–9; and Muḥammad Amīn b. ʿUmar Ibn ʿĀbdīn, *Ḥāshīyah radd al-muḥtār ʿalā al-Dār al-mukhtār: Sharḥ tanwīr al-abṣār* (Beirut, 1979), 1:79–123.

6. Muḥammad b. ʿAbd al-Bāqī al-Zurqānī, *Sharḥ al-Zurqānī ʿalā Muwaṭṭaʾ al-Imām Mālik* (Beirut, 1990), 1:129.

7. Abū al-Walīd Muḥammad b. Aḥmad Ibn Rushd, *Bidāyat al-mujtahid wa nihāyat al-muqtaṣid,* ed. ʿAlī Muḥammad Maʿūd and ʿĀdil Aḥmad ʿAbd al-Wujūd (Beirut, 1996), 1:496.

8. Ibn Rushd, *Bidāyat al-mujtahid,* 1:491. For reports used to support the Shāfiʿī position, see al-Shāfiʿī, *Kitāb al-umm,* 1:29–30.

9. For these reports, see al-Bukhārī, *Ṣaḥīḥ,* 8:382; Muslim, *Ṣaḥīḥ,* 4:2; Abū Dāʾūd, *Sunan,* 2:713–714; al-Nasāʾī, *Sunan,* 1:102; and Mālik b. Anas, *al-Muwaṭṭaʾ,* 1:117. Ibn Rushd, *Bidāyat al-mujtahid,* also cites a report, given on the authority of Ḥabīb b. Abī Thābit, on the authority of ʿUrwah b. al-Zubayr, on the authority of ʿĀʾishah, that the prophet Muhammad kissed some of his wives and then went out to pray but did not perform ablution. See Abū Dāʾūd, *Sunan,* 1:179; al-Tirmidhī, *al-Jāmiʿ al-ṣaḥīḥ,* 1:86; Ibn Mājah, *Sunan,* 1:502; al-Nasāʾī, *Sunan,* 1:124; and Ibn Ḥanbal, *Musnad,* 6:210.

10. See Aḥmad b. ʿAbd al-Ḥalīm Ibn Taymīyah, *Fiqh al-ṭahārah,* ed. al-Sayyid al-Jamīlī (Beirut, 1987), 171–191.

11. See ʿAbdallāh b. ʿAbd al-Raḥmān Ibn Abī Zayd, *al-Risālah al-faqīh,* ed. al-Hādī Ḥamū and Muḥammad Abū al-Ajfān (Beirut, 1986; reprint, Beirut, 1997), 83–84.

12. See Aḥmad b. Aḥmad Zarrūq, *Sharḥ ʿalā matn al-Risālah,* and Qāsim b. ʿĪsā Ibn Nājī, *Sharḥ ʿalā matn al-Risālah,* published together (Beirut, 1982), 1:78–79, where the different opinions of Mālik and Mālikī jurists are discussed in relation to the text of Ibn Abī Zayd.

13. Al-Shāfiʿī, *Kitāb al-umm,* 1:33–34.

14. Ismāʿīl b. Yaḥyāʾ al-Muzanī, *Mukhtaṣar,* published with al-Shāfiʿī, *Kitāb al-umm,* 8:96. Also, see the commentary on this section in Aḥmad b. Muḥammad Ibn al-Maḥāmilī, *Kitāb al-lubāb fī al-fiqh al-Shāfiʿī* (Cairo, 1274; reprint, Medina, 1286–1315); and the related comments in Abū Zurʿa al-ʿIrāqī, *Tanqīh al-lubāb,* with an abridgment by Zakrīyāʾ b. Muḥammad al-Anṣārī, entitled *Taḥrīr tanqīḥ al-lubāb,* published in the margins of his *Tuḥfat al-ṭullāb* (Cairo, 1340).

15. See Ibn Qudāmah, *al-Mughnī,* 1:242–243. Those who require *wuḍūʾ* for touching the penis unintentionally include al-Awzāʿī (Abū ʿAmr ʿAbd al-Raḥmān

b. ʿAmr), al-Shāfiʿī, Isḥāq (Abū Yaʿqūb Isḥāq b. Ibrāhīm), Abū Ayyūb, and Abū Khaythamah (Zahīr b. Muʿāwīyah b. Ḥudayj). Both al-Awzāʿī and ʿAṭāʾ (b. Abī Rabāḥ) maintain that there is no distinction between touching the penis with the palm and touching it with the back of the hand.

16. See Ibn Qudāmah, *al-Mughnī,* 1:243–244. The quote is taken from 1:244. Along with al-Shāfiʿī, Ibn Qudāmah also cites Mālik, ʿAṭāʾ, and (Muḥammad b. Muslim) al-Zuhrī as maintaining the position that the area around the anus is to be included in the definition of "genitals." Ibn Qudāmah mentions, without giving names, that some jurists consider touching a severed penis to also require ablution.

17. See ʿUmar b. al-Ḥusain al-Khiraqī, *al-Mukhtaṣar fi al-fiqh,* ed. M. Zuhair al-Shāwīsh (Damascus, 1378; reprint, Beirut, 1384), 23.

18. See Ibn Qudāmah, *al-Mughnī,* 1:246.

19. Muḥammad b. al-Ḥasan al-Shaybānī, *Kitāb al-Āthār,* ed. Abū al-Wafā al-Afghānī (Beirut, 1993), 1:35–38. The first and second reports are also cited in al-Shaybānī's recension of the *Muwaṭṭaʾ*, and in his *al-Ḥujjah fi ikhtilāf ahl al-Kūfah wa ahl al-Madīnah* (Lucknow, 1888), 55–58. Also see al-Ṭaḥāwī, *Sharḥ maʿānī al-āthār,* 1:47.

20. This report is cited in Abū Dāʾūd, *Sunan,* 1:182; al-Tirmidhī, *al-Jāmiʿ al-ṣaḥīḥ,* 1:85; al-Nasāʾī, *Sunan,* 1:101; Ibn Mājah, *Sunan,* 1:483; Ibn Ḥanbal, *Musnad,* 4:23; al-Ṭaḥāwī, *Sharḥ maʿānī al-āthār,* 1:76; and Ibn Rushd, *Bidāyat al-mujtahid,* 1:503–505.

21. See, for example, see the discussion of the things that invalidate ablution in Ayātallāh Khomeinī, *Taḥrīr al-wasīlah* (Beirut, 1985), 1:25–26.

22. On the general notion of purity in Islamic law, comparative scholarship has produced a number of conflicting theories, all of which interpret purity laws as symbolic in character. For the earliest attempts to interpret Muslim purity laws from a comparative perspective, see Ignaz Goldziher, "Wasser als Dämonen abwehrendes Mittel," *Archiv für Religionswissenschaft* 13 (1910): 20–46; and Karl Voller, "Die Symbolik des masḥ," *Archiv für Religionswissenschaft* 8 (1905): 97–. Also see the related works of Arent Jan Wensinck, "Die Entstehung der muslimischen Reinheitsgesetzgebung," *Der Islam* 5 (1914): 62–80; and his "Der Herkunft der gesetzlichen Bestimmungen die Reinigung (istinjāʾ oder istitāba) betreffend," *Der Islam* 1 (1910): 101–102. More recently, see Georges-Henri Bousquet, "La pureté rituelle en Islam: Étude de fiqh et de sociologie religieuse," *Revue de l'Histoire des Religions* 138 (1950): 53–71; A. A. Kevin Reinhart, "Impurity/No Danger," *History of Religions* 30 (1990–1991): 1–24; and Marion Holmes Katz, *Body of Text: The Emergence of the Sunnī Law of Ritual Purity* (Albany, 2002). Related analysis can be found in Traki Zannad, *Les lieux du corps en Islam* (Paris, 1994).

23. Al-Qudūrī, *Mukhtaṣar fī al-fiqh,* 20. Also see the discussion of this passage in Ibn al-Humām, *Sharḥ fatḥ al-qadīr ʿalā al-Hidāyah: Sharḥ bidāyat al-mubtadā, maʿa sharḥ al-ʿināyah ʿalā al-Hidāyah* (Cairo, 1389), 1:36–55.

24. See Ibn Rushd, *Bidāyat al-mujtahid,* 1:479–490. For general reports on urine and feces, see al-Bukhārī, *Ṣaḥīḥ,* 4:15–17, 48, 56, 60, 8:7; Muslim, *Ṣaḥīḥ,* 2:72–73, 75–79, 3:20, 4:105; Abū Dāʾūd, *Sunan,* 1:61, 64; al-Nasāʾī, *Sunan,* 1:86–87, 112–113; Ibn Mājah, *Sunan,* 1:94; Mālik b. Anas, *al-Muwaṭṭaʾ,* 2:11; al-Dārimī, *Sunan,* 1:10; and ʿAlī b. ʿUmar al-Dāraquṭnī, *Sunan* (Beirut, 1980), 1:56.

For reports on gas, see al-Bukhārī, *Ṣaḥīḥ,* 4:4; Muslim, *Ṣaḥīḥ,* 3:98–99; Abū Dāʾūd, *Sunan,* 1:67; al-Nasāʾī, *Sunan,* 1:114; al-Tirmidhī, *al-Jāmiʿ al-ṣaḥīḥ,* 1:56; Ibn Mājah, *Sunan,* 1:74; al-Dārimī, *Sunan,* 1:47; Ibn Khuzaymah, *Ṣaḥīḥ* (Beirut, 1970), 1:18 (27); Aḥmad b. al-Ḥusayn al-Bayhaqī, *al-Sunan* (Karachi, 1989), 1:117; ʿAbd al-Razzāq, *al-Muṣannaf,* 534; Ibn Abī Shaybah, *Kitāb al-muṣannaf al-aḥādīth wa al-āthār,* 2:429; and al-Ṭabarānī, *al-Muʿjam al-kabīr,* 7:166. Many of these reports include the distinction that ablution is required only for gas when it makes a sound or has an odor.

On other substances issuing from the urethal and anal openings, such as prostatic fluid, see Mālik b. Anas, *al-Muwaṭṭaʾ,* 2:13; al-Bukhārī, *Ṣaḥīḥ,* 4:13; Muslim, *Ṣaḥīḥ,* 3:4; Abū Dāʾūd, *Sunan,* 1:6; al-Nasāʾī, *Sunan,* 1:7; Ibn Mājah, *Sunan,* 1:13; al-Dārimī, *Sunan,* 1:49; al-Bayhaqī, *al-Sunan,* 1:115; Ibn Khuzaymah, *Ṣaḥīḥ,* 18–22; Aḥmad b. ʿAlī Abū Yaʿlā, *al-Muʿjam* (Beirut, 1989), 1, 266 (314); Ibn Ḥibbān, *Ṣaḥīḥ* (Cairo, 1952), 1087–1090; ʿAbd al-Razzāq, *al-Muṣannaf,* 1:610; and al-Ṭaḥāwī, *Sharḥ maʿānī al-āthār,* 1:47.

25. On blood, see Mālik b. Anas, *al-Muwaṭṭaʾ,* 2:11–12; al-Dāraquṭnī, *Sunan,* 1:56; and Ibn Rushd, *Bidāyat al-mujtahid,* 1:484–485. On pus, see Ibn Ḥanbal, *Musnad,* 3:17, 5:431, 6:117; and al-Dāraquṭnī, *Sunan,* 1:56. On vomit, see al-Tirmidhī, *al-Jāmiʿ al-ṣaḥīḥ,* 1:64; al-Dārimī, *Sunan,* 4:24; Abū Dāʾūd, *Sunan,* 14:32; Ibn Ḥanbal, *Musnad,* 5:431; al-Dāraquṭnī, *Sunan,* 1:56; al-Ṭaḥāwī, *Sharḥ maʿānī al-āthār,* 2:96; ʿAbdallāh b. ʿAlī Ibn al-Jārūd, *Muntaqā min al-sunan al-musnadah ʿan Rasūl Allāh* (Beirut, 1952), 150; Ibn Khuzaymah, *Ṣaḥīḥ,* 1958; and al-Bayhaqī, *al-Sunan,* 1:144.

26. See Ibn Rushd, *Bidāyat al-mujtahid,* 1:485–518.

27. Al-Qudūrī, *Mukhtaṣar fī al-fiqh,* 21; Ibn al-Humām, *Sharḥ fatḥ al-qadīr,* 1:56–68.

28. See Ibn Rushd, *Bidāyat al-mujtahid,* 1:483–485.

29. See ibid., 1:484–485.

30. This is also evident from legal opinions concerning the purification of people with incontinence of urine or unhealing wounds which continually bleed. According to jurists from different schools, such people can be considered "not impure" for the period following their ablution until the end of their perfor-

mance of the ritual for which they performed the ablution. In effect, most people without such conditions most likely would require ablution more than one time a day. For a discussion of these cases, see Ibn Rushd, *Bidāyah al-mujtahid,* 2:82–90; and Ibn Qudāmah, *al-Mughnī,* 1:421–427.

31. Al-Ṭabarī, *Taʾrīkh al-rusul wa al-mulūk,* 1:108; Rosenthal, *The History of al-Ṭabarī,* 270; al-Ṭabarī, *Jāmiʿ al-bayān fī tafsīr al-Qurʾān,* on Q 6:98. Also see Ismāʿīl b. ʿUmar Ibn Kathīr, *Qiṣaṣ al-anbiyāʾ,* ed. Yūsuf ʿAlī Budaywī (Damascus and Beirut, 1992), 20.

32. For reports on the lack of defecation associated with the Israelites' eating of the manna in the wilderness of wandering, see Ibn Kathīr, *Tafsīr al-Qurʾān al-ʿaẓīm,* on Q 2:57. On the use of terminology, see Aḥmad b. Fāris al-Qazwīnī, *Ḥulīyat al-fuqahāʾ,* ed. ʿAbdallāh b. ʿAbd al-Muḥsin al-Turkī (Beirut, 1403); and Muḥammad b. Aʿlā b. ʿAlī al-Tahānawī, *Kashshāf iṣṭilāḥāt al-funūn,* ed. Aloys Sprenger and others (Calcutta, 1862), 112.

33. For the report that Adam and Eve were clothed with feathers, like wild birds, given on the authority of Muḥammad b. Qays, see al-Ṭabarī, *Taʾrīkh al-rusul wa al-mulūk,* 1:82. For the report, given on the authority of Wahb b. Munabbih, that Adam and Eve's genitals were covered by light, see Ibn Kathīr, *Tafsīr al-Qurʾān al-ʿaẓīm,* on Q 7:26. For the report that Adam and Eve had fingernails covering their genitals, see al-Ṭabarī, *Jāmiʿ al-bayān fī tafsīr al-Qurʾān,* on Q 7:22; and al-Thaʿlabī, *Qiṣaṣ al-anbiyāʾ,* 32. For comparative works on the significance of Adam and Eve's coverings in the garden of Eden, see Stephen Lambden, "From Fig Leaves to Fingernails: Some Notes on the Garments of Adam and Eve," in *A Walk in the Garden,* ed. Paul Morris and Debora Sawyer, Journal for the Study for the Old Testament Supplemental Series 136 (Sheffield, 1992), 74–91; and Sebastian P. Brock, "Clothing Metaphors as a Means of Theological Expression in Syriac Tradition," in *Typus, Symbol, Allegorie bei den östlichen Vätern und ihren Parallelen im Mittelalter,* ed. Margot Schmidt (Eichstatt, 1981), 11–40.

34. Ibn Kathīr, *Tafsīr al-Qurʾān al-ʿaẓīm,* on Q 7:22. Ibn Kathīr remarks that this report is considered less reliable because it does not go back to the time of the prophet Muḥammad. On celibacy in the garden of Eden, see Simonetta Calderini, "Woman, 'Sin' and 'Lust': The Fall of Adam and Eve according to Classical and Modern Muslim Exegesis," in *Religion and Sexuality,* ed. Michael A. Hayes, Wendy Porter, and David Tombs, Studies in Theology and Sexuality 2, Roehampton Institute London Papers 4 (Sheffield, 1998), 49–63; and Gary Anderson, "Celibacy or Consummation in the Garden? Reflections on Early Jewish and Christian Interpretations of the Garden of Eden," *Harvard Theological Review* 82 (1989): 121–148.

According to the *Umm al-kitāb,* trans. P. Filippani-Ronconi (Naples, 1966), question 7:220 (p. 97), Adam and Eve were endowed with genitals and breasts only after being cast down to earth. Also see W. Ivanow, "Umm al-kitab," *Der Islam* 23 (1936): 1–13.

35. See al-Ṭabarī, *Taʾrīkh al-rusul wa al-mulūk,* 1:85–87. A similar account mentioning Muzdalifah and Jamʿ is found only in Muḥammad b. ʿAlī al-Shawkānī, *Fatḥ al-qadīr* (Beirut, 1998), on Q 2:35–39. The account in al-Shawkānī is also attributed to Ibn ʿAbbās by Ibn Saʿd and Ibn ʿAsākir.

36. See al-Ṭabarī, *Taʾrīkh al-rusul wa al-mulūk,* 1:132–133; Rosenthal, *The History of al-Ṭabarī,* 303.

37. See, for example, al-Qurṭubī, *al-Jāmiʿ li-aḥkām al-Qurʾān*, on Q 7:20 and 20:120.

38. See al-Ṭabarī, *Jāmiʿ al-bayān fī tafsīr al-Qurʾān,* on Q 2:36; al-Ṭabarī, *Taʾrīkh al-rusul wa al-mulūk,* 1:109–110; Rosenthal, *The History of al-Ṭabarī,* 280–281; and Ibn Kathīr, *Tafsīr al-Qurʾān al-ʿaẓīm,* on Q 2:36–38. On the first pilgrimage of Adam to Mecca, see the ḥadīth reports collected in al-Suyūṭī, *al-Durr al-manthūr,* on Q 2:36. Also see al-Azraqī, *Akhbār Makkah,* 1:36–44, on both incidents.

39. See al-Ṭabarī, *Taʾrīkh al-rusul wa al-mulūk,* 1:107; Rosenthal, *The History of al-Ṭabarī,* 278; and al-Thaʿlabī, *Qiṣaṣ al-anbiyāʾ*, 32. See the English translation in William Brinner, *ʿArāʾis al-Majālis fī Qiṣaṣ al-Anbiyāʾ; or, "Lives of the Prophets" as Recounted by Abū Isḥāq Aḥmad ibn Muḥammad ibn Ibrāhīm al-Thaʿlabī* (Leiden, 2002), 55.

40. Al-Ṭabarī, *Taʾrīkh al-rusul wa al-mulūk,* 1:128–129; Rosenthal, *The History of al-Ṭabarī,* 299. Rosenthal translates *sunbulah* or *sunbalah* as "wheat" but notes (299n814) that it also means "ear of corn." The term and its plurals are found in the Quran five times, twice in Q 2:261 in a parable, and three times in the Joseph story (Q 12:43, 46, 47) as the seven "grains" which the seven cows eat in the dream interpreted by Joseph. Whether the term refers to "corn" or "wheat," it is employed with the connotation of cultivated produce.

41. See al-Ṭabarī, *Taʾrīkh al-rusul wa al-mulūk,* 1:127–128; Rosenthal, *The History of al-Ṭabarī,* 298. There is another parallel here with the seven grains of wheat in the Joseph story (Q 12:46–47).

42. See the report given on the authority of Qatādah in al-Ṭabarī, *Taʾrīkh al-rusul wa al-mulūk,* 1:123–124; Rosenthal, *The History of al-Ṭabarī,* 294–295, in which God provides Adam with cattle for the purpose of sacrifice and the making of clothing.

43. See al-Ṭabarī, *Taʾrīkh al-rusul wa al-mulūk,* 1:127–128; Rosenthal, *The History of al-Ṭabarī,* 298. Also see al-Ṭabarī, *Jāmiʿ al-bayān fī tafsīr al-Qurʾān,* on Q 2:36; and al-Masʿūdī, *Murūj al-dhahab,* 1:61.

44. See Abū Dāʾūd, *Sunan,* 14:28; Ibn Mājah, *Sunan,* 7:18; al-Dārimī, *Sunan,* 4:26; ʿAbd al-Razzāq, *al-Muṣannaf,* 7522; Ibn Khuzaymah, *Ṣaḥīḥ,* 3:226 (1963); al-Ṭaḥāwī, *Sharḥ maʿānī al-āthār,* 2:98–99; al-Bayhaqī, *al-Sunan,* 4:265; and Ibn

al-Jārūd, *Muntaqā min al-sunan al-musnadah ʿan Rasūl Allāh*, 386. On this ḥadīth report, see the comments of Muḥammad b. ʿAbdallāh al-Ḥākim, *al-Mustadrak ʿalā al-Ṣaḥīḥayn*, 5 vols. (Cairo, 1997), 1:427; and Ibn Ḥibbān, *Ṣaḥīḥ*, 899.

45. For a discussion of these positions relative to the ḥadīth reports of Thawbān and Rāfiʿ bt. Khudayj, see Ibn Rushd, *Bidāyat al-mujtahid*, 3:164–173.

46. See Mālik b. Anas, *al-Muwaṭṭaʾ*, 18:30–32. This is also the position of al-Shāfiʿī and Sufyān al-Thawrī, based on the ḥadīth report transmitted by ʿIkrimah on the authority of Ibn ʿAbbās that the prophet Muhammad cupped himself while he was fasting. For this ḥadīth report, see al-Bukhārī, *Ṣaḥīḥ*, 30:32; Abū Dāʾūd, *Sunan*, 14:29; al-Tirmidhī, *al-Jāmiʿ al-ṣaḥīḥ*, 6:61; al-Bayhaqī, *al-Sunan*, 4:267; and Ibn Abī Shaybah, *Kitāb al-muṣannaf al-aḥādīth wa al-āthār*, 2:163. For the claim that the ḥadīth of Ibn ʿAbbās abrogates that given by Thawbān, see Ibn Rushd, *Bidāyat al-mujtahid*, 3:172–173; and al-Shawkānī, *Nayl al-awṭār* (Beirut, 1998), 11:6. See al-Shāfiʿī, *Kitāb al-umm*, 1:106, who holds that bleeding does not break the fast but that it is better not to participate in bloodletting if it is not necessary. The Ḥanafīs hold that cupping does not break the fast, and they do not consider it to be reprehensible for the person fasting. See al-Ṭaḥāwī, *Sharḥ maʿānī al-āthār*, 1:350.

47. On the issue of menstruating and breaking the fast, see al-Bukhārī, *Ṣaḥīḥ*, 6:6–8, 19–20, 24, 28–29, 30:41; Muslim, *Ṣaḥīḥ*, 3:62–66; Abū Dāʾūd, *Sunan*, 1:104, 107–109, 112, 114–116; al-Tirmidhī, *al-Jāmiʿ al-ṣaḥīḥ*, 1:93–96; al-Nasāʾī, *Sunan*, 1:133–134, 137, 3:2; Ibn Mājah, *Sunan*, 1:114, 115; al-Dārimī, *Sunan*, 1:80, 84, 90, 93; Mālik b. Anas, *al-Muwaṭṭaʾ*, 2:97, 98, 100, 104, 105; and al-Shawkānī, *Nayl al-awṭār*, 2:19.

48. See Khomeinī, *Taḥrīr al-wasīlah*, 262.

49. See al-Shawkānī, *Nayl al-awṭār*, 2:19, where the distinction made for menstruation and its connection to the religion of women is attributed to the prophet Muhammad in a ḥadīth report given on the authority of Abū Saʿīd. The same account is related in al-Thaʿlabī, *Qiṣaṣ al-anbiyāʾ*, 33; Brinner, *ʿArāʾis al-Majālis fī Qiṣaṣ al-Anbiyāʾ; or, "Lives of the Prophets"*, 55. According to ʿAbdallāh b. al-Shaykh Muḥammad al-Nawawī, *Saḥīḥ Muslim bi-sharḥ Muḥyī al-Dīn al-Nawawī*, 19 vols. (Beirut, 1994), the difference between missed prayers (which the menstruating women does not make up) and missed fast days (which the menstruating woman does make up) relates to the frequency of the prayer relative to that of the fast. See al-Shāfiʿī, *Kitāb al-umm*, 1:63–64.

50. On these ḥadīth reports and the discussion of their relation, see Abū Dāʾūd, *Sunan*, 14:32; al-Tirmidhī, *al-Jāmiʿ al-ṣaḥīḥ*, 6:24–25; Ibn Mājah, *Sunan*, 7:16; Ibn Ḥanbal, *Musnad*, 2:498; al-Dārimī, *Sunan*, 4:26; Ibn al-Jārūd, *Muntaqā min al-sunan al-musnadah ʿan Rasūl Allāh*, 140; al-Dāraquṭnī, *Sunan*, 2:184; al-Ḥākim, *al-Mustadrak*, 15:22; al-Bayhaqī, *al-Sunan*, 4:219; Ibn Khuzaymah, *Ṣaḥīḥ*,

3:226; Ibn Ḥibbān, *Ṣaḥīḥ,* 907; al-Ḥusayn b. Masʿūd al-Baghawī, *Sharḥ al-sunnah,* 5 vols. (Beirut, 1971), 3:488; and al-Shawkānī, *Nayl al-awṭār,* 11:7.

51. See Mālik b. Anas, *al-Muwaṭṭaʾ,* 18:47; al-Zurqānī, *Sharh al-Zurqānī ʿalā Muwaṭṭaʾ al-Imām Mālik,* 18:202; and ʿAbd al-Salām b. Saʿid Saḥnūn, *al-Mudawwanah al-kubrā* (Beirut, 1994), 1:271, where the ḥadīth of Ibn ʿUmar is attributed to the prophet Muhammad, and another report given on the authority of Abū Saʿīd al-Khudrī. The same position is stated in Ibn Abī Zayd, *al-Risālah,* 160.

52. For an overview of the positions, see Ibn Rushd, *Bidāyat al-mujtahid,* 3:173–175. Also see al-Shāfiʿī, *Kitāb al-umm,* 1:106; and Ibn Qudāmah, *al-Mughnī,* 4:368–369.

53. For this report, see Ibn Mājah, *Sunan,* 7:20; al-Dāraquṭnī, *Sunan,* 2:184; and al-Ṭaḥāwī, *Sharḥ maʿānī al-āthār,* 2:88–89, who says that the report is weak.

54. For this report, see al-Bukhārī, *Ṣaḥīḥ,* 30:23; Muslim, *Ṣaḥīḥ,* 13:12; Ibn Mājah, *Sunan,* 7:20; Abū Dāʾūd, *Sunan,* 14:34; al-Tirmidhī, *al-Jāmiʿ al-ṣaḥīḥ,* 6:32; Ibn Khuzaymah, *Ṣaḥīḥ,* 3:246; Ibn al-Jārūd, *Muntaqā min al-sunan al-musnadah ʿan Rasūl Allāh,* 794; al-Bayhaqī, *al-Sunan,* 4:229–230; al-Baghawī, *Sharḥ al-sunnah,* 3:479, and al-Ṭaḥāwī, *Sharḥ maʿānī al-āthār,* 2:92.

55. See al-Shāfiʿī, *Kitāb al-umm,* 1:108.

56. See Mālik b. Anas, *al-Muwaṭṭaʾ,* 18:19. This is also discussed in Ibn Rushd, *Bidāyat al-mujtahid,* 3:173–175.

57. See Mālik b. Anas, *al-Muwaṭṭaʾ,* 18:18, and see 18:13, 14, 16. See the discussion of this in al-Zurqānī, *Sharḥ al-Zurqānī ʿalā Muwaṭṭaʾ al-Imām Mālik,* 2:218–222. Ibn Abī Zayd, *al-Risālah,* 160–162, simply states that kissing out of passion is forbidden during the daylight hours of the month of Ramadan, and ʿAbd al-Majīd b. Ibrāhīm al-Sharnūbī, *Taqrīb al-maʿānī ʿalā matn al-Risālah li-Abī Zayd al-Qayrawānī,* 99, explains that kissing down out of mercy or kindness is not prohibited.

58. See Ibn Qudāmah, *al-Mughnī,* 4:360–364 (489).

59. See Muḥammad b. ʿAlī Ibn Bābūyah, *ʿIlal al-sharāʾiʿ* (Qum, 1957–1958), 2:80.

60. Al-Qudūrī, *Mukhtaṣar fī al-fiqh,* 20. Also see Ibn al-Humām, *Sharḥ fatḥ al-qadīr,* 1:56–68.

61. See al-Qudūrī, *Mukhtaṣar fī al-fiqh.* Also see Ibn al-Humām, *Sharḥ fatḥ al-qadīr,* 1:56–68. For a more detailed discussion of the different conditions in which sexual intercourse (which might not include the emission of semen) with something other than the vagina of a woman, such as an anus or the vagina of an animal, breaks the fast, see Ibn Qudāmah, *al-Mughnī,* 4:372–380.

62. See Khomeinī, *Taḥrīr al-wasīlah,* 262–263.

63. On the requirement of completing the fast of a person who has died, see

al-Bukhārī, *Ṣaḥīḥ,* 30:42; Muslim, *Ṣaḥīḥ,* 13:153–158; Abū Dā᾿ūd, *Sunan,* 14:42; al-Tirmidhī, *al-Jāmiʿ al-ṣaḥīḥ,* 5:31, 6:22; al-Nasā᾿ī, *Sunan,* 5:116; Ibn Ḥanbal, *Musnad,* 1:239, 5:359; al-Shawkānī, *Nayl al-awṭār,* 11:22; Mālik b. Anas, *al-Muwaṭṭa᾿,* 18:42–43; and al-Shāfiʿī, *Kitāb al-umm,* 2:114.

64. On the understanding of *zakāt* as offering, see the definitions of the word in Ibn Manẓūr, *Lisān al-ʿArab,* 3:1849, s.v. "Zakāt"; al-Fīrūzābādī, *Qāmūs al-muḥīṭ,* 2:464; and Aḥmad b. Muḥammad al-Fayyūmī, *al-Miṣbāḥ al-munīr,* 2 vols. (Beirut, 1978), 1:346. Also see the discussions in Ibn al-Humām, *Sharḥ fatḥ al-qadīr,* 2:153; Muḥammad b. Aḥmad al-Shirbīnī, *Mughnī al-muḥtāj ilā maʿrifat maʿānī alfā᾿ al-minhāj* (Beirut, 1994) 1:367; and Aḥmad b. Ghunaym al-Nafrāwī, *al-Fawākih al-dawānī,* 2 vols. (Cairo, 1955), 1:378. Also see the remarks of the editor of Ibn Rushd, *Bidāyat al-mujtahid,* 3:56–58n1.

65. Ibn Rushd, *Bidāyat al-mujtahid,* 3:71.

66. For an example of items apparently excluded for practical purposes, see the exemption on giving offering for gold and silver used as ornamentation in Ibn Rushd, *Bidāyat al-mujtahid,* 3:71–74. There are two ḥadīth reports relative to this position. One, transmitted on the authority of Jābir b. ʿAbdallāh, records that the prophet Muhammad said: "There is no offering for ornamentation." On this ḥadīth report, see ʿAbd al-Raḥmān b. ʿAlī Ibn al-Jawzī, *al-Taḥqīq,* 8 vols. (Cairo, 2001), 2:374; Ibn Abī Shaybah, *Kitāb al-muṣannaf al-aḥādīth wa al-āthār,* 3:155; and al-Shāfiʿī, *Kitāb al-umm,* 1:228. A longer ḥadīth, reported on the authority of the grandfather of ʿUmar b. Shuʿayb, can be found in Abū Dā᾿ūd, *Sunan,* 9:3; al-Tirmidhī, *al-Jāmiʿ al-ṣaḥīḥ,* 5:10 (632); al-Nasā᾿ī, *Sunan,* 23:19; Ibn Abī Shaybah, *Kitāb al-muṣannaf al-aḥādīth wa al-āthār,* 3:153; al-Dāraquṭnī, *Sunan,* 2:112; and al-Bayhaqī, *al-Sunan,* 4:140.

67. Al-Qudūrī, *Mukhtaṣar fī al-fiqh,* 55. Also see the text with commentary in Ibn al-Humām, *Sharḥ fatḥ al-qadīr,* 2:183–186. That this is also the opinion of Zufar is found in al-Marghīnānī, *al-Hidāyah,* 1:108. Compare al-Sarakhsī, *Kitāb al-mabsūṭ,* 2:149–188.

68. See Ibn Rushd, *Bidāyat al-mujtahid,* 3:73–74.

69. For the first ḥadīth, see al-Bukhārī, *Ṣaḥīḥ,* 24:45; Muslim, *Ṣaḥīḥ,* 12:8–9; Abū Dā᾿ūd, *Sunan,* 9:11; al-Tirmidhī, *al-Jāmiʿ al-ṣaḥīḥ,* 5:3, 8; al-Nasā᾿ī, *Sunan,* 23:16, 18; Ibn Mājah, *Sunan,* 8:4, 15; Ibn Abī Shaybah, *Kitāb al-muṣannaf al-aḥādīth wa al-āthār,* 3:151; al-Dāraquṭnī, *Sunan,* 2:127; and al-Bayhaqī, *al-Sunan,* 4:117. For the second ḥadīth, see al-Marghīnānī, *al-Hidāyah,* 1:108; and Ibn al-Humām, *Sharḥ fatḥ al-qadīr,* 2:183–184.

70. This detail is mentioned by Muḥammad b. Maḥmūd al-Bābartī in his *Sharḥ ʿināyah ʿalā al-Hidāyah,* printed in Ibn al-Humām, *Sharḥ fatḥ al-qadīr,* 2:184.

71. See al-Marghīnānī, *al-Hidāyah,* 1:108; and Ibn al-Humām, *Sharḥ fatḥ al-qadīr,* 2:183–184.

72. See Ibn Rushd, *Bidāyat al-mujtahid,* 3:74–76. The different opinions are based upon the interpretation of a ḥadīth report which says offering is required for free-grazing sheep and goats. See Abū Dā᾽ūd, *Sunan,* 9:4; al-Tirmidhī, *al-Jāmi*ʿ *al-ṣaḥīḥ,* 5:4; Ibn Mājah, *Sunan,* 8:9; Ibn Abī Shaybah, *Kitāb al-muṣannaf al-aḥādīth wa al-āthār,* 3:121–122; al-Ḥākim, *al-Mustadrak,* 1:392–393; and al-Bayhaqī, *al-Sunan,* 4:88.

73. See al-Qudūrī, *Mukhtaṣar fī al-fiqh,* 55; and Ibn al-Humām, *Sharḥ fatḥ al-qadīr,* 2:186–189.

74. On the requirement of *zakāt* for these three types of animals, see Ibn Ḥanbal, *Musnad,* 5:179, 230, on cows; Abū Dā᾽ūd, *Sunan,* 9:12; al-Tirmidhī, *al-Jāmi*ʿ *al-ṣaḥīḥ,* 5:5; al-Nasā᾽ī, *Sunan,* 23:8; Ibn Mājah, *Sunan,* 8:12, 16; al-Dārimī, *Sunan,* 3:5; and Mālik b. Anas, *al-Muwaṭṭa*᾽, 17:24, on cattle; al-Bukhārī, *Ṣaḥīḥ,* 24:36–38; Abū Dā᾽ūd, *Sunan,* 9:4–5, 12; al-Tirmidhī, *al-Jāmi*ʿ *al-ṣaḥīḥ,* 5:4; al-Nasā᾽ī, *Sunan,* 23:4–5, 7, 10; Ibn Mājah, *Sunan,* 8:9–10, 16; al-Dārimī, *Sunan,* 3:3, 6, 35; and Mālik b. Anas, *al-Muwaṭṭa*᾽, 17:23, on camels; and al-Bukhārī, *Ṣaḥīḥ,* 24:37; Abū Dā᾽ūd, *Sunan,* 9:5, 12; al-Tirmidhī, *al-Jāmi*ʿ *al-ṣaḥīḥ,* 5:4; al-Nasā᾽ī, *Sunan,* 23:5, 10, 15, Ibn Mājah, *Sunan,* 8:13, 16; al-Dārimī, *Sunan,* 3:4, and Mālik b. Anas, *al-Muwaṭṭa*᾽, 17:23, on goats and sheep.

75. See al-Qudūrī, *Mukhtaṣar fī al-fiqh,* 55; and Ibn al-Humām, *Sharḥ fatḥ al-qadīr,* 2:186–189.

76. See Ibn Rushd, *Bidāyat al-mujtahid,* 3:78–81.

77. See Mālik b. Anas, *al-Muwaṭṭa*᾽, 17:19–22; al-Suyūṭī, *Tanwīr al-ḥawālik: Sharḥ Muwaṭṭa*᾽ *al-Imām Mālik,* 2 vols. (Cairo, 1969), 17:19–22; al-Zurqānī, *Sharḥ al-Zurqānī* ʿ*alā Muwaṭṭa*᾽ *al-Imām Mālik,* 17:19–22; Saḥnūn, *al-Mudawwanah al-kubrā,* 1:377–382; Ibn Abī Zayd, *al-Risālah,* 169–171; and al-Shāfiʿī, *Kitāb al-umm,* 1:37–40.

78. See al-Qudūrī, *Mukhtaṣar fī al-fiqh,* 58; al-Sarakhsī, *Kitāb al-mabsūṭ,* 2:149–188, 3:1–15; and Ibn al-Humām, *Sharḥ fatḥ al-qadīr,* 2:241–257.

79. On requiring *zakāt* for olive oil, see Ibn Rushd, *Bidāyat al-mujtahid,* 3:80, where the decisive factor is whether or not olive oil is used for food. See Mālik b. Anas, *al-Muwaṭṭa*᾽, 17:20; and al-Shāfiʿī, *Kitāb al-umm,* 1:34–36.

80. On honey, see Ibn Rushd, *Bidāyat al-mujtahid,* 3:77, where a single ḥadīth report is cited in al-Tirmidhī, *al-Jāmi*ʿ *al-ṣaḥīḥ,* 5:9, requiring a skin of honey for every ten skins harvested. This ḥadīth is also found in al-Bayhaqī, *al-Sunan,* 4:126, but is also dismissed as weak and compared to reports in which the prophet states that offering is required on honey. See Abū Dā᾽ūd, *Sunan,* 9:12; and Mālik b. Anas, *al-Muwaṭṭa*᾽, 17:39.

81. See Abū Bakr al-Ḥaddād, *Jawharat al-nayyirah* (Istanbul, 1885), 1:153.

82. In addition to the reports already cited, see al-Tirmidhī, *al-Jāmi*ʿ *al-ṣaḥīḥ,* 5:13; and Abū Dā᾽ūd, *Sunan,* 9:17.

83. On onions, see al-Ḥaddād, *Jawharat al-nayyirah,* 1:153. On figs, see Ibn

Rushd, *Bidāyat al-mujtahid,* 3:80, where the opinion of Ibn Ḥabīb is cited, based on the exegesis of Q 6:141. For a general overview and lists of what produce is and is not subject to *zakāt,* see al-Zurqānī, *Sharḥ al-Zurqānī ʿalā Muwaṭṭaʾ al-Imām Mālik,* 2:182–183; and Ibn Qudāmah, *al-Mughnī,* 4:155–167.

84. For a sample listing of the foods to be given, see, Mālik b. Anas, *al-Muwaṭṭaʾ* 17:3; Ibn Ḥanbal, *Musnad,* 5:179, 228; Ibn Mājah, *Sunan,* 8:16; and Ibn Rushd, *Bidāyat al-mujtahid,* 3:78–80.

85. See, for example, the exegesis on Q 20:117–119. Also see al-Ṭabarī, *Taʾrīkh al-rusul wa al-mulūk,* 123–124; Rosenthal, *The History of al-Ṭabarī,* 294–295, on the thirty types of fruit coming down from the garden of Eden to Adam.

86. See, for example, the account of the first domesticated animals sent down to Adam and Eve so that they could make clothing from them in al-Ṭabarī, *Taʾrīkh al-rusul wa al-mulūk,* 123–124; Rosenthal, *The History of al-Ṭabarī,* 294–295.

87. See Mālik b. Anas, *al-Muwaṭṭaʾ,* 17:9. Neither is offering incumbent upon categories of people representing a social stratification that did not exist in the garden of Eden. See Muslim, *Ṣaḥīḥ,* 44:37; Abū Dāʾūd, *Sunan,* 9:25; al-Tirmidhī, *al-Jāmiʿ al-ṣaḥīḥ,* 5:23; Ibn Mājah, *Sunan,* 8:27; Mālik b. Anas, *al-Muwaṭṭaʾ,* 17:29; and Ibn Rushd, *Bidāyat al-mujtahid,* 3:59–62.

88. For this account, see al-Shawkānī, *Fatḥ al-qadīr,* on Q 2:35–39.

89. See, for example, Ibn Mājah, *Sunan,* 8:3; Abū Dāʾūd, *Sunan,* 9:4; al-Tirmidhī, *al-Jāmiʿ al-ṣaḥīḥ,* 5:3; al-Nasāʾī, *Sunan,* 23:18–19; al-Dārimī, *Sunan,* 3:7; and Mālik b. Anas, *al-Muwaṭṭaʾ,* 17:5, 7, 11.

90. See al-Bukhārī, *Ṣaḥīḥ,* 24:1; and Ibn Ḥajar, *Fatḥ al-bārī,* 2:202–207.

91. Ibn Mājah, *Sunan,* 7:44.

92. See al-Bukhārī, *Ṣaḥīḥ,* 30:2, 9, 77:78; Muslim, *Ṣaḥīḥ,* 13:158, 162–164; and al-Tirmidhī, *al-Jāmiʿ al-ṣaḥīḥ,* 6:54.

93. See al-Bukhārī, *Ṣaḥīḥ,* 30:2, 97:35, 50; Muslim, *Ṣaḥīḥ,* 13:164–165; and Zayd b. ʿAlī, *Majmuʿ al-fiqh,* ed. E. Griffini (Milan, 1919), 420.

94. See al-Tirmidhī, *al-Jāmiʿ al-ṣaḥīḥ,* 6:23; Ibn Mājah, *Sunan,* 7:50; and Ibn Rushd, *Bidāyat al-mujtahid,* 3:65–66.

95. On *zakāt* and the fast as a means to subdue carnal desires, see al-Bukhārī, *Ṣaḥīḥ,* 30:10, 67:3; Muslim, *Ṣaḥīḥ,* 16:1; al-Nasāʾī, *Sunan,* 22:43, 26:3; and Ibn Mājah, *Sunan,* 9:1. On prayer during the fast as forgiveness of sins, see al-Bukhārī, *Ṣaḥīḥ,* 2:27, 28, 30:6, 31:1, 32:1; Muslim, *Ṣaḥīḥ,* 6:173–175; Abū Dāʾūd, *Sunan,* 6:1; al-Tirmidhī, *al-Jāmiʿ al-ṣaḥīḥ,* 6:1, 82; al-Nasāʾī, *Sunan,* 20:3, 22:39–40, 47:21; Ibn Mājah, *Sunan,* 5:173, 7:2; al-Dārimī, *Sunan,* 4:54; and Mālik b. Anas, *al-Muwaṭṭaʾ,* 6:1–2.

96. See al-Azraqī, *Akhbār Makkah,* 1:39. Ibn Isḥāq reports that after arriving in Mecca, Adam stayed there until the time of his death. For other reports that Adam wanted to return to the garden of Eden, see al-Azraqī, *Akhbār Makkah,*

1:41; and al-Ṭabarī, *Taʾrīkh al-rusul wa al-mulūk,* 1:132–134; Rosenthal, *The History of al-Ṭabarī,* 302–304.

97. See al-Azraqī, *Akhbār Makkah,* 1:36.

98. See Ibn Kathīr, *Tafsīr al-Qurʾān al-ʿaẓīm,* on Q 2:39; and al-Zamakhsharī, *al-Kashshāf ʿan ḥaqāʾiq ghawāmiḍ al-tanzīl wa ʿuyūn al-aqāwīl fī wujūh al-taʾwīl,* on Q 2:39.

99. See al-Ṭabarī, *Taʾrīkh al-rusul wa al-mulūk,* 1:132–134; Rosenthal, *The History of al-Ṭabarī,* 302–304.

100. On Adam's being made custodian of the jeweled Kaʿbah, see the report of Wahb b. Munabbih in al-Azraqī, *Akhbār Makkah,* 1:37–38. Ibn ʿAbbās reports that the angels had circumambulated this Kaʿbah for one thousand years before Adam's arrival. Kaʿb al-Aḥbār also describes this jeweled Kaʿbah when asked by ʿUmar b. al-Khaṭṭāb about it. Another report by Wahb gives more details on the description of the jewels out of which the Kaʿbah was constructed. For these reports, see al-Azraqī, *Akhbār Makkah,* 1:39–41. On Adam's role in initiating the pilgrimage to Mecca, see al-Azraqī, *Akhbār Makkah,* 1:43–44, citing ʿUthmān b. Sājj, Abū Hurayrah, and ʿAbdallāh b. Abī Sulaymān, a client of the Banī Makhzūm.

101. Al-Qudūrī, *Mukhtaṣar fī al-fiqh,* 66–67. Also see Ibn al-Humām, *Sharḥ fatḥ al-qadīr,* 2:439–442.

102. See Ibn Qudāmah, *al-Mughnī,* 5:129–157.

103. See Ibn Bābūyah, *ʿIlal al-sharāʾiʿ,* 2:112 and 168 (on clothing), 2:159 (on perfume), and 2:164–167 (on kohl and ejaculation).

104. See Ibn Rushd, *Bidāyat al-mujtahid,* 3:277 and 392 (shoes), 3:275–279 and 392 (clothing), 3:280–284 (perfume), 3:284–289 (hunting), 3:289–291 (marriage), 3:381–383 (nails and hair), 3:386–389 (sex).

105. For the complete text translated here, see Ibn al-Humām, *Sharḥ fatḥ al-qadīr,* 2:446, where the ḥadīth report is transmitted on the authority of Ibn ʿUmar. Ibn al-Humām also cites additional reports transmitted on the authority of Abū Bakr, ʿAbdallāh, and Ibrāhīm b. Yazīd al-Jawzī. The same ḥadīth report is cited in al-Marghīnānī, *al-Hidāyah,* 2:150–151, with the interpretation that the "crying" refers to raising one's voice in the saying the ritual statement of pilgrimage (talbīyah). Ibn Mājah, *Sunan,* 25:6, cites a similar ḥadīth report in which the prophet Muhammad is first asked what is required for the pilgrimage, then what is the pilgrim, then what is the pilgrimage. Ibn Mājah, *Sunan,* 25:16, contains the ḥadīth report with only the "crying and bleeding" part. The same is cited by al-Tirmidhī, *al-Jāmiʿ al-ṣaḥīḥ,* 7:14, and in 7:4 al-Tirmidhī cites a ḥadīth report mentioning only the "provisions and luggage" portion, on the authority of Abū Bakr.

106. See, for example, al-Ṭabarī, *Jāmiʿ al-bayān fī tafsīr al-Qurʾān,* on Q 7:22; and al-Ṭabarī, *Taʾrīkh al-rusul wa al-mulūk,* 1:79–87.

107. See, for example, the reports in al-Bukhārī, *Ṣaḥīḥ,* 25:17, 26:10; Muslim, *Ṣaḥīḥ,* 15:6–10; Abū Dā'ūd, *Sunan,* 11:30; al-Nasā'ī, *Sunan,* 24:29, 42, 44; and Mālik b. Anas, *al-Muwaṭṭa',* 20:18–20.

108. See Ibn Rushd, *Bidāyat al-mujtahid,* 3:280–281. For the ḥadīth, see al-Bukhārī, *Ṣaḥīḥ,* 66:12; Muslim, *Ṣaḥīḥ,* 15:1; Abū Dā'ūd, *Sunan,* 11:11; al-Tirmidhī, *al-Jāmi' al-ṣaḥīḥ,* 7:20; al-Nasā'ī, *Sunan,* 24:6; Ibn al-Jārūd, *Muntaqā min al-sunan al-musnadah 'an Rasūl Allāh,* 447; Ibn Khuzaymah, *Ṣaḥīḥ,* 4:191–193; al-Ṭaḥāwī, *Sharḥ ma'ānī al-āthār,* 2:126–127; and al-Bayhaqī, *al-Sunan,* 5:56.

109. See the overview of these opinions in Ibn Rushd, *Bidāyat al-mujtahid,* 3:283–285. According to Abū Ḥanīfah, this prohibition is because marshmallow gives off a pleasant scent and is therefore like henna, the application of which is also prohibited. Abū Yūsuf and al-Shaybānī say that the marshmallow helps to quench the thirst and keeps away drowsiness, so both Abū Yūsuf and al-Shaybānī require the giving of alms only for the pilgrim who applies marshmallow, while Abū Ḥanīfah requires a blood offering. On this discussion, see Ibn al-Humām, *Sharḥ fatḥ al-qadīr,* 2:24–41. On the prohibition of clothing dyed with turmeric, saffron, and safflower, see al-Marghīnānī, *al-Hidāyah,* 2:150–151; and Ibn al-Humām, *Sharḥ fatḥ al-qadīr,* 2:442–443.

110. See Ibn Qudāmah, *al-Mughnī,* 5:147–150. Other ritual applications of perfume are closely tied to entrance into the garden of Eden. Perfume is applied after purification from menstruation, for Friday prayers, and to wash the dead in preparation for their entrance into the garden of Eden. Mālik b. Anas cites a report in which 'Ā'ishah states that she applied perfume to the head of the prophet Muhammad only before he entered into his sacralized state and again after he left this state. The perfume may be applied to mark the transition between one state and the next, but it must not be reapplied or noticeable from an earlier application when the pilgrim is sacralized.

For the application of perfume after purification from menstruation, see al-Bukhārī, *Ṣaḥīḥ,* 6:12–14; and al-Dārimī, *Sunan,* 1:115. For the application of perfume for Friday prayers, see al-Bukhārī, *Ṣaḥīḥ,* 11:3, 6, 19; Muslim, *Ṣaḥīḥ,* 7:7–8; al-Tirmidhī, *al-Jāmi' al-ṣaḥīḥ,* 4:29, al-Nasā'ī, *Sunan,* 14:6, 11; Ibn Mājah, *Sunan,* 5:80; al-Dārimī, *Sunan,* 2:191; and Mālik b. Anas, *al-Muwaṭṭa',* 2:113. On the use of perfume for washing the dead to prepare for entrance into the garden of Eden, see al-Bukhārī, *Ṣaḥīḥ,* 23:8–9, 13, 15, 20–22, 28:20; Muslim, *Ṣaḥīḥ,* 11:36, 40, 15:93–103; al-Tirmidhī, *al-Jāmi' al-ṣaḥīḥ,* 7:105, 8:15; al-Nasā'ī, *Sunan,* 21:28, 32, 34–46, 24:46, 85; Ibn Mājah, *Sunan,* 6:8, 25:87; and al-Dārimī, *Sunan,* 5:35.

For this report attributed to 'Ā'ishah, and other ḥadīth reports relative to this question, see al-Bukhārī, *Ṣaḥīḥ,* 25:39; Muslim, *Ṣaḥīḥ,* 15:1; Abū Dā'ūd, *Sunan,* 11:11; al-Tirmidhī, *al-Jāmi' al-ṣaḥīḥ,* 7:20; Ibn Mājah, *Sunan,* 25:18; Mālik b. Anas, *al-Muwaṭṭa',* 20:7; Ibn al-Jārūd, *Muntaqā min al-sunan al-musnadah 'an Rasūl Allāh,* 414; al-Dārimī, *Sunan,* 5:10; Ibn Ḥanbal, *Musnad,* 2:181–182, 192,

200; Ibn Khuzaymah, *Ṣaḥīḥ,* 4:155; al-Ṭaḥāwī, *Sharḥ maʿānī al-āthār,* 2:130; and al-Dāraquṭnī, *Sunan,* 2:274.

111. See Ibn Qudāmah, *al-Mughnī,* 5:119–131.

112. On this ḥadīth, see Mālik b. Anas, *al-Muwaṭṭaʾ,* 20:8; al-Bukhārī, *Ṣaḥīḥ,* 25:21; Muslim, *Ṣaḥīḥ,* 15:1; Abū Dāʾūd, *Sunan,* 11:32; al-Tirmidhī, *al-Jāmiʿ al-ṣaḥīḥ,* 7:19; Ibn Mājah, *Sunan,* 25:19; al-Nasāʾī, *Sunan,* 24:15; Ibn al-Jārūd, *Muntaqā min al-sunan al-musnadah ʿan Rasūl Allāh,* 416; al-Dārimī, *Sunan,* 5:10; al-Ṭaḥāwī, *Sharḥ maʿānī al-āthār,* 2:134–135; al-Dāraquṭnī, *Sunan,* 2:230; al-Bayhaqī, *al-Sunan,* 5:46–49; Abū Yaʿlā, *al-Muʿjam,* 9:304; Ibn Qudāmah, *al-Mughnī,* 5:119; and Ibn Rushd, *Bidāyat al-mujtahid,* 3:275.

113. See Ibn Rushd, *Bidāyat al-mujtahid,* 3:275–279. For the ḥadīth report, see Abū Dāʾūd, *Sunan,* 11:32 (1864); al-Tirmidhī, *al-Jāmiʿ al-ṣaḥīḥ,* 7:19 (833); al-Nasāʾī, *Sunan,* 24:15; and al-Bayhaqī, *al-Sunan,* 5:46–49. Also see the reports cited in al-Shāfiʿī, *Kitāb al-umm,* 2:160–163.

114. For reports linking the origins of sewing and sewn clothing to Adam and Eve's realization that they were naked and had genitals, see al-Ṭabarī, *Taʾrīkh al-rusul wa al-mulūk,* 1:82; Ibn Kathīr, *Tafsīr al-Qurʾān al-ʿaẓīm,* on Q 7:26; and al-Ṭabarī, *Jāmiʿ al-bayān fī tafsīr al-Qurʾān,* on Q 7:22.

115. See Abū Yūsuf, *Ikhtilāf Abī Ḥanīfah wa Ibn Abī Laylā,* ed. Abū al-Wafāʾ al-Afghānī (Cairo, 1357), 138–140. Also see al-Shāfiʿī, *Kitāb al-umm,* 2:229, in which the penalty of a sheep or cow is required for anyone, pilgrim or not, cutting down a tree in the sanctuary of Mecca. There is no penalty, however, for the pilgrim cutting down a tree outside the sanctuary, in contrast to a penalty for the pilgrim who hunts prey outside the sanctuary.

116. See al-Ṭaḥāwī, *Ikhtilāf al-fuqahāʾ,* published in English as *Imām Ṭaḥāwī's Disagreement of the Jurists,* ed. M. Maʿṣūmī (Islamabad, 1391), *Ikhtiṣār ikhtilāf al-fuqahāʾ,* 57. On this text, see M. Maʿṣūmī, "Imām Ṭaḥāwī fī Kitāb ikhtilāf al-fuqaqhāʾ," in *Fikr-u Naẓar* (Islamabad, 1973), 193–194.

On the sanctuary of Medina and its restrictions, see Mālik b. Anas, *al-Muwaṭṭaʾ,* 45:10–13; al-Bukhārī, *Ṣaḥīḥ,* 29:1, 4, 56:71, 74, 58:10, 17, 60:10, 70:28, 85:21, 96:5, 6; Muslim, *Ṣaḥīḥ,* 15:455–459, 462, 463, 471, 472, 478–479; Abū Dāʾūd, *Sunan,* 11:95; al-Tirmidhī, *al-Jāmiʿ al-ṣaḥīḥ,* 46:67; Ibn Mājah, *Sunan,* 25:102; and Ibn Ḥanbal, *Musnad,* 1:170. For other restrictions on activities in Medina, see Abū Zayd ʿUmar b. Shabbah, *Kitāb taʾrīkh al-madīnah al-munawwarah,* ed. ʿAlī Muḥammad Dandal and Yāsīn Saʿd al-Dīn Bayān (Beirut, 1996), 1:23–29.

117. See al-Ṭaḥāwī, *Sharḥ maʿānī al-āthār,* 57–58. There are no references in the six books to this ḥadīth report.

118. For another list of the prohibitions and the penalties associated with the pilgrim and the sanctuary at Mecca, see Aḥmad b. Yaḥyāʾ al-Murtaḍā, *ʿUyūn al-azhār fī fiqh al-aʾimmah al-aṭhār* (Beirut, 1975), 167–175.

119. See, for example, the discussion of these penalties in Aḥmad b. ʿAlī al-

Jaṣṣāṣ, *Aḥkām al-Qur'ān,* ed. ʿAbd al-Salām Muḥammad ʿAlī Shāhīn (Beirut, 1994), on Q 5:95; ʿImād al-Dīn al-Harrāsī, *Aḥkām al-Qur'ān* (Beirut, 1985), on Q 5:95; Abū Bakr Ibn al-ʿArabī, *Aḥkām al-Qur'ān,* ed. Muḥammad ʿAbd al-Qādir ʿAṭā' (Beirut, n.d.), on Q 5:95; and Ibn al-Humām, *Sharḥ fatḥ al-qadīr,* 3:49–127.

120. Ibn Abī Zayd, *al-Risālah,* 182. According to al-Sharnūbī, *Taqrīb al-maʿānī ʿalā matn al-Risālah,* 120, the choice of sacrifice is preferred when there is a domesticated animal established as being equivalent to the wild prey killed. In *Sharḥ ʿalā matn al-Risālah,* Zarrūq (365) states that the choice of which penalty to pay is left up to the pilgrim but that determining the domesticated animal equivalent to the wild prey killed is the decision of the two just men mentioned in Q 5:95. Other opinions are discussed in Ibn Nājī, *Sharḥ ʿalā matn al-Risālah,* 365–366.

121. On feeding the poor as a penalty for breaking the fast, see al-Bukhārī, *Ṣaḥīḥ,* 30:29–31, 51:20, 69:13, 84:204; Muslim, *Ṣaḥīḥ,* 13:81–82; Abū Dā'ūd, *Sunan,* 14:38; and al-Tirmidhī, *al-Jāmiʿ al-ṣaḥīḥ,* 6:28. On animal sacrifice, see al-Bukhārī, *Ṣaḥīḥ,* 27:2, 30:68; Muslim, *Ṣaḥīḥ,* 15:174; al-Nasā'ī, *Sunan,* 24:49; and Mālik b. Anas, *al-Muwaṭṭa',* 20:62–64, 155, 158–159, 255. On paying for breaking the fast, see al-Bukhārī, *Ṣaḥīḥ,* 30:39; Muslim, *Ṣaḥīḥ,* 13:149–150; Abū Dā'ūd, *Sunan,* 14:2; al-Nasā'ī, *Sunan,* 36:63; and al-Dārimī, *Sunan,* 4:29.

122. See Ibn Qudāmah, *al-Mughnī,* 5:162–165 (no marriage), 165–169 (no vaginal sex, whether ejaculating or not), 168–169 (nonvaginal sex, whether ejaculating or not), 170–171 (kissing, whether ejaculating or not), and 171–174 (lustful looking).

123. See Abū Dā'ūd, *Sunan,* 11:9; al-Tirmidhī, *al-Jāmiʿ al-ṣaḥīḥ,* 7:100; and Ibn Mājah, *Sunan,* 25:12. Also see al-Bukhārī, *Ṣaḥīḥ,* 6:27, 25:145; and al-Nasā'ī, *Sunan,* 3:23.

124. See al-Qudūrī, *Mukhtaṣar fī al-fiqh,* 72–74; al-Marghīnānī, *al-Hidāyah,* 2:173–176; Ibn al-Humām, *Sharḥ fatḥ al-qadīr,* 3:24–41; and al-Sarakhsī, *Kitāb al-mabsūṭ,* 3:118–121.

125. See Ibn Rushd, *Bidāyat al-mujtahid,* 3:289–292. Also see Mālik b. Anas, *al-Muwaṭṭa',* 20:22; and al-Zurqānī, *Sharḥ al-Zurqānī ʿalā Muwaṭṭa' al-Imām Mālik,* on 20:22, relating the ḥadīth about the marriage of Maymūnah taking place after she was out of her sacralized state according to the ḥadīth reports preserved in Muslim, Abū Dā'ūd, al-Tirmidhī, and Ibn Mājah (2:264–265).

126. See Mālik b. Anas, *al-Muwaṭṭa',* 20:48; Muslim, *Ṣaḥīḥ,* 14:9; Abū Dā'ūd, *Sunan,* 11:18; al-Nasā'ī, *Sunan,* 24:18; Ibn Mājah, *Sunan,* 9:66; Ibn al-Jārūd, *Muntaqā min al-sunan al-musnadah ʿan Rasūl Allāh,* 156; al-Ṭaḥāwī, *Sharḥ maʿānī al-āthār,* 2:268; al-Dāraquṭnī, *Sunan,* 11:14; al-Bayhaqī, *al-Sunan,* 5:65; al-Shāfiʿī, *Kitāb al-umm,* 1:316; al-Dārimī, *Sunan,* 11:2; Ibn Khuzaymah, *Ṣaḥīḥ,*

4:183; al-Baghawī, *Sharḥ al-sunnah,* 4:149; and Ibn Rushd, *Bidāyat al-mujtahid,* 3:289–292).

127. See Ibn Rushd, *Bidāyat al-mujtahid,* 1:479–518.

128. See ibid., 1:485–490.

129. See al-Shāfiʿī, *Kitāb al-umm,* 1:26.

130. See ibid., 1:26–28.

131. Ibid., 1:28. See also the long comment on this passage by the editor of *Kitāb al-umm,* 1:28–32. For a brief discussion of the two views attributed to al-Shāfiʿī, see al-Murtaḍā, *ʿUyūn al-azhār,* 44–45.

132. See Ibn Rushd, *Bidāyat al-mujtahid,* 1:489–490. For the report transmitted by ʿUmar b. al-Khaṭṭāb, see Mālik b. Anas, *al-Muwaṭṭaʾ,* 2:10. It is also transmitted on the authority of Abū Hurayrah, ʿAlī b. Abī Thābit, Ibn Masʿūd, and al-Shaʿbī. See al-Bayhaqī, *al-Sunan,* 1:120; and al-Ṭabarānī, *al-Muʿjam al-kabīr,* 9:285. For a slightly different opinion from Ḥanafī scholars, see al-Qudūrī, *Mukhtaṣar fī al-fiqh,* 20; and Ibn al-Humām, *Sharḥ fatḥ al-qadīr,* 1:36–55.

133. See Ibn Rushd, *Bidāyat al-mujtahid,* 1:490. Also see Mālik b. Anas, *al-Muwaṭṭaʾ,* 2:9–11; al-Zurqānī, *Sharḥ al-Zurqānī ʿalā Muwaṭṭaʾ al-Imām Mālik,* 75–79; Saḥnūn, *al-Mudawwanah al-kubrā,* 1:119; Ibn Abī Zayd, *al-Risālah,* 84; and al-Sharnūbī, *Taqrīb al-maʿānī ʿalā matn al-risālah,* 24.

134. This ḥadīth report is taken from Muslim, *Ṣaḥīḥ,* 3:23. The same ḥadīth report transmitted on the authority of Zayd b. Thābit is found in al-Dārimī, *Sunan,* 1:51; al-Nasāʾī, *Sunan,* 1:121–122; Ibn Ḥanbal, *Musnad,* 5:184, 188–192; and al-Ṭabarānī, *al-Muʿjam al-kabīr,* 5:139.

135. For a complete list of the transmitters and the sources, see Ibn Rushd, *Bidāyat al-mujtahid,* 1:505–515. For more recent analyses of these ḥadīth reports and their relation to purity laws, see Katz, *Body of Text,* 101–123; and Michael Cook, "Magian Cheese: An Archaic Problem in Islamic Law," *Bulletin of the School of Oriental and African Studies* 47 (1984): 449–467.

136. See Mālik b. Anas, *al-Muwaṭṭaʾ,* 2:5; and al-Shāfiʿī, *Kitāb al-umm,* 1:35. On this report, abrogating the practice of the prophet Muhammad, see ʿUthmān b. ʿAbd al-Raḥmān Ibn al-Salāḥ, *ʿUlūm al-ḥadīth* (Damascus, 1986), 277–278; and Katz, *Body of Text,* 105.

137. See Ibn Rushd, *Bidāyat al-mujtahid,* 1:515. For the report from Jābir b. ʿAbdallāh, see al-Bukhārī, *Saḥīḥ,* 70:18, 20, 26, 53, 58; Muslim, *Saḥīḥ,* 3:90; Abū Dāʾūd, *Sunan,* 1:74–75; al-Tirmidhī, *al-Jāmiʿ al-ṣaḥīḥ,* 1:58–59, 23:27–33; al-Nasāʾī, *Sunan,* 1:122; Ibn Mājah, *Sunan,* 1:65–66, 26:29; al-Dārimī, *Sunan,* 1:51–52; and al-Bayhaqī, *al-Sunan,* 1:155–156. On the abrogation, see ʿUmar b. Aḥmad Ibn Shāhīn, *al-Nāsikh wa al-mansūkh min al-ḥadīth* (Manṣūrah, 1995), 172.

138. See the analysis in Ibn Rushd, *Bidāyat al-mujtahid,* 1:516–518n69. There are a number of different chains of transmission passing through Abū Hurayrah

that go to the prophet Muhammad. Other chains pass through ʿĀʾishah, Ḥudhayfah, Abū Saʿīd, and al-Mughayrah b. Shaʿbah.

139. This ḥadīth is taken from al-Tirmidhī, *al-Jāmiʿ al-ṣaḥīḥ,* 8:17. The same ḥadīth, transmitted with this *isnād*, can be found in Ibn Mājah, *Sunan,* 6:14; ʿAbd al-Razzāq, *al-Muṣannaf,* 3:4007; and Ibn Ḥibbān, *Ṣaḥīḥ,* 751.

140. See al-Tirmidhī, *al-Jāmiʿ al-ṣaḥīḥ,* 8:17–18.

141. See Mālik b. Anas, *al-Muwaṭṭaʾ,* 16:1. Ibn Qudāmah, *al-Mughnī,* 1:256, cites the ḥadīth report of Abū Hurayrah but states that ablution is not required for carrying a corpse.

142. On exceptions made for carrion-eating animals, see al-Bukhārī, *Ṣaḥīḥ,* 59:15–17; Muslim, *Ṣaḥīḥ,* 22:43–49; Abū Dāʾūd, *Sunan,* 16:22; al-Tirmidhī, *al-Jāmiʿ al-ṣaḥīḥ,* 16:17; al-Nasāʾī, *Sunan,* 42:9; Ibn Mājah, *Sunan,* 28:1–2; and al-Dārimī, *Sunan,* 7:2–3. On animals which can be eaten, see al-Nasāʾī, *Sunan,* 42:35; Ibn Mājah, *Sunan,* 29:31; al-Dārimī, *Sunan,* 6:24, 7:5–6; and Abū Dāʾūd, *Sunan,* 26:36. For the ḥadīth which lists the five types of animals allowed to be killed in the *ḥaram* or by pilgrims outside the *ḥaram*, see Ibn Rushd, *Bidāyat al-mujtahid,* 3:370–376; and the many references to the variations of this ḥadīth in different ḥadīth collections in 3:370–375n710.

143. See Khomeinī, *Taḥrīr al-wasīlah,* 1:103.

144. See Ibn Rushd, *Bidāyat al-mujtahid,* 2:66–78, for different examples.

145. See, for example, Katz, *Body of Text,* 103.

146. See Ibn Qudāmah, *al-Mughnī,* 1:254–255.

147. Al-Tirmidhī, *al-Jāmiʿ al-ṣaḥīḥ,* 3:25.

148. See Ibn Taymīyah, *Fiqh al-ṭahārah,* 191–194.

149. See al-Shawkānī, *Nayl al-awṭār,* 1:96.

150. See Abū Dāʾūd, *Sunan,* 1:72; al-Nasāʾī, *Sunan,* 1:113; and Ibn Mājah, *Sunan,* 24:6.

151. See Ibn Rushd, *Bidāyat al-mujtahid,* 505; and Ibn Qudāmah, *al-Mughnī,* 1:254–255.

152. See, for example, al-Ṭabarī, *Jāmiʿ al-bayān fī tafsīr al-Qurʾān,* on Q 2:34–39; and Ibn Kathīr, *Tafsīr al-Qurʾān al-ʿaẓīm,* on Q 2:34–39.

153. See the reports given on the authority of Ibn ʿAbbās, Mujāhid, and al-Ḥasan al-Baṣrī in al-Ṭabarī, *Jāmiʿ al-bayān fī tafsīr al-Qurʾān,* on Q 11:40 and 23:27. Other interpretations of the "tannūr" in Q 11:40 and 23:27 include that it refers to the "face of the earth," the "breaking of the dawn," or the name of a particular location. Mujāhid and al-Shaʿbī relate it to a location in Kufah, and Ibn ʿAbbās to a place in Syria and India. Also see Ibn Manẓūr, *Lisān al-ʿArab,* s.v. "al-tannūr."

154. See Sigmund Freud, "Taboo and Emotional Ambivalence," in his *Totem and Taboo,* trans. James Strachey (New York, 1950), 18–74.

155. See Muslim, *Ṣaḥīḥ,* 3:116–119; Abū Dā'ūd, *Sunan,* 26:11–12; al-Tirmidhī, *al-Jāmiʿ al-ṣaḥīḥ,* 23:40; al-Nasā'ī, *Sunan,* 1:100; Ibn Mājah, *Sunan,* 26:5; and al-Dārimī, *Sunan,* 1:79, 8:34.

156. See al-Bukhārī, *Ṣaḥīḥ,* 30:51; Muslim, *Ṣaḥīḥ,* 13:181–182, 186, 188–193; Abū Dā'ūd, *Sunan,* 14:54, 57; al-Nasā'ī, *Sunan,* 22:76–78. For the injunction against perpetual fasting (wiṣāl), see al-Bukhārī, *Ṣaḥīḥ,* 30:20, 48–50, 86:42, 94:9, 96:5; Muslim, *Ṣaḥīḥ,* 13:55–61; Abū Dā'ūd, *Sunan,* 14:25; al-Tirmidhī, *al-Jāmiʿ al-ṣaḥīḥ,* 6:62; al-Dārimī, *Sunan,* 4:14; and Mālik b. Anas, *Muwaṭṭa',* 18:38–39.

157. The symbolic nature of ritual and its use in delimiting ideal concepts of social order is emphasized in Claude Lévi-Strauss, *Totemism,* trans. Rodney Needham (Boston, 1962), and is expanded upon in Howard Eilberg-Schwartz, *The Savage in Judaism: An Anthropology of Israelite Religion and Ancient Judaism* (Bloomington, 1990), esp. 115–140. Also see Clifford Geertz, "Deep Play: Notes on the Balinese Cockfight," in his *The Interpretation of Cultures* (New York, 1973), 412–453.

## CHAPTER THREE

1. Al-Ṭabarī, *Ta'rīkh al-rusul wa al-mulūk,* 3:262. Also see the account in ʿUthmān b. Aḥmad Ibn al-Ḥawrānī, *al-Ishārāt ilā amākin al-ziyārāt,* ed. Bassām al-Jābī, (Damascus, 1981), 46–47, trans. in Josef W. Meri, "A Late Medieval Syrian Pilgrimage Guide: Ibn al-Ḥawrānī's *al-Ishārāt ilā amākin al-ziyārāt* (Guide to Pilgrimage Places)," *Medieval Encounters* 7 (2001): 35. This account is also mentioned at the beginning of the article by David Margoliouth, "The Relics of the Prophet Mohammed," *Moslem World* 27, no. 1 (1937): 20–27.

On the burial place of Muʿāwiyah's, see Jaʿfar al-Ḥasanī, "Qabr Muʿāwiya b. Abī Sufyān," *Majallat al-Majmaʿ al-ʿIlmī al-ʿArabī* 19 (1944): 434–441. Further discussion of the prophet Muhammad's shirt, including a brief discussion of Muʿāwiyah's burial with it, can be found in August Müller, *Der Islam im Morgen- und Abendland* (Berlin, 1885–1887), 1:161–162. On clothing used as burial shrouds, see al-Bukhārī, *Ṣaḥīḥ,* 34:31, 23:78, 65:115. For examples of clothing said to have curative powers, see ʿAbd al-Raḥmān b. Aḥmad Ibn Rajab, *Kitāb al-dhayl ʿalā ṭabaqāt al-Ḥanābila,* ed. M. Ḥ. al-Fiqī (Cairo, 1952–1953), 2:27; Michael Chamberlain, *Knowledge and Social Practice in Medieval Damascus, 1190–1350,* Cambridge Studies in Islamic Civilization (Cambridge, 1994), 122; and Josef W. Meri, "Aspects of Baraka (Blessings) and Ritual Devotion among Medieval Muslims and Jews," in a special issue of *Medieval Encounters: Jewish, Christian and Muslim Culture in Confluence and Dialogue* 5 (1999): 54.

2. See Nasīm al-Riyāḍ's commentary on the margins of al-Qāḍī ʿIyyāḍ b. Mūsā, *al-Shifā'* (Cairo, 1977), 2:287, in the section on the al-Isrā' and al-Miʿrāj

of the prophet Muhammad. For a discussion of this passage, see Aḥmad Taymūr, *al-Āthār al-nabawīyah* (Cairo, 1391), 82. Also see the reference in Abū al-Faraj al-Isbahānī, *Kitāb al-aghānī* (Cairo, 1970), 16:24.

3. Percy Molesworth Sykes, "A Fourth Journey in Persia, 1897–1901," *Geographical Journal* 19 (1902): 121–173, esp. 167, reports that Iranians place etched carnelian with names of the twelve imams into the mouth of the deceased. Single carnelian beads were placed in the mouths of corpses of early Seleucid burials at Saar on Bahrain. See A. Herling, "Excavation of a Tylos Period Cemetery at Sar (Bahrain)," paper presented at the Seminar for Arabian Studies, Oxford, 1994, 246n126.

On the use of hair and nails in other cultural contexts, see "Wicked Witchery," *Limited Edition: Oxford Times,* October 2003, 17. On other examples of hair burial in the British Isles, see Christopher Hallpike, "Hair," in *Encyclopedia of Religion,* ed. M. Eliade and others (New York, 1987), 6:154–157. On hair and nails in general, see E. E. Sikes and Louis H. Gray, "Hair and Nails," in Hastings and others, *Encyclopedia of Religion and Ethics,* vol. 6, s.v. "hair"; and Edmund R. Leach, "Magical Hair," *Journal of the Royal Anthropological Institute* 88 (1958): 147–164. More specifically focused on Punjabi practices but also useful is P. Hershman, "Hair, Sex and Dirt," *Man,* n.s., 9 (1974): 274–298. A wide variety of examples can be found in Frazer, *The Golden Bough*, vol. 3, *Taboo and the Perils of the Soul,* 258ff.; and G. A. Wilken, *Über das Haaropfer und einige andere Trauergebräuche bei den Völkern Indonesiens* (Amsterdam, 1886–1887), 78ff., particularly on Arab practices involving hair and its symbolism when removed from a corpse.

4. See al-Bukhārī, *Ṣaḥīḥ,* 4:33; and Muslim, *Ṣaḥīḥ,* 15:324–326. A similar report can be found in Abū Dā'ūd, *Sunan,* 2:78. Also see the brief overview of this tradition in Ignaz Goldziher, "Veneration of Saints in Islam," in his *Muslim Studies,* 2:322–323. For information on the hair of the prophet Muhammad deposited with Umm Salamah, see Ibn Kathīr, *al-Bidāyah wa al-nihāyah fī al-ta'rīkh*, 3:19–20.

5. See Ibn Ḥajar, *Fatḥ al-bārī,* on al-Bukhārī, *Ṣaḥīḥ,* 4:33.

6. See al-Qasṭallānī, *Irshād al-sārī li-sharḥ Ṣaḥīḥ al-Bukhārī*, on al-Bukhārī, *Ṣaḥīḥ,* 4:33.

7. See Ibn Ḥanbal, *Musnad,* 4:324. There are several reports that both the prophet Muhammad's hair and his sweat were collected by his followers, but there do not appear to be any traditions regarding this sweat after the death of the prophet Muhammad. For a sample of these reports, see al-Bukhārī, *Ṣaḥīḥ,* 79:41; and Ibn Sa'd, *al-Ṭabaqāt al-kubrā,* ed. E. Sachau (Leiden, 1904–1908), 1:139, 8:313.

8. See Ibn Mājah, *Sunan,* 25:6; and al-Tirmidhī, *al-Jāmi' al-ṣaḥīḥ,* 44:6. In

this ḥadīth report, the prophet Muhammad says that a pilgrim is one who smells and has disheveled hair. For an example of the use of this ḥadīth report to explain the restrictions on cutting hair and nails, see Ibn al-Humām, *Sharḥ fatḥ al-qadīr,* 2:442–443.

9. See Ibn al-Ḥawrānī, *al-Ishārāt ilā amākin al-ziyārāt,* 148–149; Meri, "A Late Medieval Syrian Pilgrimage Guide," 67; ʿAbd al-Raḥmān Ibn al-Jawzī, *Muthīr al-Gharām bi faḍāʾil al-Quds wa al-Shām,* in *Arbaʿ rasāʾil fī faḍāʾil al-Masjid al-Aqṣā* (Nasr City, 2000), 310; and ʿAlī b. Abī Bakr al-Harawī, *Kitāb al-ishārāt ilā maʿrifat al-ziyārāt,* ed. J. Sourdel-Thomine (Damascus, 1953), 8–9. On the pinning of the hair to his hat, see al-Isbahānī, *Kitāb al-aghānī,* 15:12; and Michael Lecker, "King Ibn Ubayy and the Quṣṣāṣ," in *Method and Theory in the Study of Islamic Origins,* ed. Herbert Berg (Leiden, 2003), 29–72, esp. 63.

10. For the biographical information on al-Balawī, see Ibn Ḥajar, *al-Iṣābah fī tamyīz al-ṣaḥābah* (Beirut, 1415), no. 9940, 7:129; Ibn al-Athīr, *Usd al-ghābah* (Beirut, n.d.), no. 5915; and Ibn ʿAbd al-Barr, *al-Istīʿāb fī maʿrifat al-aṣḥāb,* ed. ʿAlī Muḥammad al-Bajāwī, 4 vols. (Cairo, n.d.), no. 3009.

11. Abū Zayd ʿAbd al-Raḥmān b. Muḥammad al-Dabbāgh, *Maʿālim al-aymān fī maʿrifat ahl al-Qayrawān* (Cairo, 1968), no. 609, 1:97. Today the shrine is called the Zāwīyah of Sidī Ṣāḥib. It is located just outside the city walls of Qayrawan.

12. See ibid. 1:97; and Taymūr, *al-Āthār al-nabawīyah,* 85.

13. See ʿAbd al-Ghanī al-Nābulsī, *al-Ḥaḍrah al-unsīyah fī riḥlah al-qudsīyah* (Beirut, 1990), 344; Goldziher, "Veneration of Saints in Islam," 330.

14. See Goldziher, "Veneration of Saints in Islam," 330–331.

15. See Ibn Ḥajar, *al-Durar al-kāminah fī aʿyān al-miʾah al-thāminah,* ed. ʿAbd al-Muʿayin Khān (Hyderabad, 1972), s.v. "ʿAlī b. Muḥammad bl al-Ḥasan al-Khalāṭī"; and Ibn Ḥajar, *Fatḥ al-bārī,* on al-Bukhārī, 71:10.

16. See Ibn Ḥajar, *Fatḥ al-bārī,* 1:139; and Goldziher, "Veneration of Saints in Islam," 327.

17. See Muḥammad b. Shakir al-Kutubī, *Fawāt al-wafayāt* (Beirut, 2000), 1:105; and Goldziher, "Veneration of Saints in Islam," 329.

18. See Goldziher, "Veneration of Saints in Islam," 329–330.

19. See Muḥammad b. ʿAbd al-Raḥmān al-Sakhāwī, *al-Ḍawʾ al-lāmiʿ li-ahl al-qarn al-tasiʿ* (Cairo, 1353–1355; reprint, Beirut, 1966), 4:1220–1221. Ibn al-Zaman was also said to have had in his possession a rock with a footprint of the prophet Muhammad. See Taymūr, *al-Āthār al-nabawīyah,* 86.

20. See ʿAbd al-Qādīr b. Muḥammad al-Nuʿaymī, *al-Dāris fī taʾrīkh al-madāris* (Damascus, 1367–1370), 2:68. Also see the condensed account in ʿAbd al-Bāsiṭ b. Mūsā, *Mukhtaṣar tanbīh al-ṭālib wa irshād al-dāris,* ed. Ṣalāḥ al-Munajjid (Damascus, 1947), 79.

21. See Goldziher, "Veneration of Saints in Islam," 330.

22. See ibid., 329–330; and N. J. G. Kaptein, *Muhammad's Birthday Festival: Early History in the Central Muslim Lands and Development in the Muslim West until the 10th/16th Century* (Leiden, 1993).

23. Al-Nasāʾī, *Sunan,* 8:11. Also see the report in Ibn Ḥanbal, *Musnad,* 4:23. For some of the other uses associated with the saliva of the prophet Muhammad, see Annemarie Schimmel, *And Muḥammad Is His Messenger* (Chapel Hill, 1985), 76; and Meri, "Aspects of Baraka," 111, especially the reports of people receiving his saliva in their dreams.

24. For an overview of these sites, see Taymūr, *al-Āthār al-nabawīyah,* 89–96.

25. Al-Sakhāwī, *al-Ḍawʾ al-lāmiʿ*, 4:437. This report is also discussed briefly by Taymūr, *al-Āthār al-nabawīyah,* 83.

26. See al-Sakhāwī, *al-Ḍawʿ al-lāmiʿ*, 3:912. In this account, the man with the hairs in Jerusalem is referred to as a "shaykh" as opposed to a "rajul ṣāliḥ" in the biography of al-Murshidī himself.

27. See ibid., 7:229.

28. See al-Qasṭallānī, *Kitāb al-shamāʾil min al-mawāhib al-ladunīyah* (Cairo, 1995), 4:254.

29. See ʿAbd al-Raḥmān b. Muḥammad Ibn Abī Ḥātim, *al-Jarḥ wa al-taʿdīl,* ed. ʿAbd al-Raḥmān b. Yaḥyā al-Muʿallimī (Beirut, 1371). For an overview of Ibn Abī Ḥātim's work, see Muḥammad Diyāʾ al-Raḥmān Aʿẓamī, *Dirāsāt fī al-jarḥ wa al-taʿdīl* (Benares, 1983), esp. 297–434.

30. Ibn Abī Ḥātim, *al-Jarḥ wa al-taʿdīl,* 1:7.

31. Ibid.

32. Ibid.

33. See Abū Isḥāq al-Shīrāzī, *Ṭabaqāt al-fuqahāʾ*, ed. Iḥsān ʿAbbās (Beirut, 1970).

34. See ibid., 40–94. This information was also included in Brannon Wheeler, *Applying the Canon in Islam: Authorization and Maintenance of Interpretive Reasoning in Ḥanafī Scholarship* (Albany, 1996).

35. For an overview of this perspective on traveling in search of knowledge, see al-Khaṭīb al-Baghdādī, *al-Riḥlah fī ṭalab al-ḥadīth,* ed. Nūr al-Dīn ʿAttar (Beirut, 1395); and Ibn ʿAbd al-Barr, *Jāmiʿ al-bayān al-ʿilm wa faḍli-hi wa mā yanbaghī fī riwāyati-hi wa ḥamli-hi,* ed. ʿAbd al-Raḥmān Muḥammad ʿUthmān (Cairo, 1968). This practice is also discussed in Goldziher, *Muslim Studies,* 2:168–185; and G. H. A. Juynboll, *Muslim Tradition: Studies in Chronology, Provenance and Authorship of Early Ḥadīth* (Cambridge, 1983), 66–70.

36. On these six books, see the work of Arent Jan Wensinck, *A Handbook of Early Muhammadan Tradition,* 7 vols. (Leiden, 1927); and S. Ali Raza Naqvi, "Prophetic Sunna in the Islamic Legal Framework," *Islamic Studies* 19 (1980): 120–133, esp. 126–128.

37. For further discussion of this point, see Bernard Weiss, *The Search for God's Law: Islamic Jurisprudence in the Writings of Sayf al-Dīn al-Āmidī* (Salt Lake City, 1992), 256–328, esp. 256–269.

38. On this genre, see Juynboll, *Muslim Tradition,* 134–160; and Aʿẓamī, *Dirāsāt fī al-jarḥ wa al-taʿdīl,* 297–434.

39. The main sources for this biographical information are ʿAbd al-Raḥmān b. Yūsuf al-Mizzī, *Tuḥfat al-ashrāf bi-maʿrifat al-aṭrāf,* ed. ʿAbd al-Ṣamad Sharaf al-Dīn (Bhiwandi, 1965–1981); Shams al-Dīn al-Dhahabī, *al-Kāshif fī maʿrifat man la-hu riwāyat fī al-kutub al-sittah,* ed. ʿIzzat ʿAlī ʿĪd ʿAṭiyyah and Mūsā Muḥammad ʿAlī al-Mawshī (Cairo, 1963); and Ibn Ḥajar, *Tahdhīb al-tahdhīb* (Hyderabad, 1325).

40. For the weak transmitters, see al-Bukhārī, *Kitāb al-ḍuʿafāʾ al-ṣaghir* (Allahabad, 1325); al-Nasāʾī, *Kitāb al-ḍuʿafāʾ wa al-matrūkīn* (Beirut, 1985); Muḥammad b. ʿAmr al-ʿUqaylī, *Kitāb al-ḍuʿafāʾ al-kabīr,* ed. ʿAbd al-Muʿṭī Amīn Qalʿajī (Beirut, 1404); Muḥammad Ibn Ḥibbān, *Maʿrifat al-majrūḥīn wa al-ḍuʿafāʾ min al-muḥaddithīn,* ed. ʿAzīz Baygh al-Nawshabāndī al-Qadirī (Hyderabad, 1390); ʿAbdallāh Ibn ʿAdī, *al-Kāmil fī ḍuʿafāʾ al-rijāl,* ed. Suhayl Zakkār (Beirut, 1988); and Ibn Ḥajar, *Lisān al-mīzān* (Hyderabad, 1329–1331; reprint, Beirut, 1407). For the trustworthy transmitters, see Aḥmad al-ʿIjlī, *Taʾrīkh al-thiqāt,* ed. ʿAbd al-Muʿṭī Amīn Qalʿajī (Beirut, 1984); and Ibn Ḥibbān, *Kitāb al-thiqāt,* ed. M. ʿAbd al-Maʿīd Khān (Hyderabad, 1393).

41. On the concept of travel and the restricting of access to authoritative texts as an important aspect of Islamic learning, see Chamberlain, *Knowledge and Social Practice in Medieval Damascus,* passim.

42. For a general overview of the footprint relics, see Shah Muḥammad ʿUmar, *Istishfāʾ wa tawassul bi-āthār al-ṣāliḥīn wa sayyid al-Rasūl* (Delhi, 1391); and René Basset, "Les empreintes merveilleuses," *Revue des Traditions Populaires* 9 (1894): 689–693. There are brief references in Goldziher, "Veneration of Saints in Islam," 330; and A. F. Mehren, *Revue des monuments funéraires du Kerafat ou de la Ville des morts hors du Caire, Mélanges asiatiques tirés du Bulletin de l'Academie imperiale des sciences de St.-Petersbourg* (St. Petersburg, 1871), 533.

43. There are numerous sources which attest to the existence and visitation of the footprint under the Dome of the Rock. See, for example, Mujīr al-Dīn ʿAbd al-Raḥmān b. Muḥammad al-Ḥanbalī, *al-Uns al-jalīl bi-taʾrīkh al-Quds wa al-Khalīl* (Amman, 1973), 2:371; Burhān al-Dīn Ibrāhīm b. Qāḍī al-Ṣalt, *Bāʿith al-nufūs li-ziyārat al-Quds al-maḥrūs,* in *Arbaʿ rasāʾil fī faḍāʾil al-Masjid al-Aqṣā* (Nasr City, 2000), 13; and Shams al-Dīn Muḥammad al-Munhājī al-Suyūṭī, "Ittiḥāf al-akhsāʾ bi-faḍāʾil al-masjid al-aqṣāʾ," *Journal of the Royal Asiastic Society,* n.s., 19 (1887): 258–259. Also see the brief discussion in Taymūr, *al-Āthār al-nabawīyah,* 64–65.

44. The footprint under the Dome of the Rock is criticized as a fake by Ibn

Taymīyah because according to him there are no ḥadīth reports which mention the existence of this relic. See Ibn Taymīyah, *al-Hidāyah al-Islāmīyah* (Cairo, 1990), 1:260; and Aḥmad b. Muḥammad al-Wafā'ī Ibn al-ʿAjamī, *Tanzīh al-muṣṭafā al-mukhtār ʿammā lam yathbat min al-akhbār* (Beirut, n.d.), 21–37. On Ibn Taymīyah's criticism of the practice of touching the footprint of the prophet Muhammad in Damascus, see Muḥammad Umar Memon, *Ibn Taymiyya and Popular Religion* (The Hague, 1976). Also see Ibn Taymīyah, *al-Jawāb al-bāhir fī zuwwāb al-maqābir,* ed. Abū Yaʿlā Muḥammad Ayman al-Shabrāwī (Beirut, 1417).

45. See Ḥasan b. ʿAlī ʿUjaymī and Yaḥyā Maḥmūd Saʿatī, *Ihdāʾ al-laṭāʾif min akhbār al-Ṭāʾif* (Ṭāʾif, 1980), 23–26, in the section on Wajj. Other reports place the footprint in different areas within al-Ṭāʾif.

46. See M. Tamisier, *Voyage en Arabie: Sejour dans le Hedjaz, campagne d'Assir* (Paris, 1840), 1:330–334, 338–339.

47. On this footprint in the village of al-Qadem, see Joseph Toussaint Reinaud, *Monumens arabes, persans et turcs* (Paris, 1828), 2:322. For the reports of the question posed by Gabriel, see al-Bukhārī, *Ṣaḥīḥ,* 8:80, 62:3, 63:45, 64:83, 65: Q4:13, 81:41; Muslim, *Ṣaḥīḥ,* 44:2; al-Tirmidhī, *al-Jāmiʿ al-ṣaḥīḥ,* 46:15; and Ibn Ḥanbal, *Musnad,* 3:91.

48. See Reinaud, *Monumens arabes, persans et turcs,* 2:322.

49. For information on Abū Ayyūb al-Anṣārī, see Shams al-Dīn al-Dhahabī, *Tajrīd asmāʾ al-Ṣaḥābah* (Hyderabad, 1315), 1:161; Ibn ʿAbd al-Barr, *Istīʿāb fī maʿrifat al-aṣḥāb* (Baghdad, 1970), 1:156; and Ibn Ḥajar, *Iṣābah fī tamyīz al-ṣaḥābah* (Baghdad, 1970), 2:98. On the discovery of the tomb, see P. Wittek, "Aywansary," *Annales de l'Histoire de Philosophie et d'Histoire Orientales et Slaves* (1951): 505–510.

50. See Corneille Trumelet, *Les Français dans le désert,* 2d ed. (Paris, 1886), 88.

51. See Joseph-Simon Galliéni, *Voyage au Soudan français (Haut-Niger et pays de Ségou), 1879–1881* (Paris, 1855), 58. The report of these footprints might be related to the cavern of Bakoui, in which were found traces of the footprints of Bechuana and a jinn who preceded humankind to earth. See Julian Girard de Rialle, *La mythologie comparée* (Paris, 1878), 1:197.

52. On this footprint, see R. Hartmann, "al-Ḳadam bei Damaskus," *Orientalische Literaturzeitung* (1913): 115–118. Later the footprint was transferred to the library of Ṣilt Ruqayyah. See M. A. Talass, *Mosquées de Damas* (Beirut, 1943), 230.

53. See the account of the footprints and the dome in ʿAbd al-Ṣamad b. ʿAbdallāh al-Miṣrī, *Manāqib al-quṭb al-nabawī wa al-sharīf al-ʿalawī Sidī Aḥmad al-Badawī: al-Jawāhir al-sanīyah wa al-karamāt Aḥmadīyah* (Cairo, 1991), 128. There is a brief discussion in Taymūr, *al-Āthār al-nabawīyah,* 63.

54. On the Qā'itbay footprints, see Nasīm al-Riyāḍ Sharḥ on the margins of al-Qāḍī ʿIyāḍ, *al-Shifā'*, 2:287. He reports, on the authority of Aḥmad Daḥlān, that the Sultan paid twenty thousand dinars for the footprint and left instructions that it be put in his tomb.

55. On the sultan ʿAbd al-Ḥamīd I, see T. W. Arnold, *The Caliphate* (Oxford, 1924), 165–166. On the footprint buried with him, see T. W. Arnold, "Ḳadam Sharīf," in *Encyclopaedia of Islam*, 4:367–368.

56. On the footprints of the prophet Muhammad in India, see John Burton-Page, "Ḳadam Sharif (India and Pakistan)," in *Encyclopaedia of Islam*, 4:368. Also see Jaʿfar Sharīf, *Qanūn-i Islām*, trans. G. A. Herklots as *Islam in India; or, The Qanun-i-Islam: The Customs of the Musalmans of India*, ed. W. Crooke (Oxford, 1921; reprint, New Delhi, 1972), s.v. "Bārah Wafāt"; Goldziher, "Veneration of Saints in Islam," 330; Edward Sell, *Faith of Islam* (Wilmington, Del., 1976), 245; and Reinaud, *Monumens arabes, persans et turcs*, 2:322n2.

57. For information on the footprints in the Masjid Āthār al-Nabī, see Taymūr, *al-Āthār al-nabawīyah*, 55–56; Basset, "Les empreintes merveilleuses," 689; and X. B. Saintine, *Histoire de l'expédition française en Egypte* (Paris, 1830), 1:461. On the Gawr Mosque footprints, see Burton-Page, "Ḳadam Sharif (India and Pakistan)," 368; and Sharīf, *Qanūn-i Islām*, s.v. "Ghawr."

Richard F. Burton, *The Land of Midian* (London, 1879), 2:83, attributes the Masjid Āthār al-Nabī in Cairo to a mistaken interpretation of the older Egyptian Athor el-Núbí, referring to the goddess "Athor the Gold."

58. On the Topkapi relics, see Taymūr, *al-Āthār al-nabawīyah*, 65. On the Qadam Rasul Building, see Burton-Page, "Ḳadam Sharif (India and Pakistan)," 368.

59. See C. Landberg, *Catalogue de manuscripts arabes provenant d'une bibliothèque privée a el-Medîna et appartenant a la maison E. J. Brill* (Leiden, 1883), 47–48 (no. 178).

60. For these references, see Aḥmad b. Muḥammad al-Maqqarī, *The History of the Mohammedan Dynasties in Spain, Extracted from the Nafhu-t-tíb min ghosni-i-Andalusi-r-rattíb táríkh Lisánu-d-Dín Ibni-i-Khattíb*, trans. Pascual de Gayangos (London, 1840–1843), 1:908; and Reinaud, *Momumens arabes, persans et turcs*, 2:321.

61. See Landberg, *Catalogue de manuscripts arabes*, 47 (no. 178).

62. See Ibn al-Faqīh, *Abrégé du livre des pays*, trans. Henri Massé (Damascus, 1972), 101; ʿAbd al-Raḥmān b. ʿUmar al-Jawbarī, *Kitāb al-mukhtar fi kashf al-asrār* (Cairo, 1898), trans. René Khawam as *Le voile arraché: L'autre visage de l'Islam* (Paris, 1979–1980), 214; Goldziher, "Veneration of Saints in Islam," 327; and Meri, "Aspects of Baraka," 109.

63. See Aḥmad b. Yaḥyā al-Wansharīsī, *al-Miʿyār al-muʿrib: Wa al-jāmiʿ al-*

*mughrib ʿan fatāwā ʿulamāʾ Ifrīqiya wa al-Andalus wa al-Maghrib,* ed. Muḥammad Ḥajjī (Beirut, 1981), 3:545–547. On this reference, see David Powers, *Law, Society, and Culture in the Maghreb, 1300–1500* (Cambridge, 2002).

64. See R. P. A. Dozy, *Dictionnaire détaillé des noms des vètements chez les Arabes* (Amsterdam, 1845; reprint, Beirut, 1969), 421–424; and Goldziher, "Veneration of Saints in Islam," 327.

65. For this account, see Mūsā b. Muḥammad al-Yūnīnī, *Dhayl mirʾāt al-zamām* (Hyderabad, 1954–1961), 2:45–46. Also see the discussion in Meri, "Aspects of Baraka," 63–69.

66. See the report by Chamberlain, *Knowledge and Social Practice in Medieval Damascus,* 49, from a Vatican manuscript of Ibn Shākir. Also see the citation of this reference in Meri, "Aspects of Baraka," 65.

67. On the confiscation by al-Mālik al-Ashraf, see Khalīl b. Aybak al-Ṣafadī, *Kitāb al-wāfī bi al-wafayāt* (Leipzig, 1931), 7:176–178; Ibn al-Jawzī, *Mirʾāt al-Zamān fī taʾrīkh al-aʿyān* (Hyderabad, 1951–1952), 8:713; and J. M. Mouton, "De quelques reliques conservées à Damas au Moyen-Âge: Stratégie politique et religiosité populaire sous les Bourides," *Annales Islamologiques* 27 (1993): 245–254, esp. 247.

68. See Ibn al-Ḥawrānī, *al-Ishārāt ilā amākin al-ziyārāt,* 30.

69. See Mouton, "De quelques reliques conservées à Damas au Moyen-Âge," 246; and Josef W. Meri, *The Cult of Saints among Muslims and Jews in Medieval Syria* (Oxford, 2002), 111n221.

70. On the sandal in the Madrasa al-Dāmāghīya, see ʿAbd al-Qādīr b. Muḥammad al-Nuʿaymī, *al-Dāris fī taʾrīkh al-madāris* (Beirut, 1990), 1:177–182. On the sandal in the Sulṭān al-Ghūrī mausoleum, see ʿAbd al-Raḥmān al-Jabartī, *ʿAjāʾib al-āthār fī al-tarājīm wa al-akhbār* (Cairo, 1959–1967). For the report in al-Nuʿaymi, see Meri, *The Cult of Saints among Muslims and Jews in Medieval Syria,* 64; and idem, "Sacred Journeys to Sacred Precincts: The Cult of the Saints among Muslims and Jews in Medieval Syria" (PhD dissertation, Oxford University, 1998).

71. For an example of these traditions, see Aḥmad b. al-Ḥusayn al-Bayhaqī, *Dalāʾil al-nubūwah* (Beirut, 1405), 1:252–275.

72. On some of these miraculous physical characteristics, see al-Ḥalabī, *al-Sīrah al-Ḥalabīyah,* 3:407; and Arnold, "Ḳadam Sharīf," 369.

73. On the curative powers of the prophet Muhammad's spittle, see Ibn Mājah, *Sunan,* 31:40, 46; al-Bukhārī, *Ṣaḥīḥ,* 4:40, 65 on Q 4:4, 75:5 and 18; Muslim, *Ṣaḥīḥ,* 4:250–253; Ibn Ḥanbal, *Musnad,* 3:486, and al-Dārimī, *Sunan,* 1:56. On the collection of the prophet Muhammad's sweat, see al-Bukhārī, *Ṣaḥīḥ,* 79:41; and Ibn Ḥanbal, *Musnad,* 3:103, 136, 212, 221, 226, 230–231, 239, 287, 6:376; and Sulaymān b. Dāʾūd al-Ṭayālisī, *Musnad* (Hyderabad, 1321), no. 2078.

74. On the Sufi cult of foot touching, see Schimmel, *Deciphering the Signs of*

*God*, 182–183; and Anastase Marie de St. Elie, "Le culte rendu par les musulmans aux sandales de Mahomet," *Anthropos* 5 (1910): 363–366.

75. On this larger list, see Margoliouth, "The Relics of the Prophet Mohammed," 20–27. There is no complete list of these artifacts, and some of those mentioned here are types of which there are multiple copies. Of the various artifacts, the most work has been done on the shoes or sandals of the prophet Muhammad. See Aḥmad b. Muḥammad al-Maqqarī's poem's on the Prophet's shoes, *Fatḥ al-mutaʿālī fī madḥ al-niʿāl* (Hyderabad, 1334). Also see Ibrāhīm b. ʿAyish Ḥamd, *Ḥaqq al-yaqīn fī muʿjizāt khaṭam al-anbiyāʾ wa al-mursalīn* (Medina, 2002); and ʿAbd al-Munʿim ʿAbd al-Rādī Hāshimī, *Muʿjizāt al-anbiyāʾ* (Kuwait, 1999).

For references to the larger caches of relics, see the collection kept by ʿUmar II in Ibn Ḥajar, *Tahdhib al-tahdhīb* (Beirut, 1968), 472. Ibn Ṭūlūn records a procession of relics from Jerusalem to Damascus. See Shams al-Din b. Muḥammad b. ʿAlī b. Ṭūlūn, *Iʿlām al-warā bi-man waliya nāʾiban min al-atrāk bi-Dimashq al-Shām al-kubrā*, ed. M. A. Duhmān (Damascus, 1964), 209. Ibn Kathīr, *al-Bidāyah wa al-nihāyah fī al-taʾrīkh*, 14:50, mentions a Quran codex, a relic (the sandal), and banners of the prophet Muhammad. Ibn Khallikān, *Wafayāt al-aʿyān wa anbāʾ abnāʾ al-zamān*, ed. Muḥammad Muḥyi al-Dīn ʿAbd al-Ḥamīd, (Cairo, 1948–1949), reports that the vizier Tāj al-Dīn b. Ḥinna purchased a cache of relics which he housed in the Ribāṭ Dayr al-Ṭīn south of Cairo. Al-Jabartī, *ʿAjāʾib al-āthār fī al-tarājīm wa al-akhbār*, reports the sudden discovery of the prophet Muhammad's relics in the mausoleum of Sultan al-Ghūrī, including shoes, handwriting, and hairs. For these and other references, see also Goldziher, "Veneration of Saints in Islam," 330–332; and Meri, "Aspects of Baraka," 243.

For references to individual items, see, on the cup, Ibn Ḥajar, *Tahdhīb al-tahdhīb*, 464; and al-Isbahānī, *Kitāb al-aghānī*, 4:189, 21:183; and on the mantle and clothing, Müller, *Der Islam im Morgen- und Abendland*, 161–162; Nurhan Atasoy, "Khirḳa-yi Sharīf," in *Encyclopaedia of Islam*, 5:18–19; and Yāqūt, *Muʿjam al-buldān*, 1, 423, 4. Ibn Baṭṭūṭah, *Riḥlah Ibn Baṭṭūṭah* (Beirut, 1964), 1:95, mentions the kohl pencil and awl. See also Goldziher, "Veneration of Saints in Islam," 327; and Corneille Trumelet, *Les saints de l'Islam: Legendes hagiologiques et croyances algeriennes* (Paris, 1881).

76. There are multiple references to the prophet Muhammad's copy of the Quran, often conflated with other famous copies of the Quran, such as those belonging to ʿAlī b. Abī Ṭālib and specific codices of ʿUthmān. For general overviews, see Meri, "Aspects of Baraka," 240–242; al-Harawī, *Kitāb al-ishārāt ilā maʿrifat al-ziyārāt*, 15:66; Ibn al-Ḥawrānī, *al-Ishārāt ilā amākin al-ziyārāt*, 22; Muḥammad b. ʿĪsā Ibn Kannān, *al-Mawākib al-islāmīya fī al-mamālik wa al-maḥāsin al-shāmīya*, ed. Ḥ. Ismāʿīl (Damascus, 1992–1993), 1:421; Ignaz Goldziher, *Die Richtungen der islamischen Koranauslegung* (Leiden, 1920; reprint, 1970), 274; Th. Nöldeke, *Geschichte des Qorâns* (Göttingen, 1860), 3:8; Ibn Baṭṭūṭah,

*Riḥlah Ibn Baṭṭūṭah*, 105; idem, *Tuḥfat al-nuẓẓār fī gharāʾib al-amṣār wa ʿajāʾib al-asfār*, ed. ʿA.-ʿA. al-Kattānī (Beirut, 1975), 1:207–208; and Muḥammad b. ʿAlī b. Shaddād, *al-Aʿlāq al-khaṭīra fī dhikr umarāʾ al-Shām wa al-Jazīra*, ed. Y. Z. ʿAbbāra (Damascus, 1991), 125. See also Aḥmad b. Yaḥyāʾ al-ʿUmayrī, *Masālik al-abṣār fī mamālik al-amṣār*, ed. A. Z. Bāshā (Cairo, 1924), 1:216; Aḥmad b. Muḥammad al-Maqqarī, *Nafkh al-ṭīb min ghuṣn al-Andalus al-raṭīb*, ed. I. ʿAbbās (Beirut, 1968), 1:605; Shams al-Dīn Dhahabī, *al-ʿIbar fī khabar man ghabar*, ed. M. Zaghlūl (Beirut, 1988), 2:463; and al-Yūnīnī, *Dhayl mirʾāt al-zamān*, 4:92–93. On a Quran shirt of the prophet Muhammad, see the *Oriental* 1, no. 5 (1873): 624; it was given as a gift to the British viceroy in 1873 and then acquired by general Tytler (d. 1813) during the siege of Delhi and sold by his widow in Calcutta, according to Goldziher, "Veneration of Saints in Islam," 330.

77. On the handwritten letters of the prophet Muhammad, see the various references in Goldziher, "Veneration of Saints in Islam," 330–332; and Meri, "Aspects of Baraka," 48. These include a letter the prophet Muhammad addressed to the ancestors of the Banū ʿUqaysh (see Muḥammad b. al-Ḥasan Ibn Durayd, *Kitāb jamharat al-lughah* [Beirut, 1987–1988], 113), a letter giving Syrian places to Tamīm al-Dārī (see Ferdinand Wüstenfeld, *Register zu den genealogischen Tabellen der arabischen Stämme und Familien* [Göttingen, 1853], 442), a letter held by Saʿīd b. Qiyād (see al-Ṭabarī, *Taʾrīkh al-rusul wa al-mulūk*, 3:1143), and a letter to Heraclius held by Alfonso of Spain (see ʿAbd al-Raḥmān b. ʿAbdallāh al-Suhaylī, *al-Rawd al-Unuf* [Cairo, 1332], 1:321; and al-Maqqarī, *The History of the Mohammedan Dynasties in Spain*, 1:684). Also on the letters, see Muhammad Hamidullah, "La lettre du prophète à Héraclius et le sort de l'original," *Arabica* (1955): 97–110; al-Bukhārī, *Ṣaḥīḥ*, 1:6, 56:102, 65:3; Ibn Ḥanbal, *Musnad*, 1:263; al-Yaʿqūbī, *Taʾrīkh al-Yaʿqūbī*, 2:84; Abū ʿUbayd al-Qāsim b. Salām, *Kitāb al-amwāl* (Cairo, 1968), 56; Abū Nuʿaym, *Dalāʾil al-nubūwah* (Hyderabad, 1977), 2:121; Aḥmad b. ʿAlī Qalqashandī, *Ṣubḥ al-aʿshā fī sināʿat al-inshāʾ* (Cairo, 1964), 6:376–377; Ibn al-Qayyim, *Zād al-maʿād fī hadī khayr al-ʿibād* (Beirut, 1979), 3:60; Shams al-Din b. Muḥammad b. ʿAlī b. Ṭūlūn, *Iʿlām al-sāʾilīn ʿan kutub sayyid al-mursalīn* (Beirut, 1983), no. 4; ʿAlī ʿAbd al-Mālik al-Muttaqī, *Kanz al-ʿummāl fī sunan al-aqwāl wa al-afʿāl* (Hyderabad, 1945), 2:5893, 5:5658, 5710, and 5712; Frants Buhl, *Das Leben Muhammeds* (Leipzig, 1930), 245; and Gustav Weil, *Mohammed der Prophet* (Stuttgart, 1843), 198–200.

78. For a brief but useful overview of the classical and contemporary sources on the tomb of the prophet Muhammad in Medina, see Muḥammad b. ʿAbdallāh, *Ayna dufina Rasūl al-Islām?* (Beirut, 1413).

79. See M. J. De Goeje, *Mémoires sur les Carmathes du Bahraïn et le Fatimides* (Leiden, 1886), 106–107; and R. P. A. Dozy, *Die Israeliten zu Mekka von Davids Zeit bis in's fünfte Jahrhundert unsrer Zeitrechnung* (Leipzig, 1864), 172.

80. See al-Ṭabarī, *Jāmiʿ al-bayān fī tafsīr al-Qurʾān*, 2:629, on Q 2:248.

81. See ibid., 2:629, on Q 2:248.

82. It is significant to note, also, that the loss of the ark and the destruction of Jerusalem coincide with the Israelites' loss of God's favor. The exegesis of Q 17:2–9 and 5:20 in Ibn Kathīr claims that the Israelites rejected and killed God's prophets. Also see some of the relevant exegesis on Q 7:142–157 and 2:47–61.

83. Ibn Kathīr, *Tafsīr al-Qurʾān al-ʿaẓīm*, 1:285, on Q 2:248. For the full reports, see al-Ṭabarī, *Jāmiʿ al-bayān fī tafsīr al-Qurʾān*, 2:627–628, on Q 2:248.

84. For some of the biblical associations of Moses and his rod with kingship and authority, see Wayne Meeks, *The Prophet-King: Moses Traditions and the Johannine Christology* (Leiden, 1967), esp. 176–215.

85. For an overview of all these traditions, see Ibn Kathīr, *Qiṣaṣ al-anbiyāʾ*, 308–444. Also see al-Ṭabarī, *Taʾrīkh al-rusul wa al-mulūk* , 1:231–256.

86. See al-Zamakhsharī, *al-Kashshāf ʿan ḥaqāʾiq ghawāmiḍ al-tanzīl wa ʿuyūn al-aqāwīl fī wujūh al-taʾwīl,* 3:319, on Q 28:21–28. In his exegesis of Q 28:21–28, al-Ṭabarī, *Jāmiʿ al-bayān fī tafsīr al-Qurʾān,* 20:43, also explicitly states that Adam took the rod from the garden of Eden.

87. See, for example, al-Zamakhsharī, *al-Kashshāf ʿan ḥaqāʾiq ghawāmiḍ al-tanzīl wa ʿuyūn al-aqāwīl fī wujūh al-taʾwīl,* 3:319–320, on Q 28:21–28.

88. Al-Ṭabarī, *Jāmiʿ al-bayān fī tafsīr al-Qurʾān,* on Q 7:22; and see al-Ṭabarī, *Taʾrīkh al-rusul wa al-mulūk,* 1:79–87.

89. Al-Ṭabarī, *Taʾrīkh al-rusul wa al-mulūk,* 1:81.

90. See Ibn Kathīr, *Tafsīr al-Qurʾān al-ʿaẓīm,* on Q 2:57. Ibn ʿAṭīyah and al-Jawharī identify manna as being like honey, on the basis of Hudhaylī poetry, like that flowing from Eden and the promised land. For the poetry associated with the Banū Hudhayl, see R. Jacobi, "Die Anfänge der arabischen Ġazalpoesie: Abū Ḏuʾaib al-Huḏalī," *Der Islam* 61 (1984): 218–250.

91. For some of these traditions, see al-Bukhārī, *Ṣaḥīḥ,* 74:12; Muslim, *Ṣaḥīḥ,* 51:26; and al-Dārimī, *Sunan,* 20:112.

92. See Ibn Kathīr, *Tafsīr al-Qurʾān al-ʿaẓīm,* on Q 2:57.

93. See al-Ṭabarī, *Jāmiʿ al-bayān fī tafsīr al-Qurʾān,* on Q 6:98. On the notion that manna does not cause defecation, see al-Ṭabarī, *Jāmiʿ al-bayān fī tafsīr al-Qurʾān*; and Ibn Kathīr, *Tafsīr al-Qurʾān al-ʿaẓīm,* on Q 2:57.

94. A number of traditions report that all the fruits of the earth originated in the garden of Eden and were brought down by Adam, either with or without God's explicit consent. See, for example, al-Ṭabarī, *Jāmiʿ al-bayān fī tafsīr al-Qurʾān,* on Q 20:117–119. In this same section, al-Ṭabarī reports that Gabriel brought Adam a bag of grains of wheat from the garden and instructed Adam to distribute the grains in the earth, sowing, harvesting, collecting, husking, winnowing, grinding, kneading, and baking by hand.

95. Ibn Kathīr, *Tafsīr al-Qurʾān al-ʿaẓīm,* on Q 2:57.

96. In a report transmitted on the authority of Ibn ʿAbbās, it is said that God

commanded Adam to slaughter a ram he had sent down from the garden so that Adam and Eve could spin and weave clothes from its wool. See al-Ṭabarī, *Taʾrīkh al-rusul wa al-mulūk,* 1:82.

97. See ibid., 1:82.

98. See Ibn Kathīr, *Tafsīr al-Qurʾān al-ʿaẓīm,* on Q 7:26.

99. See al-Ṭabarī, *Jāmiʿ al-bayān fi tafsīr al-Qurʾān,* on Q 7:22. For the fingernails as covering, also see al-Thaʿlabī, *Qiṣaṣ al-anbiyāʾ*, 32.

100. See, for example, al-Qurṭubī, *al-Jāmiʿ al-aḥkām al-Qurʾān,* on Q 7:20 and 20:120.

101. See al-Thaʿlabī, *Qiṣaṣ al-anbiyāʾ*, 23–25.

102. See al-Ḥalabī, *al-Sīrah al-Ḥalabīyah,* 1:20; and al-Kisāʾī, *Qiṣaṣ al-anbiyāʾ*, ed. Isaac Eisenberg (Leiden, 1922), 28. These traditions are discussed briefly in J. Pedersen, "Ādam," in *Encyclopaedia of Islam,* 1:176–178.

103. On these reports, and the Bayt al-Maʿmūr, see al-Ṭabarī, *Taʾrīkh al-rusul wa al-mulūk,* 1:87–88. Also see the essays reprinted in Henri Corbin, "The Configuration of the Temple of the Kaʿbah as the Secret of the Spiritual Life," in his *Temple and Contemplation,* esp. 183–262.

104. See Wensinck, "The Ideas of the Western Semites Concerning the Navel of the Earth"; and M. J. Kister, "A Booth like the Booth of Moses," *Bulletin of the School of Oriental and African Studies* 25 (1962): 150–155, reprinted in his *Studies in Jahiliyya and Early Islam* (London, 1980), chap. 8.

105. For a brief discussion of the significance of Abraham's building of the Kaʿbah from these five mountains, see Firestone, *Journeys in Holy Lands,* 91, 216n64.

106. For this and much of what follows, see al-Ṭabarī, *Taʾrīkh al-rusul wa al-mulūk,* 1:85–88; and al-Ṭabarī, *Jāmiʿ al-bayān fi tafsīr al-Qurʾān,* on Q 2:127.

107. Two reports, both transmitted on the authority of Ibn ʿAbbās, attribute the reduction of Adam's size to different causes. In the first, God reduces Adam because he is supposed to be expelled from the garden of Eden but still has access. In the second, the angels complain about the breath of Adam. For both of these, see al-Ṭabarī, *Taʾrīkh al-rusul wa al-mulūk,* 1:85–86.

108. Al-Ṭabarī, *Jāmiʿ al-bayān fi tafsīr al-Qurʾān,* on Q 2:127. In another report, it is said that every place Adam stopped on his journey to Mecca became an inhabited or cultivated (ʿimrān) area, whereas the places in between became barren desert.

109. On the concept of Mecca as the "Umm al-Qurā," see Yāqūt, *Muʿjam al-buldān,* 1:254–255, s.v. "Umm al-Qurā."

110. See R. Eklund, *Life between Death and Resurrection According to Islam* (Uppsala, 1941).

111. For an example of early Umayyad attempts to utilize relics to demarcate

territorial claims, see G. R. Hawting, "The Ḥajj in the Second Civil War," in *Golden Roads: Migration, Pilgrimage, and Travel in Medieval and Modern Islam,* ed. Ian Richard Netton (Wiltshire, 1993), 31–42; S. D. Goitein, "The Sanctity of Jerusalem and Palestine in Early Islam," in his *Studies in Islamic History and Institutions* (Leiden, 1966), chap. 7; and M. Kister, "'You Shall Only Set Out for Three Mosques': A Study of an Early Tradition," *Le Muséon* 82 (1969): 173–196.

112. On this inscription, now in the Khalīl Mosque, see Max van Berchem, "La chaire de la mosquée d'Hébron," in *Festschrift Eduard Sachau,* ed. G. Weil (Berlin, 1915), 298–310; L. H. Vincent, E. J. H. MacKay, and F. M. Abel, *Hébron: La Haram el-Khalil* (Paris, 1923); and G. Wiet, "Notes d'epigraphie syro-musulmane," *Syria* 5 (1924): 216–253, who notes that the head was considered parallel to the rock in Jerusalem. For an overview of Fatimid artifact collection, see Caroline Williams, "The Cult of ʿAlid Saints in the Fatimid Monuments of Cairo," pt. 1, "The Mosque of al-Aqmar," pt. 2, "The Mausolea," *Muqarnas* 1 (1983): 37–60.

113. See Williams, "The Cult of ʿAlid Saints in the Fatimid Monuments of Cairo," pt. 1, 38–41. On the different accounts concerning the location of the head, including Damascus, Baalbek, Homs, Aleppo, Raqqa, Medina, and Marw, see Ibn Shahrāshūb, *Manāqib Āl Abī Ṭālib;* Ibn Muyassar, *Akhbār Miṣr* (Cairo, 1981), 38; Mehren, "Tableau général des monumens religieux du Caire," *Mélanges Asiatiques, St. Petersburg* 4 (1855): 309, 338; and Goldziher, "Veneration of Saints in Islam," 322.

114. See Williams, "The Cult of ʿAlid Saints in the Fatimid Monuments of Cairo," pt. 1, 38–41. For a general overview of burial buildings in Islamic contexts, see Thomas Leisten, *Architektur für Tote: Bestattung in architecktonischem Kontext in den Kernländern der islamischen Welt zwischen 3./9. und 6./12. Jahrhundert* (Berlin, 1997); James Dickie (Yaqub Zaki), "Allah and Eternity: Mosques, Madrasas and Tombs," in *Architecture of the Islamic World,* ed. George Michell (London, 1978), 18–47.

115. On this discovery, see al-Maqrizī, *al-Mawāʾiz wa al-iʿtibar bi dhikr al-khiṭāṭ* (Cairo, 1270), 3:437–438; and Williams, "The Cult of ʿAlid Saints in the Fatimid Monuments of Cairo," pt. 1, 38–41.

116. On this, see Williams, "The Cult of ʿAlid Saints in the Fatimid Monuments of Cairo," pt. 1, esp. 37. Williams cites the existence of twenty-seven monuments of the Fatimid period, of which ten are linked to ʿAlid figures. She argues that these buildings "appeared as an architectural expression of an officially sponsored cult of ʿAlid martyrs and saints that was being used to generate support for the government of an Ismaiʿili imamate-caliphate which was being spiritually and politically discounted by historical events" (37).

For studies of pilgrimages in Faṭimid Egypt, see Y. Raghib, "Essai d'inventaire chronologique des guides à l'usage de pèlerins du Caire," *Revue des Études Islamiques* 1 (1973): 259–260; F. DeJong, "Cairene Ziyâra-Days: A Contribution to the Study of Saint Veneration in Islam," *Die Welt des Islams* 17, nos. 1–4 (1929): 26–43; M. Maḥmūd Zaytūn, *al-Qabbārī zāhid al-Iskandariyya* (Cairo, 1968); M. Shāhīn Ḥamza, *al-Sayyida Nafīsa* (Cairo, n.d.); and Ṣalāḥ ʿAzzām, *al-Sayyid ʿAbd al-Raḥīm al-Qināwī* (Cairo, 1970).

117. On this, see al-Maqrizī, *al-Mawāʾiz wa al-iʿtibar bi dhikr al-khiṭāṭ*, 3:449; Louis Massignon, "La cité des morts au Caire (Qarāfa-Darb al-Aḥmar)," *Bulletin de l'Institut Français d'Archéologie Orientale* 57 (1958): 67; and Muḥammad b. Aḥmad Ibn Jubayr, *Riḥlah,* trans. R. J. C. Broadhurst as *The Travels of Ibn Jubayr* (London, 1952). For general information on Egyptian mosques of note, see Suʾād Māhir, *Miṣr wa awliyāʾu-ha al-ṣaliḥūn* (Cairo, 1973).

118. See M. al-Ghaffār al-Hāshimī, *Ādāb ziyārat al-aḍriḥa wa al-qubūr* (Cairo, 1966); Shams al-Dīn Ibn al-Zayyāt, *al-Kawākib al-sayyāra fī tartīb al-ziyāra* (Cairo, 1907); J. Chelhod, "La baraka chez les Arabes ou l'influence bienfaisante du sacré," *Revue de l'Histoire des Religions* 147 (1955): 68–88; and Ignaz Goldziher, "Le culte des saints chez le muselmans," *Revue de l'Histoire des Religions* 2 (1891): 257–351.

119. On Nūr al-Dīn's building projects and their ideological background, see Nikita Elisséeff, "Les monuments de Nūr al-Dīn: Inventaire, notes archéologiques et bibliographiques," *Bulletin d'Études Orientales* 13 (1949): 5–43.

120. For this inventory, see Elisséef, "Les monuments de Nūr al-Dīn," 7–16. Also see M. Sovernhein, "Die arabischen Inschriften von Aleppo," *Der Islam* 15 (1926): 198–199; G. Ploix de Rotrou, *La citadelle d'Alep et ses alentours* (Chatenay-Malabry, 2001), 77; and J. Sauvaget, *Alep: Essai sur le développement d'une grande ville syrienne: Des origines au milieu du IXI siècle* (Paris, 1941), 116.

121. See Elisséef, "Les monuments de Nūr al-Dīn," 19–30; ʿAbd al-Raḥmān b. Ismāʿīl Abū Shāma, *Kitāb al-Rawḍatain fī akhbār al-dawlatain* (Cairo, 1287–1288); K. A. C. Creswell, "The Origin of the Cruciform Plan of Cairene Madrasas," *Bulletin de l'Institut Français d'Archéologie Orientale* 21 (1922): 1–54; K. A. C. Creswell and M. ʿAbd al-ʿAzīz Marqūq, *Masājid al-Qāhirah qabl ʿasr al-mamālīk* (Cairo, 1942); P. Bourgoin, *Précis de l'art arabe* (Paris, 1892); and S. Abdul Hakk and Kh. Moaz, *Aspects de l'ancienne Damas* (Damascus, 1949), 84.

122. See Elisséef, "Les Monuments de Nūr al-Dīn," 31–32.

123. On this *minbar,* which was transported to Jerusalem by Salāḥ al-Dīn, see ibid., 16; al-Masʿūdī, *Murūj al-dhahab,* 19; and Max van Berchem, *Matériaux pour un Corpus Inscriptionum Arabicarum* (Cairo, 1894), 2:393–403 and pls. 29–30.

124. On these other building projects, and on the pilgrimage of Nūr al-Dīn

to Mecca and Medina, see Elisséef, "Les Monuments de Nūr al-Dīn," 31–35; Max van Berchem and Edmond Fatio, *Voyage en Syrie* (Cairo, 1914–1915), 176; M. Sobernheim, "Ḥamāt," in *Encyclopaedia of Islam*, 3:119–121; and Richard F. Burton, *A Pilgrimage to al-Medinah and Meccah* (London, 1885), 2:185.

125. See Ibn al-Ḥawrānī, *al-Ishārāt ilā amākin al-ziyārāt*, 83–83; Meri, "A Late Medieval Syrian Pilgrimage Guide," 48. On Ibn al-Ḥawrānī and the time period when he documented the pilgrimage sites, see E. Geoffroy, *Le soufisme en Égypte et en Syrie sous les derniers Mamelouks et les premiers Ottomans: Orientations spirituelles et enjeux culturels* (Damascus, 1995). On the typology of different types of shrines commemorating different objects and activites associated with prophetic figures, see James Dickie (Yaqub Zaki), "Allah and Eternity," 36–46.

126. See Shams al-Dīn Muḥammad al-Munhājī al-Suyūṭī, *Itḥaf al-akhiṣṣā᾽ bi faḍā᾽il al-Masjid al-Aqṣā*, ed. Ahmad Ramadan Ahmad (Cairo, 1982). See also Amikam Elad, *Medieval Jerusalem and Islamic Worship: Holy Places, Ceremonies, Pilgrimage* (Leiden, 1995). On the earlier period, see M. Rosen-Ayalon, *The Early Islamic Monuments of al-Haram al-Sharif: An Iconographic Study* (Jerusalem, 1989).

127. This list is culled from a number of sources. In addition to sources already cited, see Abū al-Ḥasan ʿAlī b. Muḥammad al-Rubaʿī, *Faḍā᾽il al-Shām wa Dimashq*, ed. S. Munajjid (Damascus, 1951); Abū al-Baqā ʿAbdallāh b. Muḥammad al-Badrī, *Nuzhat al-anām fī maḥāsin al-Shām* (Cairo, 1341); Ibn Faḍlallāh al-ʿUmayrī, *Masālik al-abṣār fī mamālik al-amṣār* (Cairo, 1342/1924); Khalīl al-Ẓāhirī, *Zubda kashf al-mamālik: Tableau politique et administratif de l'Égypte, de la Syrie et du Hidjâz sous la domination des sultans mamloûks du XIIIe au XVe siècle,* ed. Ravaisse (Paris, 1894); R. Hartmann, "Die geographische Nachrichten über Palaestina und Syrien in Khalil az-Zahiris Zubda" (PhD dissertation, Tübingen University; published, Kirchlein, 1907); and Qāḍī Maḥmūd al-ʿAdawi, *Kitāb al-ziyārāt bi-Dimashq*, ed. Ṣalāḥ al-Dīn al-Munajjid (Damascus, 1956). On the pilgrimage guides, see J. Sourdel-Thomine, "Les anciens de pèlerinage damascains d'après les sources arabes," *Bulletin dè Études Orientales* 14 (1952–1954): 65–85. For other travelers' accounts, see M. Gaudefroy-Demombynes, trans., *Les voyages d'Ibn Jobair* (Paris, 1949); and E. Sirrīya, "Ziyārāt of Syria in a Riḥla of ʿAbd al-Ghanī al-Nābulusī (1050/1641–1143/1731)," *Journal of the Royal Asiatic Society* (1979): 109–122. The best overview of these sites and the pilgrimages attached to them can be found in Meri, *The Cult of Saints among Muslims and Jews in Medieval Syria,* passim; R. Hartmann, "Politische Geographie des Mamlukenreiches," *Zeitschrift der Deutschen Morgenländischen Geschellschaft* (1916): 1–40, 477–511; and M. Gaudefroy-Demombynes, *La Syrie à l'époque des Mamelouks* (Paris, 1923). An account of local monasteries, some relevant to these Muslim sites, can be found in Ḥabīb Zayyāt, "Adyār Dimashq wa burru-hā fī

al-Islām," *al-Mashriq* 43 (1949): 80–97. Also see O. Livne-Kafri, "Early Muslim Ascetics and the World of Christian Monasticism," *Jerusalem Studies in Arabic and Islam* 20 (1996): 105–129.

128. For an overview of these sites in Hama, see J. Gaulmier, "Pélerinages populairs à Hama," *Bulletin d'Études Orientales* 1 (1931): 137–152. See Louis Massignon, "Pèlerinages populaires à Bagdad," *Revue du Monde Musulman* 6–13 (December 1908): 641, for examples in Iraq.

129. On the competition over the location of the tomb of Moses, see Joseph Sadan, "Le tombeau de Moïse a Jéricho et a Damas: Une compétition entre deux lieux saints principalement à l'époque ottomane," *Revue des Études Islamiques* 49 (1981): 59–99; Joseph Sadan, "The Tomb of Moses (Maqām Nabī Mūsā): Rivalry between Regions as to Their Respective Holy Places" [in Hebrew], *Near East* (Quarterly of the Israel Oriental Society) 28, nos. 1–2 (1979): 22–38, 220–238; and A. S. Yahuda, "A Muslim Tradition about the Location of Moses' Grave," *Ha-Doar* 30 (1941): 14–15, reprinted in *ʿEver ve ʿArav* (New York, 1946), 283–288. For an overview of the sources relating to the tomb of Moses, see H. Spoer, "Das Nabī-Mūsā-Fest," *Zeitschrift des Deutschen Palästinavereins* 32 (1909): 207–221. On the physical description of the tomb near Jericho, see Sh. Tamari, "Maqām Nabī Mūsā near Jericho" [in Hebrew], *Cathedra for the History of Eretz Israel and Its Yeshuv* 11 (1979): 153–180.

130. On Khalīl and Hebron, see Heribert Busse, "Die Patriarchengräber in Hebron und der Islam," *Zeitschrift des Deutschen Paleastina-Vereins* 114 (1992): 672–687.

131. See Meri, *The Cult of Saints among Muslims and Jews in Medieval Syria,* 6. Also see ʿUmar b. Muḥamad Ibn al-ʿAdīm, *Zubdat al-Ḥalab min taʾrīkh Ḥalab,* ed. S. al-Dahhān (Damascus, 1951–1968); and ʿAbd al-Qādīr b. Muḥammad al-Nuʿaymī, *al-Dāris fī taʾrīkh al-madāris,* ed. Ibrāhīm Shams al-Dīn (Beirut, 1990).

132. On the tomb in the Iraqi village of al-Kifl, see Judah al-Ḥarizi, *Taḥkemoni,* ed. and trans. V. E. Reichert (Jerusalem, 1973), chap. 35, 2:208; twelfth-century Jewish traveler Petaḥiyah of Regensburg in E. N. Adler, *Jewish Travellers in the Middle Ages: A Treasury of Travelogues from 9 Centuries* (London, 1930; reprint, New York, 1966), 84–85; and Yāsīn al-Biqāʿī, "al-Nubdha al-laṭīfa fī al-mazārāt al-sharīfa," Damascus, Maktabat al-Asad, MS, 11386, fol. 41v–42r, cited by Meri, "Aspects of Baraka," 55. For the tomb near Aleppo, in the village of Tādhif or Taduf, see Yāqūt, *Muʿjam al-buldān,* s.v. "Tādhif"; and Rabbi Elfarra of Málaga in Avraham Yaʿari, *Maṣṣaʿot Ereẓ Yisraʾel shel ʿOlim Yehudim mi-Yemei ha Beinayim ve-ʿad Reshit Yemei Shivat Ziyon* (Ramat-Gan, 1976), 110.

133. See *Annales du Musée Guimet,* 7 (1886): 433–434; and Goldziher, "Veneration of Saints in Islam," 330.

134. See Goldziher, "Veneration of Saints in Islam," 330.

135. See Ibn Khallikān, *Wafayāt al-aʿyān wa anbāʾ abnāʾ al-zamān*, 2:191. This Ribāṭ, also known as the Bustān al-Maʿshūq, is located near the Birkat al-Ḥabash, south of Cairo.

136. See ʿAlī Bāshā Mubārak, *al-Khiṭaṭ al-tawfīqīyah al-jadīdah* (Cairo, 1969), 6:52, 11:71; and Goldziher, "Veneration of Saints in Islam," 327.

137. See Ibn Ṭūlūn, *Iʿlām al-warā bi-man waliya nāʾiban min al-atrāk bi-Dimashq al-Shām al-kubrā*, 209.

138. On the open acknowledgment of the reasons for relic acquisiton, see Mouton, "De quelques reliques conservées à Damas au Moyen-Âge," 245–254. On rivalry over the virtues of Jerusalem and Syria, see E. Sivan, "La caractère sacré de Jérusalem aux XIIe–XIIIe siècles," *Studia Islamica* 17 (1976): 149; and ʿIzz al-Dīn ʿAbd al-ʿAzīz ʿAbd al-Salām al-Sulamī, *Targhīb ahl al-Islām fī sukhnā al-Shām* (Beirut, 1998).

139. See the discussion in Meri, "Aspects of Baraka," 68; Ibn al-Ḥawrānī, *al-Ishārāt ilā amākin al-ziyārāt*, 143–147; and Janine Sourdel-Thomine, "Inscriptions arabes de Karak Nuḥ," *Bulletin d'Études Orientales* 12 (1949–1950): 71–84.

140. See Ibn al-Ḥawrānī, *al-Ishārāt ilā amākin al-ziyārāt*. 90–91; and Meri, "Aspects of Baraka," 65.

141. Al-Wansharīsī, *al-Miʿyār al-muʿrib*, 2:545.

142. On the keys, see see J. Sourdel-Thomine, *Clefs et serrures de la Kaʿba* (Paris, 1971); and Butrus Abu-Manneh, "A Note on the 'Keys of the Kaʿba'," *Islamic Quarterly* 18 (1974): 73–75.

143. On the collection as a whole, see O. Sermed Muhtar, *Müze-i Askeri-i Osmani-Rehber* (Istanbul, 1920–1922); Tahsin Öz, *Hirka-i Saadet Dairesi ve Emanat-i Mukaddese* (Istanbul, 1953); and Esin Atil, *The Age of Sultan Süleyman the Magnificent* (Washington, D.C., 1987).

144. On this Quran, see al-Umayrī, *Masālik al-abṣār fī mamālik al-amṣār*, 1:216.

145. On the body of Daniel and the tombs, see Ibn Taymīyah, *Kitāb al-iqtiḍāʾ al-ṣirāṭ al-mustaqīm* (Cairo, 1412), 339; Muḥammad Umar Memon, trans., *Ibn Taymīya's Struggle against Popular Traditions, with an Annotated Translation of his Kitāb Iqtiḍāʾ al-Ṣirāṭ al-Mustaqīm Mukhālafat Ahl al-Jaḥīm* (The Hague, 1976), 268–269; Ibn Qayyim al-Jawzīyah, *Ighathat al-lahfan min nasāyid al-shayṭān* (Cairo, 1991), 203; and Joseph Castagné, "Le culte des lieux saints de l'Islam au Turkestan," *Ethnographie*, n.s., 46 (1951): 46–124. Also see B. Scarcia Amoretti, "A proposito della mediazione giudaica nell'Islam: Il caso di Daniele," *Rivista degli studi orientali* 60 (1986): 205–211.

146. See the seven-page catalog in Faquir Saiyad Jamal al-Din, *List of the Sacred Relics Kept in the Lahore Fort Together with a Brief History of the Same* (Lahore, 1877). Also see Goldziher, "Veneration of Saints in Islam," 330.

147. See Samuel K. Eddy, *The King Is Dead: Studies in the Near Eastern Resis-*

*tance to Hellenism, 334–31 B.C.* (Lincoln, 1961), esp. 257–294, 295–323. On Edfu, see Dieter Kurth, *Edfou VIII: Die Inschriften des Tempels von Edfu*, Abteilung 1, Übersetzungen, Band 1 (Wiesbaden, 1998); and Hermann Junker, *Die Stundenwachen in den Osirismysterien, nach den Inschriften von Dendera, Edfu und Philae* (Vienna, 1910).

148. See Nadia Abu El-Haj, *Facts on the Ground: Archaeological Practice and Territorial Self-Fashioning in Israeli Society* (Chicago, 2001), esp. 130–162; and Yael Zerubavel, *Recovered Roots: Collective Memory and the Making of Israeli National Tradition* (Chicago, 1995). A general theoretical overview of national identity and its relationship to territory can be found in Benedict Anderson, *Imagined Communities* (London, 1983); and a similar treatment of kings using narrative and rituals to construct "national" identies in premodern times is A. M. Hocart, *Kings and Councillors* (Cairo, 1937).

149. The map was published by Lumā Khalaf/Nahhas (1369/1998) and is based on an earlier map produced by the Royal Jordanian Geographic Centre in Amman, and is distributed by the Jordan Tourism Board.

150. See, for example, some of the accounts reviewed in Charles Williams, *Oriental Affinities of the Legend of the Hairy Anchorite* (Urbana, 1925–1926).

151. "Elated Shiites, on a Pilgrimage, Want the U.S. Out," *New York Times*, April 22, 2003, A1, A11: "Men offered water to passing pilgrims from cast-iron bathtubs set up along the roads, and hawkers sold pales of tablets of compressed earth, the holy soil on which Hussein's blood was spilled." Also see Yitzhak Nakash, "Corpse Traffic," in his *The Shiʿis of Iraq*, new ed. (Princeton, 2003).

152. See Meri, "Aspects of Baraka," 51–52.

153. See al-Harawī, *Kitāb al-ishārāt ilā maʿrifat al-ziyārāt*, 4.

154. See Muḥammad b. Aḥmad al-Muqaddasī, *Aḥsan al-taqāsīm fi maʿrifat al-aqālīm*, ed. M. J. de Goeje, Descriptio imperii Moslemici (Leiden, 1967), 46; and Goldziher, "Veneration of Saints in Islam," 227.

155. See Yaḥyā Ḥaqqī, *Qandil Umm Hashim: The Lamp of Umm Hashim*, trans. Denys Johnson-Davies (Cairo, 2004).

156. See David Frankfurter, *Religion in Roman Egypt* (Princeton, 1998), 51 and pl. 21, for sand rubbed from columns and walls of the temple of Arensnuphisin Philae by pilgrims. Thanks to Michael Williams for this reference.

157. See the advertisement in *Jordan Times*, May 11, 2004, 6: "The Hashemite Kingdom of Jordan Baptism Site Commission Expression of Interest for Filling, Packaging, and Marketing the Sacred Water at the Baptism Site of Jesus Christ." Also see the Web site at the Ministry of Tourism and Antiquities: baptismsite@mota.gov.jo.

158. An overview of the Theravāda understanding of the bodies of the Buddha can be found in Frank E. Reynolds, "The Several Bodies of the Buddha:

Reflections on a Neglected Aspect of Theravāda Tradition," *History of Religions* 16 (1977): 374–389. Other useful information can be found in Paul Mus, "Où finit Puruṣa?" in *Mélanges d'indianisme à la mémoire de Louis Renou* (Paris, 1968), 539–563; and John Strong, "The Transforming Gift: An Analysis of Devotional Acts of Offering in Buddhist Avadāna Literature," *History of Religions* 18 (1979): 221–237. Note the important instances of the Buddha relics' being a substitute for the Buddha in his absence. See, for example, Ananda and the Buddha in the Kalingabodhi Jataka in E. B. Cowell, ed., *The Jataka* (Cambridge, 1895–1907), and Mahinda's seeing of the Buddha relic. For these references, I am indebted to Kirstin Scheible, "Stealing, Hoarding, Guarding: Nagas and the Three Types of Buddha Relics in the Pali Vamsas," paper presented at the annual meeting of the American Academy of Religion, November 2003.

159. The best-known account of the distribution of the remains of the Buddha and the building of the stupas is to be found in the Asokavadana and the Mahavamsa. For an English translation and commentary on the Asokavadana, see John Strong, *The Legends of King Asoka: A Study and Translation of the Asokavadana,* Princeton Library of Asian Translations (Princeton, 1983). For an English translation of the Mahavamsa, see Wilhelm Geiger, trans., *The Mahavamsa; or, The Great Chronicle of Ceylon* (London, 1912).

160. See further Etienne Lamotte, *Histoire du bouddhisme indien* (Louvain, 1958), 182; John Strong, *The Legends of King Asoka,* 109–119; and Mus, *Barabudur,* vol. 1, passim.

161. See See Philip P. Arnold, "Sacred Landscapes of New York State and the Problem of Religion in America," paper presented at the Comparative Religion Colloquium, University of Washington, November 2002. Haiawatha discovers the first wampum, a quahog shell at the time of the creation of the world. Note also that the logo of the Tree of Peace Society represents territory with objects of war thrown into the ground at its base. This central tree is an Onondaga representation for the law of peace and represents the land. See Philip P. Arnold and Ann Grodzins Gold, eds., *Sacred Landscapes and Cultural Politics* (Aldershot, 2001). On the Hiawatha figure in other mythologies, see Ernest J. Moyne, *Hiawatha and Kalevala* (Helsinki, 1963).

162. See Arent Jan Wensinck, "Arabic New Year and the Feast of Tabernacles," *Uitgave van de Koninklijke Akademie van Wetenschappen te Amsterdam,* vol. 25 (1925); idem, "Some Semitic Rites of Mourning and Religion: Studies on their Origin and Mutual Relation," *Verhandelingen der Koninklijke Akademie van Wetenschappen te Amsterdam,* Afdeling Letterkunde, n.r., 18, no. 1 (1918); and idem, "Tree and Bird as Cosmological Symbols in Western Asia," *Uitgave van de Koninklijke Akademie van Wetenschappen te Amsterdam*, vol. 22 (1921). Islamic rituals are no different in substance from these actions and actually may be con-

tinuations of them but are set apart as "Islamic" because of the new referents attached to them in Islamic law. Also see Mary Douglas, *Natural Symbols: Explorations in Cosmology* (New York, 1982).

163. See Bruce Lincoln, *Authority: Construction and Corrosion* (Chicago, 1994), esp. his defintion of authority as "given" as opposed to coerced or convinced.

## CHAPTER FOUR

1. There exists a great deal of work on the architecture of Muslim tombs, funerary rites, and the visitation of tombs. For general studies on architecture, see Leisten, *Architektur für Tote*, passim; John Simpson, "Death and Burial in the Late Islamic Near East: Some Insights from Arachaeology and Ethnography," in *The Archaeology of Death in the Ancient Near East,* ed. Stuart Campbell and Anthony Green (Oxford, 1995), 240–252; Y. Raghib, "Structure de la tombe d'après le droit musulman," *Arabica* 39 (1992): 393–403; and L. Trümpelmann, "Muslimische Gräber," in *Antike Welt: Zeitschrift für Archäologie und Kulturgeschichte* 15 (1991): 4–16.

On the City of the Dead in Cairo, see Massignon, "La cité des morts au Caire (Qarāfa-Darb al-Aḥmar)"; and Christopher Taylor, *In the Vicinity of the Righteous: Ziyāra and the Veneration of Muslim Saints in Late Medieval Egypt* (Leiden, 1999). On South Asia, see John Burton-Page, "Muslim Graves of the 'Lesser Tradition': Gilgit, Puniāl, Swāt, Yūsufzai," *Journal of the Royal Asiatic Society* (1986): 248–254; and M. S. Ahluwalia, "Mughal Tombs at Bahlopur: An Architectural Study," in *Contacts between Cultures: South Asia,* ed. K. I. Koppedrayer (Lewiston, 1992), 222–224. For the Indian Ocean coast of Kenya, see James S. Kirkman, "Mnarani of Kilifi: The Mosques and Tombs," *Ars Orientalis* 3 (1959): 95–111; James S. Kirkman, *The Arab City of Gedi, Excavations at the Great Mosque, Architecture and Finds* (Oxford, 1954); idem, "Excavations at Kilepwa: An Introduction to the Medieval Archaeology of the Kenya Coast," *Antiquaries Journal* 32 (1953): 168–184; and S. A. Strong, "History of Kilwa," *Journal of the Royal Asiatic Society*, April 1895. On Zanzibar, see Jean-Claude Penrad, "The Social Fallout of Individual Death: Graves and Cemeteries in Zanzibar," in *The History and Conservation of Zanzibar Stone Town*, ed. Abdul Sherif, 82–90 (Zanzibar, 1995); and Amina Ameir Issa, "The Burial of the Elite in Nineteenth-Century Zanzibar Stone Town," in Sherif, *The History and Conservation of Zanzibar Stone Town*, 67–80. For Iran, see Tadeusz Dzierzykray-Rogalski, "Islamic Graves from Faras," *Nubica* 1–2 (1987–1988): 505–509. On the Ḥaḍramawt and Yemen, see R. B. Serjeant, "The Cemeteries of Tarîm (Ḥaḍramawt) (with Notes on Sepulture)," *Le Muséon* 62 (1942): 232–234; and idem, *The Saiyids of Hadramawt* (London, 1957). On Sarajevo Muslim saints' tombs, see Alija Bejtic, "Jedno videnje sarajevskih evlija i njihovih grobova kao kultnih mjesta," *Prilozi za Orientalnu Filologiju* 31 (1981): 111–129.

For examples of information about burials from archaeological excavations in the Near East and South Asia, see J. K. Eakins, *Tell el-Hesi: The Muslim Cemetery in Field V and VI/IX (Statum II)* (Winona Lake, Ind., 1993); H. Kamada and T. Ohtsu, "Report on the Excavations at Songor A: Isin-Larsa, Sassanian and Islamic Graves," *al-Rafidan* 9 (1988): 135–172; G. A. Wilhelm, "Excavations at Tell Khirbet Salih," in *Tell Karrana 3: Tell Jikan, Tell Khirbet Salih,* ed. G. Wilhelm and C. Zaccagnini (Mainz, 1993), 261–262; S. J. Saller, *Excavations at Bethany (1949–1953)* (Jerusalem, 1957); B. Mershen, "The Islamic Cemetery of Abu an-Naml," *Annual of the Department of Antiquities of Jordan* 34 (1990): 331–332; H. Curvers, "The Middle Habour Salvage Operation: Excavation at Tell al-Raqai, 1986," *Akkadica* 55 (November/December 1987): 1–29; M. Kervran, "Preliminary Report on the Excavation of Qal'at al-Bahrain," *Fouilles a Qal'at al-Bahrain: 1ère partie (1977–1979),* ed. M. Kervran and others (Manama, 1982), 59–84, esp. 75–76; A. Fakhry, *The Egyptian Deserts: Bahria Oasis* (Cairo, 1950); E. F. Schmidt, *The Alishar Hüyük Seasons of 1928 and 1929* (Chicago, 1933), esp. 118–120; and L. Halbert, "The Mohammedan Graves," in *Rang Mahal: The Swedish Archaeological Expedition to India, 1952–1954,* ed. H. Rydh and others, Acta Archaeologica Ludiensia (Lund, 1959), 185–188.

For examples of recent scholarship on funerary rites, see See H. Granqvist, *Muslim Death and Burial: Arab Customs and Traditions Studied in a Village in Jordan* (Helsinki, 1965); and M. Galal, "Essai d'observations sur les rites funéraires en Égypte actuelle" *Revue des Études Islamiques* 11 (1937): 131–299. For specifically Shiʿi rituals associated with funerals and tombs, see Percy Molesworth Sykes, *Khan Bahadur Khan, the Glory of the Shia World* (London, 1910), 102–118; and Stanley Lane-Poole, "Death and Disposal of the Dead (Muhammadan)," in Hastings and others, *Encyclopedia of Religion and Ethics,* 4:500–502. Also see the analysis of Richard Eaton, *Sufis of Bijapur, 1300–1700: Social Roles of Sufis in Medieval India* (Princeton, 1978), describing an Urs at a tomb observed by Abbé Carré published in *The Travels of the Abbé Carré in India and the Near East, 1672 to 1674,* ed. Charles Fawcett, trans. Lady Fawcett (London, 1947), 2:323–325; and Sharif, *Islam in India; or, The Qanun-i-Islam*, esp. 39–45 and 135.

Firsthand observations can be found in Meer Hassan Ali, *Observations of the Mussulmauns of India, Descriptive of Their Manners, Customs, Habits, and Religious Opinions Made during a Twelve Years' Residence in Their Immediate Society*, 2d ed., ed. W. Crooke (London, 1917), giving reports on the visit to the prophet Muhammad's tomb during the Ḥajj (123–124) and visits to the tombs of ʿAlī, Ḥasan, and Ḥusain (124–125). On Egypt and the Arabian Peninsula, see Edward William Lane, *Arabian Society in the Middle Ages: Studies from the Thousand and One Nights*, ed. Stanley Lane-Poole (London, 1883), for pilgrimage to saint tombs (68–72), death ceremonies, and grave rituals (262–264).

More comparative and sociologically informed analysis can be found in

Georges-Henri Bousquet, "Le rituel du culte des saints (à propos du livre de T. Canaan)," *Revue Africain* 93 (1949): 277–290; and A. D. H. Bivar, "Seljūqid Ziyārats of Sar-i Pul (Afghanistan)," *Bulletin of the School of Oriental and African Studies* 29 (1966): 57–63; E. Dermenghem, *Le culte des saints dans l'Islam maghrébin* (Paris, 1954); and Meri, *The Cult of Saints among Muslims and Jews in Medieval Syria.*

For examples of scholarship on the legality of visiting tombs, see Henri Laoust, *La profession de foi d'Ibn Baṭṭah* (Damascus, 1958), esp. 80, 149; idem, *Le précis de droit d'Ibn Qudāma* (Beirut 1950), esp. 21; A. Parrot, *Malédictions et violation des tombes* (Paris, 1939); Ch. D. Matthews, "A Muslim Iconoclast (Ibn Taymiyyah) on the 'Merits' of Jerusalem and Palestine," *Journal of the American Oriental Society* 56 (1936): 1–21, including Ibn Taymīyah's "Qā'idah fī ziyārat Bayt al-Maqdis"; N. H. Olesen, *Culte des saints et pèlerinages chez Ibn Taymiyya (661/1268–728/1328)* (Paris, 1991); Muḥammad Umar Memon, *Ibn Taymīya's Struggle against Popular Traditions*; G. Makdisi, *Ibn ʿAqīl, Religion and Culture in Classical Islam* (Edinburgh, 1997), esp. 210–212; Christopher Taylor, *In the Vicinity of the Righteous,* 195–218; and Meri, *The Cult of Saints among Muslims and Jews in Medieval Syria,* 126–138.

2. For general comments on the nau-gaz tombs, see John Burton-Page, "Makbara," in *Encyclopaedia of Islam,* 6:125–128, esp. 127; and Friedrich Wetzel, *Islamische Grabbauten aus Indien aus der Zeit der Soldatenkaiser, 1320–1540* (Leipzig, 1918). On the nau-gaz tombs in Southeast Asia, especially in Java (Wali Songo), see Glenn Smith, "The Making and Unmaking of Madura's Sacred Tombs," *Review of Indonesian and Malaysian Affairs* 32, no. 2 (1998): 211–249.

3. Theodore Bent, *Southern Arabia* (London, 1900; reprint, London, 1994), 131–132.

4. See W. H. Ingrams, "Hadhramaut: A Journey to the Seiʿar Country and through the Wadi Maseila," *Geographic Journal* 88 (1936): 524–551, esp. 535. Ingrams also mentions that there were fossils laid on the tomb, as described by Bent, and the local tradition that these fossils would return to the tomb on their own if taken from it. Ingrams reports that his group took one of these fossils back to the British Museum for analysis before mailing it back to the Ḥaḍramawt through the postal service (535). For Doughty's visit to this tomb of Salih, see Robin Bidwell, *Travellers in Arabia* (London, 1976), 84–85.

5. See Ingrams, "Hadhramaut: A Journey to the Seiʿar Country and through the Wadi Maseila," 554; and the mention of the Hud's tomb in W. H. Ingrams, "The Hadhramaut: Present and Future," *Geographical Journal* 92 (1938): 289–312, esp. 298. On the cleft in the rock, see al-Hamadānī, who cites a ḥadīth report in which a man claimed to have squeezed through the crack at the tomb of Hud and seen a man with a long face and thick beard lying down. On his head was

an inscription stating: "I am Hud who believed in God." See al-Ḥasan b. Aḥmad al-Hamadānī, *Kitāb al-iklil* (Beirut, 1986), 8:206–207.

6. See, for example, D. van der Meulen and H. von Wissmann, *Ḥaḍramaut: Some of Its Mysteries Unveiled* (Leiden, 1932): "Hud must have been a very big man, for his grave is about 120 feet long. The qubba is built on the spot where his head is said to rest, the place where, also, the rock was cleft open" (159). Bent, *Southern Arabia,* reports that Hud's tomb was forty feet in length, piled with rocks in the shape of an elongated cairn like the tomb of Salih, though he admits he did not see the tomb himself (133).

Muḥammad ʿAbd al-Qādir BāMaṭraf visited the tomb in 1954 and found it to be a pile of small stones about ninety-two feet long and four feet high. See M. ʿAbd al-Qādir BāMaṭraf, *Mulāḥaẓāt ʿalā mā dhikr al-Hamadānī ʿan Jighrāfiyah Ḥaḍramawt* (Aden, 1984), 12–13. Nicholas Clapp, *The Road to Ubar: Finding the Atlantis of the Sands* (Boston, 1998), visited Hud's tomb in the spring of 1995: "He was evidently a very tall man, for his sarcophagus extended beyond the confines of the building and a good ninety feet up the hillside behind it" (268).

7. See Shaykh ʿAbd al-Qādir Muḥammad al-Ṣabbān, *Visits and Customs: The Visit to the Tomb of the Prophet Hud,* ed. and trans. Linda Boxberger and Awad Abdelrahim Abu Hulayqa, American Institute for Yemeni Studies, Yemeni Translation Series 2 (Ardmore, Pa., 1998); and François de Keroualin and Ludovic Schwarz, "Hud, un pélerinage en Hadramaout," *Quaderni di studi arabi* 13 (1995): 181–189.

For classical references to Hud's tomb, see al-Muqaddasī, *Aḥsan al-taqāsīm fi maʿrifat al-aqālīm,* 67, 102; Muḥammad Ibn Ḥawqal, *Ṣūrat al-arḍ,* ed. J. H. Kramers, Opus Geographicum (Leiden, 1967), 25; Ibn Jubayr, *Riḥlat Ibn Jubayr* (Beirut, 1964), 237; and al-Harawī, *Kitāb al-ishārāt ilā maʿrifat al-ziyārāt,* trans. into French by J. Sourdel-Thomine as *Guide des lieux de pèlerinage* (Damascus: Institut français de Damas, 1957), 15.

For reports on the different locations of the tombs of these two Arab prophets, see Joseph Toussaint Reinaud, *Géographie d'Aboulféda: Allgemeine Einleitung und französische Übersetzung des Taqwīm al-buldān von Abūʾl-Fidāʾ (gest. 732 H./1331 n. Chr.),* ed. Fuat Sezgin (Frankfurt, 1985), 2:1:135.

On the tomb of Hud in Damascus, see ʿAlī b. Muḥammad al-Rabaʿī, *Faḍāʾil al-Shām* (Damascus, 1999), 34–35. On the maqām of Nabi Hud, near Jerash, see Charles Doughty, *Travels in Arabia Deserta* (Cambridge, 1888; reprint of 3d ed., New York, 1979), 1:49: "For Mohammedans there is a grave of their prophet Hud, who lies buried in more places of Arabia." Also see Ghazi Bin Mohammed, ed., *Maqāmāt al-Urdun: Holy Sites of Jordan* (Amman, 1995), 28–29.

On the shrine of Salih in Acre, see Ibn Jubayr, *Riḥlat Ibn Jubayr,* 276; Haim Schwartzbaum, *Biblical and Extra-biblical Legends in Islamic Folk-Literature*

(Walldorf-Hessen, 1982), 158n180; T. Canaan, *Mohammedan Saints and Sanctuaries in Palestine* (London, 1927), 329; and Yoel Koch, "The Jamiʿ, Nabi Ṣāleḥ's Tomb and Ayn al-Baqar in Acre in the Middle Ages" [in Hebrew], *Arabic and Islamic Studies* (Ramat-Gan) 2 1978): 102–114. On Acre, see F.-M. Abel, *Géographie de la Palestine* (Paris, 1967), 2:235–237.

8. On the tomb of al-Galsad and the giant tomb near Shabwah, see Bent, *Southern Arabia,* 134, citing Yāqūt, *Muʿjam al-buldān,* s.v. "Jalsad," and an unidentified "Makrisi." On the second giant tomb, whose exact location and name are not identified, see Ingrams, "Hadhramaut: A Journey to the Seiʿar Country and through the Wadi Maseila," 549.

9. See Muqātil b. Sulaymān, *Tafsīr Muqātil b. Sulaymān,* ed. ʿAbdallāh Maḥmūd Shiḥātah (Cairo, 1979), on Q 2:125. Also see the reports in al-Azraqī, *Akhbār Makkah,* 39; and Muḥammad b. Aḥmad al-Fāsī, *Shifāʾ al-gharām bi-akhbār al-balad al-ḥarām* (Cairo, 1956), 1:197. Also see the discussion of these references in Rubin, "The Kaʿba," 110–111.

10. See al-Suyūṭī, *al-Darr al-manthūr,* on Q 2:125.

11. See al-Ḥalabī, *al-Sīrah al-Ḥalabīyah,* 14. For other references to the burial of prophets in the Meccan sanctuary, see ʿAbdallāh b. Muslim b. Qutaybah, *al-Maʿārif* (Cairo, 1959), 14; and Ibn Saʿd, *al-Ṭabaqāt al-kubrā* (Leiden, 1904–1908), 1:52.

12. On the use of stelae in Nabataean contexts, see John F. Healey, *The Religion of the Nabataeans: A Conspectus* (Leiden, 2001). On pillars in Hatra and Palmyra, see Basile Aggoula, *Inventaire des inscriptions hatréennes* (Paris, 1991); and J. Teixidor, *Inventaire des inscriptions de Palmyre* (Beirut, 1965). On the cairns of the Safaitic Arabs in the basalt desert, see Willard Oxtoby, *Some Inscriptions of the Safaitic Bedouin* (New Haven, 1968), esp. 20–25. On monoliths, see Arnaud, P. "Naïskoi monolithes du Hauran," in *Hauran I: Recherches archéologiques sur la Syrie du sud à l'époque hellénistique et romaine,* ed. J.-M. Dentzer, 2:373–386 (Paris, 1985).

For general comments, see Wellhausen, *Reste arabischen Heidentums,* 73–94; H. Lammens, *L'Arabie occidentale avant l'Hégire* (Beirut, 1928), 101–179, esp. 167, 173–176; Dominique Sourdel, *Les cultes du Hauran à l'époque Romaine* (Pairs, 1952), esp. 19–112; J. Teixidor, *The Pagan God: Popular Religion in the Greco-Roman Near East* (Princeton, 1977), 62–99; K. Dijkstra, *Life and Loyalty: A Study in the Socio-religious Culture of Syria and Mesopotamia in the Graeco-Roman Period Based on Epigraphic Evidence* (Leiden, 1995); and U. Avner, "Ancient Cult Sites in the Negev and Sinai Deserts," *Tel Aviv* 11 (1984): 115–131.

13. See, for example, Arent Jan Wensinck, "Some Semitic Rites of Mourning and Religion," passim; Edward William Lane, *An Account of the Manners and Customs of the Modern Egyptians* (London, 1890); and Gustave E. von Grunebaum, *Muhammadan Festivals* (New York, 1951).

14. See the description in van der Meulen and von Wissmann, *Ḥaḍramaut,* 160. Also see the diagrams and pictures in al-Ṣabbān, *Visits and Customs,* esp. 49–51.

15. See James de Vere Allen and Thomas H. Wilson, *Swahili Houses and Tombs on the Coast of Kenya,* Art and Archaeology Research Papers (London, 1979), 14–21; and Thomas H. Wilson, "Swahili Funerary Architecture on the North Kenya Coast," in Allen and Wilson, *Swahili Houses and Tombs,* 33–46, esp. for the pillar tomb at Takwa (33–34) and the pillar tomb at Mwana (figs. 7B and 8). On the "mosque of the pillar" at Takwa, see J. S. Kirkan, "Takwa: The Mosque of the Pillar," *Ars Orientalis* 2 (1957): 175–182.

16. See Wetzel, *Islamische Grabbauten in Indien aus der Zeit der Soldatenkaiser, 1320–1540,* 16; Salome Zajadacz-Hastenrath, *Chaukhandigräber: Studien zur Grabkunst in Sind und Balunchistan* (Wiesbaden, 1978), 15; K. Jettmar, "The Middle Asiatic Heritage of Dardistan: Islamic Collective Tombs in Punyal and Their Background," *East and West* 17 (1967): 59–82; M. P. Grjaznov, "Minusinskie kamennye baby v svjazi s nekotorymi novymi materialami," *SA* 12 (1950): 128–157; and F. Bergman, *Archaeological Researches in Sinkiang* (Stockholm, 1939), passim.

17. See Alexander Cunningham, *Report for the Year 1872–1873,* Archaeological Survey of India 5 (Calcutta, 1873; reprint, Varanasi, 1966), 5:130; and idem, *Four Reports Made during the Years 1862–63–64–65,* Archaeological Survey of India 1 (Simla, 1871; reprint, Varanasi, 1972), 323–324.

18. See Cunningham, *Report for the Year 1872–1873,* 130, who states that this is the westernmost example of a nau-gaz tomb that he has observed. The name Lamech might also be a reference to the Lamech of Genesis 4:18–24, who was in the seventh generation from Adam and the father of Jabal, Jubal, Tubal-Cain, and Naamah. On this genealogy, see J. Gabriel, "Die Kainitengenealogie: Gn 4,17–24," *Biblica* 40 (1959): 409–427. Lamech, the father of Noah, is of the seventh generation from Enosh in the line of Seth, according to Gen 5:25–31. Also see B. Jacob, *Das Erste Buch der Tora: Genesis übersetzt und erklärt* (Berlin, 1934), 166–167; and Richard Hess, "Lamech," in *The Anchor Bible Dictionary,* 4:136–137.

19. See W. Crooke, *An Introduction to the Popular Religion and Folklore of Northern India* (Allahabad, 1894), 140–141; and *Gazetteer of the Province of Oudh* (Lucknow, 1877–1878), 1:11. Crooke's account is taken from Cunningham, *Four Reports Made during the Years 1862–63–64–65,* 324, where the same measurements are provided.

20. Al-Balādhūrī, *Futūḥ al-buldān,* 124. Also see Ahmad Nabi Khan, *Multan: History and Architecture* (Islamabad, 1403/1983). This temple of Multan is also mentioned by the Chinese pilgrim Hieuen Tsang, who visited Multan in 641 CE, and ʿAlī Kūfī mentions a golden idol in Multan at the time of the Arab conquests.

21. On the tomb of Job in Turkestan, see Castagné, "Le culte des lieux saints de l'Islam au Turkestan," 80–81. For other examples of shrines in South and Central Asia associated with prominent prophetic figures from the Quran and Bible, see T. Hungerford Holdich, *The Indian Borderland, 1880–1900* (London, 1901; 2d ed., London, 1909), 73–74, on the Throne of Solomon (takht-i-Suliman), said to be the mountain on which king Solomon sat to look over India. There is a shrine on a ledge below the southernmost cliff of this mountain. Castagné, "Le culte des lieux saints de l'Islam au Turkestan," 106, lists the Throne of Jesus (takht Gokhi Hazretti Issa Paigambar) in the village of Jam in Turkestan as the place of the throne of the prophet Jesus and, according to local tradition, the place where Jesus walked on water.

22. On the tomb of Daniel at Sus, see al-Muqaddasī, *Aḥsan al-taqāsīm fī maʿrifat al-aqālīm,* 3:417; Aḥmad b. Dāʾūd al-Dīnawarī, *Kitāb al-akhbār al-ṭiwāl,* ed. Aḥmad b. Dāʾūd (Beirut, 1959), 49; al-Harawī, *Kitāb al-ishārāt ilā maʿrifat al-ziyārāt,* 69; idem, *Guide des lieux de pèlerinage,* 154; al-Bakrī, *Das Geographische Wörterbuch des Abu ʿObeid ʿAbdallah,* 94; M. Streck and C. E. Bosworth, "Sūs," in *Encyclopaedia of Islam,* 9:898–899; Reinaud, *Géographie d'Aboulféda,* 2:85; and M. Schreiner, "Beiträge zur Geschichte der theologischen Bewegungen," in *Zeitschrift der Deutschen Morgenländischen Gesellschaft* 43 (1890): 58–59. On the archeological site of Susa, see Sylvia A. Matheson, *Persia: An Archaeological Guide,* 2d ed. (London, 1976), 147–152.

On Bukhara and Samarqand under the Timurids and thereafter, see Guy Le Strange, *The Lands of the Eastern Caliphate* (Cambridge, 1905), esp. 313–315 (Bukhara), 316–318 (Samarqand); Ibn Ḥawqal, *Ṣūrat al-arḍ,* 362–364 (Bukhara), 365–368 (Samarqand); al-Muqaddasī, *Aḥsan al-taqāsīm fī maʿrifat al-aqālīm,* 281–282 (Bukhara), 278–279 (Samarqand); Yāqūt, *Muʿjam al-buldān,* s.v. "Bukhāra," "Samarqand"; and Ibn Baṭṭūṭah, *Tuḥfat al-nuẓẓār fī gharāʾib al-amṣār wa ʿajāʾib al-asfār,* ed. A. A. al-Kattānī (Beirut, 1975), 3:27 (Bukhara), 3:52 (Samarqand). Also see the account of the Spanish ambassador Clavijo to the city of Samarqand in 1405, Ruy González de Clavijo, *Narrative of the Spanish Embassy to the Court of Timur at Samarkand in the Years 1403–1406,* trans. Guy Le Strange (London, 1928), 169.

23. This account is repeated by pilgrims visiting the shrine and other locals, including the matriarch of the family responsible for providing the cloth covering for the tomb itself. On Timur's policy of legitimation, see Beatrice Forbes Manz, "Tamerlane and the Symbolism of Sovereignty," *Iranian Studies* 21 (1987): 105–122. On Timur's campaigns in Iran, Iraq, and Syria, see, idem, *The Rise and Rule of Tamerlane* (Cambridge, 1989), 71–73.

24. See Amoretti, "A proposito della mediazione giudaica nell'Islam: il caso di Daniele." Amoretti remarks (206–207) that Daniel might also be a local Iranian saint.

On other Central Asian tombs and shrines, see O. Olufsen, "Muhamedanske gravminder i Transkaspein, Khiva, Bokhara, Turkestan og Pamir," *Geografisk tidskrift* (Copenhagen) 17 (1903): 110–120, 146–159. On sacred places in historic Kirghizstan, see I. G. Petrash, *Sviatye mesta obmana* (Frunze, 1961). On the legends and shrine of Pahlavān Maḥmūd in Khiva, see T. Dzhalalov, "Khaiiam Khorezma," *Zvezda Vostoka* (Tashkent), 1962, 141–144; A. M. Piemontese, "La leggenda del santo-lottatore Pahlavān Maḥmūd Xvārezmi 'Puryā-ye Vali' (m. 722/1322)," *Annali dell'Istituto orientale di Napoli,* n.s., 15 (1965): 167–213.

25. In addition to the tomb of the prophet Daniel in Sūs, there is a mosque associated with him in Alexandria, Egypt. On this Mosque of Daniel in Alexandria, see Leszek Dabrowski, "La citerne a eau sous la mosquée de Nébi Daniel," *Bulletin of the Faculty of Arts, Alexandria University* 12 (1958): 40–48; and E. Breccia, "Les sondages près de la mosquée Nébi Daniel," *Bulletin de Musée Gréco-Romain* (1925–1931): 48. Also see G. Botti, "Les citernes d'Alexandrie," *Bulletin de la Société Archéologique d'Alexandrie* 2 (1899): 15; and Herz Maux, "Les citernes d'Alexandria," *Monumentes de l'Art Arabe* (1898): 81–86 with pls. 5–7.

26. On the tomb of Job in Palestine, see ʿAbd al-Ghanī al-Nābulsī, *al-Ḥaqīqah wa al-majāj fī riḥlah bilād al-Shām wa Miṣr wa al-Ḥijāz,* ed. Riyāḍ ʿAbd al-Ḥamīd Murād (Damascus, 1989), 194–195, who reports that it is near the wadi of the Ayn Silwān in Jerusalem, and that the name of this wadi goes back to the prophet Job. Al-Nābulsī cites al-Ḥanbali, who states in his history that the one who wrote the *Uns* relates about this well also (see to 195). Ibn Jubayr, *Riḥlat Ibn Jubayr,* 247, also mentions this tomb in his travels. On the tomb of Job in Oman, see Philip Ward, *Travels in Oman: On the Track of the Early Explorers* (Cambridge, 1987), who describes the tomb as being housed in a new mosque, a place for family picnics. This tomb is also mentioned by Bertram Thomas, who traveled there in 1928. See Bertram Thomas, "Among Some Unknown Tribes of Saudi Arabia," *Journal of the Royal Anthropological Institution* (1929): 97–111. On the maqām of Job in al-Salṭ in Jordan, see Ghazi Bin Mohammed, *Maqāmāt al-Urdun: Holy Sites of Jordan,* 46–47.

27. For some of the accounts on the discovery of the tomb of Daniel in Sūs, see al-Dinawarī, *Kitāb al-akhbār al-ṭiwāl,* 130; Ibn Taymīyah, *Majmūʿ fatāwā Shaykh al-Islām Aḥmad b. Taymīya,* ed. A. al-ʿĀṣimī (Riyadh, 1991), 27:120–121; and Meri, *The Cult of Saints among Muslims and Jews in Medieval Syria,* 127.

28. ʿAbd al-Ghanī al-Nābulsī, *Riḥlatān ilā Lubnān: Zwei Beschreibungen des Libanon: ʿAbdalganī an-Nābulsīs Reise durch die Biqāʿ und al-ʿUṭaifīs Reise nach Tripolis,* ed. Ṣalāḥaddīn al-Munajjid and Stefan Wild (Beirut, 1979), day 4, pp. 67–68. In this same text, al-Nābulsī mentions the tomb of David (day 10, pp. 103–104), which he describes as a "long tomb," but he also notes that it is well known that the tomb of David is in Jerusalem. On day 11 (p. 107) al-Nābulsī visits the tomb of the prophet Zurayq, which he also describes as "big and long."

For another brief mention of the tomb of Seth, see al-Nābulsī, *al-Ḥaqīqah wa al-majāj fī riḥlah bilād al-Shām wa Miṣr wa al-Ḥijāz,* 168. On the travels of al-Nābulsī, see Sirrīya, "Ziyārāt of Syria in a Riḥla of ʿAbd al-Ghanī al-Nābulusī (1050/1641–1143/1731)."

29. See Ibn Jubayr, *Riḥlat Ibn Jubayr,* 253.

30. See ibid., 253. Ibn Jubayr also claims that the tomb of Noah's son is adjacent to the tomb of Noah, though he provides no specifics and this is not mentioned in other accounts. For the tomb, or maqām, of the prophet Noah in Kerak in Jordan, see Ghazi Bin Mohammed, *Maqāmāt al-Urdun: Holy Sites of Jordan,* 26–27.

31. For the anonymous Hebrew account, see L. Grünhut and M. N. Adler, eds., *Eleh ha-Massaʿot* (Frankfurt, 1903), which is in part based upon the *Toẓaʾot Ereẓ Yisraʾel* attributed to Moshe b. Mordecai Bassola, *Massaʿot ereẓ Yisraʾel le-Rabbi Moshe Bassola,* ed. E. Y. Ben-Ẓevi (Jerusalem, 1938), trans. D. Ordan as In Zion and Jerusalem: The Itinerary of Rabbi Moses Basola (1521-1523), ed. A. David (Jerusalem, 1999). The *Eleh ha-Massaʿot* also refers to the tombs of Eldad and Modad in the town of Nabi Zaruʿa.

For Lord Curzon's account, see G. N. Curzon, *Leaves from a Viceroy's Notebook* (London, 1926), 363–364. According to Castagné, "Le culte des lieux saints de l'Islam au Turkestan," the shrine of the prophet Idris, the Mazar Idris Paigambar, in the Valley of Tchatkal in the district of Namangan, is considered by many to be the tomb of Noah. Castagné reports that the site is popular for pilgrims from Tashkent and Ferghana (71).

32. On the tomb of the Abel, see Shawqī Abū Khalīl, *Aṭlas al-Qurʾān* (Damascus, 2003), 16, who reports the tomb to be about fifteen meters in length.

33. See Meri, "A Late Medieval Syrian Pilgrimage Guide,"54. Meri's translation is based on the edition of Ibn al-Ḥawrānī's *al-Ishārāt ilā amākin al-ziyārāt* by Bassām al-Jābī, 97. See also al-Harawī, *Kitāb al-ishārāt ilā maʿrifat al-ziyārāt,* 11; ʿAlī b. Hibatallāh b. ʿAsākir, *Taʾrīkh madīnat Dimashq,* ed. S. al-Munajjid (Damascus, 1951–1954), partially trans. N. Élisséeff as *La description de Damas d'Ibn ʿAsākir* (Damascus, 1959), 1:104–105; and Ibn Jubayr, *Riḥlat Ibn Jubayr,* 247.

Ibn al-Ḥawrānī also states that the hidden tablets of Seth were found in a cave on Mount Qāsiyūn, that John the Baptist and his mother lived on the mountain for forty years, that saints are buried at the foot of the mountain, that the mountain is where Jesus took refuge with his mother, and that nearby is the tomb of the prophet Moses and the maqām of the prophet Abraham and the cave where he discovered God (105/56–122/63). On the tomb of Ibn ʿArabī, at the base of Qāsiyūn, see P. B. Fenton, "The Hidden Secret Concerning the Shrine of Ibn ʿArabī: A Treatise by ʿAbd Ghanī al-Nābulusi," *Journal of the Muhyiddin ibn ʿArabi Society* 22 (1997): 1–40.

34. See Meri, *The Cult of Saints among Muslims and Jews in Medieval Syria,* 52, citing Louis Ginzberg, *The Legends of the Jews,* 5:19. The Greek or Syrian Antioch legend of the giant can also be found in Photius, *Bibliotheca,* ed. Bekker (Berlin, 1824–1825), 348.13, where it is explained that because the name Dam means conquerer, and Askos means wineskin, there grew up a myth that a giant (Gigas) named Askos was defeated by Zeus or Dionysius and was thus flayed to make a wineskin, and the defeat of this giant Askos was the founding of the city of Damascus. See David MacRitchie, "Giants," in Hastings and others, *Encyclopedia of Religion and Ethics,* 6:189–197.

35. On this tomb, sometimes associated with the prophet Hosea, see Selah Merrill, *East of the Jordan: A Record of Travel and Observation in the Countries of Moab, Gilead, and Bashan* (London, 1881; reprint, London, 1986), 306; and Ghazi Bin Mohammed, *Maqāmāt al-Urdun: Holy Sites of Jordan,* 40–41.

36. John Lewis Burckhardt, *Travels in Syria and the Holy Land* (London, 1822; reprint, New York, 1983), 353.

37. On this tomb, see Ghazi Bin Mohammed, *Maqāmāt al-Urdun: Holy Sites of Jordan,* 36–37.

38. See John Lewis Burckhardt, *Travels in Syria and the Holy Land,* 431. The Egyptian Jewish pilgrim Yitgadel visited the tomb of Aaron in 1371 but did not enter what he describes as the "inner cave" where the body is housed. See Z. Ilan, *Qivrei ẓaddiqim be-ereẓ Yisra'el* (Jerusalem, 1997), 135; and Meri, *The Cult of Saints among Muslims and Jews in Medieval Syria,* 244. Abū al-Ḥasan ʿAlī al-Masʿūdī, *Kitāb al-tanbīh wa al-ishrāf,* ed. M. J. de Goeje (Leiden, 1894), 143–144, mentions Mount Hārūn as a mountain holy to Christians.

According to Robert Schick, "Ecclesiastical History of Petra," in *The Petra Church,* ed. Patricia Bikai (Amman, 2001), 1–5, the Muslim shrine to the prophet Aaron was constructed in the fourteenth century. See Glen Peterman and Robert Schick, "The Monastery of Saint Aaron," *Annual of the Department of Antiquities of Jordan* 40 (1996): 473–480, esp. 477–478. There are two translations of the date of the extant dedicatory inscription. E. H. Palmer, *The Desert of the Exodus* (Cambridge, 1871), 435, says 739 AH, which is 1338–1339 CE. F. G. Peake, *A History of Jordan and Its Tribes* (Coral Gables, Fla., 1958), 82, 135, says 728 AH, which is 1327–1328. Also on the inscription, see C. Clermont-Ganneau, "L'inscription de Nebî Hâron et le 'dharīh' funéraire des Nabatéens et des Arabes," *Recueil d'Archéologie Orientale* 2 (1898): 362–366. A Jewish pilgrim visited the shrine around 1238–1244. See Adler, *Jewish Travellers in the Middle Ages,* 127. See also Theodor Wiegand, *Sinai* (Berlin, 1920), 136–145; and M. R. Savignac, "Sur les pistes de Transjordanie méridionale," *Revue Biblique* 45 (1936): 235–262, esp. 259–262.

39. See ʿAlī Aḥmad ʿAlī Maḥāsh al-Shaḥrī, "Grave Types and 'Triliths' in

Dhofar," *Arabian Archaeology and Epigraphy* 2 (1991): 182–195, esp. 185, fig. 4. For another site attributed to the prophet ʿUmrān, just south and east of Tyre in Lebanon, see Ali Khalil Badawi, *Tyre and It's* [*sic*] *Region* (Beirut, n.d.), 82.

40. On other graves in Oman that are not particularly long, see Ward, *Travels in Oman*, esp. 535, where he does report seeing large, ovoid, flat slabs of rock for graves, the largest of them being sixteen paces long and six to seven paces wide.

41. On ʿImrān as the father of Moses, see al-Suyūṭī, *al-Itiqān fī ʿulūm al-Qurʾān*, ed. Muṣṭafā Dīb al-Bughā (Beirut, 1421/2000), on Q 12, citing Ibn Asākir; Ibn Kathīr, *Qiṣaṣ al-anbiyāʾ*, s.v. "Moses," "Shuʿayb"; and idem, *Tafsīr al-Qurʾān al-ʿaẓīm*, on Q 19:51–53. On the discrepancy concerning the identity of the Moses mentioned in Q 18:60–82, see Fakhr al-Dīn al-Rāzī, *Mafātīḥ al-ghayb* (Cairo, n.d.), on Q 18:60–65. On Ezra as a descendant of ʿImrān through Aaron, see al-Suyūṭī, *al-Itiqān fī ʿulūm al-Qurʾān*, on Q 9:30, citing Ibn ʿAsākir. On ʿImrān b. Mathan as the father of Mary the mother of Jesus, see al-Ṭabarī, *Jāmiʿ al-bayān fī tafsīr al-Qurʾān*, on Q 3:33–41; al-Ṭabarī, *Taʾrīkh al-rusul wa al-mulūk*, 711–712; Ibn Kathīr, *Tafsīr al-Qurʾān al-ʿaẓīm*, on Q 3:33–34; and Gordon Newby, *The Making of the Last Prophet: A Reconstruction of the Earliest Biography of Muhammad* (Columbia, 1989).

42. Doughty, *Travels in Arabia Deserta*, 1:434.

43. See Curzon, *Leaves from a Viceroy's Notebook*, 363–364; and D. van der Meulen, *Aden to the Hadhramaut: A Journey in South Arabia* (London, 1947), 194–195. Also see Lammens, *L'Arabie occidentale avant l'Hegire*, 129. Classical sources mention the tradition that when Eve fell from Eden she landed in Jedda but do not refer to her tomb's being there. See, for example, al-Ṭabarī, *Taʾrīkh al-rusul wa al-mulūk*, 120; idem, *Jāmiʿ al-bayān fī tafsīr al-Qurʾān*, on Q 2:38 and 20:128; Ibn Kathīr, *Tafsīr al-Qurʾān al-ʿaẓīm*, on Q 2:38; and Ibn Jubayr, *Riḥlat Ibn Jubayr*, 53.

44. See Ibn Kathīr, *Qiṣaṣ al-anbiyāʾ*, 23–24.

45. See al-Ṭabarī, *Taʾrīkh al-rusul wa al-mulūk*, 162–163. The cave on Abū Qubays is also mentioned by Ibn Ḥawqal, *Ṣūrat al-arḍ*, 102. Yāqūt, *Muʿjam al-buldān*, s.v. "Abū Qubays," mentions a number of traditions regarding the origins of the name of the mountain, including that Adam acquired from this mountain fire (iqtabasa) that had come down from the heavens. Yāqūt (s.v. "Ghār") also mentions the Cave of the Treasure as being located on Mount Abū Qubays, where Adam buried his books. Al-Yaʿqūbī, *Taʾrīkh al-Yaʿqūbī*, 1:6, also mentions Adam's being buried in the Cave of the Treasure, and the preparation of Adam's body by his son Seth.

The pseudepigraphical Life of Adam and Eve mentions the tablets of stone and clay which Eve commanded her children to make and bury, tablets which were later uncovered by Solomon. See Johnson, "Life of Adam and Eve," 2:249–295;

and L. S. A. Wells, "The Books of Adam and Eve," in *The Apocrypha and Pseudepigrapha of the Old Testament,* ed. R. H. Charles (Oxford, 1913), 2:123–154. The Testament of Adam states that Seth buried secret books or stelae in the Cave of the Treasure along with the things Adam had removed from the garden of Eden, including the gold, myrrh, and frankincense which the Magi would remove and offer as gifts to Jesus at the time of his birth.

For the Testament of Adam, see Robinson, "Testament of Adam"; and idem, *The Testament of Adam.* For the Arabic text, see Gibson, *Apocrypha Arabica,* 1–58. For the Three Steles of Seth, see Robinson and Wisse, "The Three Steles of Seth (NHC VII,5)." For the Syriac text entitled "The Book of the Cave of Treasures" [Meʿārath gazzē], attributed to Ephraim the Syrian, see Budge, *The Book of the Cave of Treasures*; and Bezold, *Die Schatzhohle (Meʿārath Gazzē)*

On the hiding and recovery of secret books in the Arabic hermetical tradition, see some of the traditions associated with Appolonius of Tyre and Alexander the Great, in J. Ruska, *Tabula Smaragdina* (Heidelberg, 1926); and Sivestre de Sacy, *Kitāb al-ʿilal; or, Sirr al-khalīqah*; and Weisser, *Kitāb al-ʿilal; or, Sirr al-khalīqah.* Also see Ibn Wahshiyya, *al-Filāḥa al-Nabaṭīyah,* containing an account of the secret knowledge revealed by the Sun, Moon, and Saturn to Adam and Seth.

46. Al-Ṭabarī, *Taʾrīkh al-rusul wa al-mulūk,* 162.

47. See ibid., 121–122; al-Ṭabarī, *Jāmiʿ al-bayān fī tafsīr al-Qurʾān,* on Q 2:127; and Ibn Kathīr, *Tafsīr al-Qurʾān al-ʿaẓīm,* on Q 2:34–39. Ibn ʿAbbās also reports that the distance between the footsteps of Adam would be a journey of three days for a normal person. See al-Ṭabarī, *Jāmiʿ al-bayān fī tafsīr al-Qurʾān,* on Q 2:127.

48. Personal communication, February 2004.

49. See Ingrams, "Hadhramaut: A Journey to the Seiʿar Country and through the Wadi Maseila," who postulates that the giant tombs were probably sanctuaries of "the old religion" (534).

50. Ibid., 531.

51. Ibid., 549.

52. Bent, *Southern Arabia,* 133. On possible links between Hellenistic sites and later Islamic tombs, see Nina Jidejian, *Tyre: Through the Ages* (Beirut, 1969); and C. Clermont-Ganneau, "L'inscription phénicienne de Maʿsoub," *Recueil d'Archéologie Orientale* 1 (1888): 81–86.

53. *Moyen-Orient: Liban, Syrie, Jordanie, Iraq, Iran: Les Guides Bleus* (Paris, 1965), 122.

54. Personal communication, February 2004.

55. Personal communication, March 2004.

56. For an example of a nau-gaz tomb that was enlarged by later patronage in Multan, in Sind, see Henry Cousens, *The Antiquities of Sind: With Historical Outline,* Archaeological Survey of India 46 (Calcutta, 1929; reprint, Karachi, 1975),

345, who reports on the tomb of Shahbaz Shaykh Usmān Marwandī. He died in 1274 in Sehwān, and his mausoleum was built in 1356 and then enlarged in 1639. On tomb architecture affecting the perception of the size of the body buried in the tomb in this same area, see Zajadacz-Hastenrath, *Chaukhandigräber,* 16–18.

57. See Cunningham, *Report for the Year 1872–1873,* 5:130–131.

58. See Ibid., 130.

59. See ibid., 131.

60. See ibid., 106.

61. See ibid., 104.

62. See Alexander Cunningham, *Report of a Tour in the Punjab in 1878–79,* Archaeological Survey of India 14 (Calcutta, 1887; reprint, Varanasi, 1970), 41; and H. B. W. Garrick and A. Cunningham, *Report of a Tour in the Panjâb and Râjpûtâna in 1883–84,* Archaeological Survey of India 23 (Calcutta, 1887; reprint, Varanasi, n.d.), 63.

63. On the nau-gaz tombs in Ahmadabad, see Philip Davies, *The Penguin Guide to the Monuments of India: Islamic, Rajput, European* (New York, 1989), 2:343. On the city of Ahmadabad and its monuments, see George Michell and Snehal Shah with John Burton-Page, eds., *Ahmadabad* (Bombay, 1988); M. A. Chaghatai, *Muslim Monuments of Ahmadabad through Their Inscriptions* (Poona, 1934); and Ratnamanirao Bhimrao Jote, *Gujarat-nun-Patnagar Amdavad* (Ahmedabad, 1928). For more general works on the Muslim monuments of the area, see Percy Brown, *Indian Architecture: Islamic Period* (Bombay, 1965–1968); John Marshall, "The Monuments of Muslim India," in *Cambridge History of India* (Cambridge 1936), vol. 3, chap. 23; and S. K. Saraswati, "Art," in *History and Culture of the Indian People: The Delhi Sultanate,* ed. Ramesh Chandra Majumdar (Bombay, 1960), vol. 4, chap. 19.

64. See Crooke, *An Introduction to the Popular Religion and Folklore of Northern India,* 140–141.

65. See ibid., 140.

66. See Cunningham, *Report for the Year 1872–1873,* 131, 104.

On the earliest Muslim invasions of Sind, see C. E. Bosworth and T. W. Haig, "Sind," in *Encyclopaedia of Islam,* 9:632–635; F. Gabrieli, "Muhammad ibn Qāsim ath-Thaqafī and the Arab Conquest of Sin," *East and West,* n.s., 15 (1964–1965): 281–295; Y. Friedmann, "A Contribution to the Early History of Islam in India," in *Studies in Memory of Gaston Wiet,* ed. Myriam Rosen-Ayalon (Jerusalem, 1977), 309–333; D. N. McLean, *Religion and Society in Arab Sind* (Leiden, 1989); Richard F. Burton, *Scinde; or, the Unhappy Valley* (London, 1851); idem, *Scinde Revisited* (London, 1877); A. Wink, *al-Hind: The Making of the Indo-Islamic World* (Leiden, 1990); H. M. Ishaq, "A Peep into the First Arab Expeditions to India under the Companions of the Prophet," *Islamic Culture* 19 (1945): 109–114;

and B. M. B. K. As-Sindi, "The Probable Date of the First Arab Expeditions to India," *Islamic Culture* 20 (1946): 250–266.

67. On these long graves, see Hasan Muarif Ambary, "Epigraphical Data from 17th–19th Century Muslim Graves in East Java," in *Cultural Contact and Textual Interpretation: Papers from the Fourth European Colloquium on Malay and Indonesian Studies Held in Leiden in 1983,* ed. C. D. Grijns and S. O. Robson, Verhandelingen van het Koninklijk Instituut voor Taal-, Land- en Volkenkunde 115, 24–37 (Dordrecht, 1986).

68. On this date, see Sir T. S. Raffles, "On the Malayu Nation: Translation of a Maláyu Manuscript Entitled A History of Former Times Containing an Account of the First Arrival of the Portuguese at Malacca," *Asiatick Researches* 12 (1816): 116–122; Th. W. Juynboll, "De datum Maandag 12 Rabīʿ I op den grafsteen van Malik Ibrāhīm," *TBS* 53 (1922): 605–608; J. P. Moquette, "De datum op den grafsteen van Malik Ibrahim te Grissee," *TBS* 54 (1912): 208–214; idem, "De grafstenen te Pasé en Grissee vergeleken met dergelijke monumenten uit Hindoestan," *TBS* 54 (1912): 536–648; V. Monteil, *Indonésie* (Paris, 1970), 95–125; and N. A. Baloch, *The Advent of Islam* (Islamabad, 1980).

69. See Ambary, "Epigraphical Data from 17th–19th Century Muslim Graves in East Java," 25–26.

Long tombs are also reported along the coast of Kenya. Allen and Wilson, *Swahili Houses and Tombs on the Coast of Kenya,* mention a number of large tombs, ranging from five meters wide by nine meters long. Figure 15 shows a tomb nine meters long by five meters wide. Figure 7 shows a tomb eleven meters long by two meters wide. Figure 4 shows a tomb nine meters long by four meters wide.

On tombs in this area, see G. Matthew, "The East African Coast until the Coming of the Portuguese," in *History of East Africa,* ed. R. Oliver and G. Matthew (Oxford, 1963), 95–127; James S. Kirkman, *Men and Monuments on the East African Coast* (London, 1964), esp. 90; R. Wilding, "The Ancient Buildings of the North Kenya Coast," *Plan East Africa* 2 (1971): 41–46, esp. 44–45; R. Lewcock, "Architectural Connections between Africa and Parts of the Indian Ocean Littoral," *Art and Archaeology Research Papers* 9 (1976): 13–23, esp. 16–17; and J. S. Trimingham, *Islam in East Africa* (Oxford, 1964). On Takwa, see T. H. Wilson, "Takwa: An Ancient Swahili Settlement of the Lamu Archipelago," *Kenya Past and Present* 10 (1979): 6–16; and J. S. Kirkan, "Takwa: The Mosque of the Pillar."

70. On this tomb and the question of the antiquity of the inscription, see Ahmad Nabi Khan, *Islamic Architecture of Pakistan: An Analytical Exposition,* vol. 1, *Arab and Central Asian Contribution* (Islamabad, 1411/1900).

71. For information on documentary sources and the dating of tombs by ar-

chitectural and archeological means, see M. H. Panhwar, *Source Material on Sind, and the Culture of Sind* (Karachi, 1980); A. A. Brohi, *A History of Tombstones: Sind and Baluchistan* (Lahore, 1986); and Salome Zajadacz-Hastenrath, "Islamic Funerary Enclosures in Sind," *Islamic Art* 4 (1992). On South Asian Muslim remains under the ʿAbbasids, see Muhammad Abdul Ghafur, "Fourteen Kufic Inscriptions of Banbhore, the Site of Debal," *Pakistan Archaeology* 3 (1966): 81–83. For a general overview of the Muslim shrines in India, see Christian W. Troll, ed., *Muslim Shrines in India: Their Character, History and Significance* (Delhi, 1989; reprint, New Delhi, 2003); and R. E. Enthoven, *The Folklore of Bombay* (Oxford, 1924), esp. 141–167.

72. On tombs of companions of the prophet Muhammad in Central Asia, see Castagné, "Le culte des lieux saints de l'Islam au Turkestan," describing Mazar of Abu Jalil in the village of Kara-Mazar (77–78) and the tomb of Nour Ata, dated to 261 AH (874 CE) (103–105). On the tombs of the earliest Muslims in China, see Dru C. Gladney, "Muslim Tombs and Ethnic Folklore: Charters for Hui Identity," *Journal of Asian Studies* 46 (1987): 495–532. These include the Linghan Muslim tombs in the Quanzhou mosque, founded 1009–1010, said to house two Muslim saints sent to China by the prophet Muhammad; He Qiaoyun's Minhsu, housing two of four saints sent from Medina during the reign of the Tang emperor Wu De (618–626 CE); the "bell tomb" of the third of those saints, Wahb Abu Kabcha; and the burial place of the fourth, in Yangzhou. See Liu Binru and Chen Dazuo, "Yangzhou 'Huihui tang' he yuandai alabowen de mubei" [Yangzhou 'Huihui temple' and the Yuan dynasty Arabic gravestones], reprinted in *Huizu shilun ji,* 1949–1979 [Hui history collection, 1949–1979], ed. Chinese Academy of Social Sciences Ethnology Department and Central Nationalities Institute Ethnology Department, Hui History Team (Yinchuan, 1984); Chen Dasheng, "Quanzhou yisilanjiaopai yu yuanmou yisiba xizhanluan zingzhi shishen" [Tentative inquiry into the Islamic sects at Quanzhou and the 'isbah' disturbance toward the end of the Yuan dynasty], in *Symposium on Quanzhou Islam,* ed. Quanzhou Maritime Museum (Quanzhou, 1983), 167–176; idem, ed., *Islamic Inscriptions in Quanzhou* (Yinchuan, 1984), 95–101; Yang Hongzun, "A Preliminary Discussion on the Building Year of Quanzhou Holy Tomb and the Authenticity of Its Legend," in *The Islamic Historic Relics in Quanzhou,* ed. Committee for Protecting Islamic Historical Relics in Quanzhou and the Research Centre for the Historical Relics of Chinese Culture (Quanzhou, 1985), 16–38; Zhi Cheng, "'Fanke mu' ji qi qouguan wen ti shitan" [A tentative inquiry into 'barbarian guests' graves' and related problems]," in *Symposium on Quanzhou Islam* (Quanzhou, 1985); and Wu Wenliang, *Religious Inscriptions in Quanzhou* (Quanzhou, 1957).

On tombs of prominent Muslims in Oman which are not reported to be overly long, see John Carter, "Graves of Three Descendants of Badr Bū Ṭuwayriq in Ẓafār of Oman," *Arabian Studies* 2 (1975): 211–212. On tombs of Muslim martyrs in Asia Minor, see F. W. Hasluck, "Graves of the Arabs in Asia Minor," *Annual of the British School at Athens* 19 (1912–1913): 182–190.

73. See Cunningham, *Four Reports Made during the Years 1862–63–64–65*, 323.

74. See Crooke, *An Introduction to the Popular Religion and Folklore of Northern India*, 140–141; W. Simpson, *Journal of the Royal Asiatic Society of Bengal*, 205; and D.G.B., "Naugaza Tombs," *Panjab Notes and Queries* 1 (1884): 109.

75. See Cousens, *The Antiquities of Sind*, esp. 12–13.

76. On these temples, see George Michell, ed., *Brick Temples of Bengal: From the Archives of David McCutchion* (Princeton, 1983). For studies on the similarity of the Buddhist stupa and the Muslim dome, see Jas. Burgess, *The Buddhist Stupas of Amaravati and Jaggayyapeta in the Krishna District, Madras Presidency, Surveyed in 1882*, Archaeological Survey of Southern India (London, 1887; reprint, Varanasi, 1970); and idem, *Report on the Buddhist Cave Temples and Their Inscriptions: Being Part of the Results of the Fourth, Fifth, and Sixth Seasons' Operations of the Archaeological Survey of Western India, 1876–77, 1877–78, 1878–79*, Archaeological Survey of Western India 4 (London, 1883; reprint, Varanasi, 1964).

For the study of the Muslim dome as representing the sky or the heavens, see Paul Wheatley, *The Places Where Men Pray Together* (Chicago, 2001), 300, 465n25; and Charles Wendell, "Baghdād: *Imago Mundi*, and Other Foundation Lore," *International Journal of Middle East Studies* 2 (1971): 119–120. Some useful information can also be found in E. B. Smith, *The Dome: A Study in the History of Ideas* (Princeton, 1950).

For links between Buddhist and Muslim tomb architecture in the Orissa hill shrines, see W. W. Hunter, *Orissa* (London, 1872). On the comparison of Muslim and Buddhist tomb symbolism in the Maldives, see John Carswell, "Mosques and Tombs in the Maldive Islands," *Art and Archaeology Research Papers* 9 (1976): 26–30, esp. 27–28.

77. Henry Cousens, *The Architectural Antiquities of Western India* (London, 1926), 59, and his note on the use of baked mud bricks in Sind, 82–83.

78. On the baked mud brick of Indian Muslim tombs, see Sharīf, *Islam in India; or, The Qanun-i-Islam*, 280–284. Also see the general treatment of Rita Taploo, "The Origin and Development of Islamic Tombs in India (II)," *Quarterly Review of Historical Studies* 15, no. 1 (1975–1976): 20–30; and Ziauddin Desai, "Principle Mosques and Tombs of India," *Indo-Asian Culture* 14 (1965): 332–342. For an example from the Near East, see Kamada and Ohtsu, "Report on the Excavations at Songor A," 151, pl. 44B.

79. On the stupas and the relics of the Buddha, see the references in chap. 3 above.

80. For a review of the different texts and architectural features related to the notion of the building as a stone embodiment of the otherwise absent person

or deity, see Prasanna Kumar Acharya, *Hindu Architecture in India and Abroad* (Oxford, 1965), esp. vols. 6 and 7.

81. See Stella Kramrisch, *The Hindu Temple,* 2 vols. (Calcutta, 1946). On the baked bricks as a symbolic substance related to the flesh of the deity, see the Matsyapurana, chap. 269; Taitt. Samh. 4:4.9; and S.B. VI.1.2.22f.

82. See the references in Kramrisch, *The Hindu Temple,* 104.

83. On the dismemberment of Purusa and its cosmogonic significance, see the references and analysis in Lincoln, *Myth, Cosmos, and Society*; and Grottanelli and others, "Sacrificio, organizzazione del cosmo, dinamica sociale."

84. See Kramrisch, *The Hindu Temple,* 1:67–99; and Ananda Coomaraswamy, *Elements of Buddhist Iconography* (Cambridge, Mass., 1935), pls. 1 and 2.

85. See Wetzel, *Islamische Grabbauten in Indien aus der Zeit der Soldatenkaiser, 1320–1540*. See esp. the example of the tomb at the cemetery of Lakho Pir near Jerruck from the fifteenth century (16, fig. 3). Also see the examples in Zajadacz-Hastenrath, *Chaukhandigräber*, esp. 15.

86. See Jettmar, "The Middle Asiatic Heritage of Dardistan"; Grjaznov, "Minusinskie kamennye baby v svjazi s nekotorymi novymi materialami"; and Bergman, *Archaeological Researches in Sinkiang.*

87. For studies on some of the early connections between Muslims and Indian religious ideas, see Y. Friedmann, "The Temple of Multan: A Note on Early Muslim Attitudes to Idolatry," *Israel Oriental Studies* 2 (1972): 176–182; idem, "A Contribution to the Early History of Islam in India"; idem, "The Origins and Significance of the Chach Nāma," in *Islam in Asia*, vol. 1, ed. R. Israeli and A. Johns (Jerusalem, 1984); V. B. Mishra, *Religious Beliefs and Practices of North India during the Early Medieval Period* (Leiden, 1973); V. B. Mishra, *The Hindu Sahis of Afghanistan and the Punjab, A.D. 865–1026* (Patna, 1972); G. R. Tibbetts, "Pre-Islamic Arabia and Southeast Asia," *Journal of the Malayan Branch of the Royal Asiatic Society* 25, no. 3 (1956); and T. Watters, *On Yuan Chwang's Travels in India, 629–645 A.D.*, 2 vols. (London, 1904–1905).

88. van der Meulen, *Aden to the Hadhramaut*, 193.

89. See Walter Harris, *A Journey through the Yemen* (Edinburgh, 1903), 318. Yāqūt, *Muʿjam al-buldān*, s.v. "Ṣanʿāʾ," reports that the city of Sanʿa was named after Ṣanʿāʾ b. Azāl b. Yaqṭan b. ʿĀbir (Eber) b. Shāliḥ (Shelah). The biblical names Shelah and Eber are associated with the prophets Salih and Hud, making Sanʿa a descendant of Salih and Hud.

90. See Ibn al-Faqīh, *Kitāb al-buldān,* ed. Yūsuf al-Hādī (Beirut, 1996), 74–78. Yāqūt, *Muʿjam al-buldān,* s.v. "Bakkah," relates another report on the authority of ʿAmr b. al-ʿĀṣ that associates the name "Bakkah" with the giants.

91. See Doughty, *Travels in Arabia Deserta,* 1:434, 1:668, where he mentions the tomb of "al-Sānī" (which he translates as "the smith"), near Ḥāʾil, measuring three fathoms in length. On the three heroic cycles of the Banū Hilāl, see

A. Vaissière, "Cycle héroïque des Ouled-Hilal," *Revue Afrique* 36 (1892): 242–243, 312–324; A. Bel, "La Djâzya, chanson arabe précédée d'observations sur quelques légendes arabes et sur la geste des Banū Hilāl," *Journal Asiatique* (1902–1903): 289–347; and H. R. Idris and J. Schleifer, "Hilāl," in *Encyclopaedia of Islam,* 3:385–387.

92. For an overview of these discoveries and their association with giants and heroes, see the expansive work of John Boardman, *The Archaeology of Nostalgia: How the Greeks Re-created Their Mythical Past* (London, 2002). Many of the references that follow are cited by Boardman in the course of his analysis.

93. See Solinus, *Collectanea Rerum Memorabilium,* ed.Theodor Mommsen (Berlin, 1895; reprint, 1958), trans. into German by H. Walter as *Die Collectanea Rerum Memorabilium des Gaius Iulius Solinus* (Wiesbaden, 1968), 9.6.

94. See Pausanias, *Description of Greece,* ed. and trans. W. H. S. Jones (Cambridge, Mass., 1971), 8.32.5. On Asklepios and the origins of human beings, see Angela Maria Mazzanti, *L'uomo nella cultura religiosa del tardo-antico: Tra etica e ontologia* (Bologna, 1990), esp. 67–74.

95. See Philostratus, *Heroicus,* trans. J. K. B. Maclean and E. B. Aitken (Atlanta, 2001), 8.13–17. On the Aloadai brothers and the giants, see Erika Simon, "Otos und Ephialtes," *Antike Kunst* 5 (1962): 43–44; and idem, "Aloadai," in *Lexicon Iconographicum Mythologiae Classicae* (Zurich, 1981), vol. 1, pt. 1:570–572. On Alkyoneus and his battle with Heracles, see B. Andreae, "Herakles und Alkyoneus," *Jahrbuch des Deutschen Archäologischen Instituts* 77 (1962): 130–210; F. Croissant, "Remarques sur la métope de la Mort d'Alkyoneus à l'Héraion du Silaris," *Bulletin de Correspondance Hellénique* 89 (1965): 390–399; and C. Robert, "Alkyoneus," *Hermes* 19 (1884): 473–485.

96. See Plutarch, *Vitae,* ed. and trans. Bernadotte Perrin as *Plutarch's Lives* (Cambridge, Mass., 1989), 8 (of Cimon), 36 (of Theseus). On this account, see F. Frost, "Plutarch and Theseus," *Classical Bulletin* 60 (1984): 65–73. On Theseus, see C. Dugas, "L'évolution de la légende de Thésée," *Revue des Etudes Grecques* 56 (1943): 1–24, reprinted in *Recueil Charles Dugas* (Paris, 1960), 93–107; C. Dugas and R. Flacelière, *Thésée: Images et récits* (Paris, 1958); and H. A. Shapiro, "Theseus in Kimonian Athens: The Iconography of Empire," *Mediterranean Historical Review* 7 (1992): 29–49.

97. See Plutarch, *Vitae Parallelae,* ed. C. Lindoskog and K. Ziegler (Leipzig, 1960), Life of Sertorius, 9; and Strabo, *Geography,* ed. and trans. H. L. Jones (London, 1917–1932), 829, who places it at Lynx, in Morocco. On Antaios and his defeat by Heracles, see Fr. Vian, *La guerre des Géants* (Paris, 1952), 21.43–44. On Greek and Roman burial customs, see Donna C. Kurtz and John Boardman, *Greek Burial Customs* (Ithaca, 1971); and Jocelyn M. C. Toynbee, *Death and Burial in the Roman World* (Ithaca, 1971).

98. See Pausanius, *Description of Greece,* 1.35.5. On the giant Asterios or Aster,

see Vian, *La Guerre des Géants,* 262–264; and Gratia Berger-Doer, "Aster," in *Lexicon Iconographicum Mythologiae Classicae,* vol. 2, pt. 1:903.

99. See Pausanius, *Description of Greece,* 8.29.4.

100. See Philostratus, *Heroicus,* 8.3.

101. See Phlegon, *De Mirabilibus,* cited in W. Hansen, *Phlegon of Tralles' Book of Marvels* (Exeter, 1996), 17.

102. On Greek heroes, see Angelo Brelich, *Heros: Il culto greco degli eroi e il problema degli esseri semi-divini* (Rome, 1957).

103. See Diodorus Siculus, *Bibliotheca Historica,* ed. and trans. C. H. Oldfather and others, 7 vols. (Cambridge, Mass., 1933–1967), 1.24.2; and Pausanius, *Description of Greece,* 1.35.5. On Ajax, see P. Von der Mühll, *Der große Aias* (Basel, 1930).

104. See Philostratus, *Heroicus,* 7.9; and Homer, *Iliad,* ed. T. W. Allen (Oxford, 1931), 3.226–229. Also see L. R. Farnell, *Greek Hero-Cults and Ideas of Immortality* (Oxford, 1921), 307–308.

105. See Herodotus, *Historiae,* ed. C. Hude (Oxford, 1908, 1927), 1.67–68. See also G. L. Huxley, "Bones for Orestes," *Greek, Roman, and Byzantine Studies* 20 (1979): 145–48.

106. Pausanius, *Description of Greece,* 5.13:4–6. On Pelops, see O. Berger, *La légende de Pélops et d'Oinomaos* (Louvain, 1935); and Ismène Triantis, "Pelops," in *Lexicon Iconographicum Mythologiae Classicae,* vol. 7, pt. 1:282–287.

107. Phlegon, *De Mirabilibus,* in Hansen, *Phlegon of Tralles' Book of Marvels,* 11. On the strength of Idas, see Homer, *Iliad,* trans. A. T. Murray (Cambridge, Mass., 1999), 9.558.

108. See Ptolemaeus Chennus of Alexandria, *Kaine Historia,* cited in Photius, *Bibliotheca,* 147a–b. Also see the memorial to the lost finger of Orestes in Pausanius, *Description of Greece,* 8.34.2–3; and the discussion in Walter Burkert, *The Creation of the Sacred: Tracks of Biology in Early Religions* (Cambridge, Mass., 1996), 34–40.

Other body parts commonly mentioned include heads. Conon in F. Jacoby, *Fragmente der griechischen Historiker* (Berlin, 1923), 26, F1:45, mentions the head of Orpheus, which was washed up at the mouth of the river Meles near Smyrna before being reburied neaby. Lucianus of Samosata, *Adversus Indoctum: Verae Historiae* (Biponti, 1789–1793), 11–12, says the head of Orpheus was buried at Bacheion in Lebos. Stobaeus, 64.14, says the lyre was buried with the head, and Myrsilus of Lesbos, *Historika Paradoxa,* F2, says the head of Orpheus is buried at Antiss (Lesbos).

109. See R. Plot, *The Natural History of Oxfordshire* (Oxford, 1677); and Boardman, *The Archaeology of Nostalgia,* 35.

110. See Boardman, *The Archaeology of Nostalgia,* 34–35; J. Westwood, *Albion:*

*A Guide to Legendary Britain* (Salem, 1985); W. Field, *An Historical and Descriptive Account of the Town and Castle of Warwick and of the Neighbouring Spa of Leamington* (Warwick, 1815), 24–27, 232–233; and Henry T. Cooke, *A Guide to Warwick, Kenilworth, Stratford-on-Avon, Coventry, and the Various Places of Interest in the Neighbourhood* (Warwick, 1870), esp. 99–101.

For ancient examples of monster bones, see Pausanius, *Description of Greece,* 2.10.2, concerning bones in the sanctuary of Asklepios. Diodorus Siculus, *Bibliotheca Historica,* 1.26.6–7, relates an Egyptian tradition that Osiris defeated multi-bodied creatures, called giants by the Greeks. Pliny, *Historia Naturalis,* 11.111, reports on ants as big as wolves in northern India, and the horns of these ants are said to have been displayed in the temple of Heracles at Erythrai. Sir John Maundevile mentioned the "Pismire" ants of Sri Lanka, as big as dogs, which mined gold. See A. Layard and others, *The Marvellous Adventures of Sir John Maundevile Kt: Being His Voyage and Travel Which Treateth of the Way to Jerusalem and of the Marvels of Ind with Other Islands and Countries* (Westminster, 1895), chap. 30.

111. See Boardman, *The Archaeology of Nostalgia,* 34–35; and Kenneth Oakley, "Folklore of Fossils," *Antiquity* 39 (1965): 9–16, 117–125, esp. 123.

112. See the references listed in Reidar Th. Christiansen, *The Migratory Legends: A Proposed List of Types with a Systematic Catalogue of the Norwegian Variants,* vol. 71, no. 175 (Helsinki, 1958), 81–88.

113. See Oakley, "Folklore of Fossils," 123.

114. Al-Qurṭubī, *al-Jāmiʿ li-aḥkām al-Qurʾān,* on Q 7:69. Also see Ibn Kathīr, *Tafsīr al-Qurʾān al-ʿaẓīm,* on Q 7:69, who says that God made the people of ʿĀd taller than ordinary people.

115. See al-Qurṭubī, *al-Jāmiʿ li-aḥkām al-Qurʾān,* on Q 7:69; al-Ṭabarī, *Jāmiʿ al-bayān fī tafsīr al-Qurʾān,* on Q 7:69; and al-Thaʿlabī, *Qiṣaṣ al-anbiyāʾ,* 105.

116. See al-Thaʿlabī, *Qiṣaṣ al-anbiyāʾ,* 105.

117. Yāqūt, *Muʿjam al-buldān,* s.v. "Iram." Also see the account in Ibn Kathīr, *Qiṣaṣ al-anbiyāʾ,* 87; and Muḥammad Mutawalī al-Shaʿrāwī, *Qiṣaṣ al-anbiyāʾ,* ed. Merkaz al-Turāth li-l-khidma al-Kitāb wa al-Sunnah (Cairo, 1997), 1:389.

118. See al-Ṭabarī, *Jāmiʿ al-bayān fī tafsīr al-Qurʾān,* on Q 26:128–129; Ibn Kathīr, *Tafsīr al-Qurʾān al-ʿaẓīm,* on Q 26:128–129; Ibn Kathīr, *Qiṣaṣ al-anbiyāʾ,* 87; and al-Shaʿrāwī, *Qiṣaṣ al-anbiyāʾ,* 1:390–391.

119. See al-Ṭabarī, *Taʾrīkh al-rusul wa al-mulūk,* 244, who gives the genealogy as Salih b. ʿUbayd b. Asif b. Masikh b. Ubayd b. Khadir b. Thamūd b. Gether b. Aram b. Shem b. Noah and Salih b. Asif b. Kamashij b. Iram b. Thamūd b. Gether b. Aram b. Shem b. Noah. ʿAbd al-Raḥmān b. Abī Bakr al-Suyūṭī, *al-Itiqān fī ʿulūm al-Qurʾān,* gives the genealogy, on the authority of Wahb b. Munabbih, as Salih b. ʿUbayd b. Hayir b. Thamūd b. Hayir b. Shem b. Noah. Al-Thaʿlabī, *Qiṣaṣ al-anbiyāʾ,* gives the genealogy as Salih b. ʿUbayd b. Asif b.

Mashij b. Ubayd b. Hadhir b. Thamūd b. ʿĀd b. Uz b. Aram b. Shem b. Noah, making Salih a direct descendant of the ʿĀd.

The genealogy of Hud is given as much closer to Noah. Ibn Kathīr, *Qiṣaṣ al-anbiyāʾ*, 80, gives the genealogy as Hud b. Shelah b. Arpachshad b. Shem b. Noah. Al-Qurṭubī, *al-Jāmiʿ li-aḥkām al-Qurʾān,* cites Ibn Isḥāq as saying that Hud was the son of Uz (Aws) b. Aram b. Shelah b. Arpachshad b. Shem b. Noah. Al-Ṭabarī, *Taʾrīkh al-rusul wa al-mulūk,* 231, gives the genealogy as Hud b. Abdallah b. Rabah al-Khalud b. ʿĀd b. Uz (Aws) b. Aram b. Shem b. Noah.

120. For this ḥadīth report, see Ibn Ḥibbān, *Ṣaḥīḥ Ibn Ḥibbān* (Beirut, 1984), 1:125.

121. On this distinction, see Ibn Kathīr, *Qiṣaṣ al-anbiyāʾ*, 80–81. There is some dispute over the genealogy of Shuʿayb. Al-Ṭabarī, *Jāmiʿ al-bayān fī tafsīr al-Qurʾān,* on Q 7:85, cites Ibn Isḥāq, ʿAṭā b. Abī Rabāḥ, and others as saying that Shuʿayb was the son of Mikil (or Mikaʾil) b. Issachar (Yashjar) b. Midian b. Abraham. He cites Sharqī b. al-Quṭāmī as saying that Shuʿayb was Ephah b. Jashbub (Yawbab) b. Midian b. Abraham. In both cases, he is related to Abraham through his son Midian. This is also repeated in Ibn Kathīr, *Qiṣaṣ al-anbiyāʾ*, 177–178. Al-Ṭabarī and Ibn Kathīr also cite another genealogy which makes Shuʿayb a descendant of Abraham through the line of Isaac: Shuʿayb b. Jazi b. Issachar (Ayfa) b. Levi b. Jacob b. Isaac b. Abraham (al-Ṭabarī), and Shuʿayb b. Issachar b. Levi b. Jacob (Ibn Kathīr). In any case, the inclusion of Issachar in both genealogies makes Shuʿayb share in the lines of both Isaac (Gen 30:17–18) and Midian.

122. Al-Ṭabarī, *Taʾrīkh al-rusul wa al-mulūk,* 214–215. Also see Ferdinand Wüstenfeld, *Genealogische Tabellen der arabischen Stämme und Familien,* 2 vols. (Göttingen, 1852–1853).

123. See Ibn Kathīr, *Qiṣaṣ al-anbiyāʾ*, 80–81; al-Kisāʾī, *Qiṣaṣ al-anbiyāʾ*, trans. W. M. Thackston as *The Tales of the Prophets* (Boston, 1978), 109–117.

124. See Ibn Kathīr, *Qiṣaṣ al-anbiyāʾ*, 189–190.

125. For further details, see Brannon Wheeler, "al-Anbiyāʾ al-ʿarabīyah wa qubūr al-jabābirah," *al-Nashra* 30 (Spring 2004): 19–23.

126. On the flood as an epoch divider, see Isaac M. Kikawada, "Noah and the Ark," in *The Anchor Bible Dictionary,* ed. David Noel Freeman and others (New York, 1992), 4:1123–1131; and A. D. Kilmer, "The Mesopotamian Concept of Overpopulation and Its Solution as Reflected in the Mythology," *Orientalia* 41 (1972): 160–177.

127. See Thorkild Jacobsen, *The Sumerian King List,* Assyriological Studies 11 (Chicago, 1942); and Pritchard, *Ancient Near Eastern Texts Relating to the Old Testament,* 265–266. On life span reduction, see D. L. Petersen, "Yahweh and the Organization of the Cosmos," *Journal for the Study of the Old Testament* 13 (1979): 47–64, esp. 58–59; and J. Schreiner, "Gen 6, 1–4 und die Problematik von Leben

und Tod," in *De la Tôrah au Messie*, ed. M. Carrez and others (Paris, 1981), 65–74, esp. 70–72.

128. See, for example, Christensen, *Les types du premier homme et du premier roi*; W. G. Lambert and A. R. Millalrd, *Atra-hasis: The Babylonian Story of the Flood* (London, 1969); R. Humphries, *Ovid: Metamorphoses* (Bloomington, 1958); and Suryakanta, *The Flood Legend in Sanskrit Literature* (Delhi, 1950).

129. See, for example, Ibn Kathīr, *Tafsīr al-Qurʾān al-ʿaẓīm,* on Q 28:19 and Q 40:35. Also see the account, attributed to Ibn ʿAbbās, of the prophet Muhammad's night journey, during which he sees in hell the giants who do not believe in the Day of Reckoning. See ibid., on Q 17:1.

130. Ibid., on Q 5:20–26. Also see Ibn Kathīr, *Qiṣaṣ al-anbiyāʾ* (Beirut, 1312/1992), 71. Al-Thaʿlabī, *Qiṣaṣ al-anbiyāʾ*, 75, gives an account on the authority of Jaʿfar al-Ṣādiq that ʿAnāq was the name of the first daughter born to Adam and Eve after the fall from Eden, and the first person to fornicate.

131. See al-Ṭabarī, *Taʾrīkh al-rusul wa al-mulūk,* 498–499. See the accounts mentioned in Ibn al-Jawzī, *al-Muntaẓam fī tawārīkh al-mulūk wa al-umam* (Beirut, 1995), 1:236.

132. Taken from al-Ṭabarī, *Taʾrīkh al-rusul wa al-mulūk,* 501.

133. See Ibn Kathīr, *Tafsīr al-Qurʾān al-ʿaẓīm,* on Q 5:20–26; and idem, *Qiṣaṣ al-anbiyāʾ*, 382–388.

134. See al-Ṭabarī, *Taʾrīkh al-rusul wa al-mulūk,* 548; and Ibn al-Jawzī, *al-Muntaẓam fī tawārīkh al-mulūk wa al-umam,* 257–264. On the relation of the Amalekites to the Ṭasm, Jadīs, Jurhum, Thamūd, and ʿĀd, see ʿAbd al-Mālik Ibn Hishām, *Kitāb al-tijān* (Hyderabad, 1928), 29–30; al-Azraqī, *Akhbār Makkah,* 44–56; and Th. Nöldeke, *Über die Amalekiter und einige andere Nachbarvölker der Israeliten* (Göttingen, 1864). For a different biblical context for conflict between the Israelites and the Amalekites (1 Sam 15), see D. Edelman, "Saul's Battle against Amaleq (1 Sam 15)," *Journal for the Study of the Old Testament* 35 (1986): 71–84.

135. For a possible historical reference to the Anakim in the Egyptian Execration texts, see Pritchard, *Ancient Near Eastern Texts Relating to the Old Testament,* 328–329; and W. F. Albright, "The Egyptian Empire in Asia in the Twenty-first Century BC," *Journal of the Palestine Exploration Society* 8 (1928): 223–256.

136. For the references to Og as one of the Rephaim, see Deut 3:11, 13, and Josh 12:4, 13:12. On the epithet "Raphite" applied to the Rephaim, see C. E. L'Heureux, "The yelîdê hārāpāʾ: A Cultic Association of Warriors," *Bulletin of the American Schools of Oriental Research* 221 (1976): 83–85. On the Rephaim in general, see W. Horwitz, "The Significance of the Rephaim," *Journal of Northwest Semitic Languages* 7 (1979): 37–43.

The "Valley of the Rephaim" (ʿēmeq repāʾîm) is rendered into Greek in the Septuagint as (2 Sam 5:18) "Valley of the Titans" (titanōn) and (1 Chron 11:15,

14:9) "Valley of the Giants" (gigantōn). See Gershom Edelstein, "Rephaim, Valley of," in *The Anchor Bible Dictionary* (1992), 5:676–677.

For giants as enemies in European traditions and folkore, see Strabo, *Geography,* 248; Pindar, *Pythia,* ed. and trans. W. H. Race (Cambridge, Mass., 1997), 1:15–22; J. Wood, *Giants and Dwarfs* (London, 1868); and O. L. Jiriczek, "Faeröische Märchen und Sagen," *Zeitschrift des Vereins für Volkskunde* 2 (1892), 1–23, esp. 18 on "trolls" and "seehunsfell." For Danish examples, see Evald Tang Kristensen, *Danske sagn* (Copenhagen, 1892–1901; reprint, Hassing, 1963–1968), esp. 3:13–15, 8–12. On Finnish examples, see V. E. V. Wessman, *Förteckning över Sägentyperna* (Helsinki, 1931). On German examples, see John R. Broderius, "The Giant in Germanic Tradition" (PhD dissertation, University of Chicago, 1933), esp. sec. 12. For Icelandic examples, see Jón Arnason, *Legends of Iceland* (London, 1864), 1:40–53.

137. Most versions of the Bible translate the Hebrew "nepilīm" as "giants." The Septuagint and Vulgate use *gigantes.* The Peshiṭta, Samarian Pentateuch, Targum Onkelos, and Targum Neofiti use variations of the root G-B-R. See P. S. Alexander, "The Targumim and Early Exegesis of 'Sons of God' in Genesis 6," *Journal of Semitic Studies* 23 (1972): 60–71. On the general significance of the passage in Genesis, see D. J. A. Clines, "The Significance of the 'Sons of God' Episode (Genesis 6:1–4) in the Context of the 'Primeval History' (Genesis 1–11)," *Journal for the Study of the Old Testament* 13 (1979): 33–46; and Richard Hess, "Nephilim," in *The Anchor Bible Dictionary* (1992), 4:1072–1073.

138. Josephus, *Jewish Antiquities,* 5.ii.3 (pp. 58–59).

139. See Jerome in E. Klostermann, *Eusebius Werke,* vol. 3, pt. 1, *Das Onomastikon der Biblischen Ortsnamen, mit der lateinischen Übersetzung des Hieronymus* (Leipzig, 1904), 21:21–23 (Ashdod), 7:11–18 (Hebron, described as a dwelling place of giants [habitaculum gigantum]), 73:16–23 (Gaza). Also see the references in Michele Piccirillo and Eugenio Alliata, eds., *The Madaba Map Centenary, 1897–1997: Travelling through the Byzantine Umayyad Period* (Jerusalem, 1998), 96, 78, 123.

140. See Eucherius, *Letter to Faustus,* ed. I. Fraipont, Corpus Scriptorum Latinorum (Turnhout, 1958), 128, trans. Wilkinson in his *Jerusalem Pilgrims before the Crusades,* 53. See Adomnan, *The First Book on the Holy Places,* ed. L. Bieler, Corpus Scriptorum Latinorum 175, 235 (Turnhout, 1958), 259; Wilkinson, *Jerusalem Pilgrims before the Crusades,* 105.

141. Theodosius, *The Topography of the Holy Land,* ed. P. Geyer (Turnhout, 1958), 148, trans. Wilkinson in his *Jerusalem Pilgrims before the Crusades,* 70.

142. See Bernard the Monk, "Travels," in *Itinera Hierosolymitana et Descriptiones Terrae Sanctae Bellis Sacris Anteriora: Latina Lingua Exarata Sumptibus Societatis Illustrandis Orientis Latini Monumentis,* ed. T. Tobler and others (Osnabrück, 1966), 309–320, esp. 313; Wilkinson, *Jerusalem Pilgrims before the Crusades,* 142.

143. See al-Ṭabarī, *Taʾrīkh al-rusul wa al-mulūk,* 121–122; idem, *Jāmiʿ al-bayān fī tafsīr al-Qurʾān,* on Q 2:127; and Ibn Kathīr, *Tafsīr al-Qurʾān al-ʿaẓīm,* on Q 2:34–39.

144. See Castagné, "Le culte des lieux saints de l'Islam au Turkestan," 85–86. For another possible example of this growth of the body in the tomb, see Castagné's (63–64) description of the Mazar Khorkhoutt-Ata venerated by the Kazakhs and Kirghiz. He reports that pilgrims discovered the feet of the saint sticking out of the tomb because of his great stature. Also see V. Veliaminov-Zernov, *Bulletins de la Section Orientale des Archives Russes,* vol. 9:272.

145. On the special significance of Daniel and his body, see U. Monnerret de Villard, *Le leggende orientali sui Magi evangelici* (Vatican City, 1952); Louis Massignon, "Elie et son rôle transhistorique, Khadiriyya en Islam," *Opera Minora* 1 (1969): 142–161, esp. 154–147; G. Vajda, "Deux 'Histoires de prophètes' selon la tradition des Shīʿites duodécimains," in *Biblical and Other Studies in Memory of S. D. Goitein,* ed. R. Ahroni (Columbus, 1986), 124–133; B. Heller, "Daniel in der islamischen Legende," in *Encyclopaedia Judaica,* ed. Cecil Roth (Jerusalem, 1972), 833–835; Sophia Grotzfeld, "Dāniyāl in der arabischen Legende," in *Festgabe für Hans Wehr,* ed. W. Fischer (Wiesbaden, 1969), 72–85; and A. Fodor, "Malḥamet Daniyal," in *The Muslim East: Studies in Honour of Julius Germanus,* ed. Gyula Kaldy-Nagy and Gyula Germanus (Budapest, 1974), 85–160.

146. See Ibn Qayyim al-Jawzīyah, *Ḥādī al-arwāḥ ilā bilād al-afrāḥ,* ed. ʿAbd al-Laṭīf Āl Muḥammad al-Fawāʾir (Amman, 1987), 164.

147. On Jesus and the Dajjāl, see Q 18:94–99. Al-Bukhārī, *Ṣaḥīḥ,* gives an overview of events (92:76–77) and describes how Jesus uses a sword (92:88–89) and the Dajjāl is killed by Jesus (92:93); al-Tirmidhī, *al-Jāmiʿ al-ṣaḥīḥ,* describes Jesus coming as morning prayer is called to slay the Dajjāl with his hand and showing the people the sword of the Dajjāl on his sword (31:10), Gog and Magog (31:23), the sword used (31:33), Jesus returning (31:54), the Dajjāl (31:55–62), and Jesus killing the Dajjāl (31:62); see also Ibn Mājah, *Sunan,* 36:11.

On the Dubbat al-Arḍ, al-Fīrūzābādī, *Qāmūs al-muḥīṭ,* s.v. "Dabb" records that the Dabbat al-Arḍ appears at the end of time, appearing to make a pilgrimage to Mecca. In its possession is the rod of Moses and the ring of Solomon with which he strikes each believer.

148. On the burial mounds of the ancient Gulf region, see Michael Rice, *The Archaeology of the Arabian Gulf, c. 5000–323 BC* (London, 1994), esp. 234–256; D. T. Potts, *The Arabian Gulf in Antiquity* (Oxford, 1990), esp. 1:192–231, 237–249; Geoffrey Bibby, *Looking for Dilmun* (New York, 1969), esp. figs. 1–2; and Brendt Alster, "Dilmun, Bahrain, and the Alleged Paradise in Sumerian Myth and Literature," in *Dilmun: New Studies in the Archaeology and Early History of Bahrain,* ed. D. T. Potts (Berlin, 1983), 39–74. On the cairns with Safaitic inscriptions, see F. V. Winnett and G. Lankester Harding, *Inscriptions from Fifty Safaitic*

*Cairns* (Toronto, 1978), esp. 3–32; Oxtoby, *Some Inscriptions of the Safaitic Bedouin,* 20–25; and William Lancaster and Fidelity Lancaster, "Graves and Funerary Monuments of the Ahl al-Gahl, Jordan," *Arabian Archaeology and Epigraphy* 4 (1993): 151–169. On cairns, burial mounds, and triliths in Oman, see D. T. Potts, *A Prehistoric Mound in the Emirate of Umm al-Qaiwain: U.A.E. Excavations at Tell Abraq in 1989* (Copenhagen, 1990), esp. 53; al-Shaḥrī, "Grave Types and 'Triliths' in Dhofar," esp. 190–191; and idem, "Recent Epigraphic Discoveries in Dhofar," *Proceedings of the Seminar for Arabian Studies* 21 (1991): passim. For burial mounds in Hasa, see P. B. Cornwall, "Ancient Arabia: Explorations in Hasa, 1940–41," *Geographical Journal* 107 (1946): 28–50. On cairn burials in Afghanistan and India, see Halbert, "The Mohammedan Graves," 187–188; and Vincent A. Smith, "European Graves at Kabul," *Indian Antiquary,* August 1909, 232. For other European tombs in Muslim areas, see Joan du Plat Taylor, "Medieval Graves in Cyprus," *Ars Islamica* 5 (1938): 35–86.

149. See Edward Westermarck, *Ritual and Belief in Morocco* (London, 1926), 1:56–60. For other accounts of the rituals related to cairns, see Peake, *A History of Jordan and its Tribes*; John Lewis Burckhardt, *Notes on the Bedouins and Wahabys* (London, 1831), esp. 17–18; J. G. Wetzstein, *Reisebericht über Hauran und die Trachonen* (Berlin, 1860), esp. 2; A. Musil, *Arabia Deserta* (New York, 1927), esp. 88; W. O. Lancaster, *The Rwala Bedouin Today* (Cambridge, 1981); and R. B. Serjeant, "The White Dune at Abyan, an Ancient Place of Pilgrimage in Southern Arabia," *Journal of Semitic Studies* 6 (1971): 74–83.

150. See Zajadacz-Hastenrath, *Chaukhandigräber*; trans. Michael Robertson as *Chaukhandi Tombs: Funerary Art in Sind and Baluchistan* (Karachi, 2003); citing Richard F. Burton, *Sindh and the Races That Inhabit the Valley of the Indus, with Notices of the Topography and History of the Province* (London, 1851; reprint, Karachi, 1973), 415n31, on the folklore that stones are though to intercede for the deceased on the Day of Judgment, and that extra stones may be placed on the tomb by visitors.

151. On the mountain symbolism of the burial mounds and cairnlike tombs, see Tamara M. Green, "Tombs," in *Encyclopedia of Religion,* esp. 14: 553. Goldziher, *Muslim Studies,* 254, claims that the dome structure developed out of the less permanent tent which was pitched over the dead body. In some places in the Arabian Peninsula and Jordan desert, the cairn or dome is simply represented by a ring of stones (rawḍah) or low-walled enclosure (ḥawṭah) with or without a roof (56).

152. On examples of burial mounds with grave goods, see Mohd. Abdul Waheed Khan, "Excavation of a Medieval Site near Quṭb Shāhi Tombs (Golconda)," *Islamic Culture* 44 (1970): 227–231; B. Guz-Sibertsein and K. Raveh, "Tel Dor: Maritime Archaeology—1987/1988," *Excavations and Surveys in Israel 1988/89,* 7/8 (1990): 51; D. Ussishkin and J. Woodhead, "Excavations at Tel Jezreel, 1990–

1991: Preliminary Report," *Tel Aviv* 18 (1991): 72–92; 19 (1992): 3–70, esp. 29–31; Kervran, "Preliminary Report on the Excavation of Qalʿat al-Bahrain," 75; E. D. Oren, *Explorations in the Negev and Sinai* (Beersheba, 1976), esp. 11, 13, and 250–251 (appendix) for a detailed listing of objects including beads, bells, pendants, anklets, headdresses, pins, combs, mirrors, knife blades, glass bottles, ceramics, and colored stones. For knife blades, see B. De Vries, "The Fortifications at El-Lejjun," in *The Roman Frontier in Central Jordan: Interim Report on the Limes Arabicus Project, 1980–1985,* ed. S. T. Parker (Oxford, 1987), 311–351, esp. 344.

For examples of weapons and jewelry depicted on tombs, see Zajadacz-Hastenrath, *Chaukhandigräber,* esp. fig. 56, p. 82, for the fifteenth-century tomb at the Hassani Sirhani graveyard. For evidence in Luristan, see Muhammad Abdul Ghafur, *The Calligraphers of Thatta* (Karachi, 1968), esp. 25; Wilhelm Eilers, *Lurische Gravsteine als Zeugnisse des Weiterlebens kassitischer Motive in der Gegenwart: Aus der Welt der islamischen Kunst* (Berlin, 1959), esp. 267–274. Also see Charles Masson, *Narrative of Various Journeys in Balochistan, Afghanistan and the Panjab* (London, 1842; reprint, Karachi, 1974), 2:275; and Katherina Otto-Dorn, "Türkische Gravsteine mit figurenreliefs aus Kleinasien," *Ars Orientalis* 3 (1959): 63–76, on figurative Seljuk depictions.

153. See Castagné, "Le culte des lieux saints de l'Islam au Turkestan," 85–86; and Edward Westermarck, *Pagan Survivals in Muhammadan Civilization* (London, 1933), 63.

154. See John Lewis Burckhardt, *Travels in Arabia: An Account of Those Territories in Hedjaz Which the Mohammedans Regard as Sacred* (London, 1829; reprint, London, 1968): 333–334; and Zahra Freeth and H. V. F. Winstone, *Explorers of Arabia: From the Renaissance to the End of the Victorian Era* (New York, 1978), 114.

155. For a striking example of this, consider the different types of jewelry reported to have been placed on the stone from Golgotha in Jerusalem by Christian pilgrims: armlets, bracelets, necklaces, rings, tiaras, girdles, crowns, belts. See Paul Geyer, ed., *Itinera Hierosolymitana saeculi IV–VIII,* Corpus Scriptorum Ecclesiasticorum Latinorum 39 (Vindobonae, 1898), 175, 171; and Wilkinson, *Jerusalem Pilgrims before the Crusades,* 83. Also see P. Geyer, *Kritische und sprachliche Erlaüterungen zu Observations sur le Vocabulaire du Pèlerinage chez Egérie et chez Antonin de Plaisance* (Nijmegen, 1965).

156. See Cunningham, *Report for the Year 1872–1873,* 106, pl. 33, figs. 6–8, and the other travelers' accounts he cites.

157. For Turkish examples of weapons carved on tombs, see Katherina Otto-Dorn, "Türkische Gravsteine mit Figurenreliefs aus Kleinasien," *Ars Orientalis* 3 (1959): 63–76. Also see the examples cited in Masson, *Narratives of Various Journeys,* 2:275; and H. A. Rose, *Glossary of the Tribes and Castes of the Punjab and North-West Frontier Province* (Lahore, 1911–1919), 3:182.

For the frequent association of weapons with the burials of heroes and gods in Greek contexts, see John Strong, "Relics," in *Encyclopedia of Religion*, 11:7686–7692; and Pausanius, *Description of Greece*, 3.iii.6–7, on the weapons of a number of heroes, including the ax of Peisander, arrow of Meriiones, spear of Achilles, and sword of Memnon. Virgil, *Georgics*, ed. and trans. H. R. Fairclough and others (Cambridge, Mass., 1999–2000), 493–497, refers to a time when farmers will plough up rusty spears and helmets and wonder at the big bones uncovered. Suetonius, *De Vita Caesarum*, ed. and trans. J. C. Rolfe (Cambridge, Mass., 1997–1998), on Augustus, 72, says Augustus collected giants' bones and the weapons of ancient heroes. Procopius, *De Bello Gothico*, trans. H. B. Dewing (London, 1914–1940), 4.22, reports on the incredible size of Aeneas's ship displayed in Rome.

The lance that pierced the side of Jesus is reported to have been hung in the Holy Sepulchre in Jersualem. See Adomnan, *The First Book on the Holy Places*, 235; and Wilkinson, *Jerusalem Pilgrims before the Crusades*, 97.

158. For examples of such elaborate necropolises, see H. Basset and Lévi-Provençal, "Chella, une nécropole mérinide," *Hespéris* 2 (1922): 1–92, 255–316, 385–425, which describes one built by the Marīnid sultans Abu Saʿīd and Abu al-Ḥasan in the fourteenth century; and G. Deverdun, *Marrakech des origines à 1912* (Rabat, 1959), esp. 381–395, on the Saʿdian tombs of Marrakesh of the sixteenth century. Also see J. Bourrilly and E. Laoust, *Stèles funéraires marocaines* (Paris, 1927). For necropolises in South Asia, see M. A. Chaghatai, "The So-Called Gardens and Tombs of Zeb-un-Niza at Lahore," *Islamic Culture* 9 (1935): 610–620; H. Goetz, "The Pathan Tombs of Sarhind," *Islamic Culture* 13 (1939): 313–318; and Siddique G. Memon, *The Tombs of the Kalhora Chiefs in Hyderabad* (Karachi, 1994). For Bijapur, see Richard Eaton and Saiyid Muhyi al-Din bin Mahmud Qadiri, *Sahifat-i Ahl-i Huda*, ed. and trans. M. Akbaruddin Siddiqi (Hyderabad, 1966). On Chinese Muslim necropolises, see Dru C. Gladney, "The Hui, Islam, and the State: A Sufi Community in China's Northwest Corner," in *Muslims in Central Asia: Expressions of Identity and Change*, ed. Jo-Ann Gross (Durham, 1992), 501–510.

159. On the stone piles for noble and royal burials, see V. I. Abaev, *Skifo-evropejskie izoglossy na styke vostoka i zapada* (Moscow,1965), esp. 136–139, also on the big burial mounds in Central Asia, perhaps related to Bronze Age catacomb tombs, some with up to fifty thousand cubic meters of earth and stone. On pillared and tower tombs in the Red Sea hills, see A. Paul, "Ancient Tombs in Kassala Province," *Sudan Notes and Records* 33 (1952): 54–57, describing tower tombs at Maman from the fifteenth century; and J. W. Crowfoot, *Sudan Notes and Records* 5 (1922): 87, describing tombs resembling pyramid-like towers. Thomas H. Wilson, "Swahili Funerary Architecture of the North Kenya Coast," in *Swa-*

*hili Houses and Tombs of the Coast of Kenya,* by James de Vere Allen and Thomas H. Wilson, Art and Archaeology Research Papers (London, 1979), 34, argues that pillared "tombs therefore functioned as symbols of hereditary succession and supernatural authority, the foundatins upon which rested, to use Trimingham's observation, the leadership systems of the coastal communities."

160. See A. Burnes, *Travel in Bokhara* (London, 1834; reprint, Karachi, 1973), 3:137, who measures the tomb at eighteen feet in length; and Cunningham, *Report for the Year 1872–1873,* 106, who says it is forty-six feet long.

161. Cunningham, *Four Reports Made during the Years 1862–63–64–65,* 323. And see Crooke, *An Introduction to the Popular Religion and Folklore of Northern India,* 140–141. The smaller size is reported by Abul Fazl, as recorded in Francis Gladwin, *Ayeen Akbery; or, The Institutes of the Emperor Akber* (London, 1800; reprint, London, 2000), 2:33.

162. van der Meulen, *Aden to the Hadhramaut,* 194–195.

163. See Eaton and Qadiri, *Sahifat-i Ahl-i Huda,* 88; and Richard Eaton, *Sufis of Bijapur, 1300–1700,* fig. 11, p. 140.

164. See Elizabeth Merklinger, *Indian Islamic Architecture: The Deccan, 1347–1686* (Warminster, 1981); and idem, "Seven tombs at Holkonda: A Prelimary Survey," *Kunst des Orients* 10 (1975): 187–197. Henry Cousens, *A List of Antiquarian Remains in His Highness the Nizam's Territories,* Archeological Survey of India 31 (Calcutta, 1900), 187–196, also surveys the seven tombs at Holkonda and states that they were rebuilt so that those of the saints were larger than the tombs of others, including royalty.

165. See Cousens, *A List of Antiquarian Remains in His Highness the Nizam's Territories,* 141. Flags, poles, and other tall structures are often used to designate the tomb of a particularly important person. See, for example, Burton-Page, "Makbara"; and idem, "Muslim Graves of the 'Lesser Tradition': Gilgit, Puniāl, Swāt, Yūsufzai," in which are described the tombs of pirs marked by a white flag, or a green flag in the case of a descendant of the prophet Muhammad. Tombs in Central Asia often feature tall poles of wood or metal topped with representations of hands.

166. On the special practices for the burial of women, see John Simpson, "Death and Burial in the Late Islamic Near East," esp. 242–243; A. Musil, *The Manners and Customs of the Rwala Bedouins* (New York, 1928), 670; E. S. Drower, *Peacock Angel: Being Some Account of Votaries of a Secret Cult and Their Sanctuaries* (London, 1941), 185; H. R. P. Dickson, *The Arab of the Desert: A Glimpse into Badawin Life in Kuwait and Sauʿdi Arabia* (London, 1949), 212; and P. J. Watson, *Archaeological Ethnography in Western Iran* (Tucson, 1979), 215.

On cemetery organization, see John Simpson, "Death and Burial in the Late Islamic Near East," 244. Separate areas for children and infants are reported in

C. Kramer, *Village Ethnoarchaeology: Rural Iran in Archaeological Perspective* (New York, 1982), 76; and K. Prag, "Preliminary Report on the Excavations at Tell Iktanu, Jordan, 1987," *Levant* 21 (1989): 33–45, esp. 42.

On the burial of religious leaders near mosques, see S. Yeivin, *First Preliminary Report on the Excavations at Tel 'Gat' (Tell Sheykh Ahmed el-'Areyny): Seasons 1956–1958* (Jerusalem, 1961), 3; F. Barth, *Nomads of South Persia: The Basseri Tribe of the Khamseh Confederacy* (Oslo, 1980), 142; M. Haiman, *Archaeological Survey of Israel: Map of Har Hamran—Southwest (198) 10-00* (Jerusalem, 1986), 127; and J. Schaefer, "Archaeological Remains for the Medieval Islamic Occupation of the Northwest Negev Desert," *Bulletin of the American Schools for Oriental Research* 274 (May, 1989): 33–60, 59). For the practice of burying the most pious Muslims first in the case of multiple deaths, see Hamid Algar, "Burial in Islam," in *Encyclopedia Iranica* (Costa Mesa, Calif., 1990), 4:563–565, esp. 564.

167. On the footprint of Adam in Sri Lanka, also associated with the Buddha and Vishnu, see Reinaud, *Géographie d'Aboulféda,* 2:1:88–89; James Low, *Transactions of the Royal Asiatic Society of Great Britain and Ireland* 3 (1835): 57; and Ibn Baṭṭūṭah, *Riḥlah Ibn Baṭṭūṭah,* 4:170.

168. See al-Nābulsī, *al-Ḥaḍrah al-unsīyah fī al-riḥlah al-qudsīyah,* 127. Al-Nābulsī also mentions the footprint of Adam in Sri Lanka, which, he claims, is washed every day by rain (128).

169. On the footprint of Perseus at Chemmis in Egypt, see Herodotus, *Historiae,* 2.91. On the footprint of Heracles in Scythia, see ibid., 4.82. For the footprint of Dionysius and Heracles in the far west, see Lucianus of Samosata, *Adversus Indoctum: Verae Historiae,* 1.7. Other remains associated with the gigantic size of Heracles include the lake he made at Agyrion (Sicily) and some footprints located near there. See Diodorus Siculus, *Bibliotheca Historica,* 4.24.3–4; and Aristotle, *De Mirabilibus Auscultationibus,* ed. and trans. W. D. Ross (Oxford, 1908–1952), 97.

170. On the footprints of the Buddha, see John Strong, "Relics," 277. On the tooth relic of the Buddha in Sri Lanka, see Jack Finegan, *An Archaeological History of Religions of Indian Asia* (New York, 1989): 317; and A. M. Hocart, *The Temple of the Tooth in Kandy* (London, 1931).

171. For examples of excellent studies in analogous cases, see H. L. Seneviratne, *Rituals of the Kandyan State* (Cambridge, 1978); and A. Weingrod, "Saints, Shrines, and Politics in Contemporary Israel," in *Religious Regimes and State-Formation: Perspectives from European Ethnology*, ed. E. R. Wolf, 73–83 (Albany, 1991).

172. For examples, see Josef Strzygowski, "Ruins of Tombs of the Latin Kings on the Haram in Jerusalem," *Speculum* 11 (1936): 499–508; Carl Ernst, *Eternal Garden: Mysticism, History, and Politics at a South Asian Sufi Center* (Albany, 1992), 225; John Simpson, "Death and Burial in the Late Islamic Near East," 247–248;

and G. F. Dales, "Hissar IIIC Stone Objects in Afghan Sistan," in *Mountains and Lowlands: Essays in the Archaeology of Greater Mesopotamia,* ed. L. D. Levin and T. Cuyler Young (Malibu, Calif., 1977), 17–27.

173. For examples of tomb "discovery" and territorial claims, see Glenn Smith, "The Making and Unmaking of Madura's Sacred Tombs," esp. 217–234; Hasluck, "Graves of the Arabs in Asia Minor," esp. 189, on the discovery of tomb of the ghazi Ayoub during the siege of Constantinople in 1453 and the tomb of Abū Ḥanīfah during the siege of Baghdad under Suleiman in 1534. For studies on the relation of identity formation and its connection with tombs, see some of the articles in Gross, *Muslims in Central Asia,* including Jo-Ann Gross, "Approaches to the Problem of Identity Formation," 1–26; Gladney, "The Hui, Islam, and the State," 498–511; and Hamid Algar, "Shaykh Zaynullah Rasulev: The Last Great Naqshbandi Shaykh of the Volga-Urals Region," 112–133.

174. On the use of shrines as markers of territorial claims, see Marx, "Communal and Individual Pilgrimage," esp. 31–45, on the shrines and tombs of ʿAlī b. Abī Ṭālib, the prophets Salih and Aaron, and local holy men and ancestors. For other references on the rituals of the Sinai Bedouin relative to tombs, see Gustave E. von Grunebaum, *Beduei Sanai* (Beersheba, 1962); Y. Kapara, "Ziyarat Skeikh Abu Taleb," *Teva ve-Aretz* 17 (1975): 192–194; G. W. Murray, *Sons of Ishmael: A Study of the Egyptian Bedouin* (London, 1935); and E. L. Peters, "From Particularism to Universalism in the Religion of the Cyrenaica Bedouin," *Bulletin of the British Society for Middle Eastern Studies,* vol. 13 (1976).

175. See Peter Metcalf, *A Borneo Journey into Death* (Philadelphia, 1982); R. Bowen, "Death and the History of Islam in Highland Aceh," *Indonesia* 38 (1984): 21–38; idem, "Graves, Shrines and Power in a Highland Sumatran Society," in *Manifestations of Sainthood in Islam,* ed. Grace Martin Smith and Carl W. Ernst (Istanbul, 1993), 1–14; and R. E. Enthoven, *Folklore of the Konkan,* Indian Folklore (Delhi, 1976), esp. 40–48.

176. On the cosmogonic aspects of tombs, see Bejtic, "Jedno videnje sarajevskih evlija i njihovih grobova kao kultnih mjesta," 42; Gladney, "The Hui, Islam, and the State," 513–516; Elizabeth G. Traube, *Cosmology and Social Life: Ritual Exchange among the Mambai of East Timor* (Chicago, 1986); and Ernst, *Eternal Garden,* 237. On the ritual treatment of tombs with water and rocks, and its connection to cosmogonic notions, see M. W. Cavendish, "The Custom of Placing Pebbles on Nubian Graves," *Sudan Notes and Records* 47 (1966): 151–156; W. B. Emery, *Nubian Treasure* (London, 1948); C. G. Seligman and B. Z. Seligman, "The Bari," *Journal of the Royal Anthropological Institute* (London) 58 (1928): 463–465; Westermarck, *Pagan Survivals in Muhammadan Civilization,* 213; and Wellhausen, *Reste arabischen Heidentums,* 182–185. On connections between saint tombs and the sanctuary in Mecca, see Westermarck, *Pagan Survivals in Muhammadan Civilization,* 189–192; and Serjeant, "Ḥaram and Ḥawṭah."

177. On this pattern, see John Wansbrough, *Quranic Studies* (Oxford, 1977), 21–25; and Andrew Rippin, "Ṣāliḥ," in *Encyclopaedia of Islam,* 8:984.

178. See Ibn Qayyim al-Jawzīyah, *Ḥādī al-arwāḥ ilā bilād al-afrāḥ*, 163; Ibn Ḥanbal, *Musnad,* 2:315; and Muslim, *Ṣaḥīḥ*, 51:11.

179. See Schwarzbaum, *Biblical and Extra-biblical Legends in Islamic Folk-Literature*, 49; al-Kisāʾī, *Qiṣaṣ al-anbiyāʾ*, 65; al-Damīrī, *Ḥayāt al-Ḥayawān* (Damascus, 1989), trans. A. S. G. Jayakar as *Ad-Damîrî's Ḥayat al-Ḥayawân: A Zoological Lexicon* (Frankfurt, 2001), 2:296; Aḥmad Ibshihi, *al-Mustaṭraf* (Beirut, 1983), 2:125; Gustav Weil, *The Bible, the Koran, and the Talmud; or, Biblical Legends of the Mussulmans* (London, 1846), 25–26; and Ginzberg, *The Legends of the Jews*, 1:112, 5:141–142.

For related discussion on Greek heroes and the golden age, see See Marcel Detienne, *The Gardens of Adonis: Spices in Greek Mythology,* trans. J. Lloyd (Princeton, 1977).

180. Note that the prophet Muhammad is not considered to have been of gigantic size. On his tomb and the mosque in Medina, see Ghazi I. Bisheh, "The Mosque of Madīnah throughout the First Century A.H." (PhD dissertation, University of Michicagan, 1979). On other important tombs in Medina, see Aḥmad b. ʿAbd al-Ḥamīd al-ʿAbbāsī, *Kitāb ʿumdat al-akhbār fī madīnat al-mukhtār* (Cairo, nd), esp. 147–162; and Y. Raghib, "Les premiers monuments funéraires de l'Islam," *Annales Islamologiques* 9 (1970): 21–22.

## CONCLUSION

1. J. Z. Smith, *To Take Place,* 54–55. Smith's remarks are drawn primarily from Louis Dumont, *Homo hierarchicus: Essai sur le système des castes* (Paris, 1966), trans. Mark Sainsbury, Louis Dumont, and Basia Gulati as *Homo Hierarchicus: The Caste System and Its Implications,* 2d ed. (Chicago, 1980).

2. See J. Z. Smith, *To Take Place,* 56. Smith concedes that Dumont does not make this distinction between two separate axes: pure and impure, sacred and profane. Smith claims that such a distinction is implied by Dumont, although Dumont seems rather to emphasize that the distinction of pure and impure is the differentiation of the sacred. See Dumont, *Homo Hierarchicus,* xxxviii–xxxix, 364–365n32; and Louis Dumont and D. Pocock, "Pure and Impure," *Contributions to Indian Sociology* 3 (1959): 9–39. This is clearly the implication taken by Valerio Valeri, *Kingship and Sacrifice: Ritual and Society in Ancient Hawaii,* trans. Paula Wissing (Chicago, 1985), 89–90. Valeri's definition of impurity as a loss of integrity (84–89), which ultimately relies on a theory of sympathetic magic going back to Marcel Mauss, is different from the concept employed by Dumont. See Marcel Mauss and Henri Hubert, *Sacrifice: Its Nature and Function,* trans. W. D. Hall (Chicago, 1964); and Marcel Mauss, "Esquisse

d'une théorie générale de la magie," *Année Sociologique* 7 (1902–1903), trans. D. Pocock as *A General Theory of Magic* (London, 1972).

Valeri also cites Jean-Pierre Vernant, "The Pure and the Impure," in his *Myth and Society in Ancient Greece*, trans. Janet Lloyd (Sussex, 1980), 110–129, originally published in *L'Année Sociologique* (1953–1954): 331–352. For more on Greek notions of impurity, see L. Moulinier, *Le pur et l'impur dans la pensée et la sensibilité des Grecs jusqu'à la fin du IVe siècle avant J.-C.* (Paris, 1950). On the Maori definitions, see Jean Smith, *Tapu Removal in Maori Religion* (Wellington, 1974).

Stanley Tambiah, *World Conqueror and World Renouncer: A Study of Buddhism and Polity in Thailand against a Historical Background* (Cambridge, 1976), whom Smith also cites (*To Take Place*, 151n42), maintains that a clearer distinction between the two systems is to be understood as a conscious and ironic redefinition of the Vedic structure on the part of Buddhist theorists. See esp. 19–22. A similar argument is made for linking the performance of certain rituals to the endurance of the Moroccan state in M. E. Combs-Schilling, *Sacred Performances: Islam, Sexuality, and Sacrifice* (New York, 1989).

3. See, for example, Zayd b. ʿAlī, *Majmuʿ al-fiqh*, 62; Ibn Taymīyah, *Fiqh al-taḥārah*, 168–169; al-Bukhārī, *Ṣaḥīḥ*, 65:25; al-Tirmidhī, *al-Jāmiʿ al-ṣaḥīḥ*, 6:21; al-Nasāʾī, *Sunan*, 22:51, 62, 64; Ibn Mājah, *Sunan*, 7:12; Mālik b. Anas, *al-Muwaṭṭaʾ*, 18:52; Zayd b. ʿAlī, *Majmuʿ al-fiqh*, 437; and al-Shawkānī, *Nayl al-awṭār*, 11:20.

4. See al-Bukhārī, *Ṣaḥīḥ*, 6:20, 30:41; Muslim, *Ṣaḥīḥ*, 3:67–69; Abū Dāʾūd, *Sunan*, 1:104, 119; al-Tirmidhī, *al-Jāmiʿ al-ṣaḥīḥ*, 1:97, 6:68; al-Nasāʾī, *Sunan*, 3:17, 22:64; Ibn Mājah, *Sunan*, 1:118; and al-Dārimī, *Sunan*, 1:102. On hair, see Abū Dāʾūd, *Sunan*, 2:85; al-Tirmidhī, *al-Jāmiʿ al-ṣaḥīḥ*, 2:165; al-Nasāʾī, *Sunan*, 12:57; Ibn Mājah, *Sunan*, 5:64; and al-Dārimī, *Sunan*, 2:105.

5. See the statements in Muslim, *Ṣaḥīḥ*, 3:11–13; Abū Dāʾūd, *Sunan*, 1:103; al-Nasāʾī, *Sunan*, 1:172–173, 3:18–19; Ibn Mājah, *Sunan*, 1:119; al-Dārimī, *Sunan*, 1:82, 108; and Mālik b. Anas, *al-Muwaṭṭaʾ*, 2:88. Also see statements in which the mouth of the menstruating woman is specified, including those in Muslim, *Ṣaḥīḥ*, 3:14; Abū Dāʾūd, *Sunan*, 1:102; al-Tirmidhī, *al-Jāmiʿ al-ṣaḥīḥ*, 1:100–101; al-Nasāʾī, *Sunan*, 1:55, 176–177, 2:10, 3:14–15; Ibn Mājah, *Sunan*, 1:124; and al-Dārimī, *Sunan*, 1:108.

6. See Ibn Rushd, *al-Bidāyat al-mujtahid*, 2:57–77, on these substances. Also see the ḥadīth reports mentioned in Ibn Ḥazm, *al-Muḥallā bi-l-athār*, ed. ʿAbd al-Ghafār Sulayman al-Bandārī (Beirut, n.d.), 1:121–122; and Ibn Qudāmah, *al-Mughnī*, 1:208–211.

7. Compare with the conclusions of Eilberg-Schwartz, *The Savage in Judaism*, passim; and Katz, *Body of Text*, esp. 21–24.

8. On women and men praying together as a group, see al-Bukhārī, *Ṣaḥīḥ*, 10:164; Muslim, *Ṣaḥīḥ*, 4:132, 5:269; Abū Dāʾūd, *Sunan*, 2:69–70, 141, 196; al-Tirmidhī, *al-Jāmiʿ al-ṣaḥīḥ*, 2:59; al-Nasāʾī, *Sunan*, 9:16, 10:32, 44, 13:77; Ibn

Mājah, *Sunan,* 5:54; al-Dārimī, *Sunan,* 2:52; and Ibn Ḥanbal, *Musnad,* 6:301, 371. On the congregational prayer in particular, see Ibn Rushd, *Bidāyat al-mujtahid,* 2:323–356. On further distinctions between men and women during prayer, see al-Bukhārī, *Ṣaḥīḥ,* 21:5, 16, 22:9, 93:26; Muslim, *Ṣaḥīḥ,* 4:102–107; Abū Dā'ūd, *Sunan,* 2:168; al-Tirmidhī, *al-Jāmiʿ al-ṣaḥīḥ,* 2:155; al-Nasā'ī, *Sunan,* 13:15–16, 49:24; Ibn Mājah, *Sunan,* 5:65; al-Dārimī, *Sunan,* 2:85; and Mālik b. Anas, *al-Muwaṭṭa',* 9:61.

9. Al-Qudūrī, *Mukhtaṣar fī al-fiqh,* 35. On these distinctions, also see Ibn al-Humām, *Sharḥ fatḥ al-qadīr,* 1:315–320; Ibn Rushd, *Bidāyat al-mujtahid,* 2:286–299; Ibn Qudāmah, *al-Mughnī,* 1:674–681, 2:149–222; and Ibn Ḥazm, *al-Muḥallā bi-l-athār,* 2:395–404.

10. Al-Qudūrī, *Mukhtaṣar fī al-fiqh,* 36. Also see see al-Bukhārī, *Ṣaḥīḥ,* 8:2, 10, 12, 77:20; Muslim, *Ṣaḥīḥ,* 4:275; Abū Dā'ūd, *Sunan,* 2:77; al-Nasā'ī, *Sunan,* 9:18; al-Dārimī, *Sunan,* 2:100; Ibn al-Humām, *Sharḥ fatḥ al-qadīr,* 1:274–321; and Ibn Rushd, *Bidāyat al-mujtahid,* 2:300–322.

11. See Ibn al-Humām, *Sharḥ fatḥ al-qadīr,* 2:49–69; Ibn Rushd, *Bidāyat al-mujtahid,* 2:323–356; Ibn Qudāmah, *al-Mughnī,* 2:87–142; and Muḥammad b. Muḥammad al-Ghazālī, *al-Wasīṭ fī al-madhhab,* ed. Muḥammad M. Tāmir and Aḥmad M. Ibrāhīm (Beirut, 1997), 2:241–260.

12. On *tayammum,* see Ibn al-Humām, *Sharḥ fatḥ al-qadīr,* 1:121–142; Ibn Rushd, *Bidāyat al-mujtahid,* 2:3–56; al-Ghazālī, *al-Wasīṭ fī al-madhhab,* 1:351–394; and Ibn Qudāmah, *al-Mughnī,* 1:266–290.

13. See Ibn al-Humām, *Sharḥ fatḥ al-qadīr,* 2:27–48; Ibn Rushd, *Bidāyat al-mujtahid,* 2:357–366; Ibn Qudāmah, *al-Mughnī,* 2:87–142; and al-Ghazālī, *al-Wasīṭ fī al-madhhab,* 2:241–260.

14. On these prohibitions, see Ibn al-Humām, *Sharḥ fatḥ al-qadīr,* 6:400–458, 486–493; and Ibn Qudāmah, *al-Mughnī,* 5:110.

15. See Ibn al-Humām, *Sharḥ fatḥ al-qadīr,* 5:434–465. Also note the prohibition against carrying a copy of the Quran into the Dār al-Ḥarb, and the prohibition against unprotected women in the Dār al-Ḥarb, in Ibn Ḥanbal, *Musnad,* 2:76, 1:385–390, 420; and al-Bukhārī, *Ṣaḥīḥ,* 67:6, 65:Q 5:9.

16. Compare also with the separation of powers described in Stuart Cohen, *The Three Crowns: Structures of Communal Politics in Early Rabbinic Jewry* (Cambridge, 1990); and Ernst Hartwig Kantorowicz, *The King's Two Bodies: A Study in Medieval Political Theology* (Princeton, 1957).

17. See al-Māwardī, *al-Aḥkām al-sulṭānīyah* (Cairo, 1973), 5. For an English translation, see al-Māwardī, *The Ordinances of Government: Al-Aḥkām al-Sulṭāniyya w'al-Wilāyāt al-Dīniyya,* trans. Wafaa H. Wahba, Great Books of Islamic Civilization (Reading, 1996), 3.

18. See al-Māwardī, *al-Aḥkām al-sulṭānīyah,* 6; idem, *The Ordinances of Gov-*

*ernment*, 3. For this concept of authority and its definition in al-Māwardī, also see Hanna Mikhail, *Politics and Revelation: Māwardī and After* (Edinburgh, 1995).

19. On Douglas's attempt to develop the Durkheimian model, which can accommodate a more complex social system, see Louis Gernet, *The Anthropology of Ancient Greece,* trans. John Hamilton and Blaise Nagy (Baltimore, 1981), esp. "The Mythical Ideal of Value in Greece," 73–111, originally published in *Journal de Psychologie* 41 (October–December 1948): 415–462; and M. Granet, *Danses et légendes de la chine ancienne,* 2 vols. (Paris, 1926, 1959).

20. Mary Douglas, *Impurity and Danger* (New York, 1966), 209. For a more detailed analysis of the Lele, see Douglas, *The Lele of the Kasai* (London, 1963), esp. 209–213, on initiation rites of the Pangolin cult. See also idem, "Animals in Lele Religious Symbolism," *Africa* 27, no. 1 (1957): 46–58.

21. Douglas, *Impurity and Danger,* 210.

22. Douglas's remarks, which seem to interpret this disjunction as something the Lele seek to overcome through their rituals (as a means of atonement), is misleading given her emphasis upon the persistence of rituals and rules acknowledged to be arbitrary and fictive. See Douglas, *Impurity and Danger*, 209. For other such interpretations, see Evans-Pritchard, *Nuer Religions;* and Eliade, *The Sacred and the Profane.*

23. See von Grunebaum, *Muhammadan Festivals*; and Abdellah Hammoudi, *Victime et ses masques* (Paris, 1988), trans. Paula Wissing as *The Victim and Its Masks: An Essay on Sacrifice and Masquerade in the Maghreb* (Chicago, 1993). There is a useful discussion of this point in Fred Denny, "Pilgrimage and the History of Religions: Theoretical Approaches to the Hajj," in *Approaches to Islam in Religious Studies,* ed. Richard Martin (Tucson, 1985).

24. Also see Douglas, *Natural Symbols,* esp. 1–19.

25. On the ethnography of surfing, see Hugo Veriomme, *Surf Saga: Cowabunga!* (Paris, 1976); Ellis William, *Narrative of a Tour of Hawaii; or, Owhyhee, with Remarks on the History, Traditions, Manners, Customs and Language of the Inhabitants of the Sandwich Islands* (London, 1826); and Mark Twain, *Roughing It* (Hartford, 1872). On the history, see Drew Kampion and Bruce Brown, *Stoked: A History of Surf Culture* (Los Angeles, 1997; reprint, Köln, 1998); Nick Carroll, ed., *The Next Wave: A Survey of World Surfing* (London, 1991); Midget Farrelly and Craig McGregor, *This Surfing Life* (London, 1965), 106–112; and Robert Young and Rod Holmes, *The History of Surfing,* 2d ed. (Angourie, 1994).

26. On the surfing of Hawaiian kings, see Andy Martin, *Walking on Water* (London, 1991; reprint, London, 1992), 138–141; Malcolm Gault-Williams, *Legendary Surfers: A Definitive History of Surfing's Culture and Heroes* (www.legendarysurfers.com, 2003); Tom Blake, *Hawaiian Surfriding: The Ancient and Royal Pastime* (Flagstaff, 1961); William H. Chickering, *Within the Sound of These*

*Waves: The Story of the Kings of Hawaii Island* (New York, 1941); Ben Finney and James Houston, *Surfing, the Sport of Hawaiian Kings* (Rutland, 1966); David Kalakaua, *The Legends and Myths of Hawaii: The Fables and Folklore of a Strange People* (New York, 1888); Sandra Kimberley Hall and Greg Ambrose, *Memories of Duke: The Legend Comes to Life: Duke Paoa Hahanamoku, 1890–1968* (Honolulu, 1995); Mark Blackburn, *Surf's Up: Collecting the Longboard Era* (Atglen, Pa., 2001); and idem, *Hula Girls and Surfer Boys* (Atglen, Pa., 2000). On travel in search of the wave, in the footsteps of ancestors, see Carroll, *The Next Wave,* 15–30. On travel in surfing, see John Conway, *Adventure Sports: Surfing* (London, 1988), 17–32; Rick Abbott, *The Science of Surfing* (Cardiff, 1972); the novelized accounts of Paul Harvey, *Surfer!* Penguin Readers (Harlow, 1999); and Allan Weisbecker, *In Search of Captain Zero: A Surfer's Road Trip beyond the End of the Road* (New York, 2001).

27. Original boards were "logs" taken from a special tree. On the logs, see Tommy Holmes, *The Hawaiian Canoe* (Honolulu, 1997); and Tom Blake, *Hawaiian Surfboard* (Honolulu, 1935). General overviews of boards can be found in Howard Jennar, *Making a Surfboard: The Complete Manual* (Darlinghurst, 1985). On vintage longboards, see Sam Ryan, *1960s Surfboard Guide* (Leucadia, 1994). For a relevant discussion of the use of surfboards in amusement park rides, see Bernard LeMehaute, *Surfing Carrousel,* 2 vols. (Pasadena, Calif., 1980–1989).

28. See Kampion and Brown, *Stoked,* 23–53.

29. See the statement of Bear in the film *Big Wednesday* (Warner Bros., 1978): "Nobody surfs forever. One day the big swell will come and wipe away everything that came before it." This is illustrated at other points in the film: when Matt Johnson gives Bear's log to a younger surfer after wiping out on the big swell; when Bear is asked if he is a surfer and he replies that he is just a trashman.

In the movie *In God's Hands* (Tri-Star Pictures, 1998), the narrator asks: "How good do you want to be? How far are you willing to go?" The ultimate limit is the last scene in the film, where the Mexican swell is surfed all alone. Other surfers in the film, such as Bob, cannot achieve this, as is illustrated by his death when trying to surf the fifty-foot waves in Hawaii without being pulled in by a motorized craft.

30. On rebel surfing culture, see Kampion and Brown, *Stoked,* 82–85; Kent Pearson, *Surfing Subcultures of Australia and New Zealand* (St. Lucia, 1979), 184–189; Stephen Hull, "A Sociological Study of the Surfing Subculture in the Santa Cruz Area," master's thesis, San Jose State University, 1976; John Irwin, *Scenes* (Beverly Hills, Calif., 1977); John Irwin, "A Study of the Growth of a Deviant Subculture," master's thesis, University of California, Berkeley, 1965; and Matt Warshaw, *Above the Roar: 50 Surfer Interviews* (Santa Cruz, Calif., 1997). On the loner subculture of surfing, see Carroll, *The Next Wave,* 205; Ricky Grigg, *Big Surf, Deep Dives and the Islands: My Life in the Ocean* (Honolulu, 1998); Nachum

Shifren, *Surfing Rabbi: A Kabbalistic Quest for Soul* (Los Angeles, 2001); and Joseph Scures, "The Social Order of the Surfing World," master's thesis, University of Washington, 1986.

For specialty studies on surf lingo, see Peter Neely, *Indo Surf and Lingo* (Noosa Heads, , 1990–2000); Trevor Cralle, *The Surfin'Ary: A Dictionary of Surfing Terms and Surfspeak* (Berkeley, 1991); and Phil Jarratt, *Surfing: The Dictionary* (South Melbourne, 1985).

31. On the use of the terms "surf punk" and "surf nazis" see John Blair, *The Illustrated Discography of Surf Music, 1959–1965* (Riverside, Calif., 1978); idem, *The Illustrated Discography of Surf Music, 1961–1965* (Riverside, Calif., 1983); and Stephen J. McParland, *Beach, Street and Strip: The Albums* (Sydney, 1983). Also see the lyrics of the typical surf-punk tune, such as Agent Orange, "Bite the Hand That Feeds," from the album *This Is the Voice* (El Segundo, 1997).

32. See Claude Lévi-Strauss, *Homme nu* (Paris, 1971); *The Naked Man*, 679; and idem, *The Savage Mind*, 90–91. Also see Normand Roy, *L'analyse du rituel chez Claude Lévi-Strauss: Le finale de l'Homme nu dans la perspective du structuralisme* (Montreal, 1995).

33. ʿAbd al-Raḥmān b. Muḥammad Ibn Khaldūn, *al-Muqaddimah*, trans. Franz Rosenthal as *The Muqaddimah: An Introduction to History*, 3 vols., Bollingen Series 43 (Princeton, 1967), 1:70. Also see Aziz al-Azmeh, *Ibn Khaldūn: An Essay in Reinterpretation* (London, 1982), esp. 27–47; and and ʿA. Ḥilw, *Ibn Khaldūn: Muʾassis ʿilm al-ijtimāʿ* (Beirut, 1969).

34. Ibn Khaldūn, *al-Muqaddimah;* Rosenthal, *The Muqaddimah*, 1:90. On this concept, also see Charles Issawi, *An Arab Philosophy of History: Selections from the Prolegomena of Ibn Khaldun of Tunis (1332–1406)* (London, 1950; reprint, London, 1963), esp. chap. 6, pp. 99–130; and M. ʿA. al-Jabirī, *al-ʿAṣabīya wa al-dawlah: Maʿālim naẓarīya Khaldūnīya fī al-taʾrīkh al-Islāmī* (Casablanca, 1971).

35. See the useful work of James C. Scott, *Weapons of the Weak: Everyday Forms of Peasant Resistance* (New Haven, 1985); and idem, *Domination and the Arts of Resistance: Hidden Transcripts* (New Haven, 1990). Also helpful is David Laitin, *Hegemony and Culture: Politics and Religious Change among the Yoruba* (Chicago, 1986). See the related works of Richard Horsely, *Hidden Transcripts and the Arts of Resistance: Applying the Work of James C. Scott to Jesus and Paul* (Atlanta, 2004); William Leggett, "Hegemony and National Identity in Indonesia" (PhD dissertation, Northern Illinois University, 1994); Matt Long, "Skipping Church: Applying James C. Scott's *Domination and the Arts of Resistance* to Late Medieval England" (PhD dissertation, Emory and Henry College, 2002).

# *Works Cited*


Abaev, V. I. *Skifo-evropejskie izoglossy na styke vostoka i zapada*. Moscow: Nauka, Glav. red. vostochnoi lit-ry,1965.

ʿAbbāsī, Aḥmad b. ʿAbd al-Ḥamīd. *Kitāb ʿumdat al-akhbār fī madīnat al-mukhtār*. Cairo: al-Maktabah al-Tijarīyah al-Kubrā, n.d.

Abbott, Rick. *The Science of Surfing*. Cardiff: John Jones Cardiff, 1972.

ʿAbd al-ʿAzīz, Nabīl Muḥammad. *Khizānat al-silāḥ: Maʿa dirāsah ʿan khazāʾin al-silāḥ wa muhtawīyagi-hā ʿalā ʿaṣr al-Ayyūbīyīn wa al-Mamālik*. Cairo: Maktabat al-Anjul al-Miṣrīyah, 1978.

ʿAbd al-Razzāq, Ibn Hammām al-Ṣanʿānī. *al-Muṣannaf fī al-ḥadīth*. Beirut: Dār al-Kutub al-ʿIlmīyah, 2000.

Abdul Hakk, S., and Kh. Moaz. *Aspects de l'ancienne Damas*. Damascus: Institut français de Damas, 1949.

Abel, F. M. *Géographie de la Palestine*. Paris: J. Gabalda, 1967.

Abel, O., and G. Kyrle. *Die Drachenhöhle bei Mixnitz*. Vienna: Verlag Öster. Staatsdruckerei, 1931.

Abel, Othenio, and Wilhelm Koppers. "Eiszeitlich Bärendarstellungen und Bärenkult in paläobiologischer und prähistorisch-ethnologischer Beleuchtung." *Palaeobiologica* 7 (1939): 7–64.

Abercromby, J. *The Pre- and Proto-historic Finns*. 2 vols. London: D. Nutt, 1898.

Abū Dāʾūd al-Sijistānī. *Sunan*. Ed. Muḥammad Muḥyī al-Dīn ʿAbd al-Ḥamīd. Beirut: Dār al-Kutub al-ʿIlmīyah, 1980.

Abu El-Haj, Nadia. *Facts on the Ground: Archaeological Practice and Territorial Self-Fashioning in Israeli Society*. Chicago: University of Chicago Press, 2001.

Abū Khalīl, Shawqī. *Aṭlas al-Qurʾān*. Damascus: Dār al-Fikr, 2003.

Abu-Manneh, Butrus. "A Note on the 'Keys of the Kaʿba.'" *Islamic Quarterly* 18 (1974): 73–75.

Abū Nuʿaym, Aḥmad b. ʿAbdallāh. *Dalāʾil al-nubūwah.* Hyderabad: Majlis Dāʾirat al-Maʿārif al-ʿUthmānīyah, 1977.

Abū Shāma, ʿAbd al-Raḥmān b. Ismāʿīl. *Kitāb al-Rawḍatain fī akhbār al-dawlatain.* Cairo, 1287–1288.

Abū Yaʿlā, Aḥmad b. ʿAlī. *al-Muʿjam.* Beirut: Dār al-Maʾmūn li-l-Turāth, 1989.

Abū Yūsuf, Yaʿqūb. *Ikhtilāf Abī Ḥanīfah wa Ibn Abī Laylā.* Ed. Abū al-Wafāʾ al-Afghānī. Cairo, 1357.

Acharya, Prasanna Kumar. *Hindu Architecture in India and Abroad.* Oxford: Oxford University Press, 1965.

ʿAdawī, Qāḍī Maḥmūd. *Kitāb al-ziyārāt bi-Dimashq.* Ed. Ṣalāḥ al-Dīn al-Munajjid. Damascus: al-Majmaʿ al-ʿIlmī al-ʿArabī bi-Dimashq, 1956.

Adler, E. N. *Jewish Travellers in the Middle Ages: A Treasury of Travelogues from 9 Centuries.* London, 1930; reprint, New York: Hermon Press, 1966.

Adomnan. *The First Book on the Holy Places.* Ed. L. Bieler. Corpus Scriptorum Latinorum 175, 235. Turnhout: Paravia, 1958.

Agent Orange. *This Is the Voice.* El Segundo, Calif.: Enigma Records, 1997.

Aggoula, Basile. *Inventaire des inscriptions hatréennes.* Paris: Paul Geuthner, 1991.

Aharoni, Y. "The Solomonic Temple, the Tabernacle, and the Arad Sanctuary." In *Orient and Occident: Essays Presented to Cyrus H. Gordon on the Occasion of His Sixty-fifth Birthday,* ed. H. A. Hoffman, Alter Orient und Altes Testament 22, 1–8. Neukirchen: Verlag Butzen and Becker Kevelaer, 1973.

Ahluwalia, M. S. "Mughal Tombs at Bahlopur: An Architectural Study." In *Contacts between Cultures: South Asia,* ed. K. I. Koppedrayer, 222–224. Lewiston: Edwin Mellen Press, 1992.

Ahlwardt, W., ed. *The Divans of the Six Ancient Arabic Poets.* London: Trübner, 1870.

Ahmed, Salahuddin. *A Dictionary of Muslim Names.* New York: New York University Press, 1999.

Akademie der Wissenschaft und der Literatur. *Keilschrifturkunden aus Boghazköi.* Berlin: Gebr. Mann, 1921.

Albright, W. F. "The Egyptian Empire in Asia in the Twenty-first Century BC." *Journal of the Palestine Exploration Society* 8 (1928): 223–256.

Alekseenko, E. A. "The Cult of the Bear among the Ket (Yenisei Ostyaks)." In *Popular Beliefs and Folklore Tradition in Siberia,* ed. V. Diószegi, 175–192. Budapest: Akadémiai Kiadó, 1968.

Alexander, David. *The Arts of War: The Nasser D. Khalili Collection of Islamic Art.* Oxford: Oxford University Press, 1992.

Alexander, David. "Dhu al-fakār." PhD dissertation, Institute of Fine Arts, New York University, 1984.

Alexander, G. "The Story of the Kaʿba." *Muslim World* 28 (1938): 43–53.

Alexander, P. S. "The Targumim and Early Exegesis of 'Sons of God' in Genesis 6." *Journal of Semitic Studies* 23 (1972): 60–71.

Algar, Hamid. "Burial in Islam." In *Encyclopedia Iranica,* ed. Ehsan Yarshater, 4:563–565. Costa Mesa, Calif.: Mazda Publishers, 1990.

Algar, Hamid. "Shaykh Zaynullah Rasulev: The Last Great Naqshbandi Shaykh of the Volga-Urals Region." In *Muslims in Central Asia: Expressions of Identity and Change,* ed. Jo-Ann Gross, 112–133. Durham: Duke University Press, 1992.

Ali, Meer Hassan. *Observations of the Mussulmauns of India, Descriptive of Their Manners, Customs, Habits, and Religious Opinions Made during a Twelve Years' Residence in Their Immediate Society.* 2d ed. Ed. W. Crooke. London: Oxford Univeristy Press, 1917.

Allen, James de Vere, and Thomas H. Wilson. *Swahili Houses and Tombs on the Coast of Kenya.* Art and Archaeology Research Papers. London: AARP, 1979.

Alster, Brendt. "Dilmun, Bahrain, and the Alleged Paradise in Sumerian Myth and Literature." In *Dilmun: New Studies in the Archaeology and Early History of Bahrain,* ed. D. T. Potts, 39–74. Berlin: D. Reimer Verlag, 1983.

Altheim, F., and R. Stiehl. *Die Araber in der alten Welt.* Berlin: De Gruyter, 1968.

Ambary, Hasan Muarif. "Epigraphical Data from 17th–19th Century Muslim Graves in East Java." In *Cultural Contact and Textual Interpretation: Papers from the Fourth European Colloquium on Malay and Indonesian Studies Held in Leiden in 1983,* ed. C. D. Grijns and S. O. Robson, Verhandelingen van het Koninklijk Instituut voor Taal-, Land- en Volkenkunde 115, 24–37. Dordrecht, 1986.

ʿĀmid, al-Sayyid. *al-Qarābah ʿinda Ibn Khaldūn wa Rūbirtsūn Smith.* Alexandria: al-Markaz al-ʿArabī li-l-Nashr wa al-Tawzīʿ, 1984.

Amoretti, B. Scarcia. "A proposito della mediazione giudaica nell'Islam: Il caso di Daniele." *Rivista degli studi orientali* 60 (1986): 205–211.

ʿAmr b. al-Ahtam. *Die Mufaḍḍalîjât.* Ed. Heinrich Thorbecke. Leipzig: Brockhaus, 1885.

Andersen, F. I. "2 (Slavonic Apocalypse of) Enoch." In *The Old Testament Pseudepigrapha,* ed. James H. Charlesworth, 1:91–221. Garden City, N.Y.: Doubleday, 1983.

Anderson, Benedict. *Imagined Communities.* London: Verso, 1983.

Anderson, Gary. "Celibacy or Consummation in the Garden? Reflections on Early Jewish and Christian Interpretations of the Garden of Eden." *Harvard Theological Review* 82 (1989): 121–148.

Anderson, Gary. *Sacrifices and Offerings in Ancient Israel: Studies in Their Social and Political Importance.* Atlanta: Scholars Press, 1987.

Anderson, Robert T. "Samaritans." In *The Anchor Bible Dictionary,* ed. David Noel Freedman and others, 5:940–947. New York: Doubleday, 1992.

Anderson, Robert T. *Studies in Samartian Manuscripts and Artifacts: The Chamberlain-Warren Collection.* Cambridge, Mass.: Harvard University Press, 1978.

Andreae, B. "Herakles und Alkyoneus." *Jahrbuch des Deutschen Archäologischen Instituts* 77 (1962): 130–210.

Ansari, Shahabuddin. "How Kaʿba Came to Be Defiled with Idols." *Studies in Islam* 19 (1982): 39–45.

Anṣārī, Zakarīyāʾ b. Muḥammad. *Tuḥfat al-ṭullāb.* Cairo: Muṣṭafā al-Bābī al-Ḥalabī, 1340.

Antoninus Placentinus. "Itinerarium." In *Itinera Hierosolymitana saeculi IV–VIII,* ed. Paul Geyer, Corpus Scriptorum Ecclesiasticorum Latinorum 39, 157–218. Vindobonae: F. Tempsky, 1949; reprint, New York: Johnson Reprint, 1964.

Aristotle. *De Mirabilibus Auscultationibus.* Trans. W. D. Ross. 12 vols. Oxford: Clarendon Press, 1908–1952.

Árnason, Jón. *Icelandic Legends.* London: Richard Bentley, 1864.

Arnaud, P. "Naïskoi monolithes du Hauran." In *Hauran I: Recherches archéologiques sur la Syrie du sud à l'époque hellénistique et romaine,* ed. J.-M. Dentzer, 2:373–386. Paris: Paul Geuthner, 1985.

Arnold, Philip P. "Sacred Landscapes of New York State and the Problem of Religion in America." Paper presented at the Comparative Religion Colloquium, University of Washington, November 2002.

Arnold, Philip P., and Ann Grodzins Gold, eds. *Sacred Landscapes and Cultural Politics.* Aldershot: Ashgate, 2001.

Arnold, T. W. *The Caliphate.* Oxford: Oxford University Press, 1924.

Arnold, T. W. "Ḳadam Sharīf." In *Encyclopaedia of Islam,* 2d ed., ed. H. A. R. Gibb and others, 4:367–368. Leiden: E. J. Brill, 1960–2002.

As-Sindi, B. M. B. K. "The Probable Date of the First Arab Expeditions to India." *Islamic Culture* 20 (1946): 250–266.

Atallah, W. "Aymu-l-Lāh: Vestige d'un culte chtonien." *Arabica* 22 (1975): 162–169.

Atasoy, Nurhan. "Khirḳa-yi Sharīf." In *Encyclopaedia of Islam,* 2d ed., ed. H. A. R. Gibb and others, 5:18–19. Leiden: E. J. Brill, 1960–2002.

Atil, Esin. *The Age of Sultan Süleyman the Magnificent.* Washington, D.C.: National Gallery of Art, 1987.

Augustin, Bernd. "Arms." In *Oriental Splendour: Islamic Art from German Private Collections,* ed. Claus-Peter Haase and others, 182–224. Hamburg: Museum für Kunst und Gewerbe, 1993.

Avner, U. "Ancient Cult Sites in the Negev and Sinai Deserts." *Tel Aviv* 11 (1984): 115–131.

Awzāʿī, ʿAbd al-Raḥmān. *Sunan al-Awzāʿī.* Ed. and compiled by Marwān Muḥammad al-Shaʿār. Beirut: Dār al-Nafāʾis, 1993.

Aʿẓamī, Muḥammad Diyāʾ al-Raḥmān. *Dirāsāt fī al-jarḥ wa al-taʿdīl*. Benares: al-Jāmiʿah al-Salafīyah, 1983.

Azmeh, Aziz. *Ibn Khaldūn: An Essay in Reinterpretation*. London: Cass, 1982.

Azraqī, Muḥammad b. ʿAbdallāh. *Akhbār Makkah*. Ed. Rushdī al-Ṣāliḥ Malḥas. Beirut, 1983. Published in German as *Chroniken der Stadt Mecca,* ed. F. Wüstenfeld (Leipzig, 1858; reprint, Beirut: Maktabat Khayyat, 1964).

ʿAzzām, Ṣalāḥ. *al-Sayyid ʿAbd al-Raḥīm al-Qināwī*. Cairo: Muʾassasat Dār al-Shaʿb, 1970.

Badawi, Ali Khalil. *Tyre and It's* [*sic*] *Region*. Beirut, n.d.

Badrī , Abū al-Baqā ʿAbdallāh b. Muḥammad. *Nuzhat al-anām fī maḥāsin al-Shām*. Cairo: al-Maktabah al-ʿArabīyah, 1341.

Baghawī, al-Ḥusayn b. Masʿūd. *Sharḥ al-sunnah*. 5 vols. Beirut: al-Maktab al-Islāmī, 1971.

Bakrī, Abū ʿUbayd ʿAbdallāh. *Kitāb muʿjam mā istaʿjam*. Published as *Das Geographische Wörterbuch des Abu ʿObeid ʿAbdallah*, ed F. Wüstenfeld Göttingen: Deuerlich'sche Buchhandlung, 1876–1877.

Balādhūrī, Aḥmad b. Yaḥyā. *Futūḥ al-buldān*. Ed. M. J. de Goeje. Leiden: E. J. Brill, 1968.

Baloch, N. A. *The Advent of Islam*. Islamabad: National Institute of Historical and Cultural Research, 1980.

BāMaṭraf, M. ʿAbd al-Qādir. *Mulāḥaẓāt ʿalā mā dhikr al-Hamadānī ʿan Jighrāfiyah Ḥaḍramawt*. Aden, 1984.

Baqi, F. R. "Kitāb faḍāʾil al-ramy fī sabīl Allāh." *Islamic Culture* 34, no. 3 (1960): 195–218.

Bar-Adon, Pessaḥ. *The Cave of the Treasure: The Finds from the Caves in Naḥal Mishmar.* Jerusalem: Israel Exploration Society, 1980.

Barth, F. *Nomads of South Persia: The Basseri Tribe of the Khamseh Confederacy*. Oslo: University Press, 1980.

Barton, G. A. *The Royal Inscriptions of Sumer and Akkad.* New Haven: Yale University Press, 1929.

Basset, H., and Lévi-Provençal. "Chella, une nécropole mérinide." *Hespéris* 2 (1922): 1–92, 255–316, 385–425.

Basset, René. "Les empreintes merveilleuses." *Revue des Traditions Populaires* 9 (1894): 689–693.

Bassola, Moshe b. Mordecai. *Massaʿot erez Yisraʾel le-Rabbi Moshe Bassola.* Ed. E. Y. Ben-Ẓevi. Jerusalem: ha-Hevrah ha-ʿIvrit la-Hakirat Erets-Yisraʾel ve-ʿAtikoteha, 1938. Trans. D. Ordan as *In Zion and Jerusalem: The Itinerary of Rabbi Moses Basola (1521-1523),* ed. A. David (Jerusalem, 1999).

Batchelor, John. *The Ainu and Their Folklore*. London: Religious Tract Society, 1901.

Bayhaqī, Aḥmad b. al-Ḥusayn. *Dalāʾil al-nubūwah*. Beirut: Dār al-Kutub al-ʿIlmīyah, 1405.

Bayhaqī, Aḥmad b. al-Ḥusayn. *Dalāʾil al-nubūwah*. Cairo, s.n., 1970.

Bayhaqī, Aḥmad b. al-Ḥusayn. *Musnad*. Beirut: Dār al-Kutub al-ʿIlmīyah, n.d.

Bayhaqī, Aḥmad b. al-Ḥusayn. *al-Sunan*. Karachi: Jāmiʿat Dirāsāt al-Islāmīyah, 1989.

Becker, C. H. "Die Kanzel im Kultus des alten Islam." *Islam* 3 (1912): 451–469. Reprinted in his *Islam Studien* (Leipzig, 1924; reprint, Hildesheim: G. Olms, 1967).

Bediako, Gillian. *Primal Religion and the Bible: William Robertson Smith and His Heritage*. Sheffield: Sheffield Academic Press, 1997.

Beeston, A. F. L. "Appendix on the Inscriptions Discovered by Mr. Philby." In *Sheba's Daughters*, ed. H. St. J.B. Philby, 448–452. London: Methuen and Co., 1939.

Beeston, A. F. L. "The Oracle Sanctuary of Jar al-Labbaʾ." *Le Muséon* 62 (1949): 207–228.

Beeston, A. F. L. "The Ritual Hunt: A Study in Old South Arabian Religious Practice." *Le Muséon* 61 (1948): 183–196.

Beeston, A. F. L. *Warfare in Ancient South Arabia (2nd–3rd Century AD)*. London: Luzac, 1976.

Beidelman, O. *W. Robertson Smith and the Sociological Study of Religion*. Chicago: University of Chicago Press, 1974.

Bejtic, Alija. "Jedno videnje sarajevskih evlija i njihovih grobova kao kultnih mjesta." *Prilozi za Orientalnu Filologiju* 31 (1981): 111–129.

Bel, A. "La Djâzya, chanson arabe précédée d'observations sur quelques légendes arabes et sur la geste des Banū Hilāl." *Journal Asiatique* (1902–1903): 289–347.

Belaiew, Colonel N. "Damascene Steel." Pts. 1 and 2. *Journal of the Iron and Steel Institute* 97 (1918): 417; 104 (1921): 181.

Benito, C. "Enki and Ninmah and Eni and the World Order." PhD dissertation, University of Pennsylvania, 1969.

Benn, James. "Where Text Meets Flesh: Burning the Body as an Apocryphal Practice in Chinese Buddhism." *History of Religions* 37, no. 4 (1998): 295–321.

Bent, Theodore. *Southern Arabia*. London: Smith, Elder and Co., 1900; reprint, London: Garnet Publishing, 1994.

Berger, O. *La légende de Pélops et d'Oinomaos*. Louvain, 1935.

Berger-Doer, Gratia. "Aster." In *Lexicon Iconographicum Mythologiae Classicae*, vol. 2, pt. 1:903. Zurich: Artemis, 1981–1999.

Bergman, F. *Archaeological Researches in Sinkiang*. Stockholm: Bokförlags Aktiebolaget Thule, 1939.

Bernard the Monk. "Travels." In *Itinera Hierosolymitana et Descriptiones Terrae Sanctae Bellis Sacris Anteriora: Latina Lingua Exarata Sumptibus Societatis*

*Illustrandis Orientis Latini Monumentis,* ed. T. Tobler and others, 309–320. Osnabrück: Zeller, 1966.
Bezold, C., ed. and trans. *Die Schatzhohle (Meʿārath Gazzē).* Leipzig: J. C. Hinrisch'sche Buchhandlung, 1883–1888; reprint, Amsterdam: Philo Press, 1981.
Bibby, Geoffrey. *Looking for Dilmun.* New York: Knopf, 1969.
Bidwell, Robin. *Travellers in Arabia.* London: Hamlyn, 1976.
*Big Wednesday.* Burbank: Warner Bros., 1978.
Bin Mohammed, Ghazi. *Maqāmāt al-Urdun: Holy Sites of Jordan.* Amman: Turab, 1995.
Bīrūnī, Muḥammad b. Aḥmad. *Kitāb al-jawāhir fī maʿrifat al-jawāhir.* Hyderabad: Jamiʿat Daʾirat al-Maʿārif al-ʿUthmānīyah, 1355.
Biqāʿī, Yāsīn. "al-Nubdha al-laṭīfa fī al-mazārāt al-sharīfa." Damascus, Maktabat al-Asad, MS, 11386.
Bisheh, Ghazi I. "The Mosque of Madīnah throughout the First Century A.H." PhD dissertation, University of Michicagan, 1979.
Bivar, A. D. H. "Seljūqid Ziyārats of Sar-i Pul (Afghanistan)." *Bulletin of the School of Oriental and African Studies* 29 (1966): 57–63.
Black, John Sutherland, and George Chrystal. *The Life of William Robertson Smith.* London: A. and C. Black, 1912.
Blackburn, Mark. *Hula Girls and Surfer Boys.* Atglen, Pa.: Schiffer, 2000.
Blackburn, Mark. *Surf's Up: Collecting the Longboard Era.* Atglen, Pa.: Schiffer, 2001.
Blair, John. *The Illustrated Discography of Surf Music, 1959–1965.* Riverside, Calif.: J. Bee Productions, 1978.
Blair, John. *The Illustrated Discography of Surf Music, 1961–1965.* Riverside, Calif.: J. Bee Productions, 1983.
Blake, Tom. *Hawaiian Surfboard.* Honolulu: Paradise of the Pacific Press, 1935.
Blake, Tom. *Hawaiian Surfriding: The Ancient and Royal Pastime.* Flagstaff: Northland Press, 1961.
Boardman, John. *The Archaeology of Nostalgia: How the Greeks Re-created Their Mythical Past.* London: Thames and Hudson, 2002.
Boas, Franz. *The Jesup North Pacific Expedition,* vol. 5, pt. 2, *The Kwakiutl of Vancouver Island.* Leiden: E. J. Brill, 1898; reprint, New York: AMS Press, 1975.
Boas, Franz. *The Religion of the Kwakiutl Indians.* Columbia University Contributions to Anthropology 10. New York: Columbia University Press, 1930.
Bogoras, Waldemar. "Le mythe de l'Animal-Dieu mourant et ressuscitant." In *XXIIIe Congrès International des Américanistes, Rome 1926* (Rome, 1926).
Borgehammar, S. *How the Holy Cross Was Found: From Event to Medieval Legend.* Stockholm: Almqvist and Wiksell International, 1991.
Bosworth, C. E., and T. W. Haig, "Sind." In *Encyclopaedia of Islam,* 2d ed., ed. H. A. R. Gibb and others, 9:632–635. Leiden: E. J. Brill, 1960–2002.

Botti, G. "Les citernes d'Alexandrie." *Bulletin de la Société Archéologique d'Alexandrie* 2 (1899): 15.

Boucher, Daniel. "The Pratityasamutpadagatha and Its Role in the Medieval Cult of the Relics." *Journal of the International Association of Buddhist Studies* 14 (1991): 399–411.

Boudot-Lamotte, A., and F. Vire. "Contribution a l'étude de l'archerie musulmane: Notes complémentaires." *Arabica* 17, no. 1 (1970): 47–68.

Bourgoin, P. *Précis de l'art arabe*. Paris: E. Leroux, 1892.

Bourrilly, J., and E. Laoust. *Stèles funéraires marocaines*. Paris: Librairie Larose, 1927.

Bousquet, Georges-Henri. "La pureté rituelle en Islam: Étude de fiqh et de sociologie religieuse." *Revue de l'Histoire des Religions* 138 (1950): 53–71.

Bousquet, Georges-Henri. "Le rituel du culte des saints (à propos du livre de T. Canaan)." *Revue Africain* 93 (1949): 277–290.

Bousset, W. *The Antichrist Legend*. London: Hutchinson and Co., 1896.

Bowen, R. "Death and the History of Islam in Highland Aceh." *Indonesia* 38 (1984): 21–38.

Bowen, R. "Graves, Shrines and Power in a Highland Sumatran Society." In *Manifestations of Sainthood in Islam*, ed. Grace Martin Smith and Carl W. Ernst, 1–14. Istanbul: Isis Press, 1993.

Bowman, J. "Early Samaritan Eschatology." *Journal of Jewish Studies* 6 (1955): 63–72.

Bowman, J. "Samaritan Studies." *Bulletin of the John Rylands Library* 40 (1957–1958): 298–327.

Braunholtz, H. J., and A. S. Fulton. "An Inscribed Turkish Sword." *British Museum Quarterly* 1 (1927): 106–107.

Bréant, "Description à un procédé à l'aide duquel on obtient une espèce d'acier fondu, semblable à celui des lames damassées orientales." *Bulletin de la Société d'Encouragement pour l'Industrie Nationale* 21 (1823): 222–227.

Breccia, E. "Les sondages près de la mosquée Nébi Daniel." *Bulletin de Musée Gréco-Romain* (1925–1931): 48.

Brelich, Angelo. *Heros: Il culto greco degli eroi e il problema degli esseri semi-divini*. Rome: Ediziioni dell'Ateneo, 1957.

Breton, J. F. "Religious Architecture in Ancient Hadramawt." *Proceedings of the Seminar for Arabian Studies* 10 (1980): 5–16.

Breton, J. F. "Les temples de Maʿin et du Jawf (Yémen): État de la question." *Syria* 75 (1998): 61–80.

Breton, J. F., and C. Robin. "Le sanctuaire préislamique du Gabal al-Lawd (Nord-Yémen)." *Comptes Rendus de l'Académie des Inscriptions et Belles-Lettres* (1982): 590–629.

Brinner, William. *ʿArāʾis al-Majālis fī Qiṣaṣ al-Anbiyāʾ; or, "Lives of the Prophets"*

*as Recounted by Abū Isḥāq Aḥmad ibn Muḥammad ibn Ibrāhīm al-Thaʿlabī.* Leiden: E. J. Brill, 2002.
Brock, Sebastian P. "Clothing Metaphors as a Means of Theological Expression in Syriac Tradition." In *Typus, Symbol, Allegorie bei den östlichen Vätern und ihren Parallelen im Mittelalter,* ed. Margot Schmidt, 11–40. Eichstatt: F. Pustet Regensburg, 1981.
Broderius, John R. "The Giant in Germanic Tradition." PhD dissertation, University of Chicago, 1933.
Brohi, A. A. *A History of Tombstones: Sind and Baluchistan.* Lahore: Sindhi Adabi Board, 1986.
Brookes, D. S. "Of Swords and Tombs: Symbolism in the Ottoman Accession Ritual." *Turkish Studies Association Bulletin* 17 (1993): 1–22.
Brown, Percy. *Indian Architecture: Islamic Period.* Bombay: D. B. Taraporevala Sons, 1965–1968.
Budge, E. A. W., ed. and trans. *The Book of the Cave of Treasures.* London: Religious Tract Society, 1927.
Buhl, Frants. *Das Leben Muhammeds.* Leipzig: Quelle and Meyer, 1930.
Bukhārī, Muḥammad b. Ismāʿīl. *Kitāb al-ḍuʿafāʾ al-ṣaghir.* Allahabad: Maṭbaʿat Anwār al-Ḥamd, 1325.
Bukhārī, Muḥammad b. Ismāʿīl. *Ṣaḥīḥ.* Damascus: Dār al-Qalam, 1981.
Bulliet, Richard. *The Camel and the Wheel.* Cambridge, Mass.: Harvard University Press, 1975.
Bulqīnī, ʿUmar b. Raslān. *Maḥāsin al-iṣṭilāḥ wa tadmīn kitāb Ibn al-Ṣalāḥ.* In *Muqaddimat Ibn al-Ṣalāḥ wa Maḥāsin al-iṣṭilāḥ.* Cairo: Wizārat al-Thaqāfah, 1974.
Burckhardt, John Lewis. *Notes on the Bedouins and Wahabys.* London: H. Colburn and R. Bentley, 1831.
Burckhardt, John Lewis. *Travels in Arabia: An Account of Those Territories in Hedjaz Which the Mohammedans Regard as Sacred.* London: H. Colburn, 1829; reprint, London: Cass, 1968.
Burckhardt, John Lewis. *Travels in Syria and the Holy Land.* London: J. Murray, 1822; reprint, New York: AMS Press, 1983.
Burckhardt, T. "The Symbolism of the Mirror." *Symbolon* 4 (1954): 117–123.
Burgess, Jas. *The Buddhist Stupas of Amaravati and Jaggayyapeta in the Krishna District, Madras Presidency, Surveyed in 1882.* Archaeological Survey of Southern India. London: Trübner and Co., 1887; reprint, Varanasi: Indological Book House, 1970.
Burgess, Jas. *Report on the Buddhist Cave Temples and Their Inscriptions: Being Part of the Results of the Fourth, Fifth, and Sixth Seasons' Operations of the Archaeological Survey of Western India, 1876–77, 1877–78, 1878–79.* Archaeological

Survey of Western India 4. London: Trübner and Co., 1883; reprint, Varanasi: Indological Book House, 1964.

Burkert, Walter. *The Creation of the Sacred: Tracks of Biology in Early Religions.* Cambridge, Mass.: Harvard University Press, 1996.

Burkert, Walter. *Homo Necans: The Anthropology of Ancient Greek Sacrificial Ritual and Myth.* Berkeley: University of California Press, 1983.

Burnes, Alexander. *Travels into Bokhara.* London: J. Murray, 1834; reprint, Karachi: Oxford University Press, 1973.

Burnside, Carol Emma. "W. Robertson Smith and Louis Dumont: 'Fundamental Institutions' and 'Ideologies.'" PhD dissertation, Committee on the History of Culture, University of Chicago, 1987.

Burton, Richard F. *The Book of the Sword.* London: Chatto and Windus, 1884; reprint, New York: Dover, 1987.

Burton, Richard F. *The Land of Midian.* London: C. K. Paul and Co., 1879.

Burton, Richard F. *A Pilgrimage to al Medinah and Meccah.* London, 1885.

Burton, Richard F. *Sindh and the Races That Inhabit the Valley of the Indus, with Notices of the Topography and History of the Province.* London: W. H. Allen, 1851; reprint, Karachi: Oxford University Press, 1973; reprint, Ottowa: Laurier Books, 1997.

Burton, Richard F. *Scinde; or, The Unhappy Valley.* London: R. Bentley and Son, 1851.

Burton, Richard F. *Scinde Revisited.* London: R. Bentley and Son, 1877.

Burton-Page, John. "Ḳadam Sharif (India and Pakistan)." In *Encyclopaedia of Islam,* 2d ed., ed. H. A. R. Gibb and others, 4:368. Leiden: E. J. Brill, 1960–2002.

Burton-Page, John. "Makbara." In *Encyclopaedia of Islam,* 2d ed., ed. H. A. R. Gibb and others, 6:125–128. Leiden: E. J. Brill, 1960–2002.

Burton-Page, John. "Muslim Graves of the 'Lesser Tradition': Gilgit, Puniāl, Swāt, Yūsufzai." *Journal of the Royal Asiatic Society* (1986): 248–254.

Busink, T. *Der Tempel von Jerusalem: Von Salomo bis Herodes.* 2 vols. Leiden: E. J. Brill, 1970–1980.

Busse, Heribert. "Jerusalem and Mecca, the Temple and the Kaaba: An Account of Their Interrelation in Islamic Times." In *The Holy Land in History and Thought,* ed. M. Sharon, 236–246. Leiden: E. J. Brill, 1988.

Busse, Heribert. "Die Patriarchengräber in Hebron und der Islam." *Zeitschrift des Deutschen Paleastina-Vereins* 114 (1992): 672–687.

Caetani, Leone. *Annali dell'Islam.* Milan: U. Hoepli, 1905–1926.

Cahen, Claude. "Tabṣirah al-albāb fī kaifayah al-nijjāh min al-ḥurūb min al-aswā': Un traité d'Armurerie composé pour Saladin." *Bulletin d'Etudes Orientales* (Beirut) 12 (1947–1948): 103–163.

Cahill, Suzanne. "The Word Made Bronze: Inscriptions on Medieval Chinese Bronze Mirrors." *Archives of Asian Art* 38 (1985): 62–70.

Calderini, Simonetta. "Woman, 'Sin' and 'Lust': The Fall of Adam and Eve according to Classical and Modern Muslim Exegesis." In *Religion and Sexuality*, ed. Michael A. Hayes, Wendy Porter, and David Tombs, Studies in Theology and Sexuality 2, Roehampton Institute London Papers 4, 49–63. Sheffield: Sheffield Academic Press, 1998.

Canaan, T. *Mohammedan Saints and Sanctuaries in Palestine.* London: Luzac and Co., 1927.

Canova, Giovanni. "Il serpente della Kaʿba: Una nota sulla Mecca preislamica." *Annali di Carl Foscari: Rivista della Racolta di lingue e letterature straniere dell'Università di Venezia* 25 (1994): 421–425.

Carré, Abbé. *The Travels of the Abbé Carré in India and the Near East, 1672 to 1674.* Ed. Charles Fawcett. Trans. Lady Fawcett. London: Hakluyt Society, 1947.

Carroll, Nick, ed. *The Next Wave: A Survey of World Surfing.* London: Macdonald and Queen Anne, 1991.

Carswell, John. "Mosques and Tombs in the Maldive Islands." *Art and Archaeology Research Papers* 9 (1976): 26–30.

Carter, John. "Graves of Three Descendants of Badr Bū Ṭuwayriq in Ẓafār of Oman." *Arabian Studies* 2 (1975): 211–212.

Castagné, Joseph. "Le culte des lieux saints de l'Islam au Turkestan." *Ethnographie*, n.s., 46 (1951): 46–124.

Castrén, M. A. "Journey into Siberia in 1845–1849." *Magazin zemlevedenia u pyteoestvia* 6, no. 2 (1860).

Cavendish, M. W. "The Custom of Placing Pebbles on Nubian Graves." *Sudan Notes and Records* 47 (1966): 151–156.

Chaghatai, M. A. *Muslim Monuments of Ahmadabad through Their Inscriptions.* Poona, s.n., 1934.

Chaghatai, M. A. "The So-Called Gardens and Tombs of Zeb-un-Niza at Lahore." *Islamic Culture* 9 (1935): 610–620.

Chamberlain, Michael. *Knowledge and Social Practice in Medieval Damascus, 1190–1350.* Cambridge Studies in Islamic Civilization. Cambridge: Cambridge University Press, 1994.

Chelhod, J. "La baraka chez les Arabes ou l'influence bienfaisante du sacré." *Revue de l'Histoire des Religions* 147 (1955): 68–88.

Chen Dasheng. "Quanzhou yisilanjiaopai yu yuanmou yisiba xizhanluan zingzhi shishen" [Tentative inquiry into the Islamic sects at Quanzhou and the "isbah" disturbance toward the end of the Yuan dynasty]. In *Symposium on Quanzhou Islam*, ed. Quanzhou Maritime Museum, 167–176. Quanzhou: Quanzhou Maritime Museum, 1983.

Chen Dasheng, ed. *Islamic Inscriptions in Quanzhou.* Yinchuan: Ningxia ren min chu ban she, 1984.

Chesnut, G. F. *The First Christian Histories: Eusebius, Socrates, Sozomen, Theodoret, and Evagrius.* 2d ed. Macon, Ga.: Mercer University Press, 1986.
Chickering, William H. *Within the Sound of These Waves: The Story of the Kings of Hawaii Island.* New York: Harcourt, Brace and Co., 1941.
Christensen, Arthur. *Les types du premier homme et du premier roi.* Archives d'études orientales 14.2. 2 vols. Stockholm: P. A. Norstedt, 1917; Leiden: E. J. Brill, 1934.
Christiansen, Reidar Th. *The Migratory Legends: A Proposed List of Types with a Systematic Catalogue of the Norwegian Variants.* FF Communications, vol. 71, no. 175. Helsinki: Suomalainen Tiedeakatemia, 1958.
Clapp, Nicholas. *The Road to Ubar: Finding the Atlantis of the Sands.* Boston: Houghton Mifflin, 1998.
Clermont-Ganneau, C. "L'inscription de Nebî Hâron et le 'dharīh' funéraire des Nabatéens et des Arabes." *Recueil d'Archéologie Orientale* 2 (1898): 362–366.
Clermont-Ganneau, C. "L'inscription phénicienne de Maʿsoub." *Recueil d'Archéologie Orientale* 1 (1888): 81–86.
Clermont-Ganneau, C., and Jean-Baptise Chabot, eds. *Répertoire d'épigraphie sémitique.* Paris: Imprimerie Nationale, 1900–1968.
Clifford, R. J. *The Cosmic Mountain in Canaan and the Old Testament.* Cambridge, Mass.: Harvard University Press, 1972.
Clines, D. J. A. "The Significance of the 'Sons of God' Episode (Genesis 6:1–4) in the Context of the 'Primeval History' (Genesis 1–11)." *Journal for the Study of the Old Testament* 13 (1979): 33–46.
Coedès, George. *Pour mieux comprendre Angkor.* Paris: A. Maisonneuve, 1947.
Cohen, J. A. *A Samaritan Chronicle.* Leiden: E. J. Brill, 1981.
Cohen, Stuart. *The Three Crowns: Structures of Communal Politics in Early Rabbinic Jewry.* Cambridge: Cambridge University Press, 1990.
Colebrooke, T. E. "On the Proper Names of the Mohammadans." *Journal of the Royal Asiatic Society of Great Britain and Ireland* 11 (1879): 210.
Collins, J. J. "Sibylline Oracles." In *The Old Testament Pseudepigrapha,* ed. James H. Charlesworth, 1:317–472. Garden City, N.Y.: Doubleday, 1983.
Collins, Marilyn F. "The Hidden Vessels in Samaritan Traditions." *Journal for the Study of Judaism* 3, no. 1 (1972): 97–116.
Combs-Schilling, M. E. *Sacred Performances: Islam, Sexuality, and Sacrifice.* New York: Columbia University Press, 1989.
Connelly, J. B. "Votive Offerings from Hellenistic Failaka." In *L'Arabie préislamique et son environement historique et culturel,* ed. T. Fahd, 145–158. Strasbourg: Université des Sciences Humaines des Strasbourg, 1989.
Conway, John. *Adventure Sports: Surfing.* London: Salamander, 1988.
Cook, Michael. "Magian Cheese: An Archaic Problem in Islamic Law." *Bulletin of the School of Oriental and African Studies* 47 (1984): 449–467.

Cooke, G. A. *A Text-Book of North-Semitic Inscriptions.* Oxford: Clarendon Press, 1903.

Cooke, Henry T. *A Guide to Warwick, Kenilworth, Stratford-on-Avon, Coventry, and the Various Places of Interest in the Neighbourhood.* Warwick: H. T. Cooke and Son, 1870.

Coomaraswamy, Ananda. *Elements of Buddhist Iconography.* Cambridge, Mass.: Harvard University Press, 1935.

Coon, Carleton S. *The Hunting Peoples.* London: J. Cape, 1971.

Corbin, Henri. *Cyclical Time and Ismaili Gnosis.* Trans. Nancy Pearson. London: Kegan Paul International, 1983.

Corbin, Henri. *L'homme de lumière dans le soufisme iranien.* Paris: Éditions Présence, 1971. Trans. Nancy Pearson as *The Man of Light in Iranian Sufism* (Boulder, Colo.: Shambhala, 1978).

Corbin, Henri. *Temple et contemplation.* Paris: Flammarion et Cie., 1980. Trans. Philip and Liadain Sherrard as *Temple and Contemplation* (London: Kegan Paul International, 1986).

Corbin, Henri. *Terre céleste et corps de résurrection.* Paris: Buchet, 1979. Trans. Nancy Pearson as *Spiritual Body and Celestial Earth: From Mazdean Iran to Shiʿīte Iran* (Princeton: Princeton University Press, 1977).

Cornwall, P. B. "Ancient Arabia: Explorations in Hasa, 1940–41." *Geographical Journal* 107 (1946): 28–50.

*Corpus Inscriptionum Semiticarum.* Paris: Imprimerie Nationale, 1881–.

Cour, A. "Jaysh." In *Encyclopaedia of Islam,* 2d ed., ed. H. A. R. Gibb and others, 2:504. Leiden: E. J. Brill, 1960–2002.

Cousens, Henry. *The Antiquities of Sind: With Historical Outline.* Archaeological Survey of India 46. Calcutta: Government of India, 1929; reprint, Karachi: Oxford University Press, 1975.

Cousens, Henry. *The Architectural Antiquities of Western India.* London: India Society, 1926.

Cousens, Henry. *A List of Antiquarian Remains in His Highness the Nizam's Territories.* Archeological Survey of India 31. Calcutta: Office of the Superintendent of Government Printing, 1900.

Cowell, E. B., ed. *The Jataka.* Cambridge: Cambridge University Press, 1895–1907.

Cowley, Arthur. "The Samaritan Doctrine of the Messiah." *Expositor,* 5th ser., 1 (1895): 161–174.

Cralle, Trevor. *The Surfin'Ary: A Dictionary of Surfing Terms and Surfspeak.* Berkeley: Ten Speed Press, 1991.

Crawford, H., and others, eds. *The Dilmun Temple at Saar.* London: Kegan Paul International, 1997.

Crawley, A. E. "Mirror." In *Encylopedia of Religion and Ethics,* ed. James Hastings and others. New York: Charles Scribner's Sons, 1951.

Creswell, K. A. C. "The Origin of the Cruciform Plan of Cairene Madrasas." *Bulletin de l'Institut Français d'Archéologie Orientale* 21 (1922): 1–54.

Creswell, K. A. C. "The Kaʿba in A.D. 608." *Archaeologia* 94 (1951): 97–102.

Creswell, K. A. C., and M. ʿAbd al-ʿAzīz Marqūq. *Masājid al-Qāhirah qabl ʿaṣr al-mamālīk.* Cairo: Dār al-Maʿārif, 1942.

Croissant, F. "Remarques sur la métope de la Mort d'Alkyoneus à l'Héraion du Silari." *Bulletin de Correspondance Hellénique* 89 (1965): 390–399.

Crone, Patricia. *Meccan Trade and the Rise of Islam.* Princeton: Princeton University Press, 1987.

Crooke, W. *An Introduction to the Popular Religion and Folklore of Northern India.* Allahabad: Government Press, 1894.

Cross, F. M. "The Priestly Tabernacle." *Biblical Archaeologist Reader* 1 (1961): 201–228.

Crowfoot, J. W. "Wedding Customs in the Northern Sudan." *Sudan Notes and Records* 5 (1922): 182–208.

*Cuneiform Texts from Babylonian Tablets . . . in the British Museum.* London: Trustees of the British Museum, 1896.

Cunningham, Alexander. *Four Reports Made during the Years 1862–63–64–65.* Archaeological Survey of India 1. Simla: Government Central Press, 1871; reprint, Varanasi: Indological Book House, 1972.

Cunningham, Alexander. *Report for the Year 1872–1873.* Archaeological Survey of India 5. Calcutta: Office of the Superintendent of Government Printing, 1873; reprint, Varanasi: Indological Book House, 1966.

Cunningham, Alexander. *Report of a Tour in the Punjab in 1878–79.* Archaeological Survey of India 14. Calcutta: Superintendent of Government Printing, 1887; reprint, Varanasi: Indological Book House. 1970.

Curvers, H. "The Middle Habour Salvage Operation: Excavation at Tell al-Raqai, 1986." *Akkadica* 55 (November/December 1987): 1–29.

Curzon, G. N. *Leaves from a Viceroy's Notebook.* London: Macmillan and Co., 1926.

Dabbāgh, Abū Zayd ʿAbd al-Raḥmān b. Muḥammad. *Maʿālim al-aymān fī maʿrifat ahl al-Qayrawān.* Cairo: Maktabat al-Khanjī, 1968.

Dabrowski, Leszek. "La citerne a eau sous la mosquée de Nébi Daniel." *Bulletin of the Faculty of Arts, Alexandria University* 12 (1958): 40–48.

Dales, G. F. "Hissar IIIC Stone Objects in Afghan Sistan." In *Mountains and Lowlands: Essays in the Archaeology of Greater Mesopotamia,* ed. L. D. Levine and T. Cuyler Young, 17–27. Bibliotheca Mesopotamia 7. Malibu, Calif.: Undena Publications, 1977.

Damīrī, Muḥammad b. Mūsā. *Ḥayāt al-ḥayawān.* Damascus: Dār Ḥalās, 1989. Trans. A. S. G. Jayakar as *Ad-Damîrî's Ḥayat al-Ḥayawân: A Zoological Lexicon*

(Frankfurt: Institute for the History of Arabic-Islamic Science at the Johann Wolfgang Goethe University, 2001).

Dāraquṭnī, ʿAlī b. ʿUmar. *Sunan*. Beirut: ʿAlam al-Kutub, 1980.

Dārimī, ʿAbdallāh b. ʿAbd al-Raḥmān. *Sunan al-Dārimī*. Ed. Khālid al-Sabʿ al-ʿAlamī. Beirut: Dār al-Kitāb al-ʿArabī, 1407.

Davies, Philip. *The Penguin Guide to the Monuments of India: Islamic, Rajput, European*. New York: Penguin Books, 1989.

Day, John. "William Robertson Smith's Hitherto Unpublished Second and Third Series of Burnett Lectures on the Religion of the Semites." In *William Robertson Smith: Essays in Reassessment,* Journal for the Study of the Old Testament Supplemental Series 189, ed. William Johnstone, 190–202. Sheffield: Sheffield Academic Press, 1995.

de Clavijo, Ruy González. *Narrative of the Spanish Embassy to the Court of Timur at Samarkand in the Years 1403–1406.* Trans. Guy Le Strange. London: Harper, 1928.

Dedering, S. *Apocalypse of Baruch.* Peshiṭta Institute 4.3. Leiden: E. J. Brill, 1973.

De Goeje, M. J. *Mémoires sur les Carmathes du Bahraïn et le Fatimides*. Leiden: E. J. Brill, 1886.

de Heusch, Luc. *Sacrifice in Africa: A Structualist Approach.* Bloomington: Indiana University Press, 1985.

DeJong, F. "Cairene Ziyâra-Days: A Contribution to the Study of Saint Veneration in Islam." *Die Welt des Islams* 17, nos. 1–4 (1929): 26–43.

de Jonge, M. "Christelijke Elementen in de Vitae Prophetarum." *Nederlands Theologisch Tijdschrift* 16 (1961–1962): 161–178.

de Keroualin, François, and Ludovic Schwarz. "Hud, un pélerinage en Hadramaout." *Quaderni di studi arabi* 13 (1995): 181–189.

Deniker, Joseph. *Les Ghiliaks: D'après les derniers renseignements*. Paris: E. Leroux, 1884.

Denny, Fred. "Pilgrimage and the History of Religions: Theoretical Approaches to the Hajj." In *Approaches to Islam in Religious Studies,* ed. Richard Martin. Tucson: Arizona State University Press, 1985.

Deraniyagala, P. E. P. "Sinhala Weapons and Armour." *Journal of the Ceylon Branch of the Royal Asiatic Society* 35 (1942): 57–142, plates I–V.

de Rialle, Julian Girard. *La mythologie comparée*. Paris: C. Reinwald, 1878.

Dermenghem, E. *Le culte des saints dans l'Islam maghrébin*. Paris: Gallimard, 1954.

de Rotrou, G. Ploix. *La citadelle d'Alep et ses alentours*. Chatenay-Malabry: Alteredit 2001.

Desai, Ziauddin. "Principle Mosques and Tombs of India." *Indo-Asian Culture* 14 (1965): 332–342.

de Sarzec, E., and L. Heuzey. *Découvertes en Chaldée*. Paris: E. Leroux, 1884.
de Savignac, J. "Le sens du terme Ṣâphôn." *Ugarit Forschungen* 16 (1984): 273–278.
de St. Elie, Anastase Marie. "Le culte rendu par les musulmans aux sandales de Mahomet." *Anthropos* 5 (1910): 363–366.
Detienne, Marcel. *The Gardens of Adonis: Spices in Greek Mythology*. Trans. J. Lloyd. Princeton: Princeton University Press, 1977.
Deverdun, G. *Marrakech des origines à 1912*. Rabat: Éditions techniques nord-africaines, 1959.
De Vries, B. "The Fortifications at El-Lejjun." In *The Roman Frontier in Central Jordan: Interim Report on the Limes Arabicus Project, 1980–1985*, ed. S. T. Parker, 311–351. Oxford: B. A. R., 1987.
D.G.B. "Naugaza Tombs." *Panjab Notes and Queries* 1 (1884): 109.
Dhahabī, Shams al-Dīn. *al-ʿIbar fī khabar man ghabar*. Ed. M. Zaghlūl. Beirut: Dār al-Kutub al-ʿIlmīyah, 1988.
Dhahabī, Shams al-Dīn. *al-Kāshif fī maʿrifat man la-hu riwāyat fī al-kutub al-sittah*. Ed. ʿIzzat ʿAlī ʿĪd ʿAṭiyyah and Mūsā Muḥammad ʿAlī al-Mawshī. Cairo: Dār al-Kutub al-Ḥadīthah, 1963.
Dhahabī, Shams al-Dīn. *Siyar aʿlām al-nubalāʾ*. Ed. Bashār ʿAwwād Maʿrūf. Beirut: Muʾassasat al-Risālah, 1992.
Dhahabī, Shams al-Dīn. *Tajrīd asmāʾ al-ṣaḥābah*. Hyderabad: Majlis Dāʾirat al-Maʿārif al-ʿUthmānīyah, 1315.
Dickie, James (Yaqub Zaki). "Allah and Eternity: Mosques, Madrasas and Tombs." In *Architecture of the Islamic World*, ed. George Michell, 18–47. London: Thames and Hudson, 1978.
Dickson, H. R. P. *The Arab of the Desert: A Glimpse into Badawin Life in Kuwait and Sau'di Arabia*. London: George Allen and Unwin, 1949.
Dieterlen, G., and S. de Ganay. "Le génie des eaux chez les Dogons." *Miscellanaea Africana* 5 (Paris, 1942): 61ff.
Dijkstra, K. *Life and Loyalty: A Study in the Socio-religious Culture of Syria and Mesopotamia in the Graeco-Roman Period Based on Epigraphic Evidence*. Leiden: E. J. Brill, 1995.
Dikshitar, V. R. *War in Ancient India*. Calcutta: Macmillan and Co., 1944.
Dīnawarī, Aḥmad b. Dāʾūd. *Kitāb al-akhbār al-ṭiwāl*. Ed. Aḥmad b. Dāʾūd. Beirut: Dār al-Kutub al-ʿIlmīyah, 1959.
Diodorus Siculus. *Bibliotheca Historica*. Ed. and trans. C. H. Oldfather and others. 7 vols. Cambridge, Mass.: Harvard University Press, 1933–1967.
Donner, K. *Ethnological Notes about the Yenisei Ostyaks*. Helsinki: Suomalais-ugrilainen Seura, 1933.
Dossin, G. "L'inscription de fondation de Iahdun-Lim, roi de Mari." *Syria* 32 (1935): 1–28, pls. 1–2.

Doughty, Charles. *Travels in Arabia Deserta*. Cambridge: Cambridge University Press, 1888; reprint of 3d. ed., New York: Dover Publications, 1979.

Douglas, Mary. "Animals in Lele Religious Symbolism." *Africa* 27, no. 1 (1957): 46–58.

Douglas, Mary. *Impurity and Danger.* New York: Praeger, 1966.

Douglas, Mary. *The Lele of the Kasai*. London: International African Institute, 1963.

Douglas, Mary. *Natural Symbols: Explorations in Cosmology*. New York: Pantheon Books, 1982.

Dozy, R. P. A. *Dictionnaire détaillé des noms des vètements chez les Arabes.* Amsterdam: J. Müller, 1845; reprint, Beirut: Librairie du Liban, 1969.

Dozy, R. P. A. *Die Israeliten zu Mekka von Davids Zeit bis in's fünfte Jahrhundert unsrer Zeitrechnung.* Leipzig: W. Engelmann, 1864.

Dozy, R. P. A. *Supplément aux dictionnaires arabes*. Leiden: E. J. Brill, 1927.

Dozy, R. P. A., and Engelmann. *Glossaire des mots espagnols et portugais dérivés de l'arabe*. Leiden: E. J. Brill, 1869.

Drake, H. A. "Eusebius and the True Cross." *Journal of Ecclesiastical History* 36 (1985): 1–22.

Drake, H. A., and others. *Eudoxia and the Holy Sepulchre: A Constantinian Legend in Coptic*. Testi e documenti per lo studio dell'antichità 47. Milan: Cisalpino-Goliardica, 1980.

Drijvers, H. J. W. "Inscriptions from Allat's Sanctuary." *Aram* 7 (1995): 109–119.

Drijvers, H. J. W., and J. W. Drijvers. *The Finding of the True Cross: The Judas Kyriakos Legend in Syriac*. Corpus Scriptorum Christianorum Orientalium 565, Subsidia 93. Louvain: Peeters, 1997.

Drijvers, J. W. *Helena Augusta: The Mother of Constantine the Great and Her Finding of the True Cross*. Leiden: E. J. Brill, 1992.

Drower, E. S. *Peacock Angel: Being Some Account of Votaries of a Secret Cult and Their Sanctuaries*. London: J. Murray, 1941.

Dugas, C. "L'évolution de la légende de Thésée." *Revue des Etudes Grecques* 56 (1943): 1–24. Reprinted in *Recueil Charles Dugas* (Paris: E. de Boccard,1960), 93–107.

Dugas, C., and R. Flacelière. *Thésée: Images et récits*. Paris: E. de Boccard, 1958.

Dumont, Louis. *Homo hierarchicus: Essai sur le système des castes.* Paris: Gallimard, 1966. Trans. Mark Sainsbury, Louis Dumont, and Basia Gulati as *Homo Hierarchicus: The Caste System and Its Implications,* 2d ed. (Chicago: University of Chicago Press, 1980).

Dumont, Louis, and D. Pocock. "Pure and Impure." *Contributions to Indian Sociology* 3 (1959): 9–39.

Durkheim, Émile. *The Elementary Forms of the Religious Life.* Trans. Joseph Ward Swain. London, 1915; reprint, New York: Free Press, 1965.

Dussaud, René. *Les monuments palestiniens et judaïques.* Paris: E. Leroux, 1912.

Dyrenkova, N. P. "Bear Worship among Turkish Tribes of Siberia." In *Proceedings of the 23rd International Congress of Americanists*, 437–445. New York: Science Press Print Co., 1928–1930.

Dzhalalov, T. "Khaiiam Khorezma." *Zvezda Vostoka* (Tashkent), 1962, 141–144.

Dzierzykray-Rogalski, Tadeusz. "Islamic Graves from Faras." *Nubica* 1–2 (1987–1988): 505–509.

Eakins, J. K. *Tell el-Hesi: The Muslim Cemetery in Field V and VI/IX (Statum II)*. Winona Lake, Ind.: Scholars Press, 1993.

Eaton, Richard. *Sufis of Bijapur, 1300–1700: Social Roles of Sufis in Medieval India*. Princeton: Princeton University Press, 1978.

Eaton, Richard, and Saiyid Muhyi al-Din bin Mahmud Qadiri. *Sahifat-i Ahl-i Huda*. Ed. and trans. M. Akbaruddin Siddiqi. Hyderabad: Majlis Dāʾirat al-Maʿārif al-ʿUthmānīyah, 1966.

Eddy, Samuel K. *The King Is Dead: Studies in the Near Eastern Resistance to Hellenism, 334–31 B.C.* Lincoln: University of Nebraska Press, 1961.

Edelman, D. "Saul's Battle against Amaleq (1 Sam 15)." *Journal for the Study of the Old Testament* 35 (1986): 71–84.

Edelstein, Gershom. "Rephaim, Valley of." In *The Anchor Bible Dictionary*, ed. David Noel Freedman and others, 5:676–677. New York: Doubleday, 1992.

Edsman, Carl-Martin. "Bärenfest." In *Die Religion in Geschichte und Gegenwart*, ed. Kurt Galling and Hans Campenhausen. Tübingen: Mohr, 1957.

Edsman, Carl-Martin. "Bear Rites among the Scandinavian Lapps." In *Proceedings of the 9th International Congress for the History of Religions*, Tokyo, 1960, 25–32.

Edsman, Carl-Martin. "The Story of the Bear Wife in Nordic Tradition." *Ethnos* (Stockholm) 21 (1956): 1–2.

Eilberg-Schwartz, Howard. *The Savage in Judaism: An Anthropology of Israelite Religion and Ancient Judaism*. Bloomington: Indiana University Press, 1990.

Eilers, Wilhelm. *Lurische Gravsteine als Zeugnisse des Weiterlebens kassitischer Motive in der Gegenwart: Aus der Welt der islamischen Kunst*. Berlin, 1959.

Eissfeldt, O. *Baal Zaphon, Zeus Kasios und der Durchzug der Israeliten durchs Meer*. Halle: M. Niemeyer, 1932.

Eklund, R. *Life between Death and Resurrection According to Islam*. Uppsala: Almqvist and Wiksells, 1941.

Elad, Amikam. *Medieval Jerusalem and Islamic Worship: Holy Places, Ceremonies, Pilgrimage*. Leiden: E. J. Brill, 1995.

"Elated Shiites, on a Pilgrimage, Want the U.S. Out." *New York Times*, April 22, 2003.

Elgood, Heather. *Hinduism and the Religious Arts*. London: Cassells, 1998.

Elgood, Robert Francis Willard. "A Study of the Origin, Evolution and Role in Society of a Group of Chiselled Steel Hindu Arms and Armour from Southern India, c. 1400–1865 A.D." PhD dissertation, Linacre College, Oxford University, 1998.

Elgood, Robert. *Arms and Armour of Arabia in the 18th, 19th, and 20th Centuries.* London: Scolar Press, 1994.

Elgood, Robert. *Firearms of the Islamic World in the Tareq Rajab Museum, Kuwait.* London: I. B. Taurus, 1995.

Elgood, Robert, ed. *Islamic Arms and Armour.* London: Scolar Press, 1979.

Eliade, Mircea. *Forgerons et alchimistes.* Paris: Flammarion, 1956. Trans. Stephen Corrin as *The Forge and the Crucible,* 2d ed. (Chicago: University of Chicago Press, 1956).

Eliade, Mircea. *The Sacred and the Profane.* Trans. Willard R. Trask. New York: Harcourt, Brace, 1959.

Elisséeff, Nikita. "Les monuments de Nūr al-Dīn: Inventaire, notes archéologiques et bibliographiques." *Bulletin d'Études Orientales* 13 (1949): 5–43.

Elliger, K. "Die grosser Tempelsakristeien im Verfassungsentwurf des Ezechiel." In *Festschrift Albrecht Alt zum 70. Geburtstag gewidmet,* ed. Albrecht Alt, 79–103. Leipzig: Karl-Marx Universität, 1954.

Emery, W. B. *Nubian Treasure.* London: Methuen, 1948.

Enthoven, R. E. *Folklore of the Konkan.* Indian Folklore. Delhi: S. Chand, 1976.

Enthoven, R. E. *The Folklore of Bombay.* Oxford: Clarendon Press, 1924.

Ephʿal, Israel. *The Ancient Arabs: Nomads on the Borders of the Fertile Crescent, 9th–5th Centuries B.C.* Leiden: E. J. Brill, 1982.

Epiphanius. *Haereses.* Ed. Karl Holl. Berlin: Akademie-Verlag, 1980–1985.

Epstein, I., ed. *The Babylonian Talmud.* London: Soncino Press, 1948.

Ernst, Carl. *Eternal Garden: Mysticism, History, and Politics at a South Asian Sufi Center.* Albany: State University of New York Press, 1992.

Ernst, Carl. *Following Muhammad: Rethinking Islam in the Contemporary World.* Chapel Hill: University of North Carolina, 2003.

Ettinghausen, Richard. "Die bildliche Darstellung der Kaʿba im islamischen Kulturkreis." *Zeitschrift der Deutschen Morgenländischen Gesellschaft* 12 (1933): 111–137.

Eucherius. *Letter to Faustus.* Ed. I. Fraipont. Corpus Scriptorum Latinorum. Turnhout, 1958.

Evans-Pritchard, E. E. *Nuer Religion.* Oxford: Oxford University Press, 1956.

Fahd, Toufic. *La divination arabe.* Leiden: E. J. Brill, 1966.

Fahd, Toufic. *Le panthéon de l'Arabie centrale à la veille de l'Hégire.* Paris: P. Geuthner, 1968.

Fahd, Toufic. "Une partique cléromantique à la Kaʿba préislamique." *Semitica* 8 (1958): 55–79. Originally published in *Proceedings of the 27th International Congress of Orientalists* 24 (1957): 246–248.

Fakhry, A. *The Egyptian Deserts: Bahria Oasis.* Cairo: Government Press, 1950.

Falkenstein, A. *Die Inschriften Gudeas von Lagash.* Rome: Pontificium Institutum Biblicum, 1966.
Faraday, M. "An Analysis of Wootz, or Indian Steel." *Quarterly Journal of Science, Literature and the Arts* 7 (1819): 288–290.
Farber-Flügge, G. "Inanna und Enki." In *Der Mythos "Inanna und Enki" unter besonderer Berücksichtingung der Liste der Me,* ed. G. Farber-Flügge, Studia Pohl 10, 16–65. Rome: Biblical Institute Press, 1973.
Farès, Bishr. *Une miniature religieuse de l'École arabe de Baghdad.* Cairo: Institut français d'archéologie orientale, 1948.
Farnell, L. R. *Greek Hero-Cults and Ideas of Immortality.* Oxford: Clarendon Press, 1921.
Farrelly, Midget, and Craig McGregor. *This Surfing Life.* London: Angus and Robertson, 1965.
Fāsī, Muḥammad b. Aḥmad. *Shifāʾ al-gharām bi-akhbār al-balad al-ḥarām.* Cairo, s.n. 1956.
Fatimi, S. Q. "Malaysian Weapons in Arabic Literature: A Glimpse of Early Trade in the Indian Ocean." *Islamic Studies* (Karachi) 3, no. 2 (1964): 199–228.
Fayyūmī, Aḥmad b. Muḥammad. *al-Miṣbāḥ al-munīr.* 2 vols. Beirut: Dār al-Kutub al-ʿIlmīyah, 1978.
Fenton, P. B. "The Hidden Secret Concerning the Shrine of Ibn ʿArabī: A Treatise by ʿAbd Ghanī al-Nābulusi." *Journal of the Muhyiddin ibn ʿArabi Society* 22 (1997): 1–40.
Ferrand, G. *Relations de voyages et textes géographiques arabes, persans et turcs relatifs a l'Extrême-Orient.* Paris: E. Leroux, 1914.
Field, W. *An Historical and Descriptive Account of the Town and Castle of Warwick and of the Neighbouring Spa of Leamington.* Warwick: H. Sharpe, 1815.
Figulla, H. H., and others. *Keilschrifttexte aus Boghazköi.* Leipzig: J. C. Hinrichs, 1921.
Finegan, Jack. *An Archaeological History of Religions of Indian Asia.* New York: Paragon House, 1989.
Finney, Ben, and James Houston. *Surfing, the Sport of Hawaiian Kings.* Rutland: C. E. Tuttle Co., 1966.
Firestone, Reuven. *Journeys in Holy Lands: The Evolution of the Abraham-Ishmael Legends in Islamic Exegesis.* Albany: State University of New York Press, 1990.
Fīrūzābādī, Muḥammad b. Yaʿqūb. *Qāmūs al-muḥīṭ.* 4 vols. Cairo: ʿIsā al-Bābī al-Ḥalabī, 1971–1973.
Flusser, D. *The Josippon.* 2 vols. Jerusalem: Merkaz Zalman Shazar, 1978–1980.
Fodor, A. "Malḥamet Daniyal." In *The Muslim East: Studies in Honour of Julius Germanus,* ed. Gyula Kaldy-Nagy and Gyula Germanus, 85–160. Budapest: Loránd Eotvos University, 1974.

Frankfort, Henri. *Kingship and the Gods*. Chicago: University of Chicago Press, 1948.

Frankfurter, David. *Religion in Roman Egypt*. Princeton: Princeton University Press, 1998.

Frantzen, Allen J. *Bloody Good: Chivalry, Sacrifice, and the Great War*. Chicago: University of Chicago Press, 2004.

Frazer, J. G. *The Golden Bough*. New York: Macmillan, 1922.

Fredricksson, H. *Jahwe als Krieger*. Lund: C. W. K. Gleerup, 1945.

Freeth, Zahra, and H. V. F. Winstone. *Explorers of Arabia: From the Renaissance to the End of the Victorian Era*. New York: Holmes and Meier, 1978.

Freud, Sigmund. "Taboo and Emotional Ambivalence." In his *Totem and Taboo*, trans. James Strachey, 18–74. New York: W. W. Norton, 1950.

Freudenthal, J. *Alexander Polyhistor und die von ihm erhaltenen Reste jüdischer und samaritanischer Geschichtswerke*. Breslau: H. Skutsch, 1874.

Friedmann, Y. "A Contribution to the Early History of Islam in India." In *Studies in Memory of Gaston Wiet*, ed. Myriam Rosen-Ayalon, 309–333. Jerusalem: Institute of Asian and African Studies, Hebrew University, 1977.

Friedmann, Y. "The Origins and Significance of the Chach Nāma." In *Islam in Asia*, vol. 1, ed. R. Israeli and A. Johns. Jerusalem: Magnes Press, 1984.

Friedmann, Y. "The Temple of Multan: A Note on Early Muslim Attitudes to Idolatry." *Israel Oriental Studies* 2 (1972): 176–182.

Frish, Daniyel, ed. *Sefer ha-Zohar Ḥadash*. Jerusalem: Mekhon Daʿat Yosef, 1999. Trans. Harry Sperling and Maurice Simon as *The Zohar* (London: Soncino, 1970).

Frost, F. "Plutarch and Theseus." *Classical Bulletin* 60 (1984): 65–73.

Gabriel, J. "Die Kainitengenealogie: Gn 4,17–24." *Biblica* 40 (1959): 409–427.

Gabrieli, F. "Muhammad ibn Qāsim ath-Thaqafī and the Arab Conquest of Sin." *East and West*, n.s., 15 (1964–1965): 281–95.

Gahs, A. "Kopf-, Schädel- und Langhochenopfer bei Rentiervölkern." In *Festschrift: Publication d'hommage offerte au P. W. Schmidt*, ed. W. Koppers, 231–268. Vienna: Mechitharisten-Congregations-Buchdr., 1928.

Galal, M. "Essai d'observations sur les rites funéraires en Égypte actuelle." *Revue des Études Islamiques* 11 (1937): 131–299.

Galliéni, Joseph-Simon. *Voyage au Soudan français (Haut-Niger et pays de Ségou), 1879–1881*. Paris: Hachette, 1855.

Garbe, Richard. *Die indischen Mineralien ihre Namen und die ihnen zugbeschriebenen Kräfte*. Hildesheim: Gerstenberg, 1974.

Garrick, H. B. W., and A. Cunningham. *Report of a Tour in the Panjâb and Râjpûtâna in 1883–84*. Archaeological Survey of India 23. Calcutta: Superintendent of Government Printing, 1887; reprint, Varanasi: Indological Book House, n.d.

Gaudefroy-Demombynes, M. *La Syrie à l'époque des Mamelouks*. Paris: P. Geuthner, 1923.
Gaudefroy-Demombynes, M. "La Voile de la Kaʿba." *Studia Islamica* 2 (1954): 5–21.
Gaudefroy-Demombynes, M., ed. and trans. *Les voyages d'Ibn Jobair*. Paris: P. Geuthner, 1949.
Gaulmier, J. "Pélerinages populairs à Hama." *Bulletin d'Études Orientales* 1 (1931): 137–152.
Gault-Williams, Malcolm. *Legendary Surfers: A Definitive History of Surfing's Culture and Heroes*. www.legendarysurfers.com, 2003.
*Gazetteer of the Province of Oudh*. Lucknow: Oudh Government Press, 1877–1878.
Geertz, Clifford. "Deep Play: Notes on the Balinese Cockfight." In his *The Interpretation of Cultures*, 412–453. New York: Basic Books, 1973.
Geiger, Wilhelm, trans. *The Mahavamsa; or, The Great Chronicle of Ceylon*. London: Pali Text Society, 1912.
Geoffroy, E. *Le soufisme en Égypte et en Syrie sous les derniers Mamelouks et les premiers Ottomans: Orientations spirituelles et enjeux culturels*. Damascus: Institut français d'études arabes de Damas, 1995.
Gernet, Louis. *The Anthropology of Ancient Greece*. Trans. John Hamilton and Blaise Nagy. Baltimore: Johns Hopkins University Press, 1981.
Geyer, P. *Kritische und sprachliche Erlaüterungen zu Observations sur le Vocabulaire du Pèlerinage chez Egérie et chez Antonin de Plaisance*. Nijmegen, 1965.
Geyer, Paul, ed. *Itinera Hierosolymitana saeculi IV–VIII*. Corpus Scriptorum Ecclesiasticorum Latinorum 39. Vindobonae: F. Tempsky, 1898.
Ghafur, Muhammad Abdul. "Fourteen Kufic Inscriptions of Banbhore, the Site of Debal." *Pakistan Archaeology* 3 (1966): 81–83.
Ghafur, Muhammad Abdul. *The Calligraphers of Thatta*. Karachi: Pakistan-Iran Cultural Association, 1968.
Ghazālī, Muḥammad b. Muḥammad. *al-Wasīṭ fī al-madhhab*. Ed. Muḥammad M. Tāmir and Aḥmad M. Ibrāhīm. Beirut: Dār al-Kutub al-ʿIlmīyah, 1997.
Gibson, M. D. *Apocrypha Arabica*. Studia Sinaitica 8. London: C. J. Clay and Sons, 1901.
Gifford, E. H., ed. and trans. *Eusebii Pamphili Evangelicae Preparationis*. Oxford: Oxford University Press, 1903.
Gil, Moshe. "The Medinan Opposition to the Prophet." *Jerusalem Studies in Arabic and Islam* 10 (1987): 65–96.
Gil, Moshe. "The Origin of the Jews of Yathrib." *Jerusalem Studies in Arabic and Islam* 4 (1984): 203–224.
Ginzberg, L. "Apocalypse of Baruch (Syriac)." In *Jewish Encyclopedia*, ed. I. Singer, cols. 1215–1236. New York, 1902.

Ginzberg, Louis. *The Legends of the Jews.* Philadelphia: Jewish Publication Society of America, 1909–1938; reprint, Baltimore: Johns Hopkins University Press, 1998.

Gladney, Dru C. "The Hui, Islam, and the State: A Sufi Community in China's Northwest Corner." In *Muslims in Central Asia: Expressions of Identity and Change,* ed. Jo-Ann Gross. Durham: Duke University Press, 1992.

Gladney, Dru C. "Muslim Tombs and Ethnic Folklore: Charters for Hui Identity." *Journal of Asian Studies* 46 (1987): 495–532.

Gladwin, Francis. *Ayeen Akbery; or, The Institutes of the Emperor Akber.* London, 1800; reprint, London: Routledge, 2000.

Glaser, E. *Skizze der Geschichte und Geographie Arabiens von den ältesten Zeiten bis zum Propheten Muḥammad.* Berlin: Weidmannsche Buchhandlung, 1890.

Glassner, Jean-Jacques. "Inannat et les me." In *Nippur at the Centennial: Papers Read at the 35e Rencontre Assyriologique Internationale, Philadelphia, 1988,* ed. Maria deJong Ellis, 55–76. Philadelphia: Occasional Publications of the Samuel Noah Kramer Fund, 1992.

Goetz, H. "The Pathan Tombs of Sarhind." *Islamic Culture* 13 (1939): 313–318.

Goitein, S. D. "From Aden to India: Specimens of the Correspondence of Indian Traders of the Twelfth Century." *Journal of the Economic and Social History of the Orient* 23 (1980): 43–66.

Goitein, S. D. "The Sanctity of Jerusalem and Palestine in Early Islam." In his *Studies in Islamic History and Institutions*, chap. 7. Leiden: E. J. Brill, 1966.

Golden, J., trans. *The Fathers according to Rabbi Nathan.* New Haven: Yale University Press, 1955.

Goldman, Irving. *The Mouth of Heaven: An Introduction to Kwakiutl Religious Thought.* London: Wiley, 1975.

Goldziher, Ignaz. "Der Chatib bei den alten Arabern." *Weiner Zeitschrift für die Kunde des Morgenlandes* 6 (1892): 97–102.

Goldziher, Ignaz. "Le culte des saints chez le muselmans." *Revue de l'Histoire des Religions* 2 (1891): 257–351.

Goldziher, Ignaz. *Muhammedanische Studien.* Halle: M. Niemeyer, 1889–1890. Trans. C. R. Barber and S. M. Stern as *Muslim Studies* (London: Allen and Unwin, 1971).

Goldziher, Ignaz. *Die Richtungen der islamischen Koranauslegung.* Leiden: E. J. Brill, 1920; reprint, 1970.

Goldziher, Ignaz. "Wasser als Dämonen abwehrendes Mittel." *Archiv für Religionswissenschaft* 13 (1910): 20–46.

Gorelik, Michael. "Oriental Armour of the Near and Middle East from the Eight to the Fifteenth Centuries as Shown in Works of Art." In *Islamic Arms and Armour,* ed. Robert Elgood, 30–63. London: Scolar Press, 1979.

Goris, R. "The Position of the Blacksmiths." In *Studies in Bali Life, Thought and Ritual,* ed. W. F. Wertheim, 291–297. The Hague: W. van Hoeve, 1960.
Grabar, Oleg. "Notes sur les ceremonies umayyades." In *Studies in Memory of Gaston Wiet,* ed. M. Rosen-Ayalon, 51–60. Jerusalem: Institute of Asian and African Studies, Hebrew University, 1977.
Granet, M. *Danses et légendes de la chine ancienne.* 2 vols. Paris: Presses Universitaires de France, 1926, 1959.
Granqvist, H. *Muslim Death and Burial: Arab Customs and Traditions Studied in a Village in Jordan.* Helsinki, n.p., 1965.
Green, Tamara M. "Tombs." In *Encyclopedia of Religion,* ed. Mircea Eliade and others. New York: Macmillan, 1987.
Grigg, Ricky. *Big Surf, Deep Dives and the Islands: My Life in the Ocean.* Honolulu: Editions Limited, 1998.
Grjaznov, M. P. "Minusinskie kamennye baby v svjazi s nekotorymi novymi materialami." *Sovetskaja Arkheologija* 12 (1950): 128–157.
Gross, Jo-Ann. "Approaches to the Problem of Identity Formation." In *Muslims in Central Asia: Expressions of Identity and Change,* ed. Jo-Ann Gross, 1–26. Durham: Duke University Press, 1992.
Gross, Jo-Ann. *Muslims in Central Asia: Expressions of Identity and Change.* Durham: Duke University Press, 1992.
Grottanelli, C., and others, eds. "Sacrificio, organizzazione del cosmo, dinamica sociale." *Studi storici* 25 (1984): 829–956.
Grotzfeld, Sophia. "Dāniyāl in der arabischen Legende." In *Festgabe für Hans Wehr,* ed. W. Fischer, 72–85. Wiesbaden: Harrassowitz, 1969.
Grünhut, L., and M. N. Adler, eds. *Eleh ha-Massaʿot.* Frankfurt: J. Kauffmann, 1903.
Guz-Sibertsein, B., and K. Raveh, "Tel Dor: Maritime Archaeology—1987/1988." *Excavations and Surveys in Israel 1988/89* 7/8 (1990): 49–53.
Ḥaddād, Abū Bakr. *Jawharat al-nayyirah.* Istanbul: Maṭbaʿat Maḥmūd Bik, 1885.
Haiman, M. *Archaeological Survey of Israel: Map of Har Hamran—Southwest (198) 10-00.* Jerusalem: Agaf ha-ʿAtikot ve ha-Muzeʾonīm, ha-Aguda le-Seker Arkheologi shel Yisraʾel, 1986.
Ḥākim, Muḥammad b. ʿAbdallāh. *al-Mustadrak ʿalā al-Ṣaḥīḥayn.* 5 vols. Cairo: Dār al-Ḥaramayn li-l-Ṭibāʿah wa al-Nashr wa al-Tawzīʿ, 1997.
Ḥalabī, ʿAlī b. Burhān al-Dīn. *al-Sīrah al-Ḥalabīyah.* Cairo: al-Maṭbaʿah al-Bahīyah, 1300.
Halbert, L. "The Mohammedan Graves." In *Rang Mahal: The Swedish Archaeological Expedition to India, 1952–1954,* ed. H. Rydh and others, Acta Archaeologica Ludiensia, 185–188. Lund: Gleerup, 1959.

Hall, Sandra Kimberley, and Greg Ambrose. *Memories of Duke: The Legend Comes to Life: Duke Paoa Hahanamoku, 1890–1968*. Honolulu: Bess Press, 1995.

Hallowell, A. Irving. "Bear Ceremonialism in the Northern Hemisphere." *American Anthropologist*, n.s., 28 (1926): 1–175, esp. 53–61.

Hallpike, Christopher. "Hair." In *Encyclopedia of Religion*, ed. M. Eliade and others, 6:154–157. New York: Macmillan, 1987.

Halm, Heinz. *The Empire of the Mahdi: The Rise of the Fatimids*. Trans. Michael Bonner. Leiden: E. J. Brill, 1996.

Hamadānī, al-Ḥasan b. Aḥmad. *Kitāb al-iklil*. Beirut, 1986.

Hamayon, R. *La chasse à l'âme: Esquisse d'une théorie du chamanisme sibérien*. Nanterre: Société d'ethnologie, 1990.

Ḥamd, Ibrāhīm b. ʿAyish. *Ḥaqq al-yaqīn fī muʿjizāt khaṭam al-anbiyāʾ wa al-mursalīn*. Medina: Waqf al-Barakah al-Khayrī, 2002.

Hamidullah, Muhammad. "La lettre du prophète à Héraclius et le sort de l'original." *Arabica* (1955): 97–110.

Hammad, M. "L'evolution de la chaire dans la vie religieuse en Egypte." *Cahiers d'Histoire Egyptienne* 8 (1956): 117–129.

Hammond, P. *The Temple of the Winged Lions, Petra*. Fountain Hills, Ariz.: Petra, 1996.

Hammoudi, Abdellah. *Victime et ses masques*. Paris: Éditions du Seuil, 1988. Trans. Paula Wissing as *The Victim and Its Masks: An Essay on Sacrifice and Masquerade in the Maghreb* (Chicago: University of Chicago Press, 1993).

Ḥamza, M. Shāhīn. *al-Sayyida Nafīsa*. Cairo: n.d.

Hansen, W. *Phlegon of Tralles' Book of Marvels*. Exeter: University of Exeter Press, 1996.

Ḥaqqī, Yaḥyā. *Qandil Umm Hashim: The Lamp of Umm Hashim*. Trans. Denys Johnson-Davies. Cairo: American University of Cairo Press, 2004.

Haran, M. "The Priestly Image of the Tabernacle." *Hebrew Union College Annual* 36 (1965): 191–226.

Harawī, ʿAlī b. Abī Bakr. *Kitāb al-ishārāt ilā maʿrifat al-ziyārāt*. Ed. J. Sourdel-Thomine. Damascus, 1953. Trans. J. Sourdel-Thomine as *Guide des lieux de pèlerinage* (Damascus: Institut français de Damas, 1957).

Hare, D. R. A. "The Lives of the Prophets." In *The Old Testament Pseudepigrapha*, ed. James H. Charlesworth, 2:379–399. Garden City, N.Y.: Doubleday, 1983.

Ḥarizi, Judah *Taḥkemoni*. Ed. and trans. V. E. Reichert. Jerusalem: R. H. Cohen's Press, 1973.

Harnisch, W. *Verhängnis und Verheissung der Geschichte: Untersuchungen zum Zeit- und Geschichtsverständnis im 4. Buch Esra und in der syr. Baruchapokalypse*. Göttingen: Vandenhoek und Ruprecht, 1969.

Harrāsī, ʿImād al-Dīn. *Aḥkām al-Qurʾān*. Beirut: Dār al-Kutub al-ʿIlmīyah, 1985.

Harris, Walter. *A Journey through the Yemen*. Edinburgh: University of Edinburgh, 1903.

Harrison, Paul, trans. *The Pratiyutpanna Samadhi Sutra*. Berkeley: University of California Press, 1998.

Hartmann, R. "Die geographische Nachrichten über Palaestina und Syrien in Khalil az-Zahiris Zubda." PhD dissertation, University of Tübingen. Kirchlein: Schmersow, 1907.

Hartmann, R. "al-Ḳadam bei Damaskus." *Orientalische Literaturzeitung* (1913): 115–118.

Hartmann, R. "Politische Geographie des Mamlukenreiches." *Zeitschrift der Deutschen Morgenländischen Geschellschaft* (1916): 1–40, 477–511.

Harvey, Paul. *Surfer!* Penguin Readers. Harlow: Longman, 1999.

Ḥasan, Zakī M. *Kunūz al-Fāṭimiyyīn*. Cairo, 1937.

Ḥasanī, Jaʿfar. "Qabr Muʿāwiyah b. Abī Sufyān." *Majallat al-Majmaʿ al-ʿIlmī al-ʿArabī* 19 (1944): 434–441.

Hāshimī, ʿAbd al-Munʿīm ʿAbd al-Rādī. *Muʿjizāt al-anbiyāʾ*. Kuwait: Maktabat Ibn Kathīr, 1999.

Hāshimī, M. al-Ghaffār. *Ādāb ziyārat al-aḍriḥa wa al-qubūr*. Cairo: s.n., 1966.

Hasluck, F. W. "The Girding of the Sultan." In *Christianity and Islam under the Sultans*. Oxford: Clarendon Press, 1929; reprint, New York: Octagon Books, 1973.

Hasluck, F. W. "Graves of the Arabs in Asia Minor." *Annual of the British School at Athens* 19 (1912–1913): 182–190.

Hawting, G. R. "The Disappearance and Rediscovery of Zamzam and the 'Well of the Kaʿba.'" *Bulletin of the School of Oriental and African Studies* 43 (1980): 44–54.

Hawting, G. R. "The Ḥajj in the Second Civil War." In *Golden Roads: Migration, Pilgrimage, and Travel in Medieval and Modern Islam,* ed. Ian Richard Netton, 31–42. Wiltshire: Curzon Press, 1993.

Hawting, G. R. *The Idea of Idolatry and the Emergence of Islam: From Polemic to History.* Cambridge Studies in Islamic Civilization. Cambridge: Cambridge University Press, 1999.

Hawting, G. R. "The 'Sacred Offices' of Mecca from Jāhiliyya to Islam." *Jerusalem Studies in Arabic and Islam* 13 (1990): 62–84.

Healey, John F. *The Religion of the Nabataeans: A Conspectus*. Leiden: E. J. Brill, 2001.

Heller, B. "Daniel in der islamischen Legende." In *Encyclopaedia Judaica,* ed. Cecil Roth, 833–835. Jerusalem: Encyclopedia Judaica, 1972.

Henninger, Joseph. *Arabica sacra: Aufsätze zur religionsgeschichte Arabiens und seiner Randgebiete.* Göttingen: Vandenhoeck and Ruprecht, 1981.

Henninger, Joseph. "Das Opfer in den altsüdarabischen Hochkulturen." *Anthropos* 37–40 (1946–1947): 779–810.

Henninger, Joseph. "La religion bédouine préislamique." In *L'antica società beduina,* ed. Gabrieli Francesco. Rome: Centro di Studi Semitici, Instituto di Studi Orientali, 1959 Published in English as "Pre-Islamic Bedouin Religion," in *The Arabs and Arabia on the Eve of Islam,* ed. F. E. Peters, 109–128 (Brookfield, Vt.: Variorum, 1999).

Henninger, Joseph. "Le sacrifice chez les Arabes." *Ethnos* (Stockholm) 13 (1948): 1–16.

Herling, A. "Excavation of a Tylos Period Cemetery at Sar (Bahrain)." Paper presented at the Seminar for Arabian Studies, Oxford, 1994.

Herodotus. *Historiae.* Ed. C. Hude. Oxford: Clarendon Press, 1908, 1927. Trans. A. D. Godley as *The Histories* (London: W. Heinemann, 1924–1928).

Hershman, P. "Hair, Sex and Dirt." *Man,* n.s., 9 (1974): 274–298.

Hess, Richard. "Nephilim." In *The Anchor Bible Dictionary,* ed. David Noel Freedman and others, 4:1072–1073. New York: Doubleday, 1992.

Hess, Richard. "Lamech." In *The Anchor Bible Dictionary,* ed. David Noel Freedman and others, 4:136–137. New York: Doubleday, 1992.

Hiltebeitel, Alf. *The Ritual of Battle.* Ithaca: Cornell University Pres, 1976.

Ḥilw, ʿA. *Ibn Khaldūn: Muʾassis ʿilm al-ijtimāʿ.* Beirut: Bayt al-Ḥikmah, 1969.

Hirschberg, H. Z. *Yisraʾel be-ʿArav.* Tel Aviv: Mosad Byalik and Masadah, 1946.

Hjärpe, J. "The Symbol of the Centre and Its Religious Function in Islam." In *Religious Symbols and Their Functions,* ed. H. Biezais, 30–40. Stockholm: Almqvist and Wiksell, 1979.

Hocart, A. M. *Kings and Councillors.* Cairo: P. Barbey, 1937.

Hocart, A. M. *The Temple of the Tooth in Kandy.* London: Luzac and Co., 1931.

Hoffmeyer, Ada Bruhn. "Middelalderens islamiske svaerd." *Vaabenhistoriske Aarboger* 8 (1956): 63–80.

Holdich, T. Hungerford. *The Indian Borderland, 1880–1900.* London: Methuen and Co., 1901; 2d ed., London: Methuen, 1909.

Holl, Karl, ed. *Epiphanius.* Berlin: Akademie-Verlag, 1980–1985.

Holmes, Tommy. *The Hawaiian Canoe.* Honolulu: Editions Limited, 1997.

Homer. *Iliad.* Ed. T. W. Allen. Oxford, 1931. Trans. A. T. Murray as *Iliad* (Cambridge. Mass.: Harvard University Press, 1999).

Hominer, H., and Menahem Amelander, eds. *Sefer sheʾerit Yisraʾel ha-shalem: Ve-hu helek sheni mi-Sefer Yosipon.* Jerusalem: Hotsa'at Hominer, 1971.

Hong, Yang, ed. *Weapons in Ancient China.* New York: Science Press, 1993.

Hooke, S. H. *Middle Eastern Mythology: From the Assyrians to the Hebrews.* New York: Penguin, 1963.

Horsely, Richard. *Hidden Transcripts and the Arts of Resistance: Applying the Work*

*of James C. Scott to Jesus and Paul.* Atlanta: Society for Biblical Literature, 2004.
Horwitz, W. "The Significance of the Rephaim." *Journal of Northwest Semitic Languages* 7 (1979): 37–43.
Howard, G. *Doctrina Addai.* Texts and Translations 16, Early Christian Literature Series 4. Chico, Calif.: Scholars Press, 1981.
Hoyland, Robert. *Arabia and the Arabs: From the Bronze Age to the Coming of Islam.* New York: Routledge, 2002.
Hull, Stephen. "A Sociological Study of the Surfing Subculture in the Santa Cruz Area." Master's thesis, San Jose State University, 1976.
Huminer H., ed. *Josiphon.* Jerusalem, 1971.
Humphries, R. *Ovid: Metamorphoses.* Bloomington: Indiana University Press, 1958.
Hunter, W. W. *Orissa.* London: Smith, Elder, and Co., 1872.
Huxley, G. L. "Bones for Orestes." *Greek, Roman, and Byzantine Studies* 20 (1979): 145–148.
Ibn ʿAbd al-Barr, Yūsuf b. ʿAbdallāh. *Istīʿāb fī maʿrifat al-aṣḥāb.* Baghdad: Maktabat al-Muthannā, 1970.
Ibn ʿAbd al-Barr, Yūsuf b. ʿAbdallāh. *al-Istīʿāb fī maʿrifat al-aṣḥāb.* Ed. ʿAlī Muḥ ammad al-Bajāwī. 4 vols. Cairo, n.d.
Ibn ʿAbd al-Barr, Yūsuf b. ʿAbdallāh. *Jāmiʿ al-bayān al-ʿilm wa faḍli-hi wa mā yanbaghī fī riwāyati-hi wa ḥamli-hi.* Ed. ʿAbd al-Raḥmān Muḥammad ʿUthmān. Cairo: al-Maktabah al-Salafīyah, 1968.
Ibn ʿAbdallāh, Muḥammad. *Ayna dufina Rasūl al-Islām?* Beirut, 1413.
Ibn ʿAbd al-Wahhāb, Ḥusayn. *ʿUyūn al-muʿjizāt.* Najaf: al-Maṭbaʿah al-Ḥaydarīyah, 1950.
Ibn ʿĀbdīn, Muḥammad Amīn b. ʿUmar. *Ḥāshīyah radd al-muḥtār ʿalā al-Dār al-mukhtār: Sharḥ tanwīr al-abṣār.* Beirut: Dār al-Fikr, 1979.
Ibn Abī Ḥātim, ʿAbd al-Raḥmān b. Muḥammad. *al-Jarḥ wa al-taʿdīl.* Ed. ʿAbd al-Raḥmān b. Yaḥyā al-Muʿallimī. Beirut: Muʾassasat al-Risālah, 1371.
Ibn Abī Shaybah, ʿAbdallāh b. Muḥammad. *Kitāb al-muṣannaf al-aḥādīth wa al-āthār.* Beirut: Dār al-Tāj, 1989.
Ibn Abī Zayd, ʿAbdallāh b. ʿAbd al-Raḥmān. *al-Risālah al-faqīh.* Ed. al-Hādī Ḥamū and Muḥammad Abū al-Ajfān. Beirut: Dār al-Gharb al-Islāmī, 1986; reprint, Beirut: Dār al-Gharb al-Islāmī, 1997.
Ibn ʿAdī, ʿAbdallāh. *al-Kāmil fī ḍuʿafāʾ al-rijāl.* Ed. Suhayl Zakkār. Beirut: Dār al-Fikr, 1988.
Ibn al-ʿAdīm, ʿUmar b. Muḥammad. *Zubdat al-ḥalab min taʾrīkh Ḥalab.* Ed. S. al-Dahhān. Damascus: Institut français d'études arabes de Damas, 1951–1968.
Ibn al-ʿAjamī, Aḥmad b. Muḥammad al-Wafāʾī. *Tanzīh al-muṣṭafā al-mukhtār ʿammā lam yathbat min al-akhbār.* Beirut, n.d.

Ibn al-ʿArabī, Abū Bakr. *Aḥkām al-Qurʾān*. Ed. Muḥammad ʿAbd al-Qādir ʿAṭāʾ. Beirut: Dār al-Kutub al-Ilmīyah, n.d.

Ibn al-Athīr, ʿIzz al-Dīn, *Kāmil fī al-taʾrīkh*. Ed. C. J. Tornberg. Leiden: E. J. Brill, 1868; reprint, Beirut: Dār al-Kutub al-ʿIlmīyah, 1995.

Ibn al-Athīr. *Usd al-ghābah*. Beirut: Dār al-Kutub al-ʿIlmīyah, n.d.

Ibn al-Faqīh, Aḥmad b. Muḥammad al-Hamadhānī. *Kitāb al-buldān*. Ed. Yūsuf al-Hādī. Beirut: ʿAlam al-Kutub, 1996. Trans. Henri Massé as *Abrégé du livre des pays* (Damascus: Institute français de Damas, 1972).

Ibn al-Ḥawrānī, ʿUthmān b. Aḥmad. *al-Ishārāt ilā amākin al-ziyārāt*. Ed. Bassām al-Jābī. Damascus: Maṭbaʿat al-Maʿārif, 1981.

Ibn al-Humām, Muḥammad b. ʿAbd al-Waḥīd. *Sharḥ fatḥ al-qadīr ʿalā al-Hidāyah: Sharḥ bidāyat al-mubtadā, maʿa sharḥ al-ʿināyah ʿalā al-Hidāyah*. Cairo: Muṣṭafā al-Bābī al-Ḥalabī, 1389.

Ibn al-Jārūd, ʿAbdallāh b. ʿAlī. *Muntaqā min al-sunan al-musnadah ʿan Rasūl Allāh*. Beirut: Dār al-Qalam, 1987.

Ibn al-Jawzī, ʿAbd al-Raḥmān b. ʿAlī. *Mirʾāt al-Zamān fī taʾrīkh al-aʿyān*. Hyderabad: Majlis Dāʾirat al-Maʿārif al-ʿUthmānīyah, 1951–1952.

Ibn al-Jawzī, ʿAbd al-Raḥmān b. ʿAlī. *Mirʾāt al-zamān fī taʾrīkh al-aʿyān*. Beirut: Dār al-Shurūq, 1985.

Ibn al-Jawzī, ʿAbd al-Raḥmān b. ʿAlī. *al-Muntaẓam fī tawārīkh al-mulūk wa al-umam*. Beirut: Dār al-Kutub al-ʿIlmīyah, 1995.

Ibn al-Jawzī, ʿAbd al-Raḥmān b. ʿAlī. *Muthīr al-Gharām bi faḍāʾil al-Quds wa al-Shām*. In *Arbaʿ rasāʾil fī faḍāʾil al-Masjid al-Aqṣā*. Nasr City: Dār al-Nadā, 2000.

Ibn al-Jawzī, ʿAbd al-Raḥmān b. ʿAlī. *al-Taḥqīq*. 8 vols. Cairo: al-Fārūq al-Ḥadīthah, 2001.

Ibn al-Jawzī, ʿAbd al-Raḥmān b. ʿAlī. *Zād al-musīr fī ʿilm al-tafsīr*. Ed. ʿAbd al-Razzāq al-Mahdī. Beirut: Dār al-Kitāb al-ʿArabī, 2001.

Ibn al-Kalbī, Hishām. *Kitāb al-aṣnām*. Trans. Nabih Amin Faris as *The Book of Idols: Being a Translation from the Arabic of the Kitāb al-Aṣnām by Hishām Ibn-al-Kalbi* (Princeton: Princeton University Press, 1952). Ed. and trans. into French by W. Atallah as *Les idoles de Hicham Ibn al-Kalbi* (Paris: C. Klincksieck, 1969).

Ibn al-Maḥāmilī, Aḥmad b. Muḥammad. *Kitāb al-lubāb fī al-fiqh al-Shāfiʿī*. Cairo, 1274; reprint, Medina: Nashr wa Tawzīʿ Dār al-Bukhārī, 1286–1315.

Ibn al-Salāḥ, ʿUthmān b. ʿAbd al-Raḥmān. *ʿUlūm al-ḥadīth*. Damascus: Dār al-Fikr, 1986.

Ibn al-Zayyāt, Shams al-Dīn. *al-Kawākib al-sayyāra fī tartīb al-ziyāra*. Cairo: s.n., 1907.

Ibn al-Zubayr, al-Qāḍī al-Rashīd. *Kitāb al-hadāyā wa al-tuḥaf*. Trans. Ghāda al-

Ḥijjāwī al-Qaddūmī as *Book of Gifts and Rarities* (Cambridge, Mass.: Harvard University Press, 1996).
Ibn ʿAsākir, ʿAlī b. Abī Muḥammad al-Ḥasan. *Taʾrīkh madīnat Dimashq.* Ed. S. al-Munajjid. Damascus: Maṭbuʿat al-Majmaʿ al-ʿIlmī al-ʿArabī, 1951–1954. Partially trans. N. Élisséeff as *La description de Damas d'Ibn ʿAsākir* (Damascus: Institut français de Damas, 1959).
Ibn Bābūyah, Muḥammad b. ʿAlī. *ʿIlal al-sharāʾiʿ.* 2 vols. Qum: Maktabat al-Ṭabāṭ abāʾī, 1957–1958.
Ibn Badrūn, ʿAbd al-Mālik b. ʿAbdallāh. *Jawāhīr al-afkār wa maʿdin al-asrār.* Ed. Zuhayr al-Shāwīsh. Beirut: al-Maktab al-Islāmī, 1999.
Ibn Baṭṭūṭah, *Riḥlah Ibn Baṭṭūṭah.* Beirut: Dār Ṣādir, 1964.
Ibn Baṭṭūṭah. *Tuḥfat al-nuẓẓār fī gharāʾib al-amṣār wa ʿajāʾib al-asfār.* Ed. A. A. al-Kattānī. Beirut, Muʾassasat al-Risālah, 1975. Trans. H. A. R. Gibb and others as *The Travels of Ibn Baṭṭūṭah, A.D. 1325–1354* (London: Hakluyt Society, 1958–1994).
Ibn Durayd, Muḥammad b. al-Ḥasan. *Kitāb jamharat al-lughah.* Beirut: Dār al-ʿIlm li-l-Malayīn, 1987–1988.
Ibn Faḍlallāh al-ʿUmayrī, Aḥmad b. Yaḥyā. *Masālik al-abṣār fī mamālik al-amṣār.* Ed. A. Z. Basha. Cairo: Institut français d'archéologie orientale, 1924.
Ibn Ḥajar, Aḥmad b. ʿAlī. *al-Durar al-kāminah fī aʿyān al-miʾah al-thāminah.* Ed. ʿAbd al-Muʿayin Khān. Hyderabad: Majlis Dāʾirat al-Maʿārif al-ʿUthmānīyah, 1972.
Ibn Ḥajar, Aḥmad b. ʿAlī. *Fatḥ al-bārī bi-sharḥ Ṣaḥīḥ al-Bukhārī.* Cairo, 1301; reprint, Beirut: Dār Iḥyā al-Turāth al-ʿArabī, 1408.
Ibn Ḥajar, Aḥmad b. ʿAlī. *Iṣābah fī tamyīz al-ṣaḥābah.* Baghdad: Maktabat al-Muthannā, 1970; Cairo Dār Nahʿat Miṣr, 1970–1972; Beirut: Dār al-Kutub al-ʿIlmīyah, 1415.
Ibn Ḥajar, Aḥmad b. ʿAlī. *Lisān al-mīzān.* Hyderabad: Majlis Dāʾirat al-Maʿārif al-Niẓāmīyah, 1329–1331; reprint, Beirut: Muʾassasat al-Aʿlamī, 1407.
Ibn Ḥajar, Aḥmad b. ʿAlī. *Tahdhīb al-tahdhīb.* Hyderabad: Majlis Dāʾirat al-Maʿārif al-Niẓāmīyah, 1325.
Ibn Ḥanbal, Aḥmad. *Musnad.* Cairo: al-Maṭbaʿah al-Maymanīyah, 1895.
Ibn Ḥawqal, Muḥammad. *Ṣūrat al-arḍ.* Ed. J. H. Kramers. Opus Geographicum. Leiden: E. J. Brill, 1967.
Ibn Ḥazm, Abū Muḥammad ʿAlī. *Jawāmiʿ al-sīrah al-nabaqīyah.* Ed. Nāʾyf al-ʿAbbās. Beirut: Dār al-Kutub al-ʿIlmīyah, 1986.
Ibn Ḥazm, Abū Muḥammad ʿAlī. *al-Muḥallā bi-l-athār.* Ed. ʿAbd al-Ghafār Sulayman al-Bandārī. Beirut, n.d.
Ibn Ḥibbān, Muḥammad. *Kitāb al-thiqāt.* Ed. M. ʿAbd al-Maʿīd Khān. Hyderabad: Majlis Dāʾirat al-Maʿārif al-ʿUthmānīyah, 1393.

Ibn Ḥibbān, Muḥammad. *Maʿrifat al-majrūḥīn wa al-ḍuʿafāʾ min al-muḥaddithīn*. Ed. ʿAzīz Baygh al-Nawshabāndī al-Qadirī. Hyderabad: Majlis Dāʾirat al-Maʿārif al-ʿUthmānīyah, 1390.

Ibn Ḥibbān, Muḥammad. *Ṣaḥīḥ*. Cairo: Dār al-Maʿārif, 1952.

Ibn Ḥibbān, Muḥammad. *Ṣaḥīḥ Ibn Ḥibbān*. Beirut: Dār al-Kutub al-ʿIlmīyah, 1984.

Ibn Hishām, ʿAbd al-Mālik. *Kitāb al-tijān*. Hyderabad: Majlis Dāʾirat al-Maʿārif al-ʿUthmānīyah, 1928.

Ibn Hishām, ʿAbd al-Mālik. *al-Sīrah al-nabawīyah*. Ed. Ṭaha ʿAbd al-Rūf Saʿd. Beirut, n.d. Trans. A. Guillaume as *The Life of Muhammad* (Karachi: Oxford University Press, 1955; reprint, 1982).

Ibn Jubayr, Muḥammad b. Aḥmad. *Riḥlat Ibn Jubayr*. Beirut: Dār Sadir, 1964. Trans. R. J. C. Broadhurst as *The Travels of Ibn Jubayr* (London: J. Cape, 1952).

Ibn Kannān, Muḥammad b. ʿĪsā, *al-Mawākib al-islāmīya fī al-mamālik wa al-maḥāsin al-shāmīya*. Ed. Ḥ. Ismāʿīl. Damascus: al-Jumhūrīyah al-ʿArabīyah al-Sūrīyah, 1992–1993.

Ibn Kathīr, Ismāʿīl b. ʿUmar. *al-Bidāyah wa al-nihāyah fī al-taʾrīkh*. Cairo, 1351–1358.

Ibn Kathīr, Ismāʿīl b. ʿUmar. *al-Fuṣūl fī sīrah al-rasūl*. Ed. Muḥammad al-ʿId al-Khaṭ rāwī and Muhī al-Dīn Matū. Beirut: Dār al-Kutub al-ʿIlmīyah, 1999.

Ibn Kathīr, Ismāʿīl b. ʿUmar. *Qiṣaṣ al-anbiyāʾ*. Ed. Yūsuf ʿAlī Budaywī. Damascus and Beirut: Dār Ibn Kathīr, 1992.

Ibn Kathīr, Ismāʿīl b. ʿUmar. *Tafsīr al-Qurʾān al-ʿaẓīm*. Beirut: Dār al-Jīl, n.d.

Ibn Khaldūn, ʿAbd al-Raḥmān b. Muḥammad. *al-Muqaddimah*. Trans. Franz Rosenthal as *The Muqaddimah: An Introduction to History*, 3 vols., Bollingen Series 43 (Princeton: Princeton University Press, 1967).

Ibn Khallikān, Aḥmad b. Muḥammad. *Wafayāt al-aʿyān*. Ed. Iḥsān ʿAbbās. Beirut: Dār Assakafa, 1968–1972.

Ibn Khallikān, Aḥmad b. Muḥammad. *Wafayāt al-aʿyān wa anbāʾ abnāʾ al-zamān*. Ed. Muḥammad Muḥyi al-Dīn ʿAbd al-Ḥamīd. 6 vols. Cairo, 1948–1949.

Ibn Khuzaymah, Muḥammad b. Isḥāq. *Ṣaḥīḥ*. Beirut: al-Maktab al-Islāmī, 1970.

Ibn Mājah. *Sunan*. Ed. Muḥammad Fuʾād ʿAbd al-Bāqī. Cairo: Maṭbaʿah al-Tazīyah, 1952.

Ibn Manẓūr, Muḥammad b. Mukarram. *Lisān al-ʿArab*. Beirut: Dār al-Kutub al-ʿIlmīyah, 1990.

Ibn Mūsā, ʿAbd al-Bāsiṭ. *Mukhtaṣar tanbīh al-ṭālib wa irshād al-dāris*. Ed. Ṣalāḥ al-Munajjid. Damascus: Mudīrīyat al-Āthār al-Qadīmah al-ʿAmmah, 1947.

Ibn Muyassar. *Akhbār Miṣr*. Cairo: Institut français, 1981.

Ibn Nājī, Qāsim b. ʿĪsā. *Sharḥ ʿalā matn al-Risālah*. Beirut: Dār al-Fikr, 1982.

Ibn Qayyim al-Jawzīyah. *Ḥādī al-arwāḥ ilā bilād al-afrāḥ*. Ed. ʿAbd al-Laṭīf Āl Muḥammad al-Fawāʿīr. Amman, 1987.

Ibn Qayyim, Muḥammad b. Abī Bakr al-Jawzīyah. *Zād al-maʿād fī hadī khayr al-ʿibād*. Beirut: Muʾassasat al-Risālah, 1979.

Ibn Qayyim al-Jawzīyah. *Ighathat al-lahfan min nasāyid al-shayṭān*. Cairo: Maktabat ʿAtif, 1991.

Ibn Qudāmah, Abū Muḥammad ʿAbdallāh b. Aḥmad. *al-Mughnī*. Ed. ʿAbdallāh b. ʿAbd al-Muḥsin al-Turkī and ʿAbd al-Fattāḥ Muḥammad al-Ḥilw. Cairo: Hajr, 1986; reprint, 1992.

Ibn Qutaybah, ʿAbdallāh b. Muslim. *al-Maʿārif*. Cairo: Dār al-Maʿārif, 1959.

Ibn Rajab, ʿAbd al-Raḥmān b. Aḥmad, *Kitāb al-dhayl ʿalā ṭabaqāt al-Ḥanābila*. Ed. M. Ḥ. al-Fiqī. Cairo, s.n. 1952–1953.

Ibn Rushd, Abū al-Walīd Muḥammad b. Aḥmad. *Bidāyat al-mujtahid wa nihāyat al-muqtaṣid*. Ed. ʿAlī Muḥammad Maʿūd and ʿĀdil Aḥmad ʿAbd al-Wujūd. Beirut: Dār al-Kutub al-ʿIlmīyah, 1996.

Ibn Saʿd, Aḥmad. *al-Ṭabaqāt al-kubrā*. Ed. E. Sachau. Leiden: E. J. Brill, 1904–1908.

Ibn Saʿd, Aḥmad. *al-Ṭabaqāt al-kubrā*. Ed. Muḥammad ʿAbd al-Qādir ʿAṭā. Beirut: Dār al-Kutub al-ʿIlmīyah, 1990.

Ibn Salām, Abū ʿUbayd al-Qāsim. *Kitāb al-amwāl*. Cairo: Maktabat al-Kulliyat al-Azhar, 1968.

Ibn Salām, Abū ʿUbayd al-Qāsim. *Kitāb al-silāḥ*. Ed. Ḥātim Ṣāliḥ al-Dāmin. Beirut: Muʾassasat al-Risālah, 1985.

Ibn Shabbah, Abū Zayd ʿUmar. *Kitāb taʾrīkh al-Madīnah al-munawwarah*. Ed. ʿAlī Muḥammad Dandal and Yāsīn Saʿd al-Dīn Bayān. Beirut: Dār al-Kutub al-ʿIlmīyah, 1996.

Ibn Shaddād, Muḥammad b. ʿAlī. *al-Aʿlāq al-khaṭīra fī dhikr umarāʾ al-Shām wa al-Jazīrah*. Ed. Y. Z. ʿAbbāra. Damascus: Wizārat al-Thaqāfah, 1991.

Ibn Shāhīn, ʿUmar b. Aḥmad. *al-Nāsikh wa al-mansūkh min al-ḥadīth*. Manṣūrah: Dār al-Wafāʾ, 1995.

Ibn Shahrāshūb, Muḥammad. *Manāqib Āl Abī Ṭālib*. Najaf: al-Maktabah al-Ḥaydarīyah, 1956.

Ibn Taymīyah, Aḥmad b. ʿAbd al-Ḥalīm. *Fiqh al-ṭahārah*. Ed. al-Sayyid al-Jamīlī. Beirut: Dār al-Fikr al-Lubnānī, 1987.

Ibn Taymīyah, Aḥmad b. ʿAbd al-Ḥalīm. *al-Hidāyah al-Islāmīyah*. Cairo: al-Dār al-Ḥusaynīyah li-l-Kitāb, 1990.

Ibn Taymīyah, Aḥmad b. ʿAbd al-Ḥalīm. *al-Jawāb al-bāhir fī zuwwāb al-maqābir*. Ed. Abū Yaʿlā Muḥammad Ayman al-Shabrāwī . Beirut: Dār al-Jīl, 1417.

Ibn Taymīyah, Aḥmad b. ʿAbd al-Ḥalīm. *Kitāb al-iqtidāʾ al-ṣirāṭ al-mustaqīm*. Cairo: s.n., 1412.

Ibn Taymīyah, Aḥmad b. ʿAbd al-Ḥalīm. *Majmūʿ fatāwā Shaykh al-Islām Aḥmad b. Taymīya.* Ed. A. al-ʿĀṣimī. Riyadh: Dār al-ʿĀṣimah, 1991.

Ibn Ṭūlūn, Shams al-Din b. Muḥammad b. ʿAlī. *Iʿlām al-warā bi-man waliya nāʾiban min al-atrāk bi-Dimashq al-Shām al-kubrā.* Ed. M. A. Duhmān. Damascus: al-Maṭbaʿah al-Jarīdah al-Rasmīyah, 1964.

Ibn Ṭūlūn, Shams al-Din b. Muḥammad b. ʿAlī. *Iʿlām al-sāʾilīn ʿan kutub sayyid al-mursalīn.* Beirut: Muʾassasat al-Risalah, 1983.

Ibn Wahshiyya, Aḥmad b. ʿAlī. *al-Filāḥa al-Nabaṭīyah.* Damascus: Institut français d'études arabes, 1993.

Ibshihi, Aḥmad. *al-Mustaṭraf.* Beirut: Dār al-Kutub al-ʿIlmīyah, 1983.

Idris, H. R., and J. Schleifer. "Hilāl." In *Encyclopaedia of Islam,* 2d ed., ed. H. A. R. Gibb and others, 3:385–387. Leiden: E. J. Brill, 1960–2002.

Idrīs, ʿImād al-Dīn. *ʿUyūn al-akhbār.* Ed. M. Ghālib. Beirut: Dār al-Andalus, 1975.

Idrīsī, Muḥammad b. Muḥammad. *Kitāb nuzhat al-mushtāq fī ikhtirāq al-afāq.* Trans. P. A. Jaubert as *Géographie d'Edrisi traduite de l'arabe en français d'après deux manuscrits de la Bibliothèque du roi et accompagnée de notes* (Paris: Impr. Royale, 1836–1840).

ʿIjlī, Aḥmad. *Taʾrīkh al-thiqāt.* Ed. ʿAbd al-Muʿṭī Amīn Qalʿajī. Beirut: Dār al-Kutub al-ʿIlmīyah, 1984.

Ilan, Z. *Qivrei ẓaddiqim be-ereẓ Yisraʾel.* Jerusalem, 1997.

Imru al-Qays. *Dīwān Imruʾ al-Qays wa muhhaqātuh: Bi-sharḥ Abī Saʿīd al-Sukkarī.* Ed. Anwār ʿAylān Abū Suwaylam. al-ʿAyn: Markzaz Zayid li-l-Turāth wa al-Taʾrīkh, 2000.

*In God's Hands.* Culver City: Tri-Star Pictures, 1998.

Ingrams, W. H. "Hadhramaut: A Journey to the Seiʿar Country and through the Wadi Mascila." *Geographic Journal* 88 (1936): 524–551.

Ingrams, W. H. "The Hadhramaut: Present and Future." *Geographical Journal* 92 (1938): 289–312.

Irwin, John. *Scenes.* Beverly Hills, Calif.: Sage Publications, 1977.

Irwin, John. "A Study of the Growth of a Deviant Subculture." Master's thesis, University of California, Berkeley, 1965.

Isbahānī, Abū al-Faraj. *Kitāb al-aghānī.* Cairo: al-Ḥayah al-Miṣrīyah al-ʿĀmmah li-l-Kitāb, 1970.

Ishaq, H. M. "A Peep into the First Arab Expeditions to India under the Companions of the Prophet." *Islamic Culture* 19 (1945): 109–114.

Issa, Amina Ameir. "The Burial of the Elite in Nineteenth-Century Zanzibar Stone Town." In *The History and Conservation of Zanzibar Stone Town,* ed. Abdul Sherif, 67–80. Athens: Ohio University Press, 1995.

Issawi, Charles. *An Arab Philosophy of History: Selections from the Prolegomena of Ibn Khaldun of Tunis (1332–1406).* London, 1950; reprint, London: Murray 1963.

Isser, Stanley J. *The Dositheans.* Leiden: E. J. Brill, 1976.
Isser, Stanley J. *The Sword of Goliath: David in Heroic Literature.* Studies in Biblical Literature 6. Atlanta: Scholars Press, 2003.
Ivanow, W. "Umm al-kitab." *Der Islam* 23 (1936): 1–13.
Jabartī, ʿAbd al-Raḥmān. *ʿAjāʾib al-āthār fī al-tarājīm wa al-akhbār.* Cairo: Lajnat al-Bayān al-ʿArabī, 1959–1967.
Jabirī, M. ʿA. *al-ʿAṣabīya wa al-dawlah: Maʿālim naẓarīya Khaldūnīya fī al-taʾrīkh al-Islāmī.* Casablanca: Dār al-Thaqāfah, 1971.
Jackson, H. C. *Behind the Modern Sudan.* London: St. Martin's Press, 1955.
Jacob, B. *Das Erste Buch der Tora: Genesis übersetzt und erklärt.* Berlin: Schocken Verlag, 1934.
Jacobi, R. "Die Anfänge der arabischen Ġazalpoesie: Abū Ḏuʾaib al-Huḏalī." *Der Islam* 61 (1984): 218–250.
Jacobsen, Thorkild *The Sumerian King List.* Assyriological Studies 11. Chicago: University of Chicago Press, 1942.
Jacoby, F. *Fragmente der griechischen Historiker.* Berlin: Weidmann, 1923.
Jāḥiẓ, ʿAmr b. Baḥr. *Kitāb al-ḥayawān.* Ed. ʿAbd al-Salām Muḥammad Hārūn. Beirut: Dār al-Jīl, 1992.
Jamal al-Din, Faquir Saiyad. *List of the Sacred Relics Kept in the Lahore Fort Together with a Brief History of the Same.* Lahore, 1877.
Jamme, A. *Sabaean Inscriptions from Mahram Bilqis.* Baltimore: Johns Hopkins University Press, 1962.
Jamme, A. *The al-ʿUqlah Texts.* Washington, D.C.: Catholic University of America Press, 1963.
Jarratt, Phil. *Surfing: The Dictionary.* South Melbourne: Sun Books, 1985.
Jaṣṣāṣ, Aḥmad b. ʿAlī. *Aḥkām al-Qurʾān.* Ed. ʿAbd al-Salām Muḥammad ʿAlī Shāhīn. Beirut: Dār al-Kutub al-Ilmīyah, 1994.
Jawbarī, ʿAbd al-Raḥmān b. ʿUmar. *Kitāb al-mukhtar fī kashf al-asrār.* Cairo: s.n., 1898. Trans. René Khawam as *Le voile arraché: L'autre visage de l'Islam* (Paris: Phébus, 1979–1980).
Jennar, Howard. *Making a Surfboard: The Complete Manual.* Darlinghurst: Mason Stuart, 1985.
Jettmar, Karl. "The Gilgit Manuscripts: Discovery by Installments." *Journal of Central Asia* 4, no. 2 (1981): 1–18.
Jettmar, Karl. "The Middle Asiatic Heritage of Dardistan: Islamic Collective Tombs in Punyal and Their Background." *East and West* 17 (1967): 59–82.
Jewitt, J. R. *A Narrative of the Adventures and Suffering of J. R. Jewitt.* London, 1820.
Jidejian, Nina. *Tyre: Through the Ages.* Beirut: Dar el-Mashreq Publishers, 1969.
Jiriczek, O. L. "Faeröische Märchen und Sagen." *Zeitschrift des Vereins für Volkskunde* 2 (1892): 1–23.

Johnson, M. D. "Life of Adam and Eve." In *The Old Testament Pseudepigrapha,* ed. James H. Charlesworth, 2:249–295. Garden City, N.Y.: Doubleday, 1983.

Johnstone, William, ed. *William Robertson Smith: Essays in Reassessment.* Journal for the Study of the Old Testament Supplemental Series 189. Sheffield: Sheffield Academic Press, 1995.

Josephus. *Jewish Antiquities.* Ed. and trans. H. Thackeray and others. Cambridge, Mass.: Harvard University Press, 1962–1965.

Jote, Ratnamanirao Bhimrao. *Gujarat-nun-Patnagar Amdavad.* Ahmedabad, 1928.

Juel, Eric. "Notes on Seal-Hunting Ceremonialism in the Arctics." *Ethnos* (1945): 2–3.

Junker, Hermann. *Die Stundenwachen in den Osirismysterien, nach den Inschriften von Dendera, Edfu und Philae.* Vienna: A. Hölder, 1910.

Juynboll, Th. W. "De datum Maandag 12 Rabīʿ I op den grafsteen van Malik Ibrāhīm." *TBS* 53 (1922): 605–608.

Juynboll, G. H. A. *Muslim Tradition: Studies in Chronology, Provenance and Authorship of Early Ḥadīth.* Cambridge: Cambridge University Press, 1983.

Kaizer, Ted. *The Religious Life of Palmyra.* Oriens et Occidens 4. Stuttgart: Steiner, 2002.

Kalakaua, David. *The Legends and Myths of Hawaii: The Fables and Folklore of a Strange People.* New York: C. L. Webster and Co., 1888.

Kamada, H., and T. Ohtsu. "Report on the Excavations at Songor A: Isin-Larsa, Sassanian and Islamic Graves." *al-Rafidan* 9 (1988): 135–172.

Kampion, Drew, and Bruce Brown. *Stoked: A History of Surf Culture.* Los Angeles: General Publishing Group, 1997; reprint, Köln: Evergreen, 1998.

Kang, S. M. *Divine War in the Old Testament and in the Ancient Near East.* Berlin: W. de Gruyter, 1987.

Kantorowicz, Ernst Hartwig. *The King's Two Bodies: A Study in Medieval Political Theology.* Princeton: Princeton University Press, 1957.

Kapara, Y. "Ziyarat Skeikh Abu Taleb." *Teva ve-Aretz* 17 (1975): 192–194.

Kaptein, N. J. G. *Muhammad's Birthday Festival: Early History in the Central Muslim Lands and Development in the Muslim West until the 10th/16th Century.* Leiden: E. J. Brill, 1993.

Kashānī, Muḥsin al-Malaqqab al-Ghayḍ. *Tafsīr al-ṣāfī.* Tehran, n.d.

Katz, Marion Holmes. *Body of Text: The Emergence of the Sunnī Law of Ritual Purity.* Albany: State University of New York Press, 2002.

Kennedy, Hugh, ed. *An Historical Atlas of Islam.* 2d ed. Leiden: E. J. Brill, 2002.

Kervran, M. "Preliminary Report on the Excavation of Qal'at al-Bahrain." In *Fouilles a Qal'at al-Bahrain: 1ère partie (1977–1979),* ed. M. Kervran and others, 59–84. Manama: Ministry of Information, 1982.

Khan, Ahmad Nabi. *Islamic Architecture of Pakistan: An Analytical Exposition.*

Vol. 1, *Arab and Central Asian Contribution.* Islamabad: National Hijra Council, 1411/1900.
Khan, Ahmad Nabi. *Multan: History and Architecture.* Islamabad: Institute of Islamic History, Culture and Civilization, 1403/1983.
Khan, Mohd. Abdul Waheed. "Excavation of a Medieval Site near Quṭb Shāhi Tombs (Golconda)." *Islamic Culture* 44 (1970): 227–231.
Khaṭīb al-Baghdādī. *al-Riḥlah fī ṭalab al-ḥadīth.* Ed. Nūr al-Dīn ʿAttar. Beirut: Dār al-Kutub al-ʿIlmīyah, 1395.
Khaṭīb al-Baghdādī. *Taʾrīkh Baghdād.* Ed. ʿAbd al-Raḥmān b. Yaḥyāʾ al-Muʿallimī. Hyderabad: Dāʾirat al-Maʿarif al-ʿUthmānīyah, 1959.
Khawarizmī, Muḥammad b. Aḥmad. *Mafātīḥ al-ʿulūm.* Cairo: Dār al-Nahḍah al-ʿArabīyah, 1978.
Khiraqī, ʿUmar b. al-Ḥusain. *al-Mukhtaṣar fī al-fiqh.* Ed. M. Zuhair al-Shāwīsh. Damascus, 1378; reprint, Beirut, 1384.
Khomeinī, Ayātallāh. *Taḥrīr al-wasīlah.* Beirut: Dār al-Mantaẓar, 1985.
Khomich, L. V. "Religioznye kul'ti nentsev." *Pamiatniki kul'tury narodov Sibiri i severa* (Leningrad) (1977): 5–28.
Khoury, Nuha N. N. "The Dome of the Rock, the Kaʿba and Ghumdan: Arab Myths and Umayyad Monuments." *Muqarnas* 10 (1993): 57–65.
Kikawada, Isaac M. "Noah and the Ark." In *The Anchor Bible Dictionary,* ed. David Noel Freedman, 4:1123–1131. New York, N.Y.: Doubleday, 1992.
Kilmer, A. D. "The Mesopotamian Concept of Overpopulation and Its Solution as Reflected in the Mythology." *Orientalia* 41 (1972): 160–177.
Kindaichi, Kyōsuke. "The Concepts behind the Ainu Bear Festival (Kumamatsuri)." Trans. Minori Yoshida. *Southwestern Journal of Anthropology* 5 (1949): 345–350. Originally published in *Gakusō Zuihitsu* (Kyoto: Jinbun Shoin, 1936).
Kindī, Yaʿqūb b. Isḥāq. "al-Suyūf wa ajnāsu-hā." Arab. Mss. Leiden 287. Published by A. R. Zaki in *Bulletin of the Faculty of Arts, University of Cairo* 14, no. 2 (December 1952): 1–36.
Kindī, Yaʿqūb b. Isḥāq. *al-Suyūf wa ajnāsu-hā.* Ed. ʿAbd al-Raḥmān Zakī. Cairo: Maktabat al-Thaqāfah al-Dīnīyah, 1952.
King, L. W. *Letters and Inscriptions of Hammurabi.* London: Luzac and Co., 1898.
Kippenberg, H. G. *Garizim und Synagoge.* Berlin: W. de Gruyter, 1971.
Kirkan, J. S. "Takwa: The Mosque of the Pillar." *Ars Orientalis* 2 (1957): 175–182.
Kirkman, James S. "Excavations at Kilepwa An Introduction to the Medieval Archaeology of the Kenya Coast." *Antiquaries Journal* 32 (1953): 168–184.
Kirkman, James S. *The Arab City of Gedi: Excavations at the Great Mosque, Architecture and Finds.* Oxford: Oxford University Press, 1954.
Kirkman, James S. *Men and Monuments on the East African Coast.* London: Lutterworth, 1964.

Kirkman, James S. "Mnarani of Kilifi: The Mosques and Tombs." *Ars Orientalis* 3 (1959): 95–111.

Kisā'ī. *Qiṣaṣ al-anbiyā'*. Ed. Isaac Eisenberg. Leiden: E. J. Brill, 1922. Trans. W. M. Thackston as *The Tales of the Prophets* (Boston: Twayne, 1978).

Kister, M. J. "A Booth like the Booth of Moses." *Bulletin of the School of Oriental and African Studies* 25 (1962): 150–155. Reprinted in his *Studies in Jahiliyya and Early Islam* (London: Variorum, 1980), chap. 8.

Kister, M. J.. "The Massacre of the Banū Qurayẓa: A Re-examination of a Tradition." *Jerusalem Studies in Arabic and Islam* 8 (1986): 61–96. Reprinted in his *Society and Religion from Djāhiliyya to Islam* (Brookfield, Vt.: Variorum, 1990), chap. 8.

Kister, M. J. "'You Shall Only Set Out for Three Mosques': A Study of an Early Tradition." *Le Muséon* 82 (1969): 173–196.

Kitagawa, Joseph. "Ainu Bear Festival (Iyomante)." *History of Religions* 1 (1961): 95–151.

Klein, S. "'Al ha-sefer Vitae Prophetarum." In *Sefer Klozner*, ed. H. Torczyner, 198–208. Tel Aviv: Va'ad ha-Yovel, 1937.

Klijn, A. F. J. "The Sources and the Redaction of the Syriac Apocalypse of Baruch." *Journal of Semitic Studies* 1 (1970): 65–76.

Klijn, A. F. J. "2 (Syriac Apocalypse of) Baruch." In *The Old Testament Pseudepigrapha*, ed. James H. Charlesworth, 1:615–652. Garden City, N.Y.: Doubleday, 1983.

Klostermann, E. *Eusebius Werke*. Vol. 3, pt. 1, *Das Onomastikon der Biblischen Ortsnamen, mit der lateinischen Übersetzung des Hieronymus*. Leipzig: J. C. Hinrichs, 1904.

Kmosko, M. *Epistola Baruch filli Neriae*. Patrologia Syriaca 1.2. Paris, 1907.

Koch, Yoel. "The Jami', Nabi Ṣāleḥ's Tomb and Ayn al-Baqar in Acre in the Middle Ages." [In Hebrew.] *Arabic and Islamic Studies* (Ramat Gan) 2 (1978): 102–114.

Kohlberg, E. "Some Shi'i Views of the Antediluvian World." *Studia Islamica* 52 (1980): 41–66.

Koppers, Wilhelm. "Eiszeitlich Bärendarstellungen und Bärenkult in paläobiologischer und prähistorisch-ethnologischer Beleuchtung." *Palaeobiologica* 7 (1939): 7–64.

Kramer, C. *Village Ethnoarchaeology: Rural Iran in Archaeological Perspective*. New York: Academic Press, 1982.

Kramrisch, Stella. *The Hindu Temple*. 2 vols. Calcutta: University of Calcutta, 1946.

Kramrisch, Stella. "The Rgvedic Myth of the Craftsmen (the Rbhus)." *Artibus Asiae* 22 (1959): 113–120.

Kreinovich, E. A. "Rozhdenie i smert' cheloveka po vozzreniiam giliakov." *Etnografiia* 9 (1930): 89–113.

Krickeberg, Walter. "Bauform und Weltbild im alten Mexico." In *Mythe, Mensch und Umwelt.* Beiträge zur Religion, Mythologie und Kulturgeschichte, ed. Adolf Jensen, 295–333. Bamberg: Bamberger Verlagshaus, 1950.

Kristensen, Evald Tang. *Danske sagn.* 6 vols. Copenhagen, 1892–1901; reprint, Hassing, 1963–1968.

Kurokawa, Y. "A Newly Found Sasanian Silver Plate with Royal Bear Hunt." *Kodai oriento Hakubutsukan Kiyo* [Bulletin of the Ancient Orient Museum] 17 (1996): 65–87.

Kurth, Dieter. *Edfou VIII: Die Inschriften des Tempels von Edfu.* Abteilung 1, Übersetzungen, Band 1. Wiesbaden: Harrassowitz, 1998.

Kurtz, Donna C., and John Boardman. *Greek Burial Customs.* Ithaca: Cornell University Press, 1971.

Kutubī, Muḥammad b. Shākir. *Fawāt al-wafayāt.* Beirut: Dār al-Kutub al-ʿIlmīyah, 2000.

Kwon, Heonik. "Play the Bear: Myth and Ritual in East Siberia." *History of Religions* 38 (1999): 373–387.

Laitin, David. *Hegemony and Culture: Politics and Religious Change among the Yoruba.* Chicago: University of Chicago Press, 1986.

Lambden, Stephen. "From Fig Leaves to Fingernails: Some Notes on the Garments of Adam and Eve." In *A Walk in the Garden,* ed. Paul Morris and Debora Sawyer, Journal for the Study for the Old Testament Supplemental Series 136, 74–91. Sheffield: Journal for the Study of the Old Testament Press, 1992.

Lambert, W. G., and A. R. Millalrd. *Atra-hasis: The Babylonian Story of the Flood.* Oxford: Clarendon Press, 1969.

Lammens, H. *L'Arabie occidentale avant l'Hégire.* Beirut: Imprimerie Catholique, 1928.

Lammens, H. "La Mecque à la veille de l'Hégir." *Mélanges de l'Université Saint-Joseph* 9 (1924): 97–439.

Lammens, H. "Les sanctuaires préislamites dans l'Arabie occidentale." *Mélanges de l'Université Saint-Joseph* 11 (1926): 39–173.

Lamotte, Etienne. *Histoire du bouddhisme indien.* Louvain: Institut Orientliste, 1958.

Lancaster, W. O. *The Rwala Bedouin Today.* Cambridge: Cambridge University Press, 1981.

Lancaster, William, and Fidelity Lancaster. "Graves and Funerary Monuments of the Ahl al-Gahl, Jordan." *Arabian Archaeology and Epigraphy* 4 (1993): 151–169.

Landberg, C. *Catalogue de manuscripts arabes provenant d'une bibliothèque privée a el-Medîna et appartenant a la maison E. J. Brill.* Leiden: E. J. Brill, 1883.

Lane, Edward William. *An Account of the Manners and Customs of the Modern Egyptians*. London: Ward, Lock and Co., 1890.
Lane, Edward William. *Arabian Society in the Middle Ages: Studies from the Thousand and One Nights*. Ed. Stanley Lane-Poole. London: Catto and Windus, 1883.
Lane-Poole, Stanley. "Death and Disposal of the Dead (Muhammadan)." In *Encyclopedia of Religion and Ethics,* ed. James Hastings and others, 4:500–502. New York: Charles Scribner's Sons, 1951.
Lansdell, Henry. *Through Siberia.* 4th ed. London: S. Low, Marston, Searle and Rivington, 1883.
Laoust, Henri. *Le précis de droit d'Ibn Qudāma*. Beirut, s.n., 1950.
Laoust, Henri. *La profession de foi d'Ibn Baṭṭah*. Damascus: Institut français de Damas, 1958.
Lascu, Cristian, Florian Baciu, Mihai Gligan, and Servan Sarbu. "A Mousterian Cave Bear Worship Site in Translyvania, Roumania." *Journal of Prehistoric Religion* 10 (1996): 17–27.
Lassner, Jacob. *Demonizing the Queen of Sheba: Boundaries of Gender and Culture in Postbiblical Judaism and Medieval Islam.* Chicago: University of Chicago Press, 1993.
Latham, J. D., and W. F. Paterson, eds. *Saracen Archery: An English Version and Exposition of a Mameluke Work of Archery (c. AD 1368)*. London: Holland P., 1970.
Lauterbach, Jacob, ed. and trans. *Mekhilta de Rabbi Ishmael.* Philadelphia: Jewish Publication Society of America, 1933; reprint, 2001.
Layard, A., and others. *The Marvellous Adventures of Sir John Maundevile Kt: Being His Voyage and Travel Which Treateth of the Way to Jerusalem and of the Marvels of Ind with Other Islands and Countries.* Westminster: A. Constable and Co., 1895.
Leach, Edmund R. "Magical Hair." *Journal of the Royal Anthropological Institute* 88 (1958): 147–164.
Lecker, Michael. "King Ibn Ubayy and the Quṣṣāṣ." In *Method and Theory in the Study of Islamic Origins,* ed. Herbert Berg, 29–72. Leiden: E. J. Brill, 2003.
Lecker, Michael. *Muslims, Jews and Pagans: Studies on Early Islamic Medina.* Leiden: E. J. Brill, 1995.
Lefkovits, Judah K. *The Copper Scroll 3Q15: A Reevaluation: A New Reading, Translation, and Commentary.* Leiden: E. J. Brill, 2000.
Leggett, William. "Hegemony and National Identity in Indonesia." PhD dissertation, Northern Illinois University, 1994.
Leisten, Thomas. *Architektur für Tote: Bestattung in architecktonischem Kontext in den Kernländern der islamischen Welt zwischen 3./9. und 6./12. Jahrhundert.* Berlin: D. Reimer, 1997.

LeMehaute, Bernard. *Surfing Carrousel.* 2 vols. Pasadena, Calif.: Tetra Tech, 1980–1989.

Le Strange, Guy. *The Lands of the Eastern Caliphate.* Cambridge: Cambridge University Press, 1905.

Leszynsky, R. *Die Juden in Arabien zur Zeit Mohammeds.* Berlin: Mayer and Müller, 1910.

Levenson, J. *Program of Restoration in Ezekiel 40–48.* Missoula, Mont.: Scholars Press, 1976.

Levin, M. G., and L. P. Potapov. *Narody Sibiri.* Moscow: Izd-vo Akademii nauk SSSR, 1956. Trans. Stephen P. Dunn as *The Peoples of Siberia* (Chicago: University of Chicago Press, 1964).

Lévi-Strauss, Claude. *Homme nu.* Paris: Plon, 1971. Trans. J. and D. Weightman as *The Naked Man* (New York: Harper and Row, 1981).

Lévi-Strauss, Claude. *The Savage Mind.* The Nature of Human Society Series. London: Weidenfeld and Nicolson, 1966.

Lévi-Strauss, Claude. *Totemism.* Trans. Rodney Needham. Boston: Beacon Press, 1962.

Lewcock, R. "Architectural Connections between Africa and Parts of the Indian Ocean Littoral." *Art and Archaeology Research Papers* 9 (1976): 13–23.

L'Heureux, C. E. "The yelîdê hārāpā᾽: A Cultic Association of Warriors." *Bulletin of the American Schools of Oriental Research* 221 (1976): 83–85.

Lidzbarski, M. *Handbuch der nordsemitischen Epigraphik.* Weimar: E. Felber, 1898.

Lidzbarski, M. *Kanaanäischen Epigraphik.* Giessen: Alfred Töpelmann, 1907.

Lincoln, Bruce. *Authority: Construction and Corrosion.* Chicago: University of Chicago Press, 1994.

Lincoln, Bruce. *Myth, Cosmos, and Society: Indo-European Themes of Creation and Destruction.* Cambridge, Mass.: Harvard University Press, 1986.

Lincoln, Bruce. *Priests, Warriors, and Cattle: A Study in the Ecology of Religions.* Berkeley: University of California Press, 1981.

Lincoln, Bruce. *Theorizing Myth: Narrative, Ideology, and Scholarship.* Chicago: University of Chicago Press, 1999.

Littleton, C. Scott. "From Swords in the Earth to the Sword in the Stone: A Possible Reflection of an Alano-Sarmatian Rite of Passage in the Arthurian Tradition." In *Homage to Georges Dumézil,* ed. Edgar C. Polomé, 53–68. Washington, D.C.: Journal of Indo-European Studies, Institute for the Study of Man, 1982.

Littleton, C. Scott. "Susa-nö-wo versus Ya-mata nö woröti: An Indo-European Theme in Japanese Mythology." *History of Religions* 20 (1981): 269–280.

Liu Binru and Chen Dazuo. "Yangzhou 'Huihui tang' he yuandai alabowen de mubei" [Yangzhou 'Huihui temple' and the Yuan dynasty Arabic gravestones].

Reprinted in *Huizu shilun ji,* 1949–1979 [Hui history collection, 1949–1979], ed. Chinese Academy of Social Sciences Ethnology Department and Central Nationalities Institute Ethnology Department, Hui History Team. Yinchuan, 1984.

Livne-Kafri, O. "Early Muslim Ascetics and the World of Christian Monasticism." *Jerusalem Studies in Arabic and Islam* 20 (1996): 105–129.

Löfgren, Oscar. "Ambrosian Fragments of an Illustrated Manuscript Containing the Zoology of Al-Gahiz." *Uppsala Universitets Årsskrift* (1946): 5.

Lombard, M. *Les metaux dans l'ancien monde du Ve au XIe siècle.* Paris: Mouton, 1979.

Long, Matt. "Skipping Church: Applying James C. Scott's *Domination and the Arts of Resistance* to Late Medieval England." PhD dissertation, Emory and Henry College, 2002.

Lot-Falck, Eveline. *Les rites de chasse chez les peuples sibériens.* Paris: Gallimard, 1953.

Low, James. *Transactions of the Royal Asiatic Society of Great Britain and Ireland* 3 (1835): 1–62.

Lucianus of Samosata. *Adversus Indoctum: Verae Historiae.* Biponti: Ex Typographia Societatis, 1789–1793.

Lundquist, J. M. "The Common Temple Ideology of the Ancient Near East." In *The Temple in Antiquity,* ed. T. G. Madsen, 53–76. Provo, Utah: Religious Studies Center, Brigham Young University, 1984.

Lutzky, Harriet. "Deity and the Social Bond: Robertson Smith and the Psychoanalytic Theory of Religion." In *William Robertson Smith: Essays in Reassessment,* ed. William Johnstone, Journal for the Study of the Old Testament Supplemental Series 189, 320–330. Sheffield: Sheffield Academic Press, 1995.

Macdonald, J. *Memar Marqah.* Berlin: A. Töpelmann, 1963.

Macdonald, J. *The Samaritan Chronicle II.* Berlin: W. De Gruyter, 1969.

Macksey, Kenneth. *The Penguin Encyclopedia of Weapons and Military Technology: Prehistory to the Present Day.* New York: Penguin Books, 1993.

MacRitchie, David. "Giants." In *Encyclopedia of Religion and Ethics,* ed. James Hastings and others, 6:189–197. New York: Charles Scribner's Sons, 1951.

Māhir, Suʾād. *Miṣr wa awliyaʾu-ha al-ṣaliḥūn.* Cairo: s.n., 1973.

Mahmud, Firoz. "A Sword of Nawab Siraj-ud-Davlah in the Dacca Museum." *Bangladesh llalil Kal J. Dacca Museum* 1 (1975): 127–130.

Mājid, A. M. *Nuẓūm al-Fāṭimiyyīn wa rusūmu-hum fi Miṣr.* Cairo: s.n., 1973.

Majlisī, Muḥammad. *Bihār al-Anwār.* Tehran: s.n., 1887.

Makdisi, G. *Ibn ʿAqīl, Religion and Culture in Classical Islam.* Edinburgh: University of Edinburgh Press, 1997.

Malamat, A. "Campaigns to the Mediterranean by Iahdunlim and Other Early Mesopotamian Rulers." *Assyriological Studies* 16 (1965): 365–372.

Mālik b. Anas. *al-Muwaṭṭaʾ*. Ed. Muḥammad Fuʿād ʿAbd al-Bāqī. Beirut: Dār al-Kutub al-ʿIlmīyah, n.d.

Mandelbaum, Bernard, ed. *Pesikta de Rab Kahana*. New York: Jewish Theological Seminar of America, 1962.

Manz, Beatrice Forbes. *The Rise and Rule of Tamerlane*. Cambridge: Cambridge University Press, 1989.

Manz, Beatrice Forbes. "Tamerlane and the Symbolism of Sovereignty." *Iranian Studies* 21 (1987): 105–122.

Maqqarī, Aḥmad b. Muḥammad. *Fatḥ al-mutaʿālī fī madḥ al-niʿāl*. Hyderabad: Majlis Dāʾirat al-Maʿārif al-ʿUthmānīyah, 1334.

Maqqarī, Aḥmad b. Muḥammad. *The History of the Mohammedan Dynasties in Spain, Extracted from the Nafhu-t-tíb min ghosni-i-Andalusi-r-rattíb táríkh Lisánu-d-Dín Ibni-i-Khattíb*. Trans. Pascual de Gayangos. London: Oriental Translation Fund of Great Britain and Ireland, 1840–1843.

Maqqarī, Aḥmad b. Muḥammad. *Nafkh al-ṭīb min ghuṣn al-Andalus al-raṭīb*. Ed. I. ʿAbbās. Beirut: Dār Ṣadr, 1968.

Maqrīzī, Aḥmad b. ʿAlī. *Kitāb al-khiṭaṭ al-Maqrīzī*. Cairo: s.n., n.d.

Maqrizī, Aḥmad b. ʿAlī. *al-Mawāʾiz wa al-iʿtibar bi dhikr al-khiṭāṭ*. Cairo: Maktabat Madbulī, 1270.

Marghīnānī, ʿAlī b. Abī Bakr. *al-Hidāyah: Sharḥ bidāyat al-mubtadā*. Multān: Maktabah-i Shīrkat ʿIlmīyah, 1980.

Margoliouth, David. "The Relics of the Prophet Mohammed." *Moslem World* 27, no. 1 (1937): 20–27.

Marshall, John. "The Monuments of Muslim India." In *Cambridge History of India*, vol. 3, chap. 23. Cambridge: Cambridge University Press, 1936.

Martin, Andy. *Walking on Water*. London: J. Murray, 1991; reprint, London: Minerva, 1992.

Martin, W. L. *Tribut und Tributleistungen bei den Assyrern*. Helsinki: Societas Orientalils Fennica, 1936.

Marx, Emanuel. "Communal and Individual Pilgrimage: The Region of Saints' Tombs in South Sinai." In *Regional Cults*, ed. R. P. Werbner, ASA Monograph 16, 29–51. London: Academic Press, 1977.

Massignon, Louis. "Pèlerinages populaires à Bagdad." *Revue du Monde Musulman* 6–13 (December 1908): 641.

Massignon, Louis. "La cité des morts au Caire (Qarāfa-Darb al-Aḥmar)." *Bulletin de l'Institut Français d'Archéologie Orientale* 57 (1958): 25–79.

Massignon, Louis. "Elie et son rôle transhistorique, Khadiriyya en Islam." *Opera Minora* 1 (1969): 142–161.

Masson, Charles. *Narrative of Various Journeys in Balochistan, Afghanistan and the Panjab*. London, 1842; reprint, Karachi: Oxford University Press, 1974.

Masʿūdī, Abū al-Ḥasan ʿAlī. *Kitāb al-tanbīh wa al-ishrāf.* Ed. M. J. de Goeje. Leiden: E. J. Brill, 1894.
Masʿūdī, Abū al-Ḥasan ʿAlī. *Murūj al-dhahab wa maʿādin al-jawhar.* 7 vols. Beirut: Dār al-Andalus, 1965–1966.
Maʿṣūmī, M. "Imām Ṭaḥāwī fi Kitab Ikhtilāf al-fuqaqhā'." In *Fikr-u Naẓar.* Islamabad, 1973.
Matheson, Sylvia A. *Persia: An Archaeological Guide.* 2d ed. London: Faber, 1976.
Matthew, G. "The East African Coast until the Coming of the Portuguese." In *History of East Africa,* ed. R. Oliver and G. Matthew, 95–127. Oxford: Clarendon Press, 1963.
Matthews, Ch. D. "A Muslim Iconoclast (Ibn Taymiyyah) on the 'Merits' of Jerusalem and Palestine." *Journal of the American Oriental Society* 56 (1936): 1–21.
Mauss, Marcel. "Esquisse d'une théorie générale de la magie." *Année Sociologique* 7 (1902–1903). Trans. D. Pocock as *A General Theory of Magic* (London: Routledge, 1972).
Mauss, Marcel, and Henri Hubert. *Sacrifice: Its Nature and Function.* Trans. W. D. Hall. Chicago: University of Chicago Press, 1964.
Maux, Herz. "Les citernes d'Alexandria." *Monumentes de l'Art Arabe* (1898): 81–86 with plates 5–7.
Māwardī, ʿAlī b. Muḥammad. *al-Aḥkām al-sulṭānīyah.* Cairo: Maktabah al-Tawfiqīyah, 1973. Trans. Wafaa H. Wahba as *The Ordinances of Government: Al-Aḥkām al-Sulṭāniyya w'al-Wilāyāt al-Dīniyya,* Great Books of Islamic Civilization (Reading: Center for Muslim Contribution to Civilization, 1996).
Mayer, L. A. *Islamic Armourers and Their Works.* Geneva: Kundig, 1962.
Mazzanti, Angela Maria. *L'uomo nella cultura religiosa del tardo-antico: Tra etica e ontologia.* Bologna: Patron, 1990.
McDonald, M. V., and W. Montgomery Watt. *The History of al-Ṭabarī: The Foundation of the Community.* Albany: State University of New York Press, 1987.
McLean, D. N. *Religion and Society in Arab Sind.* Leiden: E. J. Brill, 1989.
McParland, Stephen J. *Beach, Street and Strip: The Albums.* Sydney: PTB Productions, 1983.
Meeks, Wayne. *The Prophet-King: Moses Traditions and the Johannine Christology.* Leiden: E. J. Brill, 1967.
Mehren, A. F. *Revue des monuments funéraires du Kerafat ou de la Ville des morts hors du Caire, Mélanges asiatiques tirés du Bulletin de l'Académie impériale des sciences de St.-Pétersbourg.* St. Petersburg: Impr. de l'Académie impériale des sciences, 1871.
Mehren, A. F. "Tableau général des monumens religieux du Caire." *Mélanges Asiatiques, St. Petersburg* 4 (1855): 309, 338.

Memon, Muḥammad Umar, trans. *Ibn Taymīya's Struggle against Popular Traditions, with an Annotated Translation of his Kitāb Iqtiḍā' al-Ṣirāṭ al-Mustaqīm Mukhālafat Ahl al-Jaḥīm.* The Hague: Mouton, 1976.

Memon, Siddique G. *The Tombs of the Kalhora Chiefs in Hyderabad.* Karachi: Oxford University Press, 1994.

Meri, Josef W. "Aspects of Baraka (Blessings) and Ritual Devotion among Medieval Muslims and Jews." In a special issue of *Medieval Encounters: Jewish, Christian and Muslim Culture in Confluence and Dialogue* 5 (1999): 46–69.

Meri, Josef W. *The Cult of Saints among Muslims and Jews in Medieval Syria.* Oxford: Oxford University Press, 2002.

Meri, Josef W. "Sacred Journeys to Sacred Precincts: The Cult of the Saints among Muslims and Jews in Medieval Syria." PhD dissertation, Oxford University, 1998.

Meri, Josef W. "A Late Medieval Syrian Pilgrimage Guide: Ibn al-Ḥawrānī's *al-Ishārāt ilā amākin al-ziyārāt* (Guide to Pilgrimage Places)." *Medieval Encounters* 7 (2001): 3–78.

Merklinger, Elizabeth. *Indian Islamic Architecture: The Deccan, 1347–1686.* Warminster: Aris and Phillips, 1981.

Merklinger, Elizabeth. "Seven Tombs at Holkonda: A Prelimary Survey." *Kunst des Orients* 10 (1975): 187–197.

Merrill, Selah. *East of the Jordan: A Record of Travel and Observation in the Countries of Moab, Gilead, and Bashan.* London: Richard Bentley and Son, 1881. Reprinted, London: Darf, 1986.

Mershen, B. "The Islamic Cemetery of Abu an-Naml." *Annual of the Department of Antiquities of Jordan* 34 (1990): 331–332.

Merx, Adalbert. *Der Messias oder Ta'eb der Samaritaner.* Beihefte zur Zeitschrift für die alttestamentliche Wissenschaft 17. Giessen: A. Töpelmann, 1909.

Metcalf, Peter. *A Borneo Journey into Death.* Philadelphia: University of Pennsylvania Press, 1982.

Meuli, K. "Griechische Opferbräuche." In *Phyllobolia für Peter von der Muhll zum 60 Geburtstag am 1. August 1945,* ed. Olof Gigon and others, 185–288. Basel: B. Schwabe, 1945.

Michell, George, ed., *Brick Temples of Bengal: From the Archives of David McCutchion.* Princeton: Princeton University Press, 1983.

Michell, George, and Snehal Shah, with John Burton-Page, ed. *Ahmadabad.* Bombay: Marg Publications, 1988.

Mikhail, Hanna. *Politics and Revelation: Māwardī and After.* Edinburgh: University of Edinburgh Press, 1995.

Miles, C. "Miḥrāb and 'Anazah." In *Archaeologica Orientalia in Memoriam Ernst Herzfeld,* ed. C. Miles, 156–171. Locust Valley, N.Y.: J. J. Augustin, 1952.

Milik, J. T. *Dédicaces faites par des dieux (Palmyre, Hatra, Tyr) et des thiases sémi-*

*tiques à l'époque romaine*. Recherches d'épigraphie proche-orientale 1. Paris: P. Geuthner, 1972.

Miller, P. D. *The Divine Warrior in Early Israel.* Cambridge, Mass.: Harvard University Press, 1973.

Mirkin, M., ed. *Midrash Rabbah: Bereshit-Devarim.* 11 vols. Tel Aviv: Hotsaʿat Yavneh, 1986.

Mishra, V. B. *The Hindu Sahis of Afghanistan and the Punjab, A.D. 865–1026.* Patna: Vaishali Bhavan, 1972.

Mishra, V. B. *Religious Beliefs and Practices of North India during the Early Medieval Period.* Leiden: E. J. Brill, 1973.

Miṣrī, ʿAbd al-Ṣamad b. ʿAbdallāh. *Manāqib al-quṭb al-nabawī wa al-sharīf al-ʿalawī Sidī Aḥmad al-Badawī: al-Jawāhir al-sanīyah wa al-karamāt Aḥmadīyah.* Cairo: al-Maṭbaʿah al-ʿAmirah al-ʿUthmānīyah, 1991.

Mittwoch, E. "Zur Entstehungs-geschichte des islamischen Gebets und Kultus." *Abhandlungen der preussischen Akademie der Wissenschaft* 2 (1913): 1–42.

Mizzī, Yūsuf b. ʿAbd al-Raḥmān. *Tuḥfat al-ashrāf bi-maʿrifat al-aṭrāf.* Ed. ʿAbd al-Ṣamad Sharaf al-Dīn. Bhiwandi: al-Dār al-Qayyimah, 1965–1981.

Mizzī, Yūsuf b. ʿAbd al-Raḥmān. *Tahdhīb al-kamāl.* Damascus: s.n., n.d.

Modi, J. J. "Archery in Ancient Persia." *Journal of the Royal Asiatic Society* 25 (1917–1921): 175–186.

Momigliano, A. "Pagan and Christian Historiography in the Fourth Century A.D." In *The Conflict between Paganism and Christianity in the Fourth Century,* ed. A. Momigliano, 79–99. Oxford: Clarendon Press, 1963.

Monnerret de Villard, U. *Le leggende orientali sui Magi evangelici.* Vatican City: Biblioteca apostolica vaticana, 1952.

Monteil, V. *Indonésie.* Paris: Horizons de France, 1970.

Moquette, J. P. "De datum op den grafsteen van Malik Ibrahim te Grissee." *TBS* 54 (1912): 208–214.

Moquette, J. P. "De grafstenen te Pasé en Grissee vergeleken met dergelijke monumenten uit Hindoestan." *TBS* 54 (1912): 536–648.

Moreen, Vera B. "Is(h)maʿīliyat: A Judeo-Persian Account of the Building of the Kaʿba." In *Judaism and Islam: Boundaries, Communication, and Interaction: Essays in Honor of William M. Brinner,* ed. Benjamin H. Hary and others, 185–202. Leiden: E. J. Brill, 2002.

Mosshammer, A. A. *The Chronicle of Eusebius and Greek Chronographic Tradition.* Lewisburg, Pa.: Bucknell University Press, 1979.

Moulinier, L. *Le pur et l'impur dans la pensée et la sensibilité des Grecs jusqu'à la fin du IVe siècle avant J.-C.* Paris: Louis-Jean, 1950.

Mouton, J. M. "De quelques reliques conservées à Damas au Moyen-Âge: Statégie politique et religiosité populaire sous les Bourides," *Annales Islamologiques* 27 (1993): 245–254.

*Moyen-Orient: Liban, Syrie, Jordanie, Iraq, Iran: Les Guides Bleus*. Paris: Hachette, 1965.
Moyne, Ernest J. *Hiawatha and Kalevala*. Helsinki: Suomalainen Tiedeakatemia, 1963.
Mubārak, ʿAlī Bāshā. *al-Khiṭaṭ al-tawfiqīyah al-jadīdah*. Cairo: Maṭbaʿat Dār al-Kutub, 1969.
Muhtar, O. Sermed. *Müze-i Askeri-i Osmani-Rehber*. Istanbul: Necm-i Istikbal Matbaasi, 1920–1922.
Muḥyī al-Dīn, A. "ʿIbādat al-arwāḥ fī al-mujtamaʿ al-ʿarabī al-jāhilī." In *Studies in the History of Arabia*, ed. A. T. Ansary, 2:153–164. Riyadh: University of Riyadh Press, 1984.
Mujīr al-Dīn ʿAbd al-Raḥmān b. Muḥammad al-Ḥanbalī. *al-Uns al-jalīl bi-taʾrīkh al-Quds wa al-Khalīl*. Amman: Muḥtasab, 1973.
Müller, August. *Der Islam im Morgen- und Abendland*. Berlin: G. Grote, 1885–1887.
Mumford, L. *The City in History*. New York: Harcourt, Brace and World, 1961.
Mundkur, B. *The Cult of the Serpent: An Interdisciplinary Survey of Its Manifestations and Origins*. Albany: State University of New York Press, 1983.
Munshi, K. M. *Glory That Was Gujara-Desa*. 2 vols. Bombay: Bharatiya Vidya Bhavan, 1955.
Muqaddasī, Muḥammad b. Aḥmad. *Aḥsan al-taqāsīm fī maʿrifat al-aqālīm*. Ed. M. J. de Goeje. Descriptio imperii Moslemici. Leiden: E. J. Brill, 1967.
Muqātil b. Sulaymān. *Tafsīr Muqātil b. Sulaymān*. Ed. ʿAbdallāh Maḥmūd Shiḥātah. Cairo: Muʾassasat al-Ḥalabī, 1979.
Murray, G. W. *Sons of Ishmael: A Study of the Egyptian Bedouin*. London: G. Routledge and Sons, 1935.
Murtaḍā, Aḥmad b. Yaḥyāʾ. *ʿUyūn al-azhār fī fiqh al-aʾimmah al-aṭhār*. Beirut, 1975.
Mus, Paul. *Barabudur: Equisse d'une histoire du bouddhisme fondée sur la critique archéologique des textes*. Hanoi: Impr. d'Extrême-Orient, 1935–1955.
Mus, Paul. "Où finit Puruṣa?" In *Mélanges d'indianisme à la mémoire de Louis Renou*, 539–563. Paris: Éditions de Boccard, 1968.
Mus, Paul. "Symbolisme à Angkor Thom: Le 'grand miracle' du Bayon." *Académie des Inscriptions et Belles-Lettres: Comptes-Rendus des Séances* (1936): 57–68.
Musil, A. *Arabia Deserta*. New York: American Geographical Society, 1927.
Musil, A. *The Manners and Customs of the Rwala Bedouins*. New York: American Geographical Society, 1928.
Muslim b. al-Hajjāj. *al-Jāmiʿ al-ṣaḥīḥ*. Beirut: Dāl al-Jīl, n.d.
Muttaqī, ʿAlī ʿAbd al-Mālik. *Kanz al-ʿummāl fī sunan al-aqwāl wa al-afʿāl*. Hyderabad: Majlis Dāʾirat al-Maʿārif al-ʿUthmānīyah, 1945.

Muzanī, Ismāʿīl b. Yaḥyāʾ. *Mukhtaṣar.* In *Kitāb al-umm,* by al-Shāfiʿī. Beirut: Dār Qutaybah, 1996.

Nābulsī, ʿAbd al-Ghanī. *al-Ḥaḍrah al-unsīyah fī riḥlah al-qudsīyah.* Beirut, 1990.

Nābulsī, ʿAbd al-Ghanī. *al-Ḥaqīqah wa al-majāj fī riḥlah bilād al-Shām wa Miṣr wa al-Ḥijāz.* Ed. Riyāḍ ʿAbd al-Ḥamīd Murād. Damascus: Dār al-Maʿrifah, 1989.

Nābulsī, ʿAbd al-Ghanī. *Riḥlatān ilā Lubnān: Zwei Beschreibungen des Libanon: ʿAbdalganī an-Nābulsīs Reise durch die Biqāʿ und al-ʿUṭaifīs Reise nach Tripolis.* Ed. Ṣalāḥaddīn al-Munajjid and Stefan Wild. Beirut: al-Maʿhad al-Almanī li-l-Abḥath al-Sharqīyah, 1979.

Nafrāwī, Aḥmad b. Ghunaym. *al-Fawākih al-dawānī.* 2 vols. Cairo: Muṣṭafā al-Bābī al-Ḥalabī, 1955.

Nakash, Yitzhak. *The Shīʿis of Iraq.* New ed. Princeton: Princeton University Press, 2003.

Nanji, Azim, ed. *Mapping Islamic Studies: Genealogy, Continuity and Change.* Berlin: Mouton de Gruyter, 1997.

Naqvi, S. Ali Raza. "Prophetic Sunna in the Islamic Legal Framework." *Islamic Studies* 19 (1980): 120–133.

Narr, Karl J. "Bärenzeremoniell und Schamanismus in der Älteren Steinzeit Europas." *Saeculum* 10 (1959): 233–272.

Nasāʾī, ʿAbd al-Raḥmān. *Kitāb al-ḍuʿafāʾ wa al-matrūkīn.* Beirut: Muʾassasah al-Kutub al-Thaqafīyah, 1985.

Nasāʾī, ʿAbd al-Raḥmān. *Sunan.* Beirut: Dār al-Kutub al-ʿIlmīyah, n.d.

Nawawī, ʿAbdallāh b. al-Shaykh Muḥammad. *Ṣaḥīḥ Muslim bi-sharḥ Muḥyī al-Dīn al-Nawawī.* 19 vols. Beirut: Dār al-Maʿrifah, 1994.

Neely, Peter. *Indo Surf and Lingo.* Noosa Heads: Indo Surf and Lingo, 1990–2000.

Nehmé, Leila, and C. Rubin. "Le temple de Nakrah à Yathill (Baraqish)." *Comptes Rendus de l'Académie des Inscriptions et Belles-Lettres* (1993): 427–496.

Neusner, Jacob, trans. *Genesis Rabbah: The Judaic Commentary to the Book of Genesis.* Providence: Scholars Press, 1985.

Nevo, Yehuda D., and Judith Koren. "The Origins of the Muslim Descriptions of the Jāhilī Meccan Sanctuary." *Journal of Near Eastern Studies* 49, no. 1 (1990): 23–44.

Newby, Gordon. *The Making of the Last Prophet: A Reconstruction of the Earliest Biography of Muhammad.* Columbia: University of South Carolina Press, 1989.

Nigam, M. L. "Some Literary References to the History of the Gujara-Pratihāras Mahendrapāla and Mahipāla." *Journal of the Royal Asiatic Society* (1964): 14–17.

Nissen, H. *Das Templum: Antiquarische Untersuchungen.* Berlin: Weidmann, 1869.

Noegel, Scott, and Brannon Wheeler. *Historical Dictionary of Prophets in Islam and Judaism.* Lanham, Md.: Scarecrow Press, 2002.

Nöldeke, Th. *Geschichte des Qorâns.* Göttingen: Verlag der Dieterichshen Buchhandlung, 1860.

Nöldeke, Th. "Der Gott mrʾ bytʾ und die Kaʿba." *Zeitschrift für Assyriologie* 23 (1909): 184–186.

Nöldeke, Th. "Die Schlange nach arabischem Volksglauben." *Zeitschrift für Völkerpsychologie* 1 (1860): 416.

Nöldeke, Th. *Über die Amalekiter und einige andere Nachbarvölker der Israeliten.* Göttingen: Dieterich, 1864.

Novikova, K. A. *Evenskii fol'klor.* Magadan: Magadanskoe knizhnoe izd-vo, 1958.

Nuʿaymī, ʿAbd al-Qādīr b. Muḥammad. *al-Dāris fī taʾrīkh al-madāris.* Damascus: Maṭbaʿat al-Taraqqī, 1367–1370.

Nuʿaymī, ʿAbd al-Qādīr b. Muḥammad. *al-Dāris fī taʾrīkh al-madāris.* Ed. Ibrāhīm Shams al-Dīn. Beirut: Dār al-Kitāb al-Jadīd, 1990.

Oakley, Kenneth. "Folklore of Fossils." *Antiquity* 39 (1965): 9–16, 117–125.

Obayashi, Taryo. "On the Origin of the 'Inau' Cult-Sticks of the Ainu." *Japanese Journal of Ethnology* (Tokyo) 24 (1960): 16–27.

Obayashi, Taryo, and H. Paproth. "Das Bärenfest der Oroken auf Sachalin." *Zeitschrift für Ethnologie* 91 (1966): 218.

Olesen, N. H. *Culte des saints et pèlerinages chez Ibn Taymiyya (661/1268–728/1328).* Paris: P. Geuthner, 1991.

Olufsen, O. "Muhamedanske gravminder i Transkaspein, Khiva, Bokhara, Turkestan og Pamir." *Geografisk tidskrift* (Copenhagen) 17 (1903): 110–120, 146–159.

Oppert, G. *On the Weapons, Army Organization, and Political Maxims of the Ancient Hindus.* Madras: Higginbotham, 1880.

Oren, E. D. *Explorations in the Negev and Sinai.* Beersheba: Ben Gurion University of the Negev, 1976.

Otto-Dorn, Katherina. "Türkische Gravsteine mit Figurenreliefs aus Kleinasien." *Ars Orientalis* 3 (1959): 63–76.

Oxtoby, Willard. *Some Inscriptions of the Safaitic Bedouin.* New Haven: Yale University Press, 1968.

Öz, Tahsin. *Hirka-i Saadet Dairesi ve Emanat-i Mukaddese.* Istanbul: Ismail Akgün Matbaasi, 1953.

Palmer, E. H. *The Desert of the Exodus.* Cambridge: Bell, 1871.

Panhwar, M. H. *Source Material on Sind, and the Culture of Sind.* Karachi: Institute of Sindhology, 1980.

Panseri, C. "Damascus Steel in Legend and in Reality." *Gladius* 4 (1965): 5–66.

Pant, G. N. *A Catalogue of Arms and Armours in Bharat Kala Bhavan.* Delhi: Parimal Publications, 1995.

Pant, G. N. "A Study of Indian Swords." In "Itihasa-Chayanika: Dr. Sampurnanand Felicitation Volume," special issue, *Journal of the Uttar Pradesh Provinces Historical Society* 11–13, pt. 2 (1965): 75–86.

Paproth, H. *Studien über Bärenzeremoniell.* Vol. 1, *Bärenjagdriten und Bärenfest bei den Tungusischen Völkern.* Uppsala: K. Renner, 1976.

Parrot, A. *Malédictions et violation des tombes.* Paris: Paul Geuthner, 1939.

Pârvulescu, Adrian. "The Name of the Great Bear." *Journal of Indo-European Studies* 16 (1988): 95–120.

Paul, A. "Ancient Tombs in Kassala Province." *Sudan Notes and Records* 33 (1952): 54–57.

Paulson, Ivar. *Schutzgeister und Gottheiten des Wildes (Der Jagdtiere und Fische in Nordeurasien): Eine religionsethnographische und religionsphänomenologische Untersuchung jägerischer Glaubensvorstellungen.* Acta universitatis stockholmiensis 2. Stockholm : Almqvist and Wiksell, 1961.

Pausanias. *Description of Greece.* Ed. and trans. W. H. S. Jones. Cambridge, Mass.: Harvard University Press, 1971.

Peake, F. G. *A History of Jordan and Its Tribes.* Coral Gables, Fla.: University of Miami Press, 1958.

Pearson, Kent. *Surfing Subcultures of Australia and New Zealand.* St. Lucia: University of Queensland Press, 1979.

Pedersen, J. "Ādam." In *Encyclopaedia of Islam,* 2d ed., ed. H. A. R. Gibb and others, 1:176–178. Leiden: E. J. Brill, 1960–2002.

Penrad, Jean-Claude. "The Social Fallout of Individual Death: Graves and Cemeteries in Zanzibar." In *The History and Conservation of Zanzibar Stone Town,* ed. Abdul Sherif, 82–90. Zanzibar: Department of Archives, Museums and Antiquities, 1995.

Peterman, Glen, and Robert Schick. "The Monastery of Saint Aaron." *Annual of the Department of Antiquities of Jordan* 40 (1996): 473–480.

Peters, E. L. "From Particularism to Universalism in the Religion of the Cyrenaica Bedouin." *Bulletin of the British Society for Middle Eastern Studies* 13 (1976): 5–14.

Petersen, D. L. "Yahweh and the Organization of the Cosmos." *Journal for the Study of the Old Testament* 13 (1979): 47–64.

Petrash, I. G. *Sviatye mesta obmana.* Frunze: Kyrgyzstan Basmasy, 1961.

Petrov, Alexandr A. "The Bear Taboo in Even Language and Folklore." *Inuit Studies* 13, no. 1 (1989): 131–133.

Philo. *De Vita Mosis.* Ed. F. H. Colson and G. H. Whitaker. Loeb Classical Library. Cambridge, Mass.: Harvard University Press, 1929–1953. Trans. C. D. Yonge as *The Works of Philo,* new ed. (Peabody, Mass., 1993).

Philostratus. *Heroicus.* Trans. J. K. B. Maclean and E. B. Aitken. Atlanta: Scholars Press, 2001.

Photius. *Bibliotheca*. Ed. I. Bekker. Berlin: G. Reimeri, 1824–1825.

Piaskowski, J. "Metallographic Examination of Two Damascene Steel Blades." *Journal of the History of Arab Science* 2 (1973): 3–30.

Piccirillo, Michele, and Eugenio Alliata, eds. *The Madaba Map Centenary, 1897–1997: Travelling through the Byzantine Umayyad Period*. Jerusalem: Studium Biblicum Franciscanum, 1998.

Piemontese, A. M. "La leggenda del santo-lottatore Pahlavān Maḥmūd Xvārezmi 'Puryā-ye Vali' (m. 722/1322)." *Annali dell'Istituto orientale di Napoli,* n.s., 15 (1965): 167–213.

Pindar. *Pythia*. Ed. and trans. W. H. Race. Cambridge, Mass.: Harvard University Press, 1997.

Pliny. *Historia Naturalis*. Ed. and trans. H. Rackham. Cambridge, Mass.: Harvard University Press, 1938–1963.

Plot, R. *The Natural History of Oxfordshire*. Oxford: s.n., 1677

Plutarch. *Vitae*. Ed. and trans. Bernadotte Perrin as *Plutarch's Lives*. Cambridge, Mass.: Harvard University Press, 1989.

Plutarch. *Vitae Parallelae*. Ed. C. Lindoskog and K. Ziegler. Leipzig, 1960.

Porphyry. *On Images*. Trans. A. H. Armstrong. Cambridge, Mass.: Harvard University Press, 1966.

Potts, D. T. *The Arabian Gulf in Antiquity*. Oxford: Clarendon Press, 1990.

Potts, D. T. "Late Sasanian Armament from Southern Arabia." *Electrum* 1 (1997): 127–137.

Potts, D. T. *A Prehistoric Mound in the Emirate of Umm al-Qaiwain: U.A.E. Excavations at Tell Abraq in 1989*. Copenhagen: Muksgaard, 1990.

Potts, D. T. "Some Issues in the Study of Pre-Islamic Weaponry of Southeastern Arabia." *Arabian Archaeology and Epigraphy* 9 (1998): 182–208.

Powers, David. *Law, Society, and Culture in the Maghreb, 1300–1500*. Cambridge: Cambridge University Press, 2002.

Prag, K. "Preliminary Report on the Excavations at Tell Iktanu, Jordan, 1987." *Levant* 21 (1989): 33–45.

Pritchard, James, ed. *Ancient Near Eastern Texts Relating to the Old Testament*. 3d ed. Princeton: Princeton University Press, 1969.

Procopius. *De Bello Gothico*. Trans. H. B. Dewing. 7 vols. London: W. Heinemann, 1914–1940.

Przyluski, Jean. "Pradakshina et prasavya en Indochine." In *Festschrift für Moriz Winternitz, 1863–23. dezember 1933,* ed. Otto Stein and Wilhelm Gampert. Leipzig: Otto Harrassowitz, 1933.

Puhvel, Jaan. "Remus et Frater." *History of Religions* 15 (1975): 146–157.

Qāḍī al-Nuʿmān b. Muḥammad. *Kitāb al-himma fī ādāb atbāʿ al-aʾimmah*. Ed. M. Kāmil Ḥusayn. Cairo, n.d.

Qāḍī al-Nuʿmān b. Muḥammad. *al-Majālis wa al-musāyarāt*. Ed. al-Ḥabīb al-Faqqī and others. Tunis: al-Jāmiʿah al-Tūnsīyah, 1978.
Qāḍī ʿIyyāḍ b. Mūsā. *al-Shifāʾ*. Cairo: ʿIsā al-Bābī al-Ḥalabī, 1977.
Qalqashandī, Aḥmad b. ʿAlī. *Ṣubḥ al-aʿshā fī sināʿat al-inshāʾ*. Cairo: al-Muʾassasah al-Miṣrīyah al-ʿĀmmah, 1964.
Qasṭallānī, Aḥmad b. Muḥammad. *Irshād al-sārī li-sharḥ Ṣaḥīḥ al-Bukhārī*. Cairo, 1304; reprint, Beirut: Dār Iḥyā al-Turāth al-ʿArabī, n.d.
Qasṭallānī, Aḥmad b. Muḥammad. *Kitāb al-shamāʾil min al-mawāhib al-ladunīyah*. Cairo: Maktabat al-Turāth al-Islāmī, 1995.
Qazwīnī, Aḥmad b. Fāris. *Ḥulīyat al-fuqahāʾ*. Ed. ʿAbdallāh b. ʿAbd al-Muḥsin al-Turkī. Beirut, 1403.
Qazwīnī, Zakarīyā b. Muḥammad. *Āthār al-bilād wa akhbār al-ʿibād*. Ed. Ferdinand Wüstenfeld. Göttingen: Verlag der Dieterischen Buchhandlung, 1848; reprint, Beirut: s.n., 1960–1961.
Qudūrī, Aḥmad b. Muḥammad. *Mukhtaṣar fī al-fiqh*. Cairo: Maṭbaʿat al-Khayyīrah, 1324.
Qummī, ʿAlī b. Ibrāhīm. *Tafsīr al-Qummī*. Beirut: Dār al-Surūr, 1991.
Qurṭubī, Muḥammad b. Aḥmad. *al-Jāmiʿ li-aḥkām al-Qurʾān*. Beirut: Dār al-Kitāb al-ʿArabī, 1997.
Rabaʿī, ʿAlī b. Muḥammad. *Faḍāʾil al-Sham*. Damascus: Maṭbaʿat al-Ṭarqī, 1999.
Raffles, T. S. "On the Malayu Nation: Translation of a Maláyu Manuscript Entitled A History of Former Times Containing an Account of the First Arrival of the Portuguese at Malacca." *Asiatick Researches* 12 (1816): 116–122.
Raghib, Y. "Essai d'inventaire chronologique des guides à l'usage de pèlerins du Caire." *Revue des Études Islamiques* 1 (1973): 259–260.
Raghib, Y. "Les premiers monuments funéraires de l'Islam." *Annales Islamologiques* 9 (1970): 21–22.
Raghib, Y. "Structure de la tombe d'après le droit musulman." *Arabica* 39 (1992): 393–403.
Rawson, P. S. *The Indian Sword*. Copenhagen: Danish Arms and Armour Society, 1967; rev. ed., London: Jenkins, 1968.
Rāzī, Fakhr al-Dīn. *Mafātīḥ al-ghayb*. Cairo, n.d.
Reinaud, Joseph Toussaint. *Géographie d'Aboulféda: Allgemeine Einleitung und französische Übersetzung des Taqwīm al-buldān von Abūʾl-Fidāʾ (gest. 732 H./1331 n. Chr.)*. Ed. Fuat Sezgin. Frankfurt: Institut für Geschichte der Arabisch-Islamischen Wissenschaften an der Johann Wolfgang Goethe-Universität, 1985.
Reinaud, Joseph Toussaint. *Monumens arabes, persans et turcs*. Paris: Dondey-Dupré, 1828.
Reinhart, A. A. Kevin. "Impurity/No Danger." *History of Religions* 30 (1990–1991): 1–24.

Reynolds, Frank E. "The Several Bodies of the Buddha: Reflections on a Neglected Aspect of Theravāda Tradition." *History of Religions* 16 (1977): 374–389.
Rice, D. S. "The Aghānī Miniatures and Religious Painting in Islam." *Burlington Magazine* 45 (April 1953): 128–136.
Rice, Michael. *The Archaeology of the Arabian Gulf, c. 5000–323 BC.* London: Routledge, 1994.
Riḍā, Fawād ʿAlī. *Umm al-qurā: Makkah al-mukarramah.* Beirut: Maktabat al-Maʿārif, 1987.
Rippin, Andrew. "Ṣāliḥ." In *Encyclopaedia of Islam,* 2d ed., ed. H. A. R. Gibb and others, 8:984. Leiden: E. J. Brill, 1960–2002.
Robert, C. "Alkyoneus." *Hermes* 19 (1884): 473–485.
Robinson, James M., and Frederik Wisse. "The Three Steles of Seth (NHC VII,5)." In *The Nag Hammadi Library,* ed. James M. Robinson, 362–267. San Francisco: Harper and Row, 1978.
Robinson, S. E. "Testament of Adam." In *The Old Testament Pseudepigrapha,* ed. James H. Charlesworth, 1:989–995. Garden City, N.Y.: Doubleday, 1983.
Robinson, S. E. *The Testament of Adam: An Examination of the Syriac and Greek Traditions.* Chico, Calif.: Scholars Press, 1982.
Rompay, Lucas Van. "Memories of Paradise: The Greek 'Life of Adam and Eve' and Early Syriac Tradition." *Aram* 5 (1993): 555–570.
Rose, H. A. *Glossary of the Tribes and Castes of the Punjab and North-West Frontier Province.* Lahore, 1911–1919.
Rosen-Ayalon, M. *The Early Islamic Monuments of al-Haram al-Sharif: An Iconographic Study.* Jerusalem: Institute of Archeology, Hebrew University, 1989.
Rosenthal, Franz, trans. *The History of al-Ṭabarī: From the Creation to the Flood.* Albany: State University of New York Press, 1989.
Roy, Normand. *L'analyse du rituel chez Claude Lévi-Strauss: Le finale de l'Homme nu dans la perspective du structuralisme.* Montreal: Université de Montréal, 1995.
Rubaʿī, Abū al-Ḥasan ʿAlī b. Muḥammad. *Faḍāʾil al-Shām wa Dimashq.* Ed. S. Munajjid. Damascus: s.n., 1951.
Rubin, Uri. *Between Bible and Quran: The Children of Israel and the Islamic Self-Image.* Princeton: Darwin Press, 1999.
Rubin, Uri. "Ḥanīfiyya and Kaʿba: An Inquiry into the Arabian Pre-Islamic Background of Dīn Ibrāhīm." *Jerusalem Studies in Arabic and Islam* 13 (1990): 85–112.
Rubin, Uri. "The Kaʿba: Aspects of Its Ritual Functions and Position in Pre-Islamic and Early Islamic Times." *Jerusalem Studies in Arabic and Islam* 8 (1986): 97–131.
Rupert, Brian. *Jewel in the Ashes: Buddha Relics and Power in Early Medieval Japan.* Cambridge, Mass.: Harvard University Press, 2000.
Ruska, J. *Tabula Smaragdina.* Leipzig: C. Winter's Universitätsbuchhandlung, 1926.

Ryan, Sam. *1960s Surfboard Guide*. Leucadia: Breakers House, 1994.

Ryckmans, G. *Les religions arabes préislamiques*. Louvain: Universitaires, 1951.

Ryckmans, G. "Le sacrifice DBH dans les inscriptions safaîtiques." *Hebrew Union College Annual* 23 (1950–1951): 431–438.

Ryckmans, Jacques. "La chasse rituelle dans l'Arabie du Sud ancienne." In *al-Bahit: Festschrift Joseph Henninger*, ed. J. Henninger, Studia Instituti Anthropos 28, 259–308. St. Augustin bei Bonn: Verlag des Anthropos-Instituts, 1976.

Ryckmans, Jacques. "Sacrifices, offrandes et rites connexes en Arabie du Sud préislamique." In *Ritual and Sacrifice in the Ancient Near East*, ed. J. Quaegebeur, 355–380. Louvain: Universitaires, 1993.

Ṣabbān, Shaykh ʿAbd al-Qādir Muhammad. *Visits and Customs: The Visit to the Tomb of the Prophet Hud*. Ed. and trans. Linda Boxberger and Awad Abdelrahim Abu Hulayqa. American Institute for Yemeni Studies. Yemen Translation Series 2. Ardmore, Pa.: American Institute for Yemeni Studies, 1998.

Ṣābī, Hilāl b. al-Muḥassin. *Rusūm dār al-khilāfa*. Ed. M. ʿAwwād. Baghdad, 1964. Trans. Elie A. Salem as *The Rules and Regulations of the ʿAbbasid Court* (Beirut: Lebanese Commission for the Translation of Great Works, 1977).

Sadan, Joseph. "Le tombeau de Moïse a Jéricho et a Damas: Une compétition entre deux lieux saints principalement à l'époque ottomane." *Revue des Études Islamiques* 49 (1981): 59–99.

Sadan, Joseph. "The Tomb of Moses (Maqām Nabī Mūsā): Rivalry between Regions as to Their Respective Holy Places." [In Hebrew.] *Near East* (quarterly of the Israel Oriental Society) 28, nos. 1–2 (1979): 22–38, 220–238.

Ṣafadī, Khalīl b. Aybak. *Kitāb al-wāfī bi al-wafayāt*. Leipzig: Deutsche Morgenländische Gesellschaft, 1931.

Saḥnūn, ʿAbd al-Salām b. Saʿid. *al-Mudawwanah al-kubrā*. 5 vols. Beirut: Dār al-Kutub al-ʿIlmīyah, 1994.

Saintine, X. B. *Histoire de l'expédition française en Egypte*. Paris: A.-J. Dénain, 1830.

Sakhāwī, Muḥammad b. ʿAbd al-Raḥmān. *al-Ḍawʾ al-lāmiʿ li-ahl al-qarn al-tasīʿ*. Cairo: Maktabat al-Qudsī, 1353–1355; reprint, Beirut: Dār Maktabat al-Ḥayāt, 1966.

Saldarini, A., trans. *The Fathers according to Rabbi Nathan*. Leiden: E. J. Brill, 1975.

Saller, S. J. *Excavations at Bethany (1949–1953)*. Jerusalem: Franciscan Press, 1957.

Salmāsīzāda, ʿAlī Akhbar. *Taʾrīkhca-i wakf dar Islām*. Tehran, 1964.

Salomon, Richard. *Ancient Buddhist Scrolls from Gandhara*. Seattle: University of Washington Press, 1999.

Ṣalt, Ibrāhīm b. Qāḍī. *Bāʿith al-nufūs li-ziyārat al-Quds al-maḥrūs*. In *Arbaʿ rasāʾil fī faḍāʾil al-Masjid al-Aqṣā*. Nasr City: Dār al-Nadā, 2000.

Samarqandī, Abū al-Layth. *Tafsīr al-Qurʾān al-karīm.* Baghdad: Maṭbaʿat al-Irshād, 1985.
Samhūdī, ʿAlī b. ʿAbdallāh. *Wafāʾ al-wafā.* Beirut: Dār Iḥyāʾ Turāth al-ʿArabī, 1971.
Sarakhsī, Muḥammad b. Aḥmad. *Kitāb al-mabsūṭ.* Cairo: Maṭbaʿat al-Saʿādah, 1378.
Saraswati, S. K. "Art." In *History and Culture of the Indian People: The Delhi Sultanate,* ed. Ramesh Chandra Majumdar, vol. 4, chap. 19. Bombay: Bharatiya Vidya Bhavan, 1960.
Sauvaget, J. *Alep: Essai sur le développement d'une grande ville syrienne Des origines au milieu du XIX siècle.* Paris: P. Geuthner, 1941.
Sauvaget, J. "Les epitaphes royales de Gao." *Bulletin de l'Institut Français d'Afrique Noire* 13 (1950): 418–440.
Sauvaget, J. "Notes preliminaires sur les epitaphes royales de Gao." *Revue des Études Islamiques* 21 (1948): 5–12.
Savignac, M. R. "Le sanctuaire d'Allat à Iram." *Revue Biblique* 41 (1932): 413; 43 (1934): 588.
Savignac, M. R. "Sur les pistes de Transjordanie méridionale." *Revue Biblique* 45 (1936): 235–262.
Schaefer, J. "Archaeological Remains for the Medieval Islamic Occupation of the Northwest Negev Desert." *Bulletin of the American Schools for Oriental Research* 274 (May 1989): 33–60.
Schaeffer, C. "The Bear Foster Parent Tale: A Kutenai Version." *Journal of American Folklore* 60 (1947): 286–288.
Schechter, S., ed. *Maseket Abōt de-Rabbi Natan.* Vienna: Ch. D. Lippe, 1887.
Scheffer, J. *History of Lapland.* Frankfort: Ex officina Christiani Wolffii, Typis Joannis Andreae, 1673; reprint, Oxford: G. West and A. Curtein, 1674.
Scheible, Kirstin. "Stealing, Hoarding, Guarding: Nagas and the Three Types of Buddha Relics in the Pali Vamsas." Paper presented at the annual meeting of the American Academy of Religion, November 2003.
Schermann, T. *Prophetarum Vitae Fabulosae Indices Apostolorum Discipulorumque Domini Dorotheo, Epiphanio, Hippolyto Aliisque Vindicate.* Leipzig: B. G. Teubneri, 1907.
Schick, Robert. "Ecclesiastical History of Petra." In *The Petra Church,* ed. Patricia Bikai, 1–5. Amman: American Center of Oriental Research, 2001.
Schimmel, Annemarie. *And Muḥammad Is His Messenger.* Chapel Hill: University of North Carolina Press, 1985.
Schimmel, Annemarie. *Deciphering the Signs of God: A Phenomenological Approach to Islam.* Albany: State University of New York Press, 1994.
Schimmel, Annemarie. *Islamic Names.* Edinburgh: Edinburgh University Press, 1989.

Schmidt, E. F. *The Alishar Hüyük Seasons of 1928 and 1929*. Chicago: University of Chicago Press, 1933.
Schmidt, W. "Das Primitialopfer in der Urkultur." In *Corona Amicorum: Festgabe für Emil Bächler,* ed. Emil Egli, 81–92. St. Gallen: Tschudy-Verlag, 1948.
Schopen, Gregory. *Bones, Stones, and Buddhist Monks.* Honolulu: University of Hawaii Press, 1997.
Schreiner, J. "Gen 6, 1–4 und die Problematik von Leben und Tod." In *De la Tôrah au Messie,* ed. H. Carrez and others, 65–74. Paris: Desclée, 1981.
Schreiner, M. "Beiträge zur Geschichte der theologischen Bewegungen." *Zeitschrift der Deutschen Morgenländischen Gesellschaft* 43 (1890): 58–59.
Schwartz, B. "A Hittite Ritual Text (KUB 29.1 = 1780/c)." *Orientalia,* n.s., 16 (1947): 23–55.
Schwartzbaum, Haim. *Biblical and Extra-biblical Legends in Islamic Folk-Literature.* Walldorf-Hessen, 1982.
Schwarzlose, F. W. *Die Waffen der alten Araber aus ihren Dichtern dargestellt.* Leipzig: J. C. Hinrichs, 1886; reprint, Hildesheim: Georg Olms Verlag, 1982.
Scott, James C. *Domination and the Arts of Resistance: Hidden Transcripts.* New Haven: Yale University Press, 1990.
Scott, James C. *Weapons of the Weak: Everyday Forms of Peasant Resistance.* New Haven: Yale University Press, 1985.
Scures, Joseph. "The Social Order of the Surfing World." Master's thesis, University of Washington, 1986.
Sedov, A. V., and A. Batayiʿ. "Temple of Ancient Hadramawt." *Proceedings of the Seminar for Arabian Studies* 24 (1994): 183–196.
Seligman, C. G. *Pagan Tribes of the Nilotic Sudan.* London: Routledge, 1932.
Seligman, C. G., and B. Z. Seligman. "The Bari." *Journal of the Royal Anthropological Institute* (London) 58 (1928): 463–465.
Sell, Edward. *Faith of Islam.* Wilmington, Del.: Scholarly Resources, 1976.
Seneviratne, H. L. *Rituals of the Kandyan State.* Cambridge: Cambridge University Press, 1978.
Serjeant, R. B. "The Cemeteries of Tarîm (Hadramawt) (with Notes on Sepulture)." *Le Muséon* 62 (1942): 232–234.
Serjeant, R. B. "Ḥaram and Ḥawṭah: The Sacred Enclave in Arabia." In *Mélanges Ṭāhā Ḥusain: Offerts par ses amis et ses disciples a l'occasion de son 70ième anniversaire,* ed. Abdurrahman Badawi, 41–58. Cairo: Dār al-Maʿārif, 1962.
Serjeant, R. B. *The Saiyids of Hadramawt.* London: School of Oriental and African Studies, 1957.
Serjeant, R. B. *South Arabian Hunt.* London: Luzac, 1976.
Serjeant, R. B. "The White Dune at Abyan, an Ancient Place of Pilgrimage in Southern Arabia." *Journal of Semitic Studies* 6 (1971): 74–83.

Sermed Muhtar, O. *Müze-i Askeri-i Osmani-Rehber.* 3 vols. Istanbul: Imprimerie Ndjmi-Istikbal, 1920–1922.

Sethe, K. *Beiträge zur ältesten Geschichte Ägyptens.* Leipzig: J. C. Hinrichs, 1903.

Shāfiʿī, Muḥammad b. Idrīs. *Kitāb al-umm.* Beirut: Dār Qutaybah, 1996.

Shaḥrī, ʿAlī Aḥmad ʿAlī Maḥāsh. "Grave Types and 'Triliths' in Dhofar." *Arabian Archaeology and Epigraphy* 2 (1991): 182–195.

Shaḥrī, ʿAlī Aḥmad ʿAlī Maḥāsh. "Recent Epigraphic Discoveries in Dhofar." *Proceedings of the Seminar for Arabian Studies* 21 (1991): 173–191.

Shapiro, H. A. "Theseus in Kimonian Athens: The Iconography of Empire." *Mediterranean Historical Review* 7 (1992): 29–49.

Shaʿrāwī, Muḥammad Mutawalī. *Qiṣaṣ al-anbiyāʾ.* Ed. Merkaz al-Turāth li-l-Khidma al-Kitāb wa al-Sunnah. Cairo: al-Dār al-ʿAlimīyah li-l-Kutub wa al-Nashr, 1997.

Sharīf, Jaʿfar. *Qanūn-i Islām.* Trans. G. A. Herklots as *Islam in India; or, The Qanun-i-Islam: The Customs of the Musalmans of India,* ed. William Crooke (London: H. Milford, 1921; reprint, New Delhi: Oriental Books Reprint, 1972).

Sharnūbī, ʿAbd al-Majīd b. Ibrāhīm. *Taqrīb al-maʿānī ʿalā matn al-Risālah li-Abī Zayd al-Qayrawānī.* Beirut: Dār al-Kutub al-ʿIlmīyah, 1998.

Shawkānī, Muḥammad b. ʿAlī. *Fatḥ al-qadīr.* 5 vols. Beirut: Dār Iḥyā al-Turāth al-ʿArabī, 1998.

Shawkānī, Muḥammad b. ʿAlī. *Nayl al-awṭār.* Beirut: Dār al-Khayr, 1998.

Shaybānī, Muḥammad b. al-Ḥasan. *al-Ḥujjah fī ikhtilāf ahl al-Kūfah wa ahl al-Madīnah.* Lucknow: Lajnat Iḥyāʾ al-Maʿārif al-Nuʿmānīyah, 1888.

Shaybānī, Muḥammad b. al-Ḥasan. *Kitāb al-āthār.* Ed. Abū al-Wafā al-Afghānī. Beirut: Dār al-Kutub al-ʿIlmīyah, 1993.

Shifren, Nachum. *Surfing Rabbi: A Kabbalistic Quest for Soul.* Los Angeles: Heaven Ink, 2001.

Shīrāzī, Abū Isḥāq. *Ṭabaqāt al-fuqahāʾ.* Ed. Iḥsān ʿAbbās. Beirut: Dār al-Rāʾid al-ʿArabī, 1970.

Shirbīnī, Muḥammad b. Aḥmad. *Mughnī al-muḥtāj ilā maʿrifat maʿānī alfāʾ al-minhāj.* 6 vols. Beirut: Dār al-Kutub al-ʿIlmīyah, 1994.

Shirokogoroff, S. M. *Psychomental Complex of the Tungus.* London: K. Paul, Trench, Truebner, 1935.

Siddiqi, Abdussattar. *Studien über die persischen Fremdwörter im klassischen Arabisch.* Göttingen: Vandenhoeck and Ruprecht, 1919.

Sikes, E. E., and Louis H. Gray. "Hair and Nails." In *Encyclopedia of Religion and Ethics,* ed. James Hastings and others. Edinburgh: T. and T. Clark, 1913.

Silvestre de Sacy, ed. and trans. *Kitāb al-ʿilal; or, Sirr al-khalīqah.* In *Notices et Extraits* 4 (1798–1799): 108ff.

Simon, Erika. "Aloadai." In *Lexicon Iconographicum Mythologiae Classicae,* vol. 1, pt. 1:570–572. Zurich: Artemis, 1981–1999.

Simon, Erika. "Otos und Ephialtes." *Antike Kunst* 5 (1962): 43–44.

Simpson, John. "Death and Burial in the Late Islamic Near East: Some Insights from Archaeology and Ethnography." In *The Archaeology of Death in the Ancient Near East,* ed. Stuart Campbell and Anthony Green, 240–252. Oxford: Oxford University Press, 1995.

Sirrīya, E. "Ziyārāt of Syria in a Riḥla of ʿAbd al-Ghanī al-Nābulusī (1050/1641–1143/1731)." *Journal of the Royal Asiatic Society* (1979): 109–122.

Sivan, E. "La caractère sacré de Jérusalem aux Xiie-Xiiie siècles." *Studia Islamica* 17 (1976): 149.

Sladek, W. R. "Inanna's Descent to the Netherworld." PhD dissertation, Johns Hopkins University, 1974.

Slawik, Alexander. "Kultische Geheimbünde der Japaner und Germanen." *Wiener Beiträge zur Kulturgeschichte* (Salzburg and Leipzig) 4 (1936): 675–764.

Slawik, Alexander. "Zum Problem des Bärenfestes bei den Ainu und Giliaken." *Kultur und Sprache: Wiener Beiträge zur Kulturgeschichte und Linguistik* 9 (1952): 189–203.

Slawik, Alexander. "Zur Etymologie des japanischen Terminus marebito 'Sakraler Besucher.'" *Wiener Völkerkundliche Mitteilungen* 2 (1954): 44–58.

Smith, E. B. *The Dome: A Study in the History of Ideas.* Princeton: Princeton University Press, 1950.

Smith, Glenn. "The Making and Unmaking of Madura's Sacred Tombs." *Review of Indonesian and Malaysian Affairs* 32, no. 2 (1998): 211–249.

Smith, Jean. *Tapu Removal in Maori Religion.* Wellington: Polynesian Society, 1974.

Smith, Jonathan Z. "The Bare Facts of Ritual." In *Imagining Religion: From Babylon to Jonestown*, 53–65. Chicago: University of Chicago Press, 1982.

Smith, Jonathan Z. "The Domestication of Sacrifice." In *Violent Origins,* ed. G. Hamerton-Kelly, 85–93. Stanford: Stanford University Press, 1987.

Smith, Jonathan Z. *To Take Place: Toward Theory in Ritual.* Chicago: University of Chicago Press, 1987.

Smith, Sidney. *Babylonian Historical Texts Relating to the Capture and Downfall of Babylon.* London: Methuen and Co., 1924.

Smith, Vincent A. "European Graves at Kabul." *Indian Antiquary,* August 1909, 232.

Smith, William Robertson. *Kinship and Marriage in Early Arabia.* Cambridge: Cambridge University Press, 1885.

Smith, William Robertson. *Lectures on the Religion of the Semites: The Fundamental Institutions.* 3d ed., ed. Stanley A. Cook. London: A. and C. Black, 1927. Trans. into German by R. Stübe as *Die Religion der Semiten* (Freiburg, 1899).

Smith, William Robertson. *The Religion of the Semites: Lectures on the Religion of the Semites (Second and Third Series) by William Robertson Smith.* Ed. John Day.

Journal for the Study of the Old Testament Supplemental Series 183 (Sheffield: Sheffield Academic Press, 1995).
Sobernheim, M. "Ḥamāt." In *Encyclopaedia of Islam,* 2d ed., ed. H. A. R. Gibb and others, 3:119–121. Leiden: E. J. Brill, 1960–2002.
Sollberger, E. "The Temple in Babylonia." In *Le temple et le culte,* 31–34. Leiden: E. J. Brill, 1975.
Solinus. *Collectanea Rerum Memorabilium.* Ed. Theodor Mommsen. Berlin: Apud Wiedmannos, 1895; reprint, 1958. Trans. into German by H. Walter as *Die Collectanea Rerum Memorabilium des Gaius Iulius Solinus* (Wiesbaden: F. Steiner, 1969).
Solomon, W. E. G. "The Sword of Aurangzebe: A Study of Arms and Art." *Islamic Culture* 8 (1934): 179–199.
Sourdel, Dominique. *Les cultes du Hauran à l'époque romaine.* Paris, 1952.
Sourdel-Thomine, J. "Les anciens de pèlerinage damascains d'après les sources arabes." *Bulletin d'Études Orientales* 14 (1952–1954): 65–85.
Sourdel-Thomine, J. *Clefs et serrures de la Kaʿba.* Paris: P. Geuthner, 1971.
Sourdel-Thomine, J. "Inscriptions arabes de Karak Nuḥ." *Bulletin d'Études Orientales* 12 (1949–1950): 71–84.
Sovernhein, M. "Die arabischen Inschriften von Aleppo." *Der Islam* 15 (1926): 198–199.
Spoer, H. "Das Nabī-Mūsā-Fest." *Zeitschrift des Deutschen Palästinavereins* 32 (1909): 207–221.
Stenhouse, P. *The Kitab al-Tarikh of Abu'l-Fath.* Sydney: Mandelbaum Trust, 1985.
Stenhouse, P. "Samaritan Chronicles." In *The Samaritans,* ed. A. D. Crown, 218–265. Tübingen: J. C. B. Mohr, 1989.
Sternberg, Leo. "Die Religion der Giljaken." *Archiv fur Religionswissenschaft* 8 (1905): 244–274, 456–473.
Stöcklein, Hans. "Die Waffenschätze im Topkapu Sarayi Müzesi zu Istanbul." *Ars Islamica* 1 (1934): 200–218.
Stone, George Cameron. *A Glossary of the Construction, Decoration and Use of Arms and Armor in All Countries and in All Times.* New York: Jack Brussel, 1934.
Stone, Michael, and John Strugnell, ed. and trans. *The Books of Elijah.* Missoula: Scholars Press, 1979.
Strabo. *Geography.* Ed. and trans. H. L. Jones. London: W. Heinemann, 1917–1932.
Streck, M. "Kalah." In *Encyclopaedia of Islam,* 2d ed., ed. H. A. R. Gibb and others, 4:467–468. Leiden: E. J. Brill, 1960–2002.
Streck, M., and C. E. Bosworth. "Sūs." In *Encyclopaedia of Islam,* 2d ed., ed. H. A. R. Gibb and others, 9:898–899. Leiden: E. J. Brill, 1960–2002.

Strong, John. *The Legends of King Asoka: A Study and Translation of the Asokavadana.* Princeton Library of Asian Translations. Princeton: Princeton University Press, 1983.

Strong, John. "Relics." In *Encyclopedia of Religion*, ed. Mircea Eliade and others, 11:7686–7692. New York: Macmillan, 1987.

Strong, John. "The Transforming Gift: An Analysis of Devotional Acts of Offering in Buddhist Avadāna Literature." *History of Religions* 18 (1979): 221–237.

Strong, S. A. "History of Kilwa." *Journal of the Royal Asiatic Society*, April 1895, 3–17.

Strzygowski, Josef. "Ruins of Tombs of the Latin Kings on the Haram in Jerusalem." *Speculum* 11 (1936): 499–508.

Suetonius. *De Vita Caesarum.* Ed. and trans. J. C. Rolfe. 2 vols. Cambridge, Mass.: Harvard University Press, 1997–1998.

Suhaylī, ʿAbd al-Raḥmān b. ʿAbdallāh. *al-Rawd al-unuf.* Cairo: Dār al-Kutub al-Ḥadīthah, 1332.

Suidas. *Lexicon.* Ed. A. Adler. Leipzig: B. G. Teubner, 1928–1938.

Sulamī, ʿIzz al-Dīn ʿAbd al-ʿAzīz ʿAbd al-Salām. *Targhīb ahl al-Islām fī sukhnā al-Shām.* Beirut: Dār al-Fikr al-Muʿasir, 1998.

Sulimirski, T. *The Sarmatians.* New York: Praeger, 1970.

Suryakanta. *The Flood Legend in Sanskrit Literature.* Delhi: S. Chand, 1950.

Suyūṭī. ʿAbd al-Raḥmān b. Abī Bakr. *al-Durr al-manthūr fī tafsīr al-maʾthūr.* Beirut: Dār al-Kutub al-ʿIlmīyah, 1990.

Suyūṭī, ʿAbd al-Raḥmān b. Abī Bakr. *al-Itiqān fī ʿulūm al-Qurʾān.* Ed. Muṣṭafā Dīb al-Bughā. Beirut: Muʾassasat al-Kutub al-Thaqafīyah, 1421/2000.

Suyūṭī, ʿAbd al-Raḥmān b. Abī Bakr. *Tanwīr al-ḥawālik: Sharḥ Muwaṭṭaʾ al-Imām Mālik.* 2 vols. Cairo: al-Maktabah al-Tijarīyah al-Kubrā, 1969.

Suyūṭī, Shams al-Dīn Muḥammad al-Munhājī. "Ittiḥāf al-akhsāʾ bi-faḍāʾil al-masjid al-aqṣāʾ." *Journal of the Royal Asiastic Society*, n.s., 19 (1887): 258–259.

Suyūṭī, Shams al-Dīn Muḥammad al-Munhājī. *Itḥaf al-akhiṣṣāʾ bi fadāʾil al-Masjid al-Aqṣā.* Ed. Ahmad Ramadan Ahmad. Cairo: al-Hayʿah al-Miṣrīyah al-ʿĀmmah li-l-Kitāb, 1982.

Swemer, S. M. "The Sword of Mohammed and Ali." *Moslem World* 21, no. 2 (1931): 109–121.

Sykes, Percy Molesworth. "A Fourth Journey in Persia, 1897–1901." *Geographical Journal* 19 (1902): 121–173.

Sykes, Percy Molesworth. *Khan Bahadur Khan, the Glory of the Shia World.* London: Macmillan and Co., 1910.

Ṭabarānī, Sulaymān b. Aḥmad. *al-Muʿjam al-kabīr.* Baghdad: al-Jumhūrīyah al-ʿIrāqīyah, 1978.

Ṭabarī, Muḥammad b. Jarīr. *Jāmiʿ al-bayān fī tafsīr al-Qurʾān.* Beirut: Dār al-Kutub al-ʿIlmīyah, 1412.

Ṭabarī, Muḥammad b. Jarīr. *Dalāʾil al-imāmah.* Najaf: al-Maṭbaʿah al-Haydarīyah, 1949.

Ṭabarī, Muḥammad b. Jarīr. *Taʾrīkh al-rusul wa al-mulūk.* Ed. M. J. de Goeje. Leiden: E. J. Brill, 1879–1901.

Ṭabarsī, Abū ʿAlī al-Faḍl b. al-Ḥasan. *Majmaʿ al-bayān fī tafsīr al Qurʾān.* Beirut: Dār Maktabah al-Ḥayāh, n.d.

Ṭabāṭabāʾī, Muḥammad Ḥusayn. *al-Mizān fī tafsīr al-Qurʾān.* Beirut: Muʾassasat al-Aʿlamī li-l-Maṭbūʿāt, 1970–1974.

Tahānawī, Muḥammad b. Aʿlā b. ʿAlī. *Kashshāf iṣṭilāḥāt al-funūn.* Ed. Aloys Sprenger and others. Calcutta: Asiatic Society of Bengal, 1862.

Ṭaḥāwī, Aḥmad b. Muḥammad. *Ikhtilāf al-fuqahāʾ*. Published in English as *Imām Ṭaḥāwī's Disagreement of the Jurists,* ed. M. Maʿṣūmī (Islamabad, 1391).

Ṭaḥāwī, Aḥmad b. Muḥammad. *Sharḥ maʿānī al-āthār.* Ed. Muḥammad Sayīd Jādd al-Ḥaqq. Cairo: Maṭbaʿat al-Anwār al-Muḥammadīyah, 1391.

Tal, A. "Samaritan Literature." In *The Samaritans,* ed. A. D. Crown, 313–367. Tübingen: J. C. B. Mohr, 1989.

Talass, M. A. *Mosquées de Damas.* Beirut: s.n., 1943.

*Talmud Yerushalmī.* 7 vols. Jerusalem: Peri Megadim, 1998.

Tamari, Sh. "Maqām Nabī Mūsā near Jericho." [In Hebrew.] *Cathedra for the History of Eretz Israel and Its Yeshuv* 11 (1979): 153–180.

Tambiah, Stanley. *World Conqueror and World Renouncer: A Study of Buddhism and Polity in Thailand against a Historical Background.* Cambridge: Cambridge University Press, 1976.

Tamisier, M. *Voyage en Arabie: Sejour dans le Hedjaz, campagne d'Assir.* Paris: L. Desessart, 1840.

Taploo, Rita. "The Origin and Development of Islamic Tombs in India (II)." *Quarterly Review of Historical Studies* 15, no. 1 (1975–1976): 20–30.

Tarassuk, Leonid, and Claude Blair, eds. *The Complete Encyclopaedia of Arms and Weapons.* New York: Simon and Schuster, 1979.

Ṭarsūsī, Marḍī b. ʿAlī b. Marḍī. *Mawsūʿah al-islaḥah al-qadīmah: al-Mawsūm tabṣirat arbāb al-albāb.* Ed. Karen Sader. Beirut: Dār Ṣadr, 1998.

Tawil, H. M. "Early Arab Icons: Literary and Archaeological Evidence for the Cult of Religious Images in Pre-Islamic Arabia." PhD dissertation, University of Iowa, 1993.

Ṭayālisī, Sulaymān b. Dāʾūd. *Musnad.* Hyderabad: Majlis Dāʾirat al-Maʿārif al-ʿUthmānīyah, 1321.

Ṭaybughā. "Kitāb ghunyat al-ṭullāb fī maʿrifat ramī al-nushshāb." British Museum. Ms. Add. 233489.

Taylor, Christopher. *In the Vicinity of the Righteous: Ziyāra and the Veneration of Muslim Saints in Late Medieval Egypt.* Leiden: E. J. Brill, 1999.

Taylor, Joan du Plat. "Medieval Graves in Cyprus," *Ars Islamica* 5 (1938): 35–86.

Taymūr, Aḥmad. *al-Āthār al-nabawīyah.* Cairo: ʿĪsā al-Bābī al-Ḥalabī, 1391.

Tegnaeus, Harry. *Le héros civlisateur: Contribution à l'étude ethnologique de la religion et de la sociologie Africaines.* Uppsala: s.n., 1950.

Teixidor, J. *Inventaire des inscriptions de Palmyre.* Beirut: Imprimerie catholique, 1965.

Teixidor, J. *The Pagan God: Popular Religion in the Greco-Roman Near East.* Princeton: Princeton University Press, 1977.

Thaʿlabī, Aḥmad b. Muḥammad. *Qiṣaṣ al-anbiyā'.* Cairo: Maktabat al-Jumhūrīyah al-ʿArabīyah, n.d.

Thalbitzer, Wiliam. "Die kultischen Gottheiten der Eskimos." *Archiv für Religionswissenschaft* 26 (1928).

Theodoret. *Interpretatio Quatuordecim Epistolarum s. Pauli Apostoli.* Ed. Jacques Sirmond and Johann August Nösselt. Halae Magdeburgicae: Impensis Orphanotrophei, 1771.

Theodosius. *The Topography of the Holy Land.* Ed. P. Geyer. Turnhout: Paravia, 1958.

Tholbecq, L. "Les sanctuaires des Nabatéens." *Topoi* 7 (1997): 1069–1095.

Thomas, Bertram. "Among Some Unknown Tribes of Saudi Arabia." *Journal of the Royal Anthropological Institution* (1929): 97–111.

Thompson, Campbell. *Semitic Magic: Its Origins and Development.* London: Luzac, 1908.

Thureau-Dangin, F. *Rituels accadiens.* Paris: E. Leroux, 1921.

Thurneysen, Rudolf. *Die irische Helden- und Königsage bis zum siebzehnten Jahrhundert.* 2 vols. Halle: M. Niemeyer, 1921.

Tibbetts, G. R. "Pre-Islamic Arabia and Southeast Asia." *Journal of the Malayan Branch of the Royal Asiatic Society* 25, no. 3 (1956): 182–208.

Tihāmī, Muḥammad Ḥasan Muḥammad. *Suyūf al-rasūl wa ʿuddah ḥarbi-hi.* Cairo: Hajr, 1992.

Tirmidhī, Muḥammad b. ʿĪsā. *al-Jāmiʿ al-ṣaḥīḥ.* Ed. Aḥmad Muḥammad Shākir, Muḥammad Fu'ād ʿAbd al-Bāqī, and Ibrāhīm ʿAṭwah ʿIwaḍ. Delhi: Kutub Khānah Rashīdīyah, 1937.

Torrey, C. C. *The Lives of the Prophets: Greek Text and Translation.* Philadelphia: Society of Biblical Literature and Exegesis, 1946.

Tottoli, Roberto. *I profeti biblici nella tradizione islamica.* Brescia, 1999. Trans. Michael Robertson as *Biblical Prophets in the Qur'ān and Muslim Literature* (Richmond: Curzon, 2002).

Toynbee, Jocelyn M. C. *Death and Burial in the Roman World.* Ithaca: Cornell University Press, 1971.

Traube, Elizabeth G. *Cosmology and Social Life: Ritual Exchange among the Mambai of East Timor.* Chicago: University of Chicago Press, 1986.

Triantis, Ismène. "Pelops." In *Lexicon Iconographicum Mythologiae Classicae,* vol. 7, pt. 1:282–287. Zurich: Artemis, 1981–1999.
Trimingham, J. S. *Islam in East Africa.* Oxford: Clarendon Press, 1964.
Troll, Christian W., ed. *Muslim Shrines in India: Their Character, History and Significance.* Delhi: Oxford University Press, 1989; reprint, New Delhi: Oxford University Press, 2003.
Trumelet, Corneille. *Les saints de l'Islam: Legendes hagiologiques et croyances algerienne.* Paris: Librairie Académique Didier, 1881.
Trumelet, Corneille. *Les Français dans le désert.* 2d ed. Paris: Challamel Ainé, 1886.
Trümpelmann, L. "Muslimische Gräber." In *Antike Welt: Zeitschrift für Archäologie und Kulturgeschichte* 15 (1991): 4–16.
Twain, Mark. *Roughing It.* Hartford: American Publishing Company, 1872.
ʿUjaymī, Ḥasan b. ʿAlī, and Yaḥyā Maḥmūd Saʿatī. *Ihdāʾ al-laṭāʾif min akhbār al-Ṭāʾif.* Ṭāʾif: Dār Thaqif, 1980.
ʿUmar, Shah Muḥammad. *Istishfāʾ wa tawassul bi-āthār al-ṣāliḥīn wa sayyid al-Rasūl.* Delhi: s.n., 1391.
ʿUmayrī, Aḥmad b. Yaḥyāʾ. *Masālik al-abṣār fī mamālik al-amṣār.* Ed. A. Z. Bāshā. Cairo: Dār al-Kutub al-Miṣrīyah, 1924.
*Umm al-kitāb.* Trans. P. Filippani-Ronconi. Naples: Istituto Univesiario Orientale, 1966.
Ungnad, A. "Datenlisten." In *Reallexikon der Assyriologie,* ed. Erich Ebelling and Bruno Meissner, 1:178–187. Berlin: W. de Gruyter, 1928.
ʿUqaylī, Muḥammad b. ʿAmr. *Kitāb al-ḍuʿafāʾ al-kabīr.* Ed. ʿAbd al-Muʿṭī Amīn Qalʿajī. Beirut: Dār al-Kutub al-ʿIlmīyah, 1404.
Ussishkin, D., and J. Woodhead. "Excavations at Tel Jezreel, 1990–1991: Preliminary Report." *Tel Aviv* 18 (1991): 72–92; 19 (1992): 3–70.
Vaissière, A. "Cycle héroïque des Ouled-Hilal." *Revue Afrique* 36 (1892): 242–243, 312–324.
Vajda, G. "Deux 'Histoires de prophètes' selon la tradition des Shīʿites duodécimains." In *Biblical and Other Studies in Memory of S. D. Goitein,* ed. R. Ahroni, 124–133. Columbus: Ohio State University Press, 1986.
Valeri, Valerio. *Kingship and Sacrifice: Ritual and Society in Ancient Hawaii.* Trans. Paula Wissing. Chicago: University of Chicago Press, 1985.
van Berchem, Max. "La chaire de la mosquée d'Hébron." In *Festschrift Eduard Sachau,* ed. G. Weil, 298–310. Berlin: G. Reimer, 1915.
van Berchem, Max. *Matériaux pour un corpus inscriptionum arabicarum.* Cairo: Institut français d'archéologie orientale, 1894.
van Berchem, Max, and Edmond Fatio. *Voyage en Syrie.* Cairo: Institut français d'archéologie orientale, 1914–1915.

van der Meulen, D. *Aden to the Hadhramaut: A Journey in South Arabia*. London: J. Murray, 1947.
van der Meulen, D., and H. von Wissmann. *Ḥaḍramaut: Some of Its Mysteries Unveiled*. Leiden: E. J. Brill, 1932.
Van Esbroek, M. "Hélène à Èdesse et la Croix." In *After Bardaisan: Studies on Continuity and Change in Syriac Christianty in Honour of Professor Han J. W. Drijvers*, ed. G. J. Reinink and A. C. Klugkist, 107–115. Louvain: Uitgeverij Peeters en Dep. Oosterse Studies, 1999.
Vasil'ev, B. A. "Medvezhii prazdnik." *Sovetskaia etnografiia* 4 (1948): 78–104.
Velázquez, Diego. *Apollo in the Forge*. Littleton, Colo.: Saskia, n.d.
Velázquez, Diego. *The Forge of Vulcan*. New York: McGraw-Hill, 1965.
Veriomme, Hugo. *Surf Saga: Cowabunga!* Paris: Chêne, 1976.
Vernant, Jean-Pierre. "The Pure and the Impure." In his *Myth and Society in Ancient Greece*, trans. Janet Lloyd, 110–129. Sussex: Harvester Press, 1980. Originally published in *L'Année Sociologique* (1953–1954): 331–352.
Veselovskii, A. *Razyskaniia v oblasti russkago dukhovnykh stikhov*. St. Petersburg, 1889.
Vian, Fr. *La guerre des Géants*. Paris: Librairie C. Klincksieck, 1952.
Vilkuna, Kustaa. *Volkstümliche Arbeitsfeste*. FF Communications, no. 191. Helsinki: Suomalainen Tiedeakatemia Academica Scientiarum Fennica, 1963.
Vinaver, E. "King Arthur's Sword." *Bulletin of the John Rylands Library* 60 (1958): 511–520.
Vincent, L. H., E. J. H. MacKay, and F. M. Abel. *Hébron: La Haram el-Khalil*. Paris: E. Leroux, 1923.
Virgil. *Georgics*. Ed. and trans. H. R. Fairclough and others. Cambridge, Mass.: Harvard University Press, 1999–2000.
Voegelin, Eric. *Order and History*. Baton Rouge: Louisiana State University Press, 1956.
Voller, Karl. "Die Symbolik des masḥ." *Archiv für Religionswissenschaft* 8 (1905): 97–103.
Von der Mühll, P. *Der große Aias*. Basel: F. Reinhardt, 1930.
von Grunebaum, Gustave E. *Beduei Sanai*. Beersheba: Ben-Gurion University of Negev, 1962.
von Grunebaum, Gustave E. *Muhammadan Festivals*. New York: Schuman, 1951.
von Grunebaum, Gustave E. "The Sacred Character of Islamic Cities." In *Mélanges Ṭāhā Ḥusain: Offerts par ses amis et ses disciples a l'occasion de son 70ième anniversaire*, ed. Abdurrahman Badawi. Cairo, 1962.
von Heine-Geldern, Robert. "Weltbild und Bauform in Südostasien." *Wiener Beiträge zur Kunst- und Kulturgeschichte Asiens* (Vienna) 4 (1930): 28–78.

von Schrenck, Leopold. *Reisen und Forschungen im Amur-Lande in den Jahren 1854–1856*. Vol. 3, *Die Völker des Amur-Landes*. Geographisch-historischer und anthropologisch-ethnologischer theil. St. Petersburg: Buchdruckerei der Kaiserlichen Akademie der Wissenschaften, 1881.

Vullers, Johann Augustus. *Lexicon Persico-Latinum Etymologicum*. Bonn: A. Marci, 1855–1864.

Waardenburg, J. *L'Islam dans le miroir de l'Occident*. 3d ed. Paris: Mouton, 1970.

Wales, H. G. Quaritch. *Siamese State Ceremonies: Their History and Function*. London: B. Quaritch, 1931.

Wallace, J. "Islamic Arms and Armour." *Discovering Antiques* 23 (1993): 548–552.

Wansbrough, John. *Quranic Studies*. Oxford: Oxford University Press, 1977.

Wansharīsī, Aḥmad b. Yaḥyā. *al-Miʿyār al-muʿrib: Wa al-jāmiʿ al-mughrib ʿan fatāwā ʿulamāʾ Ifrīqiya wa al-Andalus wa al-Maghrib*. Ed. Muḥammad Ḥajjī. Beirut: Dār al-Maghrib al-Islāmī, 1981.

Wāqidī, Muḥammad b. ʿUmar. *Kitāb al-maghāzī*. Ed. Marsden Jones. Oxford: Oxford University Press, 1966.

Ward, Philip. *Travels in Oman: On the Track of the Early Explorers*. Cambridge: Oleander Press, 1987.

Warshaw, Matt. *Above the Roar: 50 Surfer Interviews*. Santa Cruz, Calif.: Waterhouse, 1997.

Wasserstrom, Steven. *Between Muslim and Jew: The Problem of Symbiosis under Early Islam*. Princeton: Princeton University Press, 1995.

Wasserstrom, Steven. *Religion after Religion: Gershom Scholem, Mircea Eliade, and Henry Corbin at Eranos*. Princeton: Princeton University Press, 1999.

Watson, P. J. *Archaeological Ethnography in Western Iran*. Tucson: University of Arizona Press, 1979.

Watt, William Montgomery, and M. V. McDonald, trans. *The History of al-Ṭabarī: Muḥammad at Mecca*. Albany: State University of New York Press, 1988.

Watt, William Montgomery. *Muḥammad at Medina*. Oxford: Clarendon, 1956.

Watters, T. *On Yuan Chwang's Travels in India, 629–645 A.D.* 2 vols. London: Royal Asiatic Society, 1904–1905.

Weil, Gustav. *The Bible, the Koran, and the Talmud; or, Biblical Legends of the Mussulmans*. London: Brown, Green, and Longmans, 1846.

Weil, Gustav. *Mohammed der Prophet*. Stuttgart: Metzler'schen Buchhandlung, 1843.

Weingrod, A. "Saints, Shrines, and Politics in Contemporary Israel." In *Religious Regimes and State-Formation: Perspectives from European Ethnology*, ed. E. R. Wolf, 73–83. Albany: State University of New York Press, 1991.

Weisbecker, Allan. *In Search of Captain Zero: A Surfer's Road Trip beyond the End of the Road*. New York: Jeremy P. Tarcher and Putnam, 2001.

Weiss, Bernard. *The Search for God's Law: Islamic Jurisprudence in the Writings of Sayf al-Dīn al-Āmidī*. Salt Lake City: University of Utah Press, 1992.

Weissbach, F. H., ed. *Babylonische Miscellen*. Leipzig: J. C. Hinrichs, 1930.

Weisser, Ursula, ed. and trans. *Kitāb al-ʿilal; or, Sirr al-khalīqah*. Aleppo: Maʿhad al-Turāth al-ʿIlmī al-ʿArabī, 1979. Reprinted as *Das "Buch über das Geheimnis der Schöpfung" von Pseudo-Apollonios von Tyana* (Berlin: W. de Gruyter, 1980).

Wellhausen, Julius. *Der arabische Josippon*. Berlin: Weidmannsche Buchhandlung, 1897.

Wellhausen, Julius. *Reste arabischen Heidentums: Gesammelt und Erläutert*. Berlin: G. Reimer, 1897; reprint, Berlin: W. de Gruyter, 1927.

Wells, L. S. A. "The Books of Adam and Eve." In *The Apocrypha and Pseudepigrapha of the Old Testament,* ed. R. H. Charles, 2:123–154. Oxford: Clarendon Press, 1913.

Wendell, Charles. "Baghdād: *Imago Mundi,* and Other Foundation Lore." *International Journal of Middle East Studies* 2 (1971): 119–120.

Wensinck, Arent Jan. "Arabic New Year and the Feast of Tabernacles." *Uitgave van de Koninklijke Akademie van Wetenschappen te Amsterdam* 25 (1925).

Wensinck, Arent Jan. "Die Entstehung der muslimischen Reinheitsgesetzgebung." *Der Islam* 5 (1914): 62–80.

Wensinck, Arent Jan. *A Handbook of Early Muhammadan Tradition.* 7 vols. Leiden: E. J. Brill, 1927.

Wensinck, Arent Jan. "Der Herkunft der gesetzlichen Bestimmungen die Reinigung (istinjāʾ oder istitāba) betreffend." *Der Islam* 1 (1910): 101–102.

Wensinck, Arent Jan. "The Ideas of the Western Semites Concerning the Navel of the Earth." *Verhandelingen der Koninklijke Akademie van Wetenschappen te Amsterdam,* Afdeling Letterkunde, n.s., 17, no. 1 (1916); reprint, Amsterdam: J. Müller, 1917.

Wensinck, Arent Jan. *Mohammed en de Joden te Medina*. Leiden: E. J. Brill, 1908.

Wensinck, Arent Jan. "The Ocean in the Literature of the Western Semites." *Verhandelingen der Koninklijke Akademie van Wetenschappen te Amsterdam,* Afdeling Letterkunde, n.s., 19, no. 2 (1918).

Wensinck, Arent Jan. "Some Semitic Rites of Mourning and Religion: Studies on Their Origin and Mutual Relation." *Verhandelingen der Koninklijke Akademie van Wetenschappen te Amsterdam,* Afdeling Letterkunde, n.r., 18, no. 1 (1918); reprint, Amsterdam: J. Müller, 1917.

Wensinck, Arent Jan. "Tree and Bird as Cosmological Symbols in Western Asia." *Uitgave van de Koninklijke Akademie van Wetenschappen te Amsterdam*, vol. 22 (1921).

Wensinck, Arent Jan, and J. Jomier. "Kaʿba." In *Encyclopaedia of Islam,* 2d ed., ed. H. A. R. Gibb and others, 4:317–322. Leiden: E. J. Brill, 1960–2002.

Wensinck, Arent Jan, and R. Paret. "Kaynukā‘." In *Encyclopaedia of Islam,* 2d ed., ed. H. A. R. Gibb and others, 4:824. Leiden: E. J. Brill, 1960–2002.

Wessman, V. E. V. *Förteckning över Sägentyperna.* Helsinki: Svenska Litteratursällskapets i Finland Förlag, 1931.

Westermarck, Edward. *Pagan Survivals in Muhammadan Civilization.* London: Macmillan and Co., 1933.

Westermarck, Edward. *Ritual and Belief in Morocco.* London: Macmillan and Co., 1926.

Westwood, J. *Albion: A Guide to Legendary Britain.* Salem: Salem House, 1985.

Wetzel, Friedrich. *Islamische Grabbauten in Indien aus der Zeit der Soldatenkaiser 1320–1540.* Leipzig: J. C. Hinrichs, 1918.

Wetzstein, J. G. *Reisebericht über Hauran und die Trachonen.* Berlin: D. Reimer, 1860.

Wheatley, Paul. *The City as Symbol.* London: H. K. Lewis, 1969.

Wheatley, Paul. *The Pivot of the Four Quarters: A Preliminary Enquiry into the Origins and Character of the Ancient Chinese City.* Chicago: University of Chicago Press, 1971.

Wheatley, Paul. *The Places Where Men Pray Together.* Chicago: University of Chicago Press, 2001.

Wheeler, Brannon. "al-Anbiyā’ al-‘arabīyah wa qubūr al-jabābirah." *al-Nashra* 30 (Spring 2004): 19–23.

Wheeler, Brannon. *Applying the Canon in Islam: Authorization and Maintenance of Interpretive Reasoning in Ḥanafī Scholarship.* Albany: State University of New York Press, 1996.

Wheeler, Brannon. *Moses in the Quran and Islamic Exegesis.* London: Curzon, 2002.

"Wicked Witchery." *Limited Edition: Oxford Times,* October 2003.

Widengren, Geo. *The Ascension of the Apostle and the Heavenly Book: King and Saviour 3.* Uppsala Universitets Årsskrift 1950:7. Uppsala: Lundequistska Bokhandeln, 1950.

Widengren, Geo. *The Great Vohu Mana and the Apostle of God.* Uppsala Universitets Årsskrift 1951:4. Uppsala: Lundequistska Bokhandeln, 1945.

Widengren, Geo. *The King and the Tree of Life in Ancient Near Eastern Religion: King and Saviour 4.* Uppsala Universitets Årsskrift 1951:4. Uppsala: Lundequistska Bokhandeln, 1951.

Widengren, Geo. *Mespotamian Elements in Manichaeism:* King and Saviour 2. Uppsala Universitets Årsskrift 1946:3. Uppsala: Lundequistska Bokhandeln, 1946.

Widengren, Geo. *Muhammad, the Apostle of God, and His Ascension: King and Saviour 5.* Uppsala Universitets Årsskrift 1951:4. Uppsala: Lundequistska Bokhandeln, 1955.

Widengren, Geo. *Religionens värld: Religionsfenomenologiska studier och översikter.* Stockholm: Svenska Kyrkans Diakonistyrelses, 1952. Trans. into German by Rosemarie Elgnowski as *Religionsphänomenologie* (Berlin: de Gruyter, 1969).

Widengren, Geo. *Sakrales Königtum im Alten Testament und im Judentum.* Stuttgart: Kohlhammer, 1955.

Wiegand, Theodor. *Sinai.* Berlin: Wissenschaftlichen Veröffentlichungen des Deutsch Türkish Denkmalschutz-Kommandos, 1920.

Wiet, G. "Notes d'epigraphie syro-musulmane." *Syria* 5 (1924): 216–253.

Wilding, R. "The Ancient Buildings of the North Kenya Coast." *Plan East Africa* 2 (1971): 41–46.

Wilhelm, G. A. "Excavations at Tell Khirbet Salih." In *Tell Karrana 3: Tell Jikan, Tell Khirbet Salih,* ed. G. Wilhelm and C. Zaccagnini, 261–262. Mainz: Philipp von Zabern, 1993.

Wilken, G. A. *Über das Haaropfer und einige andere Trauergebräuche bei den Völkern Indonesiens.* Amsterdam: J. H. de Bussy, 1886–1887.

Wilkinson, J., trans. *Jerusalem Pilgrims before the Crusades.* Warminster: Aris and Phillips, 1977; and Jerusalem: Ariel, 1977.

William, Ellis. *Narrative of a Tour of Hawaii; or, Owhyhee, with Remarks on the History, Traditions, Manners, Customs and Language of the Inhabitants of the Sandwich Islands.* London: H. Fiser and P. Jackson, 1826.

Williams, Caroline. "The Cult of ʿAlid Saints in the Fatimid Monuments of Cairo." Pt. 1, "The Mosque of al-Aqmar"; pt. 2, "The Mausolea." *Muqarnas* 1 (1983): 37–60.

Williams, Charles. *Oriental Affinities of the Legend of the Hairy Anchorite.* Urbana: University of Illinois Press, 1925–1926.

Wilson, Thomas H.. "Swahili Funerary Architecture of the North Kenya Coast." In *Swahili Houses and Tombs of the Coast of Kenya,* by James de Vere Allen and Thomas H. Wilson, Art and Archaeology Research Papers. London: AARP, 1979.

Wilson, Thomas H. "Takwa: An Ancient Swahili Settlement of the Lamu Archipelago." *Kenya Past and Present* 10 (1979): 6–16.

Wink, A. *al-Hind: The Making of the Indo-Islamic World.* Leiden: E. J. Brill, 1990.

Winnett, F. V., and G. Lankester Harding. *Inscriptions from Fifty Safaitic Cairns.* Toronto: University of Toronto Press, 1978.

Wittek, P. "Aywansary." *Annales de l'Histoire de Philosophie et d'Histoire Orientales et Slaves* (1951): 505–510.

Witzel, M. *Perlen sumerischen Poesie.* Keilinschriftliche Studien 5. Fulda: Verlag des Verfassers für den Buchhandel, 1925.

Wolters, Albert M. "Apocalyptic and the Copper Scroll." *Journal of Near Eastern Studies* 19 (1990): 145–154.

Wolters, Albert M. "History and the Copper Scroll." *Annals of the New York Academy of Sciences* 722 (1994): 285–298.

Wood, J. *Giants and Dwarfs*. London: Bentley, 1868.

Wu Wenliang. *Religious Inscriptions in Quanzhou*. Quanzhou, 1957.

Wüstenfeld, Ferdinand. *Genealogische Tabellen der arabischen Stämme und Familien.* 2 vols. Göttingen: Deiterich, 1852–1853.

Wüstenfeld, Ferdinand. *Register zu den genealogischen Tabellen der arabischen Stämme und Familien*. Göttingen: Dieterichschen Buchhandlung, 1853.

Yaʿari, Avraham. *Maṣṣaʿot ereẓ Yisraʾel shel ʿolim Yehudim mi-yemei ha Beinayim ve-ʿad reshit yemei shivat Ziyon*. Ramat-Gan: Masadah, 1976.

Yadin, Y. *The Temple Scroll.* 3 vols. Jerusalem: Israel Exploration Society, 1977–1983.

Yahuda, A. S.. "A Muslim Tradition about the Location of Moses' Grave." *Ha-Doar* 30 (1941): 14–15. Reprinted in *Ever ve ʿArav* (New York: ʿOgen, 1946), 283–288.

Yang Hongzun. "A Preliminary Discussion on the Building Year of Quanzhou Holy Tomb and the Authenticity of Its Legend." In *The Islamic Historic Relics in Quanzhou,* ed. Committee for Protecting Islamic Historical Relics in Quanzhou and the Research Centre for the Historical Relics of Chinese Culture. Quanzhou, 1985.

Yaʿqūbī, Aḥmad b. Abī Yaʿqūb. *Taʾrīkh al-Yaʿqūbī.* Ed. ʿAbd al-Amīr Muhannā. Beirut: Dār Sadr, 1993.

Yāqūt, Abū ʿAbdallāh. *Muʿjam al-buldān.* Beirut: Dār Iḥyāʾ al-Turāth al-ʿArabī, 1979.

Yeivin, S. *First Preliminary Report on the Excavations at Tel 'Gat' (Tell Sheykh Ahmed el-'Areyny): Seasons 1956–1958*. Jerusalem: Gat Expedition, 1961.

Yonge, D. *The Roman History of Ammianus Marcellinus*. London: G. Bell and Sons, 1902.

Young, Robert, and Rod Holmes. *The History of Surfing*. 2d ed. Angourie: Palm Beach Press, 1994.

Yücel, Ünsal. *Islamic Swords and Swordsmiths.* Istanbul: Research Centre for Islamic History, Art and Culture, 2001. Trans. into Arabic by Taḥsayn ʿAmr Tahaoglu as *al-Suyūf al-islāmīyah wa ṣannāʿu-hā* (Kuwait: Munazzamat al-Muʾtamar al-Islāmī, 1988).

Yule, Henry, and A. C. Burnell. *Hobson-Jobson: A Glossary of Colloquial Anglo-Indian Words and Phrases.* 2d ed. New Delhi: Rupa and Co., 1986.

Yūnīnī, Mūsā b, Muḥammad. *Dhayl mirʾāt al-zamām*. Hyderabad: Majlis Dāʾirat al-Maʿārif al-ʿUthmānīyah, 1954–1961.

Zabīdī, Muḥammad Murtaḍā. *Tāj al-ʿarūs min jawāhir al-qāmūs.* Kuwait: Maṭbaʿat Ḥukūmat al-Kuwayt, 1965.

Zāhirī, Khalīl. *Zubda kashf al-mamālik: Tableau politique et administratif de l'Égypte,*

*de la Syrie et du Hidjâz sous la domination des sultans mamloûks du XIIIe au XVe siècle.* Ed. Ravaisse. Paris: E. Leroux, 1894.
Zajadacz-Hastenrath, Salome. *Chaukhandigräber: Studien sur Grabkunst in Sind und Baluchistan.* Wiesbaden: Steiner, 1978. Trans. Michael Robertson as *Chaukhandi Tombs: Funerary Art in Sind and Baluchistan* (Karachi: Oxford University Press, 2003).
Zajadacz-Hastenrath, Salome. "Islamic Funerary Enclosures in Sind." *Islamic Art* 4 (1992).
Zaki, A. R. "Centres of Islamic Sword Making in Middle Ages." *Bulletin de l'Institut d'Egypte* 38 (1955–1956): 285–295.
Zaki, A. R. "Introduction to the Study of Islamic Arms and Armour." *Gladius* 1 (1961): 17–29.
Zaki, A. R. "Islamic Armour: An Introduction." *Gladius* 2 (1963): 69–74.
Zaki, A. R. "Islamic Swords in Middle Ages." *Bulletin de l'Institut d'Egypte* 36 (1954): 365–397.
Zaky, ʿA. "Baʿḍ qaṭʿa al-islaḥah al-islāmīyah fī Istānbūl." *al-Muqataṭaf* 97 (April 1940): 393–397.
Zamakhsharī, Abū al-Qāsim Maḥmūd b. ʿUmar. *al-Kashshāf ʿan ḥaqāʾiq ghawāmiḍ al-tanzīl wa ʿuyūn al-aqāwīl fī wujūh al-taʾwīl.* Ed. Muḥammad ʿAbd al-Salām Shāhīn. 5 vols. Beirut: Dār al-Kutub al-ʿIlmīyah, 1995.
Zannad, Traki. *Les lieux du corps en Islam.* Paris: Publisud, 1994.
Zarrūq, Aḥmad b. Aḥmad. *Sharḥ ʿalā matn al-Risālah.* Beirut: Dār al-Fikr, 1982.
Zawadowski, G. "Note sur l'origine magique de Dhou-Faqar." *En Terre d'Islam* 1 (1943): 36–40.
Zayd b. ʿAlī. *Majmuʿ al-fiqh.* Ed. E. Griffini. Milan, 1949.
Zaytūn, M. Maḥmūd. *al-Qabbārī zāhid al-Iskandariyya.* Cairo: Dār al-Maʿārif, 1968.
Zayyāt, Ḥabīb. "Adyār Dimashq wa burru-hā fī al-Islām." *al-Mashriq* 43 (1949): 80–97.
Zeitlin, Solomon. "The Dead Sea Scrolls." Pt. 1, "The Lamech Scroll: A Medieval Midrash"; pt. 2, "The Copper Scrolls"; pt. 3, "Was Kando the Owner of the Scrolls?" *Jewish Quarterly Review,* n.s., 47 (1956–1957): 245–268.
Zelenin, D. K. *Kul't ongonov v Sibiri.* Moscow: Izd-vo Akademii nauk SSSR, 1936. Trans. into French by G. Welter as *La culte des idoles en Sibérie* (Paris: Payot, 1952).
Zelenin, D. K. "Tabu slov u narodov vostochnoi Evropy: Severnoi Azii." *Sbornik Muzeia antropologii i etnografii* (Leningrad) 8 (1929): 1–144.
Zerubavel, Yael. *Recovered Roots: Collective Memory and the Making of Israeli National Tradition.* Chicago: University of Chicago Press, 1995.
Zhi Cheng. "'Fanke mu' ji qi qouguan wen ti shitan" [A tentative inquiry into "bar-

barian guests' graves" and related problems]. In *Symposium on Quanzhou Islam*, ed. Quanzhou Maritime Museum. Quanzhou: Quanzhou Maritime Museum, 1985.

Zolotarev, A. M. "The Bear Festival of the Oltcha." *American Anthropologist* 39 (1939): 113–130.

Zurqānī, Muḥammad b. ʿAbd al-Bāqī. *Sharḥ al-Zurqānī ʿalā Muwaṭṭaʾ al-Imām Mālik.* Beirut: Dār al-Kutub al-ʿIlmīyah, 1990.

# *General Index*

Atlas, 28
ʿAwj, 115
Aws b. Aws al-Thaqafī, 89
Awzāʿī, 59, 77
Ayan Evenk, 9
Ayātallāh Khomeinī (d. 1989), 59, 60, 68
Ayn Silwān, 102
Ayub Paigambar, 102
ʿAyyanah b. Ḥism al-Fazārī, 40
Ayyubid, 74, 88
Azitawadda of Adana, 27
Azraqī, Muḥammad b. ʿAbdallāh (d. 921), 19, 24, 26, 28

Baʿalbek, 90
Bābāk b. Sāsān, 25
Babur, 91
Babylon, 27, 41
Babylonian Talmud, 22
Badawī, Sayyid Aḥmad, 79
Badr, 33, 34, 35, 38, 39
Badr al-Jamālī, 87
Baghdad, 77
Bahrain, 26, 118
Bahrām Chobin, 42
Bahubal, 74
Bakkah, 110
Balaam b. Beor, 116
Balādhūrī, Aḥmad b. Yaḥyā (d. 892), 102
Balawīyah, 73
Banū Hāshim, 34
Banū Hilāl, 110
Banū Ibrāhīm, 90
Banū Qaynuqāʿ, 38–39
Banū Qurayẓah, 38–39
banners, 33, 81
Baqāʿa Valley, 102, 106
barakah, 72
Bar-Kokhba, 23
2 Baruch, 22
Bashan, 116
Basrah, 77
bastards, 126
Battār, 33–39
Bavanni, 107, 108
Bayḍāʾ, 34, 37
Bayt al-Maʿmūr, 85
Bear, 244n29
beards, 55, 64, 102
bears, 2, 5–10, 11, 14, 130
Bedouin, 100
Bengal, 99
Bent, Theodore (d. 1897), 100, 106
Bernard the Monk, 117
Bhīamāla, 42
Bible, 13, 17, 21–22, 29, 43, 112
*Big Wednesday*, 244n29
Bilāl b. Hamāmah, 89
Bilāl b. Rabāh, 92
Bilqis, 88
Birmawī, 89
Bīrūnī, Muḥammad b. Aḥmad (d. 1048), 26, 31, 32
bīt Akītu, 25
bleeding, 60, 65
blood, 1, 29, 52, 56, 58, 59, 125, 177n25
bows, 6, 33, 34, 37, 81, 172n205
Branch Davidians, 131
Britain, 112
British government, 91, 106
British travelers, 103
bronze, 23, 26, 111, 148–49n28
Buddha, 14, 96, 97, 109, 120
Buddhism, 24, 97, 131; monuments of, 109; relics of, 89
Buddhist traditions, 14
Bukhārī, Muḥammad b. Ismāʿīl (d. 870), 32, 33, 34–35, 36, 40, 63, 72, 102, 216n22
Bulqīnī, 32
Burckhardt, John Lewis (d. 1817), 103, 104
Burton, Richard (d. 1890), 118, 197n57
Busrah bt. Sufwān, 48, 49, 50, 52, 53, 54
Byzantium, 27, 29, 42

Cain, 88, 103
cairns, 101, 118, 119, 214n12, 234n151
Cairo, 37, 74, 79, 87, 90, 96, 210n1
Caleb, 116
caliphs, 26, 27, 41, 42, 72, 78
Cambodia, 158n86
camel, 3–5, 10–11, 12, 26, 33, 61, 62, 78, 106
Castagné, Joseph, 102, 118
cattle, 9, 61
Cave of Blood, 103

Cave of Treasure, 15, 24, 105
Cave of Treasures, 23
Central Asia, 2, 17, 101, 102, 106, 108, 109, 224n72
Chalcolithic period, 23
chaos, 43
chiefs, 24, 26, 116
chieftains, 5, 8, 28
China, 23, 29, 30, 31, 32, 108, 224n72
Christianity, 13, 129; sites of, 93, 117; texts of, 22, 23
Christians, 22, 91, 103
1 Chronicles (20:4–8), 116
Chukchi, 8
Cimon, 111
circumambulation, 26, 101
City of the Dead, 210n1
clothes, 84
clothing, 4, 9, 10, 12, 62, 64, 65, 66, 71, 84, 85, 86, 97, 99, 101, 130, 178n33, 184n86, 185n104
Coelo-Syria, 103
coffins, 82, 96, 103, 104, 111
Combs-Schilling, M. E., 241n2
Constantinople, 78
contagion, 69–70
copper, 7, 23
Copper Scroll (3Q15), 23
Coptic, 23, 90
Corbin, Henry, 136n3
corpses, 48, 56, 68, 125, 192n3
cosmos, 171n203
Cousens, Henry, 108, 109
crescent, 26
Crooke, W. (d. 1923), 102, 107–8, 119
crowns, 23
Crusader, 88, 89
Cunningham, Alexander (d. 1893), 102, 106–7, 108, 119
curiosity shops, 14
Curzon, Lord G. N. (d. 1925), 103, 105

Dabbāgh, ʿAbd al-Raḥmān b. Muḥammad (d. 1300), 73
Dabbat al-Arḍ, 117
Ḍaḥḥāk, 82
Dāhir, 42
Daḥya al-Kalbī, 89
Dajjāl, 40, 86, 117
Damarmenus, 111–12
Damascus, 73, 74, 78, 79, 80, 88, 90, 96, 103, 213n7
Daniar, 102
Daniel, 41, 91, 102, 117
Dār al-ʿAdl, 88
dār al-ḥadīth, 80, 88
Dār al-Ḥadīth al-Ashrafiyah, 80
Dār al-Ḥarb, 127
Dār al-Islām, 12, 127
Dār al-Nadwah, 28
Dār al-Ṣilāḥ, 37
Dār al-Tābūt, 37
Daraya, 88
Dargah, 119
dates, 61, 62
David, 39, 40, 41, 81, 82, 89, 116
Day of Judgment, 117
Deccan, 119
defecation, 58, 69, 70
Delphi, 79, 111–12
Denmark, 232n136
desert, 86
Deuteronomy (2:10, 2:20–21), 116
Dhahabī, Muḥammad b. ʿUthmān (d. 1348), 32, 33, 34, 36, 37, 79, 89
dhakar, 49
dharma-kaya, 96
dharmarājikā, 96
Dhāt al-Fuḍūl, 34
Dhāt al-Ḥawāshī, 38
Dhāt al-Wishāḥ, 38, 40
Dhofar, 103, 104
Dhū al-Faqār, 33–39
Dhū al-Qarnayn, 27
Dhū al-Shāra, 29
Dhū Jadan, 42
dinars, 85, 91
dinosaurs, 112
Diodorus Siculus, 111, 229n110
Dionysius, 120
divination, 9
dogs, 8, 54
Dome of the Rock, 105, 195–96nn43–44
Don Valley, 112
Doughty, Charles (d. 1926), 104, 110
Douglas, Mary, 14, 124, 128–30

dreams, 29, 67
Duke Paoa Hahanamoku, 244n26
Dumont, Louis, 124
Dun Cow, 112
Durkheim, Emile, 3, 128
Dushara, 26

East Asia, 2
eating, 59, 60, 70
Eber, 100, 113, 115
Edfou, 208n147
Egil, 112
Egypt, 14, 29, 45, 76, 77, 79, 91, 112, 113, 157–58n86
Egyptians, 83
eight-legged lamb, 93, 94
ejaculation, 56, 60, 64, 66, 67, 185n103, 188n122
Eleh ha-massaʿot, 103
Elijah, 22, 121
Emim, 116
Emīr Ṣārim al-Dīn al-Nābulsī, 89
Enki, 14, 44, 45
Enlil, 153n63
Enoch, 43
2 Enoch, 23
Enosh, 114
entrails, 8
Epiphanius, 156n77
Eretria, 111
Eridu, 44
Eskimo, 8
Euboea, 111
Eucherius, 117
Eudoxia, 157n85
Europe, 14, 17, 27, 31, 99, 101, 232n136
Eusebius, 23
Evans-Pritchard, E. E., 137n10
Eve, 15, 23, 47, 56–58, 62, 63–67, 69, 71, 84, 85–87, 95, 97, 104, 105, 119
Evenk, 8
Ezekiel (40–42), 28
Ezra, 89, 121

faḍāʾil, 88
Faḍālah b. ʿUbayd, 89
Faḥl, 92
Faqṭash, 40–41
farj, 49, 52
fars al-ghāzī, 61
Farwa b. ʿUmayr al-Judhamī, 92
fasting, 47, 59–61, 63, 70
Fatḥ Khān, 79
Fāṭimah, 34, 91
Faṭimah bint Maimūn, 108
Fatimid, 34, 42, 87, 88, 165n145
fatwā, 79, 90
Fayrūz, 42
feathers, 57
feces, 55, 177n24
feet, 80
Fez, 79
Fiḍḍah, 34, 38
fingernails, 57, 58, 84, 94, 95, 178n33
fire, 56, 68, 69, 80, 109
Firestone, Reuven, 145n11
Fīrūzābādī, Muḥammad b. Yaʿqūb (d. 1415), 31
Fīrūz Shāh Rajab, 79
flags, 33
flood, 69, 115, 117
folklore, 17, 112
food, 9, 29, 62, 64, 66, 68, 84, 86, 132. *See also individual foods*
footprints, 71, 78–80, 90, 95, 99
fornication, 24
frankincense, 23
Frazer, J. G. 140n27
freeze-dried cat, 93, 94
Freud, Sigmund, 69–70
fundamentalism, 131
fuṣlān, 62

Gabriel, 35, 36, 44, 57, 78, 84
Gad, 92
Galsad, 101
gas, 52, 55, 60, 177n24
Gawr Mosque, 79
Gaza, 116, 117
gazelles, 11, 19–47
Gea, 111
gems, 26
Genesis: (10:22–24) 113, (5) 114, (11:10–31, 25:7) 115, (6:1–4) 117, (2:16, 3:15, 4:4) 183n16
Genesis Rabbah, 23

genitalia, 47–70; of hermaphrodite, 49; severed, 48
genitals, 84; of animals, 52, 53, 55; of corpse, 55; of youth, 53, 55
Gentile, 38, 44
Gether, 114
Ghassānid, 36
ghāzī, 99, 107, 117
Ghumdān, 42
Ghur al-Safi, 91
ghusl, 47, 125
Gilyak, 6
gnosticism, 131
goats, 118
gold, 19, 23, 25, 26, 41, 61, 63, 113, 151n45
Goliath, 39, 116
Gospel, 90
grass, 62, 66
Greece, 115
Greek language, 31
Greek legends, 4, 28, 103
Greek sources, 17, 110–12, 120
Grottanelli, C., 157n86
Gudea, 27
guffaws, 55
Gurjarra, 42
Guy of Warwick, Sir, 112

ḥadath, 57
Hadbeen, 104
Ḥaḍḍāḍ, Abū Bakr b. ʿAlī (d. 1398), 62
ḥadīth, 12, 15, 32, 34, 45, 63, 68, 69, 70, 71, 75–78, 80, 83, 88, 95, 96, 97, 99, 105, 110, 117, 121
Ḥaḍramawt, 101, 113, 118, 210n1
Ḥaḍramī, 26
Hagar, 19
Haiawatha, 209n161
Ḥāʾil, 226n91
hair, 10, 12, 64, 65, 71–75, 80, 81, 89, 90, 95, 97, 105, 125, 185n104, 192n3, 192–93n7, 193n9
ḥajar al-rukn, 24, 28
ḥajj, 12, 47
Ḥalabī, ʿAlī b. Burhān al-Dīn (d. 1635), 85, 101
Ḥalabī, Quṭb al-Dīn, 79
Hallowell, Irving, 8
Ham, 89
Hama, 88, 89
Ḥamād b. Ibrāhīm, 54
ḥammām, 60
Hammurabi, 27
Han, 23
Handala, 119
ḥaram, 25, 64
Ḥaram al-Sharīf, 88
Harapa, 107
Harawī, ʿAlī b. Abī Bakr, (d. 1215), 95, 103
Ḥārith b. ʿUmayr al-Azdī, 92
Ḥārith b. Shamr, 37
Ḥasanayn Mosque, 89
Ḥasan b. ʿAlī, 68
Hasan Muarif Ambary, 108
Hashemite Kingdom, 91, 96
Hasik, 104
Ḥatf, 33–39
Hawaii, 130, 131
ḥawṭah, 231n151
Hawting, G. R., 20–24, 29
head, 8, 34, 38, 39, 87, 93, 94, 102, 228n108
Hebrew, 4, 103
Hebron, 89, 117
Hellenistic sources, 14
henna, 186n109
Heracles, 111, 112
Heraclius, 42
hermaphrodite, 49
Hermes, 103
Hermetical tradition, 24
Hesiod, 138n17
ḥijāba, 28
Ḥijāz, 76, 104
Hijrah, 34
Ḥimṣ, 73, 96
Ḥimyarī, 42
Hindu architecture, 107, 109
Ḥirāʾ, 85
Ḥirār b. al-Aqwar, 92
Hishām b. ʿAmr al-Taghlibī, 42
Hittites, 116
Hocart, A. M., 208n148
Holy Land, 95, 99, 115, 116, 117, 121
Holy Sepulchre, 236n157
honey, 62, 183n80
Hopladamos, 111

horns, 26, 118
horses, 26, 61, 81, 118
Horus, 14, 110
Hosea, 103
Hud, 12, 88, 91, 100–101, 110, 113, 114, 116, 118, 119, 131, 152n52
Hudson's Bay, 8
Ḥughr b. ʿAdī, 89
Hul, 114
hula girls, 244n26
Ḥulwān, 31
Ḥumaymah, 92
ḥumlān, 62
hunting, 2, 5–10, 14, 25, 26, 130
Hurmuz, 42
Ḥusayn b. ʿAlī, 27, 37, 68, 87, 89, 91, 95
Ḥusayn Mosque, 37, 87

ʿibādāt, 127
Ibn ʿAbbās, 35, 44, 57, 58, 60, 64, 82, 84, 105, 112, 117
Ibn Abī al-Dunyā, 41
Ibn Abī al-Ḥadīd, 79
Ibn Abī Burdah, 41
Ibn Abī Ḥātim, ʿAbd al-Raḥmān (d. 939), 76
Ibn Abī Laylā, 62
Ibn Abī Mālik, 68
Ibn Abī Zayd al-Qayrawānī, 53, 66
Ibn al-Athīr, Abū al-Ḥasan ʿAlī (d. 1233), 33
Ibn al-Faqīh (fl. 903), 110
Ibn al-Ḥawrānī, ʿUthmān b. Aḥmad (d. 1705), 80, 88, 103
Ibn al-Jawzī, ʿAbd al-Raḥmān b. ʿAlī b. Muḥammad (d. 1201), 38, 41, 116
Ibn al-Kalbī, 25, 29
Ibn al-Mubārak, 62
Ibn al-Zaman, 73
Ibn ʿAnaq, 115
Ibn ʿArabī, 218n33
Ibn ʿAsākir, ʿAlī b. Abī Muḥammad al-Ḥasan (d. 1176), 105
Ibn ʿAṭīyah, 84
Ibn Bābūyah, Muḥammad b. ʿAlī (d. 991), 60, 64
Ibn Fāris al-Qazwīnī, 33
Ibn Ḥajar, Aḥmad b. Nūr al-Dīn ʿAlī (d. 1448), 34, 72, 79
Ibn Ḥanbal, Aḥmad (d. 856), 35, 44, 59, 72, 121
Ibn Ḥazm, ʿAlī b. Aḥmad (d. 1064), 37
Ibn Hishām, ʿAbd al-Mālik (d. 834), 19
Ibn Isḥāq, Muḥammad (d. 768), 19, 38, 41, 64
Ibn Jubayr, Muḥammad b. Aḥmad (d. 1217), 103
Ibn Kathīr, ʿImād al-Dīn Ismāʿīl (d. 1373), 26, 33, 35, 44, 57, 84, 89, 105, 114, 116
Ibn Khaldūn, Abū al-Raḥmān b. Muḥammad (d. 1382), 132
Ibn Khallikān, Aḥmad b. Muḥammad (d. 1282), 90
Ibn Khurradādhbih, 31
Ibn Mājah, Muḥammad b. Yazīd (d. 887), 32, 33, 36, 63, 65, 73
Ibn Mālik, 89
Ibn Manẓūr, Muḥammad b. Mukarram (d. 1312), 30
Ibn Qayyim al-Jawzīyah, 89
Ibn Qudāmah, ʿAbdallāh b. Aḥmad (d. 1223), 53, 60, 65, 66, 68, 69, 89
Ibn Rajab, 89
Ibn Rushd, Abū al-Walīd Muḥammad b. Aḥmad (d. 1126), 50, 51, 52, 53, 61, 64, 65, 67, 68, 69
Ibn Saʿd, Aḥmad, (ca. 784–845), 19, 33
Ibn Shahrāshūb, Abū ʿAbdallāh Muḥammad (d. 1192), 36, 44
Ibn Sīrīn, 32
Ibn Suhayl, 34
Ibn Taymīyah, Aḥmad (d. 1328), 51, 52, 69, 80
Ibn Ṭūlūn, 90
Ibn ʿUmar, 19, 44, 59, 64
Ibn Zayd, 57
Ibrāhīm b. Abī al-Mahājir, 110
Ibrāhīm b. al-Mahdī, 42
Iceland, 232n136
Idas, 112
idols, 3, 36–37
Idris, 12, 113, 121
Idrīsī, Muḥammad b. Muḥammad (d. 1165), 31
ifḍāʾ, 50
ihlāl, 72, 73
iḥrām, 64

Ikhshīdid, 73
ʿIkrimah, 25, 34, 82, 84, 92
Iliad, 111
implements, 8, 11, 21, 33, 44, 71, 86
ʿImrān, 104
Imruʾ al-Qays, 137n13
Inanna, 44
incense, 22, 83
Inder, 112
India, 30–31, 57, 83, 86, 89, 91, 99, 102, 105, 109, 115, 119, 124, 160n100
Indian sources, 96, 127
Indus, 102
*In God's Hands*, 244n29
Ingrams, W. H. (d. 1897), 100–101, 106
instruments, 80
Intichiuma, 128
Iram dhat al-ʿImād, 113
Iran, 11, 25, 28, 29, 43, 76
Iraq, 31, 43, 76, 89, 95
iron, 43, 44, 83, 84, 85
Iroquois, 14, 97
ʿĪsā b. ʿAbdallāh, 40
ʿĪsā b. Abī Jaʿfar al-Manṣūr, 42
Isḥāq b. Ibrāhīm, 53
Ishmael, 19, 24, 26, 46, 101, 114, 152n52
Ismāʿīl b. Muḥammad, 48
Ismāʿīl b. Muḥammad b. Saʿd, 49, 50–51, 53
Ismāʿīlī, 36
Isrāʾ, 78
Israel, 91
Israelites, 11, 12, 22, 29, 37–39, 40, 41, 57, 82, 84, 91, 99, 115, 116, 117, 121
Issachar, 230n121
istaka-nyasa, 109
Istanbul, 34, 79, 80, 90
iʿtikāf, 129
ivory, 23
Iyomante, 141n35
izār, 72

jabābirah, 110, 115
Jabal al-Akhḍar, 104
Jabal al-Minqār, 42
Jabal Hārūn, 104
Jabal Qara, 102
Jabartī, ʿAbd al-Raḥmān (d. 1825), 89
jabbār, 115
Jābir b. ʿAbdallāh, 68, 92
Jābir b. Samurah, 69
Jāburq, 40–41
Jādūr, 92
Jaʿfar al-Muqtadir, 27
Jaʿfar al-Ṣādiq, 36, 37, 89
Jaʿfar al-Ṭayyār, 89
Jaʿfar b. Abī Ṭālib, 92
Jaʿfar b. Khinzāb, 73
Jāḥiẓ, 152n55
Jake the alligator man, 93–94
Jalabad, 102
Jamʿ, 57
Janussan, 26
Japheth, 42
Jared, 114
jarḥ wa al-taʿdīl, 77
jars, 23
Jāsim, 114
Java, 99, 108
javelins, 81
Jawharī, 84
Jazirah, 77
Jebusites, 116
Jedda, 57, 104
Jerash, 91
Jeremiah, 21, 22, 23, 121
Jerome, 117
Jerusalem, 9, 22, 23, 30, 39, 41, 74, 75, 78, 80, 82, 88, 89, 102, 105
Jerusalem Talmud, 22
Jesus, 23, 38–40, 85, 86, 88, 92, 93, 96, 104, 117, 121, 218n33
jewelry, 7, 118
Jewish texts, 22, 23
Jewish tradition, 20, 21, 43
Jews, 37–39, 41, 89
Jhanjhana, 119
Jidda, 119
jihād, 126
jihād fī sabīl allāh, 82
Jinn, 34, 44
Job, 91, 102, 119, 120
John, 38, 39, 88, 92, 93, 218n33
Jonah, 89
Jordan, 91–93, 96, 103, 116, 118
Jordan River, 92, 96
*Jordan Times*, 208n157

madness, 55
Madrasah al-Dāmāghīya, 80
Madrasah al-Manjakīyah, 74
Maghrib, 41, 50, 79
Magi, 23
Mahalalel, 114
Mahdī, 78
mā'idah, 41
Maʿīn, 27
makam panjang, 108
Makroseiris, 111
Mālik al-Ashraf, 79, 80
Mālik b. Anas (d. 795), 48, 59, 60, 62, 65, 66, 67
Malik Ibrahim, 108
Malinowski, Bronislaw, 138–39n19
mallet, as tool of civilization sent to Adam, 83
Mamluk, 34, 88
manna, 82, 84, 178n32
Manṣūr, 42, 87
maqām, 89
maqām Ibrāhīm, 81
Mari, 27
Marj Qalʿah, 30
marshmallow, 64
Marsh's Free Museum, 93–94
Marwān b. al-Ḥakam b. Abī al-ʿĀsī, 49
Marwān b. Muḥammad, 41
Mary, 88, 104
mashhad, 87
Mashhad al-Ḥusaynī, 74
masjid, 127
Masjid al-Ḥusayn, 74
Masjid al-Jazzār Pasha, 74
Masjid al-Qadam, 78
Masjid Āthār al-Nabī, 79
masturbation, 48, 49, 51, 53, 54
Masʿūdī, Abū al-Ḥasan ʿAlī (d. 956), 25
Ma'thūr al-Fijār, 34–39
Maundevile, Sir John, 229n110
Māwardī, Abū al-Ḥasan ʿAlī (d. 1058), 127
Mayfaʿah, 93
Maymūnah bt. Saʿd, 60
Maysara b. Masrūq, 92
Mazar, 102
Mazar al-Shamali, 91
mazārāt, 89
Me, 14, 44–45
meat, 4, 26, 69
Medina, 73, 76, 77, 78, 81, 88, 118
Megalopolis, 110
Mekhilta de Rabbi Ishmael, 22
Memar Marqah, 22
menstruation, 56, 58, 59, 66, 84, 125, 186–87n110
metal, 25, 84, 97, 118
metallurgy, 44, 173n207
Methuselah, 114
Mezar Osho, 103
Middle East, 16, 17, 87, 90, 91, 101, 102
Middot, 28
Midian, 83, 230n121
Mikhdham, 33–39
Mina, 73
Minaean, 27
Mināh, 37
minbar, 81
Ministry of Religious Endowments, 91
Ministry of Tourism, 91
Mirʿāj, 78
mirrors, 14, 23, 40, 41, 81, 148–49n28
Misʿar b. Muhlahal, 30
Mishnah, 28
Mishrāf, 31
miṣr, 126, 127
Mistassini, 8
Moab, 116
Moabite Stone, 27
Mola Matar, 105
Mongol attacks, 108
monkey, 54
Morris, the freeze-dried cat, 93, 94
Moses, 38, 39, 81, 82–85, 87, 88, 89, 92, 104, 116, 117, 206n129
Mosul, 88
Mount Budh, 86
Mount of Olives, 85
Mount Qāsiyūn, 88, 103, 218n33
Mount Sinai, 85, 117
mouth, in questions of ablution, 55
Muʿādh b. Jabal, 92
muʿāmalāt, 127
Muʿāwiyah b. Abī Sufyān, 72, 87, 89, 92, 113
Muʿāwiyah, b. Hudayj, 73

Muḍāḍ b. ʿAmr, 24, 25
Muḍarī, 114
Mudrik, 89
Mughal India, 91
Muḥammad b. al-Qāsim al-Thaqafī, 108
Muḥammad b. Qays, 84
Muḥammad b. Saʿd b. Abī Waqqāṣ, 48
Muḥammad Nahār, 89
Muḥammad Shah, 107
Muʿizz, 87
Mujāhidīyah Madrasah, 79
Mujhāhid, 84
Mukarrib, 154–55n70
Mukawir, 91
*Mukhtaṣar*, 52
Muktafī, 27
Multan, 102, 107, 108, 118
Munabbih b. al-Ḥajjāj, 34
Muqātil b. Sulaymān (d. 767), 38, 101
Muqawqas, 90
Murshidī, Abū ʿAbdallāh Muḥammad b. Abī Bakr (d. 1435), 74
Murshidī, Abū Ḥamīd, 75
Murshidī, ʿUmar b. Muḥammad, 75
*Murūj al-dhahab*, 42
Musʿab, 49, 55
Muscat, 104
musk, 27
Muslim, Muḥammad b. al-Ḥajjāj (d. 875), 35, 63, 69, 72
Mustanṣir, 27
Muʾtah, 92
Muʿtaṣim, 26
Mutawakkil, 42
Muṭṭalibī, 42
*Muwaṭṭaʾ*, 48, 49
Muẓaffar, 89
Muzaffargarh, 108
Muzaffarnagar, 119
Muzanī, Ibrāhīm (d. 878), 52, 53
Muzdalifah, 57
Mycenaean tombs. *See* tholoi
myrrh, 23, 83

nabʿ, 34
Nabataean gods, 29
Nabataean sites, 104, 214n12
Nabīh b. al-Ḥajjāj b. Āmir al-Sahmī, 35
Nabonidus, 27
Nabt, 24
Nābulsī, ʿAbd al-Ghanī b. Ismāʿīl (d. 1731), 73, 102, 119–20
Nagaur, 107
Naḥal Mishmar, 23
Nahiyah, 77
Nahor, 115
nails, 10, 12, 64, 65, 71–75, 97, 185n104, 192n3
najas, 54
najāsah, 68, 125
naʿl al-nabī, 79
naʿl karīmah, 90
Narayan, 107
Nasāʾī, ʿAḥmad b. ʿAlī (d. 915), 74
Nasīm b. al-Riyāḍ, 72
Naṣrid, 74
nau-gaz tombs, 17, 99–100, 106–10, 117, 119
navel of the earth, 21
Nawf b. Faḍālah, 116
Nawī, 120
Near East, 14, 15, 25, 26, 27, 28, 29, 43, 44, 46, 115, 129
Negev, 116
Nemean lion, 112
Nentsi, 8
*New York Times*, 208n151
Nibbana, 96, 97
Niẓām al-Dīn, 80
Noah, 12, 23, 46, 69, 84, 85, 89, 90, 91, 101, 103, 105, 106, 112–15, 121
Nod, 86
nomad, 126
noncoital sexual contact, 51
Nootka, 8
North Africa, 87
North Arabia, 26
nose, in questions of ablution, 55
nosebleed, 56
Nuʿaymī, ʿAbd al-Qādir b. Muḥammad, 74
Nuʿmān, 42
Numbers: (13:27–33) 116, (13:33) 116–17
Nuer, 4
Nūr al-Dīn Maḥmūd, 74, 88, 90
Nūr Shah, 107, 119
Nuwayrī, Aḥmad b. ʿAbd al-Wahhāb (d. 1333), 79

Sayyad Mahmud, 119
Sayyida Nafisa, 89
Sayyidna Zaynab, 96
Schick, Robert, 219n38
Scott, James C., 245n35
seashells, 97, 94
Sefer Yosippon, 146n12
semen, 55, 56, 60
seminal fluid, 52
Semites, 1–10
Semitic sanctuaries, 21, 26, 30
Senegal, 79
serpent cult, 153n59
Sertorius, 111
Serug, 115
Seth, 12, 23, 92, 101, 102, 103, 106, 113, 119, 218n33
Seven Sleepers, 92
sex, 10, 30, 42, 47–70, 72, 84
Shabwah, 26, 101, 152n51
Shāfiʿī, Muḥammad b. Idris (d. 820), 51, 52, 53, 62, 66, 67
Shah Amīn al-Dīn Aʿla (d. 1675), 119
Shah-i-Zindah, 102
Shaḥrī, ʿAlī, 104
Shamash, 27
Sharḥabīl b. Khusnah, 40
Sharīf al-Dīn al-Dimyāṭī, 34, 35
Shawkānī, Muḥammad b. ʿAlī (d. 1834), 69
Shawth al-Aʿẓam ʿAbd al-Qādir Gīnānī, 91
Shaybah b. Mālik, 35
Shaybānī, Muḥammad b. al-Ḥasan (d. 804), 54, 61
sheep, 61
Shelah, 113, 115
Shem, 113, 114, 115
shield, 27, 33, 151n47
*Shifāʾ*, 72
Shiʿī, 15, 16, 54, 55, 87, 88, 95
Shīrāzī, Abū Isḥāq (d. 1083), 76, 77, 89
shoes, 80, 82, 89, 90, 97, 185n104
Shuʿayb, 83, 101, 113, 121
Shurḥabīl b. Ḥasna, 92
Siberia, 8, 109
Sibylline Oracles, 22
sidāna, 28
Sidi Shaykh, 78
silver, 23, 41, 61, 63, 113, 151n45
Sinai, 136n5
Sind, 102, 109, 222–23n66
siqāyah, 28
Sirfa, 91
Sis Paigambar, 102
siwāk, 55
siyār, 126
Siyāwukhs, 42
Skyros, 111
slaves, 126
Smith, Jonathan Z., 2, 5–10, 14, 124, 130
Smith, William Robertson, 1–10, 13, 128
smiths, 85, 172–73n207
Smyrna, 228n108
Solinus, 110
Solomon, 23, 38, 39, 40–41, 81, 82, 85, 91
Solot, 104
soteriology, 132
South Arabia, 26, 27, 28, 100
South Asia, 17, 99, 106, 108, 109, 210–11n1
Southeast Asia, 17, 29, 106, 108
souvenirs, 93, 94
Spartans, 111
spears, 27, 151n47
Sri Lanka, 119, 160n100, 229n110, 238n167
statue, 25
stele, 25
Stephanus Byzantinus, 103
Stobaeus, 228n108
stone, 25, 27, 41–42, 79, 83, 90
Strabo, 111
stupa, 96
Ṣubayb al-Rūmī, 89
Suddī, 44, 82, 84
Suetonius, 236n157
Sufi, 119
Sufism, 80
Sufyān al-Thawrī, 62
Suidas, 29
Sulaymān Abū al-Ḥadīd, 79
Sulaymānīyah sword, 170n197
Sulṭān al-Ghūrī, 80, 90
Sumerian King List, 115
Sumerian myth of distribution of Me, 14, 44–45
Sunnah, 51, 75, 76, 77, 96
sunnah, 55

# Index of Quran Citations